PRAISE FOR

WHITE TRASH

"An eloquent synthesis of the country's history of class stratification, one that questions whether the United States is indeed a place where all are created equal. *White Trash* powerfully unites four centuries of history—economic, political, cultural, and pseudoscientific—to show how thoroughly the notion of class is woven into the national fabric."
—THE BOSTON GLOBE

"This eye-opening investigation into our country's entrenched social hierarchy is acutely relevant."   —O, THE OPRAH MAGAZINE

"Formidable and truth-dealing…An eloquent volume that is more discomforting and more necessary than a semitrailer filled with new biographies of the founding fathers and the most beloved presidents."
—THE NEW YORK TIMES

"[*White Trash*] sheds bright light on a long history of demagogic national politicking, beginning with Jackson. It makes Donald Trump seem far less unprecedented than today's pundits proclaim."   —SLATE

"Isenberg…has written an important call for Americans to treat class with the same care that they now treat race.…Her work may well help that focus lead to progress."   —TIME

"Fascinating and unsettling . . . traces the long-standing codependency between America's wealthy elites and the white underclass who have been a source of cheap labor since the founding of our country . . . [a] meticulously researched survey of the class system in America." —*The Atlanta Journal-Constitution*

"Isenberg . . . has written an important call for Americans to treat class with the same care that they now treat race. . . . Her work may well help that focus lead to progress." —*Time*

"Formidable and truth-dealing . . . an eloquent volume that is more discomforting and more necessary than a semitrailer filled with new biographies of the founding fathers and the most beloved presidents." —*The New York Times*

"[*White Trash*] sheds bright light on a long history of demagogic national politicking, beginning with Jackson. It makes Donald Trump seem far less unprecedented than today's pundits proclaim." —*Slate*

"Engaging . . . After reading this book you will never think of a trailer park the same way again." —*Providence Journal*

"Written with the grace of a superb novel and the forensic fervor of our finest historians, *White Trash* pokes and prods in the nooks and crannies of the American psyche, and travels the backroads and backwaters of our national self-image, in search of how class has been made and reshaped over the decades. This is breathtaking social history and dazzling cultural analysis at its best."
—Michael Eric Dyson, author of *Tears We Cannot Stop* and *The Black Presidency*

"An eloquent synthesis of the country's history of class stratification, one that questions whether the United States is indeed a place where all are created equal. *White Trash* powerfully unites four centuries of history—economic, political, cultural, and pseudoscientific—to show how thoroughly the notion of class is woven into the national fabric." —*The Boston Globe*

"With her strong academic background and accessible voice, Isenberg takes pains to reveal classism's deep-seated roots." —*Entertainment Weekly*

"A dizzying, dazzling four-hundred-year-long tour of American history from Pocahontas to Sarah Palin, seen from a vantage point that students of American history occupy all too rarely: that of the disposable citizens whose very presence disrupts what Isenberg calls our 'national hagiography.'"
—*The New Republic*

"A book that strikes blow after blow against our foundational myth of equality and boundless opportunity for he (and, much later, she) who would seize it . . . [Isenberg's] erudition is stunning." —*The Dallas Morning News*

"A carefully researched indictment of a particularly American species of hypocrisy, and it's deeply relevant to the pathologies of contemporary America."
—*The Christian Science Monitor*

"*White Trash* is certain to be controversial. No debate, however, can minimize the rigor of Isenberg's research, the clarity of her prose, or her courage in exploring this fraught subject. Hers is a book that should forever change the way we think and talk about class, which Isenberg suggests is the rotting stage upon which American democracy will either stand or fall."
—*The American Scholar*

"*White Trash* provides an honest (and therefore important) look at four centuries of misrepresentation and exploitation—complete with the conventional wisdom, pseudoscience, and armchair anthropology that sustains it."
—Rural American, *In These Times*

"From the eugenics movement to the rise of the proud redneck, Isenberg portrays a very real and significant history of class privilege in the United States. A riveting thesis supported by staggering research."
—*Kirkus Reviews* (starred review)

"From John Locke's plans for the colonies to twentieth-century eugenics, from the rise of Andrew Jackson to the modern Republican party, *White Trash* will change the way we think about our past and present."
—T. J. Stiles, Pulitzer Prize–winning author of *Custer's Trials*

"To any and all who want to understand, and understand deeply, our present age of brutal inequality, here is a timely and essential book."
—Marcus Rediker, author of *The Slave Ship: A Human History*

"In *White Trash*, Nancy Isenberg reveals a dark and tangled American secret at the core of our history: the pervasive persistence of white poverty. She deftly explores the interplay of mockery and denial in treatments, historical and fictional, of hardships and limits in a supposed land of equal and abundant opportunity. Drawing upon popular media as well as historical sources, from past and present, she exposes harsh realities long kept hidden in plain sight."
—Alan Taylor, Pulitzer Prize–winning author of
American Colonies and *The Internal Enemy*

PENGUIN BOOKS

WHITE TRASH

Nancy Isenberg is the author of *Fallen Founder: The Life of Aaron Burr*, which was a finalist for the Los Angeles Times Book Prize in biography and won the Oklahoma Book Award for best book in non-fiction. She is the coauthor, with Andrew Burstein, of *Madison and Jefferson*. She is the T. Harry Williams Professor of American History at Louisiana State University and writes regularly for Salon.com. She lives in Baton Rouge, Louisiana, and Charlottesville, Virginia.

BY NANCY ISENBERG

Fallen Founder: The Life of Aaron Burr
Sex and Citizenship in Antebellum America

BY NANCY ISENBERG WITH ANDREW BURSTEIN

Madison and Jefferson

NANCY ISENBERG

WHITE TRASH

The 400-Year Untold History of Class in America

PENGUIN BOOKS

PENGUIN BOOKS

An imprint of Penguin Random House LLC
375 Hudson Street
New York, New York 10014
penguin.com

First published in the United States of America by Viking,
an imprint of Penguin Random House LLC, 2016
Published with a new preface in Penguin Books 2017

ISBN 9780670785971 (hardcover)
ISBN 9780143129677 (paperback)
ISBN 9781101608487 (ebook)

Printed in the United States of America
1 3 5 7 9 10 8 6 4 2

Set in New Caledonia LT Std
Designed by Francesca Belanger

In memory of Gerda Lerner and Paul Boyer

CONTENTS

LIST OF ILLUSTRATIONS

PREFACE TO THE PAPERBACK EDITION

This book was originally published in the middle of the contentious 2016 presidential election season. By describing historical patterns, it had the effect of bringing some clarity to the otherwise feverish rhetorical muddle. And yet, in the aftermath of the election, conventional wisdom did little to improve upon the preelection confusion. As ABC reported, Donald Trump's shocking electoral success represented the "triumph of class over identity." It made no sense otherwise to analysts caught short. If the undeniable factors of racism and misogyny did not tilt the balance at the polls, then "the surging return of class in politics" must have. Searching for explanations is natural, but ABC did as punditry is wont to do and produced a false dichotomy in its effort to find a simple answer. The truth is, it's not one or the other: class and identity politics operate in tandem.[1]

While it is true that the major candidates who competed in 2016 all fell back on some form of a class-conscious vocabulary in advancing their positions, it cannot be said that identity politics disappeared in the face of "surging" class issues. From the outset of the Democratic primary process, while Senator Bernie Sanders of Vermont was calling for a "class revolution," he drew in enormous numbers of millennials across the social spectrum who felt the weight of college loans. Despite Sanders's claims that his opponent was asking women to vote for her on the basis of her gender alone, front-runner Hillary Clinton directed her appeal to voters on economic issues common to "all working families." From early on in the primary, she focused alike on the pocketbook issue of child care and the racial and class roots of inner-city violence.[2]

Yet both the Democratic contenders had to make themselves likeable and familiar. Sanders looked like a rumpled professor and sounded like a vintage sixties radical, speaking truth to power. No wonder students liked him. Clinton drew in some of the younger Lean In audience, and also won over older African American women because of her proven loyalty to the black community. Emotional bonds dominate the imagined "conversation" between candidate and voter, with little overt reference to class.[3]

And yet, in the immediate analytic (or pundit-driven) aftermath, it was class all the way. Going against the grain, in a widely cited op-ed, Columbia University professor Mark Lilla wrote in the *New York Times* just after the election that it was not class at all that lay at the root of Hillary Clinton's loss to Donald Trump. He blamed her defeat on a Left-friendly version of identity politics. Trump's rise was not about class-inflected racism or "whitelash," he insisted, but served instead to expose liberals' obsessive need to grant anyone who wanted it membership in a disadvantaged group: black, gay, female, and others. He argued that the Democrats, by their reductionist tendency, had caused "white, rural, religious Americans" to see themselves as ignored, even threatened. The liberal agenda was fueling a hostility toward political correctness; therefore, if the Democratic Party wished to do better, it would have to recover a "pre-identity" politics and reemphasize Americans' shared values.[4] Once again, it was a narrowly defined view of voting, and of identity.

Owing to Trump's eccentricities, blaming Clinton was inevitable. But the flaws in Professor Lilla's logic run deeper. His assumption that there was a time when democratic politics was "pre-identity" reflects the larger problem of many respected commentators: attachment to an idealized conception of American democracy. American party politics has exploited the rhetoric of identity at least as far back as Andrew Jackson and Thomas Jefferson. Given the resilience of the white trash slur, rural working-class whites hardly needed liberal lingo to feel alienated.

Illogically, Lilla uses Bill Clinton's candidacy as one of his examples of identity-free politics. Yet as I detail in these pages, Clinton was a poster child of self-marketing. At the time, Republicans engaged in an unrelenting campaign to challenge Clinton's legitimacy as president, making every effort to label him a southern bumpkin. In response, Clinton cleverly refashioned himself as the "Arkansas Elvis" and admitted, at times, to being a beer-drinking "Bubba." He played "Heartbreak Hotel" on the saxophone and posed with a mule on the campaign trail. For the poor white kid from Hope, Clinton's public image conjured nostalgia for the 1950s Elvis. No one was more skilled than the "comeback kid" in constructing an identity for himself that bridged North and South and in repackaging his personality so as to make him acceptable to working-class white men. The Yale liberal wore blue suede shoes.

If a serious scholar such as Lilla could get Bill Clinton wrong, it's no surprise that Trump would succeed in confounding so many smart people, too. Journalists throughout 2016 scrambled to figure out what the attraction was to this loud, endlessly self-promoting New Yorker. They were sure it was some brand-new phenomenon born of reality TV and social media. But conventional wisdom was again wrong to see the 2016 election as a break from the past. Like many before him, Trump had tapped into a rich vein of identity politics: the embrace of the common man, the working stiff, the forgotten rural American.

American democracy's quirky past haunted the Trump campaign. He was not the first cranky businessman to run for high office, even in recent memory. Ross Perot was, capturing 19 percent of the popular vote in 1992. Nor was Trump the first millionaire mogul with Hollywood ties to seek the presidency. That was William Randolph Hearst, a century ago. And he certainly can't claim to be the first outsider who promised to clean up Washington and embody the hopes and dreams (and fears) of the common man. That honor belongs to Andrew Jackson. As critically, he was not the first politician to question the pedigree of a sitting president either. James Vardaman did that in spades, when he insulted President Theodore Roosevelt. Trump's rhetorical appeal to the "silent majority" was stolen from Richard Nixon. Sarah Palin paved the way for him as an earlier version of a Republican reality TV populist. Trump's favorite slogan, "Make America Great Again," was, of course, Ronald Reagan's first.

The argument of this book is that America's class history is a more complicated story than we've previously considered. The past informs the present. Presidential candidates are not masters of their own destiny; rather, they are often a patchwork of rhetorical scripts, familiar gestures, political styles inherited from their predecessors, and whatever else they happen to borrow from the grab bag of popular culture.

Critics lament that our twenty-four-hour news cycle turned the 2016 election into a horse race or a sideshow, and they're right. It was treated as a kind of sporting event. But democratic politicians have always had to lure in voters. In the early nineteenth century, southern backcountry voters came for the free food, the fistfights, and such rowdy forms of entertainment as the "gander pull." In this indelicate contest, two men on horseback competed for the honor of yanking off the head of a goose. As in the "Squatter's Tale" about "Old Sug," men at the polls expected to get a serving of whiskey and brown sugar as they listened to long-winded speeches. It is in the nature of democratic politics for office seekers to appeal with little subtlety to the tastes of the electorate. In the early twentieth century, in his run for governor and the U.S. Senate, Jeff Davis of Arkansas gained the favor of his working-class audiences by ripping off his collar and rolling up his sleeves. He intentionally imitated the uncouth, ungrammatical speech of the lower classes. Even Lyndon Johnson had to canvass in Texas for his Senate seat with a traveling band. Governor "Big Jim" Folsom of Alabama strutted across the stage barefoot.[5]

Trump's antics mirror this long tradition. One of his campaign managers, Paul Manafort, admitted at one point that Trump was simply "projecting an image." Who's surprised? Americans have a taste for a "democracy of manners," which is different from real democracy. Voters accept huge disparities in wealth, while expecting their elected leaders to appear to be no different from the rest of us. By talking tough, by boasting that he'd love to throw a punch at a protester, candidate Trump pretended he was stepping down from his opulent Manhattan penthouse to commingle with the unwashed masses. Wearing his not-so-classy bright red Bubba cap, and crooning at one rally, "I love the poorly educated," he built upon a recognizable strain of American populism.[6]

Campaigns have long relied on shallow ploys and vicious rhetoric. In the first decade of the twentieth century, William Randolph Hearst's campaign strategist, Arthur Brisbane, said: "The American people, like all people, are interested in PERSONALITY." Even then they knew. The earlier billionaire (worth seven times what Forbes says Trump is worth; three times what Trump says Trump is worth) was a more credible populist. He was a staunch union supporter who said: "Wide and equitable distribution of wealth is essential to a nation's prosperous growth and intellectual development. And that distribution is brought about by the labor union more than any other agency of our civilization." Yes, he said *that* while running for president in 1904. Politicians have learned to appeal to (and exploit!) the class discontents of the ordinary voter. An astute observer wrote in 1924 that American voters preferred to "cherish the unrealities they have absorbed" based upon "the primal instinct to defeat the side they hate or fear." It is just as true today. To his supporters, Trump's tactlessness and personal vindictiveness scored points, while his lack of policy understanding was overlooked. His fans reveled in his promise to "stick it" to "Crooked Hillary," and her imagined core base of Washington insiders and too-smart-for-their-own-good Ivy League professionals.[7]

Many Trump supporters said they were drawn to him because he "speaks his mind," and voiced a "raw honesty." As New York Times columnist Ross Douthat concluded early on, Trump was the anti-candidate, totally unpredictable. He wasn't just playing a part but was refusing to be anything like a scripted politician. The nasty nicknaming of his opponents ("Low-Energy Jeb," "Little Marco") was one-half schoolyard bully bravado and one-half public relations branding. Yet his most consistent pitch was to speak for the "forgotten Americans," those whose class identity and Middle-America sensibilities put them at odds with all politically correct liberals. His utter lack of civility made him the voice of the non-elite outsider.[8]

That is where the Sarah Palin model came in. The half-term Alaska governor was the ultimate outsider. She was selected as the GOP's 2008 vice presidential nominee because John McCain's camp bought into the conceit of reality TV, that anyone could be turned into a viable candidate if given the right makeover. She both intrigued and flabbergasted, whether she was pictured shooting caribou from a helicopter or tripping over standard syntax in her Fargoesque accent. Her appeal was the opposite of Barack Obama's: whereas she was associated with the rural backwater of Wasilla, he was a hip, savvy Chicagoan.[9]

Trump seemed to want it both ways—a man of means and glamour and a man of the people; on the first front, though, he was a most ironic example of urban sophistication. The New Yorker bragged about his Wharton MBA degree, but he sounded like a working stiff from Queens. He loved to describe himself as classy, but his outlandish way of showing off his wealth put him squarely in the camp of the nouveau riche. He ignored his inherited wealth and status and proclaimed himself a self-made millionaire. His trophy wives, his gold-accented Louis XIV furniture, and his passion for seeing his name plastered on anything and everything undermined any effort to project the highbrow appeal of old money or the intellectualism of Ivy League graduates. His bragging ways first led him into TV camp as an occasional player in WrestleMania, before going on to star in *The Apprentice*. None of this activity (or its contradictions) bothered his working-class voters. Just the opposite: it forged a bond. Every time he spoke, he rejected PC etiquette. He was "one of them."[10]

This hurling of insults is nineteenth-century political theater revivified. Trump's tweeting frenzy resembled nothing so much as Andrew Jackson responding to critics by invoking the code duello. Revenge was the Jacksonian recourse in an era when perceived slights led to brawls and shoot-outs. In the fall of 2016, anticipating defeat at the polls, Trump asserted that the election had already been "rigged." In 1825, Jacksonians similarly attributed their hero's loss to a "Corrupt Bargain," because Congress refused to ratify popular opinion. Those who lionized Jackson adored him for his unpolished backcountry manner and uncompromising positions. He has been referred to as a "democratic autocrat." For the next century or more, he was democracy incarnate.[11]

That other Trump-like politician who leaps from the past, Mississippian James Vardaman, was known in the first decade of the twentieth century as "The White Chief." He, too, was the darling of angry lower-class whites, combining a cruel racist bent with a proclivity for trash-talking. Readers are reminded that when Theodore Roosevelt dined with African American leader Booker T. Washington in the White House, Vardaman went ballistic. Though Roosevelt was the scion of the proud and wealthy New York family going back to the colonial Dutch settlers, Vardaman used his own brand of birtherism to smear the president's pedigree. His unfiltered reaction was to allude to "Old Lady Roosevelt" having been frightened by a dog during her pregnancy; in a moment of alchemy, "qualities of the male pup" were transferred to the embryo, which was all that explained Roosevelt's embrace of a black man. It is worth adding that Vardaman was equally notable for his distinctive dark locks as for his wicked tongue. Democracy, no matter how dirty, belonged to the people, he held, and the people had the right to broadcast whatever they were feeling. The twenty-first-century Vardaman speaks without self-censoring when he feels cornered by a disabled journalist or a blonde Fox News host with "blood coming out of her whatever."[12]

In spite of the founders' noble dream of an informed public, the American political landscape has never been able to sustain itself as a place for sound deliberation. Nor does American democracy consistently confer power to a calm problem solver. Outrageous language spoken by grandiose public men of all shapes and sizes and educational backgrounds, in and out of the halls of government, prefigured the passion-filled diatribes of the Civil War era. Then as now, the national media stoked the fires of popular discontent. Throughout the first half of the nineteenth century, print culture was huge, and newspapers across the country carried complete transcripts of bombastic speeches. One of the best-known practitioners of the democratic art of overstatement was Virginia planter-politician John Randolph of Roanoke, who often drowned out the practiced logic of his colleagues with oratorical detours drenched in comic indecision. Gawky to look at, this lifelong bachelor was an attack engine, thought clinically mad by many; yet the theatrically generated outrage he churned up drew crowds, and newspaper readers devoured all that he had to say. Appearance was part of Randolph's shrill charm, as were his mocking faces and rude antics: tall, impossibly thin, with a high, childlike voice, he took slugs from a flask on the floor of Congress; he loved to hear the sound of his own voice. His biographer Henry Adams said of his verbal combativeness, "He could gouge and kick, bite off an ear or a nose, or hit below the waist." Randolph asserted of his own "unprosperous" life that it was "the fruit of an ungovernable temper." The states' rights advocate was elected and reelected repeatedly over the course of decades; President Jackson named him ambassador to Russia. Like his anger-prone patron Jackson or the later Vardaman, John Randolph embodied an element in American democracy that still lives, and evidently thrives, and does not advertise for the founding generation's sobriety and deliberative spirit.[13]

What history teaches us about the true character of American democracy is that it cannot be generalized, and it cannot be defined scientifically. One cannot effectively lump voters together into arbitrary blocs based on demographic statistics and have it mean anything: there is no reductionist, easily definable women's vote, or black or Latino vote, or Evangelical vote, or youth vote. And as *White Trash* has sought to make clear, the so-called white, working-class vote is an inaccurate designation as well. Class matters, as identity politics matters, but neither is sufficient alone to define categories of voting behavior.

Something else matters that rarely gets talked about: an amorphous, intangible something we might call "embodied appeal." It is the candidate's *metaphoric* identity, not a "true" identity, that citizens are met with in video clips and edited interviews. Whether the person running is a Democrat, a Republican, or an Independent, and coming from a professional background as lawyer, doctor, military officer, or fame-chasing businessman, any individual who runs for national office is compelled to perform a kind of stage act. He or she becomes associated with a pet phrase, a slogan, a staged look, a zinger, a moniker—in short, the candidate exudes an appeal designed to push the emotional buttons of the broadest voter base imaginable. Optics matter. The size of crowds becomes a rallying point. The viability of detailed plans that the problem-solving, would-be legislator or would-be executive has studied, compared, and compiled is never as memorable as the performance dimension of the campaign.

Language rules. It is oft remarked that negative ads predominate because they work on the impressionable minds of voters. This is one of the sadder facts of modern electoral politics, yet the will does not exist to alter the increasingly expensive, all-out attack mode of saturation commercial bombing, in favor of measures that would be more amenable to the calmer vision of the framers of the Constitution who, as it happens, did not even address the prospect of the formation of organized political parties. (The original "Greatest Generation" was not composed of as many geniuses as we've been taught.) One of the reasons why the pollsters are often wrong is the widespread failure to account for the ways in which voters are convinced by what they are hearing. Selective belief, preference for one "truth" over another, explains, for instance, how someone can dismiss the vast majority of scientists who see incontrovertible evidence of dangerous trends in climate change. Political choices are hardly rational choices. An unconscious linguistic relationship forms between candidate and voter, and choice metaphors preoccupy a voter's thoughts.

Presidential elections are battles over worldviews. The symbols that mattered most to Trump voters were about class, but the metaphoric meaning played out in a more expansive rhetoric that divided constituencies by competing markers of identity. The unspoken and spoken themes of the political contest were:

Clinton Democrats	Trump Republicans
Pedigreed Elites	Disinherited
Urban Insider	Rural Outsider
Cosmopolitan	Provincial
Professionals	Working Stiffs
Meritocracy	Hard Work
Faith in Upward Mobility	Fear of Losing Class Status

Both Trump at his inaugural and President Obama in his farewell remarks called for solidarity, but their visions of what constitutes togetherness are completely at odds. President Obama and Hillary Clinton celebrated American exceptionalism, which for them was bound up in education and economic opportunity, cultural diversity, and the promise that "all men are created equal." Democrats, in general, endorse the liberal ideal of meritocracy, in which talent is rewarded through the acquisition of earned academic credentials. Yet this dream is not possible for all Americans. Only 32.5 percent of Americans today graduate college, which means that the majority does not imagine this path up the social ladder as its ticket to success. Trump, in contrast, would appear to envision solidarity in terms of an "America First" patriotism.[14]

Back in 2004, campaigning for the Democratic nomination, South Carolina Democrat John Edwards capitalized on a powerful image when he continually hammered the existence of "two Americas." The same imagery was put to use in 2016 by the nominee of the Republican Party, who painted the country he sought to rule as an economically war-torn wasteland, lacking in the vitality and the productivity that had made it dominant in the past. (In his 2017 inaugural, Trump described the "rusted-out factories scattered like tombstones across the landscape of America.") In this metaphoric construction, recovering greatness meant replenishing the strength of an all-American workforce, returning it to its accustomed (and deserved) position at the top of the food chain.

Hardworking breadwinners who had come to see diminishing returns, their pride in performance outstripped by foreign manufacturing, found their candidate. You, the disinherited, have lost ground, he said, and are at a standstill in your lives, because your federal government has *allowed* this terrible decline to occur. Whereas Senator Edwards had directed his slogan at gross inequality, shining a light on *all* the poor and underrepresented, Trump courted the predominantly white workforce, whose percentage of the population was evidently in decline; thus, immigrants and refugees became targets—"the usual suspects," if one goes back to attacks on the Irish, southern Europeans, Chinese, Jews, and others, in past generations.[15]

The election has opened up festering wounds. The deepest of these exposes how we measure the value of civic virtue and hard work. Many successful Americans believe they have made it on their own and have little patience for the complaints of those left behind. Trump perceived a world of winners and losers, and many of his supporters want to reinforce the old stigmas that separated the productive worker from the idle. They wanted the boundaries between the unemployed and employed to be firmly enforced, not weakened. "Make America Great Again" is another way of saying that hard work is no longer automatically rewarded as a virtue. It tapped the anxieties of all who resented government for handing over the country to supposedly less deserving classes: new immigrants, protesting African Americans, lazy welfare freeloaders, and Obamacare recipients asking for handouts. Angry Trump voters were convinced that these classes (the "takers") were not playing by the rules (i.e., working their way up the ladder) and that government entitlement programs were allowing some to advance past more deserving (white, native-born) Americans. This was how many came to feel "disinherited."[16]

The phenomenon of social and political alienation cannot be easily cured. Even Vice President Joe Biden remarked in 2016 that Democrats had placed too much emphasis on "pedigree." He meant intellectual pedigree, class pedigree. This simmering resentment made it easier for Trump to widen the cleavage by suggesting that the federal government had been hijacked by the first African American president, who remained illegitimate in the eyes of many in the GOP. Trump had not only dominated headlines by challenging President Obama to produce his birth certificate, but he also, significantly, questioned his Harvard credentials. Racial pedigree was used to undercut intellectual pedigree.[17]

"Taking our country back," as the Tea Party harangued after 2010, became a convenient slogan for Trump to use against the Obama administration and its surrogate Hillary Clinton. By 2016, Trump's "I will bring the jobs back" seemed a winning concept. Distrust of fluid class boundaries made many voters fear competition from below. They lacked faith in the promised social mobility of the meritocratic system. As one Trump supporter from Pennsylvania who attended the inauguration explained as he imagined his son's future: "Where I'm from, we see kids get engineering degrees and end up working at McDonald's." Anecdotal evidence suggested a rigged system and a zero-sum game for success. If there were undeserving winners, there must be losers.[18]

Trump's statements, up to and including his inaugural address, may have been short on specific policy prescriptions; but no moment was lost whenever the incoming president saw a chance to promise that he alone could restore the American dream. "We will bring back our wealth. And we will bring back our dreams." He repeated the word *dream* at least four times on January 20, 2017.[19]

Dreams may make the heart beat faster, but they do not improve social conditions or ensure fairness in the workplace or secure the family farm. So, once again, it is the language deployed by the politician that obscures patterns we have seen before but that strikes voters as new and urgent. This is what professional historians are called on to do: to look backward and uncover what is missing in current popular conceptions. Hopefully, then, this book has achieved its goal of historicizing the plight of the underclass over four centuries. Perhaps, too, it is clearer to more Americans that the rural as well as postindustrial wasteland can no longer be overlooked as a site of meaningful social and political discontent. The prevailing mood among those whose manners have been mocked since colonial times—whether called waste people, mudsills, rednecks, or white trash—should matter to us. They are a factor in American history, because class is as American as it ever was British.

Punditry has tended to reduce the reality of class, which crosses lines of racial and gender identity, and to replace it with an all-encompassing marker of dispossession that exclusively features the once ascendant, now aggrieved "white working-class male." Such an artificial, monolithic designation of working class reinforces the idea of voting blocs as fixed categories. As a result, politicians are said to appeal to one or another preset group. We need to see beyond.[20]

We need to look honestly at the real perils of our electoral system in this age of media celebrity and instantaneous communication, especially when compounded lies cease to shock and a cacophony of voices among insistent ideologues compromise constitutional principles and make it harder and harder to know which policies stand the best chance of improving the lives of more citizens. We need to stop thinking that some Americans are the real Americans, the deserving, the talented, the most patriotic and hardworking, while others can be dismissed as less deserving of the American dream.

One thing we can do in the interest of national self-improvement is to further the conversation about the manipulations of class identity by political aspirants, who game the system each time they sell unreal expectations to people whose interests they only pretend to represent. If we do not study ourselves with due attention to disturbing patterns in our history, we will be learning little, and democracy can scarcely claim to be the best form of government.

PREFACE

One of the most memorable films of all time is *To Kill a Mockingbird* (1962), a classic portrait of the legacy of slavery and racial segregation in the South. It is a film that I have been teaching for over two decades, and is one of President Obama's favorite movies. Yet when my students watch this film (even if they were exposed to it in high school), they see for the first time that the drama within has not one but two disturbing messages.

One plotline is about the brave, principled lawyer Atticus Finch, who refuses to perpetuate the racial double standard: despite opposition, he agrees to defend an African American, Tom Robinson, on the charge of raping a poor white girl, Mayella Ewell. Though the court finds Robinson guilty, we the viewers know he is innocent. An honorable, hardworking family man, he stands well above the degraded Ewells, his accusers. The shabbily attired Mayella is cowed by her bully of a father, a scrawny man seen in overalls, who is devoid of merit or morality. Bob Ewell demands that the all-white jury of common men take his side, which they do in the end. He insists that they help him avenge his daughter's honor. Not satisfied when Robinson is killed trying to escape from prison, he attacks Atticus Finch's two children on Halloween night.

Bob Ewell's full name is Robert E. Lee Ewell. But he is not an heir of one of the aristocratic families of the Old South. As Harper Lee described them in the novel from which the classic film was adapted, the Ewells were members of the terminally poor, those whose status could not be lifted or debased by any economic fluctuation—not even the Depression. They were human waste. In the author's words, "No truant officers could keep their numerous offspring in school; no public health officer could free them from congenital defects, various worms, and diseases indigenous to filthy surroundings." They lived behind the town dump, which they combed every day. Their run-down shack was "once a Negro cabin." Garbage was strewn everywhere, making the cabin look like the "playhouse of an insane child." No one in the neighborhood knew how many children lived there: some thought nine, others six. To the town of Maycomb, Alabama, the Ewell children were simply "dirty-faced ones at the windows when anyone passed."[1] The Ewells are unmistakably what southerners (and a lot of other people) called white trash.

Americans today have a narrow and skewed understanding of white trash. One of the most powerful and most familiar symbols of backward attitudes associated with this unfavored group is that captured in newspapers and in television footage of 1957, showing the angry white faces of protest amid school integration in Little Rock, Arkansas. In 2015, tattooed KKK protestors defending the Confederate flag outside the Columbia, South Carolina, statehouse evoked similar feelings, demonstrating the persistence of an embarrassing social phenomenon. The stock of the Food Network's popular performer Paula Deen, a Georgia native known for her cholesterol-rich recipes, suddenly took a nosedive in 2013, when it was revealed that she used the "N word"; almost overnight, her down-home reputation sank and she was rebranded as a crude, unsophisticated redneck. At the other extreme, television viewers have been treated to such repackaged vaudeville characters as Jefferson Davis "Boss" Hogg in *The Dukes of Hazzard* (1979–85), which could be seen in reruns until 2015, when it was dropped because of the Confederate flag painted on Bo and Luke Duke's car, "General Lee." The very title of this show was a pun on class identity, since the Dukes are poor Georgia mountain folk and moonshiners, yet their name implies English royalty.[2]

These white trash snapshots offer an incomplete picture of a problem that is actually quite old and regularly goes unrecognized. In their conversations about viral events such as those noted above, Americans lack any deeper appreciation of class. Beyond white anger and ignorance is a far more complicated history of class identity that dates back to America's colonial period and British notions of poverty. In many ways, our class system has hinged on the evolving political rationales used to dismiss or demonize (or occasionally reclaim) those white rural outcasts seemingly incapable of becoming part of the mainstream society.

The Ewells, then, are not bit players in our country's history. Their history starts in the 1500s, not the 1900s. It derives from British colonial policies dedicated to resettling the poor, decisions that conditioned American notions of class and left a permanent imprint. First known as "waste people," and later "white trash," marginalized Americans were stigmatized for their inability to be productive, to own property, or to produce healthy and upwardly mobile children—the sense of uplift on which the American dream is predicated. The American solution to poverty and social backwardness was not what we might expect. Well into the twentieth century, expulsion and even sterilization sounded rational to those who wished to reduce the burden of "loser" people on the larger economy.

In Americans' evolving attitudes toward these unwanted people, perhaps the most dramatic language attached to the mid-nineteenth century, when poor rural whites were categorized as somehow less than white, their yellowish skin and diseased and decrepit children marking them as a strange breed apart. The words "waste" and "trash" are crucial to any understanding of this powerful and enduring vocabulary. Throughout its history, the United States has always had a class system. It is not only directed by the top 1 percent and supported by a contented middle class. We can no longer ignore the stagnant, expendable bottom layers of society in explaining the national identity.

The poor, the waste, the rubbish, as they are variously labeled, have stood front and center during America's most formative political contests. During colonial settlement, they were useful pawns as well as rebellious troublemakers, a pattern that persisted amid mass migrations of landless squatters westward across the continent. Southern poor whites figured prominently in the rise of Abraham Lincoln's Republican Party, and in the atmosphere of distrust that caused bad blood to percolate among the poorer classes within the Confederacy during the Civil War. White trash were dangerous outliers in efforts to rebuild the Union during Reconstruction; and in the first two decades of the twentieth century, when the eugenics movement flourished, they were the class of degenerates targeted for sterilization. On the flip side, poor whites were the beneficiaries of rehabilitative efforts during the New Deal and in LBJ's "Great Society."

At all times, white trash remind us of one of the American nation's uncomfortable truths: the poor are always with us. A preoccupation with penalizing poor whites reveals an uneasy tension between what Americans are taught to think the country promises—the dream of upward mobility—and the less appealing truth that class barriers almost invariably make that dream unobtainable. Of course, the intersection of race and class remains an undeniable part of the overall story.

The study presented here reveals a complicated legacy. It's not just a question of labeling the bottom at any given time. Rationalizing economic inequality has been an unconscious part of the national credo; poverty has been naturalized, often seen as something beyond human control. By this measure, poor whites had to be classified as a distinct breed. In other words, breeding was not about the cultivation of social manners or skills, but something far more sinister: an imposed inheritance. The language of class that America embraced played off English attitudes toward vagrancy, and marked a transatlantic fixation with animal husbandry, demography, and pedigree. The poor were not only described as waste, but as inferior animal stocks too.

Over the years, populist themes have emerged alongside more familiar derogatory images, but never with enough force to diminish the hostility projected onto impoverished rural whites. We have seen in recent decades the rise of tribal passions through the rediscovery of "redneck roots," a proud movement that coursed through the 1980s and 1990s. More than a reaction to progressive changes in race relations, this shift was spurred on by a larger fascination with identity politics. Roots implied that class took on the traits (and allure) of an ethnic heritage, which in turn reflected the modern desire to measure class as merely a cultural phenomenon. But as evidenced in the popularity of the "reality TV" shows *Duck Dynasty* and *Here Comes Honey Boo Boo* in recent years, white trash in the twenty-first century remains fraught with the older baggage of stereotypes of the hopelessly ill bred.

A host of well-known and lesser-known figures contributed to the long saga of America's embattled lowly breed. These include Benjamin Franklin, Thomas Jefferson, Davy Crockett, Harriet Beecher Stowe, Jefferson Davis, Andrew Johnson, W. E. B. Du Bois, Theodore Roosevelt, Erskine Caldwell, James Agee, Elvis Presley, Lyndon Baines Johnson, James Dickey, Billy Carter, Dolly Parton, William Jefferson Clinton, and Sarah Palin, to name a few. Examining their ideas, shifting public images, and self-images helps us to make greater sense of the curious and complicated story of American class identity.

This book tells many stories, then. One is the importance of America's rural past. Another, and arguably the most important, is the one we as a people have trouble embracing: the pervasiveness of a class hierarchy in the United States. It begins and ends with the concepts of land and property ownership: class identity and the material and metaphoric meaning of land are closely connected. For much of American history, the worst classes were seen as extrusions of the worst land: scrubby, barren, and swampy wasteland. Home ownership remains today the measure of social mobility.

My interest in this topic goes back to graduate school, where I was fortunate to have worked with two remarkable scholars whose approach to history shaped my professional career in significant ways. Gerda Lerner, my doctoral dissertation adviser, had a keen passion for demystifying ideologies, and she instilled in me a wariness for the limits of conventional wisdom. Paul Boyer was an intellectual historian with an amazing range, who wrote with subtlety and grace about Puritan New England, nineteenth-century moral reformers, and twentieth-century religious fundamentalists. The border town of San Benito, Texas, figures into my interest in this topic as well. It was my mother's birthplace. Her father, John MacDougall, was a modern-day colonist, bringing settlers from Canada to farm the land.

Friends and colleagues have helped this book along in crucial ways. I wish to thank those who read chapters, gave suggestions, or sent along sources: Chris Tomlins, Alexis McCrossen, Liz Varon, Matt Dennis, Lizzie Reis, Amy Greenberg, and my LSU colleague Aaron Sheehan-Dean. Lisa Francavilla, managing editor of The Papers of Jefferson: Retirement Series, Charlottesville, Virginia, called my attention to a valuable letter; Charles Roberts graciously shared with me a crucial newspaper article on the resettlement community of Palmerdale, Alabama. My Viking editor, Wendy Wolf, with roots in New Orleans, was instrumental in tightening the argument and policing the prose. Wendy put an extraordinary amount of time, skill, and care into the manuscript; her thoughtful editing has taken a complex history and made it far more reader friendly, proving that academic rigor does not have to limit accessibility. Most of all, I have to thank Andy Burstein, my dearest confidant and fellow historian, whose critical eye made this a much better book.

WHITE TRASH

Fables We Forget By

We know what class is. Or think we do: economic stratification created by wealth and privilege. The problem is that popular American history is most commonly told—dramatized—without much reference to the existence of social classes. It is as though in separating from Great Britain, the United States somehow magically escaped the bonds of class and derived a higher consciousness of enriched possibility. After all, the U.S. Senate is not the House of Lords. Schoolbooks teach the national narrative along the lines of "how land and liberty were won" or "how ordinary folks seized opportunity." The hallowed American dream is the gold standard by which politicians and voters alike are meant to measure quality of life as each generation pursues its own definition of happiness unfettered by the restraints of birth (who your parents are) or station (the position you start out from in the class system).

Our cherished myths are at once bolstering and debilitating. "All men are created equal" was successfully employed as a motto to define the promise of America's open spaces and a united people's moral self-regard in distinguishing themselves from a host of hopeless societies abroad. The idea of America was presented by its chief promoters with great panache, a vision of how a modern republic might prove itself revolutionary in terms of social mobility in a world dominated by monarchy and fixed aristocracy.

All that is bolstering. However, the reality on the ground was and is considerably different. In the most literal terms, as we shall see, British colonists promoted a dual agenda: one involved reducing poverty back in England, and the other called for transporting the idle and unproductive to the New World. After settlement, colonial outposts exploited their unfree laborers (indentured servants, slaves, and children) and saw such expendable classes as human waste. The poor, the waste, did not disappear, and by the early eighteenth century they were seen as a permanent breed. This way of classifying human failure took hold in the United

States. Every era in the continent's vaunted developmental story had its own taxonomy of waste people—unwanted and unsalvageable. Each era had its own means of distancing its version of white trash from the mainstream ideal.

By thinking of the lower classes as incurable, irreparable "breeds," this study reframes the relationship of race and class. Class had its own singular and powerful dynamic, apart from its intersection with race. It starts with the rich and potent meaning that came with the different names given the American underclass. Long before they were today's "trailer trash" and "rednecks," they were called "lubbers" and "rubbish" and "clay-eaters" and "crackers"—and that's just scratching the surface.

Lest the reader misconstrue the book's purpose, I want to make the point unambiguously: by reevaluating the American historical experience in class terms, I expose what is too often ignored about American identity. But I'm not just pointing out what we've gotten wrong about the past; I also want to make it possible to better appreciate the gnawing contradictions still present in modern American society.

How does a culture that prizes equality of opportunity explain, or indeed accommodate, its persistently marginalized people? Twenty-first-century Americans need to confront this enduring conundrum. Let us recognize the existence of our underclass. It has been with us since the first European settlers arrived on these shores. It is not an insignificant part of the vast national demographic today. The puzzle of how white trash embodied this tension is one of the key questions the book presumes to answer.

America's class language and thinking began with the forceful imprint left by English colonization. The generations of the 1500s and 1600s that first envisioned the broad-scale English exploitation of America's natural environment employed a vocabulary that was a mix of purposeful description and raw imagery. They did not indulge in pretty talk. The idea of settlement had to be sold to wary investors; the planting of New World American colonies had to serve Old World purposes. In grand fashion, promoters imagined America not as an Eden of opportunity but as a giant rubbish heap that could be transformed into productive terrain. Expendable people—waste people—would be unloaded from England; their labor would germinate a distant wasteland. Harsh as it sounds, the idle poor, dregs of society, were to be sent thither simply to throw down manure and die in a vacuous muck. Before it became that fabled "City upon a Hill," America was in the eyes of sixteenth-century adventurers a foul, weedy wilderness—a "sinke hole" suited to ill-bred commoners. Dark images of the New World accompanied more seductive ones. When early English promoters portrayed North America as a rich and fertile landscape, they grossly and perhaps knowingly exaggerated. Most were describing a land they never had seen, of course. Wary investors and state officials had to be convinced to take the plunge into a risky overseas venture. But most important, it was a place into which they could export their own marginalized people.

The idea of America as "the world's best hope" came much later. Historic memory has camouflaged the less noble origins of "the land of the free and the home of the brave." We all know what imagery springs to mind when patriots of our day seek confirmation that their country is and was always an "exceptional" place: modest Pilgrims taught to plant by generous Indians; Virginia Cavaliers entertaining guests at their refined estates along the James River. Because of how history is taught, Americans tend to associate Plymouth and Jamestown with cooperation rather than class division.

And it gets ever more misty-eyed from there, because disorder and discord serve no positive purpose in burgeoning national pride. Class is the most outstanding, if routinely overlooked, element in presuppositions about early settlement. Even now, the notion of a broad and supple middle class functions as a mighty balm, a smoke screen. We cling to the comfort of the middle class, forgetting that there can't be a middle class without a lower. It is only occasionally shaken up, as when the Occupy Wall Street movement of recent years shone an embarrassing light on the financial sector and the grotesque separation between the 1 percent and the 99 percent. And then the media giants find new crises and the nation's inherited disregard for class reboots, as the subject recedes into the background again.

An imaginary classless (or class-free) American past is the America that Charles Murray has conjured in his book *Coming Apart: The State of White America, 1960–2010* (2012). For Murray, an authority in the minds of many, the large and fluid society of 1963 was held together by the shared experiences of the nuclear family. When they watched *The

Adventures of Ozzie and Harriet, average Americans believed they were seeing their lives on the small screen.[1]

Nothing could be further from the truth. Even in its innocent youth, television caricatured people by class types. One only need consider a few of the other popular shows of those halcyon years to prove the point: *Petticoat Junction* (1963), which chronicled rural life at the Shady Rest Hotel and contrasted a simpler people with their savvier city relations; *The Farmer's Daughter* (1963), featuring a Swedish American maid from the farm who goes to work for a U.S. congressman; *Green Acres* (1965), where Arnold the pig is the smartest resident of the hick town of Hooterville; and, finally, that classic satire of social mobility, *The Beverly Hillbillies* (1962), whose mountain-bred oil millionaires seem like evolutionary throwbacks in the eyes of city folk. And lest we forget, *Ozzie and Harriet* began its long run at the same time as *The Honeymooners,* a brilliant send-up of a bus driver, a sewer worker, and their poor working-class wives. Everyone who tuned in understood perfectly well that Ozzie and Harriet's world bore no resemblance to Ralph and Alice Kramden's. Parody was one way Americans safely digested their class politics.

Selective memory allows us to romanticize a golden age that functions as a timeless talisman of American identity. For Charles Murray, who ignores the country's long history, the golden age is 1963, when the essence of the American creed was somehow captured in a Gallup poll in which respondents refused to self-identify as either poor or rich: approximately half said that they were working class, while the other half perceived themselves as middle class. As if a single statistic could possibly tell a comprehensive story, the social scientist writes, "Those refusals reflected a national conceit that had prevailed *from the beginning of the nation: America didn't have classes,* or, to the extent that it did, Americans should act as if we didn't" (emphasis added). Murray's fable of class denial can only exist by erasing a wealth of historical evidence that proves otherwise. The problem is, the evidence has never been effectively laid out, allowing gross misrepresentations to stand.[2]

By gaining first a better understanding of the colonial context and, next, charting the steps by which modern definitions of class were established, we will be able to see how ideas and ideals combined over time. By acknowledging the ongoing influence of older English definitions of poverty and class, we will come to recognize that class identity was apparent in America—profoundly so—long before George Gallup saw it as a creature of public opinion; indeed, class resonated long before waves of immigrants swept ashore in the nineteenth century and an awkward, often heated process of acculturation ensued. Above all, we must stop declaring what is patently untrue, that Americans, through some rare good fortune, escaped the burden of class that prevailed in the mother country of England. Far more than we choose to acknowledge, our relentless class system evolved out of recurring agrarian notions regarding the character and potential of the land, the value of labor, and critical concepts of breeding. Embarrassing lower-class populations have always been numerous, and have always been seen on the North American continent as waste people.

Historical mythmaking is made possible only by forgetting. We have to begin, then, with the first refusal to face reality: most colonizing schemes that took root in seventeenth- and eighteenth-century British America were built on privilege and subordination, not any kind of proto-democracy. The generation of 1776 certainly underplayed that fact. And all subsequent generations took their cue from the nation's founders.

A past that relies exclusively on the storied Pilgrims, or the sainted generation of 1776, shortchanges us in more ways than one. We miss a crucial historical competition between northern and southern founding narratives and their distinctive parables minimizing the importance of class. The Declaration of Independence and the federal Constitution, principal founding documents, loom large as proof of national paternity; the six-foot-three-inch Virginian George Washington stands head and shoulders above his countrymen as the figurative "father" of his nation. With Virginia's claim to an origins story in mind, another founding father, John Adams, heralded the first governor of Massachusetts Bay Colony, John Winthrop, as an earlier and stronger model for an American patrician-patriarch. The lesson is easy: then as now, origins are contested territory. What can't be denied, however, are the class origins of the anointed leaders.[3]

Beyond the web of stories the founding generation itself wove, our modern beliefs have most to do with the grand mythmakers of the nineteenth century. The inspired historians of that period were nearly all New Englanders; they outpaced all others in shaping the historical narrative, so that the dominant story of origins worked in their favor. That is how we got the primordial Puritan narrative of a sentimental community and a commendable work ethic. Of course, the twin attributes of religious freedom and hard work erase from the record all those settlers who did not live up to these high ideals. The landless, the impoverished, the progenitors of future generations of white trash conveniently disappear from the founding saga.

There were plays and poems, in addition to standard histories, flowing from the pens of Bostonians as they praised the separatists who established the early settlements. As early as 1769, New Englanders began celebrating "Forefathers Day" in Plymouth. Boston artist Henry Sargent unveiled his painting *Landing of the Fathers* in 1815. But the first volume of George Bancroft's widely praised *History of the United States* (1834) may be the best example of how the *Mayflower* and *Arbella* washed ashore and seeded the ground where love of liberty bore its ripest fruit in hubristic orations by the likes of Daniel Webster at well-attended nineteenth-century anniversary celebrations. These efforts were magnified as a result of promotional skills demonstrated by such organizations as the Colonial Dames, who worked to elevate the *Mayflower* Pilgrims and Winthrop's Puritans into some of the foremost figures in our national memory.[4]

In 1889, the Pilgrim Monument (now known as the National Monument to the Forefathers) was dedicated at Plymouth. Showing just how "colossal" the original plan was, the Boston architect and sculptor Hammatt Billings submitted a design for a 150-foot monument, which he conceived as the American version of the Colossus of Rhodes, one of the Seven Wonders of the Ancient World. It does not nullify his purpose that the final sculpture proved to be of a smaller scale and (predictably) allegorical: a female figure of Faith points to heaven and clutches a Bible, much like the Statue of Liberty with her torch.[5]

Monuments imperfectly record the past, as we all know. There is strange discrepancy between the chiseled female form (which could appear almost anywhere) and the event being recalled. John Gast's famous 1872 painting *American Progress* has an ethereal female spirit flying above the pioneers' transcontinental migratory march west across the plains; stagecoaches, wagons, railroad tracks, telegraph lines push aside Indians and buffalo that stand in their way. Billings's statue also heralds Faith, who lofts above the actual people on the *Mayflower*: their names appear less prominently on the side of the structure. Thus the first English settlers' personal motives for making the journey have been subsumed into a singular, overwhelming force of religious liberty. The settlers remain mute. The complex process of colonization is condensed and forgotten, because all human traces (the actual people tied to those names) are lost. There is no remembrance of those who failed, those without heirs or legacies. Instead, time has left subsequent generations with a hollow symbol: progress on the march.[6]

The compression of history, the winnowing of history, may seem natural and neutral, but it is decidedly not. It is the means by which grade school history becomes our standard adult history. And so the great American saga, as taught, excludes the very pertinent fact that after the 1630s, less than half came to Massachusetts for religious reasons. The tall tales we unthinkingly absorb when young somehow remain within; the result is a narrowly conceived sense of national belonging productive of the most uncompromising of satisfying myths: "American exceptionalism." We are unique and different, and the absence of class is one of our hallmarks.

Exceptionalism emerges from a host of earlier myths of redemption and good intentions. Pilgrims, persecuted in the Old World, brave the Atlantic dreaming of finding religious freedom on America's shores; wagon trains of hopeful pioneer families head west to start a new life. Nowhere else, we are meant to understand, was personal freedom so treasured as it was in the American experience. The very act of migration claims to equalize the people involved, molding them into a homogeneous, effectively classless society. Stories of unity tamp down our discontents and mask even our most palpable divisions. And when these divisions are class based, as they almost always are, a pronounced form of amnesia sets in. Americans do not like to talk about class. It is not supposed to be important in our history. It is not who we are.

Instead, we have the Pilgrims (a people who are celebrated at Thanksgiving, a holiday that did not exist until the Civil War), who came ashore at Plymouth Rock (a place only designated as such in the late eighteenth century). The quintessential American holiday was associated with the native turkey to help promote the struggling poultry industry during the Civil War. The word "Pilgrim" was not even popularized until 1794.

Nevertheless, the "first" Thanksgiving has been given a date of 1621, when well-meaning Pilgrims and fair-minded Wampanoags shared a meal. The master of ceremonies was their Indian interpreter, Squanto, who had helped the English survive a difficult winter. Left out of this story is the detail (not so minor) that Squanto only knew English because he had been kidnapped and sold as a slave to an English ship's captain. (Coerced labor of this kind reminds us of how the majority of white servants came to America.) Squanto's friendship, alas, was a far more complicated affair than the fairy tale suggests. He died of a mysterious fever the very next year while engaged in a power struggle with Massasoit, the "Great Sachem" of the Wampanoag confederation.[7]

In spite of the obvious stature of a Washington and a Jefferson, and Virginia's settlement thirteen years pre-Pilgrim, the southern states lagged behind the scribbling northerners in fashioning a comprehensive colonial myth to highlight their own cultural ascendancy in the New World. Here's what we have: Less a story than a mystery, there persists to this day a morbid curiosity about the 1587 "Lost Colony" of Roanoke, a puzzle on the order of Amelia Earhart's disappearance over the Pacific. A strange allure surrounds every vanishing people—recall the wildly popular television series *Lost*. Or Plato's Atlantis. Ghost ships and ghost colonies invoke a marvelous sense of timelessness; they exist outside the normal rules of history, which explains why Roanoke's mystery mitigates the harsh realities we instinctively know the early settlers were forced to face.[8]

If Roanoke is a tantalizing curio of a lost world, Jamestown, its more permanent offspring, grew to represent the Virginia colony's origins in a way that could compete with the uplifting story of the Pilgrims. The 1607 founding of Jamestown may lack a national holiday, but it does claim a far sexier fable in the dramatic rescue of John Smith by the "Indian princess" Pocahontas. As the story goes, in the middle of an elaborate ceremony, the eleven-year-old "beloved daughter" of "King" Powhatan rushed forward and placed her head over Smith, stopping tribesmen from smashing his skull with their clubs. A magical bond formed between the proud Englishman and the young naïf, cutting through all the linguistic and cultural barriers that separated the Old and New Worlds.

This brave girl has fascinated poets, playwrights, artists, and filmmakers. She has been called the "patron deity" of Jamestown and the "mother" of both Virginia and America. A writer in 1908 dubiously claimed that Pocahontas was actually the daughter of Virginia Dare, the youngest member of the Roanoke colony, making the Indian princess a child of European descent lost in the wilderness, much like Edgar Rice Burroughs's *Tarzan of the Apes,* published three years later.[9]

The best-known, most recent version of the story is the 1995 Walt Disney animated film. Strikingly beautiful, unnervingly buxom, and more like a pop culture diva than a member of the Tsenacommacah tribe, Disney's Pocahontas fabulously communes with nature, befriending a raccoon, talking to a tree; she is nearly identical to other Disney heroines Snow White and Cinderella, who also boast a menagerie of animal friends. Why? Communing with nature draws upon the potent romantic image of the New World as a prelapsarian classless society. Old tropes meld seamlessly with new cinematic forms: women in Western culture have been consistently portrayed as closer to Mother Nature, lushness and abundance, Edenic tranquility and fertility. There is no rancid swamp, no foul diseases and starvation, in this Jamestown recreation.[10]

Scholars have debated whether the rescue of Smith ever took place, since only his account exists and its most elaborate version was published years after Pocahontas's death. Smith was a military adventurer, a self-promoter, a commoner, who had the annoying habit of exaggerating his exploits. His rescue story perfectly mimicked a popular Scottish ballad of the day in which the beautiful daughter of a Turkish prince rescues an English adventurer who is about to lose his head. Though an Anglican minister presided over Princess Pocahontas's marriage to the planter John Rolfe, one member of the Jamestown council dismissed her as the heathen spawn of a "cursed generation" and labeled her a "barbarous[ly] mannered" girl. Even Rolfe considered the union a convenient political alliance rather than a love match.[11]

We should not expect Disney to get that right when the fundamental principle of the classless American identity—sympathetic communion— is at stake. The film builds on another mythic strand of the oft-told tale: it is John Smith (blond and brawny in his animated form), not Rolfe, who takes on the role of Pocahontas's lover. Exaggerating her beauty and highlighting her choice to save Smith and become an ally of the English is not new. When a less-than-flattering portrait appeared in 1842, making her plump and ungainly, and not the lovely and petite Indian princess, there was a storm of protest over what one critic called a "coarse and unpoetical" rendering. Her Anglicized beauty is nonnegotiable; her primitive elegance makes her assimilation tolerable. Indeed, it is all that makes acceptance of the Indian maiden possible.[12]

The Pocahontas story requires the princess to reject her own people and culture. This powerful theme has persisted, as the historian Nancy Shoemaker observes, because it contributes to the larger national rationale of the Indians' willing participation in their own demise. Yet this young girl did not willingly live at Jamestown; she was taken captive. In the garden paradise of early Virginia that never was, war and suffering, greed and colonial conquest are conveniently missing. Class and cultural dissonance magically fade from view in order to remake American origins into a utopian love story.[13]

Can we handle the truth? In the early days of settlement, in the profit-driven minds of well-connected men in charge of a few prominent joint-stock companies, America was conceived of in paradoxical terms: at once a land of fertility and possibility and a place of outstanding wastes, "ranke" and weedy backwaters, dank and sorry swamps. Here was England's opportunity to thin out its prisons and siphon off thousands; here was an outlet for the unwanted, a way to remove vagrants and beggars, to be rid of London's eyesore population. Those sent on the hazardous voyage to America who survived presented a simple purpose for imperial profiteers: to serve English interests and perish in the process. In that sense, the "first comers," as they were known before the magical "Pilgrims" took hold, were something less than an inspired lot. Dozens who disembarked from the *Mayflower* succumbed that first year to starvation and disease linked to vitamin deficiency; scurvy rotted their gums, and they bled from different orifices. By the 1630s, New Englanders reinvented a hierarchical society of "stations," from ruling elite to household servants. In their number were plenty of poor boys, meant for exploitation. Some were religious, but they were in the minority among the waves of migrants that followed Winthrop's *Arbella*. The elites owned Indian and African slaves, but the population they most exploited were their child laborers. Even the church reflected class relations: designated seating affirmed class station.[14]

Virginia was even less a place of hope. Here were England's rowdy and undisciplined, men willing to gamble their lives away but not ready to work for a living. England perceived them as "manure" for a marginal land. All that these idle men understood was a cruel discipline when it was imposed upon them in the manner of the mercenary John Smith, and the last thing they wanted was to work to improve the land. All that would keep the fledgling colony alive was a military-style labor camp meant to protect England's interests in the country's ongoing competition with the equally designing Spanish, French, and Dutch governments. That a small fraction of colonists survived the first twenty years of settlement came as no surprise back home—nor did London's elite much care. The investment was not in people, whose already unrefined habits declined over time, whose rudeness magnified in relation to their brutal encounters with Indians. The colonists were meant to find gold, and to line the pockets of the investor class back in England. The people sent to accomplish this task were by definition expendable.[15]

So now we know what happens to our colonial history. It is white-washed. Though New World settlers were supposed to represent the promise of social mobility, and the Pilgrims generated our hallowed faith in liberty, nineteenth-century Americans paradoxically created a larger-than-life cast of "democratic" royalty. These inheritors founded the first genealogical societies in the 1840s, and by the turn of the twentieth century patriotic organizations with an emphasis on hereditary descent, such as the General Society of Mayflower Descendants and the Order of the Founders and Patriots of America, boasted chapters across the nation. The highly exclusive Order of the First Families of Virginia was established in 1912, its members claiming that their lineage could be traced back to English lords and Lady Rebecca Rolfe—whom we all know as the ennobled and Anglicized Pocahontas.[16]

Statues are the companions of elite societies in celebrating paternal lineage and a new aristocracy. They tell us that some families (and some classes) have a greater claim as heirs of the founding promise. Municipal and state leaders have supported the national hagiography in bold form by constructing grand monuments to our colonial city fathers. The version of John Winthrop that the Revolutionary John Adams had favored, dressed in Shakespearean or Tudor-Stuart attire and with an ornate ruff collar and hose, first graced the Back Bay of Boston in 1880. But the largest such memorial is the twenty-seven-ton statue of William Penn perched atop City Hall in Philadelphia. After it was completed in 1901, no structure in the entire city was permitted to be taller than Penn's Quaker hat until 1987, ensuring that the founder's sovereign gaze towered over the City of Brotherly Love, commemorating the colonizing act of territorial possession. In British law, ownership was measured by standing one's ground—that is, holding and occupying the land. Land itself was a source of civic identity. This principle explains as well the totem value of "Plymouth Rock," the large stone discovered long after the last Pilgrim breathed New England air, christened in the eighteenth century as the first piece of land on which the *Mayflower* settlers stood.[17]

Commemoration of this kind begs the following questions: Who were the winners and losers in the great game of colonial conquest? Beyond parceling the land, how were estates bounded, fortunes made, and labor secured? What social structures, what manner of social relationships did the first European Americans really set in motion? Finding answers to these questions will enable us to fully appreciate how long-ago-established identities of haves and have-nots left a permanent imprint on the collective American mind.

Americans' sketchy understanding of the nation's colonial beginnings reflects the larger cultural impulse to forget—or at least gloss over—centuries of dodgy decisions, dubious measures, and outright failures. The "Lost Colony" of Roanoke was just one of many unsuccessful colonial schemes. Ambitious-sounding plans for New World settlements were never more than ad hoc notions or overblown promotional tracts. The recruits for these projects did not necessarily share the beliefs of those principled leaders molded in bronze—the John Winthrops and William Penns—who are lionized for having projected the enlarged destinies of their respective colonies.

Most settlers in the seventeenth century did not envision their forced exile as the start of a "Citty upon a Hill." They did not express undying confidence in Penn's "Holy Experiment." Dreamers dreamt, but few settlers came to America to fulfill any divine plan. During the 1600s, far from being ranked as valued British subjects, the great majority of early colonists were classified as surplus population and expendable "rubbish," a rude rather than robust population. The English subscribed to the idea that the poor dregs would be weeded out of English society in four ways. Either nature would reduce the burden of the poor through food short-ages, starvation, and disease, or, drawn into crime, they might end up on the gallows. Finally, some would be impressed by force or lured by boun-ties to fight and die in foreign wars, or else be shipped off to the colonies. Such worthless drones as these could be removed to colonial outposts that were in short supply of able-bodied laborers and, lest we forget, young "fruitful" females. Once there, it was hoped, the drones would be energized as worker bees. The bee was the favorite insect of the English, a creature seen as chaste but, more important, highly productive.[18]

The colonists were a mixed lot. On the bottom of the heap were men and women of the poor and criminal classes. Among these unheroic transplants were roguish highwaymen, mean vagrants, Irish rebels, known whores, and an assortment of convicts shipped to the colonies for grand larceny or other property crimes, as a reprieve of sorts, to escape the gallows. Not much better were those who filled the ranks of inden-tured servants, who ranged in class position from lowly street urchins to former artisans burdened with overwhelming debts. They had taken a chance in the colonies, having been impressed into service and then choosing exile over possible incarceration within the walls of an over-crowded, disease-ridden English prison. Labor shortages led some ship captains and agents to round up children from the streets of London and other towns to sell to planters across the ocean—this was known as "spiriting." Young children were shipped off for petty crimes. One such case is that of Elizabeth "Little Bess" Armstrong, sent to Virginia for stealing two spoons. Large numbers of poor adults and fatherless boys gave up their freedom, selling themselves into indentured servitude, whereby their passage was paid in return for contracting to anywhere from four to nine years of labor. Their contracts might be sold, and often were, upon their arrival. Unable to marry or choose another master, they could be punished or whipped at will. Owing to the harsh working conditions they had to endure, one critic compared their lot to "Egyptian bondage."[19]

Discharged soldiers, also of the lower classes, were shipped off to the colonies. For a variety of reasons, single men and women, and families of the lower gentry, and those of artisan or yeoman classes joined the mass migratory swarm. Some left their homes to evade debts that might well have landed them in prison; others (a fair number coming from Germany and France) viewed the colonies as an asylum from persecution for their religious faith; just as often, resettlement was their escape from economic restrictions imposed upon their trades. Still others ventured to America to leave tarnished reputations and economic failures behind. As all students of history know, slaves eventually became one of the largest groups of unfree laborers, transported from Africa and the Caribbean, and from there to the mainland British American colonies. Their numbers grew to over six hundred thousand by the end of the eighteenth century. Africans were found in every colony, especially after the British government gave full encouragement to the slave trade when it granted an African monopoly to the Company of Royal Adventurers in 1663. The slave trade grew even faster after the monopoly ended, as the American colonists bargained for lower prices and purchased slaves directly from foreign vendors.[20]

To put class back into the story where it belongs, we have to imagine a very different kind of landscape. Not a land of equal opportunity, but a much less appealing terrain where death and harsh labor conditions awaited most migrants. A firmly entrenched British ideology justified rigid class stations with no promise of social mobility. Certainly, Puritan religious faith did not displace class hierarchy either; the early generations of New Englanders did nothing to diminish, let alone condemn, the routine reliance on servants or slaves. Land was the principal source of wealth, and those without any had little chance to escape servitude. It was the stigma of landlessness that would leave its mark on white trash from this day forward.

So, welcome to America as it was. The year 1776 is a false starting point for any consideration of American conditions. Independence did not magically erase the British class system, nor did it root out long-entrenched beliefs about poverty and the willful exploitation of human labor. An unfavored population, widely thought of as waste or "rubbish," remained disposable indeed well into modern times.

Part I

TO BEGIN
THE WORLD ANEW

CHAPTER ONE

Taking Out the Trash

━━━━━◦○◦━━━━━

Waste People in the New World

Colonies ought to be Emunctories or Sinkes of States; to drayne
away the filth.

—John White, *The Planters Plea* (1630)

In the minds of literate English men and women, as colonization began
in the 1500s, North America was an uncertain world inhabited by
monstrous creatures, a blank territory skirted by mountains of gold.
Because it was a strange land that few would ever see firsthand, spectac-
ular tales had more appeal than practical observation. England's two
chief promoters of American exploration would never set foot on the continent. Richard Hakluyt the elder (1530–91) was a lawyer at Middle
Temple, a vibrant center of intellectual life and court politics in the London metropolis. His much younger cousin with the identical name (1552–
1616) trained at Christ Church, Oxford, and never hazarded a voyage
beyond the shores of France.[1]

The elder Hakluyt was a bookish attorney who happened to be well
connected to those who dreamt of profit from overseas ventures. His
circle included merchants, royal officials, and such men on the make as
Sir Walter Raleigh, Sir Humphrey Gilbert, and Martin Frobisher, all of
whom sought fame and glory from exploration. These men of action were
endowed with larger-than-life egos; they were a new breed of adventurer,
known for heroism but also for ill-tempered public behavior.[2]

Richard Hakluyt the younger was an Oxford fellow and clergyman
who devoted his life to compiling the travel narratives of explorers. In
1589, he published his most ambitious work, *Principall Navigations,* an
exhaustive catalogue of all the accounts he could track down of English
travelers to the East, the North, and of course America. In the age of
Shakespeare, everyone who was anyone read Hakluyt. The unstoppable
John Smith quoted liberally from his writings, proving himself more than
a brute soldier of fortune.[3]

Even before publishing *Principall Navigations*, the younger Hakluyt had sought royal favor. He prepared a treatise for Queen Elizabeth I and her top advisers, laying out his working theory of British colonization. "Discourse of Western Planting" (1584) was pure propaganda, designed to persuade the queen of the benefits of American settlements. Sir Walter Raleigh had commissioned the work, hoping for the state financing he never received when he launched an expedition that led to the short-lived Roanoke colony, off the Carolina coast.[4]

In Hakluyt's English colonial vision, distant America was a wilderness of an almost inconceivable dimension. For the French intellectual Michel de Montaigne, in 1580, it was the habitat of a simple and uncorrupted people whom he whimsically called "cannibals," slyly challenging the popular image of brutes gorging on human flesh. Like Hakluyt, he had never seen Native peoples, of course. Hakluyt at least was more practical (and more Anglican) than Montaigne in his outlook on the aboriginals. He believed them neither dangerous nor innocent, but empty vessels waiting to be filled with Christian—and, no less, commercial— truths. He imagined the Indians as useful allies in fulfilling English aspirations, possible trading partners, and subordinate, to be sure, but above all a natural resource to be exploited for the greater good.[5]

Attaching "empty" as a metaphor to a mysterious land served the legal purposes of the English state. Without recognized owners, the territory was available and waiting to be taken. Even for the bookish cleric Hakluyt, the trope of conquest he used presented America as a lovely woman waiting to be wooed and wed by the English. They would become her rightful owners and deserving custodians. It was all a fiction, of course, because the land was not really *inane ac uacuum*—void and vacant. As the English conceived it, however, any land had to be taken out of its natural state and put to commercial use—only then would it be truly owned.[6]

Obviously, the Indian occupants were deemed unable to possess a true title. Combing ancient laws for convincing analogies, English colonizers classified the Natives as savages, and sometimes as barbarians. The Indians did not build what the English would acknowledge as permanent homes and towns; they did not enclose the workable ground inside hedges and fences. Under their tenancy, the land appeared unbounded and untamed—what John Smith, in his accounts of Virginia, and later New England, described as "very ranke" and weedy. The Indians lived off the earth as passive nomads. Profit-seeking planters and industrious husbandmen, on the other hand, were needed to cultivate the ground for its riches, and in doing so impose a firm hand.[7]

This powerful conception of land use would play a key role in future categorizations of race and class on the experimental continent. Before they even established new and busy societies, colonizers denoted some people as entrepreneurial stewards of the exploitable land; they declared others (the vast majority) as mere occupiers, a people with no measurable investment in productivity or in commerce.

Whether barren or empty, uncultivated or rank, the land acquired a quintessentially English meaning. The English were obsessed with waste, which was why America was first and foremost a "wasteland" in their eyes. Wasteland meant undeveloped land, land that was outside the circulation of commercial exchange and apart from the understood rules of agricultural production. To lie in waste, in biblical language, meant to exist desolate and unattended; in agrarian terms, it was to be left fallow and unimproved.

Wasteland was idle land. Arable tracts of desirable property could only be associated with furrowed fields, rows of crops and fruit trees, golden waves of grain, and pasture for cattle and sheep. John Smith embraced the same ideological premise with a precise (if crude) allusion: the Englishman's right to the land was ensured by his commitment to carpeting the soil with manure. An English elixir of animal waste would magically transform the Virginia wilderness, making untilled wasteland into valuable English territory. Waste was there to be treated, and then exploited. Waste was wealth as yet unrealized.[8]

In his "Discourse of Western Planting," Hakluyt confidently described the entire continent as that "waste firm of America." Not terra firma, but *waste firm.* He saw natural resources as raw materials that could be converted into valuable commodities. Like other Englishmen of his day, he equated wastelands with commons, forests, and fens—those lands that sixteenth-century agrarian improvers eyed for prospective profits. Wasteland served the interest of private owners in the commercial marketplace, when the commons was enclosed and sheep and cattle grazed there; forests could be cut down for timber and cleared for settle-ments; fens or marshes could be drained and reconstituted as rich, arable farmland.[9]

It was not just land that could be waste. People could be waste too. And this brings us to our most important point of embarkation: Hakluyt's America required what he classified as "waste people," the corps of labor-ers needed to cut down the trees, beat the hemp (for making rope), gather honey, salt and dry fish, dress raw animal hides, dig the earth for minerals, raise olives and silk, and sort and pack bird feathers.[10]

He pictured paupers, vagabonds, convicts, debtors, and lusty young men without employment doing all such work. The "fry [young children] of wandering beggars that grow up idly and hurtfully and burdenous to the Realm, might be unladen and better bred up." Merchants would be sent to trade with the Indians, selling trinkets, venting cloth goods, and gathering more information about the interior of the continent. Artisans were needed: millwrights to process the timber; carpenters, brick mak-ers, and plasterers to build the settlement; cooks, launderers, bakers, tai-lors, and cobblers to service the infant colony.[11]

Where would these workers come from? The artisans, he felt, could be spared without weakening the English economy. But the bulk of the labor force was to come from the swelling numbers of poor and home-less. They were, in Hakluyt's disturbing allusion, "ready to eat up one another," already cannibalizing the British economy. Idle and unused, they were waiting to be transplanted to the American land to be better (albeit no more humanely) put to use.[12]

This view of poverty was widely shared. One persistent project, first promoted in 1580 but never realized, involved raising a fleet of hundred-ton fishing vessels comprising ten thousand men, half of whom were to be impoverished vagrants. The galley labor scheme was designed to beat the famously industrious Dutch at the fishing trade.[13] Leading mathema-tician and geographer John Dee was another who imagined a maritime solution to poverty. In 1577, as the British navy expanded, he proposed converting the poor into sailors. Others wished for the indigent to be swept from the streets, one way or another, whether gathered up as forced laborers building highways and fortifications or herded into pris-ons and workhouses. London's Bridewell Prison was chartered in 1553, the first institution of its kind to propose reformation of vagrants. By the

1570s, more houses of corrections had opened their doors. Their found-ers offered to train the children of the poor to be "brought up in labor and work" so they would not follow in the footsteps of their parents and become "idle rogues."[14]

In this sense, what Hakluyt foresaw in a colonized America was *one giant workhouse*. This cannot be emphasized enough. As the "waste firm of America" was settled, it would become a place where the surplus poor, the waste people of England, could be converted into economic assets. The land and the poor could be harvested together, to add to—rather than continue to subtract from—the nation's wealth. Among the first waves of workers were the convicts, who would be employed at heavy labor, felling trees and burning them for pitch, tar, and soap ash; others would dig in the mines for gold, silver, iron, and copper. The convicts were not paid wages. As debt slaves, they were obliged to repay the English commonwealth for their crimes by producing commodities for export. In return, they would be kept from a life of crime, avoiding, in Hakluyt's words, being "miserably hanged," or packed into prisons to "pitifully pine away" and die.[15]

As he saw it, the larger reward would be reaped in the next genera-tion. By importing raw goods from the New World and exporting cloth and other commodities in return, the poor at home would find work so that "not one poor creature" would feel impelled "to steal, to starve, and beg as they do." They would prosper along with the growth of colonial trade. The children of "wandering beggars," having been "kept from idle-ness, and made able by their own honest and easy labor," would grow up responsibly, "without surcharging others." Children who escaped pau-perism, no longer burdens on the state, might reenter the workforce as honest laborers. The poor fry sent overseas would now be "better bred up," making the lot of the English people better off, and the working poor more industrious. It all sounded perfectly logical and realizable.[16]

Seeing the indigent as wastrels, as the dregs of society, was certainly nothing new. The English had waged a war against the poor, especially vagrants and vagabonds, for generations. A series of laws in the four-teenth century led to a concerted campaign to root out this wretched "mother of all vice." By the sixteenth century, harsh laws and punish-ments were fixed in place. Public stocks were built in towns for runaway servants, along with whipping posts and cages variously placed around

London. Hot branding irons and ear boring identified this underclass and set them apart as a criminal contingent. An act of 1547 allowed for vagrants to be branded with a V on their breasts and enslaved. While this unusual piece of legislation appears never to have been put into practice, it was nonetheless a natural outgrowth of the widespread vilification of the poor.[17]

By 1584, when Hakluyt drafted his "Discourse of Western Planting," the poor were routinely being condemned as "thriftless" and "idle," a diseased and dangerously mobile, unattached people, everywhere running "to and fro over all the realm." Compared to swarms of insects, labeled as an "over-flowing multitude," they were imagined in language as an effluvial current, polluting and taxing England's economic health.[18]

Slums enveloped London. As one observer remarked in 1608, the heavy concentrations of poor created a subterranean colony of dirty and disfigured "monsters" living in "caves." They were accused of breeding rapidly and infecting the city with a "plague" of poverty, thus figuratively designating unemployment a contagious disease. Distant American colonies were presented as a cure. The poor could be purged. In 1622, the famous poet and clergyman John Donne wrote of Virginia in this fashion, describing the new colony as the nation's spleen and liver, draining the "ill humours of the body . . . to breed good bloud." Others used less delicate imagery. American colonies were "emunctories," excreting human waste from the body politic. The elder Richard Hakluyt unabashedly called the transportable poor the "offals of our people."[19]

The poor were human waste. Refuse. The sturdy poor, those without physical injuries, elicited outrage over their idleness. But how could vagabonds, who on average migrated some twenty to eighty miles in a month, be called idle? William Harrison, in his popular *Description of England* (1577), offered an explanation. Idleness was wasted energy. The vagabonds' constant movement led nowhere. In moving around, they failed (like the Indians) to put down healthy roots and join the settled labor force of servants, tenants, and artisans. Harrison thought of idleness in the same way we might today refer to the idling motor of a car: the motor runs in place; the idle poor were trapped in economic stasis. Waste people, like wastelands, were stagnant; their energy produced nothing of value; they were like festering weeds ruining an idle garden.[20]

Wasteland, then, was an eyesore, or what the English called a "sinke hole." Waste people were analogized to weeds or sickly cattle grazing on a dunghill. But unlike the docile herd, which were carefully bred and contained in fenced enclosures, the poor could become disruptive and disorderly; they occasionally rioted. The cream of society could not be shielded from the public nuisance of the poor, in that they seemed omnipresent at funerals, church services, on highways and byways, in alehouses, and they loitered around Parliament—even at the king's court. James I was so annoyed with vagrant boys milling around his palace at Newmarket that he wrote the London-based Virginia Company in 1619 asking for its help in removing the offensive population from his sight by shipping them overseas.[21]

As masterless men, detached and unproductive, the vagrant poor would acquire colonial masters. For Hakluyt and others, a quasi-military model made sense. It had been used in Ireland. In the New World, whether subduing the Native population or contending with other European nations with colonial ambitions, fortifications would have to be raised, trenches dug, gunpowder produced, and men trained to use bows. Militarization served other crucial purposes. Ex-soldiers formed one of the largest subgroups of English vagrants. Sailors were the vagrants of the sea, and were often drawn into piracy. The style of warfare most common in the sixteenth century involved attacks on nearly impregnable fortifications, and required prolonged sieges and large numbers of foot soldiers. Each time war revived, the poor were drummed back into service, becoming what one scholar has called a "reserve army of the unemployed."[22]

The life of the early modern soldier was harsh and unpredictable. Disbanded troops often pillaged on their way home. In the popular literature of the day, soldiers-turned-thieves were the subjects of a number of racy accounts. John Awdeley's *The Fraternity of Vagabonds* (1561) and others of its kind depicted the wandering poor as a vast network of predatory gangs. Ex-soldiers filled empty slots in the gangs as "uprightmen," or bandit leaders. "Cony-catchers" literally bagged their booty. These consummate robbers had as one tool of their trade the hook, which was jammed through open windows in order to steal valuable goods. In proposing to ship "our idle soldiers" overseas, Hakluyt aimed to turn con men into actual cony-catchers, shooting rabbits to give hearty substance to the American colonists' daily stew. In other words, sending veteran soldiers and convicts to America would reduce crime and poverty in one masterstroke.[23]

Whatever else their lives entailed, vagrants, children of beggars, and ex-soldiers who might be transported to the New World and transplanted onto its soil were thought to be fertilizing wasteland with their labor. Their value was calculated not in humane (or even human) terms, but as a disembodied commercial force. If that proposition seems cold and calculating, it was. In death, they were, to use the operative modern phrase, collateral damage. They had more value to the realm as dead colonists than as idle waste in England. In his grand scheme, Hakluyt imagined disciplined children of English beggars who survived in the colonies as nothing more than a future pool of soldiers and sailors.[24]

Planting unwanted people in American soil meant fewer temptations to take up lives of crime. Some might actually thrive in the open, vacant land of America—because surely they had no chance at all in the overpopulated labor market back home. Still, one cannot resist the conclusion that the children of the poor were regarded as recycled waste. Their destiny, once these same folk were "bred up" as soldiers and sailors, was to fill out a colonial reserve army of waste men, to be sent to die in England's wars. Brutal exploitation was the modus operandi of the English projectors who conceived an American colonial system at the end of the sixteenth century—before there were colonies.[25]

When Jamestown, the English outpost along the Chesapeake Bay, was finally founded in 1607, the hardships its settlers experienced proved the general flaw in Hakluyt's blueprint for creating real-life colonies. Defenders of the Virginia Company of London published tracts, sermons, and firsthand accounts, all trying to explain away the many bizarre occurrences that haunted Jamestown. Social mores were nonexistent. Men defecated in public areas within the small garrison. People sat around and starved. Harsh laws were imposed: stealing vegetables and blasphemy were punishable by death. Laborers and their children were virtual commodities, effectively slaves. One man murdered his wife and then ate her.[26]

After the miscarriage of Sir Walter Raleigh's Roanoke, Jamestown was christened England's first infant child. Bidding the English patience with Jamestown, the poet John Donne sermonized in 1622, "Great

Creatures lye long in the Wombe." Jamestown's was a slow, painful birth, attended by scant confidence in its future. That year, a lopsided Indian attack nearly wiped out the entire population.[27]

The pervasive traumas throughout Jamestown's early years are legend. Before 1625, colonists dropped like flies, 80 percent of the first six thousand dying off. Several different military commanders imposed regimes of forced labor that turned the fledgling settlement into a prison camp. Men drawn to Jamestown dreamt of finding gold, which did little to inspire hard work. Not even starvation awoke them from the dream. A new group arrived in 1611, and described how their predecessors wallowed in "sluggish idlenesse" and "beastiall sloth." Yet they fared little better.[28]

There were few "lusty men" in Virginia, to repeat Hakluyt's colorful term. It remained difficult to find recruits who would go out and fell trees, build houses, improve the land, fish, and hunt wild game. The men of early Jamestown were predisposed to play cards, to trade with vile sailors, and to rape Indian women. A glassblower was sent to make colored beads—trinkets to sell to the Indians. This was Hakluyt's idea. But where were the husbandmen needed to raise food?[29]

Impracticality, bad decisions, and failed recruitment strategies left the colony with too few ploughmen and husbandmen to tend the fields and feed the cattle that were being shipped from England. Jamestown lost sight of the English creed expressed in Thomas More's *Utopia* (1516): that every productive society prized its tillers of the earth. More wrote that in failing to promote husbandry, "no commonwealth could hold out a year."[30]

John Rolfe, husband of Pocahontas, took these words to heart. In 1609 he introduced the strain of tobacco from Bermuda that Virginia's settlers succeeded with, and tobacco quickly became the new gold—the ticket to wealth. Its discovery led to a boom economy, bringing high prices for the "filthy weed." Tobacco was at once both a boom and bane. Though it saved the colony from ruin, it stunted the economy and generated a skewed class system. The governing council jealously guarded what soon became the colony's most precious resource: laborers. The only one of Hakluyt's lessons to be carefully heeded was the one they applied with vengeance: exploiting a vulnerable, dependent workforce.[31]

The governor and members of his governing council pleaded with the

Virginia Company to send over more indentured servants and laborers, who, like slaves, were sold to the highest bidder. Indentured servants were hoarded, overworked, and their terms unfairly extended. Land was distributed unequally too, which increased the class divide. Those who settled before 1616, who had paid their own passage, were given one hundred acres; after that date, new arrivals who paid their own way received only fifty acres. More important, from 1618, those who brought over an indentured servant received an additional fifty acres. The head-right system, as it was known, allotted land by counting heads. More bodies in a planter's stable meant more land. Significantly, if a servant died on the voyage over, the owner of the indenture still secured all of his promised acreage. It paid to import laborers, dead or alive.[32]

Contracts of indenture were longer than servant contracts in England—four to nine years versus one to two years. According to a 1662 Virginia law, children remained servants until the age of twenty-four. Indentures were unlike wage contracts: servants were classified as chattels, as movable goods and property. Contracts could be sold, and servants were bound to move where and when their masters moved. Like furniture or livestock, they could be transferred to one's heirs.[33]

The leading planters in Jamestown had no illusion that they were creating a classless society. From 1618 to 1623, a good many orphans from London were shipped to Virginia—most indentured servants who followed in their train were adolescent boys. As a small privileged group of planters acquired land, laborers, and wealth, those outside the inner circle were hard-pressed to escape their lower status. Those who did become poor tenants found that little had changed in their condition; they were often forced do the same work they had done as servants. A sizable number did not survive their years of service. Or as John Smith lamented in his 1624 *Generall Historie of Virginia . . .*, "This dear bought Land with so much bloud and cost, hath onely made some few rich, and all the rest losers."[34]

Among the more insidious practices in the colony, wives and children were held accountable for their husband's or father's indentured period of labor. After the Natives attacked in 1622, a colonist named Jane Dickenson was held by them in captivity for ten months. When she returned to Jamestown, she was told that she owed 150 pounds of tobacco to her husband's former master. Unable to pay, she would be forced to work off her dead husband's unmet obligations. She appealed to the governor, writing that her treatment was identical to the "slavery" she experienced among the "cruel savages." Had English civilization been sacrificed in this colonial wasteland? That was Dickenson's unspoken message. Nor was her treatment unusual. John Smith acknowledged in his *Generall Historie* that "fatherless children" were left "in little better condition than slaves, for if their Parents die in debt, their children are made bondmen till the debt be discharged."[35]

The leaders of Jamestown had borrowed directly from the Roman model of slavery: abandoned children and debtors were made slaves. When indentured adults sold their anticipated labor in return for passage to America, they instantly became debtors, which made their orphaned children a collateral asset. It was a world not unlike the one Shakespeare depicted in *The Merchant of Venice,* when Shylock demanded his pound of flesh. Virginia planters felt entitled to their flesh and blood in the forms of the innocent spouses and offspring of dead servants.[36]

If civilization was to be firmly planted, Jamestown would have to be given the look of a normal English village, along with efforts to promote good habits among the people. The colony needed to shed its image as a penal colony and to plant firmer roots. It needed more than tobacco. It needed herds of cattle, fields of crops, and improved relations between masters and servants. Most of all, it needed many more marriageable women. In 1620 the Virginia Company sent to the colony fifty-seven "young, handsome, and honestlie educated Maides." Over the next three years, 157 more women made the crossing. They were thought of as emissaries of a new moral order. Company records hint at something else as well: the "greatest hindrances" to "Noble worke" rested on "want of comforts"; men deserved to "live contentedlie." The transportation of female cargo would "tye and roote the Planters myndes to Virginia by the bonds of wives and children." Sexual satisfaction and heirs to provide for would make slothful men into more productive colonists.

All that was required of the women was that they marry. Their prospective husbands were expected to buy them, that is, to defray the cost of passage and provisions. Each woman was valued at 150 pounds of tobacco, which was the same price exacted from Jane Dickenson when she eventually purchased her freedom. Not surprisingly, then, with their value calculated in tobacco, women in Virginia were treated as fertile commodities. They came with testimonials to their moral character, impressing on "industrious Planters" that they were not being sold a bad bill of goods. One particular planter wrote that an earlier shipment of females was "corrupt," and he expected a new crop that was guaranteed healthy and favorably disposed for breeding. Accompanying the female cargo were some two hundred head of cattle, a reminder that the Virginia husbandman needed both species of breeding stock to recover his English roots.[37]

Despite everything, Jamestown never became a stable agrarian community. The Virginia plantation remained strangely barren during the first half of the seventeenth century. First, the anticipated harvest of the region's natural resources did not occur. Nor did the various ranks and stations (balancing skilled laborers and manual workers) form according to plan. As late as 1663, Governor William Berkeley was still advocating for the goods Hakluyt had proposed: flax and hemp, timber and tar for ships, and exotics such as silk and olive oil. The "vicious ruinous plant of Tobacco," as Berkeley condemned it, left Virginia without a diversified economy.[38]

At the heart of the Jamestown system was the indentured contract that made laborers disposable property. In so harsh an environment, survival was difficult, and the unappreciated waste people were literally worked to death. Young men and boys who came without families were the most vulnerable and most exploited of all. Unable to plant roots, many failed to produce heirs and secure the cherished English ideal of attachment to the land.

Class divisions were firmly entrenched. The ever-widening gap in land ownership elevated large planters into a small, privileged faction. At the same time, the labor system reduced servants to debt slaves, and, living so far from home, they had little recourse to demand better treatment. Isolation, then, increased the potential for abuse. The only liberty for colonial servants came with their feet—by running away. Jamestown's founders reproduced no English villages. Instead, they fashioned a ruthless class order.

Despite Jamestown's intractable problems, a group of English investors and religious separatists secured a patent from the Virginia Company and set their sights on land near the mouth of the Hudson River. Whether by accident or, as some have speculated, by secret design, their first ship, the *Mayflower*, landed on Cape Cod, beyond the purview of the Virginia Company, in 1620. The small, struggling band lost half their number to starvation and disease during the first year. The wife of one of the leaders, William Bradford, mysteriously disappeared over the side of the *Mayflower*. It would be a full decade before the English settlers in Massachusetts made significant inroads in attracting new settlers to the region.[39]

When the mass migration of 1630 did take place, it was the well-organized John Winthrop who led a fleet of eleven ships, loaded with seven hundred passengers and livestock, and bearing a clear objective to plant a permanent community. Far more intact families migrated to the colony than had to Virginia, and a core of the settlers were Puritans who did not need the threat of a death sentence to attend church services on the Sabbath—one of the many examples of heavy-handedness practiced in the early days of Jamestown.

Land ownership was New England's most tempting lure. During its first decade, the Bay Colony received some twenty-one thousand settlers, only about 40 percent of whom came from East Anglia and the coastal towns where a high percentage of Puritan converts lived. For every religious dissenter in the exodus of the 1630s, there was one commercially driven emigrant from London or other areas of England. The majority in these years came as extended families accompanied by their servants. And almost 60 percent of the arrivals were under the age of twenty-four—one-third of them unattached males.[40]

When Winthrop defended the colony, he wanted to create a religious community that would be saved from the "corrupted" bastions of learning, Oxford and Cambridge. Beyond fighting corruption and the Catholic antichrist, however, the new governor proved himself a pragmatic man. To attract settlers, he boasted that the amount of money required for purchasing a few measly acres in England translated into hundreds of acres in Massachusetts. In overpopulated Britain, he said, the land "groaneth under her inhabitants." Nevertheless, Winthrop had no plan for redeeming all the poor, whom he referred to as the "scum of the land." His vision of vile waste people differed little from that of the Anglican cleric Richard Hakluyt's.[41]

Inequality was a given in the "Citty upon a Hill," submission was regarded as a natural condition of humankind. In "A Model of Christian Charity," Winthrop declared that some were meant to rule, others to serve their betters: "God Almightie in his most holy and wise providence hath soe disposed the Condition of mankind, as in all times some must be rich some poore, some highe and eminent in power and dignitie; others meane and in subjeccion." Lest there be any doubt, Governor Winthrop despised democracy, which he brusquely labeled "the meanest and worst of all forms of Government." For Puritans, the church and state worked in tandem; the coercive arm of the magistracy was meant to preserve both public order and class distinctions.[42]

In Puritan society, the title of "gentleman" usually applied to men with some aristocratic pedigree, though wealthy merchants who held prominent positions in the church could acquire the same designation. "Master" or "Mister" and "Mistress" were for educated professionals, clergymen, and their wives. "Goodman" attached to the honorable husbandman, who owned land but did not occupy a prominent position as magistrate or minister. New Englanders used these titles sparingly, but they were certainly conscious of them; the government they abided by, after all, imitated English county oligarchies in which the landed elite monopolized government offices.[43]

The Puritan elite depended on a menial labor force. At the top of the pecking order were apprentices and hired servants. Lower down were those forced into servitude because of debt or after having committed a crime, as we have seen in Virginia. Case in point: in 1633, Winthrop presided over the trial of a man accused of robbery. Upon conviction, his estate was sold and used to repay his victims. He was then bound for three years of service, and his daughter, as added collateral, bound for fourteen. This was typical. The 1648 *Laws and Liberties* established two classes of an even lower order who could be divested of liberty: Indians captured in "just wars," and "strangers as willingly sell themselves, or are sold to us." The "strangers," in this case, were indentured servants from *outside* the colony as well as imported African slaves.[44]

For servants, seventeenth-century New Englanders relied most heavily on exploitable youth, male and female, ages ten to twenty-one. By law, single men and women were required to reside with families and submit to family government. Children were routinely "put out" to labor in the homes of neighbors and relatives. The 1642 Massachusetts General

Court's order for the proper education of children treated apprentice, servant, and child as if all were interchangeable. Parents and masters alike assumed responsibility to "breed & bring up children & apprentices in some honest Lawfull calling." Family supervision policed those who might otherwise become "rude, stubborn & unruly."[45]

Monitoring the labor of one's own offspring became the norm, as landed families retained control over the males well into adulthood. Young men could not leave the family estate, nor escape their father's rule, without endangering their inheritance. So family members worked long hours, as did servants of various ranks. While the extended Puritan family functioned with less recurrence to acts of ruthlessness than the system adopted during the tobacco boom in Virginia, legal and cultural practices muddied the distinction between son and servant.[46]

Thus the Puritan family was at no time the modern American nuclear family, or anything close. It was often composed of children of different parents, because one or another parent was likely to die young, making remarriage quite common. Winthrop fathered sixteen children with four different wives, the last of whom he married at age fifty-nine, two years before his death. Most households also contained child servants who were unrelated to the patriarch; during harvest season, hired servants were brought in as temporary workers, and poor children were purchased for longer terms as menial apprentices for domestic service or farmwork. The first slave cargo arrived in Boston in 1638. Winthrop, for his part, owned Indian slaves; his son purchased an African.[47]

While servants were expected to be submissive, few actually were. Numerous court cases show masters complaining of their servants' disobedience, accompanied by charges of idleness, theft, rudeness, rebelliousness, pride, and a proclivity for running away. In 1696, the powerful minister Cotton Mather published *A Good Master Well Served*, which was an unambiguous attempt to regulate the Bay Colony's disorderly servant population. Directing his words toward those who served, he insisted, "You are the *Animate, Separate, Active Instruments* of other men." In language that is impossible to misunderstand, he reaffirmed, "*Servants,* your *Tongues,* your *Hands,* your *Feet,* are your *Masters,* and they should move according to the Will of your *Masters.*" Those of mean descent would learn from a sharp tongue or a ready whip that submission was expected of them.[48]

Puritan wariness did not end there. Among servants, and those of "meane condition" above them, were men and women of enlarged ambition who were deemed undeserving. At least according to anxious oligarchs. Puritans never opposed commerce or the acquisition of wealth, but they were clearly conflicted when it came to social mobility. The government enacted sumptuary laws, penalizing those who wore rich silks or gold buttons in an attempt to rise above their class station. Overly prosperous people aroused envy, and Puritan orthodoxy dictated against such exhibition of arrogance, pride, and insolence. In the 1592 tract *On the Right, Lawful, and Holy Use of Apparel,* the English Puritan clergyman William Perkins had shown how appearance demarcated one's standing in the Great Chain of Being, God's class hierarchy. Unsanctioned displays of finery were disruptive, an infraction on the same order as masters who treated servants too leniently. Both were perceived as early indicators of a society falling from grace.[49]

One had to know his or her place in Puritan Massachusetts. Church membership added a layer of privilege before the courts and elsewhere to an already hierarchical regime. Expulsion from the church carried a powerful stigma. Heretics such as Anne Hutchinson and Mary Dyer were physically banished, cut off and ostracized. Only those who begged forgiveness and humbled themselves before the dual authority of court and church returned to the community. Dyer returned unrepentant, determined to challenge the ruling order. Between 1659 and 1661, she and three other Quakers were charged with "presumptuous & incorrigible contempt" of civil authority. After trial, they were summarily hanged.[50]

Anne Hutchinson was excommunicated from the Boston congregation and expelled from the Bay Colony in 1638 for refusing to bend to the authority of the town fathers. She was sternly advised: "You have rather been a Husband than a Wife and a preacher than a Hearer, and a Magistrate than a Subject." Hutchinson had held religious classes in her home, and had acquired a large following. Turning the social order upside down, she had undermined the carefully orchestrated moral geography of the Puritan meetinghouse. Male dominance was unquestioned, and ranks so clearly spelled out, that no one could miss the power outlined in something so simple as a seating chart. Members and nonmembers sat apart; husbands and wives were divided; men sat on one side of the room, women on the other. Prominent men occupied the first two rows of benches: the first was reserved exclusively for magistrates, the second for the families of the minister and governor, as well as wealthy merchants. The more sons a man had, the better his pew. Age, reputation, marriage, and estate were all properly calculated before a church seat was assigned.[51]

Puritans were obsessed with class rank. It meant security to them, and they could not disguise the anxiety that even the thought of its disruption—or dissolution—produced. After the bloodletting of King Philip's War (1675–76), Mary Rowlandson's cautionary tale, *The Sovereignty and Goodness of God*, appeared widely in print, offering up a forceful example of the role of class at a susceptible moment of rebuilding. At the outset of the war, Narragansett Indians dragged Rowlandson from her burning house in Lancaster, Massachusetts, and held her as a prisoner for eleven weeks. Her 1682 account detailed the psychological struggle she had endured as she sought to preserve her identity as a member of the English gentry after being forced into servitude by her Indian captors. As the wife of a minister and the daughter of a wealthy landowner, Rowlandson told a double story: on one level it was a journey of spiritual redemption, on another a tale of the loss of breeding, followed by the former prisoner's restoration to her previous class rank.[52]

Rowlandson's Indian mistress is the story's villain. Weetamoo was a powerful sachem (queen) of the Pocasset Wampanoags who had inherited her station after displaying the savvy to marry three other prominent sachems. Dressed in girdles of wampum beads, wrapped in thick petticoats, and adorned with bracelets, Weetamoo spent hours on her toilette. A "severe and proud dame," she ordered Rowlandson around and slapped her. In Rowlandson's eyes, her detested mistress was the Indian equivalent of the English noblewoman, a royalist of the New World who flaunted her power. Submission—the same quality Puritans demanded of their own servants—did not come easily to Rowlandson. The once-proud minister's wife had been reduced to a lowly maidservant. In this way, she did not equate the Natives with primitive savages, as the captive Jane Dickenson did in Virginia; instead they were usurpers and posers, who grossly violated the divine order of assigned stations.[53]

The Puritans used family authority, reinforced by the law, to regulate their servant population. Distrustful of strangers and religious outsiders, they also granted privileges to the religious "Elect," or those who comprised the core constituency of the church laity. Children of the Elect gained the inherited religious privilege of an easier path to church membership. Indeed, the "halfway covenant" of 1662 established a system of religious pedigree. As Cotton Mather's long-lived father, Reverend Increase Mather, put it: God "cast the line of Election" so that it passed "through the loins of godly Parents." Excommunication alone ended this privilege, saving the flock from a corrupt lineage. Minister Thomas Shepard agreed, projecting that a child of the Elect would be pruned, nurtured, and watered so as to grow in grace. By this method, religious station reinforced class station. And by celebrating lineage, the visible saints became a recognizable breed.[54]

Colonizing schemes all drew on the language of breeding. Fertility had to be monitored, literally and figuratively, under the watchful supervision of household and town fathers. This was the case in disciplining unruly children, corralling servants, and dispensing religious membership privileges to the next generation (i.e., the offspring of the godly). Good breeding practices tamed otherwise unmanageable waste, whether it was wasteland or waste people; breeding sustained the pastoral tradition already associated with the Elizabethan age, which found its best literary expression in testaments to rustic beauty and cosmic harmony.

What separated rich from poor was that the landless had nothing to pass on. They had no heirs. This was particularly true in Jamestown, where the orphans of dead servants were sold off like the possessions of a foreclosed estate. As "beggarly spawn," the poor were detached from the land. Only proper stewards of the fertile ground deserved rights.

It was something more than a figure of speech to describe the lovely Indian princess Pocahontas, the mother of America, as a child of nature who had married into the English community. A common trope had it that English explorers "married" the land they discovered. Marriage implied custodial authority, a sovereign right to a corner of the earth. In dedicating a book to Sir Walter Raleigh in 1587, Hakluyt the younger reminded his patron of the "sweet embraces" of Virginia, "that fairest of nymphs," whom the queen had conferred upon him as his bride. The land patent was thus a marriage contract.[55]

Visual images likewise celebrated the fecundity of the land. In Flemish artist Jan van der Straet's classic drawing *The Discovery of America*

(1575), exploration was metaphorically a sexual encounter. Depicting Amerigo Vespucci's landing in the New World, the artist has the explorer standing erect, surrounded by ships and tools of navigation, while a plump, naked Indian woman lies languidly on a hammock before him, extending her hand. English writers took up the same potent theme, claiming that the feminine figure of North America was stretching out her hand (and land) to "England onelie," her favored suitor.[56]

The richest embellishment of New World fertility came from the pen of Thomas Morton, whose *New English Canaan, or New Canaan, containing an abstract of New England* (1637) offered humorous double entendres amid lush descriptions of the land. Historians are divided over what to make of the controversial Morton. Some reckon him a scoundrel and libertine, while others regard him as a populist critic of Governor John Winthrop and the Puritan establishment.[57]

He arrived in 1624, with thirty servants in tow, and set himself up on a pastoral manorial estate. From there he established an outpost to trade in furs with Native tribes. He served as a lawyer in defense of a royal patent pursued by other non-Puritan investors to the northern part of New England. But he also battled Winthrop's Puritans, was arrested three times, had his goods confiscated and his house burned down. He was banished from the colony twice, writing *New English Canaan* while in exile in England, where he worked (unsuccessfully) at getting the Massachusetts Bay Colony's patent revoked.[58]

His dislike of the Puritans is manifest in his observations about their use of the land. They were no better than "moles," he wrote, blindly digging into the earth without appreciating its natural pleasures. It bothered him that the Puritans had no real interest in the Native people beyond converting them. He dismissed Winthrop and his followers as "effeminate"—as bad husbands of the land. He satirized the Puritans in *New English Canaan* as sexually impotent second husbands to a widowed land, which Morton (who had married a widow himself) and his business associates could rescue. They were ready to move in on the incompetent Puritans—strutting nearby, attractive and decidedly more virile lovers waiting in the wings.

Morton's New England landscape contained "ripe grapes" supported by "lusty trees," "dainty fine round rising hillocks," and luscious streams that made "so sweet a murmuring noise to hear as would ever lull the senses with delightful sleep." He connected fertility to pleasure in the prevailing medical context: women, it was said, were more likely to conceive if they experienced sexual satisfaction. Morton was so consumed with the fertility of the physical environment that he marveled at the apparent ease with which Indian women became pregnant. The region's animals were especially generative too, with wild does bearing two or three fawns at a time. With fewer women and a shorter history, New England had produced more children than Virginia, at least according to Morton. He could not resist including in his *New English Canaan* the strange story of the "barren doe," a single woman from Virginia who was unable to conceive a child until she traveled north.[59]

As compelling as these passages are, Morton was actually stealing from earlier accounts. Ralph Hamor had written apocryphally in 1614 that in Virginia, lions, bears, and deer usually had three or four offspring at a time. This was the fulfillment of Hakluyt's claim that Raleigh's bride Virginia would "bring forth new and most abundant offspring." Others would repeat similar claims. In *A New Voyage to Carolina* (1709), John Lawson contended that "women long married without children in other places, have removed to Carolina and become joyful mothers." They had an "easy Travail in their child-bearing, in which they are so happy, as seldom miscarry." The argument went that happy, healthy European women moved closer to nature in America. Like deer in the wild, women in the New World became instinctive, docile breeders.[60]

Breeding had a place in more than one market. In Virginia and elsewhere in the Chesapeake region in the early seventeenth century, a gender imbalance of six to one among indentured servants gave women arriving from England an edge in the marriage exchange. Writing of Maryland in 1660, former indentured servant George Alsop claimed that women just off the boat found a host of men fighting for their attention. Females could pick and choose: even servants had a shot at marrying a well-heeled planter. Alsop called such unions "copulative marriage," through which women sold their breeding capacity to wealthy husbands. In language that was decidedly uninhibited, he wrote that women went to "market with their virginity." Another promoter, writing about Carolina, went so far as to say that a woman could find a husband in America no matter what she looked like. If, newly arrived, she appeared "Civil" and was "under 50 years of Age," some man would purchase her for his wife.[61]

"Copulative marriage" was one option, remarriage another. Men of Jamestown found they could increase their acreage and add to the sum of laborers by marrying a widow whose husband had bequeathed land to her. In the scramble to get land and laborers during the tobacco boom, members of the council devised various means to get their hands on land—and not always ethically. One man married a woman because her first husband shared the last name of a wealthier dead man. He scammed the system by confusing the two names in order to get title to the more desirable property. Widows were obvious conduits of wealth and land, and with high mortality rates prevailing throughout the seventeenth century, those who survived rampant disease would likely have married two or three times.[62]

Battles over class interests, land, and widows came naturally to Virginians, and at times grew quite deadly. Bacon's Rebellion of 1676 was one of the greatest conflicts the colony witnessed. It pitted a stubborn governor, William Berkeley, against Nathaniel Bacon, a recent immigrant of some means but also of frustrated ambition. Historians still debate the causes of the crisis and its ultimate meaning, but there is ample evidence to show that the participants made it about class warfare. Bacon wanted Berkeley to launch attacks on a tribe of Indians who ostensibly threatened the more socially vulnerable people of Virginia's frontier, and he made himself a leader of the disaffected. A power struggle ensued.

To the governor in Jamestown, only the meanest of men, those who had recently "crept" out of indentured servitude, could find common cause with the rebels. Berkeley dismissed Bacon as an upstart and a demagogue. Other prominent supporters of the governor called the rebels "ye scum of the country" and—here is where the language gets especially evocative—"offscourings" of society. "Offscourings" (human fecal waste) was one of the most common terms of derision for indentured servants and England's wandering vagrants. Meanwhile, landholders who sided with Bacon were summarily dismissed as "Idle" men, whose "debauchery" and "ill husbandry" had led them into debt. The rebels were directly compared to swine rooting around in the muck.[63]

Slaves and servants joined Bacon's force too, being promised their freedom after the expected showdown with Berkeley. Nothing like this had occurred in Virginia before. Slavery had been slow to take hold, with only around 150 slaves counted in 1640, and barely 1,000 out of a total population of 26,000 in 1670. Massachusetts and English possessions in the Caribbean, not Virginia, were the first colonies to codify slave law. By the time of Bacon's Rebellion, there were some 6,000 servants in the southern colony, and roughly one-third of all freeholders, many of them former indentured servants, were barely scraping by, weighed down by debts and unfair taxes. Indeed, Governor Berkeley had thought even before Bacon's challenge that a prospective foreign invasion or large-scale attack by Indians would automatically devolve into class warfare. The "Poor Endebted Discontented and Armed" would, he wrote, use the opportunity to "plunder the Country" and seize the property of the elite planters.[64]

The struggle also was concerned as well with the status of friendly Indians residing in the sprawling colony. Bacon claimed that Berkeley and the men around him were protecting their own lucrative trade with preferred tribes instead of saving frontier settlers from raids and reprisals. Taxing colonists for forts made of mud were not only useless, the rebels held, but were yet another means for Berkeley's "Juggling Parasites" in the Assembly to increase taxes without offering meaningful protection in return. Virginians living farther from the capital (and coast) felt they were not reaping the same advantages from the land that the wealthier planters in older parts of the colony were. As one drifted west from the seat of power, class identity felt less secure.[65]

It is likely that a fair number among Bacon's following wanted to push the Indians off desirable lands, or felt an impulse to lash out against them in retaliation for recent frontier attacks. There is little doubt that a sizable number of Bacon's men were frustrated by declining tobacco prices amid an economic downturn that made it more difficult to acquire good land. Valuable acreage was hoarded by those whom one contemporary called the "Land lopers," who bought up (or lopped off) large tracts without actually settling them. The "lopers" had inside connections to the governor. Discontent was unavoidable when men were unable to support their families on the little land they had.[66]

The problems faced in 1676 were not new, nor would they ever disappear from the American vocabulary of class. Distance from power intensified feelings of vulnerability or loss. Bacon died of dysentery the same year the rebellion began, and Berkeley was gratified to learn that his adversary met his maker covered in lice—a cruel commentary on the filth and disease that attached to an enemy of the ruling class. It is worth repeating that although Bacon himself was from an elite family, he consorted with the dregs of society; his lice-covered body proved he had become one of them. Some of his followers were executed, while others died in prison. Berkeley did not escape untarnished either. He was escorted by troops to England to face an official inquiry. He died in London, outlasting Bacon by only eight months.[67]

Nor was the power struggle confined to strong-willed men. The wives of the mutineers also assumed a prominent role in the rebellion. Elizabeth Bacon defended her husband's actions in a letter to her sister-in-law in England, hoping to build a metropolitan defense for his frontier cause. Because she came from a prominent family, her words had weight. Other women who vocally supported the resistance were heard as well. The "news wives" told everyone within their circle that the governor planned to take everything they owned (down to their last cow or pig) if they failed to pay a new round of taxes. Beyond spreading seditious rumors of this kind, women assumed a symbolic role in the conflict. At one point, Bacon rounded up the wives of Berkeley supporters—his phalanx of "white aprons"—to guard his men while they dug trenches outside the fortified capital of Jamestown. The women were meant to represent a neutral zone (white aprons standing in for a white flag, the sign of truce). They were too valuable a resource for either side to waste.[68]

One of the most dramatic moments in the trial of the rebels involved Lydia Chisman. In a scene that resembled Pocahontas's dramatic gesture (whether or not true) to save John Smith, Chisman offered up her own life for that of her husband, confessing that she had urged him to defy the governor. Her plea fell on deaf ears, and her husband, who was probably tortured, died in prison. While Berkeley damned Chisman as a whore, the female rebels were largely able to avoid the most severe penalties. In English law, the wife and children of a traitor were subject to an attainder in blood—the loss of all property and titles. But widows Bacon and Chisman were permitted to regain their estates. Both remarried, Bacon twice and Chisman once.[69]

How could such a catastrophe occur and yet the women evade punishment? Though Governor Berkeley had hoped to confiscate as much property as he could from the rebels, his reckless pursuit of vengeance led to his downfall. The royal commissioners, their authority reinforced by the ships and troops sent to quell the rebellion, quickly turned against the governor. They insisted that the king's pardon was universal, they overturned many of Berkeley's confiscations, and they called for his removal. To preserve the colony, peace and justice had to be restored. One of the ways to restore order was to show mercy to rebellious wives.[70]

These facts matter. Keeping the land and widows in circulation was more important to the royal commissioners than impoverishing unrepentant women. In 1690, English playwright Aphra Behn wrote a comedy based on Bacon's Rebellion, aptly titled *The Widow Ranter*. The plot centers on a lowborn, promiscuous, cross-dressing, tobacco-smoking widow (she wrongly thinks smoking is a sign of good breeding) who twice marries above her station. Despite her uncouth ways, she knows her worth. As she tells a newcomer to the colony, "We rich Widdows are the best Commodity this Country affords."[71]

Fertility was greatly prized in colonial America. Good male custodians were needed to husband the land's wealth. Widows were expected to quickly remarry so that their land did not go to waste. Some women used this practice to their advantage. Lady Frances Culpeper Stevens Berkeley Ludwell (1634–95) married three colonial governors, including William Berkeley. She bore no children and was consequently able to keep a tight rein on the proceeds of the estates she inherited. She husbanded the land instead of allowing her trio of husbands to control her. Nevertheless, Lady Berkeley was a highly controversial figure during Bacon's Rebellion, blamed for egging on her husband and behaving as a treacherous Jezebel by sexually manipulating the much older man.[72]

Husbanding fertile women remained central to colonial concepts of class and property. This dictate became even more fixed as Virginians began to regulate the offspring of slave women. In a law passed in 1662, a slave was defined not only by place of origin, or as a heathen, but also for being born to an enslaved woman. In the wording of the statute, a law without any British precedent, "condition of the mother" determined whether a child was slave or free. It was Roman law that provided the basis for treating slave children as the property of masters; the English law of bastardy served as a model for children following the condition of the mother. It was the case that a slave followed the condition of the mother as far back as Saint Thomas Aquinas. The analogy Aquinas used associated the womb with the land: if a man visited the island of another man, and sowed his seed in another man's land, the owner still had a right to the produce. The 1662 Virginia law could as easily have been based on a breeder's model: the calves of the cow were the property of the owner, even if the male bull belonged to someone else.[73]

Fertility played an equally significant role in defining women's and men's places in society. A woman's breeding capacity was a calculable natural resource meant to be exploited and a commodity exchanged in marriage. For slave women, fertile capacity made the womb an article of commerce and slave children chattel—movable property, like cattle. (The word "chattel" comes from the same Latin root as "cattle.") Slave children were actually listed in the wills of planters as "breedings," and a slave woman's potential to breed was denoted as "future increase," a term that applied to livestock as well.[74]

At the opening of the century of settlement, English philosopher Francis Bacon noted in 1605 that wives were for "generation, fruit, and comfort." To compare a woman's body to arable land that produced fruit made perfect sense to his readers. The act of propagation and issue encompassed children as much as calves, alike valued as the generation of good stock. Women and land were for the use and benefit of man.[75]

Land held power because of its extent, potential for settlement, and future increase. Knowing how to master the land's fruitfulness was the true definition of class power. It is important that we understand Bacon's Rebellion for what it revealed: *the most promising land was never equally available to all.* The "Parasites" who encircled Governor Berkeley held a decided advantage. Inherited station was mediated by political connections or the good fortune of marrying into a profitable inheritance. By 1700, indentured servants no longer had much of a chance to own land. They had to move elsewhere or become tenants. The royal surveyors made sure that large planters had first bids on new, undeveloped land, and so the larger tracts were increasingly concentrated in fewer hands. Then, as more shipments of slaves arrived in the colony, these too were monopolized by the major landholding families.[76]

For all their talk of loving the land, Virginians were less skilled in the art of husbandry than their English counterparts. Few ploughs were used in seventeenth-century Virginia. The simple hoe was the principal tool in the raising of tobacco, an implement that demanded considerable human labor. The majority of those who landed on American shores did not live long enough to own land, let alone to master it. Slavery was thus a logical outgrowth of the colonial class system imagined by Hakluyt. It emerged from three interrelated phenomena: harsh labor conditions, the treatment of indentures as commodities, and, most of all, the deliberate choice to breed children so that they should become an exploitable pool of workers.

Waste men and waste women (and especially waste children, the adolescent boys who comprised a majority of the indentured servants) were an expendable class of laborers who made colonization possible. The so-called wasteland of colonial America might have had the makings of a New Canaan. Instead, waste people wasted away, fertilizing the soil with their labor while finding it impossible to harvest any social mobility.

CHAPTER TWO
John Locke's Lubberland

❦

The Settlements of Carolina and Georgia

> Surely there is no place in the World where the Inhabitants live with less Labour than in N[orth] Carolina. It approaches nearer to the Description of Lubberland than any other, by the great felicity of the Climate, the easiness of raising Provisions, and the Slothfulness of the People.
>
> —William Byrd II, "History of the Dividing Line" (1728)

When Americans think of the renowned English Enlightenment thinker John Locke, what comes to mind is how Thomas Jefferson tacitly borrowed his words and ideas for the Declaration of Independence. Locke's well-known phrase "Life, Liberty and Estate" was transformed by the Virginian into "life, liberty and the pursuit of happiness." Locke was the must-read of every educated man, woman, and child in the British American colonies. Called the "great and glorious asserter of natural Rights and Liberties of Mankind," he was responsible for more than the *Two Treatises of Government* (1689), which became the playbook of American Revolutionaries. Most important for our present consideration, he authored the *Fundamental Constitutions of Carolina* (1669), which granted that "every Freeman in Carolina shall have ABSOLUTE POWER AND AUTHORITY over his Negro Slaves." As one of his loudest critics exclaimed in 1776, "Such was the language of the humane Mr. Locke!" Nor was this surprising. For Locke was a founding member and third-largest stockholder of the Royal African Company, which secured a monopoly over the British slave trade. His relationship to Carolinian slavery was more than incidental.[1]

In 1663, King Charles II of England issued a colonial charter to eight men, whom he named the "absolute Lords and proprietors" of Carolina. They were given extensive powers to fortify, settle, and govern the colony. Two years later, the first surveyor sized up the northeastern part of the colony, Albemarle County, named after one of the proprietors,

George Monck, Duke of Albemarle. But it would take another powerful proprietor, Lord Anthony Ashley Cooper, Earl of Shaftesbury, to fashion a more recognizable political design of his "darling" Carolina.[2]

Shaftesbury held a powerful position in London as head of the Council of Trade and Foreign Plantations, and he encouraged Locke to join him in the colonial venture. Through Shaftesbury, then, Locke secured the post of secretary of the Council of Trade, and he became the private secretary of the Lords Proprietors, which obliged him to open a correspondence with agents in Carolina and to forward instructions to them. Though he never set foot on American soil, Locke was given the concocted title of "Landgrave," and forty-eight thousand acres of Carolina land was conferred on him for his services. With his intimate knowledge of the colony and his wide reading on the New World generally, Locke undoubtedly had a decisive hand in drafting the inherently illiberal *Fundamental Constitutions*.[3]

The *Fundamental Constitutions* did more than endorse slavery. It was a manifesto promoting a semifeudalistic and wholly aristocratic society. Much ink was spilled in devising a colonial kingdom that conferred favor upon titled elites and manor lords. It was on the basis of a fixed class hierarchy that the precious commodity of land was allocated. Each new county was divided into sections: one-fifth of the land was automatically reserved for proprietors, another fifth for the colonial nobility, and three-fifths for untitled manor lords and freeholders.[4]

The eight proprietors comprised a supreme ruling body of the Palatine Court, which had an absolute veto over all laws. Governing powers were left in the hands of the Grand Council, run by the local nobility and the proprietors, and it was this body that had sole authority for proposing legislation. A top-heavy colonial parliament consisted of proprietors or their deputies, all of the hereditary nobility of the colony, and one freeholder from each precinct. The constitution made clear that power rested at the top and that every effort had been made to "avoid erecting a numerous democracy."[5]

Class structure preoccupied Locke the constitutionalist. He endowed the nobility of the New World with such unusual titles as landgraves and caciques. The first of these was derived from the German word for prince; the latter was Spanish for an American Indian chieftain. Both described a hereditary peerage separate from the English system, and an imperial shadow elite whose power rested in colonial estates or through commercial trade. A court of heraldry was added to this strange brew: in overseeing marriages and maintaining pedigree, it provided further evidence of the intention to fix (and police) class identity. Pretentious institutions such as these hardly suited the swampy backwater of Carolina, but in the desire to impose order on an unsettled land, every detail mattered—down to assigning overblown names to ambitious men in the most rustic outpost of the British Empire.[6]

Yet even the faux nobility was not as strange as another feature of the Locke-endorsed *Constitutions*. That dubious honor belongs to the nobility and manor lord's unique servant class, ranked above slaves but below freemen. These were the "Leet-men," who were encouraged to marry and have children but were tied to the land and to their lord. They could be leased and hired out to others, but they could not leave their lord's service. Theirs, too, was a hereditary station: "All the children of Leet-men shall be Leet-men, so to all generations," the *Constitutions* stated. The heirs of estates inherited not just land, buildings, and belongings, but the hapless Leet-men as well.[7]

More than some anachronistic remnant of the feudal age, Leet-men represented Locke's awkward solution to rural poverty. Locke did not call them villains, though they possessed many of the attributes of serfs. He instead chose the word "Leet-men," which in England at this time meant something very different: unemployed men entitled to poor relief. Locke, like many successful Britons, felt contempt for the vagrant poor in England. He disparaged them for their "idle and loose way of breeding up," and their lack of morality and industry. There were poor families already in Carolina, as Locke knew, who stood in the way of the colony's growth and collective wealth. In other words, Locke's Leet-men would not be charity cases, pitied or despised, but a permanent and potentially productive peasant class—yet definitely an underclass.[8]

But did Leet-men ever exist? Shaftesbury's Carolina plantation, which was run by his agent, had slaves, indentured servants, and Leet-men of a sort. In 1674, the absent owner instructed his agent to hire laborers as "Leet-men," emphasizing that by their concurrence to this arrangement he could retain rights to the workers' "progeny." In this way, Shaftesbury saw children as key to his hereditary class system—as did his colonial predecessors in Virginia and Massachusetts.[9]

The *Fundamental Constitutions* was really a declaration of war against poor settlers. In the 1650s, even before King Charles had issued the Carolina charter, Virginia's imperious governor, William Berkeley, had been selling land grants. The first surveyor reported that most of the Virginia émigrés in Carolina territory were not legitimate patent holders at all. They were poor squatters. The surveyor warned that the infant Carolina colony would founder if more "Rich men" were not recruited, that is, men who could build homes and run productive plantations. Landless trespassers (who were not servants) promised only widespread "leveling," by which the surveyor meant a society shorn of desirable class divisions.[10]

Locke agreed. Poor Virginians threatened to drag down the entire colony. Shaftesbury, too, believed that everything should be done to discourage "Lazy or debauched" men and their families from settling in Carolina. The proprietors definitely did not want a colony overrun with former indentured servants. They did not want Virginia's refuse. In their grand scheme, Leet-men were intended to take the place of those who lived off the land without contributing to the coffers of the ruling elite. Serfs, in short, were better than those "lazy lubbers," meaning stupid, clumsy oafs, the word that came to describe the vagrant poor of Carolina.[11]

Locke's invention of the Leet-men explains a lot. It enables us to piece together the curious history of North Carolina, to demonstrate why this colony lies at the heart of our white trash story. The difficult terrain that spanned the border with Virginia, plus the high numbers of poor squatters and inherently unstable government, eventually led Carolina to be divided into two colonies in 1712. South Carolinians adopted all the features of a traditional class hierarchy, fully embracing the institution of slavery, just as Locke did in the *Fundamental Constitutions*. The planter and merchant classes of South Carolina formed a highly incestuous community: wealth, slaves, and land were monopolized by a small ruling coterie. This self-satisfied oligarchy were the true inheritors of the old landgraves, carrying on the dynastic impulses of those who would create a pseudo-nobility of powerful families.[12]

By 1700, we should note, slaves comprised half the population of the southern portion of the Carolina colony, an imbalance that widened to 72 percent by 1740. Beginning in 1714, a series of laws required that for every six slaves an owner purchased, he had to acquire one white servant. Lamenting that the "white population do not proportionally multiply," South Carolina lawmakers had one more reason to wish that a corps of Leet-men and women had actually been formed. Encouraged to marry and multiply, tied to the land, they might have provided a racial and class barrier between the slaves and the landed elites.[13]

North Carolina, which came to be known as "Poor Carolina," went in a very different direction from its sibling to the south. It failed to shore up its elite planter class. Starting with Albemarle County, it became an imperial renegade territory, a swampy refuge for the poor and landless. Wedged between proud Virginians and upstart South Carolinians, North Carolina was that troublesome "sinke of America" so many early commentators lamented. It was a frontier wasteland resistant (or so it seemed) to the forces of commerce and civilization. Populated by what many dismissed as "useless lubbers" (conjuring the image of sleepy and oafish men lolling about doing nothing), North Carolina forged a lasting legacy as what we might call the *first white trash colony*. Despite being English, despite having claimed the rights of freeborn Britons, lazy lubbers of Poor Carolina stood out as a dangerous refuge of waste people, and the spawning ground of a degenerate breed of Americans.[14]

The rivalry between the dueling Carolinas was only part of the story. The original charter of Carolina would eventually be divided three ways, when Georgia was parceled out of the original territory in 1732. This last southern colony was the most unusual of Britain's offspring. An ex-military man, James Oglethorpe, was its guiding force, and he saw this venture as a unique opportunity to reconstruct class relations. It was a charitable endeavor, one meant to reform debtors and rescue poor men, by offering society a decidedly more humane alternative to Locke's servile Leet-men. Georgia provided an advantageous venue for the *"right disposing of the Poor"* in the colonies, which would "breed up and preserve our own Countrymen," one advocate insisted. In refusing to permit slavery, the Georgia colony promised that "free labor" would replace a reliance on indentured servants as well as African bondsmen.[15]

But Georgia meant something more. Even as South Carolinians jealously eyed the new territory as a place where they might sell slaves and control the land, the colony of free laborers offered a ready boundary (and slave-free zone) that would protect the vulnerable planter class from

Native tribes and Spanish settlers in Florida, who might otherwise offer a haven to their runaway slaves. Georgia, as we shall see, was a remarkable experiment.

North Carolina's physical terrain was crucial in shaping the character of its people. Along the boundary between Virginia and Carolina was a large and forbidding wetland known as the Dismal Swamp. The word "swamp" was derived from Low German and Dutch, though it was first used by English setters in Virginia and New England. "Dismal," on the other hand, conjured the superstitious lore of medieval times. The word was associated with cursed days, Egyptian plagues, sinister plots, and inauspicious omens. For William Shakespeare, it evoked a netherworld, as in the "dark dismal-dreaming night."[16]

Virginians viewed the twenty-two-hundred-square-mile wetland as a danger-filled transitional zone. The seemingly endless quagmire literally overlapped the two colonies. There were no obvious routes through its mosquito-ridden cypress forests. In many places, travelers sank knee-deep in the soggy, peaty soil, and had to wade through coal-colored, slimy water dotted with gnarled roots.[17]

Little sunshine penetrated the Dismal Swamp's trees and thickets, and the air gave off noxious fumes, which were colorfully described as "Noisome exhalations," arising from a "vast body of mire and nastiness." This statement comes from the travelogue of a wealthy Virginian, William Byrd II, who trekked through the bowels of the Virginia-Carolina borderland in 1728. A witty, English-educated planter, Byrd crafted a dark tale of an inhospitable landscape and weighed in on Carolina's oafish inhabitants. Thus he was the first of many writers to draw a jaded portrait of the swampy origins of white trash rural life.[18]

This bleak region became a symbol of the young North Carolina colony. The Great Dismal Swamp divided civilized Virginia planters from the rascally barbarians of Carolina. Swamps rarely have fixed borders, and so the northern dividing line was continually a point of contention during the first sixty-five years of Carolina's existence. Virginia repeatedly challenged the boundary as set forth in Carolina's 1663 charter. Jurisdictional disputes created a political climate of legal uncertainty and social instability.[19]

Byrd's solution to the Dismal Swamp was to drain it and remake it as productive farmland. Later projectors, including George Washington, got behind Byrd's idea. Teaming with other investors, Washington established a company in 1763 whose purpose was to use slaves to drain the swamp, grow hemp, and cut wood shingles. By 1790, they were working to build a canal (a "ditch," as it was more accurately called at the time) to tunnel through the morass of cypress trees, prickly briars, and muddy waterways.[20]

The Carolina coastline was nearly as uninviting, cutting off the northern part of the colony from ready access to large sailing vessels. Only New Englanders, in their low-bottomed boats, could navigate the shallow, shoal-filled inlets of the Outer Banks. Without a major harbor, and facing burdensome taxes if they shipped their goods through Virginia, many Carolinians turned to smuggling. Hidden inlets made North Carolina attractive to pirates. Along trade routes from the West Indies to the North American continent, piracy flourished in the late seventeenth and early eighteenth centuries. Several of Albermarle's governors were accused of sheltering these high-seas thieves and personally profiting from the illicit trade. The notorious Blackbeard (a.k.a. Edward Teach, or Edward Thatch) made a home here, as did the Barbados gentleman turned pirate, Major Stede Bonnet. Supposedly, both were warmly welcomed into the humble homes of North Carolinians. At least that was what the surly Blackbeard claimed, until he lost his head in a grisly clash with Virginians in 1718.[21]

The Albemarle section of North Carolina was comparable to the poorest districts in Virginia. Most of the settlements were widely scattered—something else the proprietors did not like. The settlers refused to pay their quitrents (land tax), which was one of the ways the proprietors hoped to make money.[22] By 1729, when the proprietors sold their original grant to the British government, North Carolina listed 3,281 land grants, and 309 grantees who owned almost half the land. This meant that in a population of nearly 36,000 people, the majority received small or modest grants, or owned no land at all. Most poor households lacked slaves, indentured servants, or even sons working the land. In 1709, squatters in the poorest district in Albemarle petitioned "your honers" for tax relief, pointing out that their land was nothing more than sand. A few months later, an Anglican minister reported in disgust that the colonists "were so careless and uncleanly" that there was "little difference between the corn in the horse's manger and the bread on their tables." The entire North Carolina colony was "overrun with sloth and poverty."[23]

Worthless land and equally worthless settlers had led Virginia officials to question the Virginia-Carolina boundary line as early as 1672, when Governor Berkeley initiated negotiations with the Carolina proprietors in an effort to absorb Albemarle into Virginia. That plan fell through, but it was tried again two decades later. Over the years, colonial officials rarely succeeded in collecting customs duties. The proprietors faced resistance in collecting quitrents. Disorder ruled. A British possession in name only, Albemarle County was routinely able to escape imperial rule.[24]

During its first fifty years, the errant northern part of Carolina, which had its own government, was rocked by two internal rebellions and one war with Tuscarora Indians. The misnamed Culpeper's Rebellion (1677–79) is particularly instructive. In a contest with Thomas Miller, an ambitious trader and tobacco planter who wanted to crack down on smugglers, collect customs duties, and gain favor with proprietors, Thomas Culpeper, a surveyor, sided with the poorer settlers. Theirs was a personal conflict with broad repercussions. Miller took advantage of a leadership vacuum to seize control of government. Like a petty tyrant, he surrounded himself with an armed guard, while Culpeper rallied popular support and organized an informal militia. Miller was forced to flee the colony. Back in London, he charged Culpeper with leading an uprising, and as a result in 1680 Culpeper was tried for treason.[25]

In an unexpected development, the proprietor Lord Shaftesbury came to Culpeper's defense. He delivered an eloquent oration before the Court of King's Bench, arguing that a stable government had never legally existed in North Carolina. Anticipating Locke's *Two Treatises of Government,* Shaftesbury concluded that the colony remained effectively in a state of nature. Without a genuine government, there could be no rebellion. Commentary like this merely underscored northern Carolina's outlier status.[26]

Culpeper's Rebellion was something less than a servile insurrection. The poor settlers' rallying cry of "noe Landgraves, noe Casiques" filled the air, yet we cannot call theirs strictly a war of the poor against the rich. Miller's agenda was to stop smuggling and force his fellow Englishmen to participate in the British colonial trade system. His targets were those, including modest farmers, who depended on smuggling to survive. Class power, in this instance, was about those who benefited from a greater reliance on the imperial orbit of influence. But Miller had also asserted an unconstitutional claim to the governorship and, by applying heavy-handed tactics, failed to command respect within the political community. Indeed, he was known for his foul mouth and drunken oaths against the king, which resulted in charges of sedition and blasphemy. He was at best a poseur, at worst a crude bully. In the end, North Carolina's aristocratic leadership proved as dubious as the made-up titles of landgraves and caciques.[27]

A history of misrule continued to haunt North Carolina. Governor Seth Sothell, who served from 1681 to 1689, engrossed as many as forty-four thousand acres for private gain. He was eventually banished from the colony. Nor was this unique. From 1662 to 1736, North Carolina went through forty-one governors, while its sister colony saw twenty-five. After 1691, in an effort to enhance stability, the government in South Carolina appointed the deputy governor for North Carolina. When a rebellion against Governor Edward Hyde ignited in 1708, Virginia governor Alexander Spotswood went to war against his southern neighbor. Their conflict triggered renewed hostilities from the Tuscarora Indians, who resented unceasing English encroachment on their lands.[28]

In 1711, South Carolina intervened, sending Captain John Barnwell north to put down the Tuscaroras. Barnwell expected to be awarded a large land grant for his service. With his expectations unmet, he turned the tables and incited the Indians to attack several North Carolina settlements. Even before his betrayal, though, he felt little identification with the colonists, writing that North Carolinians were the most "cowardly Blockheads [another word for lubber] that ever God created & must be used like negro[e]s if you expect any good of them."[29]

Governor Spotswood of Virginia lashed out against Albemarle County as a "common Sanctuary for all our runaway servants," and censured its "total Absence of Religion." He echoed a previous Virginia governor when he denounced the place as the "sinke of America, the Refuge of Renegadoes." He meant by this a commercial sinkhole, and with the loaded term "renegadoes," a bastion of lawless, irreligious men who literally renounced their national allegiance as well as their Christian faith. Though there were but few ministers to guide them, the real apostasy of the people was said to be their refusal to be good taxpaying Britons.[30]

Virginians constantly aimed to keep their neighbor in line. A surveying team was dispatched in 1710, but failed to settle anything. The same was attempted in 1728, when William Byrd II accepted his commission to lead a joint expedition. He endured trying months navigating the Dismal Swamp and met with residents, mocked them mercilessly, and lustily eyed their women as much as he coveted the fertile land beyond the Dismal Swamp. He instructed his men to beat drums and shoot off guns to determine the size of the swamp, and crudely compared the sound to that "prattling Slut, Echo." Such petulance reflected his general feeling that the dark, mysterious Carolina terrain would never give up her secrets. Yet Byrd was undeterred. A man of letters as well as an amateur naturalist, he wrote two versions of his adventure: one was the less censored "secret history," the other a longer, more polished tract called "The History of the Dividing Line Betwixt Virginia and North Carolina."[31]

For Byrd, Virginia was an almost Eden-like colony, and a far cry from her uncivilized neighbor. In a bemused letter of 1726, written just two years before he began his tour of North Carolina, he described himself as a man resting underneath his "fig tree," surrounded by "my Flocks and my Herds, my Bond-men and Bond-women." Part feudal squire, part modern Abraham, Byrd portrayed his colony as a bucolic retreat far from the "Vagrant Mendicants" roaming the "island of beggars"—by which he meant England. He pretended that poverty did not exist in Virginia; his slaves were both dutiful and productive. A well-ordered society, based on slavery, had not only allowed him to indulge a pastoral dream but had also kept poor whites at bay.[32]

Things were different in Carolina. Just across the ill-defined border was an alien world where class authority was severely compromised. Byrd's little band of land commissioners were "knights-errant" embarked on a grand medieval crusade. When people emerged from their huts, staring as a flock at the strangers from Virginia, "it was as if we had been Morocco ambassadors." Having brought a chaplain along on their journey, they were able to christen children and marry men and women from place to place along their route. Byrd and his party of superior Christians sprinkled holy water on the heathen Carolinians.[33]

Or so he fantasized. In fact, the Carolinians proved resistant to religion and reform. As Byrd noted, the men had an abiding "aversion" to labor of any kind. They slept (and snored) through most of the morning. On waking, they sat smoking their pipes. Rarely did they even peek outside their doors, and during the cooler months, those who did quickly returned "shivering to their chimney corners." In milder weather they got as far as thinking about plunging a hoe into the ground. But thinking turned to excuses, and nothing was accomplished. The unmotivated Carolina folk preferred, he said, to "loiter away their lives, like Solomon's sluggards." The little work that actually got done was performed by the female poor.[34]

Carolina obliged William Byrd to adjust his broader vision of America's destiny. For his example of the "wretchedest scenes of poverty" he had ever seen in "this happy part of the world," he isolated a rusticated man named Cornelius Keith, who had a wife and six children yet lived in a home without a roof. The Keiths' dwelling was closer to a cattle pen, he said, than to any human habitation. At night the family slept in the fodder stack. Byrd found it especially odd that the husband and father was more interested in protecting feed for his animals than the safety of his family. Keith had chosen this life, and that was what most shocked the wealthy explorer from Virginia. Here was a man with a skilled trade, possessing good land and good limbs, who nevertheless preferred to live worse than the "bogtrotting Irish." Byrd's choice of words was, as usual, unambiguous. English contempt for the Irish was nothing new, but "bogtrotting" was an exquisite synonym for swamp vagrant.[35]

When Byrd identified the Carolinians as residents of "Lubberland," he drew upon a familiar English folktale that featured one "Lawrence Lazy," born in the county of Sloth near the town of Neverwork. Lawrence was a "heavy lump" who sat in his chimney corner and dreamt. His dog was so lazy that he "lied his head agin the wall to bark." In Lubberland, sloth was contagious, and Lawrence had the power to put all masters under his spell so that they fell into a deep slumber. As applied to the rural poor who closed themselves off to the world around them, the metaphor of sleep suggested popular resistance to colonial rule. Byrd

found the people he encountered in Carolina to be resistant to all forms
of government: "Everyone does what seems best in his own eyes."[36]

As he further contemplated the source of idleness, Byrd was convinced that it was in the lubbers' blood. Living near the swamp, they
suffered from "distempers of laziness," which made them "slothful in
everything but getting children." They displayed a "cadaverous complexion" and a "lazy, creeping habit." The combination of climate and an
unhealthy diet doomed them. Eating swine, they contracted the "yaws,"
and their symptoms matched those of syphilis: they lost their noses and
palates, and had hideously deformed faces. With their "flat noses," they
not only looked like but also began to act like wild boars: "Many of them
seem to grunt rather than speak." In a "porcivorous" country, people
spent their days foraging and fornicating; when upset, they could be
heard yelling out, "Flesh alive and tear it." It was their "favorite exclama-
tion," Byrd said. This bizarre colloquialism suggested cannibalism, or

The *Mapp of Lubberland or the Ile of Lazye* (ca. 1670) portrayed
an imaginary territory in which sloth is contagious and normal men
lack the will to work.

perhaps hyenas surrounding a fresh kill and devouring it. How could these carnivorous swamp monsters be thought of as English?[37]

Byrd left behind few practical ideas for reforming the godforsaken wilderness he had explored. Only drastic measures would work: replacing lubbers with Swiss German settlers and draining the swamp of its vile murky waters. He mused that colonization would have had a better outcome if male settlers had been encouraged to intermarry with Indian women. Over two generations, the Indian stock would have improved, as a species of flower or tree might; dark skin blanched white, heathen ways dimmed. Here, Byrd was borrowing from the author John Lawson, who wrote in *A New Voyage to Carolina* that men of lower rank gained an economic advantage by marrying Native women who brought land to the union. While he was at it, Byrd also condemned unrefined whites for marrying promiscuous Englishwomen right off the boat. He even suggested, satirically, of course, that social problems would disappear if the poor were more like bears and spent six months each year in hibernation: "'Tis a pity our beggars and pickpockets could not do the same," he wrote.[38]

Byrd's views, if colorfully expressed, were by no means his alone. An Anglican minister named John Urmston reported that his poor white charges loved their hogs more than they did their minister. They let the hogs into their churches to avoid the heat, leaving "dung and nastiness" on the floor. In 1737, Governor Gabriel Johnson of North Carolina referred to his people as "the meanest, most rustic and squalid part of the species." As late as the 1770s, a traveler passing through North Carolina found the residents to be the most "ignorant wretches" he had ever met. They could not even tell him the name of the place where they lived, nor offer directions to the next family's home. Insular country people greeted travelers with incredulous stares and looked upon them as "strange, outlandish folks." These rural poor were a people untethered from reality.[39]

Shocking as it is for us to contemplate, large numbers of early American colonists spent their entire lives in such dingy, nasty conditions. The sordid picture conveyed here is an unavoidable part of the American past. Yet there's more. They walked around with open sores visible on their bodies; they had ghastly complexions as a result of poor diets; many were missing limbs, noses, palates, and teeth. As a traveler named Smyth recorded, the ignorant wretches he encountered wore "cotton rags" and were "enveloped in dirt and nastiness."[40]

The poor of colonial America were not just waste people, not simply a folk to be compared to their Old World counterparts. By reproducing their own kind, they were, to contemporaneous observers, in the process of creating an anomalous new breed of human. A host of travelers in Carolina in the seventeenth and early eighteenth centuries believed that class structure was tied to geography and rooted in the soil. Explorers, amateur scientists, and early ethnologists like William Byrd all assumed—and unabashedly professed—that inferior or mismanaged lands bred inferior, ungovernable people.

John Locke's influence over Carolina was mostly of an intellectual character. Not so the next southern colony to arise under the direction of an ambitious projector. Rather than a constitutional creation, Georgia was founded as a charitable venture, designed to uplift poor families and to reform debtors. One of the most important minds behind it belonged to James Edward Oglethorpe. Oglethorpe was a military adventurer who, with permission of Parliament and the colony's trustees, traveled to the American colony and helped to plant settlers. Unique among the American settlements, Georgia was not motivated by a desire for profit. Receiving its charter in 1732, the southernmost colony was the last to be established prior to the American Revolution. Its purpose was twofold: to carve out a middle ground between the extremes of wealth that took hold in the Carolinas, and to serve as a barrier against the Spanish in Florida. As such, it became the site of an unusual experiment.

Conservative land policies limited individual settlers to a maximum of five hundred acres, thus discouraging the growth of a large-scale plantation economy and slave-based oligarchy such as existed in neighboring South Carolina. North Carolina squatters would not be found here either. Poor settlers coming from England, Scotland, and other parts of Europe were granted fifty acres of land, free of charge, plus a home and a garden. Distinct from its neighbors to the north, Georgia experimented with a social order that neither exploited the lower classes nor favored the rich. Its founders deliberately sought to convert the territory into a haven for hardworking families. They aimed to do something completely unprecedented: to build a "free labor" colony.

According to Francis Moore, who visited the settlement in its second year of operation, two "peculiar" customs stood out: both alcohol and dark-skinned people were prohibited. "No slavery is allowed, nor negroes," Moore wrote. As a sanctuary for "free white people," Georgia "would not permit slaves, for slaves starve the poor laborer." Free labor encouraged poor white men in sober cultivation and steeled them in the event they had to defend the land from outside aggression. It also promised to cure settlers of that most deadly of English diseases, idleness.[41]

Though it operated with support from Parliament and was overseen by a board of twenty trustees, Georgia remained in theory a charitable enterprise. The trustees sought to inculcate the spirit of benevolence, as expressed in the colony's motto, *Non sibi sed aliis* (Not for themselves, but for others). Beyond the work of the trustees, Oglethorpe shaped the day-to-day operations of the colony, having brought over the first group of 114 English settlers, Moses-like, in 1732–33.[42]

A trustee, Oglethorpe never held the office of governor, nor did he even purchase land to enrich himself. Though a highly educated member of Parliament, he traveled without a servant and lived simply. Having fought as an officer under Prince Eugene of Savoy in the Austro–Turkish War of 1716–18, he understood military discipline. This was how he came to trust in the power of emulation; he believed that people could be conditioned to do the right thing by observing good leaders. He shared food with those who were ill or deprived. Visiting a Scottish community north of Savannah, he refused a soft bed and slept outside on the hard ground with the men. More than any other colonial founder, Oglethorpe made himself one of the people, promoting collective effort.[43]

As a free-labor buffer zone between English and Spanish territories, Georgia's circumstances were unique. In 1742, Oglethorpe led a military expedition against Spanish St. Augustine, a campaign his English neighbors to the north had balked at funding. He marveled at how the South Carolinians deluded themselves in believing they were safe, burdened as they were with a large slave population—"stupid security," he called it. Savannah's physical layout exhibited all the elements of a military camp, and recruits were put through military drills even before they landed in America. Male orphans were taught to hold a musket as soon as they were physically able.[44]

One young believer in the colony, sixteen-year-old Philip Thicknesse, wrote to his mother in 1735 that "a man may live here upon his own improvements, if he be industrious." In his grand plan, Oglethorpe wanted a colony of orderly citizen-soldiers; he subscribed to the classical agrarian ideal that virtue was acquired by cultivating the soil and achieving self-sufficiency. Productive, stable, healthy farming families were meant to anchor the colony. As he wrote in 1732, women provided habits of cleanliness and "wholesome food," and remained on hand to nurse the sick. Unlike others before him, Oglethorpe felt the disadvantaged could be reclaimed if they were given a fair chance.

Far more radical was his calculation that a working wife and eldest son could replace the labor of indentured servants and slaves. He claimed that a wife and one son equaled the labor value of an adult male. He was clearly not fond of the practice of indenture, considering it the same as making "slaves for years." While Georgia's trustees did not prohibit the use of white servants, Oglethorpe made sure their tenures were limited. Oddly, it turned out that the colonists best suited to the Georgia experiment were not English but Swiss, German, French Huguenot, and Scottish Highlander, all of whom seemed prepared for lives of hardship, arriving as whole communities of farming families.[45]

Slavery, however, could not be kept apart from future projections in Georgia. After allowing South Carolina to send over slaves to fell trees and clear the land for the town of Savannah, Oglethorpe came to regret the decision. He made a brief trip to Charles Town, and returned to discover that in the interim the white settlers had grown "impatient of Labour and Discipline." Some had sold good food for rum punch. With drunkeness came disease. And so, Oglethorpe wrote, the "Negroes who sawed for us" and encouraged white "Idleness" were sent back.[46]

Many contemporaries connected slavery to English idleness. William Byrd weighed in on the ban against slavery in Georgia in a letter to a Georgia trustee. He saw how slavery had sparked discontent among poor whites in Virginia, who routinely refused to "dirty their hands with Labour of any kind," preferring to steal or starve rather than work in the fields. Slavery ruined the "industry of our White People," he confessed, for they saw a "Rank of Poor Creatures below them," and detested the thought of work out of a perverse pride, lest they might "look like slaves." A North Carolina proprietor, John Colleton, observed in Barbados that poor whites were called "white slaves" by black slaves; it struck him that the same contempt for white field hands prevailed in the southern colonies in North America.[47]

A fair number of Georgians were less high-minded, and envious of their South Carolina neighbors. As soon as the slavery ban (it was not part of the original charter) was adopted in Georgia, petitions were sent to the trustees seeking permission to purchase slaves. Oglethorpe waged a war of words with proslavery settlers, whom he called "Malcontents." At the height of the controversy, in 1739, he argued that African slavery should never be introduced into his colony, because it went against the core principle of the trustees: "to relieve the distressed." Instead of offering a sanctuary for honest laborers, Georgia would become an oppressive regime, promoting "the misery of thousands in Africa" by permitting a "free people" to be "sold into perpetual Slavery."[48]

He had written similarly about English sailors back in 1728. Strange though it might seem to us, Oglethorpe's argument against slavery was drawn from his understanding of the abuse sailors faced as a distinct class. In the eighteenth century, seamen were imagined as a people naturally "bred" for a life at sea, whose very constitution was amenable to a hard life in the British navy. In his tract protesting the abuse of sailors, the more enlightened Oglethorpe rejected claims that men were born to such an exploited station. For him, seamen literally functioned as "slaves," deprived of the liberties granted to freeborn Britons. As poor men, they were dragged off the streets by press gangs, thrown into prison ships, and sold into the navy. Poorly fed, grossly underpaid, and treated as "captives," they were a brutalized class of laborers, and in every way coerced.[49]

According to Georgians who petitioned for slaves, Negroes were "bred up" for hard labor in the same way as sailors. Africans would survive in damp, noxious swamps as well as in the sweltering heat. They were cheap to feed and clothe. A meager subsistence diet of water, corn, and potatoes was thought adequate to keep them alive and active. One outfit and a single pair of shoes would last an entire year. White indentured servants were fundamentally different. They demanded English dress for every season. They expected meat, bread, and beer on the table, and if denied this rich diet felt languid and feeble and would refuse to work. If forced to labor as hard as African slaves through the grueling summer months, or so the petitioners claimed, white servants would run away from Georgia as if escaping a "charnel house" (a repository for rotting corpses). Proslavery Georgians were not above accusing Oglethorpe of running a prison colony.[50]

Oglethorpe was unmoved by their demands. Just as he had earlier called press gangs "little tyrants" with "great sticks" when they forcibly turned poor men into sailors, he now charged that the Georgians who fled to South Carolina preferred "whipping Negroes" to regular work. Oglethorpe pointed to those settlers who were not afraid of labor, who knew how to "subsist comfortably" without clamoring for slaves. They were the Scottish Highlanders and German settlers who had petitioned the trustees to keep slavery out of the colony. Oglethorpe felt that these folks were hardier and their predisposition to work was superior to that of Englishmen. But the truth lay in an ability to work collectively, a desire to understand and appreciate the demands of subsistence farming—a commitment to long-term survival in a sparsely settled colony. Many English settlers were unwilling to work hard, because they lacked any background in farming. Apothecaries, cheese mongers, tinkers, wig makers, and weavers abounded. There were too few who could cultivate the soil. Patrick Tailfer, who drafted one of the petitions in support of slaveholding, refused to cultivate a single acre of the land he had been granted.[51]

We should make clear that Oglethorpe was not a modern egalitarian. He did not imagine his colony as a multiracial community, nor did he surmount common prejudices with respect to Africans. He permitted there to be a small number of Indian slaves in the colony. His plan centered on class: he restricted slavery principally because he believed it would shift the balance of class power in Georgia and "starve the poor white laborer." In the larger scheme of things, his reform philosophy recognized that weak and desperate men could be led to choose a path that dictated against their own interests. A man might sell his land for a glass of rum; debt and idleness were always a temptation.[52]

Despite his good intentions, the colony failed to eliminate all class divisions. In addition to the fifty acres allotted to charity cases, settlers who paid their own way might be granted as many as five hundred acres. They were expected to employ between four and ten servants. But five hundred acres was the maximum limit for freeholders. The trustees wanted settlers to occupy the land, not to speculate in land. Absentee landholders were not welcome. Georgia also instituted a policy of keeping the land "tail-male," which meant that land descended to the eldest male child. This feudal rule bound men to their families. The tail-male provision protected heirs whose poor fathers might otherwise feel pressure to sell their land.[53]

Many settlers disliked the practice. Hardworking families worried about the fate of their unmarried daughters, who might be left with nothing. One such complaint came from Reverend Dumont, a leader of French Protestants interested in migrating to Georgia. What would happen to widows "too old to marry or beget children," he asked. And how could daughters survive, especially those "unfit for Marriage, either by Sickness or Evil Construction of their Body"?[54]

Dumont's questions went to the core of Oglethorpe's and the trustees' philosophy. Young widows and daughters were seen as breeders of the next generation of free white laborers. Georgia's policy was to nurture the natural process of "propagation," as Oglethorpe declared in one of his promotional tracts. His grand plan was to ensure that English and other Protestants would quickly outnumber the French and Spanish in North America. The war against the rival Catholic colonial powers was, at length, a battle of numbers. Georgia had to have enough free white men to field its armies, and it had to benefit from a reproductive advantage, winning the demographic war as well.[55]

Alas, Oglethorpe was fighting a losing battle. Many of the men demanding slaves were promised credit to buy slaves from South Carolinian traders. Slaves were a lure, dangled before poorer men in order to persuade them to put up their land as collateral. That is why Oglethorpe believed that a slave economy would have the effect of depriving vulnerable settlers of their land. Keeping out slavery went hand in hand with preserving a more equitable distribution of land. If the colony allowed settlers to have "fee simple" land titles (so they could sell their land at will), large-scale planters would surely come to dominate. He predicted in 1739 that, left to their own devices, the "Negro Merchants" would gain control of "all the lands in the Colony," leaving nothing for "all the laboring poor white Men."[56]

German Lutherans, who established a community in 1734, also saw the dangers of Georgia becoming like South Carolina. Without encouragement from Oglethorpe, Reverend Bolzius of their contingent observed that "a Common white Laborer in Charles Town" earned no greater wage than "a Negroe." Africans were encouraged to "breed like animals," and slaveowners would do everything possible to increase their stock. Merchants and other gentlemen hoarded the best land near the coast or along the commercial rivers, and poorer men were forced to possess remote, less desirable land. South Carolina was a poor white family's worst nightmare.[57]

Oglethorpe left the colony in 1743, never to return. Three years earlier, a soldier had attempted to murder him, the musket ball tearing through his wig. He survived, but his dream for Georgia died. Over the next decade, land tenure policies were lifted, rum was allowed to flow freely, and slaves were sold surreptitiously. In 1750, settlers were formally granted the right to own slaves.[58]

A planter elite quickly formed, principally among transplants from the West Indies and South Carolina. By 1788, Carolinian Jonathan Bryan was the most powerful man in Georgia, with thirty-two thousand acres and 250 slaves. He set up shop there in 1750, the very year slavery was made legal, and his numerous slaves entitled him to large tracts of lands. But to build his empire he had to pull the strings of Georgia's Executive Council, whose chief duty was distributing land. A long tenure on the council ensured that he acquired the most fertile land, conveniently situated along major trade routes. By 1760, only 5 percent of white Georgians owned even a single slave, while a handful of families possessed them in the hundreds. Jonathan Bryan was the perfect embodiment of the "Slave Merchants" who Oglethorpe had warned would dominate the colony.[59]

Oglethorpe's ideas did not entirely disappear. Both Benjamin Franklin and Thomas Jefferson agreed that slaveowning corrupted whites. The idea of promoting a free white labor buffer zone went into Jefferson's draft of what became the Northwest Ordinance (1787), a blueprint for the admission of new states to the Union. Franklin and Jefferson were equally passionate about mobilizing the forces of reproduction. They saw population growth as a sign of national strength. Slavery, too, was to be measured as a numbers game. As Reverend Bolzius had observed, if slaves were encouraged to "breed like animals," then poor whites could not reproduce at the same rate and hold on to their land or their freedom.

It was already apparent that slavery and class identity were inter-twined. Oglethorpe had connected free labor to the idea of a vital, secure, (re)productive society. Free white laborers, while adding to the military strength of a colony, could not compete economically with a class of land-engrossing slaveholders. What had been considered "pecu-liar" about Georgia—the banning of slavery—would ironically come to mean the precise opposite when in the nineteenth century slavery became the "peculiar institution" of the American South.

All the while, the deeply ingrained English disgust for idleness per-sisted. The rural poor, though seen as a liability, became an unbanishable part of the American experience. Not only did free laborers exist in con-trast to imported African slaves, but they also stood apart from useless white lubbers. Land was the principal source of wealth, and remained the true measure of liberty and civic worth. Hereditary titles may have gradually disappeared, but large land grants and land titles remained central to the American system of privilege. When it came to common impressions of the despised lower class, the New World was not new at all.

CHAPTER THREE

Benjamin Franklin's American Breed

The Demographics of Mediocrity

Can it be a Crime (in the Nature of Things I mean) to add to the Number of the King's Subjects, in a new Country that really wants People?

—Benjamin Franklin, "The Speech of Miss Polly Baker" (1747)

Like every educated Englishman, Benjamin Franklin was obsessed with idleness. In his *Poor Richard's Almanack* of 1741, he offered familiar advice that echoed the talk of Hakluyt, Winthrop, and Byrd: "Up sluggard, and waste not life; in the grave will be sleeping enough." There was utterly nothing new in his pitch for hard work as the way to wealth.[1]

By the 1740s and 1750s, Franklin was well positioned to contribute to the ongoing debate on class and American colonization. Born to a modest tradesman, he had established himself as a successful printer, publishing the *Pennsylvania Gazette* since 1729. His first in a series of profitable annual almanacs rolled off the presses three years later. As a public wit, he had mastered the art of ventriloquism on the page, mimicking colonial characters. The teenage Franklin had pretended to be a mature Boston widow in his "Silence Dogood" letters; Dingo, an African slave, was another of his personae. Poor Richard Saunders, the figure featured in his almanacs, was the cuckold tradesman whose pert proverbs never matched his whining over the daily struggle to make ends meet. So successful was Franklin in expanding his printing business, taking on partners, and honing his literary disguises that he retired from day-to-day management of all commercial concerns in 1748.[2]

Freed from work, he was elected to the Pennsylvania Assembly in 1751, and remained active in promoting civic enterprise. He helped to found a hospital and a young men's academy in Philadelphia. During the same decade, his electrical experiments made a strong impression in

Europe. He was awarded the prestigious Copley Medal of the Royal Society of London. Honorary degrees from Harvard, Yale, and the College of William and Mary quickly followed. Appointed deputy postmaster general, he introduced reforms for improving communication among the colonies. At the Albany Congress in 1754, he proposed an intercolonial governing body aimed at shoring up military defenses and promoting western expansion. Though approved at the Albany Congress, the plan of union was never ratified by the colonies.[3]

As the colonies' leading man of science, Franklin popularized the latest theories. Of primary interest here are his efforts to apply scientific knowledge to that most perplexing of all subjects: the creation of classes. It was an article of faith in eighteenth-century British thought that civilized societies usually formed out of the fundamental human need for security to ensure survival, but the same societies were gradually corrupted by a preoccupation with luxuries, which resulted in decadence. The rise and fall of the Roman Empire stood behind such theorizing; what Franklin did was to shift the focus to human biology. Underneath all human endeavors were gut-level animal instincts—and foremost for Franklin was the push and pull of pain and pleasure. Too much pleasure produced a decadent society; too much pain led to tyranny and oppression. Somewhere in between was a happy medium, a society that channeled humanity's better animal instincts.[4]

Did North America offer the environment to achieve this happy medium? Franklin thought so. Its unique environment could strip away the unnatural conditions of the Old World system. The vast continent would give Americans a demographic advantage in breeding quickly and more fruitfully than their English counterparts. Freed from congested cities, as well as the swelling numbers of unemployed and impoverished, Americans would escape the extremes of great wealth and grinding poverty. Instead of a frantic competition over resources, the majority would be perfectly content to occupy a middling stage, what he called a "happy mediocrity."

The industrious ant, another favorite insect of the English, provided Franklin with the evidence he needed. In 1748, as he watched one ant lead a procession of his fellows along a string to a molasses pot hanging from the ceiling, he discovered that ants communicated with each other.

His curiosity about animal behavior grew, and two years later he tried an experiment with pigeons. Arranging pairs of the birds in a box, he noted that they reproduced quickly but never permitted the box to get over-crowded. The birds engaged in natural selection, the "old and strong driving out the young and weak, and obliging them to seek new habitations." As he added more boxes, the pigeons filled them, reproducing in response to the available space and food.[5]

Ants and pigeons. Communal creatures could be easily compared to people. Reducing all human action to the overriding impulse to seek pleasure and avoid pain, the utilitarian Franklin was convinced that the driving forces of social development had little to do with religion or morality. If men and women were at their core animals, then they were instinctively driven to eat, procreate, and move. The last of these qualities, what Franklin called the feeling of "uneasy in rest," came from the apparent similarity he found between animal and human migration. People displayed the desire to roam, to move forward, and to improve their state. Unsettled land sparked the instinct to migrate, as did limited resources encourage emigration—little different from the lives of the young pigeons who were forced to seek out new habitations. Franklin's notion of "uneasy in rest" echoed Richard Hakluyt the younger, who had claimed all Englishmen to be "stirrers abroad," a people who were searchers of new places and seekers of new avenues of wealth.[6]

In "Observations Concerning the Increase of Mankind" (1751), one of his most important treatises, Franklin predicted that Americans would double in population in twenty years. Idleness would be bred out of the English constitution. Large families encouraged parents to be industrious. Children would be put to work, imitating their parents, and spurred on by the will to survive. Class formation would occur, but it would be in a state of flux and adjustment, as people spread outward and filled the available territory.[7]

People needed incentives to produce more children. Franklin reminded his readers in "Observations" that in the Roman Empire, fruitful women had been rewarded for the number of offspring they produced. Slave women were rewarded with their liberty, while freeborn widows with large broods earned property rights and the autonomy ordinarily reserved for freeborn men. His point was that great empires needed large populations (strength came in numbers) in order to people and settle new territories. The incentives that America offered were of a different kind than elsewhere: an abundance of land and the liberty to marry young.[8]

The purest expression of Franklin's reproductive philosophy came in his 1747 satire "The Speech of Miss Polly Baker." Appearing before a judge, Polly was found guilty of having borne an illegitimate child for the fifth time. Speaking in her own defense, Miss Baker described herself as an industrious woman: "I have brought Five fine Children into the World, at the Risque of my Life; I have maintain'd them well by my own Industry, without burthening the Township." Her self-confidence was bolstered by the knowledge of her patriotic service. She had added to the "Number of the King's Subjects, in a new Country that really wants People." She should be praised, not punished, was the message.

Baker's plight was not of her own doing. She wanted to be married; she wanted to display the "Industry, Frugality, Fertility, and Skill in Oeconomy, appertaining to a good Wife's Character." Was it her fault that bachelors abounded? she pleaded. How could her action be considered sinful when one gazed on the "admirable workmanship" of God in creating her beautiful children? Had she not fulfilled her higher duty, "the first and great Command of Nature, and of Nature's God, *Encrease and Multiply*?" As Franklin saw it, God and nature were on the side of Miss Baker, and foolish laws and outdated church sanctions on the other. To make his point, he added a humorous coda: the judge who heard her speech was convinced and he married her himself the next day.[9]

Franklin's offbeat story touched on all the points that he was trying to prove by demographic calculations and point-by-point reasoning in his "Observations." The two essays should be read side by side. Nor was it an accident that he named his character Baker, a sly reference to the womb as an oven, a popular jest among English writers at the time. For Franklin, a man of both science and commerce, reproductive labor was work and should be valued as such. By adding to the "numbers of the King's subjects," reproductive labor was an imperial asset.

It also made sense for Franklin to target bachelors in his tale. In the American colonies and in England, the unmarried man of means was a scandalous figure. He was ridiculed as a hermaphrodite, as half man, half woman; his prescribed punishment, as one New York newspaper demanded, should be to have half of his beard shaved from his face to indicate his diminished manliness. Others felt he should lose his inheritance. In the same way that land could be left fallow, human fertility could be wasted. Having no children, wasting their seed, bachelors indulged in the worst kind of reproductive idleness.[10]

On the other hand, bastards added to the population and increased the wealth of the empire. Franklin's own circumstances reinforced his view. His son William (later royal governor of New Jersey) was a bastard. William, too, fathered a bastard son, William Temple Franklin, and Temple, as he was known, added two known illegitimate children to the family tree. Bastards were a Franklin family tradition.[11]

Like John Locke, Franklin was certain that healthy children were the "riches of every country." Yet his promotion of natural increase in the 1750s had more to do with colonial politics than strictly scientific curiosity. More than anywhere else, he asserted unambiguously, fit and fertile children were the special assets of British North America. In "Observations," he sought to convince British policy makers that the Caribbean islands should not be the preferred colonial model. Franklin deplored the racial imbalance in the West Indies, which kept the population of laboring whites at artificially low numbers. Slaveowners, who didn't perform their own labor, suffered from physical defects: they were "enfeebled, and therefore not so generally prolific." In short, he concluded that slavery made Englishmen idle and impotent.[12]

Franklin also believed that slavery taught children the wrong lessons: "White Children become proud, disgusted with Labour, and being educated in Idleness, are rendered unfit to get a Living by Industry." His words here echoed what William Byrd had written about poor whites in Virginia. Byrd admitted to the Georgia trustees in 1726 that poor white laboring men learned to despise labor, and would rather steal than work in the fields. Franklin changed the above equation: slavery corrupted all white men, rich and poor alike.

On a larger scale than Oglethorpe, Franklin was fashioning a free-labor zone for the northern colonies. The magic elixir to achieve his idealized British America was, in a word, breeding. In his imagination, a continental expanse populated by fertile settlers would create a more stable society. Children would replace indentured servants and slaves as laborers, mirroring the system of labor that Oglethorpe had tried but failed to permanently institute in Georgia.

Franklin expanded his theory amid global war and shifting boundaries on the North American continent. By 1760, he was writing in support of Britain's claim to Canada, eager to add that large territory to the empire after the British victory over France in the Seven Years' War. British colonists would fill up the land, and the majority would remain a "middling population" happily engaged in agriculture. Unlike the structurally imbalanced sugar islands, North America's desirable "mediocrity of fortunes" would lead the growing population to rely heavily on the consumption of British-made goods. This was a win-win situation for British merchants and American colonists, because population growth would at the same time augment commerce and manufacturing back in England. Not afraid of hyperbole, Franklin offered a warning to Parliament if it tried to hem in the colonial population. By refusing to add Canada, the highest legislative authority would be no better than a cruel midwife stifling the birth of every third or fourth child in North America.[13]

Franklin's theory of breeding would remain a staple of American exceptionalism for centuries to come. He provided three irresistible arguments. First, he promised that class stability accompanied western migration. Second, he reasoned that the dispersal of people would reduce class conflict and encourage a wider distribution of wealth among the population. Third, what he called a "mediocrity of fortunes" was his belief in the growth of a middle-range class condition. His farming families were not poor or self-sufficient, but engaged in some form of commercial farming, producing enough to support their families and purchase British goods.[14]

The most startling feature of his theory was that the class contentment he described could be achieved through natural means, or, to put it more bluntly, by letting nature take its course. The British Empire, with its well-trained ground forces and powerful navy, secured the territory. From that moment forward, the unoccupied land was the lure for settlers much like the molasses pot for the ants. In a land of opportunity, procreating came more naturally, as families felt happy and secure. Rigid class distinctions and the hoarding of resources were less likely to take place. The compression of classes persisted as long as new land was acquired in which people could spread and settle. Industry, frugality, and fertility were the natural outgrowth of a happy mediocrity.

How realistic was Franklin's theory? And to what degree was his argument based on wishful thinking rather than a reasonable explanation for human behavior? To begin with, eighteenth-century American colonists—like twenty-first-century Americans—were not anything like ants or pigeons. Human nature does not follow some mechanistic model of predictable reactions to pain and pleasure. And Franklin's omnipotent and guiding hand of nature was never left unmediated by other, equally powerful forces of politics and culture. Were people really mice in a maze? Or was colonization, migration, and peopling more messy and less certain than his grand theory promised?

Franklin's own experiences belied his optimism as to the ease with which colonists moved from one place to another. As a teenager, he had run away from Boston to Philadelphia, cutting short the full term of an apprenticeship he had been contracted to serve with his elder brother. A fugitive and vagrant, he was part of the large class of servants on the lam. His movement, like so many others, was haphazard, less methodical than the ants he studied. William Moraley, who arrived in Philadelphia in the same decade as young Franklin and wrote a memoir about his experiences, may have said it best when he described himself as a "Tennis-ball of fortune," bouncing from one new master to the next. Despite his literary skills, training as a law clerk and watchmaker, the un-Franklinesque Moraley seemed to migrate in circles and never up the social ladder. There was no guarantee that restlessness ensured social mobility.[15]

Poverty was increasingly common as the eighteenth century wore on. Philadelphia had its economic slumps, brutally cold winter weather, and shortages of wood that caused the poor nearly to freeze to death. In 1784, one man who was part of the working poor in the city wrote to the local newspaper that he had six children, and though he "strove in all his power," he could not support them. Hard work by itself was not the magic balm of economic self-sufficiency, nor was Franklin correct that big families were always a boon. He was even wrong about his tabulations on American birthrates. Infant mortality in Philadelphia was surprisingly high, and comparable to English rates, proving that Franklin's prediction of a healthy and happy population was more rhetorical than it was demographic fact.[16]

The quintessential self-made man was not self-made. The very idea is ludicrous given the inescapable network of patron-client relationships that defined the world of Philadelphia. To cushion his rise, Franklin relied on influential patrons, who provided contacts and loans that enabled him to acquire the capital he needed to set up his print shop and invest in costly equipment.

For Franklin to obtain patronage and navigate contending political factions was a tricky enterprise. Pennsylvania's class structure had some unusual quirks. At the top were the proprietors, members of William Penn's family, who owned vast tracts of land and collected quitrents. Next came the wealthy Quaker landowners and merchants, bound together by family and religious ties. In the eighteenth century, the Society of Friends disowned any member who married outside the sect, which inflicted real economic hardship by depriving the expelled of important commercial resources, loans, and land sales.[17]

Franklin was neither a Quaker nor a quasi Quaker (finding some special appeal in their religious principles), but he did develop strong personal relationships with several cosmopolitan and highly educated Friends in Philadelphia and in England. He relied on Quaker patrons, especially in the early days of his business. Like another one of his sponsors, the lawyer Alexander Hamilton, a non-Quaker leader of the Quaker Party (and no relation to the later politician), he initially sided with the Friends in local and imperial politics, except that he broke ranks when it came to an orthodox stand on pacifism. His friends were liberal Friends, who were not exclusive about who should wield influence within the political faction of the Quaker Party. That was how Hamilton rose to power in Pennsylvania and saw to Franklin's appointment as clerk of the Assembly, which in turn led to his official entrance onto the local political stage.[18]

The Friends did not rule uncontested. There was a rising non-Quaker elite faction, with ties to both the proprietors and the Anglican Church. Their political influence derived from strong commercial ties with England and to the essential Scottish countinghouses. Their power was enhanced upon the purchase of thousands of acres of the most lucrative tracts of real estate, which was made possible because the land office was overseen by the powerful proprietors. They became known as the Proprietary Party—a rival group to the wealthy Quakers. Though Franklin began his rise by becoming a master tradesman and a printer, he could not ignore the colonial merchants of either party. Merchants dealt in world markets; they were wholesalers, a distinctly different class from shopkeepers or tradesmen like Franklin, and many were extremely wealthy. Sound paper money helped with overseas trade, and Franklin's contract from the Assembly to print money drew him closer to the commercial elite.[19]

Class status was still based on family name in Pennsylvania, for the top tier was dominated by the Penn, Pemberton, and Logan families—the proprietors and Quaker elites. Below them was a growing transatlantic merchant class that set itself apart by engaging in a conspicuous display of wealth. These families owned slaves and servants, and silver tea sets; they wore rich fabrics, had grand homes, and drove carriages. At the time Franklin retired from his printing operations in 1748, he was in the top tenth percentile in wealth, owning a horse and chaise and having invested in a large tract of land. Even among the plain Quakers, known for their simple dress, carriages were a status symbol. In 1774, in a city of fifteen thousand, only eighty-four Philadelphians owned a carriage.[20]

Class was about more than wealth and family name; it was conveyed through appearances and reputation. Franklin understood this. The first portrait of him, painted in 1746, did not show him in his leather apron setting print type; nor was he pushing a wheelbarrow along the street, as he described himself—a dutiful tradesman—in his *Autobiography*. He was wearing a respectable wig and a fine ruffled shirt, and assumed all the airs of the "Better Sort."[21]

If material appearances defined the proprietors and wealthy classes as the "Better Sort," then the same rule applied at the other end of the social spectrum among the "Meaner Sort." A legal distinction existed between the free and the unfree, the latter including not only slaves but also indentured servants, convict laborers, and apprentices. As dependents, they were all classified as mean, servile, and ill-bred. Thousands of unfree laborers flooded Philadelphia, so that as early as 1730, Franklin was complaining about "vagrants and idle persons" entering the colony. He wrote these words after having escaped impoverished circumstances not many years before. He had arrived in Philadelphia in 1723 as a runaway, meanly dressed in filthy, wet clothing.[22]

For better or worse, the word "sorts" was meaningful. It loosely referred to different grades of commercial goods. Buttons and tobacco were classified in "sorts." A 1733 advertisement in a New York newspaper offered "fans made and sold of richer and meaner sort." Unlike the idiom of breeding stocks, which measured value through family bloodlines, commercial sorts placed more emphasis on outward appearance, as in the separation of quality goods from cheaper ones. As a commercial people, the British were inclined to think of their social classes along the same lines. When a newspaper referred to people of the "meanest quality," it could as easily have been an appraisal of the texture of cloth, meaning something that was coarse, unfinished, composed of baser materials, and cheaply made.[23]

In general, meanness meant poverty and a disagreeable dependence, whether in the form of a reliance upon charity or forced labor in a workhouse. Philadelphia, Boston, and New York all had almshouses. But meanness also attached to the condition of servitude, and was embodied in submissiveness. There was a stigma assigned to those of the lower classes, because they allowed themselves to be looked down upon, despised, and abused. The meaner sort was thought to possess a rude appearance, dull mind, and unrefined manners, and to indulge in vulgar speech. Meanness was filth and lowliness, yet another variation of the enduring class of waste people.[24]

Franklin was not sympathetic to the plight of the poor. His design for the Pennsylvania Hospital in 1751 was intended to assist the industrious poor, primarily men with physical injuries. The permanent class of impoverished were not welcome; they were simply shooed over to the almshouse. He felt the English were too charitable, an opinion he based on observing German settlers in his own colony, who worked with greater diligence because they came from a country that offered its poor little in the way of relief. When he talked about the poor, he sounded like William Byrd. In complaining about British mobs of the poor that raided the corn wagons in 1766, he charged that England was becoming "another Lubberland."[25]

Most men wanted a "life of ease," Franklin concluded, and "freedom from care and labor." Sloth was in itself a form of pleasure. This was why he contended that the only solution to poverty was some kind of coercive system to make the indigent work: "I think the best way of doing good to the poor, is not making them easy *in* poverty, but leading or driving them *out* of it." The poor's instinct of being "uneasy in rest" had been impaired; so what they needed was a jolt (of electricity?) to work again.[26]

Here we see the double meaning inherent in Franklin's theory of forced migration. In his projected model of emigration, a continental expanse populated by fertile settlers would allow people to escape the onus of working for others. Parents and children would work for themselves, stripping away a culture of subservience that was part and parcel of being of the meaner sort. But with newfound liberty, their fate rested on the most impersonal of forces: survival of the fittest. The harsh environment of the frontier forced settlers either to work hard or perish. Only the more frugal, fertile, and industrious would succeed, while the slothful and incompetent would have to keep moving or die.

If Franklin valued the middling sort on the frontier, he was already their champion before he wrote "Observations Concerning the Increase of Mankind." The "middling people" of Pennsylvania were, he had written, the "Tradesmen, Shopkeepers, and Farmers." He had no desire to eliminate the "Better Sort," of course, but he rejected the idea that if some were "better," everyone else was automatically *the meaner Sort,* i.e., the Mob, or the Rabble."

In a pamphlet of 1747, "Plain Truth," he demonstrated that the middle had a crucial role to play for the colony. That year Delaware was invaded by an irregular French and Spanish force. Franklin wrote to warn his fellow Philadelphians, especially the Quakers, that the same fate awaited them unless they organized a voluntary militia. He called for a "militia of FREEMEN," by which he meant men of the better and middling sorts, working together to defend their property and their colony.[27]

To rally support for his militia plan, he cast the dangers of a foreign invasion in terms of class warfare. Who, he posed, could be expected to lead the attack on a civilized people? It would be those "licentious Privateers," the dregs of society: "Negroes, Mulattoes, and others of the vilest and most abandoned of Mankind." He insisted that no indentured servants would be allowed to join the army of freemen. Besides advocating for defense of the colony, what was Franklin up to? Simple. He was redrawing class lines, bringing industrious middling men up the social ladder and refortifying the line that separated the middling from the meaner sort.[28]

Franklin proved that he had little faith in human nature. From his early days in Pennsylvania, he had fulminated against the intractable poor. In 1731, he wrote a piece in the *Pennsylvania Gazette* about the "scandalous Collection" of slaves, drunks, and low white servants who gathered at the outdoor fairs. As he gazed on his fellow Philadelphians, he accepted the cynical view of humanity that virtue was a rare and malleable trait. In his *Autobiography,* he told a story of how he gave up vegetarianism as a young man after he saw the belly of a fish cut open and all the little fish fall out. This story was a class parable, the lesson being that the big fish (or powerful elites) devoured weaker men. Franklin was not a disciple of the "Sermon on the Mount," but believed instead that the poor were neither less greedy nor naturally humble compared to those above. If the little fish in his world were allowed to rise, they would be just as rapacious.[29]

If inventive, Franklin was a man of his time, expressing a natural discomfort with unrestrained social mobility. For most Americans of the eighteenth century, it was assumed impossible for a servant to shed his lowly origins; the meaner sort, as one newspaper insisted, could never "wash out the stain of servility." There were fears that the meaner sort were treading too close on the heels of those above them.[30]

Franklin certainly never endorsed social mobility as we think of it today, despite his own experience. To be accurate, he fantasized that the continent would flatten out classes, but it was clear that this condition was contingent upon keeping poor people in perpetual motion. Franklin's militia plan expressed a conservative impulse. Giving the accomplished middling sort a feeling of public respect and a sense of civic duty would yield them the solid contentment of happy mediocrity. Contentment might actually reduce the desire of more ambitious men to rise up the social ladder too quickly or recklessly.

Franklin understood that maintaining class differences had its own appeal. In the *Pennsylvania Gazette,* the newspaper he edited, an article was published in 1741 that exposed why people preferred having a class hierarchy to having none. Hierarchy was easily maintained when the majority felt there was someone below them. "How many," the author asked, "even of the better sort," would choose to be "*Slaves* to those *above* them, provided they might exercise an *arbitrary* and *Tyrannical* Rule over all *below them*?" There was something desirable, perhaps even pleasurable, to use Franklin's utilitarian axiom, in the feeling of lording over subordinate classes. To alter that measure of satisfaction required a drastic rewiring of the eighteenth-century mind. Again, for Franklin, the solution lay in a radical process of spreading people so far apart and in such sparsely settled territory that they would forget who was once above or below them. But did it make sense that the rich would sacrifice their class advantage and not hire laborers or bring along slaves as they headed west? Or was his theory premised on the belief that only the poor would seek out new habitations?[31]

Franklin knew the frontier he was theorizing was an imaginary place. But it served his purposes. As a political argument, he offered a strong defense for British North America as the demographic stronghold of the empire. Here were the breeders of British subjects, and a fast-growing pool of consumers of manufacturing goods. His demographic science also concealed the deep contempt he felt for the poor. The coercive forces of nature were more palatable than the workhouse or almshouse. As late as 1780, he warned his grandson that society divided people into "two Sorts of People," those who "live comfortably in Good Houses" and those who "are poor and dirty and ragged and vicious and live in miserable Cabins and garrets," and "if they are idle, they must go without or starve." While the foregoing assessment of an uncensored Franklin was harsh, it reminds us of the prevailing sentiment: the poor were expendable. On the frontier, too, in "miserable Cabins," poverty and hopelessness abounded.[32]

Franklin knew about white Indians, the English who were taken captive as children and never really readjusted after returning to English settlements. A wealthy young man, a former Indian captive whom Franklin claimed to know, gave up his estate, taking nothing but a gun and coat when he made his way back to the wilderness. With this parable, Franklin acknowledged that freedom from care, and laziness, would always be a temptation for some. Relying on his demographic figures, the law of averages, nevertheless made the occasional outlier less of a worry.[33]

Franklin was not blind to the fact that North America's frontier settlers would not be composed solely of the finest British stock. He was quick to call those who inhabited the Pennsylvania backcountry the "refuse" of America. But at the same time, he hoped that the forces of nature would carry the day, that the demands of survival would weed out the slothful, and that the better breeders would supplant the waste people. That was his wish, at least.[34]

Franklin's theory had traction because it was built upon the prevalent English thinking of his time. He was less an innovator than he was an ingenious popularizer. His fame was such that his ideas about demographic expansion found fertile ground as the American Revolution arrived, when the iconic propagandist Thomas Paine presented a variation of Franklin's American breed to a receptive audience. Like Franklin, Paine imagined a people forged from unique conditions of its land and resources. The American breed was endowed with an instinctive, youthful, and forward-directed spirit.

Paine's pamphlet *Common Sense* (1776) is heralded for having captured the spirit of the Revolution, replete with a potent language of natural rights and an economic justification for independence. For Paine, the unique character of America's empowered white inhabitants, supported by the unquestioned majesty of an extensive continent, was evidence of the irresistible sway of nature's law. He emphasized free trade and America's potential as a commercial empire. He celebrated the power of a burgeoning continent over the reach of distant kings, as he employed the rhetorical device of unnatural breeding to disavow monarchy. He forecast that independence would end the waste and idleness that prevailed under the colonial regime.

Paine is actually an odd choice for modern Americans to celebrate as a Revolutionary symbol. He was an Englishman born and bred; better put, an Englishman in exile. When *Common Sense* was published in January 1776, he had been in Philadelphia for little more than a year. He had arrived with a letter of introduction from Franklin, which landed him a job editing the *Pennsylvania Magazine; or American Monthly Museum,* a venture committed to everything American, despite its unmistakable London design and English editor. Adding to the irony of the situation, he had been an exciseman in England, and tax collectors did not fare well in the protests leading up to the Revolution. Though his pamphlet did not sell the 150,000 copies he claimed, it did win over George Washington, and it did reach audiences in New England, New York, Baltimore, and Charleston. Like his sponsor Franklin, Paine was fascinated by facts and figures, the stuff of political arithmetic and useful knowledge, yet at the same time he was not above quoting Aesop's fables. His pamphlet spoke a familiar language, a distinctly British language of commerce, employing a simple and direct style capable of reaching readers beyond the educated elite.[35]

Paine's writing is equally as revealing for what he does and doesn't say about class. He would not tackle the monopoly of land and wealth until 1797, after watching the French Revolution unfold, when he declared in *Agrarian Justice* that everyone had an equal and divine right to the ownership of the earth. In *Common Sense,* he pushed class, poverty, and other social divisions aside. Though he acknowledged the "distinctions of rich, of poor," he directly dismissed the "harsh ill-sounding names" that exacerbated class conflict. In two breezy paragraphs, he coupled the distinctions of class and sexual difference as phenomena beyond present political concern. They were differences derived from nature, effects that had come about by accident. They simply were. Class disparities did not rise to the level of justifying revolution.[36]

Paine's sleight of hand in concealing class reflected his preference for talking about breeds. His overarching argument was that European-descended Americans were a new race in the making, one specially bred for free trade instead of the state machinery of imperial conquest. His critique of the British political economy was centered on the enormous debts it incurred through expensive military adventures, which he blamed on the frivolous ambitions of English royalty. Over time, kings and queens had become wasteful heads of state, in and of themselves a social liability.[37]

He accused the monarchy of "engrossing the commons," that is, destroying the representative nature of the House of Commons, the one branch that embodied the will of the rising merchant class in England. The American colonies, meanwhile, were being "drained" of their collective manpower and wealth, merely to underwrite new overseas wars. Independence would allow America to "begin the world over again," Paine declared dramatically. The new nation would signal a new world order. Unburdened by constant debt and a large military, it would be a vibrant continental power erected on the ideals of free trade and global commerce.[38]

As a promoter on the order of the Hakluyts, Paine conceived of America as an experimental society through which to adjust, or recalibrate, the very meaning of empire. Like past commentators, he extolled the natural resources of America: timber, tar, iron, and hemp. Corn and other agricultural goods would give America a leading role in feeding Europe. North America's major cash crop, tobacco, was starkly missing from his discussion—he used grain-producing Pennsylvania as his model, not Virginia.[39]

Most important, he insisted that independence would benefit both America and the British nation. Free trade (as he imagined it) did not discriminate; it knew no bounds. He even assured his American readers that English merchants would be on their side, wanting to protect and advance trade with America rather than plunge the government of Great Britain into another costly war. He was right about some merchants, but dead wrong about the war.[40]

It was Paine's theory of human nature that led him to emphasize commercial alliances over class divisions. His mantra was: commerce was natural, monarchy was unnatural. In many of his writings, he argued that commerce emerged from mutual affections and shared survival impulses, while monarchy rested on plunder and overawing the "vulgar" masses. Ultimately, kings benefited no one but themselves. "Your dependence upon the crown is no advantage," he told his readers in another essay, "but rather an injury to the people of Britain, as it increases the power and influence of the King. They benefited only by trade, and this they have after you are independent of the crown." In this way, Paine saw commerce as the balm that smoothed over class differences and united the interests of British and American merchants alike.[41]

Paine knew that class tensions existed. He understood that revolutions stirred up resentments. In *Common Sense,* he adopted an ominous tone at a key point in his argument, warning readers that the time was ripe to declare independence and form a stable government. Or else. In the current state of things, "the mind of the multitude is left at random," he wrote, and "the property of no man is secure." Therefore, if the leadership class did not seize hold of the narrative, the broad appeal to political independence would be supplanted by an incendiary call for social leveling. Landless mobs were waiting in the wings if colonial leaders failed to act. For Paine, "common sense" meant preserving the basic structure of the class order, and preventing the whole from descending into a mob mentality and eventual anarchy.[42]

An effective system of commerce needed a stable class system, but what it didn't need was dull-witted kings running the show. The practice of "exalting one man so greatly above the rest" was contrary to common sense and nature. Not only were the "ignorant and unfit" routinely elevated to kings, so were ennobled infants, as yet lacking reason. A "king worn out by age and infirmity" could not be legitimately removed from power. Here was nature out of control, deformed, perverted. Paine mocked the idea that English royalty were "some new species," a "race of men" worthy of infallible stature. History did not justify any claim that the "present race of kings" had honorable (let alone divine) origins. William the Conqueror was a "French Bastard," an invader with his "armed Banditti," a "usurper," a "ruffian," Paine scoffed.[43]

In the course of desacralizing the British monarchy as an effete if not defunct breed, Paine repeated what other enlightened critics had already said. Recall that Paine had only been in America for thirteen months in January 1776, when the first edition of *Common Sense* was published, and he had not yet traveled outside of Philadelphia. His knowledge of America was based mostly on newspapers and books, the squibs and scraps he collected from the storehouse of public knowledge in circulation in England and America. Paine asked Franklin (who was still in England as war approached) for a copy of Oliver Goldsmith's *History of Earth and Animated Nature* (1774). Goldsmith, Franklin, and Paine all embraced the popular science of natural history, which divided the continents into distinct breeds or races of people.[44]

On this basis, Paine pursued two powerful arguments about breeding. One highlighted the notion that Britain's monarchy was rooted in antiquated thinking and political superstition. The other aimed to prove that Americans were a distinct people, a lineage based not on superstition but on science. The widely regarded theories of Linnaeus (1707–78) and Georges-Louis Leclerc, Comte de Buffon (1707–88), which influenced Goldsmith's treatise, divided the world into varieties and races shaped by the environment unique to each major continent. The Swedish botanist Carl von Linné, better known to history as Linnaeus, organized all of plant and animal life, and divided *Homo sapiens,* the word he coined for humans, into four varieties. The European type he said was sanguine, brawny, acute, and inventive; the American Indian he deemed choleric and obstinate, yet free; the Asian was melancholic and greedy; and the African was crafty, indolent, and negligent. This grand (and ethnocentric) taxonomy served Paine's purpose in justifying the American Revolution. To "begin the world over again," Americans of English and European descent had to be a new race in the making—perhaps a better one—as they laid claim to North America.[45]

In Paine's simple formulation, breeding was either conditioned by nature or it was corrupted through superstition. The first possibility allowed a people's fullest potential to be unleashed, while the latter only reduced their ability to grow and improve themselves. Again, he was not alone in equating monarchy with bad breeding. Paine echoed another of Franklin's friends, the Unitarian cleric and scientist Joseph Priestley, who argued in 1774 that British subjects were comparable to the "livestock on a farm," being passively transferred from "one worn out royal line to another." Even more telling, a newspaper article published in both London and Philadelphia in 1774 pointed out that the worship of kings was "absurd and unnatural" and defied "common sense." This unnamed writer sarcastically contended that "simpering Lords" in England would worship a goose if it had been endowed with all the royal trappings. The line that would have caught Paine's eye was this: that kings were "made to propagate, to supply the state with *an hereditary succession of the breed.*"[46]

But there was nothing sacred about a royal breed. Blind allegiance to what enlightened critics had reduced to a barnyard custom exposed how an intelligent, civilized people might lose their grip on reality. The natural order was greatly out of alignment: British kings were exalted above everyone else for no logical reason. Americans had a unique opportunity to break free from the relics of the past and to set a true course for a better future, one unburdened by the deadweight of kings and queens.

It was this antiauthoritarian idea that made Paine's pamphlet most radical. If kings could be seen as "ignorant and unfit," then why not royal governors, Quaker proprietors, or the "Better Sort" riding in their carriages? If monarchy was not what it was supposed to represent, other customary forms of power could be questioned too. Class appearances might be similarly seen as mere smoke and mirrors. This is why Paine was careful to downplay the distinction between the rich and the poor. He wanted his American readers to focus on distant kings, not local grandees. He wanted them to break with the Crown, not to disturb the class order.

For like reasons, he turned a blind eye to slavery. Paine's America was above all else an "asylum" for future-directed Europeans. No one else need apply. He argued against the inherited notion that America was a dumping ground for lesser humans. It was only a sanctuary for able, hardworking men and women. This overly sanguine portrait cleaned up class and ignored what was unpleasant to look at. Indentured servitude and convict labor were still very much in evidence as the Revolution neared, and slavery was a fact of life. Philadelphia had a slave auction outside the London Coffee House, at the center of town on Front and Market Streets, which was directly across from Paine's lodgings. In *Common Sense*, the propagandist mentioned "Negroes" and "Indians" solely to discredit them for being mindless pawns of the British, when they were incited to harass and kill white Americans and to undermine the worthy cause of independence. The English military had "stirred up Indians and Negroes to destroy us." Us against them. Civilized America was being pitted against the barbarous hordes set upon them by the "hellish" power of London.[47]

Paine's purpose was to remind his readers of America's greatness, drawing on the visual comparison of the continent in its size and separation from the tiny island that ruled it. "In no instance hath nature made the satellite larger than its primary planet," he declared, magnifying Newtonian optics. The existing scheme did nothing but "reverse the common order of nature." England belonged to Europe, he contended, and America belonged to none but herself. Canadians would demand their freedom too, because according to Paine's taxonomic portrait they were more American than English. They were as much the offspring of the North American continent as their forward-looking southern siblings, endowed with the same traits and ambitions.[48]

As he conjured an embryonic people, Paine gave consideration to one more element that impinges on our study of class. He was thoroughly convinced that independence would eliminate idleness. Like Franklin, he projected a new continental order in which poverty was diminished. "Our present numbers are so happily proportioned to our wants," he wrote, "that no man need be idle." There were enough men to raise an army and engage in trade: enough, in other words, for self-sufficiency. The land would only continue to be wasted if "lavished by a king on his worthless dependents." (Here, Paine did take a swipe at the old Pennsylvania proprietors.) With room to grow, the infant nation would reach new heights by displaying a manly, youthful spirit of commerce that Londoners once possessed but had since lost. The Revolution would end petty quarrels between colonies that had been nurtured in a culture of imperial dependence. Only through independence could America achieve its natural potential for commercial growth.[49]

For a long time, Great Britain "engrossed us," Paine explained, proud to be part of his adopted home, his American asylum. The government in London and the Crown were controlling land and resources of the North American continent for selfish purposes. But now the United Colonies were awake to a new reality: the British monopoly had run its course. Anything less than complete independence would be "like wasting an estate on a suit at law, to regulate the trespasses of a tenant, whose lease is just expiring." Wasting an estate. Britain's lease was up.[50]

In advocating for an American breed bent on productivity and expansion, Paine's richly evocative language of waste, idleness, breeding, and engrossing of land fed excitable minds. Knowing his impressionable audience, he compared the coming Revolution to Noah and the great flood: it would give birth to a "race of men, perhaps as numerous as all Europe," their "portion of freedom" to be passed on to future generations. Population would grow and flourish as long as Americans filled the continent and harvested its resources for export. Paine's economic heroes were overseas merchants, commercial farmers, shipbuilders, inventors, and property-owning and property-protecting Americans—but decidedly not the landless poor.[51]

"Britain and America are now distinct empires," declared Paine in 1776. Six years later, as the war was coming to an end, he would still be defending the distinct American breed. "We see with other eyes," he wrote, "we hear with other ears, and think with other thoughts than those formerly used."[52]

To his credit, Paine held nothing back in poking holes in the dogma of hereditary monarchy. But with his broad swipes at royalty, he obscured other forms of injustice. He too loosely clothed the language of class in the garb of continental races and commercial impulses. Indians and slaves are marginalized in his grand vision of a new world order. Neither did he allow the ignoble waste people to make any appearance in *Common Sense;* the vast numbers of convict laborers, servants, apprentices, working poor, and families living in miserable wilderness cabins are all absent from his prose.

For Paine, the crucial issue for Americans in 1776 was not whether but how soon a new and independent regime would advance toward its destiny as first among nations. He assumed that the mighty forces of commerce and continental expansion would eliminate idleness and correct imbalances. There was nothing wrong with cultivating Anglo-American commercial instincts and sustaining peaceful transnational trade alliances with Great Britain. But in other areas, Paine hoped that the British way of seeing and hearing would disappear from America. He presumed, incorrectly as it turns out, that class would take care of itself.

CHAPTER FOUR

Thomas Jefferson's Rubbish

A Curious Topography of Class

By this means twenty of the best geniusses will be raked from the rubbish annually, and be instructed, at the public expence, so far as the grammar schools go. . . .

The circumstance of superior beauty is thought worthy of attention in the propagation of our horses, dogs, and other domestic animals; why not in that of man?

—Thomas Jefferson, *Notes on the State of Virginia* (1787)

Like Thomas Paine and Benjamin Franklin, Thomas Jefferson thought about class in continental terms. His greatest accomplishment as president was the 1803 acquisition of Louisiana, a vast territory that more than doubled the size of the United States. He called the new western domain an "empire for liberty," by which he meant something other than a free-market economy or a guarantee of social mobility. The Louisiana Territory, as he envisioned it, would encourage agriculture and forestall the growth of manufacturing and urban poverty—*that* was his formula for liberty. It was not Franklin's "happy mediocrity" (a compression of classes across an endless stretch of unsettled land), but a nation of farmers large and small. This difference is not nominal: Franklin and Paine used Pennsylvania as their model, while Jefferson saw America's future—and the contours of its class system—through the prism of Virginia.[1]

Eighteenth-century Virginia was both an agrarian and a hierarchical society. By 1770, fewer than 10 percent of white Virginians laid claim to over half the land in the colony; a small upper echelon of large planters each owned slaves in the hundreds. More than half of white men owned no land at all, working as tenants or hired laborers, or contracted as servants. Land, slaves, and tobacco remained the major sources of wealth in Jefferson's world, but the majority of white men did not own slaves. That is why Mr. Jefferson wafted well above the common farmers who dotted the countryside that extended from his celebrated mountaintop home. By the time of the Revolution, he owned at least 187 slaves, and by the Battle of Yorktown he held title to 13,700 acres in six different counties in Virginia.[2]

Pinning down Jefferson's views on class is complicated by the seductiveness of his prose. His writing could be powerful, even poetic, while reveling in rhetorical obfuscation. He praised "cultivators of the earth" as the most valuable of citizens; they were the "chosen people of God," and they "preserved a republic in vigor" through their singularly "useful occupation." And yet Jefferson's pastoral paragon of virtue did not describe any actual Virginia farmers, and not even he could live up to this high calling. Despite efforts at improving efficiency on his farms, he failed to turn a profit or rescue himself from mounting debts. In a 1796 letter, he sadly admitted that his farms were in a "barbarous state" and that he was "a monstrous farmer." Things continued downhill from there.[3]

Though we associate Jefferson with agrarian democracy and the yeoman class, his style was that of a gentleman farmer. As a member of the upper class, he hired others or used slaves to work his land. He did not become an engaged farmer until 1795, prompted by his growing interest in treating agriculture as a science. He experimented with new techniques taken from his reading, and kept meticulous records in his farm and garden books. He owned the latest manuals on husbandry—there were fifty in Monticello's library. He could ignore what didn't spark his curiosity. His dislike of the vile weed of tobacco, which he kept growing for financial reasons, led him to admit in 1801 that he "never saw a leaf of my tobacco packed in my life." For the most part, agricultural improvement fascinated him, and he did design a new plough, with its moldboard of least resistance, in 1794, hoping in large and small ways to modernize American farming.[4]

The irony is that Jefferson's approach to improving American farming was decidedly English, and not American at all. The books he read and the kind of husbandry he admired came primarily from the English agrarian tradition and British improvers of his day. His decision to raise wheat so as not to be completely dependent on tobacco, coupled with his plan to introduce merino sheep into every Virginia county in order to produce better wool, were attempts to correct what his fellow improver George Washington lambasted as the "slovenly" habits in farmers of their state. Virginians were far behind the English in the use of fertilizers, crop rotation, and harvesting and ploughing methods. It was common for large planters and small farmers alike to deplete acres of soil and then leave it fallow and abandoned. "We waste as we please," was how Jefferson gingerly phrased it.[5]

Jefferson knew that behind all the rhetoric touting America's agricultural potential there was a less enlightened reality. For every farsighted gentleman farmer, there were scads of poorly managed plantations and unskilled small (and tenant) farmers struggling to survive. How could slaves, who did most of the fieldwork on Virginia plantations, assume the mantle of "cultivators of the earth"? For Jefferson, it seems, they were mere "tillers." Tenants, who rented land they did not own, and landless laborers and squatters lacked the commercial acumen and genuine virtue of cultivators too. In his perfect world, lower-class farmers could be improved, just like their land. If they were given a freehold and a basic education, they could adopt better methods of husbandry and pass on favorable habits and traits to their children. As we will see, however, Jefferson's various reform efforts were thwarted by those of the ruling gentry who had little interest in elevating the Virginia poor. Even more dramatically, his agrarian version of social mobility was immediately compromised by his own profound class biases, of which he was unaware.[6]

Historically hailed as a democrat, Thomas Jefferson was never able to escape his class background. His privileged upbringing inevitably colored his thinking. He could not have penned the Declaration of Independence or been elected to the Continental Congress if he had not been a prominent member of the Virginia gentry. He had the advantages of an education in the classics, and was trained in law and letters at the elite College of William and Mary. He collected books, amassing 6,487 volumes. Proficient in Latin and Greek, he enjoyed Italian, read old French and some Spanish, and was also versed in the obscure Anglo-Saxon language. He surrounded himself with European luxury goods and was an epicurean in his tastes, as displayed by his love of French sauternes. To imagine that Jefferson had some special insight into the anxious lives of the lower sort, or that he truly appreciated the unpromising conditions tenant farmers experienced, is to fail to account for the wide gulf that separated the rich and poor in Virginia.[7]

If Franklin thought of class as principally conditioned by demography—

the human compulsion to seek pleasure and avoid pain—Jefferson subscribed to a different philosophy. Though equally drawn to numbers and political arithmetic, he saw human behavior as conditional, plastic, adaptable; across generations, it would conform to shifts in the physical and social environment. If the hand of nature bestowed merit on some, so did local surroundings and the choice of a mate. But above all, what divided people into recognizable stations was the intimate relationship between land and labor. As he wrote in 1813, "the spontaneous energies of the earth are a gift of nature," but man must "husband his labor" in order to reap its greatest benefits. In Jefferson's larger scheme of things, class was a creature of topography; it was shaped by the bond forged between producers and the soil. By producers, of course, he meant husbandmen and landowners—not tenants, not slaves.[8]

The occupation he loved, the descriptor that most delighted him, was *cultivator*. This word meant more than one who earned his bread through farming; it drew upon the eighteenth-century idiom that arose from the popular study of natural history. To cultivate meant to renew, to render fertile, which thus implied extracting real sustenance from the soil, as well as good traits, superior qualities, and steady habits of mind. Cultivation carried with it rich associations with animal breeding and the idea that good soil led to healthy and hearty stocks (of animals or people). Proficiency in tapping the land's productive potential had the added benefit of improving the moral sense, which was what Jefferson meant when he described that "peculiar deposit of genuine and substantial virtue" found in the breast of every true cultivator. In this way, the soil could be regenerative, much like a deposit of calcium-rich marl, which educated farmers used to restore nutrients to the land.[9]

In Jefferson's taxonomy, then, class was less about Franklin's commercialized language of "sorts," whereby people and goods were readily equated and valued. Instead, Jeffersonian-style classes were effectively strata that mimicked the different nutritive grades within layers of the soil. To this bookish Virginian, idealizing rural society, classes were to be regarded as natural extrusions of a promising land, flesh-and-blood manifestations of an agrarian topography.

Revolutionary Virginia was hardly a place of harmony, egalitarianism, or unity. The war effort exacerbated already simmering tensions between elite Patriots and those below them. In British tradition, the American elite expected the lower classes to fight their wars. In the Seven Years' War, for example, Virginians used the infamous practice of impressment to round up vagabonds to meet quotas. During the Revolution, General Washington stated that only "the lower class of people" should serve as foot soldiers. Jefferson believed that class character was palpably real. As a member of the House of Delegates, he came up with a plan to create a Virginia cavalry regiment specifically for the sons of planters, youths whose "indolence or education, has unfitted them for foot-service."[10]

As early as 1775, landless tenants in Loudoun County, Virginia, voiced a complaint that was common across the sprawling colony: there was "no inducement for the poor man to Fight, for he had nothing to defend." Many poor white men rebelled against recruitment strategies, protested the exemptions given to the overseers of rich planters, and were disappointed with the paltry pay. Such resistance led to the adoption of desperate measures. In 1780, Virginia assemblymen agreed to grant white enlistees the bounty of a slave as payment for their willingness to serve until the end of the war. Here was an instant bump up the social ladder. Here was the social transfer of wealth and status from the upper to the lower class. But even this gruesome offer wasn't tempting enough, because few took the bait. Two years later when the Battle of Yorktown decided the outcome of the war, the situation was unchanged. Of those fighting on the American side, only a handful hailed from Virginia.[11]

There were other attempts to mollify poor white farmers. In drafting a new constitution in 1776, Virginia rebels embraced freehold suffrage: adult white men who were twenty-one and who had a freehold of twenty-five acres of cultivated land were awarded the right to vote. Yet the same Revolutionaries were stingy when it came to redressing landlessness and poverty. Jefferson's proposal to lift up the bottom ranks, granting men without any land of their own fifty acres and the vote, was dropped from the final version of the constitution.[12]

Appointed to a committee to revise Virginia's laws, Jefferson tried another tactic that aimed to shift the balance of class power in the state. He succeeded in eliminating primogeniture and entail, two legal practices that kept large amounts of land in the hands of a few powerful families. His purpose was for land to be distributed equally to all children in a family, not just vested in the eldest male. Entail, which restricted the sale of land, would be replaced with privately owned land grants. Meanwhile, the committee considered a proposal granting each freeborn child a tract of seventy-five acres as an incentive to encourage poorer men to marry and have children. Jefferson's freeholders needed children to anchor them to the land and as an incentive to turn from idleness.[13]

But reform did not take easily. Virginia's freehold republic failed to instill virtue among farmers, the effect that Jefferson had fantasized. The majority of small landowners sold their land to large planters, mortgaged their estates, and continued to despoil what was left of the land. They looked upon it as just another commodity, not a higher calling. Jefferson failed to understand what his predecessor James Oglethorpe had seen: the freehold system (with disposable land grants) favored wealthy land speculators. Farming was arduous work, with limited chance of success, especially for families lacking the resources available to Jefferson: slaves, overseers, draft animals, a plough, nearby mills, and waterways to transport farm produce to market. It was easy to acquire debts, easy to fail. Land alone was no guarantee of self-sufficiency.[14]

If the ruling elite at the Virginia constitutional convention were unwilling to grant poor men fifty acres to become freehold citizens, they were quite content to dump the poor into the hinterland. With the opening up of the land office in 1776, a new policy was adopted: anyone squatting on unclaimed land in western Virginia and Kentucky could claim a preemption right to buy it. Like the long-standing British practice of colonizing the poor, the Virginians sought to quell dissent, raise taxes, and lure the less fortunate west. This policy did little to alter the class structure. In the end, it worked against poor families. Without ready cash to buy the land, they became renters, trapped again as tenants instead of becoming independent landowners.[15]

Public education accompanied land reforms. In bill no. 79, for the "General Diffusion of Knowledge," Jefferson laid out a proposal for different levels of preparation: primary schools for all boys and girls, and grammar schools for more capable males at the public expense. For the second tier, he called for twenty young "geniusses" to be drawn from the lower class of each county. Rewarding those with merit, he devised a means of social mobility in a state where education was purely a privilege of wealthy families.[16]

Writing of his plan in *Notes on the State of Virginia*, his wide-ranging natural history of his state, he chose a rather unsavory allusion to describe the reform. His handful of lucky scholars would be "raked from the rubbish," leaving the majority to wallow in ignorance and poverty. "Rubbish" was his alliterative variation on the ever-present theme of waste people. He wasn't anticipating Teddy Roosevelt's Bunyanesque allusion to muckraking journalists, but rather was invoking the older, Elizabethan meaning of raking the muck of a bad crop. The "rubbish" designation showed contempt for the poor, a sad reminder that very few were capable of escaping the refuse heap. But the bill failed to pass: the Virginia gentry had no desire to pay for it. They had no interest in raising up a few stray kernels of genius from the wasteland of the rural poor.[17]

The education reform bill had little chance of passing, but its companion piece for funding workhouses did. As was the case with England's poor laws, the bill penalized those who "waste their time in idle and dissolute courses," loitering and wandering or deserting their wives and children: such people were "deemed vagabonds." The solution for poor children was not education, but hiring them out as apprentices. Jefferson made a minor change to the existing law, which dated to 1755: the poor would no longer wear identifying badges. But vagrants would still be punished, and their children would pay the price for their idleness in a way that was reminiscent of the exploited orphans of dead servants at Jamestown. They may have been a less visible class without badges, but they remained a powerful symbol of vice and sloth.[18]

All of Jefferson's early reforms were less about promoting equality or democracy than moderating extremes. Like the farmer's use of marl soil or peat, his approach was closer to breaking up clumps or concentrations of wealth and poverty. Virginia's social order was stagnant; it was weighed down by a top-heavy planter class and an increasingly immobile class of landless families. His powerful words, "raked from the rubbish," captured his philosophy in an unmistakable, visually compelling way. Raking was comparable to ploughing, the process of turning over tired and barren topsoil and unearthing new life from the layers below. Such improvements, though gradual in spreading benefits, promised a stronger crop of citizens in the future. ·

Jefferson's influential survey of class (as a product of topography) appeared in his *Notes on the State of Virginia*. Mostly written during his governorship of Virginia in 1780–81, the book was not published until several years later, when he was serving as the U.S. minister to France. Jefferson had been encouraged to put his ideas to paper by a series of questions posed by François Barbé-Marbois, the secretary of the French Legation in Philadelphia. His *Notes* became a kind of diplomatic intervention, offering European readers a combined defense of his home state and his new nation.

Notes offered a natural history of race and class, replete with Jefferson's own empirical observations, from facts and figures he had compiled. It was part travel narrative in the tradition of Hakluyt, and part legal brief. He imagined the opposing counsel to be the acclaimed French naturalist Georges-Louis Leclerc, the Comte de Buffon, who had offered up a highly unappealing portrait of the American continent as a backward place cursed with widespread degeneracy. In *Notes,* the only book Jefferson ever wrote, he stripped away the ugliness and replaced it with a Virginia of natural beauty and bounty. Here, in Jefferson's version of the *New English Canaan,* the continent promised unmatched resources for commercial wealth. Class was significant. The rich topography afforded a home for his "cultivators of the earth," an American breed that represented the world's best hope.

Buffon's work was troubling for a number of reasons. In his *Histoire Naturelle,* first published in 1749, he had reduced the New World to one giant and nefarious Dismal Swamp. All of America, as it were, had become North Carolina. A suffocating mixture of moisture and heat had produced stagnant waters, "gross herbiage," and miasmas of the air, which retarded the size and diversity of species. Buffon sounded at times like the colorful William Byrd, complaining of the "noxious exhalations" in America that blocked the sun, which made it impossible to "purify" the soil and air. Swamp creatures multiplied in this environment: "moist plants, reptiles, and insects, and all animals that wallow in the mire." Domestic animals shrank in size in comparison to their European counterparts, and their flesh was less flavorful. Only Carolina's prized critter, the hog, thrived in such a godforsaken terrain.[19]

Native Americans were not just savages to Buffon; they were a constitutionally enfeebled breed, devoid of free will and "activity of mind." As the forgotten stepchildren of Mother Nature, they lacked the "invigorating sentiment of love, and the strong desire for multiplying their species." They were "cold and languid," spending their days in "stupid repose," without the strong affective bonds that united people into civilized societies. Buffon had converted Indians into quasi-reptilian swamp monsters. They lurked in marshes, hunting prey, ignorant of the fate of their offspring, concerned only with the next meal or battle. The desire to reproduce, Buffon contended, was the "spark" of life and the fire of genius. This essential quality was missing from their constitution—all because they languished amid a debilitating environment.[20]

In contesting Buffon, Jefferson had to wipe the canvas clean of the swamp monsters and paint a very different, eco-friendly picture. He conjured another America, a sublime place of endless diversity. His Blue Ridge Mountains were majestic; the Mississippi River was alive with birds and fish in a way comparable to the Nile—the birthplace of Western civilization. Native Americans existed in an uncultivated state, he admitted, yet they were endowed with a manly ardor and displayed a noble mind. America was not plagued with pathetic stocks of animals or people. On the contrary, the young continent heralded one of the greatest scientific discoveries of the age: the bones of the woolly mammoth, ranked as the largest species known to man, which according to Jefferson still roamed the forests. English and European settlers had excelled, not suffered. That rare spark of genius, nurtured in Washington, Franklin, and David Rittenhouse, the Philadelphia astronomer, was solid proof, to his mind, of the invigorating and regenerative natural landscape.[21]

Jefferson fundamentally agreed with Buffon's science. He did not abandon the Frenchman's ruling premise that the physical surroundings were crucial in cultivating races and classes of people, or that land could be either regenerative or degenerative. Buffon's theory wasn't wrong then; his observations were incomplete. As Jefferson argued in 1785, in a letter to the Marquis de Chastellux, who had visited Monticello three years earlier, Native Americans were not feeble. Over time they had developed muscles to make them fleet of foot for warfare. Euro-Americans were equally adaptable to the congenial American environment. They drew upon an inbred strength passed down from generations of ancestors who had labored in the fields. Cultivation was in their blood, Jefferson was saying, and they were already engaged in transforming the land and making it their own.[22]

Jefferson's ideas of topography went beyond the natural environment.

He was equally concerned with human chorography—the way humans adapted to the land, exploited its fertility, and built social institutions. Husbandry itself was a crucial stage that elevated human societies beyond the rudiments of savagery and barbarism. The American cultivator needed some safeguards. Degeneracy was certainly possible, Jefferson admitted, but not on Buffon's scale. Dangers lurked for Americans who were too close to the wilderness, or for those too enamored with the commercial luxuries of the Old World. In one of his dreamier moments in 1785, he wrote of the hope that America would be like China, completely cut off from European commerce and manufacturing and other entanglements: "We should thus avoid all wars, and all our citizens would be husbandmen." He wished for a middle zone, between the two extremes.[23]

Jefferson was not above social engineering, believing that manners could be cultivated. His scheme for the Northwest Territory built upon his reforms for Virginia. As the chair of two congressional committees, he assumed a leading role in shaping how the land would be distributed and governed. In his report on the Land Ordinance of 1784, he devised a grid plan that would have divided the land into perfectly formed rectangles, offering individual lots, the basic unit of the family farm. He wanted the area divided into ten potential states, and gave them names. And not just any names: Sylvania, Cherronesus, Assenisipia, Metropotamia, Pelispia, to name a few. He chose fanciful names, with pseudo-classical or agrarian meanings, suggesting that in this act of state building, Congress was engaged in the regeneration or rebirth of Western civilization. He insisted that no hereditary titles be recognized in the Northwest, and after 1800 slavery and involuntary servitude would be permanently banned there. Following in the footsteps of Oglethorpe, Jefferson envisioned a free-labor zone.[24]

What was Jefferson up to? One goal was to forestall the growth of manufacturing, which in *Notes* he described as a canker on the body politic. The grid system resembled rows of garden plots, something that would have made sense to his fellow naturalist J. Hector St. John de Crèvecoeur, author of *Letters from an American Farmer* (1782). A French-born migrant who spent years in New York's Hudson Valley, and a devotee of Buffon, Crèvecoeur celebrated an "intermediary space," which created a "separate and distinct class." "Men are like plants," he believed, and the seeds of classes could be planted and cultivated. The typical class of cultivators whom he imagined filling this middle zone owned a 371-acre farm; they were not tenants or squatters, nor were they overseas merchants importing English manufactured goods. Crève-coeur's perfect farmer turned the fields into a classroom, placing his son on the plough, having him feel the up-and-down rhythm as it moved through the soil.[25]

Jefferson, too, wanted Americans tied to the land, with deep roots to their offspring, to future generations. Agrarian perfection would germinate: a love of the soil, no less than a love of one's heirs, instilled *amor patriae*, a love of country. He was not promoting a freewheeling society or the rapid commercial accumulation of wealth; nor was he advocating a class system marked by untethered social mobility. Jefferson's husband-men were of a new kind of birthright station, passed from parents to children. They were not to be an ambitious class of men on the make.[26]

Jefferson's idealized farmers were not rustics either. They sold their produce in the marketplace, albeit on a smaller scale. There was room enough for an elite gentry class, and gentleman farmers like himself. Using the latest husbandry methods, improving the soil, the wealthier farmers could instruct others, the less skilled beneath them. Education and emulation were necessary to instill virtue. American farmers required an apprenticeship of a sort, which was only possible if they were planted in the right kind of engineered environment. The Northwest Territory served that purpose, as a free-labor zone that cultivated middling aspirations and was safely decontaminated of any noxious influences. The relics of noble titles were gone, slavery was prohibited, and commercial impulses were subdued.

In one of his most ambitious plans for reform, sketched out in 1789, Jefferson thought of importing German immigrants, who were known to be superior laborers, and to place them on adjacent fifty-acre plots opposite slaves, who would be "brought up, as others, in the habits of foresight and property." At the same time, he contemplated the recruitment of Germans just to improve the caliber of Virginia's poor white farmers. The Anglo-Virginians were supposed to intermingle with and learn from the better German farmers around them.[27]

Of course, Jefferson was not always honest about the class system that surrounded him. He preferred to project an America of "tranquil permanent felicity" than confront the unpleasant reality that persisted. His most extreme statements describing the United States as the land of unparalleled opportunities usually came as responses to criticism. As he had done in *Notes*, he saw himself as a public sentry, the intellectual defender of the reputation of a rising young country.

He had a lot to defend in the aftermath of the American Revolution. The war years had taken their toll. A postwar depression created widespread suffering. States had acquired hefty debts, which caused legislatures to increase taxes to levels far higher, sometimes three to four times higher, than before the war. Most of these tax dollars ended up in the hands of speculators in state government securities that had been sold to cover war expenses. Many soldiers were forced to sell their scrip and land bounties to speculators at a fraction of the value. Wealth was being transferred upward, from the tattered pockets of poor farmers and soldiers to the bulging purses of a nouveau riche of wartime speculators and creditors—a new class of "moneyed men."[28]

The officers of the Continental Army had staged a mutiny in Newburgh, New York, in 1783, threatening to disband if Congress did not grant them full pensions. During the same year, army officers organized the Society of Cincinnati, a fraternal organization, accused of laying the foundation for a hereditary aristocracy. The society initially granted hereditary privileges to the sons of veteran officers and awarded medals as badges of membership in the highly selective club. Jefferson's prohibition on titles in the Northwest Territory was a not-so-subtle rebuke of the society's flagrant pretentions. It also explains why he banned badges previously worn by vagrants in Virginia.[29]

While Jefferson was more than willing to attack a pseudo-aristocracy, he wore rose-colored glasses when it came to acknowledging class turmoil arising from below. British papers had published reports of the mutinies and riots in the United States, which Jefferson dismissed as inconsequential. In 1784, he declared in a published response that not a single beggar could be seen "from one end to another of the continent." Poverty and class strife simply did not exist. He wrote this just a year before the Virginia bill to round up vagabonds finally passed.[30]

Jefferson had a different opinion in 1786, when Shays' Rebellion broke out across western Massachusetts. Rising taxes and mounting debts among middle-class and poor farmers had fueled a class war. Captain Daniel Shays had served in the Continental Army, and whether or not it was an accurate description, he was called the "Generalissimo" of the uprising. Shays had acquired over two hundred acres of land, only to see half of his holdings lost during the postwar depression. His supporters closed down courts that were auctioning off farms and homes, forming an ad hoc army that attempted to take over the armory in Springfield. Similar protests took place as far south as Virginia. Writing from France, Jefferson did not deny the existence of the rebellion, but treated it as a naturally recurring, even therapeutic phenomenon. In an odd twist, he calculated that such political tempests would most likely happen every thirteen years. A "little rebellion" was analogous to "storms in the physical environment"; temporarily jarring, it would settle back down, leaving society's core principles refreshed.[31]

Jefferson's language betrayed him. He envisioned rebellion as a process of regeneration, removed from human agency and, most important, devoid of class anger. For her part, Abigail Adams had little sympathy for the Shaysites. "Ferment and commotions," she curtly observed in a letter to Jefferson, had brought forth an "abundance of Rubbish." Others agreed. Captain Shays was described in newspapers as an ignorant leader, a pathetic man living in a "sty," his fellow insurgents nothing more than "brutes." Critics compared them to "Ragamuffins of the earth," lowly vagabonds who owed more than they were worth. To the naturalist Jefferson, they belonged to the sedimentary debris unearthed and let loose across the human terrain.[32]

In the same year, he wrote lengthy comments on an article entitled "Etats Unis," meant for publication in the famed *Encyclopédie Méthodique*. After summarizing the history of the Society of Cincinnati, Jefferson offered a curious explanation for the convulsions it caused. "No distinction between man and man has ever been known in America," he insisted. Among private individuals, the "poorest labourer stood on equal ground with the wealthiest Millionary," and the poor man was favored when the rights of the rich and poor were contested in the courts. Whether the "shoemaker or the artisan" was elected to office, he "instantly commanded respect and obedience." With a final flourish, Jefferson declared that "of distinctions by birth or badge," Americans "had no more idea than they had of existence in the moon or planets."[33]

Though Jefferson sold Europeans on America as a classless society, no such thing existed in Virginia or anywhere else. In his home state, a poor laborer or shoemaker had no chance of getting elected to office. Jefferson wrote knowing that semiliterate members of the lower class did not receive even a rudimentary education. Virginia's courts meticulously served the interests of rich planters. And wasn't slavery a "distinction between man and man"? Furthermore, Jefferson's freehold requirement for voting created "odious distinctions" between landowners and poor merchants and artisans, denying the latter classes voting rights.[34]

One has to wonder at Jefferson's blatant distortion, his desire to paint the Society of Cincinnati as so otherworldly to Americans that only extraterrestrials could appreciate it. He failed to recognize that many elite Americans were fond of the trappings of aristocracy.

Under the administration of George Washington, the Federalists established a "Republican Court," with rules of protocol, displays of genteel etiquette, and formal weekly levees—visits by invitation only extended to the national elite to meet with the president. Martha Washington held her drawing-room salons, and around the president emerged a cult of adulation that imitated certain aspects of royal pageantry. Powerful families in Philadelphia established dynastic marriages with European peers. Elizabeth Patterson, the daughter of a wealthy Baltimore merchant, became an international celebrity when in 1803 she married the brother of Napoleon Bonaparte. At the time, President Jefferson wrote his minister in France to inform Napoleon that his sibling had married into a family whose social rank was "with the first of the United States."[35]

In 1789, when Vice President John Adams proposed before the U.S. Senate that the president required a more daunting title, such as "Majesty," he accepted that political distinctions needed to be dressed up in pomp and circumstance. Unlike Franklin, Adams felt that the "passion for distinction" was the most powerful driving human force, above hunger and fear. Americans not only scrambled to get ahead; they needed someone to look down on. "There must be one, indeed, who is the last and lowest of the human species," Adams concluded, and even he needed his dog to love him. He also sarcastically acknowledged that while Jefferson and his brand of republicans might disdain titles and stations, they had no intention of disturbing private forms of authority; the subordinate positions of wives, children, servants, and slaves were left safely intact.[36]

Jefferson was not above his own brand of political stagecraft. Unlike Washington and Adams, who rode in fancy carriages to their inauguration ceremonies, Jefferson rode his own horse back to the President's House after delivering his inaugural address. He dispensed with the levees and greeted diplomats and guests at the executive mansion while wearing an old vest and worn slippers. He was known for his casual attire—not while he was in France, but upon his return.[37]

His version of rustic republican simplicity reflected his experience in Virginia, where the gentry lived in grand houses like Monticello, and yet dressed down when commingling with the mass of small farmers during elections. A Federalist he particularly despised, the Virginian and chief justice of the Supreme Court John Marshall, was known for his slovenly appearance. Two men's politics could not have been more different, but they dressed in the same style. Elite Virginians had a strong distaste for the nouveau riche, and believed that those with wealth, land, family names, and reputations didn't need to show off. Some observers saw Jefferson as playing a role, appearing "affectedly plain in his dress." In this climate, eliminating external signs of class did not necessarily erode expectations of deference. Dressing down just as easily masked social distinctions. The conservative art of emulation, assuming that the head of state had something to teach others, was very much a part of Jefferson's philosophy. Indeed, he allowed his sheep to graze on the lawn of the President's House, letting everyone know that a gentleman farmer occupied the highest office in the land.[38]

Jefferson may have hated artificial distinctions and titles, but he was quite comfortable asserting "natural" differences. With nature as his guide, he felt there was no reason not to rank humans on the order of animal breeds. In Notes, he wrote with calm assurance, "The circumstance of superior beauty is thought worthy of attention in the propagation of our horses, dogs, and other animals." With emphasis, he added, "why not in that of man?"[39]

Careful breeding was one solution to slavery. In his Revisal of the

Laws, Jefferson calculated how a black slave could turn white: once a slave possessed seven-eighths "white" blood, the "taint" of his or her African past was deemed gone. In 1813, he explained to a young Massachusetts lawyer how the formula worked: "It is understood in Natural history that a 4th cross of one race of animals gives an issue of equivalent for all sensible purposes to the original bloods." This was the same formula Jefferson used in breeding an original stock of merino sheep. William Byrd had earlier talked about blanching Native Americans through intermarriage with Europeans. As Buffon put it, breeding back to the "original" stock meant reconstituting blacks as white people.[40]

Jefferson's friend William Short took Buffon's ideas quite seriously. In a 1798 letter to Jefferson, he noted how blacks in the United States were becoming lighter. He admitted that this was partly due to mixing with whites, but he felt that climate mattered as well. In posing a possible scenario, he came close to endorsing Buffon's idea of regeneration: "Suppose a black family transplanted to Sweden, may we not presume . . . that in a sufficient number of succeeding generations, the color would disappear from meer effect of the climate?"[41]

It was more than a theory. Jefferson was practicing race mixing under his own roof, fathering several children with his quadroon slave Sally Hemings. What is striking about this relationship is Hemings's pedigree: her mother, Elizabeth, was half white, and her father was John Wayles, Jefferson's English-born father-in-law. Jefferson's children with Sally were the fourth cross, making them perfect candidates for emancipation and passing for white. Two of the children, Beverly and Harriet, ran away from Monticello and lived as free whites, while Madison and Eston were set free in Jefferson's will and later moved to Ohio. Eston's offspring also intermarried with whites.[42]

On his plantation, Jefferson had little difficulty in breeding slaves *as chattel*. He counted slave children in cold terms as "increase," and considered his female slaves to be more valuable than males. Men might raise food, but it was quickly consumed; women produced children that could be sold as stock. He did not shrink from saying, "I consider the labor of a breeding woman as no object, and a child raised every 2. years is of more profit than the crop of the best laboring man." Women were meant to breed, for "providence has made our interests & duties coincide perfectly."[43]

The impulse to breed played an equally significant part in Jefferson's agrarian republic. His trust of the people rested on his belief that a new kind of leadership class was bound to emerge in the United States. He laid out this theory in a series of letters he exchanged with John Adams in 1813. It was Adams who opened the friendly debate by mentioning the long human history of upholding the idea of the "Wellborn." To prove his point, he quoted the ancient Greek poet-philosopher Theognis: "When we want to purchase Horses, Asses, or Rams, We inquire for the Wellborn. And every one wishes to procure from the good breeds. A good man does not care to marry a Shrew, the Daughter of a Shrew, unless They give him a great deal of money with her." His contention was that men marry for money more than the desire for producing healthy off-spring.

Adams returned to this favorite theory that men are driven by vanity and ambition. Put a hundred men in a room, he conjectured, and soon twenty-five will use their superior talents, their cunning, to take control. This impulse would inevitably lead all kinds of men to divide into classes, and he was confident that the United States had not evolved beyond being ruled by this passion for distinction. By the eighteenth century, "wellborn" was synonymous with the landed aristocracy. Adams re-minded Jefferson of the powerful families in Massachusetts and Virginia who were bound together through kinship and property. He observed that he and Jefferson were products of the desire to marry well. Jeffer-son's lineage on his mother's side linked him to one of the First Fam-ilies of Virginia, the Randolphs, and Abigail Adams, by pedigree, was a Quincy.[44]

Jefferson was unconvinced. He interpreted Theognis differently, believing that the poet was making an ethical argument. He was actually chastising humanity for marrying the "old, ugly, and vicious" for reasons of wealth and ambition, while they more sensibly bred domestic animals "to improve the race." As Jefferson saw it, humans were animals guided by the overriding impulse (as Buffon said) of sexual desire. Nature made sure that humans would propagate the race, implanting in them lust mixed with love, through the "oestrum." The oestrum was the state of female animals in heat, and provided the capacity for sexual arousal; in *Notes*, he wrote that "love was the peculiar oestrum of poets." Sexual desire, in this way, would produce what Jefferson called a "fortuitous concourse of breeders." He meant that desire was the real engine of breeding, and according to the law of averages, unconscious lust would outflank even unbridled greed.[45]

Jefferson's model of breeding generated an "accidental aristocracy" of talent. Class divisions would form through natural selection. Men would marry women for more than money; they would consciously and unconsciously choose mates with other favorable traits. It was all a matter of probability: some would marry out of sheer lust, others for property, but the "good and wise" would marry for beauty, health, virtue, and talents. If Americans had enough native intelligence to distinguish the natural aristoi from the pseudo-aristoi in choosing political leaders, then they had reasonable instincts for selecting spouses. A "fortuitous concourse of breeders" would produce a leadership class—one that would sort out the genuinely talented from the ambitious men on the make.[46]

The question that Jefferson never answered was this: What happened to those who were not part of the talented elite? How would one describe the "concourse of breeders" living on the bottom layer of society? No matter how one finessed it, rubbish produced more rubbish, even if a select few might be salvaged. If the fortuitous breeders naturally rose up the social ladder, the unfortunate, the degenerate remained mired in the morass of meaner sorts.

In all of his musings on class, Jefferson rarely used the word "yeoman." He preferred "cultivator" or "husbandman." One time that he did use the term was in an 1815 letter to William Wirt. Born to a Maryland tavernkeeper, Wirt was one of Jefferson's apprentices whom he took under his wing, and he rose to become a noted attorney. He was one of the natural aristocracy of talent, and one of the beneficiaries of Jefferson's patronage. In 1815, Wirt was putting the finishing touches on the biography of Patrick Henry, and he asked Jefferson to paint a social picture of eighteenth-century Virginia. Conjuring a potent topographical metaphor, Jefferson contended that the colony had had a stagnant class system, whose social order resembled a slice of earth on an archeological dig. The classes were separated into "strata," which shaded off "imperceptibly, from top to bottom, nothing disturbing the order of their repose."

Jefferson divided the top tier of supposed social betters into "Aristocrats, half breeds, pretenders." Below them was the "solid independent yeomanry, looking askance at those above, yet not ventured to jostle them." On the bottom rung he put "the lowest feculum of beings called Overseers, the most abject, degraded and unprincipled race." Overseers were tasked to keep slaves engaged in labor on southern plantations. By pitting the honest yeomanry against the "feculum" of overseers, Jefferson harshly invoked the old English slur of human waste. That wasn't enough. He portrayed overseers as panderers, with their "cap in hand to the Dons"; they were vicious men without that desirable deposit of virtue, who feigned subservience in order to indulge the "spirit of domination." Jefferson endowed his Virginia class of overseers with the same vices that he attributed to those toiling in manufacturing. The twirling distaff at the workbench had been replaced with the slave driver's whip.[47]

In this strange sleight of hand, slaves became invisible laborers outside his tripartite social ranking. Jefferson made them victims of overseers, not of their actual owners. The yeomanry might be the progenitors of his noble class of cultivators, but their lineage remained unclear. The small farmers whom Jefferson knew were neither noble nor particularly independent. But he presented the upper class as an odd collection of breeds: great planters (pure-blooded Aristocrats) sat at the top, but their children might marry down and produce a class of "half breeds." The pretenders were outsiders who dared claim the station of the leading families, where they were never really welcomed. Despite his pose in his exchange with John Adams two years earlier, Jefferson's brief natural history of Virginia's classes proved that elites and upstarts married the "wellborn." The Virginia upper class was a creation of marrying for money, name, and station, in which kinship and pedigree were paramount.

In the end, though Jefferson hoped this old Virginia had disappeared, the truth was more complicated. Waste people lingered on, just as overseers did. The children of aristocrats, those of the half-breed class, and a new class that Jefferson called the "pseudo-Aristocrats" were rising to replace those who had once ruled Virginia. The composition of the strata of soil that he compared to the different classes may have changed, but the process of distinguishing the richest loam on the top and the less fertile lower layers remained in force.

Class was a permanent fixture in America. If the yeoman looked askance at those above him, the poor farmers heading west faced a new breed of aristocrats: shrewd land speculators and large cotton and sugar planters. The more cynical Adams reminded Jefferson in 1813 that the continent would be ruled by "Land jobbers" and a new class of manor lords. The glorious title of cultivator would remain beyond the reach of most backcountry settlers.[48]

CHAPTER FIVE

Andrew Jackson's Cracker Country

The Squatter as Common Man

Obsquatulate, To mosey, or to abscond.
—"Cracker Dictionary," *Salem Gazette* (1830)

B y 1800, one-fifth of the American population had resettled on its "frontier," the territory between the Appalachian Mountains and the Mississippi. Effective regulation of this mass migration was well beyond the limited powers of the federal government. Even so, officials understood that the country's future depended on controlling this vast territory. Financial matters were involved too. Government sale of these lands was needed to reduce the nation's war debts. Besides, the lands were hardly empty, and the potential for violent conflicts with Native Americans was ever present, as white migrants settled on lands they did not own. National greatness depended as much as anything upon the class of settlers that was advancing into the new territories. Would the West be a dumping ground for a refuse population? Or would the United States profit from its natural bounty and grow as a continental empire more equitably? There was much uncertainty.[1]

The western territories were for all intents and purposes America's colonies. Despite the celebratory spirit in evidence each Fourth of July beginning in 1777, many anxieties left over from the period of the English colonization revived. Patriotic rhetoric aside, it was not at all clear that national independence had genuinely ennobled ordinary citizens. Economic prosperity had actually declined for most Americans in the wake of the Revolution. Those untethered from the land, who formed the ever-expanding population of landless squatters heading into the trans-Appalachian West, unleashed mixed feelings. To many minds, the migrant poor represented the United States' re-creation of Britain's most despised and impoverished class: vagrants. During the Revolution, under the Articles of Confederation (the first founding document before the Constitution was adopted), Congress drew a sharp line between those entitled to the privileges of citizenship and the "paupers, vagabonds, and fugitives from justice" who stood outside the national community.[2]

The image of the typical poor white resident of the frontier was pathetic and striking to observers, but it wasn't new at all. He was an updated version of William Byrd's lazy lubber. He was the English vagrant wandering the countryside. If anything about him was new, it was that some observers granted him a folksy appeal: though coarse and ragged in his dress and manners, the post-Revolutionary backwoodsman was at times described as hospitable and generous, someone who invited weary travelers into his humble cabin. Yet his more favorable cast rarely lasted after the woods were cut down and settled towns and farms appeared. As civilization approached, the backwoodsman was expected to lay down roots, purchase land, and adjust his savage ways to polite society—or move on.

Whereas Franklin, Paine, and Jefferson envisioned Americans as a commercial people suited to a grand continent, those who wrote about the American breed during the nineteenth century conceived a different frontier character. This new generation of social commentators paid particular attention to a peculiar class of people living in the thickly forested Northwest Territory (Ohio, Illinois, Indiana, Michigan, and Wisconsin), along the marshy shores of the Mississippi, and amid the mountainous terrain and sandy barrens of the southern backcountry (western Virginia, the Carolinas, Georgia, plus the new states of Kentucky and Tennessee, and northern Alabama), and later the Florida, Arkansas, and Missouri Territories. In the heyday of James Fenimore Cooper (1789–1851), who gave early America the fearless forest guide known as Leatherstocking, the abstract cartography of the Enlightenment yielded to the local color of the novelist in describing the odd quirks of the rustic personality. Americans were starting to develop a mythic identity for themselves. The reading public was more attuned to travelers' accounts than they were to grid plans and demographic numbers. As Americans looked west, and many moved farther away from cities and plantations along the East Coast, they discovered a sparsely settled wasteland. In place of Jefferson's sturdy yeoman on his cultivated fields, they found the ragged squatter in his log cabin.[3]

The presumptive "new man" of the squatter's frontier embodied the best and the worst of the American character. The "Adam" of the American wilderness had a split personality: he was half hearty rustic and half dirk-carrying highwayman. In his most favorable cast as backwoodsman, he was a homespun philosopher, an independent spirit, and a strong and courageous man who shunned fame and wealth. But turn him over and he became the white savage, a ruthless brawler and eye-gouger. This unwholesome type lived a brute existence in a dingy log cabin, with yelping dogs at his heels, a haggard wife, and a mongrel brood of brown and yellow brats to complete the sorry scene.

Early republican America had become a "cracker" country. City life catered to a minority of the population, as the rural majority fanned outward to the edges of civilization. While the British had made an attempt to prohibit western migration through the Proclamation of 1763, the Revolutionary War removed such barriers and acquiesced to the flood of poorer migrants. Both crackers and squatters—two terms that became shorthand for landless migrants—supposedly stayed just one step ahead of the "real" farmers, Jefferson's idealized, commercially oriented cultivators. They lived off the grid, rarely attended a school or joined a church, and remained a potent symbol of poverty. To be lower class in rural America was to be one of the landless. They disappeared into unsettled territory and squatted down (occupied tracts without possessing a land title) anywhere and everywhere. If land-based analogies were still needed, they were not to be divided into grades of soil, as Jefferson had creatively conceived, but spread about as scrub foliage or, in bestial terms, mangy varmints infesting the land.[4]

The plight of the squatter was defined by his static nature and transient existence. With no guarantee of social mobility, the only gift he received from his country was the liberty to keep moving. Kris Kristofferson's classic lyric resonates here: when it came to the cracker or squatter, freedom was just another word for nothing left to lose.

Both "squatter" and "cracker" were Americanisms, terms that updated inherited English notions of idleness and vagrancy. "Squatter," in one 1815 dictionary, was a "cant name" among New Englanders for a person who illegally occupied land he did not own. An early usage of the word occurred in a letter of 1788 from Federalist Nathaniel Gorham of Massachusetts, writing to James Madison about his state's ratifying convention. Identifying three classes of men opposed to the new federal Constitution, he listed the former supporters of Shays' Rebellion in the western counties, the undecided who might be led astray by opinionated others, and the constituents of Maine: this last group were "squatters" who "lived upon other people's land" and were "afraid of being brought to account." Not yet a separate state, Maine was the wooded backcountry of Massachusetts, and Gorham was about to become one of the most powerful speculators in the unsettled lands of western New York State. In 1790, "squatter" appeared in a Pennsylvania newspaper, but written as "squatlers," describing men who inhabited the western borderlands of that state, along the Susquehanna River. They were men who "sit down on river bottoms," pretend to have titles, and chase off anyone who dares to usurp their claims.[5]

Interlopers and trespassers, unpoliced squatters and crackers grew crops, cut timber, hunted and fished on land they did not own. They lived in temporary huts beyond the reach of the civilizing forces of law and society and often in proximity to Native Americans. In Massachusetts and Maine, squatters felt they had a right to the land (or should be paid) if they made improvements, that is, if they cleared away the trees, built fences, homes, and barns, and cultivated the soil. Their de facto claims were routinely challenged; families were chased off, their homes burned. Squatters often refused to leave, took up arms, and retaliated: a Pennsylvania man in 1807 shot a sheriff who tried to eject him. Down Easter Daniel Hildreth, tried and convicted of attempted murder in 1800, went after the proprietor himself.[6]

Slang tends to enter the vocabulary well after the condition it describes has existed. And so the presence of squatters predated the word itself. In Pennsylvania, as early as the 1740s, colonial officials issued stern proclamations to warn off illegitimate residents who were settling on the western lands of wealthy proprietors. Twenty years later, with little success in curbing their invasion, courts made the more egregious forms of trespass a capital crime. Yet even the threat of the gallows did not stop the flow of migrants across the Susquehanna, down the Ohio, and as far south as North Carolina and Georgia.[7]

British military officers were the first to record their impressions of this irrepressible class of humanity. As early as the 1750s, they were called the "scum of nature" and "vermin"; they had no means of support except theft and license. The military condemned them, but also used them. The motley caravan of settlers that gathered around encampments such as Fort Pitt (the future Pittsburgh), at the forks of the Ohio, Allegheny, and Monongahela Rivers, served as a buffer zone between the established colonial settlements along the Atlantic and Native tribes of the interior. A semicriminal class of men, whose women were dismissed as harlots by the soldiers, they trailed in the army's wake as camp followers, sometimes in the guise of traders, other times as whole families.[8]

Colonial commanders such as Swiss-born colonel Henry Bouquet in Pennsylvania treated them all as expendable troublemakers, but occasionally employed them in attacking and killing so-called savages. Like the vagrants rounded up in England to fight foreign wars, these colonial outcasts had no lasting social value. In 1759, Bouquet argued that the only hope for improving the colonial frontier was through regular pruning. For him, war was a positive good when it killed off the vermin and weeded out the rubbish. They were "no better than savages," he wrote, "their children brought up in the Woods like brutes, without any notion of Religion, [or] Government." Nothing man could devise "improved the breed."[9]

"Squatter" or "squat" carried a range of disreputable meanings. The term suggested squashing, flattening out, or beating down; it conjured images of scattering, spinning outward, spilling people across the land. Those who recurred to the term revived the older, vulgar slur of human waste, as in "squattering a soft turd." By the late eighteenth century, in the time of the influential Buffon, squatting was uniformly associated with lesser peoples, such as the Hottentots, who reportedly convened their political meetings while squatting on the ground. During the Seven Years' War, British forces used the tactic of squatting down and hiding when fighting Native Americans—essentially imitating their foe's ambushes. Lest we overlook the obvious, squatting—sitting down—was the exact opposite of standing, which as a noun conveyed the British legal principle of securing territorial rights to the land. The word "right" came from standing erect. One's legal "standing" meant everything in civilized society.[10]

"Crackers" first appeared in the records of British officials in the 1760s and described a population with nearly identical traits. In a letter to Lord Dartmouth, one colonial British officer explained that the people called "crackers" were "great boasters," a "lawless set of rascals on the frontiers of Virginia, Maryland, the Carolinas and Georgia, who often change their places of abode." As backcountry "banditti," "villains," and "horse thieves," they were dismissed as "idle strag[g]lers" and "a set of vagabonds often worse than the Indians." By the time of the Revolution, their criminal ways had turned them into ruthless Indian fighters. In one eyewitness account from the Carolina backcountry, a cracker "bruiser" wrestled his Cherokee foe to the ground, gouged out his eyes, scalped his victim alive, and then dashed his skull with the butt of a gun. Overkill was their code of justice.[11]

Their lineage, as it were, could be traced back to North Carolina, and before that to Virginia's rejects and renegades. An Anglican minister, Charles Woodmason, who traveled for six years in the Carolina wilderness in the 1760s, offered the most damning portrait of the lazy, licentious, drunken, and whoring men and women whom he adjudged the poorest excuses for British settlers he had ever met. The "Virginia Crackers" he encountered were foolish enough as to argue over a "turd." The women were "sluttish" by nature, known to pull their clothes tightly around their breasts and hips so as to emphasize their shape. Irreligious men and women engaged in drunken orgies rather than listen to the clergyman's dull sermons. All in all, crackers were as indolent and immoral as their fellow squatters to the north.[12]

The origin of "cracker" is no less curious than "squatter." The "cracking traders" of the 1760s were described as noisy braggarts, prone to lying and vulgarity. One could also "crack" a jest, and crude Englishmen "cracked" wind. Firecrackers gave off a stench and were loud and disruptive as they snapped, crackled, and popped. A "louse cracker" referred to a lice-ridden, slovenly, nasty fellow.[13]

Another significant linguistic connection to the popular term was the adjective "crack brained," which denoted a crazy person and was the English slang for a fool or "idle head." Idleness in mind and body was a defining trait. In one of the most widely read sixteenth-century tracts on husbandry, Thomas Tusser offered the qualifying verse, "Two good haymakers, worth twenty cra[c]kers." As the embodiment of waste persons, they whittled away time, producing only bluster and nonsense.[14]

American crackers were aggressive. Their "delight in cruelty" meant they were not just cantankerous but dangerous. As "lawless rascals" of the frontier, they had a lean and mean physique, like an inferior animal. Backwoods traders were easily compared to a "rascally herd" of deer. ("Rascal" was yet another synonym for trash.) As scavengers, crackers were feisty and volatile, or they could play the fool, like Byrd's slow-witted lubbers.[15]

In 1798, Dr. Benjamin Rush, a signer of the Declaration of Independence, wrote that Pennsylvania squatters had adopted the "strong tincture of the manners" of Indians, particularly in their "violent" fits of labor, "succeeded by long intervals of rest." Perhaps their southern twins abided by the same instinctive rhythms, but the farther south one went, the more the landless indulged themselves in long periods of sloth. Rush described his state as a "sieve," leaking southbound squatters. Pennsylvania retained the heartier poor, those willing to plough the stubborn soil, whereas the truly indolent ended up in Virginia, North Carolina, and Georgia. In Rush's regional sketch, squatters from the northern states seemed to turn into crackers as soon as they crossed into the southern backcountry.[16]

The persistence of the squatter and cracker allows us to understand how much more limited social mobility was along the frontier than loving legend has it. In the Northwest (Ohio, Indiana, Illinois, Michigan, and Wisconsin Territories), the sprawling upper South (Kentucky, Tennessee, Missouri, and Arkansas Territories), and the Floridas (East and West), classes formed in a predictable manner. Speculators and large farmers—a mix of absentee land investors and landowning gentry—had the most power and political influence, and usually had a clear advantage in determining how the land was parceled out. The middling landowners had personal or political connections to the large landowning elite. In new trans-Appalachian towns such as Lexington, Kentucky, dubbed the "Athens of the West," with the addition of roads came commercial growth between 1815 and 1827, so that a new merchant middle class took root. Such towns as Lexington also supported small farmers, who had less security in retaining their land, given the fluctuations in the market, while artisans of the meaner sort hung about the town.[17]

With this flood of new settlers, squatters made their presence known. Sometimes identified as families, at other times as single men, they were viewed as a distinct and troublesome class. In the Northwest Territory, they were dismissed as unproductive old soldiers, rubbish that needed to be cleared away before a healthy commercial economy could be established. President Jefferson termed them "intruders" on public lands. Some transients found subsistence as hired laborers. All of them existed on the margins of the commercial marketplace.[18]

Educated observers feared social disorder, particularly after the financial panic of 1819, when political writers predicted in the West a "numerous population, in a state of wretchedness." Increasing numbers of poor settlers and uneducated squatters were "ripe for treason and spoil"—a familiar refrain recalling the language circulated during Shays' Rebellion in 1786. In the wake of the panic, the federal government devised a program of regulated land sales that kept prices high enough to weed out the lowest classes.[19]

By 1850, in what became a common pattern in new southwestern states, at least 35 percent of the population owned no real estate. There was no clear path to land and riches among the lower ranks. Tenants could easily be reduced to landless squatters. In the Northwest, land agents courted buyers and actively discouraged tenancy. Federal laws for purchasing land were weighted in favor of wealthier speculators. The landless west of the Appalachians were more likely to pull up stakes and move elsewhere than they were to stay in one place and work their way upward.[20]

The ubiquity of squatters across the United States turned them into a powerful political trope. They came to be associated with five traits: (1) crude habitations; (2) boastful vocabulary; (3) distrust of civilization and city folk; (4) an instinctive love of liberty (read: licentiousness); and (5) degenerate patterns of breeding. Yet even with such unappealing traits, the squatter also acquired some favorable qualities: the simple backwoodsman welcomed strangers into his cabin, the outrageous storyteller entertained them through the night. Squatters, then, were more than troublesome, uncouth rascals taking up land they didn't own. This double identity made the squatter a contested figure. By the 1830s and 1840s, he was fully a symbol of partisan politics, celebrated as the iconic common man who came to epitomize Jacksonian democracy.

Americans tend to forget that Andrew Jackson was the first westerner elected president. Tall, lanky, with the rawboned look of a true backwoodsman, he wore the harsh life of the frontier on his face and literally carried a bullet next to his heart. Ferocious in his resentments, driven to wreak revenge against his enemies, he often acted without deliberation and justified his behavior as a law unto himself. His controversial reputation made him the target of attacks that painted him as a Tennessee cracker. His wife Rachel's backcountry divorce and her recourse to both cigar and corncob pipe confirmed the couple as Nashville bumpkins, at least in the eyes of their eastern detractors.[21]

Jackson and his supporters worked on a different image. During three successive presidential campaigns (1824, 1828, 1832), General Jackson was celebrated as "Old Hickory," in sharp contrast to Crèvecoeur's tame analogy of Americans as carefully cultivated plants. Rising up in the harsh hinterland of what was once the western extension of North Carolina, the Tennessean with the unbending will and rigid style of command was a perfect match for the tough, dense wood of Indian bows and hickory switches from which he acquired his nickname.[22]

Jackson's personality was a crucial part of his democratic appeal as well as the animosity he provoked. He was the first presidential candidate to be bolstered by a campaign biography. He was not admired for statesmanlike qualities, which he lacked in abundance in comparison to his highly educated rivals John Quincy Adams and Henry Clay. His supporters adored his rough edges, his land hunger, and his close identification with the Tennessee wilderness. As a representative of America's cracker country, Jackson unquestionably added a new class dimension to the meaning of democracy.

But the message of Jackson's presidency was not about equality so much as a new style of aggressive expansion. In 1818, General Andrew Jackson invaded Florida without presidential approval; as president, he supported the forced removal of the Cherokees from the southeastern states and willfully ignored the opinion of the Supreme Court. Taking and clearing the land, using violent means if necessary, and acting without legal authority, Jackson was arguably the political heir of the cracker and squatter.

Over the two decades leading up to Andrew Jackson's election as president, the squatter and cracker gradually became America's dominant poor backcountry breed. Not surprisingly, it was their physical environment that most set them apart. In 1810, the ornithologist and poet Alexander Wilson traveled along the Ohio and Mississippi Rivers from Pittsburgh to New Orleans, cataloguing not only the sky-bound birds but

also the earth-hugging squatters, whom he found to be an equally curious species. Writing for a Philadelphia magazine, Wilson identified their
"grotesque log cabins" that scarred the otherwise picturesque wilderness.

Weeds surrounded the cabins and huts that the naturalists happened
upon. The land showed no sign of toil. Wilson described these questionable homes in mocking poetry as a "cavern'd ruin," which "frown'd a
fouler cave within." The entire family slept on a single bed, or as Wilson
put it, "where nightly kennel'd all." Kittens crawled into a broken chest, a
pig took shelter in a pot, and a leaky roof let in the rain. The squatter
patriarch stared from beneath his tattered hat, wearing a shirt "defiled
and torn," his "face inlaid with dirt and soot."[23]

For the transplanted Scotsman Wilson, habitat was the measure of a
man, marking his capacity for progress or likelihood of decay. If every
man's home was his castle, then America's backcountry squatters were
worse than peasants. With cruel irony, Wilson termed the squatter cabin
as a "specimen of the *first* order of *American Architecture*." It amazed
him that such uninspired beings could find anything to boast about, yet
they proudly spoke of America as the land of opportunity.[24]

There were many like Wilson who placed squatters below the naked
savage on the social scale. At least American Indians *belonged* in the
woods. The poor squatter's backcountry still carried the association of a
rubbish heap. There was no real social ladder emerging in the western
territories, no solid foundation for mobility under construction there, not
much rising from the bottomless basement that oozed human refuse.
From the foothills of the Appalachians into the banks of the Ohio and
Mississippi Rivers, the nation leaned backward. The squatter was frozen
in time. His primitive hut represented his underclass cage.

The distance between town and backwoods was measured in more
than miles. It had an evolutionary character, forming what some at the
time recognized as an impassable gulf between the classes. The educated
routinely wrote in disbelief that such people shared their country. In
1817, for example, Thomas Jefferson's granddaughter Cornelia Randolph
wrote to her younger sister about a trip with their grandfather to the Natural Bridge, a property that Jefferson owned ninety miles west of Monticello. Here, she said, she encountered members of that "half civiliz'd race
who lived beyond the ridge." The children she met were barely covered by
their scanty shifts and shirts, while one man strutted around before them

with his "hairy breast exposed." In this large, unruly family, she noted with disapproval, there were no more than "two or three pairs of shoes." She was especially surprised by the crude familiarity of their speech. Oblivious to social forms, they conversed with the ex-president as though he was some lost family member. As a proud member of the Virginia gentry, Cornelia was convinced that she towered above the unwashed squatters. To her further chagrin, she was astounded that the poor family exhibited not the least sense of shame over their pathetic condition.[25]

Class made its most transparent appearance by way of such contrasts. We can read volumes into the scorn expressed by the educated onlooker as he or she sized up the uncouth figures who roamed the backcountry. The need to make them into a new breed focused on more than crude living conditions, however. The backwoodsman and cracker had a telltale gait that accompanied his distinctive physiognomy. While traveling in the trans-Appalachian West in 1830, a city adventurer drolly observed of his bed companion for the night, "lantern-jawed, double-jointed backwoodsman, measuring some seven feet one in his stocking feet." A typical alligator hunter in southern Illinois bore a similar physique: "gaunt, long-limbed, lanthorn-jawed, Jonathan." ("Jonathan" simply meant "fellow" here, being a common appellation for a generic American.) The cracker women had the same protruding jaw and swarthy complexion, and were as often as not toothless.[26]

Women and children were important symbols of civilization—or the absence of it. Officers stationed in Florida in the 1830s identified "ye cracker girls" as brutes, with manners no better than sailors, and often seen smoking pipes, chewing and spitting tobacco, and cursing. Seeing their slipshod dress, dirty feet, ropy hair, and unwashed faces, one lieutenant from the Northeast dismissed them all as no better than prostitutes. In his words, everyone of the cracker class was a "swearing, lazy, idle slut!"[27]

The backwoods personality could be found as far north as Maine, as far south as Florida, and across the Northwest and Southwest Territories. They acquired localized names, such as Mississippi screamers, for their cracker-style Indian war whoop or love of squealing; Kentucky corn crackers, for their poor diet of cracked corn; and Indiana Hoosiers, for the poor in that state. "Hoosier" is a word no linguistic scholar can define with any precision. Even so, the class descriptor was the same. A Hoosier man ran off at the mouth, lied, boasted, and remained ready to harm anyone who insulted his ugly wife. They were as prone to a down-and-dirty fight as any southern cracker. Hoosier gals were no more refined than their Florida sisters. A Hoosier gal's courtship ritual, it was said, involved a lot of kicking and hair pulling.[28]

Sexual behavior was another crucial marker of class status. In a well-known poem of the era, "The Hoosier's Nest" (1833), the author harkened back to the vocabulary of the Scottish naturalist Wilson. Here again, the cabins were wild nests, a half-human, half-animal retreat perfect for indiscriminate breeding. Using a racially charged slur, the poet identified the children as "Hoosieroons"—a class variation of the mixed-race quadroons. Under their leaky roofs were none of the hearty pioneer stock. Instead, poor Indiana squatters produced a degenerate dozen of dirty yellow urchins.[29]

Filthy cabins, a lack of manners, and rampant breeding combined to make crackers and squatters a distinct class, as verified by their patterns of speech. Backwoods patois constituted a rural American version of the lower-class English cockney. In 1830, there was even a "Cracker Dictionary," preserving their vintage slang. One was "Jimber jawed," whose mouth was constantly moving, who couldn't stop talking. The cracker's protruding lower jaw carried over into his style of talking. A "ring tailed roarer" was a violent type; the descriptive "chewed up" literally referred to having one's ear, nose, or lip bitten off.[30]

But one polysyllabic word may have best captured their identity. The verb "obsquatulate" was a cracker conjugation of "squat," conveying the idea of moseying along or absconding. For a people who wouldn't settle in one place, "obsquatulate" gave an activity of sorts to the American heirs of English vagrants. They might flee like an absconding servant or amble at a slow pace without a destination in mind, but in either case it was their dirty feet and slipshod ways that defined them.[31]

Jackson was not the only Tennessean to become a national celebrity. Though by the 1830s he would come to be known as a bear hunter and "Lion of the West," David Crockett was a militia scout and lieutenant, justice of the peace, town commissioner, state representative, and finally a U.S. congressman. He was first elected to the House of Representatives in 1827. What makes the historic David Crockett interesting is that he was self-taught, lived off the land, and (most notably for us) became an ardent defender of squatters' rights—for he had been a squatter himself. As a politician he took up the cause of the landless poor.[32]

Crockett was born in the "state of Franklin," a state that was not legally a state. It had declared its independence from North Carolina in 1784 and remained unrecognized. Franklin was later incorporated into Tennessee and became a battleground as speculators and squatters scrambled to control the most arable tracts. Their activities triggered an endless series of skirmishes with the Cherokees, exacerbated by blatant treaty violations. The first governor of Tennessee territory, the prodigious land speculator William Blount, was given the Cherokee nickname "Dirt Captain." From 1797 to 1811, the federal government periodically sent troops into Tennessee to remove squatters, which only increased these ornery men's natural hostility toward Washington. To Crockett, a man of humble roots willing to stand his ground, was attributed a simple philosophy: "It's grit of a fellow that makes a man." But it wasn't grit alone that counted; an untamed physicality and fecundity was thought to be the most American of attributes. In 1830, in an unprecedented move, Crockett petitioned Congress to grant a resident of his state a tract of public land—not because of hard work, but because his wife had given birth to triplets.[33]

As that particular brand of American, the lovable outcast, Crockett acquired a reputation for spinning outrageous tall tales. In a speech he purportedly delivered in Congress (but probably never did give in these exact words) he called himself the "savagest critter you ever did see." Endowed with superhuman powers, he could "run like a fox, swim like a eel, yell like an Indian," and "swallow a nigger whole"—an absurd, racist comment that was probably meant to convey his hostility toward great slaveowning planters who pushed poor squatters off their land. The real Crockett owned slaves himself, yet in Congress he opposed large planters' engrossment of vast tracts of land. He championed a bill that would have sold land directly from the federal government to squatters at low prices. He also opposed the practice of having courts hire out insolvent debtors to work off fees—an updated variation on indentured servitude. Crockett spoke "Cracker" fluently, as was demonstrated in the 1830 dictionary that gave him full credit for coining the phrase "ring-tale roarer" to describe a violent man.[34]

Crockett's boasting carried unambiguous class accents. In 1828, he claimed that he could "wade the Mississippi with a steamboat on his back" and "whip his weight in wild cats." The one thing he said he couldn't do was to give a standard speech in Congress—which felt odd to him, given that he otherwise believed he could whip any man in the House. He lacked the eloquence that was taught, the argumentation that the educated class possessed. His humorous speeches gained public notoriety, but for many observers he remained the "harlequin," provoking laughter. According to one newspaper, queer stories and quaint sayings turned Crockett into a dancing bear, dressed up in "coat and breeches," performing a vulgar sideshow.[35]

The real Crockett was often eclipsed by the tall tales of the untutored backwoodsman. An entire cottage industry of Crockett stories were published that he never authorized. *Davy Crockett's Almanack of 1837* contains a crude engraving of a corn cracker, who appears unshaven, is dressed in buckskin, and holds a rifle in his hand. He is topped off with a grisly-looking coonskin cap, the animal's head still attached (see page 121). In another engraving, Davy's daughter is mounted on a giant alligator's back, riding the thirty-seven-foot beast like a rodeo star. Whether he fights modern-day dragons or accomplishes magical feats in a surreal hinterland, Crockett's savage instincts seem appropriate to a mock-chivalric epic. His ghostwriters and hack biographers made Crockett into a wild man and an ill-educated braggart, and yet they equally relished his over-the-top swagger in outmaneuvering steamboats, bears, and slippery town folk.[36]

His boastfulness was never seen in purely heroic terms. He might jump higher and "squat lower" than "all the fellers either side of the Alleghany hills," but his comic character actually served to mute a legitimate political voice. Representative Crockett may have compared speculators to sneaky coons in an 1824 speech before the Tennessee House, but he never lost sight of the legal ploys used to trick poorer settlers out of their land warrants. In the end, the man, not the legend, did a better job of exposing class conflict in the backcountry, where real speculators were routinely pitted against real squatters.[37]

David Crockett was an avid backer of Andrew Jackson in the 1828 election, but soon enough abandoned the imperious general. Crockett's Land Bill made enemies back in Tennessee, and he disapproved of the Indian Removal Bill, which allowed for forced expulsion of the Cherokees and other "civilized tribes" from the southeastern states. Indian removal went along with the unfair treatment of squatters, who were expelled from the public domain and were barred from securing land that they had settled and improved. Jackson's allies responded to Crockett's defection by calling him unsavory and uneducated.

Crockett accused Jackson of going back on his principles, and refused to go along with the partisan dog pack. In 1831, he wrote that he "would not wear a collar round my neck, with '*my dog*' on it, and the name of ANDREW JACKSON on the collar." Three years later he made submission to party into an ugly slur, saying he would rather "belong to a nigger, and be a raccoon dog, as the partisan of any man." In Crockett's backcountry class hierarchy, there was the free white male landowner, the squatter, the black man, the dog, and then, if his language was to be taken seriously, the party man.[38]

Democrat Andrew Jackson's stormy relationship with Crockett was replicated again and again with any number of contemporaries over the course of a career that was built on sheer will and utter impulse. Most of his loyal supporters eventually ended up on the opposition side of the partisan divide, joining the Whig Party. Controversy, large and small, seemed to follow the man. Because Jackson had relatively little experience holding political offices, his run for the presidency drew even more than the normal amount of attention to his personal character. A biography written for campaign purposes filled in the gaps in his generally combative résumé. Whether supporters portrayed him as the conquering hero or his enemies labeled him King Andrew I, all focused on his volatile emotions. He certainly lacked the education and polite breeding of his presidential predecessors.[39]

As an outsider to Washington, save for a brief, unproductive stint in Congress, his qualifications came from the field of war, where his record sparked heated criticism. His ardent backers claimed him as the spiritual successor to the sainted General Washington, but Jackson's origins lay far from the Potomac, beyond the Appalachian Mountains. Old Hickory had made his home in places where the population was thin and the law fungible. He was a slaveholding planter whose reputation situated him not in the halls of power but among the common stock. In the Tennessee backcountry, where settlement came much later than it did on the East Coast,

---

landowning and class stations ostensibly had shallower roots. As one New England journalist wondered aloud during Jackson's first run for president in 1824, who precisely were these "hardy sons of the West"?[40]

In the popular imagination, Jackson was inseparable from a wild and often violent landscape. After his celebrated victory at the Battle of New Orleans in 1815, he was identified as a "green backwoodsman" who had bested the "invincible" British foe. To another, he was "Napoleon of the woods." His political rise came through violence, having slaughtered the Red Stick faction of the Creek Nation in the swamps of Alabama in 1813–14, while leaving hundreds of British soldiers dead in the marshes of New Orleans in January 1815. Jackson bragged about the British death toll, as did American poets. One extolled, "Carnage stalks wide o'er all the ensanguin' plain." And it was no exaggeration. Bodies floated in rivers and streams, and bones of the vanquished were found by travelers decades later.[41]

Jackson did not look or act like a conventional politician, which was a fundamental part of his appeal. When Jackson arrived in Philadelphia from Tennessee to take his seat in the U.S. Senate in 1796, Pennsylvania congressman Albert Gallatin described a "tall, lank, uncouth-looking personage, with long locks hanging over his face, and a queue down his back tied in eel skin." In later years, the gaunt general struck observers as stiff in carriage, and weatherworn. Backwater diseases stalked him. Saying nothing of his external appearance, Thomas Jefferson perceived in Jackson a man of savage instincts. Once he observed him so overcome with anger that he was left speechless. (Speechlessness was the classic signifier of primitive man and untamed beast.)[42]

His fiery temper and lack of scholarly deportment permanently marked him. A sworn enemy put it best: "Boisterous in ordinary conversation, he makes up in oaths what he lacks in arguments." Not known for his subtle reasoning, Jackson was blunt in his opinions and quick to resent any who disagreed with him. Shouting curses put him in the company of both common soldiers and uncouth crackers. In "A Backwoodsman and a Squatter" (1821), one satirist captured such frontier types, folks known to "squale loose jaw and slam an angry oath."[43]

Jackson's aggressive style, his frequent resorting to duels and street fights, his angry acts of personal and political retaliation seemed to fit what one Frenchman with Jacksonian sympathies described as the westerner's "rude instinct of masculine liberty." By this code, independence came from clearing the land of potential threats. The threat could come from Native Americans, rival squatters, political adversaries, or what the corn cracker in *Davy Crockett's Almanack of 1837* described as "eel-skin" easterners who used fancy words to get what they wanted. The cracker's survivalist ethos invariably trumped legal niceties or polite decorum. It was these traits that shaded Jackson's public image in the cracker mold.[44]

After New Orleans, Jackson led his army into Spanish Florida in 1818. He began by raising troops in Tennessee without waiting for the governor's approval, then invaded East Florida under the guise of arresting a handful of Seminole Indians who were accused of attacking American settlers. When he attacked the fortified Spanish at Pensacola, what had begun as a foray to capture Indians quickly turned into a full-scale war and occupation.[45]

Jackson went beyond squatting on Spanish soil. He violated his orders and ignored international law. After overtaking several Florida towns and arresting the Spanish governor, he executed two British citizens without

In *Encounter Between a Corncracker and an Eelskin* from *Davy Crockett's Almanack of 1837*, the backwoods squatter defends his gal from the slippery, seductive words of the trader from town.

Davy Crockett's Almanack of 1837, American Antiquarian Society, Worcester, Massachusetts

real cause. The British press had a field day, calling the U.S. major general a "ferocious Yankee pirate with blood on his hands." In a devastating caricature, Jackson appeared as a swarthy, swaggering bandit flanked by a corps of militiamen who were no more than ragged, shoeless brutes, beating drums with bones and wearing skulls instead of hats.[46]

The pirate who doubled as a backcountry cracker bruiser was unrestrained and unrestrainable. In the Florida invasion, he was reportedly aided by squatters dressed up as "white savages," who may in fact have been the true catalyst behind Jackson's controversial action. The Florida conflict had all the signs of a squatters' war. Soldiers reported that Seminole warriors only attacked "cracker houses," leaving those of British or northern settlers untouched.[47]

Prominent critics insisted on a congressional investigation. The powerful Speaker of the House, Henry Clay, demanded the rogue general's censure. Jackson went to Washington, damned the established legal authorities, and told Secretary of State John Quincy Adams that the entire matter of Florida was between President Monroe and himself—and no one else. Confirmed rumors circulated that Jackson had threatened to cut off the ears of some senators because they had dared to investigate—and humiliate—him on the national stage.[48]

In Jackson's crude lexicon, territorial disputes were to be settled by violent means, not by words alone. He explained his Indian policy as the right of "retaliatory vengeance" against "inhumane bloody barbarians." In 1818, he was heralded in a laudatory biography as a kind of backcountry Moses, administering justice with biblical wrath. To those who protested his lack of regard for international law or constitutional details, defenders claimed that he was "too much a patriot in war, to suffer the scruples of a legal construction." Yet even the most devoted fans of the general had to admit he had a fiery temper. In 1825, Henry Clay's highly publicized comment that Jackson was a mere "military chieftain" suggested something tribal, primitive, and wholly unrepublican about him. When he sought the presidency in 1824 and 1828, the Seminole War remained front and center.[49]

Few of Jackson's critics were buying the chivalrous portrait his defenders presented. He was not protecting women and children so much as opening up Florida lands to squatters and roughs and other uncivilized whites. But unlike Crockett, Jackson was never a champion of squatters' rights. When ordered to remove them, he used the military to do the job. Yet at the same time he favored white possession of the land in the same way squatters had always defended their claims: those who cleared and improved the land were worthy occupants. Jackson's thinking shaped his Indian removal policy as president. He argued that Indians should not be treated as sovereign nations with special claims on the public domain, but as a dependent class. Like squatters, if Indians failed to assimilate or proved incapable of improving the land and securing land titles, they could be forcibly removed. As president, he was more than willing to use force to remove poor trespassers. Only when squatters resisted removal, as they did in Alabama in 1833, and state officials supported them, was President Jackson willing to back down and negotiate more favorable terms for white settlers.[50]

It was almost too easy for Jackson critics to publicize a counternarrative to the official campaign biography. In 1806, he had shot and killed a young lawyer named Charles Dickinson in a duel, which left him with a bullet next to his heart. While the victim's body was still warm, he made an ungentlemanly fuss when financial assistance was extended to Dickinson's widow: in his mind, the scoundrel's identity had to be permanently erased. According to the retelling of this episode in 1824, Jackson had withheld his shot, stood and watched the offending lawyer tremble, called him a "damn coward," aimed calmly, and shot him dead at close range. Another incident followed in 1813, when Jackson was party to an impromptu "O.K. Corral" gunfight with his former aide Thomas Hart Benton and his brother Jesse at the Nashville Hotel. In the election year 1828, Thomas Benton made news when he published an account about the near-fatal encounter.[51]

But nothing looked worse on Jackson's rap sheet than the so-called Coffin Handbill. He stood accused of executing six of his own men during the Creek War in 1813; six black coffins adorned the 1828 circular. Thus it was not just Indian and English blood that marked him. It was not just the dandyish lawyer Dickinson who met death at Jackson's hands. In another illustration on the same handbill, Jackson was seen in a down-and-dirty street fight, stabbing a man in the back with a sword hidden inside his cane. Like the cracker fighter who might bite, kick, and lash out indiscriminately, and hide a weapon under his coat, Jackson was seen as thoroughly ruthless—the antithesis of that studied republican gentility meant to define a sober statesman.[52]

Jackson was perturbed by the caricatures even before the Coffin Handbill made its rounds, writing to a friend in 1824, "Great pains had been taken to represent me as having a savage disposition; who allways [sic] carried a Scalping Knife in one hand & a tomahawk in the other; allways ready to knock down, & scalp, any & every person who differed with me in opinion." While denying the caricature, he could not deny his violent streak.[53]

A more appealing, sanitized version of the backwoodsman candidate surfaced in the early 1820s. It portrayed him as an outsider, a man of natural talents drawn from the "native forests," who was capable of cleaning up the corruption in Washington. His nomination provoked "sneers and derision from the myrmidons of power at Washington," wrote one avid Jackson man, who decried the "degeneracy of American feeling in that city." Jackson wasn't a government minion or a pampered courtier, and thus his unpolished and unstatesmanlike ways were an advantage.[54]

In 1819, in a speech before Congress, David Walker of Kentucky used this kind of imagery to reproach members of the House for investigating Jackson's activities in the Seminole War. Walker emphasized the class as well as cultural divide separating representatives in the capital from Americans living on a distant Florida frontier. Jackson's long experience as the "hardy and weather beaten General" had instilled in him a better sense of judging the conditions of a frontier war. He understood first-hand the suffering and hardships of besieged families. Could the members of the investigation committees fully appreciate the difficulties while sitting at home, their families safe from harm? The men censuring Jackson, whom the Kentucky congressman mocked as the "young sweet-smelling and powdered beau of the town," were out of their league. With this clever turn of phrase, he recast Jackson's foes as beaus and dandies, the classic enemies of crackers and squatters.[55]

Walker had tapped into a dominant class motif of cracker democracy, dating back at least to 1790, when the cracker-versus-beau plotline began to take shape. In its earliest literary form, the cracker buck is lured into town, plied with liquor, and swindled, after which he learns the painful lesson that his dreary cabin in the woods is "where contentment and plenty ever dwell." A similar story in 1812 told of a backwoodsman curtly dismissing a supercilious lawyer and a capering dancing master who had stood at the door of his cabin. In 1821, clergyman and backcountry historian Joseph Doddridge of western Virginia embellished these stock characters in his play *Dialogue of the Backwoodsman and the Dandy*. He summed up the peculiar virtues of rough-hewn men:

> A Backwoodsman is a queer sort of fellow. . . . If he's not a man of larnin, he had plain good sense. If his dress is not fine, his inside works are good and his heart is sound. If he is not rich or great, he knows that he is the father of his country. . . . You little dandies, and other big folk may freely enjoy the fruits of our hardships; you may feast, where we had to starve; and frolic, where we had to fight; but at peril of all of you, give the Backwoodsman none of your slack-jaw.[56]

All of this explains Congressman Walker's point-counterpoint in distinguishing General Jackson from the congressional investigators. The beau was an effete snob, and his ridicule an uncalled-for taunt. The real men of America were Jacksonian, the hearty native sons of Tennessee and Kentucky. They fought the wars. They opened up the frontier through their sacrifice and hardship. They fathered the next generation of courageous settlers. Defensive westerners thus attached to Jackson their dreams and made him a viable presidential candidate.[57]

Another way to promote their cracker president was through humorous exaggeration. As the different coffin handbills made the rounds in 1828, Jackson's men used Crockett-like humor to defend him, claiming that the general was really guilty of having eaten the six militiamen, "swallowing them all, coffins and all." When John Quincy Adams supporters circulated a note written by Jackson filled with misspellings and bad grammar, Jacksonians praised him as "self-taught." If his lack of diplomatic experience made him "homebred," this meant that he was less contaminated than the former diplomat Adams by foreign ideas or courtly pomp. The class comparison could not be ignored: Adams had been a professor of rhetoric at Harvard, while his Tennessee challenger was "sprung from a common family," and had written nothing to brag about. Instinctive action was privileged over unproductive thought.[58]

Given that his initial support in the 1824 campaign came from

Alabama, Mississippi, North Carolina, and Tennessee, Jackson was derided for having cornered the cracker vote. A humorous piece in a southern newspaper described a Georgia cracker in Crockett prose, "half alligator, half man," giving a hurrah for Jackson. By 1828, his Indiana constituency was presented as "The Backwoods Alive with Old Hickory."[59]

Jackson partisans were routinely chastised for their lack of taste and breeding. At a gathering in Philadelphia in 1828, drinkers lifted their glasses in violent toasts: "May the hickory ramrods ram down the powder of equality into our national guns, and wadded well with the voices of the people to blow Clay in the mud." Another toastmaster wished that an "Adamite head was a drum head, and me to beat it, till I would beat it in." Defending Jackson seemed to require threats that celebrated physical prowess over mental agility. If anyone dared insult the "jineral," went the story told of one Jackson fan, he would give him a "pelt." Fighting and boasting was paramount in lower-class Jacksonian circles. Or as one cracker candidate pledged as war whoops arose from his anti-Adams audience, "If so I'm elected, Gin'ral government shall wear the print of these five knuckles."[60]

In 1828, though two years in the grave, Thomas Jefferson was resurrected to prove that Jackson was of the wrong stock. Jefferson's former neighbor and longtime secretary of James Madison, Illinois governor Edward Coles, recalled Jefferson's nasty quip as the 1824 election neared: "One might as well make a sailor a cock, or a soldier a goose, as a President of Andrew Jackson." High executive office was beyond the reach of Jackson, whose questionable breeding clearly disqualified him.[61]

The candidate's private life came under equal scrutiny. His irregular marriage became scandalous fodder during the election of 1828. His intimate circle of Tennessee confidants scrambled to find some justification for the couple's known adultery. John Overton, Jackson's oldest and closest friend in Nashville, came up with the story of "accidental bigamy," claiming that the couple had married in good conscience, thinking that Rachel's divorce from her first husband had already been decreed. But the truth was something other. Rachel Donelson Robards had committed adultery, fleeing with her paramour Jackson to Spanish-held Natchez in 1790. They had done so not out of ignorance, and not on a lark, but in order to secure a divorce from her husband. Desertion was one of the few recognized causes of divorce.[62]

In the ever-expanding script detailing Jackson's misdeeds, adultery was just one more example of his uncontrolled passions. Wife stealing belonged to the standard profile of the backwoods aggressor who refused to believe the law applied to him. In failing to respect international law, he had conquered Florida; in disregarding his wife's first marriage contract, he simply took what he wanted. Jackson invaded the "sanctity of his neighbor's matrimonial couch," as the Ohio journalist Charles Hammond declared.[63]

All sorts of vicious names were used in demeaning Rachel Jackson. She was called an "American Jezebel," "weak and vulgar," and a "dirty black wench," all of which pointed to her questionable backwoods upbringing. It was pro-Adams editor James G. Dana of Kentucky who luridly painted her as a whore. She could no more pass in polite company, he said with racist outrage, than a gentleman's black mistress, even if the black wench wore a white mask. Her stain of impurity would never be tolerated among Washington's better sort. Another unpoliced critic made a similar argument. Her crude conduct might belong in "every cabin beyond the mountains," he wrote, but not in the President's House.[64]

Even without the marriage scandal, Rachel Jackson had the look of a lower-class woman. One visitor to the Jacksons' home in Tennessee thought she might be mistaken for an old washerwoman. Another described her as fat and her skin tanned, which may explain the "black wench" slur. Whiteness was a badge of class privilege denied to poor cracker gals who worked under the sun. Critics laughed at Mrs. Jackson's backcountry pronunciation; they made fun of her favorite song, "Possum Up a Gum Tree." She smoked a pipe. Alas, Rachel Jackson succumbed to heart disease shortly before she was meant to accompany her husband to Washington and take up her duties as First Lady. Her death only intensified the incoming president's hatred for his political enemies.[65]

To be sure, even beyond class issues, Jackson's candidacy changed the nature of democratic politics. One political commentator noted that Jackson's reign ushered in the "game of brag." Jacksonians routinely exaggerated their man's credentials, saying he was not just the "Knight of New Orleans," the country's "deliverer," but also the greatest general in all human history. Another observer concluded that a new kind of "talkative country politician" had arisen, who could speak for hours before having finally "exhausted the fountain of his panegyric on General Jackson."[66]

Bragging had a distinctive class dimension in the 1820s and 1830s. In a satire published in Tennessee, a writer took note of the strange adaptations of the code of chivalry in defense of honor. The story involved a duel between one Kentucky "Knight of the Red Rag" and a "great and mighty Walnut cracker" of Tennessee. The nutcracker gave himself an exalted title: "duke of Wild Cat Cove, little and big Hog Thief Creek, Short Mountain, Big Bore Cave and Cuwell's Bridge." So what did this kind of posturing mean? Like certain masters of gangsta rap in the twenty-first century, crackers had to make up for their lowly status by dressing themselves up in a boisterous verbal garb. In the Crockett manner, lying and boasting made up for the absence of class pedigree. This, too, was Andrew Jackson. He used duels, feuds, and oaths to rise in the political pecking order in the young state of Tennessee.[67]

While Jackson had little interest in squatters' rights, his party did shift the debate in their favor. Democrats supported preemption rights, which made it easier and cheaper for those lacking capital to purchase land. Preemption granted squatters the right to settle, to improve, and then to purchase the land they occupied at a "minimum price." The debate over preemption cast the squatter in a more favorable light. For some, he was now a hardworking soul who built his cabin with his own hands and had helped to clear the land, which benefited all classes. The Whig leader Henry Clay found himself on the losing side of the debate. In 1838, Clay joked in the Senate that the preemptioner might take his newfound rights and squat down in the spacious White House occupied by one "little man"—Jackson's handpicked successor, Martin Van Buren.[68]

Thomas Hart Benton, in quitting Tennessee and moving to Missouri, buried the hatchet with Jackson. As an eminent senator during and after Jackson's two terms in office, he pushed through preemption laws, culminating in the "Log Cabin Bill" of 1841. But Benton's thinking was double-edged: yes, he wished to give squatters a chance to purchase a freehold, but he was not above treating them as an expendable population. In 1839, he proposed arming squatters, giving them land and rations as an alternative to renewing the federal military campaign against the Seminoles in Florida. By this, Benton merely revived the British military tactic of using squatters as an inexpensive tool for conquering the wilderness.[69]

The presidential campaign of 1840 appears to be the moment when the squatter morphed into the colloquial common man of democratic lore. Both parties now embraced him. Partisans of Whig presidential candidate William Henry Harrison claimed that he was from backwoods stock. This was untrue. Harrison was born into an elite Virginia planter family, and though he had been briefly a cabin dweller in the Old Northwest Territory, by the time he ran for office that cabin had been torn down and replaced with a grand mansion. Kentuckian Henry Clay, who vied with him for the Whig nomination, celebrated his prizewinning mammoth hog—named "Corn Cracker," no less. The new class politics played out in trumped-up depictions of log cabins, popular nicknames, hard-cider drinking, and coonskin caps. This imagery explains why westerners and the poorer voters never fully embraced Jackson's favorite, Martin Van Buren, who was seen as a dandyish eastern bachelor. In one Whig-inspired campaign song, the Dutch-descended New Yorker was blasted as a "queer little man . . . mounted on the back of the sturdy Andy Jack."[70]

The squatter all at once became a romantic figure in popular culture. This was true in St. Louis newspaperman John Robb's *Streaks of Squatter Life*. In one of the stories in the collection, Robb introduced a poor white Missouri squatter named Sugar. Though he was dressed in rags, his personal influence over local elections was hypnotic. At the polling place, "Sug" came with a keg of whiskey, which he sweetened with brown sugar. As members of the crowd lined up for his special concoction, he told them, based on his honest opinion of the speeches he had heard, whom they should vote for. Sug had lost his girl and his farm, and yet as a landless squatter he somehow gained respect. He represented the new common man, a simple fellow who couldn't be misled by fancy rhetoric.[71]

Sug was not simply a leveling character. He actually represented a reformed, even middle-class solution to the larger debate over class and respectability. His qualities suggested a reasonable man who handed out a little whiskey and dispensed meaningful advice. He wasn't running for office. He wasn't brawling or bartering whiskey for votes. He wasn't threatening the life of a rival bidder over a tract of land. Sug knew his place as the neighborhood purveyor of common sense.[72]

The squatter may have been tamed, at least in the minds of some, but political equality did not come to America in the so-called Age of Jackson. Virginia retained property qualifications for voting until 1851; Louisiana and Connecticut until 1845; North Carolina until 1857. Tennessee did not drop its freehold restriction until 1834—after Jackson had already been elected to a second term. Eight states passed laws that disenfranchised paupers, the urban poor. Meanwhile many towns and cities adopted stricter suffrage guidelines for voting than their state legislatures did. This was true for Chicago, and for towns in Crockett's Tennessee and pro-Jackson Alabama. He could vote for a member of Congress,

STREAKS OF SQUATTER LIFE,
AND FAR-WEST SCENES.

OLD SUGAR: THE STANDING CANDIDATE.

"Old Sug" in *Streaks of Squatter Life* (1847) is a comic character whose poverty is rendered harmless. He represented a softened image of actual squatters known for brawling, drinking, and swearing at political events in the backcountry.

John Robb's *Streaks of Squatter Life* (1847), American Antiquarian Society, Worcester, Massachusetts

but in John Robb's St. Louis, his fictional pal Sug would have been denied the right to vote in municipal elections.[73]

The heralded democrat Andrew Jackson (as it was pointed out in the 1828 campaign) had actually helped draft suffrage restrictions for the Tennessee constitution in 1796. He made no effort to expand the electorate in his state—ever. As the territorial governor of Florida in 1822, he was perfectly comfortable with the new state's imposing property requirements for voting. Jackson's appeal as a presidential candidate was not about real democracy, then, but instead the attraction to a certain class of land-grabbing whites and the embrace of the "rude instinct of masculine liberty." He did not stand for universal male suffrage. Indeed, it was not the United States, but Liberia, a country founded by the British and former American slaves, that first established universal suffrage for adult men, in 1839.[74]

In the end, the cracker or squatter never resolved his paradoxical character. He could free himself of responsibility, take to the road, and start over. He could boast and brag and pelt anyone who dared to insult his favorite candidate. As many have pointed out, whiskey drinking at the polls was often more important than listening to long-winded speeches. So while some journalists defended the "country crackers" as the "bone and sinew of the country," others continued to see the cracker as a drunken fool who, as one writer put it, elevated a favorite stump speaker into a "demigod of beggars." As late as 1842, "squatter" was still considered a "term, denoting infamy of life or station," of a lesser rank than the class-neutral "settler."[75]

Thus, the cracker or squatter was never the poster child of political equality. As a figure of popular caricature, he was a vivid illustration of class distinction more than he ever was a sign of respect for the lower class. No one pretended that Sug was the equal of John Quincy Adams, William Henry Harrison, or even his local congressman. At best, a backcountry citizen might get a chance to meet President Adams, but shaking hands (in the now familiar, post-bowing fashion) did not result in an elevation in social rank. In 1828, James Fenimore Cooper observed that democratic boasting was a "cheap price" to pay for ensuring that real social leveling did not erode set-in-stone class divisions.[76]

There was one bit of lore that concerned the squatter that did take hold. He had to be wooed for his vote. He had no patience for a candidate who refused to speak his language. That was the moral of another famous squatter story of 1840, "The Arkansas Traveller," in which an elite politician canvassing in the backcountry asks a squatter for refreshment. The squatter, seated on a whiskey barrel before his run-down cabin, ignores the man's request. For a brief interlude (because it was election season), the politician was obliged to bring himself down to the level of the common man. To get his drink and the squatter's vote, the politician had to dismount his horse, grab the squatter's fiddle, and show that he could play his kind of music. Once the politician returned to his mansion, however, nothing had changed in the life of the squatter, nor for his drudge of a wife and his brood of dirty, shoeless brats.[77]

Part II

DEGENERATION OF
THE AMERICAN BREED

CHAPTER SIX

Pedigree and Poor White Trash

Bad Blood, Half-Breeds, and Clay-Eaters

Everywhere they are just alike, possess pretty much the same characteristics, the same vernacular, the same boorishness, and the same habits . . . everywhere, Poor White Trash.

—Daniel Hundley, "Poor White Trash" in
Social Relations in Our Southern States (1860)

The sectional crisis that led to America's Civil War dramatically reconfigured the democratic language of class identity. The lowly squatter remained the focus of attention, but his habitat had changed: he was now, singularly, a creature of the slave states. The terminology for poor southern whites changed too. Neither squatter nor cracker was the label of choice anymore. Dirt-poor southerners living on the margins of plantation society became even more repugnant as "sandhillers" and pathetic, self-destructive "clay-eaters." It was at this moment that they acquired the most enduring insult of all: "poor white trash." The southern poor were not just lazy vagrants; now they were odd specimens in a collector's cabinet of curiosities, a diseased breed, and the degenerate spawn of a "notorious race." A new nomenclature placed the lowly where they would become familiar objects of ridicule in the modern age.

Though "white trash" appeared in print as early as 1821, the designation gained widespread popularity in the 1850s. The shift seemed evident in 1845 when a newspaper reported on Andrew Jackson's funeral procession in Washington City. As the poor crowded along the street, it was neither crackers nor squatters lining up to see the last hurrah of Old Hickory. Instead, it was "poor white trash" who pushed the poor colored folk out of the way to get a glimpse of the fallen president.[1]

What made the ridiculed breed so distinctive? Its ingrained physical defects. In descriptions of the mid-nineteenth century, ragged, emaciated sandhillers and clay-eaters were clinical subjects, the children prematurely aged and deformed with distended bellies. Observers looked beyond dirty faces and feet and highlighted the ghostly, yellowish white tinge to the poor white's skin—a color they called "tallow." Barely acknowledged as members of the human race, these oddities with cotton-white hair and waxy pigmentation were classed with albinos. Highly inbred, they ruined themselves through their dual addiction to alcohol and dirt. In the 1853 account of her travels in the South, Swedish writer Fredrika Bremer remarked that in consuming the "unctuous earth," clay-eaters were literally eating themselves to death.[2]

White trash southerners were classified as a "race" that passed on horrific traits, eliminating any possibility of improvement or social mobility. If these *Night of the Living Dead* qualities were not enough, critics charged that poor whites had fallen below African slaves on the scale of humanity. They marked an evolutionary decline, and they foretold a dire future for the Old South. If free whites produced feeble children, how could a robust democracy thrive? If whiteness was not an automatic badge of superiority, a guarantee of the homogeneous population of independent, educable freemen, as Jefferson imagined, then the ideals of life, liberty, and the pursuit of happiness were unobtainable.

Jefferson's language of upward mobility had lost ground in the antebellum South. Jacksonian celebrations of the intrepid backwoodsman faded from view as well. By the 1850s, in the midst of fierce debates over slavery and its expansion into the West, poor whites assumed a symbolic role in sectional arguments. Northerners, especially those who joined the Free Soil Party (1848) and its successor, the Republican Party (1854), declared that poor whites were proof positive of the debilitating effects of slavery on free labor. A slave economy monopolized the soil, while closing off opportunities for nonslaveholding white men to support their families and advance in a free-market economy. Slavery crushed individual ambition, inviting decay and death, and draining vitality from the land and its vulnerable inhabitants. Poor whites were the hapless victims of class tyranny and a failed democratic inheritance. As George Weston wrote in his famous pamphlet *The Poor Whites of the South* (1856), they were "sinking deeper and more hopelessly into barbarism with every succeeding generation."[3]

Proslavery southerners took a different ideological turn, defending class station as natural. Conservative southern intellectuals became increasingly comfortable with the notion that biology was class destiny.

In his 1860 *Social Relations in Our Southern States*, Alabamian Daniel
Hundley denied slavery's responsibility for the phenomenon of poverty,
insisting that poor whites suffered from a corrupt pedigree and cursed
lineage. Class was congenital, he believed, and he used the clever analogies of "runtish forefathers" and "consumptive parents" to explain away
the plight of impoverished rural whites. For Hundley and many others, it
was bloodline that made poor whites a "notorious race." Bad blood and
vulgar breeding told the real story of white trash.[4]

Hundley's ideology appealed broadly. Many northerners, even those
who opposed slavery, saw white trash southerners as a dangerous breed.
No less an antislavery symbol than Harriet Beecher Stowe agreed with
the portrait penned by the Harvard-educated future Confederate Hundley. Though she became famous (and infamous) for her bestselling antislavery novel *Uncle Tom's Cabin* (1852), Stowe's second work told a
different story. In *Dred: A Tale of the Great Dismal Swamp* (1856), she
described poor whites as a degenerate class, prone to crime, immorality,
and ignorance. North Carolinian Hinton Rowan Helper published *The
Impending Crisis of the South* (1857), which many consider the most
important book of the nineteenth century. He sold over 140,000 copies,
making his the most popular exposé of slavery's oppression of poor
whites. Helper's South was a "cesspool of degradation and ignorance,"
and poor white trash a dwarfed, duped, and sterile population bound for
extinction. In this and other ways, the unambiguous language of class
crossed the Mason-Dixon Line and bound political opponents in surprising ways. We are taught that the Civil War was principally a contest about
the sustainability of a world predicated on black enslavement. We are not
told the whole story, then, because social insecurities and ongoing class
tensions preoccupied the politicized population too, and exerted a real
and demonstrable impact on the fractured nation—before, during, and
after those four concentrated years of unprecedented bloodletting.[5]

Poor whites were not simply a danger to the integrity of the Old South.
The unloved class conjured a special fear, that they would spread their
unique contagion into the vast domain of the West. In a remarkably short
period of time, the United States swelled by 800 million acres. Nearly
250 million acres alone came in 1845 with the Texas annexation. That year,
the "dark horse" Democrat James K. Polk captured the presidency, mainly

because he embraced an overtly aggressive course of expansion. Besides welcoming Texas, Polk promised he would provoke hostilities if Great Britain did not concede to America its claim on the Oregon Territory. Polk averted war with Britain, grudgingly accepting partition of Oregon along the forty-ninth parallel, where it stands today.

As if this acquisition of land was insufficient for "Young Hickory," the second president from Tennessee reverted to his mentor's successful rationale: Andrew Jackson had used a border skirmish in Spanish Florida as a pretext to launch a war of conquest; now Polk employed the same method to invade Mexico. When the ink dried on the Treaty of Guadalupe Hidalgo in 1848, Polk had acquired what would become the states of California, Nevada, Utah, Arizona, and New Mexico, plus portions of Colorado and Wyoming. Democratic president Franklin Pierce added to Polk's booty in 1854, when he secured the so-called Gadsden Purchase, a strip of land tacked on to the southern edge of the New Mexico Territory. This latest investment had been vigorously urged on by the alluring gamble of building a transcontinental railroad to advance southern cotton interests.[6]

Intellectual currents were affected by transcontinentalism, as a new idiom captured the public's imagination. Advancing beyond Jefferson's concept of a nation with no inherited aristocracy, Americans embraced an imperial destiny grounded in biological determinism. The new imperative held that as much as the Anglo-Saxon American's racial stock was of superior characteristics, all that was left to do was outbreed all other races. According to the political arithmetic of 1851, the United States would surpass Europe in importance by 1870, "numbering 100,000,000 of free and energetic men of our own race and blood." Those of "Anglo-Saxon descent, impregnated with its sturdy qualities of heart and brain," would put Great Britain and the United States on a course of global dominance, "as representatives of this advancing stock."[7]

Sheer demographic superiority was reinforced by the second ruling premise of the new thinking: national greatness rested on the laws of bloodlines and hereditary transmission. Learned traits such as a love of liberty, and racial exclusivity, were now assumed to be passed from one generation to the next. In the essay entitled "The Education of the Blood" (1837), one advocate asserted that the knowledge of one generation was literally retained in the atmosphere, and that the aptitude for learning entered the bloodstream and became "part of our physical constitution and is transmitted to our descendants." Simply taking the savage from his mother in the forest and placing him in civilization would fail to convert him; his "blood must be trained and educated, generation after generation must accumulate receptivity as the Anglo-Saxon race has done." The same author compared the phenomenon to the less attractive inheritance of insanity, passed on through the father's line and "imbibed with our mother's milk." Bloodlines revealed everything: a nation was only as great as its pedigree. America's destiny was determined by large land acquisitions and infused in its people's blood.[8]

This fascination with blood was pervasive in antebellum literature. Southerners were enamored with horse breeding as reflected in the periodical *American Turf Register and Sporting Magazine*. In 1834, it recorded that "American blood" (i.e., "American thoroughbreds") had achieved a quality of blood as excellent as any in the world. Avid readers knew the pedigree of the most celebrated American horses, learned the long list of sires, while breeders kept and published the records of the "American stud book" to avoid a spurious issue.[9]

Horses and humans were identical in this regard. Scottish physiologist Alexander Walker revived the debate between John Adams and Thomas Jefferson over whether human beings should breed to "improve the race." In *Intermarriage* (1838), he strongly encouraged the practice of choosing spouses according to the same natural laws that applied to horse breeding. American health reformers such as Orson Squire Fowler, in *Hereditary Descent* (1848), recommended the breeding of children with desirable qualities. He emphasized the golden rule of animal breeders: attending to pedigree. No longer measured by wealth or family name, the only pedigree that mattered was long-lived ancestors and a sound physical constitution untainted with hereditary disease or "bad blood." The rallying cry in this new advice literature extended to "hygienic" marriages: the selection of sexual partners with healthy skin, good teeth, well-formed and vigorous bodies. One had to steer clear of the "ill-born," who produced nothing but "poor and feeble stock." Could America's future be derailed through the infusion of bad blood? A would-be wit put it this way: "Noble sires, we fondly think, only to be surpassed by us, their noble sons. With what reverence we revert to our parent stock! With what pride we talk of blood! With what jealousy we guard against its contamination!"[10]

Race and healthful inheritance were part of a single discussion. In 1843, the Alabama surgeon Josiah Nott declared that the mulatto, as a hybrid, was the "offspring of two distinct species—as a mule from the horse and ass." Mulattoes were "faulty stock," a "degenerate, unnatural offspring, doomed by nature to work out its own destruction." They were doomed because, like mules, they were prone to sterility. (It was a ridiculous theory, of course.) He compared mulattoes to consumptive parents, assuming that they had inherited a defective internal organization. Not content to confine his remarks to a mixture of Anglo-Saxon and Negro, he echoed the words of the leading English authority on the subject, Sir William Lawrence, that "the intellectual and moral character of the European is deteriorated by the mixture of black or red blood."[11]

A similar doctrine of hereditary suicide had already been applied to American Indians. Jefferson's paternalistic projection of acculturated Natives was no longer endorsed by most Americans by the 1840s. A starker and dogmatic ideology took hold, arrogantly nationalistic. Native American tribes, a biologically degraded race, could no longer coexist with their Saxon superiors. In 1844, with a cold nonchalance, one writer captured the mood: "They retire before the axe and plough like the forests they once inhabited. The atmosphere of the white man is their poison. They cannot exist among us." The "red man was doomed to utter and entire extinction." This belief was not new, just more publically accepted. Henry Clay had privately voiced the same conclusion twenty years before as secretary of state.[12]

Both Texas and California loomed large in fashioning the Anglo-Saxon fantasy. Jackson subaltern Sam Houston, the first elected president of Texas, was a charismatic promoter of the region's freedom fighters. White Texans were, in his words, the embodiment of "Anglo-Saxon chivalry." Though the real force behind independence came from a filibuster, a private army of young men directed by their greed for land, Houston saw victory in racial terms. Every Texan had "imbibed the principles from his ancestry," his "kindred in blood," and was spurred on by his "superior intelligence and unsubduable courage." For many others like Houston,

Texas independence was an epochal achievement; it symbolized the passage of the "scepter" from the Old to the New World, the purest flowering of the Anglo-Saxon race.[13]

Houston was actually a strange choice to carry this banner of racial pride. Between 1829 and 1833, before he became president, he lived with the Cherokees, took two Indian wives, and sat for a portrait in full Indian garb. His presidential successor had few qualms about cleansing Texas of Indians. In 1839, the aptly named Mirabeau Buonaparte Lamar, known for his flowery poetry, pursued what he called "an exterminating war" against the Cherokees and Comanches. The Texas national constitution explicitly denied citizenship to those of African or Indian descent. The Texas legislature passed its first antimiscegenation law in 1837. It was similar to laws in force in southern states prohibiting marriage between persons of European blood and those of African ancestry.[14]

Texas could lay claim to another dubious "first." In 1849, Dr. Gideon Lincecum introduced a memorial before the Texas legislature hoping to ensure "good breeders." His solution was to castrate criminals in the manner of gelding bulls, thus literally cutting off the bloodline in order to prevent inferior people from reproducing. "Like breeds like" was the basic rule of animal breeding, and degraded stocks of animals were no different than humans. Lincecum offered a folksy analogy to make his case: "When the horse and the mare both trot, the colt seldom paces." His plan was rejected, but he was merely ahead of his time. Future eugenic policies built upon his blueprint for filtering out bad seeds from America's human breeding stock.[15]

But as Jefferson and Adams had concluded decades earlier, humans were never very careful in choosing mates. Racial mixing was consequently quite common in Texas. The American settlers who had arrived before independence were encouraged by the Mexican government to marry local Tejano women; men were granted an extra land bonus if they did. White male settlers routinely took Indian and Tejano women as concubines, and mixed-race children populated the nation and later the state. The Mexicans subscribed to a racial class and caste system, but were accustomed to racial mixing. At the top were the descendants of the old Spanish families, those claiming to have pure Castilian blood in their veins; next came the *criollos* (creoles), the locally born colonists of

Spanish heritage, who could possess up to one-eighth Indian blood; the lower castes were composed of mestizos (of mixed Spanish and Indian background), Indians, and Africans. American men who married well-born women were warmly embraced by Mexican society. As a consequence, after 1836, Texans retained the Mexican distinction between noble Castilians and inferior racially mixed classes.[16]

By the time of annexation, Anglo-Texans routinely ridiculed the dark-skinned, lower-class Tejanos as a sign of degradation among the native population. Here again, common language underscored the degradation of bloodlines. Increasingly, Mexicans were thrown together with blacks and Indians and contemptuously dismissed by Americans in general as a "mongrel race." "Mongrel" was just another word for "half-breeds" or "mulattoes," those of a "polluted" lineage. In 1844, Pennsylvania senator and future president James Buchanan crudely described an "imbecile and indolent Mexican race," insistent that no Anglo-Saxon should ever be under the political thumb of his inferior. His colleague from New Hampshire, former treasury secretary Levi Woodbury, elevated the Texas Revolution into a racial war of liberation: "Saxon blood had been humiliated, and enslaved to Moors, Indians, and mongrels." Such rhetoric had appeal far beyond the bloviated oratory of politicians. One Texas woman confidently wrote to her mother, "You feel the irresistible necessity that one race must subdue the other," and "they, of the superior race, can easily learn to look upon themselves as men of Destiny."[17]

Supporters of Texas annexation dramatized the urgent need to preserve a safely Anglo-Saxon society—continent-wide. Anglo-Texas would protect all Americans from the "semi-barbarous hordes," whose "poisonous compound of blood and color" flowed through the arteries of the mixed races in Mexico. That is what Senator Robert Walker of Mississippi argued in Congress, and reinforced with his widely influential 1844 *Letter on the Annexation of Texas*. Though a withered shell of a man, barely five feet tall and only a hundred pounds, Walker had become the most powerful Democrat in Washington. As ludicrous as it now sounds, he proclaimed that Texas would magically drain free blacks, mulattoes, and other African "mongrels" from the United States, siphoning off the dangerous dregs of slavery's past into South America. It was a racist theory with a familiar ring to it: Benjamin Rush's migratory model of 1798, in which Pennsylvania would filter out the weaker squatters by dispatching them to the lazy, cracker-filled South. Walker simply added another piece of pseudoscientific evidence to make his case: a high number of free blacks in the northern states suffered from insanity. Here was another example of political arithmetic gone awry, since the southern senator intentionally misused the U.S. census data (as Alabama's Josiah Nott had done) on black inmates in northern asylums. His main point was that free blacks were congenitally weaker in mind and body, and ill-suited for freedom, in contrast to the supposedly healthy and contented slaves in the South who did not have to aspire to liberty.[18]

The heavy-handed rhetoric cut both ways. Texas was to be rescued to strengthen America's pedigree, but the admission of too many Mexicans into an expanded Union could undermine America's racial stock. Georgia representative Alexander Hamilton Stephens, future vice president of the Confederacy, asserted that the great majority of Texans were from good stock—the right kind of people, worthy of breeding and mixing with other Americans. He employed a familiar marital metaphor from the book of Genesis to make his point: as heirs of the "Americo-Anglo-Saxon race," Texans were "from us and of us; bone of our bone, and flesh of our flesh." Opponents of the Mexican–American War used the same race-specific language in an effort to limit the amount of territory to be taken into the United States.[19]

Breeding was expected to be an increasingly important weapon in America's imperial arsenal during the one-sided war. Yankee soldiers were expected to settle in occupied territory, marry "beautiful señoritas," and achieve a new kind of "annexation." This was what had happened in California, as illustrated by the remarkable career of a young Tennessee officer, Cave Johnson Couts, a close friend of President Polk. He married a daughter of a wealthy Mexican rancher, received a large tract of land from his brother-in-law, and built a grandiose home, which he filled with his ten children. By the 1860s he owned over twenty-three thousand acres and had established himself as one of the ruling patriarchs of the new state.[20]

Yet California's early history had been as grim as that of Texas. Both of these extensive territories were overrun with runaway debtors, criminal outcasts, rogue gamblers, and ruthless adventurers who thrived in the chaotic atmosphere of western sprawl. The California gold rush attracted not only grizzled gold diggers but also prostitutes, fortune hunters, and con men selling fraudulent land titles. Among the Texas and California cutthroats who captured the American imagination was the "half-breed Mexican and white." He was known for his "mongrel dandyism," loud jewelry, and flamboyant clothing.[21]

In a certain sense, California reverted to older British colonial patterns. Though it entered the Union as a free state, prohibiting slavery, the legislature soon passed a series of byzantine laws permitting the indentured servitude of Native Americans. Between 1850 and 1854, nearly twenty thousand Indian men, women, and children were exploited as bound servants. It was John Smith's Jamestown all over again, even to its out-of-balance male-to-female ratio. The popular presses back east appealed for white women to move out west. Some of these were earnest requests, while others satirized Californians' desperate pleas for good breeders. A popular 1850 French caricature featured women packed in crates like everyday commodities, ready for export to female-starved "Californie." The *United States Magazine and Democratic Review* prophesied that if prospective wives were shipped off to California at the rate they were needed, the institution of spinsterhood would become extinct in America.[22]

The gold rush attracted more than restless white Americans looking for easy riches. Adventurers came from as far away as Australia, Chile, Hawaii, and France. Large numbers of Chinese began arriving in 1852. San Francisco quickly became the most cosmopolitan hub in all of North America. North Carolinian Hinton Rowan Helper was one of the many educated travelers to write on the racial "menagerie"—and utter degeneration of whites—that he discovered in California. His book *Land of Gold* (1855) laid the groundwork for his far more controversial polemic on poor whites, *The Impending Crisis of the South* (1857).[23]

Built tall and rail thin, Helper must have stood out among the motley assortment of émigrés. He spent three long years in California and came away hating the state. Despite all the harsh things he had to say about almost everyone he met, he was obliged to admit that most imported women had little choice but prostitution if they wished to survive in the unruly town of San Francisco.[24]

For Helper, the Digger Indians were "filthy and abominable," living like "carnivorous animals," and far worse than either "niggers" or "dogs." White men in the Golden State killed off Indians as if dispatching squirrels. The Nicaraguans Helper encountered on his return voyage to North Carolina were "feeble" and "dwarfed"—accordingly, one Kentuckian was the equal of four or five of these "hybrid denizens of the torrid zone." Free blacks likewise lived in "filth and degradation." Helper echoed Walker's racist migration theory: someday blacks would be drawn toward the equator and deposited (like waste) in the "receptacles" of South American countries.[25]

Helper complained about Californians, drawing on animal analogies whenever possible. Americans, English, French, Chinese, Indians, Negroes, and "half-breeds" could never find common cause over a gold mine any more than a panther, lion, tiger, or bear could in hovering over the body of a fresh-slain deer. The Chinese provoked contempt, for they had the gall to imagine that they were superior to Anglo-Saxons. These "semi-barbarians" shared the fate of the southern Negro: both the "copper of the Pacific" and the "ebony of the Atlantic" were destined to be permanently enslaved.[26]

As much as he was a passionate proponent of racial purity, Helper imagined himself something of a sociologist-anthropologist too. He compared the gold craze to the cotton South's single-crop economy. The conclusions drawn from his study on California reemerged in his 1857 critique of southern society. From his description of elite Californios (residents of Spanish descent), he found a western version of the cruel and self-satisfied aristocratic southern planter. The Spanish indulgence in the horror show of the bullfight struck Helper as cousin to the southern planter's wielding of his lash. The barbarous matador was akin to the "august knight" planter who lorded over slaves and poor white men. By 1857, poor white trash had taken on the traits of slain bulls, defeated beings, wallowing without hope in a state of "illiteracy and degradation" that was "purposely and fiendishly perpetuated" by callous planters.[27]

Helper easily transferred his perspective on California miners to the southern poor. The gold diggers were an updated version of squatters: they lived in squalid tents, wearing their hair long and donning scraggly beards. The majority of white men who swarmed into California became "poverty-stricken dupes." They were no different, in this way, from southern poor whites, "so basely duped, so adroitly swindled, and so damnably outraged." For Helper, economies dependent on one source of wealth created extreme class conditions. California mining was worshipped in the same way that cotton and slavery had become the false deities of the South.[28]

In *Land of Gold,* Helper actually defended slavery. But less than two years later, in *The Impending Crisis* (1857), he called for its abolition—in the same form that Abraham Lincoln and a slew of purportedly "liberal" politicians preferred: emancipation and colonization. Freed slaves would have to be expelled from the United States. The rise of the Free Soil Party in 1848, and the Republican Party in 1854, did not imply that an antislavery position was devoid of anxiety over pedigree, unnatural mixtures, and degenerate breeds. The first Republican presidential candidate was Colonel John Frémont, a man born and raised in the South who made his reputation crossing the Rockies. Like Helper, he converted to abolition in the interest of protecting the white race.[29]

Free Soil rhetoric fed the belief that freemen could not coexist with slaves—just as Anglo-Saxons could not live side by side with Indians. Slavery was a dangerous contagion spreading death and decay, and feeding a class/demographic war by "depopulating" the nation of its white inhabitants. As one clever essayist pointed out as early as 1843, poor southern whites were being forced from their homes, and pushed into exile like refugees, because they were unable to compete with those Helper called slaveowning "land-sharks." It was unfair to divest them of their land and rob them of their posterity's rightful inheritance. With "haggard features" and "emaciated forms," the poor southern families that headed west represented a new class of poverty, worse than any seen before. By "banishing her sons," the essayist of 1843 concluded, slaveowners were "warring against the vital interest of the entire non-slaveholding population in the South."[30]

Free Soilers imagined three possible scenarios in eliminating slavery. First, if the West was to remain uncontaminated, slavery had to be kept out of all new territories. Second, by prohibiting the migration of slavery into western territories and states, it seemed plausible to some that the institution would gradually die off in the Old South. Third, as in Helper's case, ending slavery would require exporting slaves elsewhere, recolonizing them in Africa, the Caribbean islands, or South America.

The Free Soil banner moved to the center of national politics in 1846.

That year, Pennsylvania Democrat David Wilmot introduced a proviso in Congress, which stipulated that all territory gained from the Mexican War must remain free soil—slavery prohibited. The wording was taken verbatim from Jefferson's 1784 draft banning slavery from the Northwest Territory. It went hand in hand with the Homestead Bill, which would have granted all men a free homestead of 160 acres. Freedom—which of course meant freedom for all whites—was only ensured through land ownership and the ability to reap sustenance from the soil. Unlike previous land policies that granted squatters preemption rights (the right to buy land they had staked out and cultivated), the new campaign turned the squatter into an entitled freeman. To be a homesteader was to be of the American people—who collectively owned as their inalienable "birthright" all the public land in the territories. Unfortunately, blocked by southern votes in Congress, the "inalienable homestead" would not become law until 1862, after secession.[31]

Free Soil politics served to underscore a class-inflected theme: southern planters were spreading slavery to the detriment of freemen. Former Kentucky congressman Benjamin Hardin captured the theme of class warfare in 1841, when he claimed that slavery was depopulating his state of the sons of its early pioneers. Recalling Daniel Boone, the most benign symbol of the old pioneer-squatter, he observed that the great man could never have imagined that his descendants were to be "driven into exile and poverty." All across Kentucky, the proud homes of freemen were being replaced by plantations and cattle. On the "turf where once sported freeborn children," "unsightly stocks" of domesticated animals and slaves now existed. Free soil revived the fight between squatters and speculators, and converted squatters into honest freemen of a "landed democracy" who stood proud against a slaveholding oligarchy.[32]

Once again, the Free Soil pledge was about saving the white man. As the Republican presidential nominee in 1856, Frémont made the crisis of the honest freeman his central platform. In barring slaveholders from the territories, he would prevent northern white laborers from being reduced to virtual slaves in the West. For nonslaveholders in the South, he offered a kind of emancipation, a promise of real independence denied to them since 1776. Still, the Free Soil doctrine raised questions over whether white trash really could ever be rescued. A Massachusetts orator put it simply: "I am a freeman, and the son of a freeman, born and reared on free soil." Poor southern whites were born in slave states, reared on unfree soil, and, according to a growing number of public commentators, they suffered from a degenerate pedigree. They did not act like freemen. In Helper's view, their ignorance and docility had made them worse than Russian serfs, when they compliantly voted the "slaveocrats" into office time and again.[33]

The new Republicans revived the old critique of Washington and Jefferson: southern agriculture depleted the soil and turned the land into waste. Helper published tables proving the North's greater productivity over the South. George Weston quoted prominent southern men in his influential pamphlet *The Poor Whites of the South* to make the case that the South was doomed to remain economically backward.[34]

All knew that poor whites were cursed because they were routinely consigned to the worst land: sandy, scrubby pine, and swampy soil. This was how they became known in the mid-nineteenth century as "sandhillers" and "pineys." Forced to the margins, often squatting on land they did not own, they were regularly identified with the decaying soil. The poor whites of "Hard-scratch" were, in the words of one, as "stony, stumpy, and shrubby, as the land they lived on." In a throwback to Buffon, Helper insisted that the "degenerate population" produced men and animals that were "dwarfed into shabby objects." In 1854, Henry David Thoreau took the same theme to its darkest corner of the imagination: the slave South was a rotting corpse, he wrote, and should at best be used to "manure" the colonizing West. Equating poor whites with human detritus, he described a people whose only function was to act as fertilizer for the territories.[35]

In her novel *Dred*, Harriet Beecher Stowe was no less harsh. Her planters dismissed the "whole race" of poor whites, "this tribe of creatures"; or as one of her characters ruefully declared, "There ought to be hunting parties got up to chase them down, and exterminate 'em, just as we do rats." The author depicted a white trash woman and her children as wounded animals hiding in the forest:

> Crouched on a pile of dirty straw, sat a miserable haggard woman, with large, wild eyes, sunken cheeks, disheveled matted hair, and long, lean hands, like bird's claws. At her skinny breast an emaciated

infant was hanging, pushing, with its little skeleton hands, as if to force nourishment which nature no longer gave; and two scared-looking children, with features wasted and pinched blue with famine, were clinging to her gown. The whole group huddled together, drawing as far as possible away from the new comer, looking up with large, frightened eyes, like hunted wild animals.[36]

Stowe's point was that poor southern whites were already exiles, whose only hope was to be lifted up by others. But would that happen? The contempt she put into the mouths of southern planters was not solely of her invention. Many planters loathed poor whites for their criminal activity, and especially the role they played alongside slaves in the trafficking of stolen goods. In the 1850s, as the poor white population swelled in numbers, a Charleston district grand jury recommended disenfranchising the poor white men who were so "degraded" that they traded alcohol with blacks.[37]

Suffrage could be stripped away from any freeman by the planter-controlled courts. In the 1840s and 1850s, North Carolina, South Carolina, Louisiana, and Virginia kept poor whites at bay by retaining property qualifications for holding office. Social ostracism was an even greater mark of shame, as planters forced poor whites to use the back door when entering the master's house. Slaves called them "stray goats" when they came begging for food or supplies. Southern reformers were just as disparaging. In a speech before the South Carolina Institute in 1851, industrial advocate and cotton mill owner William Gregg underscored the evolutionary argument in saying that "our poor white people . . . are suffered to while away an existence in a state but one step in advance of the Indian of the forest." Gregg exclusively hired poor whites to work in his factory, hoping to elevate them into a more civilized—though still a menial—station, providing steady work and granting access to schools.[38]

Few white trash squatters had any access to free soil or to homesteads. They lived instead like scavengers, vagrants, and thieves—at least according to reports by wealthy southerners. But the truth is more complicated. Many worked as tenants and day laborers alongside slaves; during harvesttime, poor men and women worked day and night for paltry wages.

In cities such as Baltimore and New Orleans, some of the most back-breaking labor—working on the railroads, paving streets, dray driving, ditch building—was chiefly performed by underpaid white laborers.[39]

By the 1850s, poor whites had become a permanent class. As non-slaveholders, they described themselves as "farmers without farms." Small-scale slaveholders tended to be related to large planters, a reminder of how much pedigree and kinship mattered. Slaveowners had unusual financial instruments that situated them above nonslaveholders: they raised slave children as an investment, as an invaluable source of collateral and credit when they sought to obtain loans.

Whether they stayed put or moved west, poor whites occupied poor land. Nearly half left the Atlantic South for Texas, Arkansas, Mississippi, and elsewhere, and still poor whites as a percentage in the original slave states remained fairly constant. The safety-valve theory did not work.[40]

The label "southern white trash" was not, as some would argue, a northern creation alone. While the "po'" in "po' white trash" may have been derived from slave vocabulary, it clearly resonated among southern elites who dismissed the poor (as Jefferson did) as "rubbish." The unlikely duo of Harriet Beecher Stowe and Daniel Hundley endorsed "good blood" to describe inherited class virtues—"veined and crossed" was the quasi-scientific description that underscored the power of intergenerational resemblance.[41]

Alabama's Hundley was never as famous as the Connecticut-born Stowe, but he was not a typical southerner either. After receiving his law degree from Harvard in 1853, he married his Virginia cousin (in the southern fashion), and was sent to Chicago by his father-in-law to manage the family's real estate. Before he wrote about poor whites, he witnessed the Panic of 1857, which flooded Chicago with the unemployed. After Lincoln was elected, he returned to Alabama, remaking himself into an ardent defender of secession and the southern way of life.[42]

Hundley claimed that genuine southern gentlemen were of Cavalier blood, an invented royal lineage superior to ordinary Anglo-Saxons. He even reduced Jefferson to a half-breed of sorts: royal Cavalier on his mother's side, hearty Anglo-Saxon on his father's. Hundley's archetypal southern gentleman was akin to an Arabian horse: six feet tall, strong and athletic, at home hunting and roaming the countryside. In his taxonomy, the white classes were divided into a descending order of bloodlines: Cavalier gentry sat at the top, Anglo-Saxons filled the middle and yeoman classes, and those he called "southern bullies" and "white trash" sat feebly at the bottom. These lowest forms traced their lineage only to the convicts and indentured servants of Jamestown; they were the befouled heirs of poor vagrants, or those from the back alleys of old London.[43]

For her part, in the plot of her novel *Dred*, Stowe divided poor southern whites into three classes. Vicious (mean) whites, like Hundley's southern bullies, were licentious beings, wallowing in a continual drunken stupor while dreaming of possessing a slave to order around. Beneath the vicious were the white trash who lived as scared animals, objects of disgust. But the most interesting class in Stowe's book were her half-breeds. The character Miss Sue was one of the Virginia Peytons ("good blood"), whose family "degenerated" as a consequence of losing its wealth. Impetuously, Sue married John Cripps, a poor white, but thanks to pedigree, their children could be saved: they were "pretty" and wore their biological inheritance on their faces, with "none of the pronunciation or manners of wild white children." After Sue's death, they were further improved in New England, attending the best schools. A healthy combination of circumstances enabled them to reassert their mother's superior class lineage.[44]

In popular depictions, poor white trash were, above all, "curious" folks whose habits were as "queer" as "any description of Chinese or Indians." Or, as a New Hampshire schoolteacher observed of clay-eaters in Georgia, the children were prematurely aged. Even at ten years old, "their countenances are stupid and heavy and they often become dropsical and loathsome to sight." Nothing more dramatically signified a dying breed than the decrepitude of wrinkled and withered children.[45]

Commentators repeatedly emphasized the odd skin color: "unnatural complexions" of a "ghastly yellowish white," or as Hundley observed, skin the color of "yellow parchment." There were "cotton-headed or flaxen-headed" children, whose unhealthy whiteness resembled the albino. There were poor white, dirt-eating urchins who bore a "cadaverous, bloodless look"; their hair, identified as "crops," took on the appearance of the soil-depleting cotton that surrounded them. The women were a "wretched specimen of maternity" rather than ideal breeders. Nor did they care properly for their offspring. The "tallow-faced gentry," as one

Kansas newspaper disapprovingly labeled them, routinely stuffed their infants' mouths with clay. The words describing poor white trash had not been quite so pronounced since the seventeenth century.[46]

"Like breeds like" continued to serve as the guiding principle etched into these damning portraits. Diarist Mary Boykin Chesnut, of a wealthy South Carolina family, offered one of the most repellent of midcentury snapshots. A woman from her neighborhood, one Milly Trimlin, was thought a witch by poor whites. "Superstitious hordes" had her bones dug up and removed from consecrated ground three times and scattered elsewhere. Despised by her own kind and living off charity, she was, Chesnut wrote, a "perfect specimen of the Sandhill tacky race." (Tacky was a degenerate breed of horse that lived in the Carolina marshlands.) Trimlin looked the part: "Her skin was yellow and leathery, even the whites of her eyes were bilious in color. She was stumpy, strong, and lean, hard-featured, horny-fisted."[47]

Few were concerned about, much less offered any solution to, their terrible poverty. Regarded as specimens more than cognitive beings, white trash sandhillers and clay-eaters loomed as abnormalities, deformities, a "notorious race" that would persist, generation after generation, unaffected by the inroads being made by social reformers. Only a minority of southerners were like William Gregg, who considered training poor white trash for factory labor. Defenders of slavery had come to argue that the system of unpaid labor was natural and necessary, and actually superior to free labor. In 1845, former governor James Henry Hammond of South Carolina insisted that slavery should be the cornerstone of all relations, and that class subordination was just as natural. Jefferson's "all men are created equal" was, Hammond insisted without shame, a "ridiculously absurd" concept. Now a circle of influential southern intellectuals were openly insisting that freedom was best achieved when people remained within their proper station.[48]

The "intellectual Caucasian" had arrived. In 1850, Professor Nathaniel Beverley Tucker of the College of William and Mary averred that this type possessed traits in the "highest perfection" and was naturally prepared for rule over both blacks and inferior whites. Six years later, the *Richmond Enquirer* restated the increasingly popular view that slavery should not be a matter of complexion but of lineage and habits. Thus it is not surprising that Harriet Beecher Stowe had slaveholders wishing for a new class of poor whites—a class of white slaves. "Like other nomadic races," Hundley wrote, white trash should "pass further and further westward and southward, until they eventually become absorbed and lost among the half-civilized mongrels who inhabit the plains of Mexico." Outward migration was the saving grace for the new elitists.[49]

Pedigree was the centerpiece of Supreme Court chief justice Roger B. Taney's majority opinion in the *Dred Scott* decision (1857). Though this case assessed whether a slave taken into a free state or federal territory should be set free, its conclusions were far more expansive. Addressing slavery in the territories, the proslavery Marylander dismissed Jefferson's prohibition of slavery in the Northwest Ordinance as having no constitutional standing. He constructed his own version of the original social contract at the time of the Revolution, the Declaration of Independence, and the Constitutional Convention: only the free white children of the founding generation were heirs to the original agreement; only pedigree could determine who inherited American citizenship and whose racial lineage warranted entitlement and the designation "freeman." Taney's opinion mattered because it literally made pedigree into a constitutional principle. In this controversial decision, Taney demonstrably rejected any notion of democracy and based the right of citizenship on bloodlines and racial stock. The chief justice ruled that the founders' original intent was to classify members of society in terms of recognizable breeds.[50]

The vagrant, the squatter, had been redrawn, yet qualitatively he/she remained the same: a piece of white trash on the margins of rural society. Observers recognized how the moving mass of undesirables in the constantly expanding West challenged democracy's central principle. California was a wake-up call. Anxious southerners focused attention not only on their slave society and slave economy, but on the ever-growing numbers of poor whites who made the permanently unequal top-down social order perfectly obvious. Who really spoke of equality among whites anymore? No one of any note. Let us put it plainly: on the path to disunion, the roadside was strewn with white trash.

CHAPTER SEVEN

Cowards, Poltroons, and Mudsills

⸺◦◊◦⸺

Civil War as Class Warfare

You have shown yourselves in no respect to be the degenerate sons of our fathers. . . . It is true you have a cause which binds you together more firmly than your fathers. They fought to be free from the usurpations of the British Crown, but they fought against a manly foe. You fight against the offscourings of the earth.

—President Jefferson Davis, January 1863

In February 1861, Jefferson Davis, the newly elected president of the Confederacy, traveled to Montgomery, Alabama, for his inauguration. Greeted by an excited crowd of men and women, he gave a brief speech outside the Exchange Hotel. Addressing his people as "Fellow Citizens and Brethren of the Confederate States of America," he invoked a tried-and-true metaphor to describe his new constituency: "men of one flesh, one bone, one interest, one purpose, and of identity of domestic institutions." As it happens, his was the same biblical allusion his vice president, Alexander Stephens of Georgia, had commandeered in Congress in 1845 when he rose in support of the annexation of Texas and its Anglo-Saxon population.[1]

The one-flesh marital trope had both a racial and a sexual dimension, presenting the desirable image of a distinct breed. Davis echoed the words of his namesake, Thomas Jefferson, when he described his new country as one that embodied "homogeneity." In *Notes on the State of Virginia,* Jefferson had made native-born stock and shared cultural values the basis of national unity and security. The idea of an "American breed" was firmly entrenched.[2]

Expositors of the "American breed" model all gravitated to an "us versus them" calculus, which became useful as territorial expansion unfolded and cultures collided. As the South seceded, further distinctions needed to be made. So when the Confederate president recurred to one of his favorite couplets, "degenerate sons," he appealed at the same time to the "days of '76," making sure his audience understood that the revolution of 1861 aimed to restore the virtuous pedigree of the founding fathers. The southern people, he assured the crowd, were heirs of the "sacred rights transmitted to us." If required, they would display "Southern valor" on the field of battle. The new nation would prove to the world that "we are not the degenerate sons" of George Washington and his noble peers, but in fact the genuine offspring and rightful lineage of the first American republic.[3]

And then there was the flip side. Davis returned to the bully pulpit in the final days of 1862, addressing the Mississippi legislature, where he openly rebuked the men who comprised the Union forces. They were nothing more than "miscreants" deployed by a government that was "rotten to the core." The war proved that North and South were two distinct breeds. Whereas southerners could lay claim to a positive pedigree, their enemy could not. Northerners were heirs to a "homeless race," traceable to the social levelers of the English civil war. What's more, the North's unflattering genealogy began in the "bogs and fens" of Ireland and England, where they were spawned from vagabond stock and swamp people. It was a delusion, Davis declared, to imagine that these two races could ever be reunited. No loyal Confederate would ever wish to lower himself and rejoin his lessers.[4]

Returning to the Confederate capital of Richmond, Davis gave another such speech in early January 1863. "You have shown yourselves in no respect to be the degenerate sons of our fathers," he repeated. Yet in one important respect, the South's cause was radically new. Their Revolutionary forebears had fought against a "manly foe." Confederates faced a different enemy: "You fight against the offscourings of the earth," the president railed. Yankees were a degenerate race, worse than "hyenas." In dehumanizing the Union troops, Davis placed them close in nature to a ravenous, cowardly species that hunted its innocent prey in whimpering packs.[5]

Wars are battles of words, not just bullets. From 1861, the Confederacy had the task of demonizing its foe as debased, abnormal, and vile. Southerners had to make themselves feel viscerally superior, and to convince themselves that their very existence depended on the formation of a separate country, free of Yankees. Confederates had to shield themselves from the odious charge of treason by fighting to preserve a core American identity that nineteenth-century northerners had corrupted.[6]

To do so, the Confederacy had to create a revolutionary ideology that concealed the deep divisions that existed among its constituent states. Tensions between the cotton-producing Gulf states and the more economically diverse border states were genuine. We tend to forget that an estimated three hundred thousand white southerners, many from the border states, fought for the Union side, and that four border states never seceded. In Georgia, throughout the war, dissent from Davis's policies was significant. Richmond was tasked with smoothing over the ever-widening division between slaveholders and nonslaveholders caused by conscription and food shortages. Claims to homogeneity were more imagined than real.[7]

The Confederacy built upon the South's prewar critiques of Yankee attributes. The Yankee gentry was allegedly composed of upstarts who lacked southern refinement. Their "freedom" was really low-class fanaticism. As one Alabama editor transparently put it in 1856:

> Free society! We sicken at the name. What is it but a conglomeration of greasy mechanics, filthy operatives, small-fisted farmers, and moon-struck theorists? All the northern, and especially the New England states, are devoid of society fitted for well-bred gentlemen. The prevailing class one meets with is that of mechanics struggling to be genteel, and small farmers who do their own drudgery, and yet are hardly fit for association with a southern gentleman's body servant.[8]

At a parade in Boston in that year, supporters of the first Republican presidential candidate, John C. Frémont, embraced the "greasy mechanic" slur as a badge of honor by displaying it on one of their banners.[9]

All the lurid name-calling had a specific purpose. Turning the free-labor debate on its head, proslavery southerners contended that the greatest failing of the North was its dependence on a lower-class stratum of menial white workers. Ten years before he became president of the Confederacy, Senator Jefferson Davis of Mississippi had argued that the slave states enjoyed greater stability. Recognizing that "distinctions between classes have always existed, everywhere, and in every country," he observed that two distinct labor systems coexisted in the United States.

In the South, the line between classes was drawn on the basis of "color," while in the North the boundary had been marked "by property, between the rich and poor." He insisted that "no white man, in a slaveholding community, was the menial servant of anyone." Like many other proslavery advocates, Davis was convinced that slavery had elevated poor whites by ensuring their superiority over blacks. He was wrong: in the antebellum period, class hierarchy was more extreme than it ever had been.[10]

James Henry Hammond, South Carolina's leading proslavery intellectual, coined the term "mudsill" to describe the essential inferiority of the North's socioeconomic system. It was "mudsill" democracy that the Confederacy would decry as it made its case against the North. By 1861, mudsill democracy had seeped into portrayals of the mudsill Union army—meant to be a foul collection of urban roughs, prairie dirt farmers, greasy mechanics, unwashed immigrants, and by 1862, with the enlistment of African American Union troops, insolent free blacks. All in all, they were Davis's waste people, the "offscourings of the earth."[11]

In 1858, Hammond had publicly aired his ideas before the U.S. Senate in a speech that proved to be widely popular. Its most enduring critique concerned the fixed character of class identity. In all societies, "there must be a class to do the menial duties, to perform the drudgery of life." With fewer skills and a "low order of intellect," the laboring class formed the base of civilized nations. Every advanced society had to exploit its petty laborers; the working poor who wallowed in the mud allowed for a superior class to emerge on top. This recognized elite, the crème de la crème, was the true society and the source of all "civilization, progress, and refinement." In Hammond's mind, menial laborers were, almost literally, "mudsills," stuck in the mud, or perhaps in a metaphoric quicksand, from which none would emerge.[12]

If all societies had their mudsills, then, Hammond went on to argue, the South had made the right choice in keeping Africa-descended slaves in this lowly station. As a different race, the darker-pigmented were naturally inferior and docile—or so he argued. The North had committed a worse offense: it had debased its own kind. The white mudsills of the North were "of your own race; you are brothers of one blood." From Hammond's perspective, their flawed labor system had corrupted democratic politics in the northern states. Discontented whites had been given the vote, and, "being the majority, they are the depositories of all your political power." It was only a matter of time, he warned ominously, before the poor northern mudsills orchestrated a class revolution, destroying what was left of the Union.[13]

Jefferson Davis and James Hammond spoke the same language. Confederate ideology converted the Civil War into a class war. The South was fighting against degenerate mudsills and everything they stood for: class mixing, race mixing, and the redistribution of wealth. By the time of Abraham Lincoln's election, secessionists claimed that "Black Republicans" had taken over the national government, promoting fears of racial degeneracy. But a larger danger still loomed. As one angry southern writer declared, the northern party should not be called "Black Republicans," but "Red Republicans," for their real agenda was not just the abolition of slavery, but inciting class revolution in the South.[14]

Confederate ideologues turned to the language of class and breeding for obvious reasons. They were invested in upholding a hierarchy rooted in the ownership of slaves. When in 1861, Jefferson Davis spoke of "domestic institutions," he meant slavery, and its protection formed the central creed of the new constitution that bound "men of one flesh" to the new nation. Vice President Alexander Stephens, in a speech given in Savannah on his return from the constitutional convention, took pains to make Hammond's mudsill theory the cornerstone of the Confederacy. The delegates had instituted a more perfect government: first, by ensuring that whites would never oppress classes of their own race; and second, by affirming that the African slaves "substratum of *our* society is made of the material fitted by nature for it." Refuting the premise of Lincoln's 1858 "House Divided" speech (that a nation cannot stand half slave, half free), Stephens equated the Confederacy with a well-constructed mansion, with slaves as its mudsill base and whites its "brick and marble" adornment. Presumably the brick represented the sturdy yeoman and the planter elite its finely polished alabaster.[15]

Class concerns never lost their potency during the war. In 1864, as defeat loomed and the South's leaders contemplated augmenting the army with slaves, some feared that the rebel nation would fall if deprived of its lowest layer. Black men would achieve a rise in status through military service, undermining general assumptions about the color-coded social hierarchy. Slaves had been impressed by state governments to build fortifications as early as 1861—a policy later adopted by the

Confederate high command and the Davis administration. But putting slaves in uniform was a far more radical move, because it elevated them (as Hammond and Stephens had argued) above their station as menial mudsills. Texas secessionist Louis T. Wigfall raged in the Confederate Senate that arming slaves was utterly unthinkable, no different than the British eradicating their landed aristocracy and putting "a market-house mob" in its place. ("Market-house mob" was another term for class revolution, and deposing the aristocracy would turn the Confederacy into another mudsill democracy—like the enfranchised rubbish of the North.) Sounding like a snobbish English lord, Wigfall added that he did not want to live in a country where "a man who blacked his boots and curried his horse was his equal." In his mind, slaves were born servants, and raising them up by making them soldiers disrupted the entire class structure. Protecting that racial and class system was why southerners had seceded. In this way, class angst suffused Confederate thinking and served to unite southern elites.[16]

Class mattered for another reason. Confederate leaders knew they had to redirect the hostility of the South's own underclass, the nonslaveholding poor whites, many of whom were in uniform. Charges of "rich man's war and poor man's fight" circulated throughout the war, but especially after the Confederate Congress passed the Conscription Act of 1862, instituting the draft for all men between the ages of eighteen and thirty-five. Exemptions were available to educated elites, slaveholders, officeholders, and men employed in valuable trades—leaving poor farmers and hired laborers the major target of the draft. Next the draft was extended to the age of forty-five, and by 1864 all males from seventeen to fifty were subject to conscription.[17]

The Union army and Republican politicians advanced a strategy aimed at further exploiting class divisions between the planter elite and poor whites in the South. Generals Ulysses S. Grant and William T. Sherman, as well as many Union officers, believed they were fighting a war against a slaveholding aristocracy, and that winning the war and ending slavery would liberate not only slaves but also poor white trash. In his memoir, Grant voiced the class critique of the Union command. There would never have been secession, he wrote, if demagogues had not swayed nonslaveholding voters and naïve young soldiers to believe that the North was filled with "cowards, poltroons, and negro-worshippers."

Convinced that "one Southern man was equal to five Northern men," Confederate soldiers saw themselves as a superior people. (The same five-to-one ratio was used by North Carolinian Hinton Rowan Helper when he defended the Anglo-Saxon race in *Land of Gold* and claimed that one Kentuckian could trounce five dwarfish and feeble Nicara-guans.) In Grant's estimation, the war was fought to liberate nonslave-holders, families exiled to poor land, who had few opportunities to better themselves or educate their children. "They too needed emancipation," he insisted. Under the "old régime," the prewar South, they were nothing but "poor white trash" to the planter aristocracy. They did as told and were accorded the ballot, but just so long as they parroted the wishes of the elite.[18]

By 1861, both sides saw the other as an alien culture doomed to extinc-tion. In a speech delivered in 1858, the same year as Hammond's famous mudsill oration, William H. Seward, the leading New York Republican who was to serve in Lincoln's cabinet, coined the term "irrepressible conflict." For Seward, free labor was a higher form of civilization, prac-ticed by the "Caucasians and Europeans." He blamed slavery on the Spanish and Portuguese, and reduced all of South America to a land of brutality, imbecility, and economic backwardness. Toppling slavery in the U.S. South, in Seward's grand historical schema, was merely an extension of the continental march of Anglo-Saxon civilization. The two class systems—slave and free—were locked in a battle for domination, and only one would survive.[19]

Of course, southern ideologues argued the exact opposite. Slavery was a vigorous and vibrant system, they insisted, and more effective than free labor. With a docile workforce, the South had eliminated conflict between labor and capital. Southern intellectuals alleged that the labor-ing class in the northern states was large, disruptive, jealous of the rich, and endowed with unwarranted political privileges. As Hammond and others saw it, the notion of equality had become the most deceptive fic-tion of the times. The very freedom "to think, feel and act," a writer warned in Charleston's *Southern Quarterly Review,* nurtures passion and provokes "unholy desire." That "unholy desire" was the longing for social mobility. Slaves were content in their menial lot, many believed. In this strange reversal of the American dream, the South's superiority arose, then, most ironically, from its absence of class mobility.[20]

Secessionists painted a dire picture of class instability above the Mason-Dixon Line. In the North, a writer contended in a Virginia magazine in 1861, "people are born, bred and educated to their leveling views," which might "reverse the condition of the rich and the poor." Education and class equality itself was seen as subversive, and Helper's *Impending Crisis of the South* was attacked as incendiary. Men were arrested, and some hanged, for peddling his book. Worried elites urged Confederate leaders to "watch and control" poor whites, "permitting them to have as little political liberty as we can, without degrading them."[21]

Not surprisingly, evidence exists to prove that southern whites lagged behind northerners in literacy rates by at least a six-to-one margin. Prominent southern men defended the disparity in educational opportunity. Chancellor William Harper of South Carolina concluded in his 1837 *Memoir on Slavery,* "It is better that a part should be fully and highly educated and the rest utterly ignorant." Inequality in education was preferable to the system in the northern states, in which "imperfect, superficial, half-education should be universal." As the Civil War arrived, editors and intellectuals called for an independent publishing industry in the Confederacy, in order to shield its people from the contamination of Union presses.[22]

Confederates openly defended the idea that the planter class was born to rule. The *"representative* blood of the South," the aristocratic elite, those of good patrician stock, were destined to have command over white and black inferiors. But for all their confidence about harmonious relations between the rich and poor in the South, many secessionists viewed nonslaveholders as the sleeping enemy within. White workingmen in places like Charleston were called "perfect drones," whose resentments could potentially be marshaled against slaveowners. Antidemocratic secessionists dismissed the poor as the hapless pawns of crass politicians, willing to sell their votes for homesteads or handouts. In 1860, Georgia governor Joseph Brown prophesied that the new Republican administration would bribe a portion of the citizens with offices, while others predicted that Lincoln would dangle bounties and cheap lands, using flattery and lures to ensnare the "lower strata of Southern society."

It was in response to such projections that small slaveholders in South Carolina organized vigilante societies and "Minute Men" companies, mainly to intimidate nonslaveholders who might try to forestall secession.[23]

Some secessionists went out of their way to allay concerns over the loyalty of nonslaveholders. In 1860, James De Bow, the influential editor of *De Bow's Review,* published a popular tract detailing the reasons why poor whites had every reason to back the Confederacy. He assured that slavery benefited all classes. Giving the mudsill theory an emphatic endorsement, he declared that "no white man at the South serves another as his body servant to clean his boots, wait on his table, and perform menial services in his household!" Besides, he wrote, wages for white workers were better in the South, and land ownership was more dispersed—which was patently untrue. He went on: class mobility was possible for nonslaveholders who scrimped and saved to buy a slave, especially a breeding female slave, whose offspring were "heirlooms" to be passed on to the next generation. If his promises of trickle-down economics were unconvincing, De Bow tacitly confirmed that slaves' elevation meant nonslaveholders' utter degradation. For these reasons, he said, the poorest nonslaveholder would readily "dig in the trenches, in defense of the slave property of his more favored neighbor." Fear of dropping to the level of slaves would lead poor whites to fight.[24]

Disunion did not alleviate such fears. In the lower South, for example, there was no popular referendum on secession except in Texas. The upper South was in no hurry to bolt. The four states that left (Virginia, North Carolina, Arkansas, Tennessee) did so only after Lincoln called for troops; all of these states contained significant numbers of pro-Union residents. West Virginians seceded from Virginia and rejoined the Union. Jefferson Davis secured the presidency without opposition, reducing his election to a symbolic vote, rubber-stamping the choice of the elite minority in the Confederate Provisional Congress.[25]

In addition to insulating the government from the people, a vocal contingent of delegates to the Confederate constitutional convention called for a repeal of the three-fifths compromise, instead counting slaves as whole persons for the purpose of representation in the Confederate legislature. This manner of representation benefited the states with the highest number of slaves. The South Carolinian novelist William Gilmore Simms, for one, thought that the border states, with their larger nonslaveholding populations, might "overslough" the cotton states. In that a slough was a swamp or mire, Simms was alluding to the mudsill-like nonslaveholders of the upper South, whose higher numbers would allow them to have more representatives than the slave-dominated states of the lower South. In the final draft of the Confederate constitution, the repeal of the three-fifths clause was voted down, but by the narrow margin of four to three states.[26]

In 1861, a nervous Georgian, who worried that slaveholders were a minority, proposed that the new state government should establish an upper house composed only of slaveholders, much like the English House of Lords. Conservative Georgia and Virginia delegates to their respective state conventions wished to curb the "swinish multitude," but in the end they refused to tamper with the right to vote. In Virginia, some elitists recognized the problem that conscription posed and sought to deal with it. Nonslaveholders might refuse to fight in a war designed to protect the slaves of the rich. Virginian Edmund Ruffin privately proposed a solution for his state: a dual system of conscription. In his two-track class system, one would require nonelite white men to take up arms, and another for planters' slaves, who would be impressed by the state and put to work for the army. Too bold and too honest in broadcasting the prevalence of social inequality, Ruffin's radical plan was never adopted.[27]

The future did not bode well for southern patricians. If they remained in the Union, or suffered defeat at the hands of the Yankees, they faced extinction. The aristocracy would be washed away in a flood of northern mudsills and liberated slaves. Their own homegrown white trash were a problem as well. Presumably, without total victory, landless laborers and poor farmers might outbreed the elite class, and if corrupted by northern democratic ideas, they might overwhelm the planter elite at the ballot box.[28]

Throughout the war, the unfair conscription policy sparked serious grievances. Early on, Florida's governor, John Milton, felt that the law could not be enforced, that poor whites would not stand for a substitution system that favored those who could buy a man to do his fighting for him. Exemptions protected the educated: teachers, ministers, clerks, politicians, as well as men in needed industries. Once the lowly conscripts were in the ranks, officers looked down on them as "food for powder," or compared them to "Tartars" and barbarians, which were the same slurs that elite southerners used to demean Lincoln's ruthless hordes. An Alabama recruit fed up with such treatment said the obvious: "They think all you are fit for is to stop bullets for them, your betters, who call you poor white trash."[29]

One odious feature of the draft was the "twenty slave law," which granted exemptions to planters with twenty or more slaves. The provision shielded the already pampered rich man and his valuable property. Some nonslaveholders refused to fight for the protection of slavery, while others thought the wealthy should pay higher taxes to subsidize a war that benefited them most. Lower-class men wanted their material interests protected. Wealthy officers were readily granted furloughs, while common soldiers were expected to endure long terms of enlistment, jeopardizing the livelihood of families left behind. As one historian has concluded, poorer soldiers thought of themselves as "conditional Confederates." This meant that poor farmers put their family's well-being before their loyalty to the Confederate nation.[30]

Southern gentlemen might be expected to fight without steady pay, but their definition of chivalry created an unrealistic standard for the lower classes. Class identity divided the ranks throughout the war. The "layouts," men who refused to volunteer or to appear for service once drafted, were rounded up by guards who were crudely called "dog catchers." Substitutes came from the poorest class of men, and were generally despised by other soldiers.[31]

Desertion was common among poor recruits, so much so that by August 1863, General Robert E. Lee was pleading with President Davis to take action to curb it. Later that year, Davis issued a general amnesty to all men who returned. In other instances, while some soldiers were executed, most companies subjected deserters instead to humiliating punishments. They were put in chains or forced to wear a barrel. Vigilantes hunted down runaway conscripts, especially in North Carolina, which had the highest rate of desertion. A community in Mississippi seceded from the Confederacy, creating the "Free State of Jones" in the middle of a swamp; it was, quite literally, a white trash Union sanctuary in President Davis's home state.[32]

Deserters stole food, raided farms, and harassed loyal soldiers and citizens. Pockets of poor men and their families had become the anarchists that upper-class southerners had long feared. In Georgia, late in the war it had reached the point that deserters were threatening to kidnap slaves or, worse, conspire with runaways. In 1865, the wives of Okefenokee renegades taunted authorities by claiming that their husbands would rise out of the swamp, armed and ready to steal as many slaves as they could round up, and then sell them to the Union navy.[33]

It is difficult to gauge what poor, illiterate soldiers thought of desertion, because they left no written records. But oral folk culture suggests that poor men openly joked about it. Desertion to them was part of the daily resistance to upper-class rule. One story making the rounds pitted a Georgia sandhiller against a North Carolina Tar-heel. Asked what he had done with a quantity of pitch, the Carolinian claimed he had sold it to Jeff Davis. Caught off guard, the sandhiller said, "What did old Davis want with all that for?" "Why," the Tar-heel jibed, "you Georgians run so that he had to buy some to make you stick."[34]

There is no way to know precisely how many men deserted. The official count from the U.S. provost marshal's report was 103,400. This was out of a total of 750,000 to 850,000 men listed as in the army by the end of the war. But these numbers are only a small part of the story. Class divided soldiers in other ways. The Confederate army dragooned at least 120,000 conscripts. There were between 70,000 and 150,000 substitutes, mostly wretchedly poor men, and only 10 percent ever reported to camp. Another 80,000 volunteers reenlisted to avoid the draft. Finally, as many as 180,000 men were at best "reluctant rebels," those who resisted joining until later in the war. Such resistance demonstrates that among average soldiers there was little evidence of a deep attachment to the Confederacy.[35]

Shortages in food fueled more discontents. As early as 1861, when planters were urged to plant more corn and grain, few were willing to give up the white gold of cotton. Consequently, food shortages and escalating inflation led to massive suffering among poor farmers, urban laborers, women, and children. One Georgian confessed that "avarice and the menial subjects of King cotton" would bring down the Confederacy long before an invading army could.[36]

More disturbing, though, the rich hoarded scarce supplies along with food. In 1862, mobs of angry women began raiding stores, storming warehouses and depots; these unexpected uprisings blanketed Georgia,

with similar protests surfacing in the Carolinas. In Alabama, forty maraud-
ing women burned all the cotton in their path as they scavenged for food.
A food riot broke out in the Confederate capital of Richmond in 1863.
When President Davis tried to calm the women, an angry female protester threw a loaf of bread at him.[37]

Female rioters were, in this way, the equivalent of male deserters.
They shattered the illusion of Confederate unity and shared sacrifice. In
1863, in the wake of the Richmond riot, *Vanity Fair* exposed the persistence of deep class divisions among the southern population. The pro-
Union magazine published a provocative image with the article, "Pity the
Poor Rebels." It described how poor men were arbitrarily rounded up as
conscripts, while the desperately poor "white trash" of the Confederacy
scratched the words "WE ARE STARVING" over the "dead wall" that
separated the North and South. The featured illustration had an unusual
caricature of Jefferson Davis, reminiscent of Jonathan Swift's antihero in
Gulliver's Travels. Here the Confederate president, in a dress and bonnet, is tied down by southern Lilliputians—tiny slaves. Either way, he is
unmanned by greedy planters or female rioters. His wrists are chained,
his dress unraveling—a sure sign that the Confederacy has had its mask
of gentility removed.[38]

Wealthy women of the South often displayed indifference to the
starving poor. When a group of deserters and poor mountain women
ransacked a Tennessee resort in 1863, Virginia French, one of the guests,
described the "slatternly, rough, barefooted women" who raced to and
fro, "eager as famished wolves for prey." Both shocked and amused, she
wrote, "Two women went into a regular fist fight & kept it up for an
hour—clawing & clutching each other because one had more than the
other!" She found it equally bizarre when another woman stole Latin
theology and French books. When asked directly, the thief justified her
booty as the act of a good mother: "She had some children who were just
beginning to read & . . . she wanted to encourage em!" An illiterate
woman thus assigned value to the literary treasures she had taken. This
might have aroused some sympathy, but for French the scene was simply
more evidence of "Democracy—Jacobinism—and Radicalism" in its
rudest form. The women were "famished" and had "tallow" faces, the men
were "gaunt" and "ill-looking," but the southern planter's wife remained

unmoved. White trash soiled all they touched, and deserved contempt, not pity.[39]

Class insularity prevailed among Richmond's elite women too. By early 1865, First Lady Varina Davis had become "unpopular with the ladies belonging to the old families," a clerk close to her husband confided to his diary. Those of "high birth" had decided to shun her and talked behind her back, remarking on her father's supposed low-class origins. There were stories widely circulated of government officials and their wives dining on delicacies while the people starved.[40]

In contemplating the demise of the Confederacy, other writers expressed more dramatic concerns. Class reorganization would reduce honored mothers to the station of "cooks for Yankee matrons," convert beloved wives into washerwomen for "Yankee butchers and libertines," and transform devoted sisters into chambermaids for "Yankee harlots." No matter how the situation was sized up, the fact that poor rural women had already lost everything scarcely mattered, because their suffering counted little compared to the unsullied women of the ruling class.[41]

A different kind of symbolism hovered over Abraham Lincoln, who in unflattering descriptions was crowned the president of the mudsills. Though he was born in Kentucky, not far from Jefferson Davis's birthplace, Honest Abe's backcountry roots became fodder for his enemies. The one thing that separated Lincoln and Davis was class origin. Southern newspapers described Davis as one "born to command." He was a West Pointer, a man of letters and polite manners. Lincoln, by contrast, was a rude bumpkin, the "Illinois ape," and a "drunken sot." Lincoln's supposed virtue, his honesty (or honest parents), was code for a suspect class background. In 1862, a close ally, Union general David Hunter, told Treasury Secretary Salmon P. Chase that Lincoln was born a "poor white in a slave state." He judged Lincoln too solicitous of slaveholders in the border states, "anxious for approval, especially of those he was accustomed to look up to." His Kentucky home made him white trash, and his chosen residence in Illinois made him a prairie mudsill. Confederates had an easy time equating midwesterners with dirt farmers; to one Virginia artilleryman, they were all "scoundrels, this scum, spawned in prairie mud."[42]

The mudslinging battle, however, ended up working in favor of the Federal side. Republicans and Union officers wore the mudsill label as a badge of pride, and made it a rallying cry for northern democracy. This strategy began even before Lincoln was elected. At a large rally in New York City, Iowa's lieutenant governor gave an impassioned speech in which he praised the "rail splitter" as the best farmer for the job—a man willing to protect the "mudsill and mechanic." And he joked that every Republican in his state had "made up their minds to cultivate mudsill ideas."[43]

The New York publication *Vanity Fair* used satire to turn the tables on Confederate class taunts. Their writers not only deflated the southerner's gallant self-image, but also had a field day defending his "groveling" foe with "lobby ears"—the mudsill. ("Lob" was another word for a rustic knave.) Imitating southern speechifiers and hack journalists, the magazine described Lincoln as the chief magistrate of the "Greasy Mechanics and Mudsills of the barbarian North."

Jefferson Davis's stilted oratory was equally subject to *Vanity Fair*'s withering satire. In a mock proclamation given after the First Battle of Bull Run, Davis issues an edict saying that his army would leave

In *Frank Leslie's Illustrated Newspaper* (1863), Lincoln, as caricatured, is literally a mudsill—stuck in the mud and unable to reach Jefferson Davis in Richmond.

Frank Leslie's Illustrated Newspaper, February 21, 1863

Washington in the dust, hang the "besotted idiot" Lincoln from the nearest tree, and topple New York City, turning the Seventh Regiment into body servants for Confederate officers. In his grandiose vision of easy victory, this parody of Davis declared that "mudsill soldiers" would offer little resistance, for "they will fly before us like sheep." Southerners' hyperbolic pronouncements were turned on their head; though begun as an insult aimed at plebian northerners, the mudsill designation proved most useful in ridiculing Confederate hubris. By 1863, *Frank Leslie's Illustrated Newspaper* had embraced the mudsill moniker, publishing a caricature of Lincoln up to his waist in mud, unable to reach the "bad bird" Davis in his Richmond nest.[44]

When General James Garfield, the future president, returned from the front in November 1863, he gave a speech at a meeting in Baltimore in defense of his fighting mudsills. He lauded the loyal men of Tennessee and Georgia who came out of "caves and rocks" to support the Union forces. The Confederacy was built, Garfield insisted, on a false idea, "not of a common government, but a government of gentlemen, of men of money, men of brains, who hold slaves." It was a government resembling that of the aristocratic Old World. His audience of commoners roared when he called the two top Confederate generals "Count Bragg" and "My Lord Beauregard." Roused by this reaction, Garfield addressed the friendly crowd as "you mudsills," for they were benefactors of a government and society that promised class mobility and a genuine respect for the workingman. For Garfield, and for many others, the mudsills were the backbone of the Union. They were those "who rejoice that God has given you strong hands and stout hearts—who were not born with silver spoons in your mouths." And proud mudsills they would remain.[45]

Because of the Confederacy's class system, and the exploitation of poor whites by the planter elite, Republican congressmen and military leaders from the outset of the war argued in favor of a confiscation policy that went at the planters' pocketbooks. It was in the border states, where allegiances were divided, that the policy of punishing rich Confederate sympathizers took shape. In Missouri, where irregular rebel guerrillas dismantled railroads and terrorized Unionist civilians, General Henry W. Halleck decided to mete out retribution in a highly selective manner. Rather than punish the entire citizenry, he ordered wealthy Missourians alone to pay reparations.[46]

In Halleck's mind, the price of war had to be felt at the top. As refugees flooded into St. Louis—poor white women and children—Halleck and his fellow officers agreed that elites should cover the costs. Street theater complemented the army's campaign, as Union officers sought to make punishments visible to the general public. Under Halleck's stern but discriminating system of assessments, Missouri Confederates who refused to pay up were publicly humiliated by having their most valuable possessions confiscated and sold at auction. Military police officers entered homes and carted off pianos, rugs, furniture, and valuable books. The contrast between the rich and poor was stark. Displaced families from the Arkansas Ozarks showed up a hundred miles west of the Mississippi in the vicinity of Rolla. Led by a former candidate for governor, they formed a strange caravan of oxcarts, livestock, and dogs, altogether numbering over two thousand. The men were categorized by observers as white trash: "tall, sallow, cadaverous, and leathery." They joined the starving, mud-covered women and barefoot children who comprised the South's forgotten poor white exiles.[47]

Public shaming was another tactic used by the Union army. In New Orleans, General Benjamin Butler's infamous Order No. 28 declared that any woman showing disrespect to a Union soldier would be treated as a prostitute, a punitive measure that denied the assumption of moral purity accorded upper-class women. More devastating was Order No. 76, by which Butler required all men and women to give an oath of allegiance; those who failed to do so had their property confiscated. Women's equal political treatment exposed what lay hidden behind the "broad folds of female crinoline," that men were hiding assets in their wives' names. A victorious officer observed that in taking Fredericksburg in 1862, Union soldiers destroyed the homes of the wealthy, leaving behind dirt from their "muddy feet." Vandalism was another way to disgrace prominent Confederates: seizing the symbols of wealth and status, smashing them, and leaving it behind as rubbish. The muddy footprint of the mudsill foot soldier was an intentionally ironic symbol of class rage.[48]

One person who took this message to heart was Andrew Johnson of Tennessee. As a military governor, Johnson became the bête noire of Confederates, the only U.S. senator from a seceding state to remain loyal to the Union. His loyalty earned him a place on the Republican ticket as Lincoln's running mate in 1864. Johnson, an old guard Jacksonian Democrat, felt no constraint in voicing his disgust with the bloated planter elite. By the time he took over as military governor, he was already known for his confrontational style, eager to duke it out with those he labeled "traitorous aristocrats." He vigorously imposed assessments to pay for poor refugee women and children, who he claimed were reduced to poverty because of the South's "unholy and nefarious rebellion." Not surprisingly, Johnson's detractors looked upon the once-lowly tailor as undeserving white trash. He had a reputation for vulgarity in the course of his stump speeches. One politician he ran against before the war went so far as to call him "a living mass of undulating filth." If Lincoln was white trash in the eyes of genteel southerners, Johnson looked worse.[49]

By the time General William T. Sherman orchestrated his famous March to the Sea in 1864, Union leaders believed that only widespread humiliation and suffering would end the war. Turning his army into one large foraging expedition, Sherman made sure his men understood the class dimension of their campaign. The most lavish destruction occurred in Columbia, South Carolina, the fire-eaters' capital, where the most conspicuous planter oligarchy held court. In tiny Barnwell, sixty miles south of Columbia, Brevet Major General Hugh Judson Kilpatrick of New Jersey staged what he called a "Nero's ball," forcing the southern belles of the town to attend and dance with Union officers while the town burned to the ground.[50]

In justifying his violent course of action, Sherman revived one of Thomas Jefferson's favorite terms for tackling class power. That word was "usufruct." Sherman contended that there was no absolute right to private property, and that proud planters only held their real estate in usufruct—that is, on the good graces of the federal government. In theory, southerners were tenants, and as traitorous tenants, they could be expelled by their federal landlords. Jefferson had used the same Roman concept to develop a political theory for weakening the hold of inherited status and protecting future generations against debts passed on by a preceding generation. Sherman went further: property did not exist without the sanction of the federal government. His philosophy not only rejected states' rights, but equated treason with a return to the state of

nature. The southern oligarchy would be shorn of its land and class privilege. The only way for elite Confederates to protect their wealth was to
submit to federal law.[51]

Union generals and their senior officers expected the cotton oligarchy
to fall along with Davis's administration. They were convinced that class
relations would radically change in the aftermath of the war. A kind of
missionary zeal shaped this strain of thinking. After the siege of Petersburg, Virginia, in 1865, Chaplain Hallock Armstrong sized up what he
called "the war against the Aristocracy," predicting in a letter to his wife
that dramatic change was coming to the Old South. It was not slavery's
demise alone that would transform society, he said, but increased
opportunities for "poor white trash." He assured her that the war would
"knock off the shackles of millions of poor whites, whose bondage was
really worse than the African." He observed their wretched conditions,
appalled that generations of families had never seen the inside of a classroom.[52]

Many others recognized that it would be an insurmountable task to
raise up the poor. A New York artillery officer named William Wheeler
encountered ragged refugees in Alabama, and found it hard to believe
that they could be classed as "Caucasians," or considered the same "flesh
and blood as ourselves." Some Union men were prepared to encounter
cadaverous poor whites in the southern backwaters, but they were surprised to see these people in the Confederate ranks. They described
deserters, prisoners, and Confederate prison guards as seedy, slouch-
ing, ignorant, and oddly attired. Soldiers in the western theater were
taken aback by the mud huts they espied along the Mississippi. The
North's mudsills seemed like royalty compared to the South's truly mud-
bespattered swamp people.[53]

Mud could well be the central image in sizing up the cost of this war
to Union and Confederate sides alike. There was no glamour, only tedious
muddy marches, food shortages, foraging (which often entailed stealing
from civilians), and the inhuman conditions that prevailed in fetid muddy
camps. Union and Confederate dead alike were hastily laid to rest in
shallow, muddy mass graves.[54]

But it was the "foul mudsill" in wartime propaganda that captured
the political imagination on both sides. "Mudsill" joined other Confederate slurs for Union men: vagabonds, bootblacks, and northern scum. And

we mustn't forget Jefferson Davis's insult of choice: "offscourings of the earth." By adopting such a vocabulary, rebels could imagine northern soldiers as Lincoln's indentured servants, low-class hirelings. To convince themselves of easy victory, Confederates insisted that the Federal army was filled with the "trash" of Europe, rubbish flushed from northern city jails and back alleys, all brought together with the clodhoppers and dirt farmers from interior sections of the Union. For their part, northerners perceived the bread riots, desertions, poor white refugees, and runaway slaves as firm evidence of a fractured Confederacy. In this way, North and South each saw class as the enemy's pivotal weakness and a source of military and political vulnerability.[55]

Both sides were partially right. Wars in general, and civil wars to a greater degree, have the effect of exacerbating class tensions, because the sacrifices of war are always distributed unequally, and the poor are hit hardest. North and South had staked so much on their class-based definitions of nationhood that it is no exaggeration to say that in the grand scheme of things, Union and Confederate leaders saw the war as a clash of class systems wherein the superior civilization would reign triumphant.

Union men had a way of identifying "white trash" with the dual bogeymen of southern poverty and elite hypocrisy. They saw secession as a fraud perpetrated against hapless poor whites. A Philadelphia journalist had the best, or at least the most original, putdown of the Confederacy's overproud social system when he directed Jeff Davis's government to put a slave on their five-cent stamp; for only then, he argued, would "poor white trash" be able to "buy the chattel cheap." But he didn't let his fellow northerners entirely off the hook either. Little separated northern mudsills from southern trash. Neither class gained much when reduced to cannon fodder.[56]

CHAPTER EIGHT

Thoroughbreds and Scalawags

Bloodlines and Bastard Stock in the Age of Eugenics

> It is better for all the world if, instead of waiting to execute degener-
> ate offspring for crime or to let them starve for their imbecility, soci-
> ety can prevent those who are manifestly unfit from continuing their
> kind. . . . Three generations of imbeciles are enough.
>
> —Justice Oliver Wendell Holmes, *Buck v. Bell* (1927)

In 1909, at the National Negro Congress in New York City, W. E. B.
Du Bois gave a provocative speech on the reception of Darwinism in
the United States. In the published version of the speech, "The Evolution
of the Race Problem," Du Bois declared that social Darwinism had
found such favor in America because the very idea of "survival of the fittest" ratified the reactionary racial politics that already prevailed. The
Harvard-trained scholar underscored, with more than a touch of irony,
how the "splendid scientific work" of Darwin endorsed an "inevitable
inequality among men and the races of men that no philanthropy ought
to eliminate." Du Bois's argument went this way: if one accepted the racist assumption that blacks are of "inferior stock," then it was pointless to
"legislate against nature"; proving the supremacy of the white race
needed no help from politicians, because any form of philanthropy would
be "powerless against deficient cerebral development."[1]

For the social critic Du Bois, it was one short step from the racism
contained in the Americanization of Darwinian selection to the realiza-
tion that white rule had corrupted the normal course of evolution.
Instead of allowing the best (whether black or white) to rise, racism had
actually undermined the Darwinian argument. It had not only *not*
improved the white race, but a false hegemony had led to "the survival of
some of the worst stocks of mankind." As much as the lower class of
whites remained where they had always been, one found throughout the
U.S. South "efficient Negroes," able and productive, being trampled
under the heels of elected officials who supported white vigilante justice

and propped up the heinous lynch law—catering to the interests of the unreconstructed white trash of the postwar South.[2]

Du Bois reasoned that by denying equal education across racial lines, in preventing the laws of evolution from operating freely in the South, white political hegemony had reapplied the "evils of class injustice." White supremacy, as a thesis, lacked any basis in science, while it wreaked more and more havoc upon a perverse, fear- and hate-based class system. Despite popular claims that the white race was destined for global dominance, it was, Du Bois assured, in decline. Among the "many signs of degeneracy" was the overall reduction in birthrates. Thus any threat of white deterioration came "from within." Yet when Democrats gained control of the southern states in 1877, after a decade of black enfranchisement, they invariably blamed Republican egalitarians for producing social chaos and triggering white downward mobility. By refusing to hold up the mirror to themselves, Du Bois contended, southern whites were failing to see their own degeneracy.[3]

In the larger scheme of things, Du Bois was retelling the history of Reconstruction and its aftermath. Much later, in 1935, he would expand his perspective into a full-length study. Yet in the 1909 speech he was already exposing several crucial connections. Above all, he understood how southern politics had set the stage for the dual appeal of Darwinism and the eugenics movement. Darwin's best-known works, *On the Origin of Species* (1859) and *The Descent of Man* (1871), scored big in America, as did the work of his cousin Francis Galton, the founder of eugenics.

Evolution rested on nature's law, whereas eugenics found nature wanting. Galton's adherents stressed the necessity for human intervention to improve the race through better breeding. Darwin himself endorsed eugenics, and he drew on the familiar trope of animal husbandry to make the case: "Man scans with scrupulous care the pedigree of his horses, cattle and dogs before he mates them; but when it comes to his marriage, he rarely, or never, takes such care." Compare Thomas Jefferson—the wording is practically identical: "The circumstance of superior beauty is thought worthy of attention in the propagation of our horses, dogs, and other domestic animals; why not that of man?" Almost as a mantra, eugenicists compared good human stock to thoroughbreds, equating the wellborn with superior ability and inherited fitness.[4]

Pseudoscience, masquerading as hereditary science, provided Americans with a convenient way to naturalize class and racial differences. The appeal of this language, which reached its zenith in the early twentieth century, first took hold during Reconstruction. Both Republicans, who wanted to rebuild the South in the image of the North, and Democrats, who wished to restore elite white rule, saw the grand scope of national reunion as part of a larger evolutionary struggle. And so Darwin's "survival of the fittest" became the watchword of politicians and journalists. They invoked a vocabulary that highlighted unnatural breeding, unfit governance, and the degenerate nature of the worst stocks. At the center of the argument was the struggle that pitted poor whites against freed slaves.

It was perhaps inevitable that poor whites would figure prominently in the debates over Reconstruction. Many northern thinkers had never for a moment bought into the old Cavalier myth of southern superiority. As one insisted in 1864, most southerners traced their lineage to the "scum of Europe," to lowly descendants of "brothels and bridewells," and could therefore dub themselves a "plebeian aristocracy" at best. When the patrician-led Confederacy collapsed, so did the illusion of the superior powers attached to southern refinement.[5]

For most Republicans, rebuilding the South meant (a) introducing a free-labor economy and (b) ensuring a loyal population. They perceived southern Unionists and freedmen as the most loyal element. The issue for Republicans was simply put: would poor whites help to transform the South into a literate society and free-market economy, or would they resist change and drag the South down?[6]

President Andrew Johnson contributed to the debate when he issued his plan for restoration of the Union. He included in his requirements disfranchisement of the wealthiest slaveholders, so that, as the *New York Herald* reported in 1865, the oligarchs of the South would be "shorn of their strength," while—and here the newspaper underscored the class dynamic—"the 'poor white trash' heretofore compelled to walk behind them and to do their bidding, are made masters of the situation." Yes, *masters*. Johnson expressed the same opinion in an address to a delegation from South Carolina: "While this rebellion has emancipated a great many negroes," he said, "it has emancipated still more white men." He would elevate the "poor white man" who struggled to till barren, sandy soil for subsistence, and who were looked down upon by the Negro and elite planter alike.[7]

The president imagined a three-tiered class system in the reconstructed states. The disenfranchised planter elite would keep their land and a certain social power, but would be deprived of any direct political influence until they regained the trust of Unionists. The middle ranks would be filled by a newly dominant poor white class. In exercising the vote and holding office, they would hold back the old oligarchy, while preventing a situation from arising in which they themselves would have to compete economically (or politically) with the freedmen. On the bottom tier, then, Johnson placed free blacks and freed slaves—the latter emancipated in fact, yet treated as resident aliens, bearing rights but still denied the franchise. The plan Lincoln's unloved successor had in mind was not a "restoration" of the old order, nor did it promise to establish a democracy. Instead, it offered America something entirely original. So let us call the Johnson plan what it would have been if actually undertaken: *a white trash republic.*

The Tennessean decidedly saw black suffrage as a low priority. He was still intent, however, on redefining the old planter elite. Despite disfranchisement, the aristocracy retained some wealth and, just as important, the power to persuade others. They would turn their former slaves, now employees, into political pawns. This was a prospect that President Johnson looked upon with some disapproval. Yet he would undermine his own design by granting individual pardons to representatives of the former ruling elite, which he may have done because he felt he needed them to win reelection.[8]

Something more dangerous loomed if blacks obtained political equality. Long-standing animosities would resurface between the two lower classes in Johnson's construct (blacks and poor whites), triggering a "war of races." Andrew Johnson's race war was not Thomas Jefferson's, however. The third president had foretold a contest of annihilation brought on by universal emancipation, once liberated slaves took their place alongside their former masters; the seventeenth president was talking about a war of racial outcasts. As he saw it, the formerly dispossessed classes, one black and one white, would wage a vicious struggle for survival. Its cause: the federal imposition of universal suffrage on the southern states.[9]

Though Johnson soon abandoned his white trash republic, his thinking allows us to better visualize the existing spectrum of ideas about Reconstruction. It is meaningful, too, that the recently established Freedmen's Bureau paired impoverished whites and freed people not as cutthroat adversaries, but as the worthy poor. From its inception in 1865, shortly before Lincoln's assassination, the bureau was specifically empowered to extend relief to "all refugees, and all freedmen," black *and* white. In debating the bureau's merits, many senators agreed that the destitution of white refugees, now "beggars, dependents, houseless and homeless wanderers," was as significant as that of the freedmen. In Alabama, Arkansas, Missouri, and Tennessee, the bureau extended twice— and in some cases four times—as much relief to whites as to blacks; in Georgia, nearly 180,000 white refugees secured food and provisions. As Republican congressman Green Clay Smith of Kentucky noted during the debate to extend the Freedmen's Bureau in 1866, "There are a large number of white people who never owned a foot of land, who never have been in possession of any property, not even a cow or a horse, yet who have been as true and devoted loyalists as anybody else." The problems of the South went deeper than the war itself, Smith acknowledged. The twin evils of poverty and vagrancy were a permanent fixture among the white population.[10]

Yet few bureau officials embraced Smith's vision of loyal, honorable poor whites. Those who visited the refugee camps, or watched what one *New York Times* correspondent called the "loafing whites" in southern towns, offered little in their favor. A skeptic in New Orleans offered this droll observation: although "poor white trash" had proven themselves incapable of doing anything before the war, they had suddenly discovered a trade in "the refugee business," by which he meant living off government handouts. In Florida, bureau agent Charles Hamilton, who later served in Congress, confessed to his superiors that freedmen were only marginally below the "white plebeians of the South" in intelligence. Widely circulated bureau reports claimed that hundreds of thousands of destitute whites lived off "Uncle Sam's rations." The typical recipients were women "covered in rags and filth, and a dozen greasy and dirty little 'innocent prattlers' in train." Perhaps the most damning assessment came from Marcus Sterling, a Union officer turned civilian administrator. After working as a bureau agent for four years in rural Virginia, he wrote a final report in 1868. While he believed that black freedmen had made great progress, were "more settled, industrious and ambitious" as a result of federal intervention, and eager to achieve literacy with "honest pride and manly integrity," the same could not be said of that "pitiable class of poor whites," the "only class which seem almost unaffected by the [bureau's] great benevolence and its bold reform." In the race for self-reliance, poor whites seemed to many bureau agents never to have left the starting gate.[11]

Agents of the Freedmen's Bureau were not alone in offering a grim prognosis for poor whites. Journalists from major newspapers headed south, sending back regular dispatches and publishing monographs for curious northern readers. Prominent articles appeared in the *Atlantic Monthly, Putnam's Magazine,* and *Harper's New Monthly Magazine.* The *New York Times* published a series of essays on the subject: in 1866, its anonymous correspondent authored a scathing exposé of white poverty, accompanied by the innocuous title "From the South: Southern Journeyings and Jottings." Writing for the *Chicago Tribune* and *Boston Advertiser,* the Illinois-based reporter Sidney Andrews expressed his unvarnished views of wretched whites, which he reissued as a book, *The South Since the War.* After having been a correspondent for the *Cincinnati Gazette,* Whitelaw Reid compiled his unsympathetic observations in a travelogue, *After the War: A Tour of the Southern States.* Finally, John Trowbridge produced *The South: A Tour of Its Battlefields and Ruined Cities,* which focused a harsh lens on rural whites.[12]

All of the above were published in the single year of 1866. Yet one of the most talked-about books in those wobbly years came out before the war had officially ended. *Down in Tennessee* (1864) was also a travel account, its author the New York cotton merchant and novelist James R. Gilmore. His argument was unique because he distinguished between "mean whites" and "common whites," arguing that the latter class was enterprising, law-abiding, and productive citizens. They stood in sharp contrast to the shiftless, thieving, and brutish mean whites, whose homes reminded him of a "tolerably-kept swine-sty or dog-kennel." Though he identified this group as a minority, they were still a dangerous class, he said, owing to their infectious character; they were a diseased segment of the prostrate South, a "fungus growth" on the body of society, "absorbing the strength and life of its other parts."[13]

All of these writers had a common desire: to unravel the enigma of the southern racial and class system in order to prognosticate about its uncertain future. If they agreed on any point, it was that which was summed up by one of Sidney Andrews's imitators: "It is now not so much a question of what is to become of poor blacks of the South, as it is one of what is to become of poor whites of the South?"[14]

The insistence of Republican-leaning journalists that poor whites languished below freedmen as potential citizens may seem startling, but it was not unexpected. Distrust was strong both of former Confederate elites and the "groveling" poor men who, like "sheep to slaughter," were dragged off to war. Whitelaw Reid felt that black children were eager to learn, while Sidney Andrews believed that blacks exhibited a "shrewd instinct for preservation," which white trash seemed to lack. In account after account, freedmen were described as capable, thrifty, and loyal to the Union. A writer for the *Atlantic Monthly* asked: why should government "disfranchise the humble, quiet, hardworking negro" and leave the North vulnerable to the vote of the "worthless barbarian"—the "ignorant, illiterate, and vicious" poor white?[15]

Thus the popular vocabulary had become more ominous. No longer were white trash simply freaks of nature on the fringe of society; they were now congenitally delinquent, a withered branch of the American family tree. As a "fungus growth," they could weaken the entire stock of southern society. More than tallow-colored skin, it was the permanent mark of intellectual stagnation, the "inert" minds, the "fumbling" speech, and the "stupid, moony glare, like that of the idiot." They were, it was said, of the "Homo genus without the sapien." Hardworking blacks were suddenly the redeemed ones, while white trash remained undeveloped, evolutionarily stagnant creatures.[16]

During Reconstruction, Republicans designated white trash as a "dangerous class" that was producing a flood of bastards, prostitutes, vagrants, and criminals. They violated every sexual norm, from fathers cohabiting with daughters, to husbands selling wives, to mothers conniving illicit liaisons for daughters. The danger came from a growing population that had stopped disappearing into the wilderness. Reid was appalled by the filthy refugees living in railroad cars, an uncomfortable foreshadowing of twentieth-century trailer trash. John W. De Forest, a bureau agent and yet another novelist, concluded that white trash were tolerable as long as Darwin's "severe law" of natural selection killed off most of them.[17]

In 1868, a writer for *Putnam's Magazine* told the "history of a family," tracing a corrupted genealogical tree back to it roots. This one basic story anticipated a host of studies that included *The Jukes* (1877), which proved the most enduring chronicle of a degenerate lineage, and which influenced Charles Davenport, the leading American eugenicist of the early twentieth century. The author of the 1868 *Putnam's* piece claimed to have discovered a real couple, with an actual name—thus going beyond Daniel Hundley's more general dismissal of southern rubbish as the heirs of indentured servants dumped in the American colonies.

One Bill Simmins was the erstwhile progenitor of this corrupt family tree. A British convict and Virginia squatter, he married a London courtesan turned "wild woman," who gave birth to a tribe of low-down, dependent people. According to the author, the only cure for white trash had to be a radical one: intervention. Take a child out of his family's hovel and place him in an asylum, where he might at least learn to work and avoid producing more inbred offspring. The genealogical link had to be cut. As we can see, the line from delinquency to eugenic sterilization was growing shorter.[18]

The idea that white trash was a measure of evolutionary progress (or lack thereof) was so pervasive in the nineteenth century that it conditioned the reception of the first federal study of soldiers. The U.S. Sanitary Commission undertook a major statistical study of some 16,000 men who had served in the Union and Confederate armies. Only a small percentage of them were nonwhite (approximately 3,000 black men and 519 Indians). When the study was published in 1869, a surgeon who had served in the Union army queried in the prestigious London *Anthropological Review* whether it was possible to draw conclusions about racial differences unless researchers actually compared blacks and poor whites. The "low down people" may have come from Anglo-Saxon stock, but they had "degenerated into an idle, ignorant, and physically and mentally degraded people." It was time to see whether intelligence was a racially specific inherited trait or not.[19]

While Republican journalists, Freedmen's Bureau agents, and Union officers published extensively, in the partisan climate of the postwar years Democrats just as painstakingly worked to rebuild an opposition party and chip away at Republican policies, and they reached for the racial arguments at hand to help. Instead of celebrating the hardworking black man and the promise of social mobility, they fretted about the loss of a "white man's government." Unconcerned with inbreeding, they focused obsessively on outbreeding, that is, the supposedly unhealthy combination of distinct races.

"Mongrel" became one of the Democrats' favorite insults in these years. The word called forth numerous potent metaphors. Both defeated Confederates and Democratic journalists in the North predicted that Republican policies would usher in a "mongrel republic." They drew paranoid comparisons to the Mexican Republic, the nineteenth-century example of racial amalgamation run amok.[20]

"Mongrel" was not the only threat Democrats perceived. The emerging cross-sectional opposition party named two more symbolic enemies: "carpetbaggers" and "scalawags." Here is how the new narrative went: When ill-bred men of suspect origins assumed power, virtue in government declined. The despised mudsill of the Civil War era was succeeded by the postwar Yankee invader. The carpetbagger, a rapacious adventurer feeding off the prostrate South, could be identified by the cheap black valise he carried. Worse than the carpetbagger, though, was the "scalawag," a betrayer. He was a southern white Republican who had sold his soul (and sold out his race) for filthy lucre.[21]

Though he did not use the word "mongrel," President Johnson was quite familiar with the danger of "mongrel citizenship"—the very phrase one newspaper used to describe what lay at the heart of Johnson's veto of the Civil Rights Act of 1866. Missouri Republican turned Democrat and avid Darwinian Francis Blair Jr. had written the president an impassioned letter against the act just days earlier. He insisted that Congress should never be allowed to inflict on the country a "mongrel nation, a nation of bastards." Johnson agreed. At the beginning of his veto message, he highlighted all the new admixtures suddenly protected under the law: "the Chinese of the Pacific States, Indians subject to taxation, the people called Gipsies, as well as the entire race designated as blacks, people of color, negroes, mulattoes and persons of African blood." In granting civil rights, the law removed racial distinctions and opened the door to equal suffrage. Johnson's veto message said that freedmen lacked something naturally endowed: fitness. Finally, the president made clear that he disapproved of any law that sanctioned interracial marriage.[22]

In 1866, President Johnson effectively abandoned the Republican Party. He had begun political life as a Jacksonian Democrat. It was as a Jacksonian, then, that he vetoed the extension of the Freedmen's Bureau and Civil Rights Act, and used his executive authority to derail federal initiatives in the South. This series of actions led Republicans in Congress to do more than override his vetoes: they searched for a more permanent constitutional solution, and found it in the impeachment process. Johnson's apostasy gave momentum to the Fourteenth and Fifteenth Amendments, which passed in 1867 and 1869, respectively. The first guaranteed equal protection under the law as a right of national citizenship, and the second prohibited discrimination in voting based on "race, color, and previous condition of servitude." Not inconsequentially, the Fourteenth Amendment also denied former Confederates the right to vote, excepting those who federal officials believed had taken the loyalty oath in good faith. Former Confederate officials were barred from holding office.[23]

For anxious social commentators, "pride of caste" and "pride of race" were under attack, the old barriers of upholding "purity of blood" and "social exclusiveness" eroding as a result of a flurry of Republican legislation. The focus turned to white women. As early as 1867, secret societies began to form, like the Knights of the White Camelia, which first organized in Louisiana. Members swore to marry a white woman, and they agreed to do everything in their power to prevent the "production of a bastard and degenerate progeny."[24]

In 1868, Francis Blair Jr., the Democratic nominee for vice president, toured the country and made the mongrel threat one of the key issues of the campaign. The next year, Chief Justice Joseph Brown of the Supreme Court of Georgia issued a monumental decision. The former rebel governor ruled that the courts had the right to dissolve all interracial marriages. "Amalgamation" was classed with incestuous unions and marriages between idiots, which the state already proscribed. By generating "sickly and effeminate" children, Brown insisted, such abhorrent marriages threatened to "drag down the superior race to the level of the inferior." He was repeating the established definition used by animal breeders to categorize a mongrel. Even more telling is Brown's eugenic logic: the state now had the right to regulate breeding in order to prevent contamination of the Anglo-Saxon stock.[25]

Still, for Democrats and Republicans alike, race could never be decoupled from class. This was why the scalawag came under venomous verbal attacks and experienced actual physical violence. The scalawag was seen as the glue that held together a fragile Republican coalition of freedmen, transplanted northerners, southern Unionists, and converted Confederates. For many southern Democrats, this white traitor was a more serious obstacle than the carpetbagger, because he was born and bred in the South, and he knew his way around the statehouse. Dismantling the Republican hold over the South demanded the figurative (and at times literal) death of the scalawag.[26]

During the election year of 1868, the scalawag was accused of inciting blacks and giving them the idea that they deserved social equality. The so-called freedmen, one angry journalist blasted, were now the "slaves of the scalawag white trash." He violated social norms by mixing freely with blacks in public and private places. He invited the black man home to dinner, wounding the sensibility of his proper wife. And yet this worthless, ill-bred creature had suddenly acquired power. The very traits they despised in him—his low-class ways, his willingness to commingle with blacks—made him the perfect party operative. In a volatile election year, the scalawag's racial and class pedigree both became issues.[27]

A brilliant piece of Democratic propaganda was "The Autobiography of a Scalawag." The protagonist, John Stubbs, had been born to a poor family of fourteen in Shifflet's Corner, Virginia, a community known for lowlifes and criminals. Joining the Confederate army, he slid from an artillery posting to teamster to cleaning Jefferson Davis's stables. He had no ambition for honor or glory; his wartime trajectory was predictably downward.

Deserting, Stubbs lied to the Yankees that he was a Union man. Returning to Virginia in 1866, he became a scalawag and found he had a talent for "nigger speaking." He defended Negro suffrage not on any high-principled stand, but on his low-down motto: "every man for himself." Stubbs knew the carpetbaggers had no respect for him, but he didn't care, as long as a generous supply of whiskey accompanied their snubs. He was rewarded with a county clerk position, without having to improve himself. In his unsentimental journey up the Republican ladder, he learned that his "rascality" was increasingly tolerated as he rose in the world.[28]

"The Autobiography of a Scalawag" was a beautiful burlesque of the self-made northern man's story of hard work and moral uplift. Stubbs was a far cry from the hereditary leadership of the Old South, whose education, refinement, and honorable bearing were legend even in defeat. He was a gross materialist, someone who lacked forethought, who lied and cheated to get ahead. He was a powerful reminder that elite southern Democrats still despised the lower classes. As one North Carolina conservative declared in 1868, the Republican Party was nothing more than the "low born scum and quondam slaves" who lorded over men of property and taste. When southern Democrats called for a "White Man's Government," they did not mean all white men.[29]

The scalawag was the Democrats' version of white trash. Just ask ex–Confederate colonel Wade Hampton, who in 1868 was still eight years from being elected governor of South Carolina. He was a hero of the "Redeemers," whose movement ultimately toppled Republican rule in the southern states, and he must be credited with the most memorable insult of all, as his words traveled all the way to England. Knowing his husbandry, Hampton invoked the best-known usage of "scalawag" as vagabond stock, "used by drovers to describe the mean, lousy, and filthy kine that are not fit for butchers or dogs." The scalawag was human waste with an unnatural ambition. He was biologically unfit, and at the same time a skilled operative who stirred the scum and thrived in the muck.[30]

Thomas Jefferson Speer, a real scalawag, gave a speech that year proudly defending his "kine." In contrast to Hampton, he was a former Confederate who had turned Republican, served in the Georgia constitutional convention, and would later sit in the U.S. Congress. Speer was unashamed of his common school education, admitting that he was "no speaker." He had opposed secession, however, and believed that the terms of defeat offered by the Union had been magnanimous. A native Georgian whose "ancestors' bones reposed beneath this soil," he asserted that he was a "friend of the colored race."[31]

Like his own rather fortunate naming, T. J. Speer understood that "scalawag" was just a name too. But southern politics thrived on such symbolism. It was rooted in the inherited revulsion to both the real and the imagined dregs of society, whether white or black. When the low-down dared to speak up, reach across the color line, the hereditary leadership class of the South simply could not stomach their overreach.

Mongrels and scalawags were conjoined twins, then, fusing the associated threats of racial and class instability. After the Civil War, and with the passage of the Thirteenth Amendment prohibiting slavery, unreconstructed white southerners imagined an almost gothic landscape in their midst, a theater of sexual deviance overseen by defective leaders. The Fourteenth Amendment appreciably added to those fears, granting equal protection under the law to black male voters, while divesting former Confederates of their right to hold office or even vote. It was a world turned upside down, as buffoons ruled the Republican kingdom. Of course, few white southern Republicans actually fit this manufactured tabloid image, yet the label stuck. Scalawags were assumed to be white trash on the inside, regardless of the wealth (or wealth of political experience) they might accrue.[32]

As the Reconstruction era ended, so-called men of inherited worth were returned to political power across the South. In the 1880s, the white North and South reconnected. The "redeemed" cracker became a hardworking farmer, while others praised the unsullied mountaineer, both capable of education and having risen enough that they would no longer be a burden on the southern economy. For a brief moment, reconciliation stories were popular, and previously warring sides in the national drama entertained bright prospects for domestic harmony.[33]

Cracker Joe (1883) was written by a New Englander. The title character's story was set in Florida, and used love and forgiveness to overcome past wrongs and resentments. Joe, a "born Cracker," runs a successful farm. He defies his heritage by exhibiting shrewd ambition. He is a "go-ahead" man, an avid reader with a phenomenal memory. He calls his wife, Luce, "the whitest woman, soul and body, I ever did see," suggesting that he is not quite white, but "only a cracker, you know." (Like the family in Harriet Beecher Stowe's *Dred,* Joe is a half-breed, his mother of "good blood.") He is forced to make amends with the son of the wealthy planter whom he had tried to murder more than a decade earlier, and for his part, the planter's son must reclaim his father's dilapidated mansion and spoiled lands, saving his legacy in the only way possible, by marrying the daughter of a New York carpetbagger. If all of this isn't improbable enough, Joe has a mulatto daughter, whom he welcomes into his home with his wife's blessing.[34]

Convenient distinctions were drawn. In the 1890s, third-generation abolitionist William Goodell Frost, president of the integrated Berea College of Kentucky, redefined his mountain neighbors: "The 'poor white' is actually degraded; the mountain white is a person not yet graded up." The latter had preserved a unique lineage for centuries, and in this important way had not lost the battle for the survival of the fittest. Frost saw the mountaineer as a modern-day Saxon, with the "flavor of Chaucer" in his speech, and a clear "Saxon temper." He was, the college president wrote, "our contemporary ancestor!" What made this isolated white the best of America's past was his "vigorous, unjaded nerve, prolific, patriotic—full of the blood of spirit of seventy-six." Mountain folk formed the very trunk of the American family tree. Frost tried. For many who did not buy what he was selling, however, mountain whites were still strange-looking moonshine hillbillies, prone to clannish feuds.[35]

It was at about this time that the term "redneck" came into wider use. It well defined the rowdy and racist followers of the New South's high-profile Democratic demagogues of the late nineteenth and early twentieth centuries: South Carolina's Ben Tillman, Arkansas's Jeff Davis, and the most interesting of the bunch, Mississippi's James Vardaman. The "redneck" could be found in the swamps. He could be found in the mill towns. He was the man in overalls, the heckler at political rallies, and was periodically elected to the state legislature. He was Guy Rencher, a Vardaman ally, who supposedly claimed the name for himself, railing on the floor of the Mississippi House about his "long red neck." One other possible explanation deserves mention: "redneck" came into vogue in the 1890s, at the same time Afrikaners were calling English soldiers "rednecks" in the Boer War in South Africa, highlighting the contrast between the Brit's sun-scored skin and his pale white complexion. Such terminology was also a staple of the sharecropper's rhythmic chant (circa 1917): "I'd druther be a Nigger, an' plow ole Beck, Dan a white Hill Billy wid his long red neck."[36]

This was the world of W. E. B. Du Bois. This was also the world of Theodore Roosevelt. The two men agreed on very little—and obviously not on evolutionary theory or the science of eugenics, to which Roosevelt was a complete convert. Certainly Du Bois found no comfort in the president's militarism or his glorification of the white settler's savagery in the Old West. But they were in total agreement on one thing: the menace of redneck politics.

Roosevelt unexpectedly became president in 1901, upon the assassination of William McKinley. Only forty-two at the time, he was known for daring military exploits during the Spanish–American War, which had earned him a place on the Republican ticket. Though his mother was born in Georgia and he could claim a Confederate pedigree, the New York politico proved himself fairly inept at navigating the rocks and shoals of southern politics. He roused the ire of many white southerners when he dared to invite Booker T. Washington of the Tuskegee Institute to dinner shortly after his inauguration as president. Reviving the script from Reconstruction, Democrats charged the new chief executive with promoting social equality between the races. For angry southerners, breaking bread with a black man in such a public and highly symbolic way was barely one step from endorsing interracial marriage. With no subtlety whatsoever, Vardaman called Roosevelt the "coon-flavored miscegenationist," describing a White House "so saturated with the odor of the nigger that the rats have taken refuge in the stables." Southern satirist Bill Arp predicted a mongrel wedding in the executive mansion. In that Booker T. Washington's daughter Portia attended Wellesley College, she too would be invited to the White House, Arp mused. And then, he sneered, she would be found to be a suitable match for one of TR's sons.[37]

In Roosevelt's opinion, Vardaman and his ilk belonged to the lowest order of demagogues. Writing the Congregationalist minister and editor Lyman Abbott, the president said that the Mississippian's "foul language" and "kennel filth" were worse than that of the lowest blackguard wallowing in the gutters of New York City. Such "unspeakable lowness" put this southerner beyond the pale of American values. In excoriating Vardaman, the president refused to repeat his hateful words, but the insult that most infuriated him was a crude birthing allusion, to the effect that "old lady Roosevelt" had been frightened by a dog while pregnant, which accounted for "qualities of the male pup that are so prominent in Teddy." Vardaman, incapable of feeling shame, joked that he was disposed to apologize to the dog but not to the president.[38]

So who was this Mississippi carnival barker, known for his white suits and white cowboy hat and long dark locks, who claimed to be the voice of "rednecks" and "hillbillies"? James Vardaman had been a newspaperman, who understood the power of invective. Southerners from Andrew Johnson to Wade Hampton had recurred to the barnyard insult when they damned their enemies. For Vardaman, democracy, no matter how dirty, belonged to "the people," and the people had the right to say whatever they felt. Friends and foes alike called him the "White Chief," partly for his white garb and partly for his supremacist rhetoric. But he was a "medicine man" to his enemies, a witch doctor who knew how to inflame the low-down tribe of white savages.[39]

He saw himself as the defender of poor whites. In his run for the governorship in 1903, Vardaman pitted poor whites against all blacks. Educating blacks was pointless and dangerous, he argued, and the state should ensure that tax dollars from white citizens should only go to white schools. The consummate showman rode to Senate victory in 1912—quite literally—on the back of an ox. When his Democratic primary opponent derided his supporters as an ignorant herd, he exploited the incident. Traveling through Mississippi giving speeches, he liked to pull up in a "cracker cart" amid a long line of cattle. At one rally he rode into town astride a single ox. The beast was adorned with flags and streamers labeled "redneck," "cattle," and "lowdown." He dramatically embraced the white trash identity.[40]

Insofar as the surviving planter elite and middle-class Mississippians despised Vardaman, he intentionally drummed up class resentments. In his reminiscence, William Percy, the son of Vardaman's Democratic opponent, LeRoy Percy, best expressed the class anger. Recalling how he surveyed the surly crowd, wondering if Vardaman's army would launch rotten eggs at his father, Percy wrote:

They were the sort of people that lynch Negroes, that mistake hood-
lumism for wit, and cunning for intelligence, that attend revivals and
fight and fornicate in the bushes afterwards. They were undiluted
Anglo-Saxons. They were the sovereign voter. It was so horrible it
seemed unreal.

Though he had no patience for the politics of hate run as a sideshow,
Percy conceded that Vardaman was a savvy politician who gave the "sovereign voter" what he wanted—red meat.[41]

Roosevelt, a patrician, had little choice but to joust with his redneck
foes. In 1905, during his southern tour, he rebuked Arkansas governor
Jeff Davis for defending the lynch mob. One newspaper joked that the
president's entourage was wise to travel through Mississippi at night, so
that Vardaman wouldn't have to shoot him. Roosevelt also ruffled the
feathers of the proud white women of the South when he had dared to
class Jefferson Davis (the Confederate president) with Benedict Arnold.
When he did that, one incensed Georgia woman declared that the president had dishonored his mother's blood.[42]

Blood was thicker than water for Roosevelt, but not in the way the
testy Georgia woman would have viewed the matter. His understanding
of race and class remained rooted in evolutionary thinking, and he
believed that blacks were naturally subordinate to the Anglo-Saxon. But
he also felt progress was possible, which was why he backed Booker T.
Washington's program for industrial education at Tuskegee Institute. If
blacks proved themselves capable of economic self-sufficiency, then they
could qualify for greater political rights. But the Harvard-educated president never abandoned the premise that racial traits were carried in the
blood, conditioned by the experiences of one's ancestors. As an ardent
exponent of "American exceptionalism," Roosevelt argued that the
nineteenth-century frontier experience had transformed white Americans
into superior stock.[43]

Roosevelt's motto can be summed up in three words: "work-fight-
breed." There is clear evidence that he was influenced by the mountaineers' myth, by which good Saxon stock was separated from the debased
southern poor white. History was written in blood, sweat, and "germ protoplasm"—the turn-of-the-century term for what we now refer to as

genes. Roosevelt believed that every middle-class American male had to stay in touch with his inner squatter; he must never lose the masculine traits that attached to the "strenuous life." Too much domestic peace, luxury, and willful sterility, as TR put it, made Americans weak, lethargic, and prone to self-indulgence.[44]

The ills attending modernity could be corrected in three ways. A man could return to the wilderness, as Roosevelt did when he hunted big game in Africa and made a harrowing trip down the Amazon River at the age of fifty-five. War—the raw fight for survival—was a second means of bringing forth ancestral Saxon traits. Breeding, however, remained the most primitive of instincts. In Roosevelt's mind, childbirth was nature's boot camp for women, a life-or-death struggle that strengthened the entire race.[45]

As for war, it did not just build character; it literally reinvigorated the best qualities of the American stock. After spending several years in the Dakotas as a rancher, Roosevelt published his voluminous *Winning of the West* (1886–96), part American history and part treatise on evolution. The author returned to New York, took up politics, and discovered a new aggressive outlet in imperialist crusading. He rallied behind the Spanish–American War in 1898 and formed his own regiment, the Rough Riders, which he filled with cowboys and mountaineers from the West, plus men like himself, athletes, who had come from Ivy League universities. He even included a number of Indians (in a separate company), a few Irish and Hispanics, one Jewish recruit, and one Italian, all in an attempt to recreate what he thought was the right mix of ethnic stocks for the new American frontier in Cuba. It is important to note that he did not include any black men, nor genuine southern crackers, in his muscular version of Darwin's Galápagos Islands experiment.[46]

Roosevelt's famed ride up San Juan Hill (actually Kettle Hill) was vividly captured by the equally famed artist Frederic Remington. Before he headed to Cuba, Remington had taken a magazine assignment in Florida. There he found the "Cracker cowboy," who was the antithesis of the pure-blooded American westerner he had earlier known. The men he encountered in Florida wore a "bedraggled appearance"; their unwashed hair, tobacco-stained beards, and sloppy dress reminded him of Spanish moss dripping off oaks in the swamps. Remington saw their lack of "fierceness" (relative to the frontiersman) and compared it to the difference between a "fox-terrier" and a "yellow cur." Pursuing the animal kingdom analogy further, he said they had no better sense of the law than "gray apes." These curlike, apish would-be conquerors stole cattle, and then showed surprise when indicted for their crime. Their ignorance was so astounding that they could not even find Texas on the map. Roosevelt would have agreed: the distinct culture of the West did not translate to the South.[47]

That said, Roosevelt did not try to resolve all the contradictions in his approach to the South. He may have defended racial purity and opposed miscegenation, but he also confessed to Owen Wister, author of *The Virginian,* that he believed that southern white men, despite their outrage over race mixing, were the first to leer at mulatto women and take black mistresses. Unimpressed by southern whites, and valuing hardworking black men, he did nothing to protect the latter's right to vote. Washington, Lincoln, and Grant were his heroes, men who lived active, virtuous lives, rejecting comfort and complacency. They weren't political tricksters, like "Br'er Vardaman," as one clever journalist called the rabid Mississippian. They weren't the aristocrats of the antebellum South either, who drank, dueled, and made "perverse" speeches. As he told Wister, white southerners had taken a wrong turn on the evolutionary ladder, using empty bombast to conceal "unhealthy traits." In the final analysis, the president opined, the Confederate generation and their heirs had contributed "very, very little toward anything of which Americans are now proud." For him, the Vardamans might be a nuisance, but their days were numbered.[48]

He could be confident in this future because Roosevelt was an unabashed eugenicist. He used the bully pulpit of his office to insist that women had a critical civic duty to breed a generation of healthy and disciplined children. He first endorsed eugenics in 1903, and two years later he laid out his beliefs in speech before the Congress of Mothers. Worried about "race suicide," as he put it, he recommended that women of Anglo-American stock have four to six children, "enough so the race shall increase and not decrease." Women's duty to suffer "birth pangs," and even face death, made the fertile female the equivalent of the professional soldier. Women who shirked their procreative duty were worse than deserters. So he pushed for passage of a constitutional amendment in 1906 that would place marriage and divorce under the control of federal law.[49]

Taking marriage and divorce laws out of the arbitrary control of the states served a larger eugenic purpose. Every die-hard eugenicist believed that citizens did not have an individual right to marry or to reproduce. As a leading eugenic organization reported in 1914, "Society must look upon germ-plasm as belonging to society and not merely to the individual who carries it." Because children produced by unfit parents could cost taxpayers if they became criminals, society had the right to protect itself. Far more dangerous was the cost to the nation's human stock if degenerates were allowed to breed. In 1913, Roosevelt wrote supportively to the leading eugenicist Charles Davenport that it was the patriotic duty of every good citizen of superior stock to leave his or her "blood behind." Degenerates, he warned, must not be permitted to "reproduce their kind."[50]

It was during the eugenic craze that reformers called for government incentives to ensure better breeding. This was when the idea of tax exemptions for children emerged. Theodore Roosevelt criticized the new income tax law for allowing exemptions for only two children, discouraging parents from having a third or fourth. He wanted monetary rewards for breeding, akin to the baby bonuses established in Australia in 1912. He also promoted mothers' pensions for widows—an idea that caught on. As one defender of pensions claimed in 1918, the widowed mother was "as much a servant of the State as a judge or general." Her child-rearing duties were no less a public service than if she had toiled on the battlefield. Like Selective Service, which weeded out inferior soldiers, the pensions were allotted exclusively to "a fit mother."[51]

Roosevelt was far from alone. Academics, scientists, doctors, journalists, and legislators all joined the "eugenic mania," as one California doctor termed the movement. Advocates believed that the way to encourage procreation of the fit was to educate the middle class on proper marriage selection. Eugenic thinking found expression in a flood of books and popular public lectures, as well as "better baby" and "fitter family" competitions at state fairs. Eugenics courses were added to college curricula. Such efforts resulted in the passage of laws imposing marriage restrictions, institutional sexual segregation of defectives, and, most dramatically, state-enforced sterilization of those designated "unfit."[52]

Charles Davenport established a research facility at Long Island's Cold Spring Harbor in 1904. His facility grew into the Eugenics Record Office. A Harvard-trained biologist and professor, Davenport, along with his team, collected inheritance data. Not surprisingly, he was also an influential member of the Eugenics Section of the American Breeders Association, a group of agricultural breeders and biologists. This group included many prominent figures, including the famed inventor Alexander Graham Bell. Davenport's second in command, Harry H. Laughlin, became the eugenics expert for the House Committee on Immigration and Naturalization, and played a crucial role in shaping the 1924 Immigration Act, one of the most sweeping and restrictive pieces of legislation in American history.[53]

When eugenicists thought of degenerates, they automatically focused on the South. To make his point, Davenport said outright that if a federal policy regulating immigration was not put in place, New York would turn into Mississippi. In *Heredity in Relation to Eugenics* (1911), he identified two breeding grounds for diseased and degenerate Americans: the hovel and the poorhouse. The hovel was familiar, whether one identified it with the cracker's cabin, the low-downer's shebang, or the poor white pigsty. Echoing James Gilmore's *Down in Tennessee* (1864), Davenport's work expressed a grave concern over indiscriminate mating that occurred in isolated shacks. Brothers slept with sisters, fathers with daughters, and the fear of an inbred stock seemed very real. His attack on the poorhouse also pointed south. Mississippi did not provide separate facilities for men and women in their asylums until 1928. Poorhouses allowed criminals and prostitutes to produce all manner of weak-minded delinquents and bastards, he believed. Finally, Davenport's antirural bias was especially potent. The survival-of-the-fittest model he subscribed to emphasized migration from the countryside to the city; as the fitter people moved, the weaker strains remained behind.[54]

Almost all eugenicists analogized human and animal breeding. Davenport described the best female breeders as women with large hips, using the same thinking that animal breeders had employed for centuries to describe cows. The biggest donor to the Eugenics Record Office was Mrs. Mary Harriman, widow of the railroad magnate Averell Harriman; she came from a family of avid horse breeders. Alexander Graham Bell imagined rearing "human thoroughbreds," saying four generations of superior parents would produce one thoroughbred. A wealthy New York horse breeder, William Stokes, published a eugenics book in 1917, and went so far as to contend that Americans could be bred to class, guaranteeing that intellectual capacity matched one's station. He popularly argued the "right of the unborn" to be born healthy. Why should one generation be punished for the bad breeding choices of the parents?[55]

Three solutions arose in the effort to "cull" American bloodlines. As in animal breeding, advocates pushed for legislation that allowed doctors and other professionals to segregate and quarantine the unfit from the general population, or they called for the castration of criminals and the sterilization of diseased and degenerate classes. If that seems a gross violation of human rights in any age, a Michigan legislator went a step further in 1903 when he proposed that the state should simply kill off the unfit. Another eugenics advocate came up with a particularly ludicrous plan to deal with a convicted murderer: execute his grandfather. Such proposals were not merely fringe ideas. By 1931, twenty-seven states had sterilization laws on the books, along with an unwieldy thirty-four categories delineating the kinds of people who might be subject to the surgical procedure. Eugenicists used a broad brush to create an underclass of the unfit, calling for the unemployable to be "stamped out," as Harvard professor Frank William Taussig wrote in *Principles of Economics* (1921). If society refused to subject hereditary misfits ("irretrievable criminals and tramps") to "chloroform once and for all," then, the professor fumed, they could at least be prevented from "propagating their kind."[56]

Eugenicists were divided over the role women should play in the national campaign. Some insisted that they remain guardians of the hearth. This ideal coincided with the traditional southern ethos that asserted planter and middle-class women possessed a "natural aversion" to associating with black men. The New York horse breeder Stokes called on women to scrutinize potential suitors, demanding family pedigrees and subjecting the man to a physical examination. (It is easy to see how he borrowed from the horse breeder's demand for pedigree papers, not to mention the proverbial "gift horse" mouth inspection.) It became popular for young women to pledge to a eugenic marriage, accepting no man who did not meet her high scientific standards. In 1908, a concerned female teacher in Louisiana started "better baby" contests, in which mothers allowed their offspring to be examined and graded. This program expanded into "fitter family" competitions at state fairs. The contests were held in the stock grounds, and families were judged in the manner of cattle. The winners received medals, not unlike prize bulls.[57]

Educated women were the gatekeepers, the guardians of eugenic marriages, though fecund poor women continued to outbreed their female betters. So-called experts contended that those who overindulged in sexual activity and lacked intellectual restraint were more likely to have feeble children. (Here they were imagining poor whites fornicating in the bushes.) Once experts like Davenport identified harlotry and poverty as inherited traits, sexually aggressive women of the lower classes were viewed as the carriers of degenerate germ protoplasm. In 1910, Henry Goddard, who ran a testing laboratory at the school for feeble-minded boys and girls in Vineland, New Jersey, invented a new eugenic

UNFIT HUMAN TRAITS SUCH AS FEEBLEMINDEDNESS EPILEPSY, CRIMINALITY, INSANITY, ALCOHOLISM, PAUPERISM and MANY OTHERS, RUN IN FAMILIES AND ARE INHERITED IN EXACTLY THE SAME WAY AS COLOR IN GUINEA-PIGS. IF **ALL MARRIAGES** WERE **EUGENIC** WE COULD **BREED OUT** MOST OF THIS UNFITNESS IN *THREE GENERATIONS*.

THE TRIANGLE OF LIFE

ENVIRONMENT — EDUCATION — HAVE — DO — WHAT YOU — ARE — HERITAGE

YOU CAN IMPROVE YOUR EDUCATION, AND EVEN CHANGE YOUR ENVIRONMENT; BUT WHAT YOU REALLY **ARE** WAS ALL SETTLED WHEN YOUR PARENTS WERE BORN. SELECTED PARENTS WILL HAVE BETTER CHILDREN THIS IS THE GREAT AIM OF EUGENICS

This 1929 chart from a Kansas fair states unequivocally that heredity determines every person's destiny. Its message is clear: unfitness must be "bred out" of the national stock.

Scrapbook, American Eugenic Society Papers, American Philosophical Society, Philadelphia, Pennsylvania

classification: the moron. More intelligent than idiots and imbeciles, morons were especially troublesome because they could pass as normal. Female morons could enter polite homes as servants and seduce young men or be seduced by them. It was thought to be a real problem.[58]

The fear of promiscuous poor women led eugenics reformers to push for the construction of additional asylums to house feebleminded white women. In this effort, they deployed the term "segregation," the same as was used by southerners to enforce white-black separation. The "passing" female was not a new trope either: it borrowed from the other southern fear of the passing mulatto, who might marry into a prominent family. Passing also conjured the old English fears of the class interloper and unregulated social mobility—the house servant seducing the lord of the manor.[59]

Even with such racial overtones, the major target of eugenicists was the poor white woman. Goddard's description of the female moron as one lacking forethought, vitality, or any sense of shame perfectly replicated Reconstruction writers' portrayal of white trash. Davenport felt the best policy was to quarantine dangerous women during their fertile years. How this policy prescription led to sterilization is rather more calculated: interested politicians and eager reformers concluded that it was cheaper to operate on women than to house them in asylums for decades. Southern eugenicists in particular argued that sterilization helped the economy by sending poor women back into the population safely neutered but still able to work at menial jobs.[60]

World War I fueled the eugenics campaign. First of all, the army refused to issue soldiers prophylactics. The top brass insisted that sexual control required a degree of internal discipline, which no army program would effectively inculcate. The army, along with local antivice groups, rounded up some thirty thousand prostitutes and placed as many as possible in detention centers and jails where they were kept out of the reach of soldiers. Thus the federal government backed a policy of sexual segregation of tainted women. At the same time, advocates for the draft argued that a volunteer force would be both unfair and uneugenic. Senator John Sharp of Mississippi insisted that without a draft only the "best blood" would go to the front, leaving behind those of an "inferior mold" to "beget the next race."[61]

The war advanced the importance of intelligence testing. Goddard had created the "moron" classification by using the Binet-Simon test, which was succeeded by the IQ (intelligence quotient) scale promoted by Stanford professor Lewis Terman and then used by the U.S. Army. The army's findings only served to confirm a long-held, unpropitious view of the South, since both poor white and black recruits from southern states had the lowest IQ scores. Overall, the study found that the mean intelligence of the soldier registered at the moron level—the equivalent of a "normal" thirteen-year-old boy. Given the results, observers wondered if poor white men were dragging down the rest of the nation.[62]

The lack of public education funding in the South made the army's intelligence test results inevitable. The gap in education levels matched what had existed between the North and South before the Civil War. Many of the men who took the test had never used a pencil before. Southern white men exhibited stunted bodies—army medical examiners found them to be smaller, weaker, and less physically fit. National campaigns to fight hookworm and pellagra (both associated with clay-eating and identified as white trash diseases) only reinforced this portrait. Beginning in 1909, the New York–based Rockefeller Institute poured massive amounts of money into a philanthropic program aimed at eliminating hookworm, while the U.S. Public Health Service tackled pellagra. The Rockefeller Foundation published shocking pictures of actual hookworm subjects, some pairing boys of similar ages, one normal and the other literally dwarfed and disfigured by the disease. It didn't help the South's image that hookworm was spread by the lack of sanitation. Outhouses were rare among the southern poor, let alone toilets.[63]

All in all, the rural South stood out as a place of social and now eugenic backwardness. Tenant farmers and sharecroppers, wandering the dusty roads with a balky mule, seemed a throwback to eighteenth-century vagrants. The "lazy diseases" of hookworm and pellagra created a class of lazy lubbers. Illiteracy was widespread. Fear of indiscriminate breeding loomed large. The stock of poor white men produced in the South were dismissed as unfit for military service, the women unfit to be mothers. In the two decades before the war, reformers had exposed that many poor white women and children worked long, grueling hours in southern textile factories. Was this another sign of "race suicide," some asked? Could they possibly produce future generations of healthy,

The 10,000 Hookworm Family (1913) from Alabama were presented as poor white celebrities who escaped the "lazy disease." They stood in contrast to the "fitter family" competitions as a perfect example of the unfit American family.

201 H Alabama, Hookworm, Box 42, Folder 1044, #1107, 1913, Rockefeller Archive Center, Sleepy Hollow, New York

This 1913 photograph from North Carolina shows the disfiguring effects of hookworm. In a shocking contrast, an undersized young man, age twenty-three, is placed alongside a normal boy, two years younger, who towers over him.

236 H North Carolina, Box 53, Folder 1269, #236 Vashti Alexander County, North Carolina, May 29, 1913, Rockefeller Archive Center, Sleepy Hollow, New York

courageous, intelligent, and fertile Americans? For many in the early twentieth century, then, the "new race problem" was not the "negro problem." It was instead a different crisis, one caused by the "worthless class of anti-social whites."[64]

It was Albert Priddy who called poor white Virginians "the shiftless, ignorant, and worthless class of anti-social whites of the South." He was the superintendent of the State Colony for Epileptics and Feebleminded in Lynchburg, Virginia. He helped shape the optimal legal test case for sterilization, a case that went to the Supreme Court in *Buck v. Bell* (1927). Priddy began building his case in 1916, targeting prostitutes. He recruited top eugenics experts, including two colleagues of Davenport's with ties to the Eugenics Record Office and the Carnegie Institution of Washington.[65]

Priddy also had the support of the University of Virginia School of Medicine, which took the lead in eugenic science and public policy. Dean Harvey Ernest Jordan saw Virginia as the "perfect laboratory" for comparing the best (Virginia's famed "First Families") and the worst stocks of poor whites. In 1912, he proposed intelligence testing of white, black, and mulatto children. He found a way to pervert the meaning of a classic phrase of the university's founder, Thomas Jefferson, into eugenic nonsense: "Man does not have an inalienable right to personal or reproductive freedom, if such freedom is a menace to society." Inalienable rights were now the inherited privileges of the superior classes, what Jordan called America's "human thoroughbreds."[66]

Eugenicists made Virginia the national test case for weeding out bad blood. Priddy recruited Arthur Estabrook of the Carnegie Institution to his campaign, getting him to offer in the Virginia courts his expert opinion on intelligence testing. But this colleague of Davenport's spread the eugenics message in yet another way. In 1926, Estabrook published *Mongrel Virginians*, a study of an isolated mountain community in Virginia known as the Win tribe. The Wins offered a curious case of inbreeding and interracial breeding; they were of "mixed races, neither black or white"—largely Indian. The portrait was damning: the community Estabrook described suffered from congenital ignorance, all springing from the licentiousness of mixed-race women. Their habit of breeding was in his words, "almost that of an animal in their freedom."[67]

The evidence in *Mongrel Virginians* was sufficient to guide passage of the Racial Integrity Act of 1924, which prohibited marriages between blacks and whites, and treated Indian blood no differently from black blood. The Virginia law defined a white person as one having "no trace" of any but Caucasian blood. Following the agenda of the eugenicists, the first draft of the law required a racial registry, tracking pedigrees in order to ensure that no light-skinned black with Indian blood might marry a white person. This regulation was removed from the final version of the bill, but the law still divided the population into white and black, fit and unfit, pure and tainted bloodlines. In the end, Virginia legislators believed they had immunized the population against mongrelism at the altar. It stopped the contagion that passed from blacks and Indians to poor whites and up the hierarchy to the unsuspecting white middle class and elites.[68]

Three years later, Justice Oliver Wendell Holmes would offer a revolutionary decision in *Buck v. Bell*, which gave the state the power to regulate the breeding of its citizens. Like Justice Taney in the *Dred Scott* decision, he believed that pedigree could be used to distinguish worthy citizens from the waste people. He ruled that sterilization was the appropriate recourse in order to curb "generations of imbeciles" from reproducing. Holmes argued that sterilization was a civic duty, saving the nation from being "swamped with incompetence." He echoed what the English had argued in the 1600s: the unfit would either starve or be executed for some crime, so sending them to be sterilized was the humane option, as being sent to the colonies had been centuries before.[69]

Carrie Buck (of *Buck v. Bell*) had been chosen for sterilization on the order of Priddy, because she was one of "these people"—that "worthless class" of southern whites. She was, in a word, a perfect specimen of white trash. While Carrie Buck was the plaintiff, her mother and daughter were on trial too. Carrie tested at the "moron level" and her mother slightly lower, according to the highly biased experts. Her illegitimate child, examined at seven months, was termed feebleminded—this was based on the observations of a Red Cross worker and on a test administered by Estabrook. The experts' pedigree chart proved degeneracy as well as sexual deviance: Carrie's mother was a prostitute, and Carrie had been raped by the nephew of her adoptive parents. Her rapist went unpunished, and yet she was sterilized.[70]

Carrie Buck and her mother, Emma (1924). Carrie, her mother,
and Carrie's illegitimate daughter were all put on trial in
Buck v. Bell (1927). Their crime was one of pedigree—
a defective breed perpetuated over three generations.

Arthur Estabrook Collection, M. E. Grenander Department
of Special Collections and Archives, University of Albany
Libraries, Albany, New York

Eugenics suffused the culture of the twenties. Social classes were ranked
according to levels of inheritable potential. At the top was the new professional "master class." Many believed that intelligence was inherited
and that tests of schoolchildren proved that the brightest pupils were
those whose parents were highly educated professionals. This elite had to
be not just mentally but also physically fit. At the Second International
Congress of Eugenics in New York, in 1921, two statues were put on display at opposite ends of Darwin Hall in the Museum of Natural History.
One was a composite of the biometric measures of the fifty most athletic
men at Harvard, the other an amalgam of one hundred thousand dough-
boys of World War I—in other words, the "average American male." The
Harvard specimen was the decidedly more impressive of the two. A new
word was coined for the cognitive elite: "aristogenic"—what we would
call a genetic leadership class. One was once again born to a station, as in
the traditional meaning of aristocracy, but it was not because of family

name or wealth. Now it was the endowment of inborn qualities that
marked off the superior class.[71]

While eugenicists made it fashionable to celebrate a hereditary ruling
class, they were as bent on organizing social classes on the basis of breeding capacity. One of the most popular eugenics lecturers, C. W. Saleeby,
spoke up for something called "eugenic feminism," insisting that the
brightest women should not only take up the suffrage cause but also
accept their patriotic duty to breed. He imagined female society organized as a bee colony: the queens of superior stock bred throughout their
fertile years, while educated sterile women (or postmenopausal) were
best suited for reform activity. Professor William McDougall at Harvard
came up with an equally radical solution. He called for a breeding colony
of "Eugenia," a separate protectorate within the United States, in which
the best and brightest would propagate a superior stock. Eugenia would
be at once a university and a stud farm. Raised as "aristocrats" in the
tradition of "noblesse oblige," the products of the special colony would go
out into the world as skilled public servants.[72]

The obsession with white trash did not lose any traction in the 1920s.
Reformers and legislators pushed their campaigns, while journalists wrote
sensational newspaper stories and published shocking photographs. The
Supreme Court ruling in *Buck v. Bell* inspired Mississippi, North Carolina, South Carolina, and Georgia to pass sterilization laws similar to the
one adopted in Virginia. Protecting and promoting "good blood" would
mean little if removing "bad blood" did not receive the same attention.[73]

The decade also saw the appearance of a new generation of novelists
who experimented with eugenic ideas. Of these, the very popular Sherwood Anderson stood out. He composed semiautobiographical tales
about small-town life, publishing the unmistakably titled *Poor White* in
1920. His character Hugh McIvey is the son of white trash, born in a
"hole" of a town on a muddy bank along the Mississippi, in Missouri. His
nature is that of a listless dreamer, his sleepy mind unable to fix on anything important. He is saved from his "animal-like stupor" when the railroad comes through town, bringing a fresh-faced New England–born
Michigander, in whose veins "flowed the blood of the pioneers," and who
becomes his schoolteacher. Almost Rousseau-like, she stimulates in him
a new intellectual vitality.[74]

Wanting to escape his past and rise socially, Hugh leaves the South behind. He wanders from town to town for three years, eventually settling in Bridewell, Ohio. There, after he takes a job in a telegraph office, technology shapes his destiny, and his dreamy nature blossoms into what the reader recognizes as good old-fashioned American ingenuity. He invents a series of machines, the most successful of which is the McIvey Corn-Cutter. Transformed into a hero in his adoptive industrializing town, Hugh meets the rebellious Clara Butterfield, a college-educated, feminist-leaning woman. She chooses him for a husband, in an act of eugenic marital selection, preferring what she describes as a "kind horse" to a "wolf or wolfhound."[75]

It is the force of reproduction that ultimately saves the couple from the tensions that arise amid the surge of modern life. After facing various dangers, Hugh becomes dark and brooding when he starts to see the machine age as nihilistic and futile. His wife pulls him back from the brink of insanity by reminding him of the son she carries in her belly. Feeling a primitive, animal impulse to reproduce allows him to carry on.[76]

Anderson's novel rejected the jingoistic optimism of the nineteenth century, but it also pointed to the eugenic idea that poor whites suffered from "childish impotence" or "arrested development," requiring the reactivation of their better Saxon qualities. Facing challenges, Hugh never reaches the level of hopelessness that infuses Erskine Caldwell's first novel, *The Bastard* (1929). Caldwell was the son of a minister in Georgia, and his father was sympathetic to eugenics. *The Bastard* seeks to prove that no human can hide from his "inborn" traits, from the imprint of his ancestors.[77]

Caldwell's protagonist is Gene Morgan ("Eugene" comes from the same root of wellborn as "eugenic"). Our ironically named hero is a bastard. He learns that his harlot mother was murdered in Louisiana, her belly slit open like a "swamp"—an allusion to the polluted wasteland inside her, from which he was spawned. Gene is a vicious white, a wanderer, and his only pleasure comes from violence. Raised by an old Negro woman and sexually attracted to a mulatto girl, he thoughtlessly transgresses the color line.[78]

Gene is lost until he meets Myra Morgan, a "clean . . . feminine woman." They marry and move to Philadelphia, where he works hard to support his new wife and the baby that soon comes along. The parents watch, to their horror, as their child transforms into a freak. His body is covered with black hair, like that of a wild animal, proving that the taint of the swamp is still present in his blood, despite Myra's purity. The doctor tells her that she can expect all of her children to be degenerate, leaving a clear message: the bastard Gene is congenitally cursed. There are hints of inbreeding, since Gene and Myra have the same last name. He contemplates murdering his son, but doesn't go through with it. He leaves his beloved wife, hoping she will marry a normal man.[79]

The rising generation of a new, modern century saw little of enduring substance in family dynasties of the Gilded Age. All they had to speak of was their money. In place of America's imperfect aristocracy, progressive reformers were eager to rear a cognitive elite, one that could deal with modern technology and bureaucracy. Class continued to matter greatly, but it wasn't going to be the flamboyant aristocracy of the effete Old World that would monitor modernity; hope lay instead with a cadre of men in white lab coats and bureaucrats in tailored suits. Professional expertise would be convincing enough evidence of inborn merit.[80]

It should seem odd to us that the high tide of eugenics coexisted with the storied glamour of the Roaring Twenties: Lindbergh's transatlantic flight, lighthearted flappers, and unpoliced speakeasies. Yet even the flappers were warned that their daring dancing style too closely resembled the ways of those who had "gypsy" (i.e., black) blood; they would be better served to settle down with a eugenically suitable mate. If ever there was time when class consciousness sank deep roots, this was it. The 1920s saw social exclusiveness masquerade as science and disdain for rural backwardness and the mongrel taint intensify. In a culture under siege, white trash meant impure, and not quite white. Like the moron who somehow passed into the middle class, the ill-bred bastard gave a watchful people a new set of social hazards to look out for, while they listened to the stock ticker and marched off a cliff with the market crash in 1929.[81]

CHAPTER NINE

Forgotten Men and Poor Folk

Downward Mobility and the Great Depression

> Shall then this man go hungry, here in lands
> Blest by his honor, builded by his hands?
> Do something for him: let him never be
> Forgotten: let him have his daily bread:
> He who has fed us, let him now be fed.
> Let us remember his tragic lot—
> Remember, or else be ourselves forgot!
>
> —Edwin Markham, "The Forgotten Man" (1932)

In 1932, three years after the stock market crash that triggered the Great Depression, Warner Brothers released *I Am a Fugitive from a Chain Gang*, the gripping story of a World War I veteran transformed into a beast of burden while working on a southern chain gang. It is a strangely powerful film that celebrates the redemptive power of work. Through no fault of their own, 20 percent of the American labor force was out of work by 1932. Average men woke to find themselves as outcasts, without the emblems of American male identity: jobs, homes, the means to provide for their families. The film's fugitive, James Allen, became a powerful symbol of the country's decline. His story is that of a patriotic, ambitious, creative, suddenly jobless northerner who becomes, in turn, a tramp, a convict, and a fugitive. He is the Depression's "Forgotten Man," exiled from the labor force. His fate is sealed when he goes south. In the last scene of the film, Allen steps back into the shadows, all hope of reclaiming his former life gone, a man forced to admit that his only recourse is to steal in order to survive. So unsettling was the scene that it was almost cut from the film.[1]

I Am a Fugitive from a Chain Gang is a grim and devastating exposé of the degraded South. The story served as a confirmation of the New Deal's conclusion that the southern economy was tragically out of step with the American dream. In 1938, six years after the film debuted,

President Franklin Roosevelt declared, "The South presents right now the Nation's No. 1 economic problem." Will Alexander, the Tennessean who headed the Farm Security Administration (FSA), argued that southern tenancy robbed men of any chance to become self-reliant. His agency engaged in "rural rehabilitation"—using the same word that was applied to physically disabled soldiers or to worn-out lands. Destitute families had to be retrained and resettled (but not coerced) into programs. For Alexander, the problem was stark and simple: success could only be achieved when the prejudice against white trash was overcome. In other words, psychological reconditioning was as necessary as educational reform.[2]

Dependency had long defined the South. Since the 1870s, impoverished sharecroppers and convict laborers, white as well as black, had clung to the bottom rung of the social order. It may be hard for us to fathom, but the convict population was no better off than southern slaves had been. A prison official said it all: "One dies, get another." Poor whites were inexpensive and expendable, and found their lot comparable to suffering African Americans when it came to the justice system. Nothing proves the point better than the fact that both black and white convicts were referred to as "niggers."[3]

Harsh sentences were common for minor offenses among this class. Robert Burns, the New Jersey man whose memoir inspired the Hollywood film, faced six to ten years hard labor for a robbery that netted him $5.80. The South's transportation infrastructure and expanded industrial base was built on the backs of chain gangs. States raked in tremendous revenues by leasing prisoners to private businesses. Historically, the majority of these laborers were black, but during the Depression more poor whites found themselves swept up in the system.[4]

Warner Brothers was said to be the most "pro-Roosevelt" studio in Tinseltown. Its top executives were committed to the bottom line, but they were not afraid of social justice issues. *I Am a Fugitive from a Chain Gang* told of the destruction of the human spirit, and how Allen's fate was sealed the moment he was thrust into the chain-gang camp. Monotony stalks the prisoners who aren't literally worked to death. They can do nothing without asking a guard's permission, not even wipe the sweat from their brows. Nothing better captures the soul-killing process than when the camera pans across the shackled men loaded on a truck and then turns the lens toward a pack of mules. Both herds are mindless beasts of burden. The mule was at the same time meant as a reminder of the backward sharecropper.[5]

As a northerner, Allen feels as if he has been thrown into alien country. He refuses to let conditions break his will. He alone among the prisoners retains the desire to escape; in time he uses his brainpower to outwit the guards. To pull off his plan, he violates a cardinal rule of the white South by soliciting help from a black convict. It is Sebastian's superior skill with the sledgehammer that bends Allen's ankle bracelets. Reversing the pattern set by the Thirteenth Amendment, a southern black man sets a northern white man free. It is a poignant scene. The larger message was crystal clear: the South is backward because of its failure to incorporate black men into the free-market economy.

Yet the talent and labor of poor whites is wasted too. James Allen's fellow white prisoners are dead on the inside. "To work out, or die out," they are told. It is the only way out. They learn to appreciate the true meaning of liberty only by watching Allen achieve it. His daring escape is accomplished not by violence but by rational planning. It proves to be a temporary success, but at least he succeeds in offering his comrades a different vision of manhood.

Allen's dream is to be an engineer. That aspiration represented the pride Americans felt in raising the Empire State Building, one of the decade's consummate achievements. In 1932, the same year that the film was released, the photographer Lewis Hine published a book about his time with the "sky boys," as the skilled men who balanced on the beams and built the iconic skyscraper were known. In *Men at Work,* now a classic, Hine vividly portrayed the courage and imagination of the workers who left their imprint on the urban landscape. "Cities do not build themselves," he pronounced, "machines cannot make machines, unless back of them all are the brains and toil of men." At the age of sixty, with an established reputation for reform, the cameraman believed that life was given power through labor. What distinguished humans from beasts was the capacity to solve problems, to create anew, and to apply cognitive energy to the labor process. The quote Hine selected as his epigraph was taken from the late philosopher William James's "What Makes a Life Significant": "Not in clanging fights and desperate marches only is heroism to be looked for, but on every bridge and building that is going up to-day, on freight trains, on vessels and lumber-rafts, in mines, among the firemen and the policemen, the demand for courage is incessant and the supply never fails." Manual laborers deserved the same respect as heroes on the battlefield. If a new breed of human arose when it gave labor enhanced social meaning, then the South, with its dull refusal to appreciate the value of work, remained caught in a primitive state of mind.[6]

If the Empire State Building, which opened in 1931, represented the highest testament to moral courage, then the tragedy that played out in Washington in the spring and summer of 1932 displayed America at its lowest ebb. Veterans of World War I formed a "Bonus Army," some twenty thousand unemployed arriving with their hurting families and setting up a shantytown across the river from Capitol Hill. They demanded of Congress their bonus pay. "We were heroes in 1917, but we're bums now," said their spokesman in a plea before the House. The House passed the Pateman Bill that would issue the bonuses, but it failed in the Senate. President Herbert Hoover labeled the marchers criminals and called out the U.S. Army to disperse those that remained after the bill failed, using bayonets, tear gas, and tanks. "The most powerful government in the world shooting its starving veterans out of worthless huts," was how John Henry Bartlett, former governor of New Hampshire, described the disturbing event in his eyewitness account.[7]

So this was how the image of the "Forgotten Man" was imprinted in the public mind, as *I Am a Fugitive from a Chain Gang* hit the theaters. Allen's status as a bumming veteran associated him with the men of the Bonus Army. In the film, he discovers that he can't pawn his war medal. The pawnbroker pulls out a box filled with such medals—by 1932, discarded junk, like the veterans themselves. The truth could hardly be denied. Class, as defined in terms of dignity, was increasingly insecure.

The Depression was associated with waste. Wasted lives, wasted land, human waste. The stock market crash unleashed a nightmarish downside to the much-vaunted American dream, its unpredictable and unpreventable downward mobility. The traditional marks of poverty were now appearing everywhere. There were Hoovervilles not just in Washington but at the New York City dump. St. Louis had the largest shantytown, with twelve hundred men; Chicago's makeshift community, on order of the mayor, was burned to the ground. The poor could no longer be considered outcasts, "untouchables," or even hoboes.[8]

The lines separating the poor from the working and middle classes seemed more permeable. The poor were simply men and women without jobs, and those who still had gainful employment sensed that they were at risk of experiencing the same fate. This fear was captured in Edward Newhouse's novel *You Can't Sleep Here* (1934), about a New York City Hooverville. On weekends, Newhouse wrote, hundreds came to watch the men in the shantytown as if they were, collectively, a "monkey in a cage." Instead of looking at them with disgust, "Sunday tourists" wondered if they might be next.[9]

Old clichés rang hollow. Upward mobility was not a destination to be reached, or a ladder to be scaled by diligence and hard work. In an autobiographical novel about bumming, called *Waiting for Nothing* (1935), Tom Kromer put it best when he wrote that his journey in life went nowhere: "What is before is the same as that which is gone. My life is spent before it started." Long admired for his competitive spirit, in the literature of the thirties the "rugged individualist" appeared ruthless and greedy. The towering giants of the business world were now "great little men." An investment banker from New York scoffed, "The American Standard of Living—the proudest boast of several administrations [is] the subject of international gibe." The "City upon a Hill" lay in ruins.[10]

Margaret Bourke-White used her camera to express the new critical outlook. Working for *Life* magazine, she shot a line of somber black men and women waiting for relief. They stood before a garish billboard that featured a ruddy-cheeked, smiling family of four driving down the road in a nice car—that's who and what hung over these real victims of an Ohio Valley flood. Irony shouted at the magazine's readers like the slogans that blared from the cartoonish billboard image of the idealized white, middle-class family: "World's Highest Standard of Living"; "There's No Way Like the American Way." By the time this provocative photograph appeared in 1937, most Americans had already come to accept the uncomfortable truth about their national situation: equal opportunity was a grand illusion. In the very same issue of *Life* were photographs of black men in chain gangs, shoring up levees in Tennessee.[11]

Bourke-White did another, similar photo essay that year. This time her aim was to dispute the myth of the classless society. Visiting Muncie, Indiana, the city made famous in the 1929 study *Middletown,* the photographer questioned the idea of "typical Americans" that the community had supposedly come to represent. She angered the residents when she featured the insides of homes, contrasting a poor white hovel of "Shedtown" with the opulent parlor of one of the wealthiest families. Her critics charged that she was focused on the upper crust and "soaked bottom," while ignoring the "middle filling" of the "community pie." But that was her point. There was no single representative American way of life.[12]

The stock market's "crash" and ensuing "Depression" invoked obvious metaphors of physical collapse. One highly cynical observer compared the bottoming out of Wall Street to a buried Egyptian tomb, "filled with the debris of delusions and false hopes." Town and country supplied competing images of ruin: boarded-up stores and banks in ghost towns, city breadlines—both symbols of idleness. In rural settings, once-prosperous farms had either dried up or become buried in dust, and fertile fields were scarred by cavernous gullies. "Depression" was another word for what the eighteenth-century governor of Virginia called his impoverished neighbor North Carolina: a "sinkhole."[13]

In the writings that suffused 1930s periodicals as well as government reports, economic failure was associated with the old notion of wasteland. When Roy Stryker was put in charge of the Historical Section of the Resettlement Administration in 1935, he hired a team of talented photographers to record images of barren land dotted with abandoned farms and long stretches of terrain destroyed by dust storms, floods, and gullies—all caused by destructive farming, irresponsible lumbering, and traditional mining techniques. In this literary and visual construction of reality on the ground, class identity was not just a slippery slope; it was closer in nature to the erratically formed, man-made furrows of the gully. People were seen in the numerous images of the FSA as scattered and anonymous, squatting along roads, worn, beaten, set adrift, washed up. The absence of active laborers conveyed its own unmistakable message— a *Life* story explained that it was hard to "see" depression because of "business not being done." Documentary photographer Arthur Rothstein took a haunting picture of an Ohio farm community. Only a few buildings

Arthur Rothstein's powerful image of erosion and wasteland (1937).
Here the Alabama land is scarred by massive gullies as a forlorn
tenant farmer stands helplessly by his barn.

Eroded land on tenant's farm, Walker County, Alabama (Arthur Rothstein, 1937),
LC-USF34-025121, Library of Congress Prints and Photographs Division, Washington, DC

were visible, and there were no people present. His camera focused on a
sign planted in the frozen mud, marking the identity of this unincorpo-
rated town. It read, "Utopia."[14]

Henry Wallace, FDR's secretary of agriculture, argued that what had
always made America unique was the constant "pressing upon social
resources" and the general belief in a "limitless and inexhaustible soil."
But the soil was not limitless, and the frontier was officially closed by the
government in 1934. Writers of all stripes, not just agricultural experts,
lamented how valuable topsoil was washing down America's rivers, the
resulting waste made worse by levees. In this way, the Depression was
an upheaval that portrayed class leveling with disordered images of
land erosion. The washing away of topsoil and debris was relatedly seen
in the washing away of different classes of people, churned up and let
loose in mass migrations caused by economic disaster. In Dorothea
Lange's *An American Exodus* (1939), a photo-essay book, images capture

the turning of the landscape into wasteland. The middle American Dust
Bowl swept up clouds of soil, and dislodged humans were driven down
the road "like particles of dust."[15]

Poor whites remained at the forefront of the American consciousness
in the thirties. The Bonus Army's Hooverville was an urban manifestation of the old squatter's shack. Tenant farmers in the southern states
continued to reside in run-down cabins, a highly mobile, migratory labor
force that was the very antithesis of self-sufficiency. After the drought
and dust bowls that hit during the middle years of the decade, "Okies"
and "Arkies" captured the media. Families in old jalopies crammed with
everything they owned headed west to California; en route, they set
up camps along major highways. They were visible on the roads in
the Golden State, taking seasonal jobs as crop pickers. As migrant workers, they called themselves "Migs," while others labeled them "rub-
ber tramps" or "shantytowns on wheels." In his "Talking Dust Bowl
Blues," the legendary folksinger Woody Guthrie expressed the mobile-
home theme with the lyric "I swapped my farm for a Ford machine."
Like the refugees from Arkansas who poured into Missouri during the
Civil War, the Migs formed a modern-day caravan of vagrants and
nomads. John Steinbeck and John Ford made this cross-country trek
famous, Steinbeck in his bestselling 1939 novel *The Grapes of Wrath*,
and Ford in his dark and disquieting 1941 Hollywood film of the same
name about the Joads' pilgrimage.[16]

Another chaotic migration was the "Back to the Land" movement
that led to numerous rural communes. Some of these had outspoken
leaders. Ralph Borsodi, who set up a subsistence homestead on the outskirts of New York City, helped to organize a cooperative village near
Dayton, Ohio. Similar ventures appeared in other states. The southern
journalist Charles Morrow Wilson described these folks as "American
peasants," but they are perhaps better described as the heirs of James
Oglethorpe's eighteenth-century Georgia colonists. One such group
from Tulsa established a community in the Ozark hills. They founded a
corporation, much like the older joint-stock companies, and adopted a set
of bylaws, in which each member was a shareholder and had a vote. They
sold timber, raised hogs and chickens, repaired the lumbering shanties
on the property, and set up a school.[17]

Unlike Arkansas tenant farmers and sharecroppers, the Tulsa colonists owned the land, albeit land of little value, which lowered them to the level of subsistence farmers. The common pattern in Arkansas was different. Here, nearly 63 percent of farmers worked as tenants. The Arkies were unlike the Tulsans, many of whom were educated, willing to work collectively, and devised a plan for the future. They might be slumming as white trash and living in shanties, but when the economy improved, the city folk would return to their former lives. For them the land was a "refuge," not a permanent source of class identity.[18]

The "Back to the Land" movement had a marked influence on New Deal policy. So it made sense when Milburn Lincoln Wilson, a trained social scientist and expert in agriculture, became the first director of the Subsistence Homesteads Division in 1933. The government's goal was to give tenants and sharecroppers the resources and skills to rise up the agricultural ladder and help city folk without jobs. Like the soil, the dispossessed had to be rehabilitated. Land, he insisted, was not just a source of profit, but was part of a "well integrated democracted [sic] community," one that knit people together by attending to the resilience of families. In Wilson's grand scheme, the homestead community was a laboratory, a demonstration of how government could ease the impact of a flagging economy and make it possible for low-income rural and urban families to become self-sufficient homeowners. The families involved were given long-term loans so that they could buy their homes. The program contributed better housing for the unemployed while acting to humanize living conditions for poor whites.[19]

At its most visionary, Wilson saw rehabilitation as the process of taking stranded coal miners in abandoned towns, displaced factory workers without jobs, and tenants trapped on unproductive land and helping them all adopt a new way of life. The modern homestead of his design was a source of a genuine democracy, producing "a sturdy rather than servile citizenry." If ever there was a proactive policy for creating the yeoman republic of Thomas Jefferson's imagination, this was it.

It was inevitable that poor southerners became a greater concern for the agency. Wilson directed attention to the South's one-crop system and "rural slum areas" in the countryside, which guaranteed the pernicious cycle of poor white and black sharecroppers' poverty from one generation to the next. Two-thirds of the nation's tenant farmers were in the South, and two-thirds were white. These facts cannot be overstated. The agricultural distress of the Depression exposed the South's long-standing dependence on submarginal land and submarginal farmers.[20]

In this way, the federal government drew national attention to the South's oppressive class environment. The homestead became a symbol of class security, sustenance, and normalcy. In 1935, the Subsistence Homesteads Division produced a pamphlet that contrasted West Virginia coal miners' dark and dismal shacks with bright new homesteads (portrayed through a published image of children playing outside on grass). A year later, the President's Committee on Tenancy made the point clearer by comparing the rungs of the agricultural ladder to prison bars. Tenancy was a cage, class status a jail. Chains tied poor whites to rotten soil and locked them away in abysmal shacks that weren't really homes at all. There was more than one chain gang in the South.[21]

Arthur Raper, one of the leading authorities on tenancy in the South, explained conditions in his 1936 study *Preface to Peasantry*. Most southern tenants were in debt to landlords, had little cash, no education; hookworm and pellagra still haunted them. Unlike the fugitive James Allen, they had no place to run. Rarely did poor whites stay on a single plantation for more than two or three years; in the winter months, they could be seen filling carts with their children and their junk and moving on. This annual phenomenon of southeastern tenant dispersion was already occurring before the mass western exodus of Okies and Arkies.[22]

The entire tenant system operated by coercion and dependence. Landowners did not want their tenants to improve, because then they would have less control over them. A hungry worker was the best worker, or so many southern cotton growers believed. No one—neither tenants nor their landlords—had any problem making children and women work in the fields. For all the above reasons, then, education remained crucial to the subsistence homestead program. Prospective clients required not only guidance in modern agricultural practices, but also schools, churches, and training in the methods of home food production. Wilson introduced a psychological element often lacking in traditional forms of charity. For poor whites, this meant they had to overcome the feeling that they were "just trash," a breed lacking the capacity for change. The homestead program would prove above all that poor whites were completely normal people.[23]

Wilson's fellow Iowan, Henry Wallace, had a similar outlook. Inferior heredity had nothing to do with rural poverty. Secretary of Agriculture Wallace predicted that if at birth one hundred thousand poor white children were taken from their "tumble-down cabins" and another hundred thousand were taken from the wealthiest families, and both groups were given the same food, education, housing, and cultural experiences, by the time they reached adulthood there would be no difference in mental and moral traits. "Superior ability" was not "the exclusive possession of any one race or any one class," he said. Reacting to Adolf Hitler's Aryan fantasy, Wallace predicted that even a "master breeder" might over generations raise a group of people with the same skin, hair, or eye color, but he would just as likely produce a group of "blond morons."[24]

Both Wilson and Wallace dismissed the notion that class (or even race) was biologically preordained. Wallace stressed the importance of understanding class insecurity. Over time, he warned, economic benefits accrued to the stronger, shrewder people in society, and if unrestrained by government, conditions would lead to "economic autocracy" and "political despotism." Sounding a lot like the critics in our present who deplore the concentration of wealth among the top 1 percent of Americans, Wallace in 1936 argued that liberty was impossible if "36 thousand families at the top of the economic pyramid get as much income as 12 million families at the bottom."[25]

The Depression revealed that liberty for some—for the select, the privileged—was not liberty for all. In a remarkable article of 1933, titled "The New Deal and the Constitution," a popular writer named John Corbin questioned the claims of Americans to an exclusive quality of freedom. He posed a rhetorical question: "Can a nation call itself free if it finds itself periodically on the verge of bankruptcy and starvation in the face of the fact that it possesses all the materials of the good life?" He meant that freedom was compromised when a nation allowed the majority of its people to suffer devastating poverty and enduring economic insecurity. Regulation, regional planning, and readjustment (the last a favorite New Deal term) were needed to correct market abuses, control the exploitation of natural resources, and adjust class imbalance, and to do so, in President Roosevelt's phrase, "not to destroy individualism but to protect it." Wilson, Wallace, and Corbin all agreed that the old laissez-faire doctrines could no longer be sustained, and that the frontier thesis—which presumed that western migration had alleviated poverty—no longer worked. For Wilson, the "great disorganizing force of the depression" was "a great, magic dark hand." Unlike Adam Smith's invisible hand of the free market, Wilson's dark hand represented the dangers of an unregulated economy: downward mobility and the ruin of countless lives.[26]

If for poor rural tenants and sharecroppers class was an inescapable cage or a prison, it was equally a source of what Henry Wallace labeled "human erosion." Human erosion was the reason for soil erosion, and not the other way around, he contended. Tenant farming was a perfect example of this process: the tenants had little reason to care for the soil as they attempted to eke out a living from it, while the landowners remained unwilling to invest in soil conservation. The willingness of Americans to tolerate waste was the real cause of human erosion. It reflected the larger social problem of devaluing human labor and human worth.[27]

Wallace had positive things to say about rural Americans, who produced more children than their urban counterparts, and played a crucial role in building up society. "The land produces the life-stream of the nation," he explained, referring to "young people bred on the farms." In unmistakable language, Wallace urged the whole country to be "concerned that its breeding stock is taken care of, that the nation does not deteriorate at the source of its life-blood." This was the warning sign John Ford sought to get across in the film version of *The Grapes of Wrath*, when Ma Joad says, "Rich fellas . . . their kids ain't no good and die out, but we keep a-comin'. . . . We'll go on forever, Pa, cos we're the people." The city folk needed "the people," needed their fecundity. It was as though Jefferson and Franklin were talking to Wallace, Steinbeck, and Ford, still promoting the old English idea that national strength was bound up with demographic growth.[28]

Unfortunately, the Subsistence Homesteads Division ran into serious difficulties. First, the funding it received was meager; second, it took time for bureaucracy to approve and build communities. On top of everything else, the Homesteads Division faced a legal challenge that threatened the entire program with termination. President Roosevelt, as a result, issued an executive order creating an entirely new agency, the Resettlement Administration (RA), in 1935. Rexford G. Tugwell, a former economics professor at Columbia, was chosen to head the new agency. A charismatic figure with a sharp mind, he had a profound influence on the New Deal's overall approach to poverty.[29]

Unlike previous programs, the RA had a clear mandate to help the rural poor. It purchased submarginal land, resettled tenants, extended relief to drought victims, arranged with local doctors cooperative medical care for farmers, restored ruined lands, and supervised camps for migrant workers, especially in California. One of its central goals was to provide loans for farm improvements, and to help tenants obtain better living conditions and learn how to become farm owners—services that greatly expanded the ongoing program that was building experimental communities. The Resettlement Administration, and its replacement, the Farm Security Administration (1937), established regional headquarters; by 1941, it had project managers in every state. What Tugwell began in 1935 carried over to his successor, Will Alexander, who as the son of an Ozark farmer was the first southerner to be put in charge of a New Deal rural poverty agency. Both the RA and FSA were politically savvy agencies, consciously orchestrating publicity campaigns. At the forefront of their effort was Roy Stryker's photographic unit, which distributed optimal images to major news outlets.[30]

Tugwell went on the lecture circuit, did radio shows, and wrote articles. In the *New York Times,* he outlined the RA's program in terms of the four "R's"—retirement of bad land, relocation of rural poor, resettlement of the unemployed in suburban communities, and rehabilitation of farm families. In his activism, though, Tugwell was not really a Jeffersonian. In his worldview, the farm was not some sacred space for cultivating virtue; it was more often an unrewarding struggle with "vicious, ill-tempered soil." As a result, farmers suffered from overwork, bad housing, and an "ugly, brooding monotony." Instead of healthy yeomen, Jefferson's theory had produced generations of "human wastage"; wishing for universal home ownership was but a foolish dream.[31]

Tugwell was nothing if not controversial. Understanding that most tenants could not vote because of poll taxes, he made their elimination one of the requirements for states to get homestead loans. Changing the South required shifting the balance of power—his agency would enable poor whites to challenge the status quo. While cynical politicians continued to dismiss them as "lazy, shiftless, no-account," Tugwell sought to make them into a politically visible constituency. Here was a proactive federal agency.[32]

The opposition to his programs came from vested interests, specifically large-scale agribusiness and southerners resistant to any attention to (or attempts to subvert) the class order. Representing this crowd was Senator Harry F. Byrd of Virginia, who mouthed the conventional wisdom that "simple mountain people" didn't deserve electricity, refrigerators, or even indoor privies. Simple meant primitive, a people incapable of aspiring to a creditable way of life.[33]

To a range of critics, Tugwell was a "parlor pink" (i.e., a liberal with communist leanings). Republicans mocked him by using lines from a popular song of 1933, "Did You Ever See a Dream Walking?" Tugwell was "a dream walking," all airy philosophy. The government's liberal darling could be seen "winking at Marx" and at the same time "kissing the foot of Madison" for having given him the idea of a super-flexible Constitution. Somehow, in combining these two disparate historical personae, Tugwell was wearing a "Russian wig under a Founder's hat." Another journalist noted that "Tugwellism" was less about the man than about the times, that is, a contest about class politics and who could claim to represent poor whites. On the surface, this forty-three-year-old Ivy Leaguer, with a cool, "carefully-studied informality of appearance," projected an air of haughtiness and seemed to regard humanity as something for "experimentation." To Tugwell's critics, then, nothing about him suggested a bona fide understanding of rural America.[34]

Tugwell, however, refused to engage in a theatrical debate over what it meant to be a "man of the people." America already had a long history of politicians pretending to identify with the earnest plowman. In the South, it was more than a pastime—it was everything. The erudite Brain Truster, though raised on a dairy farm in upstate New York, couldn't claim to be of hillbilly stock, nor did he sport farmers' red suspenders like one of the New Deal's loudest critics, Georgia governor Eugene Talmadge. He was not a rustic clown like Huey Long, who captivated audiences. He didn't have a folksy nickname either, like South Carolina senator "Cotton Ed" Smith, who went on the warpath against Tugwell's appointment as undersecretary of agriculture even before Roosevelt named him as head of the Resettlement Administration. Before his confirmation hearing, Tugwell's friends had advised him to "affect a homely democratic manner, to suggest the dear old farm." He refused to do so.[35]

In 1936, a young Washington journalist named Blair Bolles accused Tugwell of a series of crimes against America. Writing for H. L. Mencken's *American Mercury,* he shared the renowned editor's choleric rage for harebrained uplifters. Bolles claimed that the poor who were under the agency's supervision were willing to "crawl" into the "impersonal lap" of government dependency. They were all deluded and undeserving— the litany will sound familiar: "hillbilly clay-eaters," "hoe-wielders" (backward tenant farmers looking for a handout), "urban poor who see success in green pastures," and, last but not least, "desert-dwelling Indians." Each of these was presumed a breed of men with nowhere to go.[36]

Again and again, enemies of the New Deal railed against the royalist bureaucrat "Rex" Tugwell. He continued to infuriate opposing congressmen by dismissing their logic and defending government patronage with the line "nothing is too good for these people." Tugwell had no patience for the illusion of democracy, or the pretense of being a man of the people, or the empty rhetoric of equal opportunity. An urbane "voice in the wilderness," he boldly challenged the credibility of the old, illusive belief that America's class boundaries were porous and that hard work was all it took to succeed.[37]

Tugwell's class argument was simple. He summed up his views in a 1934 speech in Kansas City when he said that the old standby refrain of "rugged individualism" really meant "the regimentation of the many for the benefit of the few." The New Deal's mission was to make individualism available to those ordinarily deprived of it, freeing the many from their virtual imprisonment at the hands of the few. Like Thomas Jefferson, and like Henry Wallace, Tugwell believed that concentration of power at the top destroyed democracy. But like James Madison, the founder he most admired, he remained confident that the state could act as a neutral arbiter among contending interests—bound, in this emergency, to intercede so as to prevent a hardening of class distinctions.[38]

Tugwell felt that the extension of loans to farmers was the most successful part of the Resettlement Administration, and most Americans agreed: a Gallup poll of 1936 found that 83 percent of respondents heartily endorsed the program. But the experimental communities, nearly two-thirds of which were in the South, did not do at all well. Though not under the supervision of the Resettlement Administration, Arthurdale, in the abandoned coal-mining region of Reedsville, West Virginia, was one notable lightning rod. Constantly in the news because it was the pet project of Eleanor Roosevelt, this experimental community was accused of wasting money and Works Progress Administration man-hours. A reporter for the *Saturday Evening Post* argued that the community was not even functioning as an organ of relief because the screening process was geared toward accepting only those applicants whose success seemed assured, rather than bringing in the folks who most needed government assistance. In the end, Congress ensured the failure of Arthurdale by refusing to support a factory that would have produced furniture for the U.S. Post Office while providing the community with a steady source of employment.[39]

Arthurdale cast a long shadow. The bad publicity it received colored the reception of other planned communities, as the FSA director testified before Congress in 1943. But the deeper problem of Arthurdale was rooted in its emphasis on home ownership. Even successful communities such as those outside Birmingham and Jasper, Alabama, failed in their mission to help the poorest, ultimately retaining only middle-class residents. Without subsidies, poorer families were not a worthy credit risk. A resident of Palmerdale who worked at the *Birmingham News-Age Herald* explained that he actually had two jobs instead of one: he worked at the newspaper from 9 p.m. until early morning, and then went home to care for his fields. True, he freed his family from debt and fed his four children with canned goods, but the homestead model only served to double the labor of families like his, rather than to ease their burdens.[40]

The publicity generated by the RA and FSA contributed to unrealistic expectations and time-mangled appearances. Some photographs of Palmerdale, and Penderlea in North Carolina, showed sharp-looking homes, ornamented with children on bicycles; another showed a man with a mule-drawn stone-boat (or it might have been a plow)—an apt scene in an 1840s daguerreotype, perhaps, but out of place in depicting a modern home. Barely hanging on to his symbolic existence, the yeoman had become a quaint (and contrived) artifact of a once-pristine American life.[41]

Penderlea Homesteads in North Carolina was showcased as the government's solution to tenancy. The residents were not wealthy, but they were happy amid "pleasant, congenial, and beautiful surroundings." But perfect homes did not make perfect communities. Sabotage emerged from within the ranks of residents. Cliques formed in Penderlea, leading some to refuse to participate in community activities and to ridicule those who tried to do things "by the book." Tensions flared as residents failed—or refused—to adjust to a middle-class environment: detailed records had to be kept, parliamentary rules had to be used at meetings, and household conveniences that wives had never seen before were included in the residences. Bureaucratic missteps explained some of these troubles, but it was the artificially imposed class structure that most disturbed the peace. Middle-class behavior was not easy to teach.[42]

It took more than a village. Cooperative farming was no part of southern practice, and especially among small (or tenant) farmers. Tugwell understood the problem. Americans in general were not hostile to planned communities, which explains the popularity of Tugwell's favorite projects. The "Greenbelt towns" of Maryland (just outside Washington, DC), Milwaukee, and Cincinnati attracted an amazing twelve million visitors in 1936–37. Here, federal housing revolutionized methods of prefabrication, laying a strong foundation for the growth of suburbia in

An iconic image of Penderlea Homesteads (1936), which oddly juxtaposes a modern home and a mule-drawn stone-boat.

Homestead, Penderlea, North Carolina (1936): LC-USF33-000717-M2, Library of Congress Prints and Photographs Division, Washington, DC

the aftermath of World War II. However, the federal government could not bridge the North-South divide when it came to standards of public rural housing; southern projects were administered by southerners who were loath to spend on amenities—such as indoor plumbing. Will Alexander, the Missourian who replaced Tugwell at the RA, and then took over at the FSA, remarked on the persistence of southern backwardness: "If we could house all our low-income farm families with the same standards Danes use for their hogs, we would be a long step ahead." Southern politicians shortchanged rural Americans in another crucial way: they made sure that the New Deal's signature Social Security program excluded farm laborers.[43]

Tugwell's tenure at the RA was short—just one year—but his influence lingered. The most definitive government statement on problems facing poor farmers, *Farm Tenancy: Report of the President's Committee* (1937), showed his hand as well as that of Wilson and Wallace. No less important, the report reflected the insights of "southern regionalists" Arthur Raper and Howard Odum.[44]

More than anyone else, Howard Odum worked to change the meaning of the South and the character of "poor folk," as prominent government officials of the New Deal came to understand them. He was both a sociologist and a psychologist by training. Hired at the University of North Carolina in 1920, he headed the Department of Sociology while simultaneously serving as the first director of the School of Public Welfare. A Georgian by birth, Odum studied the classics at Emory before earning his doctorate in psychology at Clark University (a faculty made famous after Sigmund Freud's landmark visit); he then acquired his Ph.D. in sociology at Columbia University. A man of tireless energy, Odum published twenty-five books and nearly two hundred articles, founding the journal *Social Forces* as a forum for new approaches to studies of the South. In his spare time, he was a breeder of cattle.[45]

He began his close relationship with the federal government when President Hoover named him to the Research Commission on Social Trends. But it was in 1936 that Professor Odum issued his most comprehensive study, *Southern Regions of the United States*, a text of more than six hundred pages that became the New Deal's major resource for regional planning. One of his students, journalist Gerald W. Johnson, translated the massive study into a readable and popular book, momentously titled *The Wasted Land*. Another star student, Arthur Raper, wrote the definitive work on southern farm tenancy, and served as a principal researcher for the Division of Farm Population and Rural Welfare within the Bureau of Agricultural Economics. Odum collaborated with Roy Stryker of the FSA's photographic unit in overseeing a three-year sociological project of thirteen counties in North Carolina and Virginia.[46]

The real strength of Odum's work came from the amount of information he amassed. He was able to prove that the South had surrendered ninety-seven million acres to erosion (an area larger than the two Carolinas and Georgia); it had squandered the chances of millions of people by tolerating poverty and illiteracy; and it had ignored human potential by refusing to provide technological training, or even basic services, to its people. The overwhelming power of Odum's data undercut (what Odum himself called) *Gone with the Wind* nostalgia—the collective self-image elite southerners had cultivated. Here was one southerner who wanted to see some "sincere, courageous telling of the truth about the South." He was "tired of the defense complex," he said, and the unending ridicule, complacency, ignorance, and, above all, the poverty. The greatest virtue of *Southern Regions* was its quantitative weight and its objective outlook. As the southern historian Broadus Mitchell insisted at the same time, "The South does not need defense, but exposition."[47]

The primary target of Odum's research was sectionalism's destructive legacy. Mitchell interpreted Odum in such a way as to say that there was no longer a justification for using Yankee oppression for the South's refusal to change. To Odum, there were "many Souths"; what was needed now was a *regional* vision. As a cattle breeder, he compared the sectional dictate to "cultural inbreeding," and to the "stagnation" that came from resisting the "cross-fertilization of ideas" and by refusing to engage with those beyond one's state. When he looked at the Tennessee Valley Authority, he saw unmistakably the most successful of New Deal projects in regional planning; the TVA had harnessed the power of seven monumental dams, coordinating among seven states and employing nearly ten thousand people in an area that previously had suffered under tremendous poverty. Odum said he hoped the TVA "would constitute the 49th State." The straitjacket of states' rights had suffocated southern progress long enough.[48]

Odum was right about the TVA. It was a shining example of positive planning. Its dams alone were marvels of engineering, elegant and modern architectural wonders. Intelligent management resulted in soil conservation; flood, malaria, and pollution control; reforestation; and improved fertilization—all sensible land-use strategies. The TVA led to well-designed communities that supported libraries and health and recreation facilities—everything that Wilson had prescribed for the homestead villages. There were training centers in agriculture, marketing, automotive and electrical repair, mechanical work and metalwork; there were classes in engineering and mathematics at nearby colleges, plus unprecedented opportunities for adult education. A bookmobile carried libraries to workers and their families.[49]

Odum knew it would be extremely difficult to dislodge cultural prejudices. In 1938, he sent questionnaires to distinguished academics across the country, asking each to define what "poor white" meant to him. Where and when did they first hear the term? he wanted to know. Were there state and regional differences in how the term was used? Where did they think the term originated? What were its distinctive features? What other terms were prevalent that carried similar meaning?[50]

The responses revealed how slippery the label "poor white" could be. While several sociologists said outright that the term was "fuzzy," a loose example of name-calling, most of Odum's known forty-six respondents listed as many negative attributes associated with poor whites as came to mind. The most popular adjective was "shiftless." It was connected to a string of synonyms: purposeless, hand to mouth, lazy, unambitious, no account, no desire to improve themselves, inertia. All these descriptions conflated the unwillingness to work with some innate character flaw.[51]

"Shiftless" was not a new word. Chronicling his southern tour in the 1850s, Frederick Law Olmsted had used it to categorize slothful slave-owners and slaves alike. It was a favorite word among New Englanders in describing bad farmers, and was a common reproach toward tavern-keepers and other immoral characters who congregated in dens with lowly laborers. By Theodore Roosevelt's time it was the word of choice in legislation that punished deserting husbands; "shiftlessness" was a major symptom in the eugenicist's diagnosis of the degenerate. And it was of course second nature to vagrants and hoboes. W. J. Cash, in *The Mind of the South* (1941), portrayed a shiftless poor white sitting under a tree, holding a jug and surrounded by his hounds, while his wife and children were out working the fields with a kind of "lackadaisical digging."[52]

Social proximity to blacks was the second most popular explanation for their association with shiftlessness. In 1929, with his appearance in the movie *Hearts in Dixie*, the very visible African American actor known as Stepin Fetchit began a film career in which he popularized for an entire generation the crude stereotype of laziness suggested by his on-screen name. In his response to Odum on poor whites, Ira de A. Reid, a black scholar at Atlanta University, recalled that when he was growing up, "race etiquette" required that he never address a "poor white" with that name, unless he expected to be called "nigger" in return. For Reid, "white trash," "poor whites," and "niggers" all conveyed the same social stigma.[53]

Many of Odum's respondents claimed that the designation "po' white trash" derived from black vernacular. According to a Mississippian, when whites of the upper or middle class used it, they qualified it with "as blacks would say." Odum's respondents noted that poor whites lived near poor black neighborhoods, and it was virtually impossible to distinguish their dwellings. To some middle-class whites, the slight elevation in status of poor whites over poor blacks was but an empty courtesy. From outside the South, in Cincinnati, one sociologist wrote Odum that mountain whites were called "briar hoppers" and subject to de facto segregation just as urban blacks were. ("Briar hoppers" was a variation on the old English slur of "bogtrotters," aimed at the Irish.)[54]

To Odum's respondents, the twentieth century had had little effect. Poor whites were still adjudged a breed apart, an ill-defined class halfway between white and black. Under no circumstances did they ever socialize with, let alone marry, respectable whites. To another of Odum's correspondents they were like a mule to a horse or a hound to a dog; whereas dogs were "respectable," hounds were "ornery." As dyed-in-the-wool racists said of all blacks, it was said of white trash that, like the leopard, he could not change his spots.[55]

How could educated Americans have denied the effect of such persistent prejudice in distorting the southern class system? The reason is actually rather obvious: a fear of unleashing genuine class upheaval—which even the liberal elite were loath to do—led significant numbers to blame the poor for their own failure. Odum saw differently, and was instrumental in reframing the meaning of rural poverty. He argued that poor whites had a culture—what he called "folkways." He did not think that they had to remain hapless pawns. Nor did their upward path mean merely imitating the middle class; they could shape a viable existence by drawing on their own folk values, rather than striving to be a lesser version of the white-collar class. The solution for poor folk rested on giving them access to education, allowing them to become self-sufficient. This demanded restructuring the South's resource management. The region had to develop a more diverse and technologically advanced economy and agricultural system, which in turn would require a more highly skilled population of workers. But transforming every man and woman would be a long uphill battle, of course. One of Odum's respondents put it bluntly: "No one knows what to do with him." As long as he appeared stuck, he would remain no less a feature of the static South than the gully and the mule.[56]

It would take the Tennessean James Agee to probe the meaning of "poor white" on a truly meaningful level. In his powerfully drawn, enduringly evocative *Let Us Now Praise Famous Men* (1941), Agee attempted to toss the source of the white trash fetish back onto the middle class. The unusual book included the chaste still life–style photographs of Walker Evans, and addressed what Odum's slow-to-change cohort refused to do: interrogate how an interpreter imposed his values on the subject. There could be no such thing as objective journalism.

Agee opened the book by wondering out loud how a Harvard-educated, middle-class man like himself could write about poor whites without turning them into objects of pity or disgust. He did not want to be a mere gawker. How could he "pry intimately into the lives of an undefended and appallingly damaged group of human beings, an ignorant and helpless rural family, for the purpose of parading the nakedness, disadvantage and humiliation of these lives before another group of human beings, in the name of science, of 'honest journalism'"? Was it possible to convey the "cruel radiance of what is"? Probably not.[57]

So Agee experimented with different strategies, offering detailed descriptions of material objects: shoes, overalls, the sparse arrangement of furnishings in the tenant's home. With a meticulous attention to detail, he tried in words to imitate the camera's "ice-cold" vision. In another of his departures from conventional reporting, he interspersed what he imagined were the unspoken thoughts of the poor tenant with the uncensored insults he had heard from the landlord. Inside the mind of the tenant, he voiced disbelief: how did he get "trapped," how did he become "beyond help, beyond hope"? He gave his subjects real feelings, descriptive laments. The landlord's cruelty comes through his laughter over Agee's enjoyment of the tenants' "home cooking." The landlord curses a poor cropper as a "dirty son-of-a-bitch" who had bragged that he hadn't bought his family a bar of soap in five years. A woman in one of the tenant families was, in the landlord's words, the "worst whore" in this part of this country—second only to her mother. The whole bunch were, to the owner, "the lowest trash you can find."[58]

There was a method to Agee's madness. In this strangely introspective, deeply disturbing narrative, the author tries to force readers to look beyond conventional ways of seeing the poor. Instead of blaming them, he asks his audience to acknowledge their own complicity. The poor are not dull or slow-witted, he insists; they have merely internalized a kind of "anesthesia," which numbs them against the "shame and insult of discomforts, insecurities, and inferiorities." The southern middle class deserves the greater portion of shame, and especially those who excused their own callous indifference with the line, "They are 'used' to it."[59]

Despite its subsequent literary success, Agee's unsettling text reached few readers in 1941. For its part, Odum's work came under attack for speaking above (rather than to) the poor tenant farmer. One of Odum's most outspoken critics was the Vanderbilt University English professor and poet Donald Davidson, who was also hostile to the TVA, which he saw as evidence of northern meddling. As one of the contributors to *I'll Take My Stand*, Davidson defended the old agrarian ideal of the South. He dared to praise the Ku Klux Klan for defeating the "detestable" northern missionaries of the Freedmen's Bureau, and his only regret was that the KKK could not prevent the rise of the "more subtle utopians" of the New South (by which he meant Odum and his University of North Carolina crowd). The scholarly "southern regionalists" could never unify the South, Davidson declared. Odum's "indices" could not be translated into the "language of the 'ignorant man.'" What remained was an apparent paradox: Was it only the sectional demagogue who would ever be able to co-opt the poor in the South? Even if an Agee or an Odum momentarily captured the "cruel radiance of what is," wasn't it obvious that the poor whites they wished to free weren't listening? That was what Davidson believed.[60]

Somewhere between the writing styles of Agee and Odum was a new kind of southern writer. Jonathan Daniels's *A Southerner Discovers the South* (1938) not only made the bestseller list, but also won over Franklin and Eleanor Roosevelt. Here was a North Carolina journalist with an eye for irony. He avoided the density of Odum's encyclopedic study, and he steered clear of the sleepy pastoralism of the southern agrarian. With nary a hint of defensiveness, he traveled thousands of miles through the South and let the people he met talk for themselves.[61]

Daniels found evidence that disproved Davidson's critique of Howard Odum when he happened on a small-town lawyer who owned and cherished all of the sociologist's books. He visited the famous Providence Canyon, a 150-foot-deep Georgia gully, which became a strange monument to soil erosion and a natural wonder. He attacked the South's prison mentality, the idea that generation after generation of manual laborers should accept their exploitation as natural. At Cannon Mills, in North Carolina, he noted the cyclone fences that turned mills into virtual prisons. Across the street from one massive factory was a playground. The unintended lesson was to "teach the children that property is afraid of the people—their people."[62]

He offered varied portraits of poor whites, defending "restlessness" and refusing to call it shiftlessness. Daniels liked what he saw in Norris, Tennessee, a planned town that was part of the TVA. It was not the photoelectric cell lighting and heating of the big school building that impressed him so much as the "collision of children" inside the school— the "hill children of the big, poor families" alongside the children of engineers. Here was a clear-cut experiment in class desegregation. If only this was America, he thought.[63]

As Ma Joad from *The Grapes of Wrath* had put it, Daniels repeated for his southern audience: the poor are always coming. He praised the TVA for discovering that ordinary southern whites were receptive to training if given a fair chance. Some, he acknowledged, were "underfed," some "feeble-minded, perverted, insane." But they could not represent the whole poor population—*or the future*. It was not only pellagra or illiteracy that stood in the way of their rise; there was also the fear of the wealthier classes that poor whites, like blacks, might not be willing to stay in their place. Daniels refuted the "slander" that had been perpetuated by the educated classes, and he made sure his readers took heed: "The Southern Negro is not an incurably ignorant ape. The Southern white masses are not biologically degenerate."[64]

Daniels was unwavering in his belief that Jeffersonian democracy had long since died, only to be replaced by demagogues on the order of Huey Long, who, following on the heels of generations of southern patricians, plundered the people at will. He took up Odum's cautionary advice, insisting that all planning for southern revival had to start at the bottom if it was to effect anything approaching real change. "Maybe still one Reb can beat ten Yankees," wrote Daniels. But "it is irrelevant." Rebel pride had blinded all classes. "The tyrants and the plutocrats and the poor all need teaching. One of them no more than the others." Odum, Agee, and Daniels all wanted to see the South rescued from its ideological trap. They were not cynical; they were hopeful. They recognized that simple solutions—a smattering of prettified homesteads—were no cure. Something grander, on the scale of the TVA, represented the only chance to shake up the existing consensus and rearrange class structure.[65]

In the 1930s, the forgotten man and woman became a powerful symbol of economic struggle all across America. A good number of voices paid special attention to poor whites who haunted the South. The problem was not: "No one knows what to do with him." It was this: "No one wants to see him as he really is: one of us, an American."

CHAPTER TEN

The Cult of the Country Boy

Elvis Presley, Andy Griffith, and LBJ's Great Society

I'm a self-confessed raw country boy and guitar-playing fool.
—Elvis Presley (1956)

Lyndon wasn't upper class at all. Country boy, grown up in the hills.
—Virginia Foster Durr, Alabama civil rights activist (1991)

Most will remember the famous photograph of Elvis Presley standing alongside President Richard Nixon in the Oval Office. But why is it forgotten that Presley gained the friendship of Lyndon Baines Johnson? At Graceland, Presley added a three-television console like the one LBJ had in the Oval Office; "the King" also hung in his home an "All the Way with LBJ" bumper sticker from the 1964 presidential campaign, and posed for a publicity photo with the president's daughter, Lynda Bird Johnson, who at the time was dating the actor George Hamilton. Presley and Johnson at first seem to be the oddest of couples—but they had more in common than their separate celebrity worlds would suggest. Both became national figures who challenged—whose very lives disrupted—the historically toxic characterization of poor whites.[1]

When Elvis stormed onto the national scene in 1956, he seemed to be doing everything he could to act nonwhite. He openly embraced black musical style, black pompadour hair, and flashy outfits that had been associated with blacks as well. His gyrations caused his critics to compare his wildly sexualized dancing to the "hootchy-kootchy," or burlesque striptease, and the rebellious zoot suit crowd. His phenomenal fame and adoring fans helped to propel him to *The Ed Sullivan Show,* and from there to the silver screen. He soon owned a stable of Cadillacs. Elvis had achieved what no white trash working-class male had ever dreamt possible: he was at once cool and sexually transgressive and a "country boy." No longer a freakish rural outcast, as in the past, Elvis was a "Hillbilly Cat," someone many teenage boys wished they could be.[2]

Lyndon Johnson's sudden elevation to the office of chief executive on November 22, 1963, came as a great shock to the nation. Eerily replaying what had happened a century earlier, a second unelected Johnson entered the presidency after a shocking assassination. But this time, instead of the sorrow-laden, war-weary Lincoln, the nation had lost the vigorous, photogenic, East Coast elite John F. Kennedy. In the wake of tragedy, the seasoned southern politician pursued an aggressive legislative agenda in favor of civil rights and social reform—the most dramatic foray since FDR. The "Great Society," as his vast array of programs became known, called for the elimination of poll taxes and voting discrimination, the promotion of education and health care funding, and daring new programs in an effort to eradicate poverty. Yet what made LBJ different from his Democratic predecessor was the necessity that he reinvent himself by shedding the predictable trappings of a southern backwater identity—which he did without unlearning his famous Texan drawl. The accidental president had to transform how he was perceived on television, how he was judged by Washington reporters, how he was received as a national leader. Though Johnson had a proven record as a New Dealer and modern progressive, on the national stage he was still regarded as a regional figure. He refused to go easy on white rule in the South. In his 1965 inaugural address, he made progressive change a matter of national survival. He wanted to use his powers to work toward broad social equality.[3]

In many ways, Johnson's insistence on change echoed what the sociologist Howard Odum had prescribed in earlier decades: southerners had to free themselves from their misplaced nostalgia for the Old Confederacy. He wasn't afraid of modernity. "I do not believe that the Great Society is the ordered, changeless, and sterile battalion of ants," Johnson put it bluntly upon inauguration in 1965. Mindless conformity, whether Soviet or southern in style, was stifling and repressive.[4]

His heroes had not been Andrew Johnson or James K. Vardaman; Franklin Roosevelt was the politician he most admired. During the Depression, Johnson was a strong proponent of rural electrification, and he ran the jobs corps program, the National Youth Administration, in Texas. He had no patience for country-bumpkin antics either. LBJ loved modern technology, campaigned across Texas by prop plane before World War II, and was the first to use a helicopter in his Senate campaign of 1948. That year, winning in a close race, he presented himself as a worldly politician, jettisoning the folksy style of his opponent, whom a Johnson aide described as "old hat, old ways, old everything." As majority leader of the Senate, and during his vice presidency as chairman of the National Aeronautics and Space Council, it was Lyndon Johnson who first promoted "stepping into the space race" and making it a national priority to put a man on the moon.[5]

There were no red suspenders in this southern boy's closet, no blustering race-baiting to mark his career. The public had no difficulty understanding the high moral tone of LBJ's presidential oratory. He despised the false rhetoric of those Dixiecrats who feigned class solidarity with poor whites—rhetoric that typically involved angry appeals to white supremacy. As president, when he advocated civil rights, Lyndon Johnson spoke the language of brotherly love and inclusiveness. In spite of all this, the old country-boy image still haunted him.[6]

Presumably by coincidence, as President Johnson stood tall under the glare of the national spotlight, TV network executives discovered the hick sitcom. Three of the most popular shows in the 1960s were *The Andy Griffith Show; Gomer Pyle, U.S.M.C.;* and *The Beverly Hillbillies.* All revived the homespun, albeit unassimilable, traits of good old "Sug," the rural pol of the 1840s. Lyndon Johnson fondly remembered Roosevelt as "a daddy to me," and as town sheriff, Andy Griffith served as the paternal caretaker of Mayberry, North Carolina. *The Andy Griffith Show* had the feel of the thirties, not the sixties; it was a nostalgic rewrite of the Great Depression, featuring a town of misfits. Speaking about his role, Griffith insisted that he was not playing a "yokel"; the creator of the show described the sheriff as a clever man with a "wry sense of humor" on the order of the late Will Rogers, the good-natured Oklahoma humorist and film hero. As for Mayberry, most problems were solved around Andy's kitchen table—reminiscent of how Americans huddled around the radio listening to FDR's fireside chats. Outsiders were welcome in Andy's world, where the virtues of small-town democracy shone.[7]

Though the actor stopped short of saying it, Sheriff Andy was indeed surrounded by yokels, because television traded on the worst stereotypes. Mayberry's population included the gullible gas station attendant Gomer Pyle (before he got his own show) and his cousin Goober, and Ernest T. Bass, a screeching mountaineer who went on wild rampages.

As a writer for *Time* noted of Jim Nabors's Gomer, the naïve enlistee "spouts homilies out of a lopsided mouth and lopes around uncertainly like a plowboy stepping through a field of cow dung." He is a "walking disaster," who in his subsequent spin-off show single-handedly fouls up the bureaucracy of the entire Marine Corps.[8]

With the Clampetts of Beverly Hills, as the comedian Bob Hope joked, Americans had their embodiment of TV "wasteland"—a wasteland with an outhouse. Episode after episode, Granny and her kin were stymied by the science of the doorbell and the unbearable complexity of kitchen appliances, giving viewers the saddest sort of reminder of the culture shock experienced by real sharecroppers in FSA resettlement communities. Buddy Ebsen's prime-time hillbillies appeared on the cover of the *Saturday Evening Post,* sketched as characters in Grant Wood's iconic painting of 1930, *American Gothic*. This was yet another unsubtle allusion to the long-held belief that white trash were an evolutionary throwback.[9]

The Beverly Hillbillies recast as Grant Wood's famous 1930 painting, *American Gothic.*

Saturday Evening Post, February 2, 1963

The Beverly Hillbillies had its defenders. To the creator of the show, "our hillbillies" were clean and wholesome, and the network was actually doing a service in uplifting the image of rural Americans. "The word hillbilly," he insisted, "will ultimately have a new meaning in the United States as a result of our show." His optimism proved to be misplaced.[10]

Jed Clampett was no Davy Crockett, even though Buddy Ebsen had in fact played the gruff sidekick to Fess Parker's coon-capped Crockett in the fifties Disney saga. The differences between Jed and Davy were stark. Hollywood hillbillies could only be crude objects of audience laughter—mockery, not admiration. They conjured none of the frontier fantasy of the rugged individualist Crockett (or Fess Parker's TV Daniel Boone). Nothing could redeem them. The Clampetts drove a 1930s-era Ford jalopy, and Granny sat on board in a rocking chair—a camp version of John Ford's desperate Joad family.[11]

Fess Parker's buckskin champion was a jaunty country boy, a genial Gary Cooper–style suburban dad. All viewers understood that Parker's Crockett represented the best qualities imagined of early America. The 1955 Davy Crockett craze caused adoring fans to mob the actor in a way that momentarily put him in a league with Elvis; coonskin caps flew off store shelves as Disney Studios staged a publicity tour. Parker, a towering Texan, even made a stop on Capitol Hill. In a photograph distributed over the wire services, then-senator Lyndon Johnson and Speaker of the House Sam Rayburn struck up a pose with "Davy" and his rifle, Ol' Betsy.[12]

Their signature laugh track aside, sixties comedies were not purely escapist fare. They tapped into a larger anxiety amid the mass migration of poor whites who headed north and created hillbilly ghettos in cities such as Baltimore, St. Louis, Detroit, Chicago, and Cincinnati—which only fueled existing prejudice against "briar hoppers" (recalling the nomenclature of an Odum respondent). Writing about poor whites in Chicago in 1968, the syndicated columnist Paul Harvey drew a practical connection for his readers: "Suppose a real-life likeness of TV's Beverly Hillbillies should move to the big city without those millions of dollars in the bank."[13]

The trio of sitcoms tapped into suspicions that modern America had failed to create a genuine melting pot; the cultural distance between rural and urban life, between rich and poor, was immense. Don Knotts's slapstick character Barney Fife, Sheriff Andy's bumbling cousin, didn't belong in the big city any more than the corn cracker of *Davy Crockett's Almanack of 1837* did in the 1830s. Despite his drill sergeant's unrelenting badgering, Gomer, the hapless private, failed to conform to military culture; he wasn't fit for the Marines, let alone for white-collar corporate America. And the Clampetts may have bought a mansion in the heart of Hollywood, but they had not moved even one rung on the social ladder. They didn't even try to behave like middle-class Americans.

Hal Humphrey of the *Los Angeles Times* observed in 1963 that the joy of watching *The Beverly Hillbillies* was linked to the fact that "most Americans are extremely class-conscious." No matter what the plotline, every episode pitted the mercenary banker Milburn Drysdale, his "social-climbing wife," and "boob" of a son (a young man of questionable virility) against the low-down Clampetts. In Humphrey's opinion, the "Joe Doakses," or average viewers, got to see a bunch of "ragged hill people," who were "obviously . . . inferior," outsmarting equally undeserving "big shots." Theirs was, in short, a contest between "snobs" and "slobs." As far as the critic was concerned, the show's creator had come up with a formula that camouflaged class conflict with laughs. Finally, he joked, the class-bashing TV series "cashes in on Groucho Marx's theory of class struggle—or was that Karl Marx?"[14]

In the face of social upheaval, as so many old boundaries and prejudices shifted, Americans generally denied what they remained: highly class conscious. The interconnected civil rights movement and culture wars of the fifties and sixties were marked by social stratification. As ownership of a home in the suburbs came to represent the American dream, the most controversial housing option was, significantly, the trailer park. Segregation, then, was more than simply a racial issue. Zoning laws made it inevitable that housing would adhere to a class-delineated geography. The working class had its bowling alleys and diners, and "white trash" its trailer park slums, both of which contrasted sharply with the backyard barbecues of all-white neighborhoods in favored suburbs, zoned for the middle class. We forget that President Johnson's Great Society programs targeted both urban ghettos *and* impoverished white areas of Appalachia. Vietnam has been referred to as the living-room war, yet on their black-and-white television sets in 1957, Americans had already watched a racial and class war, as angry poor whites screamed curses at well-mannered black students as they tried to enter Little Rock's Central High School.

It is for reasons such as these that the poor country boy Elvis symbolized a lot of things for the generation that came of age in the fifties. While whitening African American music and challenging conservative sexual mores, he retained a social identity that was close to the story line of *The Beverly Hillbillies*. Here was a son of a white sharecropper, suddenly catapulted to a place of wealth and fame; he purchased Graceland, a mansion in Memphis, where he lived with his parents. For his beloved mother he bought a pink Cadillac, and to make the house truly a home she could appreciate, he built her a chicken coop in the backyard.[15]

As Elvis became the "country squire" of Graceland, middle-class Americans found themselves promoting the merits of suburbia more generally. Vice President Richard Nixon, for one, saw the expanding housing market as a powerful tool in waging Cold War diplomacy. In 1959, the world's two superpowers agreed to a cultural exchange: the Soviets prepared an exhibit on Sputnik and space exploration, which was put on display in New York City; for its part, the United States chose an earthbound emblem of its national pride, a typical ranch-style home, which was set up in Sokolniki Park for the edification of Russian crowds.[16]

Speaking at the opening ceremony in Moscow, Nixon took stock of the thirty-one million American families that owned homes, the forty-four million citizens who drove fifty-six million cars, and the fifty million who watched their own television sets. At this opportunistic moment, the vice president did his best to wear multiple hats, sounding on the one hand like a Madison Avenue ad man, and on the other as a prophet of the new middle class. Either way, he explicitly denied being representative of a shallow materialism. The real wonder of America's achievement, he professed, was that the "world's largest capitalist country" had "come closest to the ideal of prosperity for all in a classless society." These words strike at the heart of the matter. For Nixon, the United States was more than a land of plenty. Democratic in its collective soul, it had nearly achieved a kind of utopia. For the first time in history, capitalism was not the engine of greed, aimed at monopolizing wealth and resources; free enterprise in the 1950s was a magic elixir that was succeeding in erasing

class lines, especially through home ownership, or so he wanted it understood.[17]

The Nixons sold themselves as the perfect suburban family. Not long
before his Moscow trip, the vice president and his family took a trip to
Disneyland, which made the front pages. During the 1960 campaign,
when Nixon contested John F. Kennedy for the presidency, it was Pat
Nixon who praised her husband (and included herself) as the personifica-
tion of the American dream. In anticipation of her husband's nomination,
she told reporters that their success embodied the promise of the postwar generation, "where people of humble circumstances can go up the
ladder through sheer hard work and obtain what they work for." If she
happened to become First Lady, she said, she would be the first "working
girl" ever to inhabit the White House. Republican marketers used Pat
aggressively, producing tons of campaign materials that included badges,
flags, brochures, combs, jewelry, and a variety of buttons, all of which
boosted Pat as the ideal suburban homemaker. Party organizers stormed
the barricades of suburban shopping centers with "Patmobiles" and "Pat
Parades." Unlike a stunning young Jacqueline Bouvier Kennedy decked
out in "French couture," Pat Nixon picked her clothing off the store racks
and chose those items she could easily pack.[18]

The Nixons hailed from Whittier, in southern California, an area
of the Sunbelt that underwent dramatic changes from 1946 to 1970. As
millions of Americans bought new homes, suburban enclaves arose in
the orbit of metropolitan Los Angeles, Phoenix, Houston, Miami, and
elsewhere. One of the best-publicized housing developments of the era
grew in Levittown on the outskirts of New York City. The Levitts thought
big, putting up 17,400 houses and attracting 82,000 residents to their
Long Island development. This sweeping success led them to construct
two massive subdivisions in Bucks County, Pennsylvania, and Willing-
boro, New Jersey. As skilled promoters, the Levitts did more than simply build homes. Like their earliest progenitor, Richard Hakluyt of old
Elizabethan England, they were planting self-sustaining colonies in the
hinterland. The Levitts imagined suburbs as middle-class consumer outposts, geared for leisure activities: baseball fields, bicycle pathways, and
swimming pools complemented commercially zoned areas for shopping
centers.[19]

The key to the Levitts' system was not just cheaper housing, but homogeneous populations—in their phrasing, "stabilized" neighborhoods. They meant racial and class homogeneity, which led them to endorse "restrictive covenants" prohibiting owners from selling their homes to black families. The Levitts knew the South, because their first large-scale project was an all-white facility for wartime workers in Norfolk, Virginia. By planting suburbs in quasi-rural areas, the Levitts recognized that the value of land was not determined by industry or commerce. As isolated outposts, land values were tied to the class status of the occupants. Buying a home here required the male breadwinner to have a steady income—a mark of the new fifties middle class.[20]

Levittown was dubbed a "garden community." But the new style of tract homes uneasily occupied this rustic space. During the fifties, the pastoral image of suburbs was applied to all kinds of bedroom communities. Popular magazines featured wives tending their gardens, husbands grilling at their barbecues. This was a fanciful recasting of the Jeffersonian ideal: suburbanites were the new, let us say, "backyard yeomanry." To add to the Jeffersonian call for exurban procreative strength, the new suburbs acquired unsubtle nicknames like "Fertile Acres," owing to the high birthrates in young families. Yet many critics saw uniform homes and neat lawns as hollow symbols—a far cry from genuine democratic virtues.[21]

Instead of eliminating class distinctions, suburbs were turned into class-conscious fortresses. Zoning ordinances set lot sizes and restricted the construction of apartment buildings, emphasizing single-dwelling homes to keep out undesirable lower-class families. In Mahwah, New Jersey, for example, the local government attracted a Ford plant to the town, and then passed an ordinance that required one-acre lots containing homes in the $20,000 price range, ostensibly meaning that low-paid workers in the plant would have to live elsewhere. In New York's Westchester County, the board of education agreed to build a deluxe school in a wealthy neighborhood, while doing nothing for schools in depressed-income areas where lower-class Italian and black families lived. In Los Angeles, suburbs were appraised by the Federal Housing Authority along class lines: high marks were given to places where gardening was a popular hobby, and low marks to places where poor whites raised food in their backyards. Elvis's mother's chicken coop would have been frowned upon.[22]

In this and other ways, the federal government underwrote the growth of the new suburban frontier. Tax laws gave homeowners who took out mortgages an attractive deduction. Government made it profitable for banks to grant mortgages to upstanding veterans and to men with steady jobs. The Servicemen's Readjustment Act of 1944, better known as the GI Bill, created the Veterans Administration, which oversaw the ex-soldiers' mortgage program. Together, the FHA and the VA worked to provide generous terms: Uncle Sam insured as much as 90 percent of the typical veteran's mortgage, thereby encouraging lenders to provide low interest rates and low monthly payments. Along these same lines, when potential buyers queued up for Levittown homes, the builder initially privileged veterans. With such perks, it became cheaper for "desirable" white men to buy a home than to rent an apartment. And rather than lift up everyone, the system tended to favor those who were already middle class, or those working-class families with steady incomes.[23]

Suburban subdivisions encouraged buyers to live with their "own kind," constantly sorting people by religion, ethnicity, race, and class. The esteemed architectural critic Lewis Mumford described Levittown as a "one-class community." In 1959, the bestselling author and journalist Vance Packard summed up the suburban filtration process as "birds-of-a-feather flocking." As we have so often seen, the importance of animal stock, and of "breed" generally, remained on the tip of the American tongue when idiomatic distinctions of class identity were being made.[24]

In 1951, the Levitts opened their second development, in Bucks County, Pennsylvania, after U.S. Steel decided to build its Fairless Works in the area. It attracted steelworkers, as well as a community of construction workers who established a trailer camp. Although little actually separated the two working-class communities—the families were stable and had about the same number of children—the Levittowners felt that their community was a "symbol of middle-class attainment," while the camp's residents were labeled "trailer trash." To expel the trailer families, local officials quickly passed ordinances. Offended local residents dismissed the trailer families as "transients," saying that they should be "gotten rid of as soon as possible." One of the arguments marshaled against the trailer enclave will sound familiar: the preservation of property values. The construction workers were deemed trash not because of their class background per se, but because they lived in trailers. It was their homes on wheels that carried the stigma.[25]

The trailer occupies an important, if uncertain, place in the American cultural imagination. Representing on the one hand a symbol of untethered freedom, the mobile home simultaneously acquired its reputation as a "tin can," a small, cheap, confined way of life. When you live in a trailer, you are literally rootless, and privacy disappears. Neighbors see and hear. At their worst, such places have been associated with liberty's dark side: deviant, dystopian wastelands set on the fringe of the metropolis.

Trailers had been controversial since the 1930s. Aside from the sleek streamlined capsules that traverse the open road, these rickety boxes tend to be viewed as eyesores. Almost as soon as they were turned into permanent housing, many were associated with slums built on town dumps. As an object, the trailer is something modern and antimodern, chic and gauche, liberating and suffocating. Unlike the dull but safe middle American suburb, trailer parks contain folks who appear on the way out, not up: retired persons, migrant workers, and the troubled poor. This remains true today.

Prior to World War II, the first generation of trailers were jerry-rigged contraptions built in backyards, expressly used on hunting and fishing trips. When they hit the road in the thirties, right when Okies took to their jalopies along Route 66, one journalist called them "monstrosities," shanties on wheels. War changed that. Faced with a severe housing shortage, the federal government purchased trailers for soldiers, sailors, and defense workers. As many as thirty-five thousand trailers were drummed into service, and because military and defense installations were everywhere, trailer towns suddenly popped up in unexpected places from Maine to Michigan to Texas. In places like Hartford, Connecticut, defense workers living in "trailer villages" were easily compared to colonists and gypsies.[26]

The most remarkable account of trailer camps formed in defense centers came from the talented reporter Agnes Meyer of the *Washington Post*. Her dispatches as a "war correspondent on the home front," as she called herself, were compiled and published as a book titled *Journey Through Chaos*. Well-bred American women were not supposed to see "chaos" up close. Indeed, though her family considered higher education inappropriate for a young female, Meyer graduated from Barnard College, studied at the Sorbonne, published a scholarly work on Chinese painting, and became the first woman hired by the *New York Sun*. Momentously, she went on to marry a multimillionaire who decided to purchase the floundering *Washington Post*. Their daughter, Katharine Meyer Graham, grew up to be the most influential editor of the family's paper.[27]

In 1943, Agnes Meyer was on a fact-finding expedition when she traveled to twenty-seven war centers. From Buffalo to Detroit, and all the way out to Puget Sound, Washington, south to California, and back east by way of Texas, Louisiana, Mississippi, and Florida, she described the people she saw with unsparing detail. Her most disturbing encounters occurred, not surprisingly, in the Deep South. She shone a light on the rows of tents, trailers, and run-down shacks in Pascagoula, Mississippi, and Mobile, Alabama. She bemoaned the "neglected rural areas," and called the white trash who migrated from there pitiful, ragged, illiterate, and undernourished. They had refused to move into respectable housing projects out of fear of the law—but mostly, Meyer believed, because they feared the "restraint of being members of a decent community." Overwhelmed by the condition of their lives, by their physical and mental health and lack of prospects, she asked incredulously, "Is this America?"[28]

It was the shipyards that brought workers to Pascagoula. Nearly five thousand new workers and their families crowded the small town on the Gulf of Mexico, quickly unleashing a panic among local residents. Many of the workers were backwoods people, and their trailers were quite unsanitary. Meyer met a fifty-one-year-old man who looked eighty—a clear throwback to the 1840s, when clay-eaters were identified in the same way: old before their time. Townspeople denounced them as "vermin." The manager of the shipyards told the weary female reporter that unless these people were lifted up, "they will pull the rest of the Nation down." On to Mobile, where she learned that the illegitimacy rate was high and getting higher, and that a black-market trade in babies existed. By the time she reached Florida, she found the poor whites to be handsome on approach, but strange-looking as soon as they smiled and exposed sets of decaying teeth. Still, they were less repulsive to her than "the subnormal swamp and mountain folk" she had already encountered in Mississippi and Alabama.[29]

Trailer trash as squatters in Arizona (1950).

Photograph of mobile homes described as "squatters," in Winkelman, Arizona (1950), #02-4537, Photograph Collection of the History and Archives Division of the Arizona State Library, Archives and Public Records, Phoenix, Arizona

It was the southern war camps that set the tone, but after the war "trailer trash" became a generic term, no longer regionally specific. They appeared on the outskirts of Pittsburgh and Flint, Michigan, as well as in North Carolina and parts of the upper South. In far-off Arizona, trailer trash doubled as "squatters," photographed in weedy areas and with outhouses in their front yards. To be displaced and poor was to be white trash.[30]

Responding to bad publicity, trailer manufacturers launched a campaign to dramatically change their image. By 1947, they were calling their product a "trailer coach," emphasizing more attractive, more convenient interiors, so as to "woo the feminine trade." The determined trailer manufacturers' association pressed for improved trailer "parks"—an image that conjured well-manicured, family-friendly garden sites and was meant to cast off the temporary-sounding, refugee-bearing trailer "camps" of World War II. In sum, to make the mobile home more acceptable, manufacturers had to domesticate it. These sharp, socially attuned promoters worked hard to reinvent the trailer as a miniature suburban "bungalow-on-wheels." They did everything they could to remove "trailer trash" from the American vocabulary.[31]

It proved difficult for the trailer to compete with the tract house. Potential buyers were placed at an economic disadvantage. The FHA did not get around to insuring mortgages for mobile homes until 1971, so until then, even though trailers were cheaper, owners faced other hidden costs and penalties. Trailer parks were exiled to the least desirable lots, a sorry distance from the nicer, better-protected residential areas. Many park managers forbade children and pets, the two most obvious attractions for young couples living in suburbia. More parks emerged with smaller lots, tiny lawns—or no lawns at all. In many cities and counties, even retirees found their welcome worn out, resented because they lived on tight budgets, contributed too little to commercial growth, and failed to pay property taxes.[32]

Hollywood captured the uneasy fit between suburban ideals and life on the road in a farcical film of 1954, *The Long, Long Trailer,* which starred Lucille Ball and Desi Arnaz. The couple suffered mishap after mishap as they proved that mobile homes undermined privacy in general, and sex life in particular—not to mention providing inadequate space for the husband's treasured golf clubs. The scene that makes the mobile home problem most disconcerting occurs when the ten-foot-wide trailer flattens a relative's rosebushes, ruins her yard, and upends what began as a lovely home in a quaint neighborhood. Trailers were shown to be hazards and nuisances—out of place in the suburban dream landscape.[33]

As trailer living became increasingly popular, opposition grew apace. In the late fifties, more mobile homes were built than prefabricated homes, yet municipalities continued to look down on them. In 1962, in an important New Jersey court case, the majority ruled that a rural township could prohibit trailer parks within its limits. Still, the judge who wrote the dissent exposed the dangerous implications of this decision: "Trailer dwellers" had become a class of people, he explained, through which discrimination was tolerated under the vague language of protecting the "general welfare." For at least this one jurist, inherited social biases had reduced the owners of mobile homes to "footloose, nomadic people," a group of "migratory paupers."[34]

Retailers and real estate agents once again sought to change public perceptions. Since they could not effectively regulate the quality of mobile home parks in general, they decided to add an upscale version, and turned to advertising more exclusive mobile home communities. To separate the dumpy and dirty trailer slums from five-star dwellings, they rebranded the upscale sites as "resorts." "Trailer park" became a dirty word. Exchanging his coonskin cap for a Realtor's jacket, the actor Fess Parker became an investor in and leading promoter of high-end trailer playgrounds. "Carefree living," Parker boasted, coining a new motto for a new class. In the hands of Sunbelt speculators working hard to attract a lucrative clientele, trailer life was meant to invite comparisons to luxury hotels. Fess Parker's resort in Santa Barbara offered ocean views, a golf course, and a stock market ticker tape.[35]

Davy Crockett's call of the wild did not completely disappear either. Trailer life updated the once-catchy cry of the open road by declaring freedom from the thirty-year mortgage. In 1957, drawing on a playboy motif, a writer for *Trailer Topics* magazine promised a well-earned respite from the "well-harnessed Suburban life." (The story was accompanied by a photograph of a sexy blonde sitting coquettishly on a trailer couch.) Other mobile home dealers promised residents freedom from the suburban rut and the tedious routine of playing "nursemaid to lawns, patios, and plumbing."[36]

In Richard Nixon's birthplace of Yorba Linda, California, what was called "primordial Nixon country," a remarkable trailer community went up. (Nixon country meant Republican, conservative, and deeply class conscious.) Lake Park offered a "country club" style of living, replete with man-made lake, swimming pool, landscaped greenery, and gently winding streets; to a *New York Times* reporter, it was "suburbia in miniature." The developers, two men from Los Angeles, spent three years trying to find a city hall in Orange County that would allow them to build, and were repeatedly turned down. In order to convince Yorba Linda officials that it was not their intent to impinge upon the class consciousness of existing residents, they recast the prospective community as a "private club," highlighting the beautiful environment and ensuring that residents would pay added expenses to maintain their lots. When that was not enough, the developers added one final touch: a five-foot-high wall around the entire complex. As one city administrator observed, "We don't even know they're there." Another local resident, without any apparent shame, admitted, "We call them 'the people inside the wall,' and we're 'the people outside the wall.'" Was there any better symbol of an undisguised belief in class stratification than the construction of a wall?[37]

But the Yorba Linda trailer community hardly fit the typical profile. Further down the scale, of course, were the many low-down trailer parks that dotted the map of America. By 1968, only 13 percent of mobile homeowners held white-collar jobs, and a sizable percentage of those who lived in the poorer trailer parks came from rural, mainly southern areas. Families that could not afford to buy a new trailer were buying or renting depreciated—that is, secondhand, possibly thirdhand—trailers. A new used market emerged, fueling what two sociologists called "Hillbilly Havens" that cropped up on the periphery of cities in the Sunbelt, the Midwest, and elsewhere. Scattered along highways, often near the railroad tracks, run-down trailer parks were barely distinguishable from junkyards. Trailer trash had become America's untouchables.[38]

To make matters worse, poor and working-class trailer communities were believed to be dens of iniquity. The charge actually went back to the World War II "defense centers," to which prostitutes migrated, in a scattering of whorehouses on wheels. By the fifties, pulp fiction, with such titles as *Trailer Tramp* and *The Trailer Park Girls*, told stories of casual sexual encounters and voyeurism. In the parlance of the day, the female trailer tramp "moved from town to town—from man to man." Alongside such tales was *Cracker Girl* (1953), soft-porn pulp that titillated readers and capitalized on the thrill of crossing the tracks and getting sex on the lowdown. Tramps and trailer nomadism, like drugs and gambling, identified social disorder on the edge of town.[39]

The poor dominated the mobile home picture. In 1969, the thirteen Appalachian states were on the receiving end of 40 percent of mobile home shipments, and, not surprisingly, the cheapest models (under $5,000) headed for the hills. In 1971, New York City approved its first trailer park, after Mayor John Lindsay found support for a policy of housing the homeless in trailers. These were not Bowery bums, but people who were being uprooted as a result of urban renewal—yet somehow the solution was to stow them away in a most nonurban sort of accommodation. From Appalachia to the Big Apple, then, those without economic security and with the least political clout were seen as the most likely candidates for the trailer park.[40]

Cheap land, a plot of concrete and mud, and a junkyard trailer—the updated squatter's hovel—became the measure of white trash identity. By the 1960s, class was deeply imprinted onto most residential landscapes through zoning, housing, and school funding. As rural southerners relocated to metropolitan areas in search of work, a new kind of class tribalism emerged. Poor whites fought for a shrinking territory, and class conflict was played out in residential spaces. Which brings us to Hazel Bryan and the crystalization of the modern media circus.[41]

Nineteen fifty-seven was a crucial year of social experiment and consciousness-raising. Little Rock, Arkansas, grabbed national and international attention when Governor Orval Faubus thwarted the racial desegregation of Central High School. On September 4, fifteen-year-old Elizabeth Eckford attempted to enter the school building, but was blocked by the Arkansas National Guard. Outside the classroom building, reporters had gathered. Will Counts of the *Arkansas Democrat* and Johnny Jenkins of the *Arkansas Gazette* set the tone for how the day would be remembered. Their almost identical photographs of the lone student's stoic walk ahead of an angry crowd seemed to capture the way class and race were defined in the confrontation. Each of the photojournalists focused his lens on Eckford and the unnamed white girl behind her who was yelling insults, her face distorted. Eckford looked calm, was dressed modestly, and appeared earnest. Her white adversary wore a dress that was too tight, and as she propelled herself forward, menacingly, mouth agape, she projected the crude callousness of the recognized white trash type. That contrast was precisely what the photographers intended to record.[42]

The mysterious girl in the photo was one Hazel Bryan. A year later, at the age of sixteen, she would drop out of high school, marry, and go to live in a trailer. But it is what she was at fifteen that matters: the face of white trash. Ignorant. Unrepentant. Congenitally cruel. Only capable of replicating the pathetic life into which she was born.

Hazel and her family were part of the influx of poor whites into Little Rock after World War II. Her father was a disabled veteran, unable to work; her mother held a job at the Westinghouse plant. They had left the small rural town of Redfield in 1951, when Hazel was ten. Her mother had married at fourteen to a man twice her age. Neither of Hazel's parents had earned a high school degree, her father having joined the circus. Their Redfield home had had no indoor plumbing and an outdoor privy; the Bryans' move to the city granted basic amenities that they had not enjoyed before. The house they purchased in Little Rock was in an all-white, working-class neighborhood in the southeastern section of the state capital.[43]

The day after the photograph appeared, Hazel Bryan made herself visible once more, telling newsmen positioned outside the school that "whites should have rights, too." If black students were let into Central

Hazel Bryan is the ugly face of white trash in Will Counts's famous photograph taken on September 4, 1957.

Will Counts Collection, Indiana University Archives

High, she declared provocatively, then she would walk out. She knew enough about the social hierarchy in her adoptive hometown to understand that the reputation of working-class whites hinged on the system of segregation. Permeable racial boundaries would pull down people like her even further. A principal at Central High said that Hazel was known to have been beaten by her father, was emotionally unstable, and was not one of the "leading students" by any measure. As a troubled girl—a bad seed, one might say—she confirmed her dubious class origins by her antics.[44]

Benjamin Fine of the *New York Times* compared Hazel Bryan to one of the frenzied girls who attended Elvis Presley concerts. (Some of the reporters at Central High even egged on the high schoolers to dance rock and roll in the streets.) During the first attempt to usher the black students into the school, a student ran down the hall yelling, à la Paul Revere, "The niggers are coming." Parents outside began screaming for their children to flee. A group of girls stood at a window, shrieking. Under the direction of teachers, the majority gradually filed out of the building, though some, including Hazel's best friend, Sammie Dean Parker, later claimed to have leapt from the second-floor window.[45]

Two new schools had been built in Little Rock: Horace Mann High for black students, and R. C. Hall High (nicknamed "Cadillac High") for the wealthy families on the west side of the city. Only Central High, built in the 1920s and catering mostly to working-class families, however, was selected for desegregation. Armis Guthridge of the Capital Citizens' Council, the lead spokesman for antidesegregation forces, willfully fanned the flames of poor white resentment when he announced that the rich and well-to-do were going to see to it that the "only race-mixing that is going to be done is in the districts where the so-called rednecks live." "Redneck" was a loaded term, as he well knew. His purpose was to remind the white working class of the city that the school board elites looked down on them.[46]

Arkansas governor Orval Faubus also exploited class rift. He distanced himself from the "Cadillac crowd" and constructed himself as the victim of upper-class arrogance. The national media painted him as the "hillbilly" from Greasy Creek, in the Ozarks. *Time* caught him entertaining visitors as "milk dribbled down his chin"; he could be heard "belching gustily" like a backcountry rube. A large photograph in *Life* identified as the governor's "kinfolk" one Taylor Thornberry, a cross-eyed, crazy-looking man in overalls. At a private meeting in Newport, Rhode Island, away from the unfolding drama, President Eisenhower tried to convince Faubus to accept the court-ordered desegregation plan; the southern governor left the meeting angry and humiliated. He later admitted that he knew full well that Eisenhower's advisers had thought him as nothing more than a "country boy."[47]

From the start of the crisis, Faubus used dual fears of racial and class violence to justify ordering the Arkansas National Guard to Central High School. In his announcement the day before the school year opened, he claimed to have reports of white "caravans" ready to descend upon Little Rock from numerous outlying areas. Whether or not a race war would arise from the conflict, he let it be known that white thugs, rabble-rousers, and rednecks were contending for a place in history.[48]

Faubus loved playing the redneck card. His continued defiance

Taylor Thornberry, the cross-eyed kin of Orval Faubus, as depicted in *Life* magazine (1957). His features underscored Faubus's hillbilly and degenerate roots.

Life magazine, September 23, 1957
Francis Miller/The LIFE Picture Collection/Getty Images

infuriated Eisenhower, who dispatched the 101st Airborne Division and federalized the Arkansas National Guard. Military protection ensured that the nine black students slated to attend Central High were not barred. On the national stage, and standing before the cameras, the governor of Arkansas embodied the southern stereotype to a tee. He was a complete caricature of folly and backwardness. A reporter for *Time* accused him of "manufacturing the myth of violence" and then "whipping up" a mob to make it a reality.[49]

Little Rock was the most important domestic news story of 1957. It transformed the Central High neighborhood into a newsroom, attracting reporters from the major newspapers, magazines, and television networks. By the end of September, the number of press people had grown from a handful to 225 highly visible journalists and cameramen. The standoff between the courts and the governor—the "crisis" environment swirling about the school grounds—grabbed the world's attention. On September 24, when President Eisenhower gave a televised speech announcing that he would send troops to the Arkansas capital, 62 percent of America's television sets were tuned in. As mobs descended, reporters were themselves targeted for violence. A black journalist, Alex Wilson, was beaten and kicked, the attack recorded on film. A *Life* photographer was punched in the face and then carried off in a police wagon and charged with disorderly conduct. "Thugs in the crowd" pushed his colleagues, said newsman John Chancellor, and heckled them with nasty slurs. One reporter took the precaution of disguising himself. He rented a pickup truck and wore an old jacket and no tie. For a reporter to go undercover safely, he had to alter his class appearance, passing as a poor white workingman.[50]

The media easily slipped into southern stereotypes, depicting the "many in overalls," "tobacco-chewing white men," or as one *New York Times* article highlighted, a "scrawny, rednecked man" yelling insults at the soldiers. Local Arkansas journalists similarly dismissed the demonstrators as "a lot of rednecks." Unruly women who stood by became "slattern housewives" and "harpies." One southern reporter said it outright: "Hell, look at them. They're just poor white trash, mostly." In Nashville, mob violence erupted that same month, after the integration of an elementary school. There, a *Time* reporter had a field day trashing the women in the crowd: "vacant-faced women in curlers and loose-hanging blouses," not to mention a rock-throwing waitress with a tattooed arm. One obnoxious woman yelled to no one in particular with reference to the African American children: "Pull their black curls out!"[51]

These were all predictable motifs, serving to distance rabble-rousers from the "normal" good people of Arkansas and Tennessee. Even President Eisenhower, in his televised speech, blamed the violence on "demagogic extremists," and assumed that the core population of Little Rock was the law-abiding, taxpaying, churchgoing people who did not endorse such behavior. If the women in curlers and the waitress boasting her tattoos reminded readers of trailer trash, the rioting rednecks were more like the wild-eyed, off-his-rocker Ernest T. Bass of *The Andy Griffith Show*. By 1959, the *Times Literary Supplement* acknowledged that it was the "ugly faces" of "rednecks, crackers, tar-heels, and other poor white trash" that would be forever remembered from Central High.[52]

Despite the embarrassment he caused, Orval Faubus did not disappear. Freed from the national media spotlight, he secured reelection in 1958, and went on to serve three more terms. As a governor who refused to lay down his arms, he continued to portray himself as a staunch defender of white people's democratic right to oppose "forced integration." Praising his "doggedness," one southern journalist traced Faubus's characteristic strength to his Ozark mountain days, when he trudged five miles, dressed in overalls, to a dilapidated school. A hillbilly could get ahead down here. Thus Faubus strategically accepted a loss of support from among the better classes, who resented redneck power in any form. Like Mississippi's Vardaman and his own state's Jeff Davis before him, Orval Faubus used the threat of poor white thuggery to stay in power. And it worked.[53]

In the same year that Little Rock consumed the news media, Hollywood produced a feature-length film that capitalized on the redneck image. Starring Andy Griffith and directed by Elia Kazan, *A Face in the Crowd* was a completely different vehicle for Griffith than his subsequent television role as the friendly sheriff. It was a dark drama that followed "Lonesome Rhodes," a down-and-out man discovered playing guitar in an Arkansas jail, and traced his rapid rise into the national limelight as a powerful and ruthless TV star. For reviewers, Griffith's performance was a cross between Huey Long and Elvis Presley—a hollering, singing "redneck gone berserk with power."[54]

The plot of *A Face in the Crowd* was only a part of its story. The surrounding publicity focused on Kazan's directing technique. To get Griffith into character, he exploited the actor's childhood memories of being called white trash. In this way, it was an unusual film, and it offered a two-part message about class. First, it reminded audiences of the danger in elevating a lower-class redneck above his accustomed station and giving him power—for the redneck personality on-screen was a volatile mix of anger, cunning, and megalomania. Second, Kazan's exploitation of the backstory on Griffith delivered a stern rebuke of southern culture, where the poor were treated like dirt.[55]

Kazan tried his hand at another southern story, this time set during the Depression. *Wild River* (1960) concerned the TVA, as the construction of a dam was displacing an old matriarch and her family who were living on an island in the Tennessee River. The matriarch's sons were shown as lazy and oafish, unwilling to work or leave the island, and dependent on the black sharecroppers who farmed their fields. The daughter was a bit trampish, more than willing to sleep with the TVA agent because she saw him as her only ticket off the island. A group of surly whites beat up the agent while the local sheriff and his deputy looked on. As in the earlier film, Kazan provoked a news story when he cast real poor whites to play the extras. The "white trash squatters" of the film lived in a place called Gum Hollow, which was an existing shantytown literally situated on the town dump in Cleveland, Tennessee. Community leaders were furious at the appearance of such unappealing men in the movie. Kazan gave in to pressure and reshot the offending scenes, this time hiring what the townspeople referred to as "respectable" unemployed. In this strange episode, proud small-town arbiters of morality refused even to acknowledge the extreme poor.[56]

While Kazan's films reached middle- and upper-brow audiences, another film of the era was geared for drive-ins and became a smash hit in 1961. This was the second incarnation of *Poor White Trash,* which had first been released under the title *Bayou* in 1957 and flopped. An aggressive and slick marketing campaign turned this turkey into a hit. Exploiting the new title, the production company placed provocative ads in newspapers: "It exists Today! . . . Poor White Trash." To entice prurient adults, the cagey promoters warned local communities that no children would be permitted to see the movie. But the film turned out to be less lurid than voyeuristic. Its most fascinating scene featured a massively built poor white Cajun (played by Timothy Carey, an actor from Brooklyn) performing a wild, almost autoerotic dance. Learning his moves from Elvis, the sweaty, shaking giant doubled as a frightening ax-wielding bully from the swamps. Oversexed and violent was the featured poor white, a primal breed.[57]

Of all the films that belong to this cultural moment, *To Kill a Mockingbird* (1962) was the most highly regarded, and offered the most damning picture of poor whites. Based on Harper Lee's bestselling novel, it tells the story of a small southern town in the thirties. The movie highlights the limits of justice in a society where law and order give way to a defunct code of southern honor. A black man, Tom Robinson, is falsely accused of raping a poor white girl, Mayella Ewell. Watching the trial, the audience becomes the jury, one might say, forced to choose between the hardworking family man and the pathetic, ill-educated girl. Does race trump class, or does class trump race? This is the choice the audience must make. Robinson represents the worthy, law-abiding blacks in the community. He is honest and honorable. The Ewells are white trash.[58]

Viewers never see the Ewells' dilapidated cabin, which in the novel Harper Lee describes as the "playhouse of an insane child." Nor do viewers see the white trash family picking through the town dump. Lee's eugenic allusions are muted in the film, but the viciousness of Mayella's father, Bob Ewell, is underscored. He spits in the face of Atticus Finch, Robinson's heroic, morally impeccable defense attorney played by Gregory Peck, and he attempts to murder Finch's two children. Of course, nothing could be more insidious than child murder. There is only one possible verdict for Bob Ewell. Just as Atticus Finch shoots a "mad dog" in the street, the same fate awaits the vicious, vengeful poor white villain in the film's denouement. It is not the father who resorts to violence, though; it is his ghostly neighbor, Boo Radley. A social outcast with a troubled past, Radley acts the part of a guardian angel, saving the children on Halloween night.[59]

The Ewells may have been caricatures, as the *New York Times* movie critic directly claimed, but they were familiar ones. Hollywood did not expose the seamy economic conditions of poor whites so much as emphasize their dark inner demons. By the fifties, "redneck" had come to be synonymous with an almost insane bigotry. The actor playing Bob Ewell was scrawny, and one reviewer even called him "degenerate," suggesting the persistence of the older hereditary correlation between a shriveled body and a contracted mind. Sensationalizing redneck behavior did not just occur on the big screen, however. In Nashville, in 1957, the racist troublemaker at the head of the mob (with an affected southern accent) was a paid agitator from Camden, New Jersey.[60]

For filmmakers, the allure of redneck characters was doubled-edged. On the one hand, they were ready-made villains; on the other, they were men without inhibitions. Unrestrained and undomesticated, they stood in sharp contrast to the boxed-in suburbanite and could occasionally be appreciated for their earthy machismo. Sloan Wilson's male protagonist in *The Man in the Gray Flannel Suit* (1955), another novel made into a Hollywood film, starring Gregory Peck, was a pale imitation of the primal Cajun doing his dance to drumbeats. James Dean, Elvis Presley, Marlon Brando, and even Timothy Carey, as poor white trash, were all unreformed Americans, undomestic and unconventional. They planted a wild seed, taunting conformist male spectators who might be itching to break loose.[61]

"Redneck" and "white trash" were often used interchangeably, though not everyone agreed that the two were synonymous. In *A Southerner Discovers the South* (1938), Jonathan Daniels had insisted that not all humbly born southern men were "po' whites." He gave as examples Andrew Jackson and Abraham Lincoln, southern folk whose "necks were ridged and red with the sun." He thus divided the poor into two camps: the worthy, hardworking poor who strove to move up the social ladder, and the vulgar and hopeless who were trapped on its lowest rung. His worthy poor, having the "stout, earthy qualities of the redneck," borrowed from the older class of yeoman, a category that no longer meant what it once had. That said, Daniels's observation was not historically accurate: as we know, Jackson was vilified by his enemies as a violent, lawless cracker, and Lincoln was disparagingly termed a poor white "mudsill." But even Daniels had to admit that many other southerners defined the redneck as one who was "raised on hate." He despised blacks and demeaned "nigger lovers." In the mold of Bob Ewell, he stood prepared to stick a knife in the back of any who crossed him. That, then, was the label that stuck.[62]

And what about the hillbilly? Though redneck and hillbilly were both defined by the American Dialect Society in 1904 as "uncouth country-men," the following regional distinction was offered: "Hill-billies came from the hills, and the rednecks from the swamps." Like rednecks, hill-billies were seen as cruel and violent, but with most of their anger directed at neighbors, family members, and "furriners" (unwelcomed strangers). Like the legendary Hatfields and McCoys in the 1880s, they were known for feuding and explosive bouts of rage. When they weren't fighting, they were swilling moonshine and marrying off their daughters at seven. Like the squatter of old, they were supposedly given to long periods of sloth. Stories spread of shotgun marriages, accounts of bare-foot and pregnant women. In a 1933 study of an isolated community in the Blue Ridge Mountains of Virginia, a woman being interviewed blurted out that marriage meant she was "goin' to have her number" (of children). "I done had mine," she explained. "Fifteen. Nine living and six dead."[63]

Hollywood released *Mountain Justice* in 1938, a film based on the actual murder trial of "the Hill-billy girl" Ruth Maxwell, who had slain her father in self-defense when he came at her in a drunken rage. In coverage of the trial, Maxwell's home of Wise County, Virginia, was described as a place where "slattern women and gangling men take up the dull business of living." Warner Brothers made the film both hokey and violent. The film's technical adviser told the studio to ship in "six coon hounds, 30 corncob pipes, 43 plugs of chewing tobacco," and over a thousand yards of calico—all to make sure that a very dim portrait of mountain ways was presented. Advance promotion promised a "Gripping Melodrama of Lust and Lash." The most shocking on-screen moment occurs as Ruth's father towers over her with an enormous bullwhip.[64]

The thirties and forties saw the popularity of *Li'l Abner* as well as Paul Webb's cartoon strip *The Mountain Boys*. Webb's work was con-verted into a slapstick film, *Kentucky Moonshine* (1938), featuring the popular Ritz Brothers comedy team—it was a hillbilly version of *The Three Stooges*. A trio of New Yorkers disguise themselves as hillbillies, appearing in long, unkempt black beards while wearing tall conical hats and ragged pants (held up by ropes) exposing their dirty bare feet. The Grand Ole Opry radio station got its start in the same decade, and music groups appeared with names like the Beverly Hillbillies. Minnie Pearl, known for her famous hillbilly greeting, "Howdee," began her career on the Opry in the 1940s, and later became a star of the long-running television series *Hee Haw*. She was by no means an authentic mountain gal. "Minnie" was born into a wealthy family, was well educated, and crafted a naïve persona that made her vaudeville act a success. The hillbilly "Minnie" was so out of touch with mainstream America that she wore her trademark hat with the price tag still attached.[65]

By the forties, then, hillbilly was a stage act, and a kind of catchall name for country folk. Politicians took up the role too, offering a milder version of the theatrics of Mississippi's "White Chief" James Vardaman and Louisiana's Huey Long. A sharecropper's son named Jimmy Davis became Louisiana's governor in 1944. Though he gamely called himself "just a po' country boy," Davis was peculiarly able to straddle class divisions. He was a country crooner, a Hollywood actor (in westerns, of course), and a history professor. As one newspaper observed, the "hillbilly in Long's Chair" was a new political breed. He didn't yell, or give long harangues, or wave his arms, or make empty promises. He was, concisely put, a hillbilly with a touch of style. Of course, he was not beyond Hollywood theatrics either, riding a horse up the steps of the state capitol.[66]

As distinctive as he was, Jimmy Davis was not the only one of his kind. In 1944, Idaho matched Louisiana by electing the "Singing Cowboy" Glen Taylor to the U.S. Senate. Even earlier, Texas voters were charmed by the hillbilly ballads and good ol' radio platitudes of Wilbert Lee "Pappy" O'Daniel, a flour merchant whom they first sent to the governor's mansion, then to the U.S. Senate. It was Lyndon Johnson, in fact, whom the Ohio-reared O'Daniel defeated in the 1941 Senate race. Missouri boasted the only Republican in the bunch, a candidate named Dewey Short. He did not sing, but still earned the affectionate nickname "Hillbilly Demosthenes." As a philosophy professor, ordained preacher, and congressman, he wore several hats. His style did not borrow from the ancient Greek oratorical tradition, but relied instead on caustic, alliterative adjectives. He creatively called Congress a "supine, subservient, soporific, supercilious, pusillanimous body of nitwits," and maligned FDR's vaunted Brain Trust as "professional nincompoops." Short's constituency, described in the press as the cornpone crowd, kept reelecting him because he spiced up his prose with a fine assortment of sassy flourishes.[67]

Why this fascination with the hillbilly? In 1949, an Australian observer described this phenomenon best. Americans had a taste for what he called a "democracy of manners," which was not the same as real democracy. He meant that voters accepted huge disparities in wealth but at the same time expected their elected leaders to "cultivate the appearance of being no different from the rest of us."[68]

The positive mythology about hillbillies suited such appeals to authenticity. Beyond the image of feuding and wasting time fishing, hillbillies also tapped into a set of golden age beliefs: they were isolated, primitive, and rough on the outside yet practiced a kind of genuine democracy. They were once again William Goodell Frost's rustic Americans of pure Anglo-Saxon blood. The fantasy underwent a revival during the 1940s and 1950s, in the form of stories of plain, honest mountain people with "no respect for money, nor fame, or caste." But the vaudeville antics never lost their appeal either. Some hillbilly bands became glamorous, and a female performer named Dorothy Shay launched her career in 1950 by playing the "Park Avenue Hillbilly." She dressed as a city sophisticate while singing "happy-go-lucky" tunes.[69]

The quintessential pop icon of the 1950s, Elvis Presley, was, some believed, part hillbilly. One of his earliest performances was billed as "The Hillbilly Jamboree," and took place at Pontchartrain Beach near New Orleans in 1955, where the "Miss Hillbilly Dumplin' Contest" was also held. He also toured with Andy Griffith. In the early years, Elvis's musical style was seen as a mixture between hillbilly singing and rhythm and blues. In 1956, the music reviewer for the *Times-Picayune* was relieved to discover that the "self-confessed country boy" singing about his blue suede shoes lacked an "exaggerated hillbilly dialect." That same year, Hedda Hopper, the Hollywood gossip columnist, was just as relieved to find that Elvis had not been offered the film part of Li'l Abner.[70]

The real Elvis was not a hillbilly at all. He was a poor white boy from Tupelo, Mississippi. He was the son of a sharecropper. He was born into poverty in a shotgun shack situated in the wrong part of town. Yet when he put a guitar in his hand and millions ogled at his frenzied (some thought violent) dance moves, he was at once seen as defying middle-class norms and behaving as a sort of hillbilly—well suited to his new home of Tennessee. A friend of his confirmed the hillbilly image when he remarked to a reporter in 1956 that all Elvis had to do was "jes' show hisself and the gals git to thrashin' round and pantin' like mountain mules."[71]

And so it was in 1956 that country music, pop culture, and class politics all came together on the national stage. That year, Tennessee's governor, Frank Clement, became the Democratic Party's golden (country) boy. He was chosen to give the keynote address at the Democratic National Convention in Chicago, an honor that placed him in the running for the vice presidential nomination. In anticipation of Clement's big speech, a writer for the *Nation* called the thirty-five-year-old, six-foot-tall, dark-haired governor "one of the handsomest men in American politics." He was known for stumping in the Tennessee mountains, and folks admired him for his "barefoot boy sincerity"—a clear allusion to the "honest hillbilly" myth. Even his store-bought suits projected allegiance to the common man: the "type of rig a successful mountain man would wear on a visit to Nashville."[72]

His countrified eloquence covered the full range of registers: his voice boomed, then sank to a whisper, or, as one reporter claimed, he "sang like a mountain fiddle and died away." He used brimstone threats and usually ended with a prayerful benediction. Like Dewey Short, he lit up with alliteration. To top it all off, he had the support of the grandest hillbilly governor, "Big Jim" Folsom of Alabama, who stood six foot eight and was known for taking his shoes off onstage and campaigning with his "strawberry-pickers," as the Folsom band was called. In 1954, at a large Democratic primary gathering, he told Clement to use all his powers on the rostrum, saying he should "go out there guttin', cuttin', and struttin'." "Kissing Jim," fond of whiskey and women, gave his blessing to the flamboyant Clement.[73]

John Steinbeck, the famed author of *The Grapes of Wrath*, wrote one of the most revealing appraisals of Clement's keynote address. He adjudged that the governor had a future, whether it was in "statesmanship or musical comedy"; he saw the Democrat as part "old country boy" and part Elvis, with a dash of Billy Graham and Liberace as well. As Steinbeck put it, Clement's voice had the "frayed piercing painfulness of a square dance fiddle," and "in his most impassioned and rehearsed moments, . . . a refined bump and grind." While the author thought Clement would shake up the party in a good way, at the same time he was suggesting that the "corn-shucker" style was a regional taste that might not be so easily cultivated elsewhere.[74]

Steinbeck identified the crux of the southern politician problem: was the governor merely a rabble-rousing entertainer, or could he truly speak for the whole nation? Reflecting on his bright moment from the perspective of 1964, Clement said he knew that people were cheering his speech, but he was just as sure that some in the audience were laughing at him. That year, the Texan Horace Busby, a special assistant to President Johnson, told Bill Moyers that LBJ, with his southern drawl, should in effect be the anti-Clement when he delivered his nomination acceptance speech. "Forensics should be modern, untinged with an old fashioned style," Busby said. "Alliteration should be minimized."[75]

The Tennessee governor with the Elvis-like movements did not win the vice presidential nomination in 1956. Second place on the ticket went instead to Senator Estes Kefauver, another Tennessean, but one who expressed a somewhat softer hillbilly persona—after all, he had earned a Yale degree. Back in 1948, Kefauver had worn a coonskin cap when he ran for office, after his opponent called him a sneaky "pet coon" who was flirting with communism. In 1956, Kefauver was meant to add to the presidential ticket what one reporter aptly referred to as the "calculated common touch"—the point being that there was nothing authentic about Kefauver's pose. He was a "spurious hillbilly," a cheap ploy to offset presidential candidate Adlai Stevenson's lack of popular appeal. The Illinoisan was called an "egghead," a bore. Stevenson and Kefauver lost, of course.[76]

Meanwhile, Clement hosted Elvis at the governor's mansion, and in 1958 did the performer a good turn by speaking before a Senate Communications committee in defense of hillbilly music and rock and roll. Vance Packard, author of the bestselling *Hidden Persuaders*, was testifying before the committee, insisting that mountain music was polluting the national taste. An outraged Clement defended hillbillies as pure Elizabethans and their "nasal harmonies" as a genuine expression of the American dream. A tart Chicago reporter comically expressed his surprise that the governor "did not volunteer to fight a duel with accordions at ten paces."[77]

Kefauver of Tennessee was a traditional liberal, Folsom of Alabama a populist, and Clement of Tennessee a moderate on race issues; yet they all had to play the showman to get ahead in political life. Clement had set his sights on higher national office, only to be shut down on the night of his keynote address. It was Lyndon Baines Johnson, the seasoned Texan, who—alone among the rural southern contingent that threw their hats into the vice presidential ring during the 1950s and 1960s—eventually captured the presidency on his own accord.

As mastermind and deal maker in the Senate, Majority Leader Johnson was considered the second most powerful man in the nation after the president. He was an admirer of Henry Clay of Kentucky, the "great compromiser." (As president, he would hang Clay's portrait in the Oval Office.) Cultivating an at times paternalistic role among Senate Democrats, Johnson kept close watch on his colleagues' tastes and interests. "A man who can't smell the mood of the Senate," he professed, "has no business being leader." He seemed a cross between a schoolteacher (which he had been) and a sheriff, a tougher, more fearsome version of Andy Griffith's Mayberry character. What he had in common with the television sheriff was the rustic art of personal persuasion. His repertoire involved storytelling, verbal cudgeling, and physical contact, and he profited from an intimate knowledge of the psychology and personal quirks of every senator with whom he did business. The Senate was that "small town" over which Lyndon Johnson held sway as its modern-day lawman.[78]

When he accepted the largely thankless position of vice president in 1960, Johnson became Kennedy's dutiful lieutenant. Only his unexpected elevation to the presidency on November 22, 1963, altered the public's reception to his earthy southern persona. For a time, he acquired the kind of sympathy he had never enjoyed previously among the liberal intellectuals of his party. He was neither cool nor sophisticated like JFK, whose outward style reflected the jaunty confidence of his privileged upbringing. While some in the press continued to disparage his down-home ways, his close associates countered by insisting that he was "not some cornball rural hick." Nevertheless, like the southern politician of the hillbilly school, LBJ loved to be flamboyant. On the campaign trail, he used his Texas vernacular to forge an intimate bond with the crowds. One columnist praised him for "digging down deeply into the basic urges of ordinary people." Country-boy traits treated as liabilities before 1963 suddenly became an asset as the nation grieved the loss of its young president.[79]

Johnson's signature set of programs known as the Great Society attached to a different, and positive, variant of his southern identity. Upon passage of the Elementary and Secondary Education Act in 1965, the president flew to Stonewall, Texas, to sign the bill at the one-room schoolhouse where he had taught during the Great Depression. While there, he referred to himself as the "son of a sharecropper." His willingness to tackle poverty could be traced to his embrace of a modern South. In 1960, when he first ran for president, he echoed Howard Odum's creed: his goal was to prevent a "waste of resources, waste of lives, or waste of opportunity." By the time he launched the Great Society, the legislation he promoted focused on two distinct classes: the poor urban black population and the mountain folk of Appalachia. Seeing the Great Society as the new New Deal, Johnson connected his reform to the work of Eleanor Roosevelt, invoking her sentimental appeal to hillbillies. Lady Bird Johnson went to the Kentucky hills, where she distributed lunches and dedi-

In 1963, LBJ's tour in Kentucky included photographs of the president conversing with poor Appalachian families.

#215-23-64, Inez Kentucky, LBJ Library Photograph by Cecil Stoughton, Lyndon Baines Johnson Library, Austin, Texas

cated a new school gym; her husband sat himself down and talked with families.[80]

As they followed him on his five-state tour, cameramen captured images of the president on the porches of run-down shacks, affectionately listening to the mountain people—it was nothing if not a James Agee/Walker Evans flashback to the thirties. The problems facing Appalachia were acute: a high rate of joblessness compared to the rest of the country (in some places three or four times the national average); deteriorating housing; an uneducated workforce; and a ravaged environment wrought by strip mining. Mountain farm families had been stripped of the legal right to their property when coal-mining companies, aided by state courts, were given the prerogative to ruin fields, destroy forests, build roads wherever they chose, and pollute the water supply. In the end, the Johnson administration secured passage of the Appalachian Regional Development Act, providing infrastructure, schools, and hospitals. The president subsequently stated that seeing the poverty there firsthand had convinced him of the necessity of the Medicare amendment. And so fighting rural poverty remained a central plank in Johnson's overall "War on Poverty." But even these bold policies proved inadequate to manage the massive devastation that the blighted regional economy had already experienced.[81]

Lyndon Johnson was aware of every detail as he went about fashioning his public image. The hat he wore was not a ten-gallon cowboy, but a modified five-gallon version with a narrower brim. This was LBJ: a modified, modernized southerner. When he sought aid for Appalachia, he imagined himself as a kindly benefactor, making the "cold indifferent" government newly responsive to the "little fella." He offered homespun logic in defense of basic human decency: "No American family should settle for anything less than three warm meals a day, a warm house, a good education for their children . . . and sometimes simply to plain enjoy life." This was the Johnsonian translation of FDR's 1944 exhortation on behalf of a second Bill of Rights that included "the right to a useful and remunerative job in the industries or shops or farms or mines of the nation," "the right to earn enough to provide adequate food and clothing and recreation," "the right of every family to a decent home," and "the right to a good education."[82]

In private, though, Johnson was not always kind to poor rural whites.

He had this to say about white trash on driving through Tennessee and seeing a group of "homely" women holding up racist signs: "I'll tell you what's at the bottom of it. If you can convince the lowest white man he's better than the best colored man, he won't notice you're picking his pocket. Hell, give him somebody to look down on, and he'll empty his pockets for you." Like the Nobel Prize–winning writer William Faulkner, LBJ knew about the debilitating nature of false poor white pride. As president, he never lost sight of how central class and race were to the fractured culture of the South.[83]

Johnson's promises did not convince his critics on either the left or the right. Malcolm X called him the "head of the Cracker Party." In 1964, Barry Goldwater's campaign staff put together a fear-filled movie that showcased disturbing scenes of urban violence, pornography, topless girls, and striptease joints. Johnson's name was never mentioned, but in the middle of the thirty-minute harangue on "American Decay," a Lincoln Continental comes speeding across the dusty countryside as beer cans are jettisoned from the half-open window. It was a less-than-subtle caricature of LBJ on an aimless escapade along the perimeter of his Texas ranch, thereby reducing the tall Texan to a common redneck. (Jimmy Carter's ne'er-do-well brother Billy would later say that a redneck threw his beer cans out the window, while a good ol' boy did not.) Goldwater's campaign revived the eugenic theme of moral degeneracy, as it turned the sitting president into a symbol of white trash. LBJ's Lincoln said something. The larger-than-life president plainly indulged a defiant impulse when he drove around his ranch at high speeds while consuming beer from a paper cup. For one *Time* photographer, he posed behind the wheel and held up a squealing piglet for view. Taunting reporters was an exhibition of his country humor.[84]

The car one was seen in registered class in a very special way in the fifties and sixties and defined transgression as well as belonging. Elvis owned several Cadillacs, a Lincoln, and a Rolls-Royce. But when driven by the wrong class of people, the luxury car only exaggerated the underlying discomfort Americans felt about upward mobility. Nothing better captured this anxiety than the specially built padded seat in Elvis's favorite Cadillac that was reserved for his pet chimpanzee Scatter. The owners of beautiful vehicles were supposed to display breeding that matched the glossy magazine advertisements readers flipped through. A lower-class man did not look right exploiting the fantasy of freedom by leaving the restraints of an imposed class identity in the rearview mirror. That was Elvis and his chimp. That was LBJ too, at least for those stodgy critics who insisted on seeing him as a Texas country bumpkin and not a Washingtonian.[85]

Even Arkansas senator William Fulbright, a Johnson ally who leaned in a liberal direction, complained that Elvis symbolized the class hierarchy turned upside down: "the King" earned more than the president. George McGovern of South Dakota was disturbed that Elvis earned more than the combined annual salaries of all the faculty members at the average university. And for what? The *New York Times* movie critic Bosley Crowther lashed out: "grotesque singing" and "orgiastic" leg shaking.[86]

In mass media culture, lower-class delinquency was seen as something that could be contracted from pop idols. The "Mothers for a Moral America" that sponsored the negative campaign film about LBJ agreed, and linked his ostensible redneck ways to the danger of class disorder. As one of the Goldwater filmmakers explained, leadership at the top conditioned life at the bottom: if a president's behavior was too common, too coarse, he gave license to immoral, lower-class desires. Wealth without hard work, sex without marriage, and success without proper breeding were all danger signs. Society suffered.[87]

Goldwater supporters may have seen Johnson's behavior as that of a degenerate white trash father figure, but liberal reformers considered behaviors that attended poverty to be a matter of breeding as well. New terms reinforced pedigree: "the culture of poverty," "the poverty cycle," the "underendowed." Class still retained strong hints of the vocabulary of bloodlines and inheritance in the transformational decade of the 1960s.[88]

Nor had class wholly divorced itself from the land as a source of identity. One of the most influential intellectuals of the decade, John Kenneth Galbraith of Harvard, identified "islands" of poverty amid a society of affluence. Socialist Michael Harrington, whose book *The Other America* (1962) was instrumental in shaping policy debates, noted that the poor occupied an "invisible land," a territory hidden from the social awareness of a middle class now living in safe, segregated suburbs. Harrington discussed the economic "rejects," whom he identified as expendables, exiled from mainstream America's pleasingly productive, upwardly mobile workforce. The old English idea of dumping the poor in a distant colonial outpost was not quite buried. Out of sight, out of mind.[89]

In his consideration of the ill-served underclass, Johnson, too, thought in terms of soil. The poor were, in his words, the "little folks living on little lands who want what we already have." He had in mind the tenant farmer of history who dreamt of acquiring a meaningful tract of land. Johnson retained his own attachment to the "harsh caliche soil" of the Texas hill country, acknowledging that his strength came from the "rough, unyielding sticky clay soil." Lady Bird Johnson felt that it was the land of his youth that made him so unrelenting in his politics. Johnson reversed the older notion that living on wasteland killed the human spirit. Instead of being stuck in the clay, Johnson saw himself as having surmounted his class origins with the same drive that was needed to overcome the unforgiving land.[90]

James Reston of the *New York Times* captured Johnson on the day of his inauguration in 1965. Here was a man speaking both the "faith of the old frontier" and the new frontier of science. Here was a man who "spoke every word as if it was his last"; "nobody watching him up close could doubt his sincerity." In LBJ, Reston found a full-blown "dramatization of the American dream," the "poor boy, the country boy at the pinnacle of the world."[91]

Two weeks later, Johnson spoke to students in the Senate Youth Program. He confidently assured them that it was not important who their ancestors were, or what the color of their skin was, or whether they were born to a tenant farmer and lived in a three-room house. In fact, though, he knew that all these things did matter. The country boy might have been enjoying his moment in the sun just then, but he knew in his heart that his place among the power elite was not really secured; he was not fully accepted. A country boy might at any moment reveal some telltale sign of a white trash character. He might say something inappropriate. He could never conceal the artless drawl or dust off the sticky red clay. Indelible marks of class identity were forever stamped on him, no matter how far he wandered from the inhospitable land of his birth.[92]

Part III

THE WHITE TRASH MAKEOVER

CHAPTER ELEVEN

Redneck Roots

━━━━━━⟫◦◦◦⟪━━━━━━

Deliverance, Billy Beer, and Tammy Faye

> The first Cracker President should have been a mixture of Jimmy
> and Billy [Carter] . . . Billy's hoo-Lord-what-the-hell-get-out-the-way
> attitude heaving up under Jimmy's prudent righteousness—or Jim-
> my's idealism heaving up under Billy's sense of human limitations—
> and forming a nice-and-awful compound like life in Georgia.
> —Roy Blount Jr., *Crackers* (1980)

As identity politics rose as a force for good in the last decades of the twentieth century, authenticity was to be achieved by registering, and then heeding, the voices of previously marginalized Americans. Whites could no longer speak for people of color. Men could no long speak for women. The New Left, civil rights, and Black Power movements of the 1960s had helped to jump-start the second-wave feminist movement, yet identity politics was not the possession of the left alone. Richard Nixon rode into office in 1968 by claiming to represent the interests of the "Silent Majority" of Americans who saw themselves as hardworking, middle American homeowners dutifully paying their taxes and demanding little of the federal government.[1]

One could argue that identity has always been a part of politics, that aspiring people adopt identities the same way that they change their style of dress. Yet this is only part of the story. Some people can choose an identity, but many more have an identity chosen for them. White trash folks never took on that name for themselves, nor did the rural poor describe their plight in recognition of having been cast out of society as "waste people," "rubbish," or "clay-eaters." As we have seen, Union soldiers and Lincoln Republicans embraced the intended insult of "mudsill" when it was hurled at them from across the Mason-Dixon Line. But that was because they possessed the cultural power to shape political discourse. The dispossessed had no such power.

Eventually, self-identified "white trash" who had come up in the world began defending their depressed class background as a distinct (and perversely noble) heritage. Before the end of the 1980s, "white trash" was rebranded as an ethnic identity, with its own readily identifiable cultural forms: food, speech patterns, tastes, and, for some, nostalgic memories. If immigrants had foreign origins to reflect on, white trash invented a country of their own within the United States. In its most benign incarnation, this substratum of the amorphous American class system was no longer to be categorized as an inferior "breed" (with undesirable genetic traits) so much as a product of cultural breeding that could easily be shed and later recovered—a tradition, or identity, that one did not have to shy away from in order to gain acceptance in mainstream society. In its worst form, however, white trash identity dredged up a person's early traumatic experiences, repressed childhood memories. A not insignificant part of that was sexual deviance, a problem that still hovers over white trash America today. Hollywood gave the country an enduring symbol of that deviance, and the unwanted's recourse to barbarism, in its adaptation of James Dickey's violent thriller *Deliverance* (1970). Set in rural Georgia near the South Carolina border, the film, released in 1972, seared into the national imagination its devastating portrait of white trash ugliness and backwoods debauchery.

No matter whether it is cast as urban or rural, religious or secular, Anglo- or other hyphenate, the search for national belonging is never new. Despite the nasty cultural memory jarred loose by the retrogressive message in *Deliverance* (and especially the horrific rape of Ned Beatty's character), the backcountry of America never completely lost its regenerative associations. Appalachia remained in the minds of many a lost island containing a purer breed of Anglo-Saxon. Here, in this imaginary country of the past, is where the best of Jefferson's yeoman "roots" could be traced. Most of all, there was a raw masculinity to be found in the hills. A larger trend was turning America into a more ethnically conscious nation, one in which ethnicity substituted for class. The hereditary model had not been completely abandoned; instead, it was reconfigured to focus on transmitted cultural values over inbred traits.

An inherent paradox added to the confusion over the nature of cultural identity. Modern Americans' largely blind pursuit of the authentic, stable self was taking place in a country where roots could be, and often were, discarded. In the American model, assimilation preceded social mobility, which required either adoption of a new identity or assumption of a class disguise in order to insert oneself into the desired category of middle class. Yet by the late 1960s the middle class had become the most *inauthentic* of places: the suburbs provided indelible images of foil-covered TV dinners, banal Babbittry, and bad sitcoms. People took part in staid dinner parties, evocatively portrayed in *The Graduate,* where the talk was of a career-making investment in plastics—and what better stood for inauthenticity than unnatural products invented by chemists? There was a growing awareness that middle-class comfort was an illusion. Two sociologists ironically concluded that the few authentic identities still claimable in 1970 existed in the isolated pockets of the rural poor: Appalachian hillbillies in Tennessee, marginal dirt farmers in the upper Midwest, and "swamp Yankees" in New England.[2]

The broadcast of *An American Family* on PBS in 1973 gave millions of viewers a palpable sense of middle-class life. As television's first attempt at a "reality" show, the Loud family saga was a study in dysfunction—a decade removed from Ozzie and Harriet, and emotional light-years from the tame, kid-friendly Brady Bunch. Three hundred hours of taping over the course of a year was edited down to twelve hours of riveting television.

Outsiders may have cared about the new TV family, but a *New York Times Magazine* article on the Louds described their world as a cultural vacuum: they had few hobbies, cared little about suffering in the world at large, and seemed emotionally short-circuited when attempting to deal with one another. The parents, Bill and Pat, were getting separated, but to the husband, who avoided conflict and admitted to no failures, their pending divorce came devoid of introspection. In the words of commentator Anne Roiphe, the breakup of a marriage was experienced by him as "a minor toothache." Amid filming, the Louds' house burned down, and even that barely fazed them. They floated through life like "jellyfish," transparent and unresponsive; they valued "prettiness" and gave no attention to any but their outwardly attractive and successful neighbors; they were nonplussed when it came to "those who do not make it."

As Roiphe sublimely put it, with reference to Mario Puzo's *Godfather* clan, "Maybe it's better to be a Corleone than a Loud." At least the Sicilians' tribal, violent character got the blood flowing. (She might just as well have used "redneck" in place of "Corleone.") Blind to their blandness, the Louds were adrift, like so many others of the seventies middle class. Roiphe's updated motto for the family sampler: "Be it ever so hollow, there's no place like home."[3]

Historical fictions provided a solution for cultural longing. Alex Haley's *Roots* (1976) created a media sensation. It spent twenty-two weeks atop the *New York Times* bestseller list before becoming a twelve-hour mini-series that won nine Emmys. Haley had done something few imagined possible: he had traced his African American family's history back to a village in Gambia.

The author's success was based wholly on his claims to have discovered his paternal ancestor, Kunta Kinte, who acquired the name Toby in America. Haley insisted that he had spent long years doing careful research that had enabled him to prove that his family's oral history (and that told by an African storyteller) could be corroborated with archival documentation. The dialogue in his book may have been made up, but the family saga was a true slice of history.

Impressed by this gargantuan effort, the *New York Times* praised Haley for his "wealth of authentic detail," and for having instilled his narrative with the "feel of history." The most prominent review in the newspaper of record averred, "Its truths have been quarried by a mountain of facts." *Newsweek* likewise lauded the work as an "extraordinary social document, grounded in exhaustive research and animated by a grand passion for personal and historical truth." But it was all a lie.[4]

Far from uncovering his real roots, it was discovered that the megaselling author had invented his lineage. Controversy over his historical claims hit the news in 1977, as prominent journalists and scholars called his work a "fraud," and the full story unfolded over the next five years. He had manipulated his family oral accounts and embellished his family tree in order to tell a grand tale of an exceptional heritage that never existed. For starters, the Gambian storyteller he relied upon merely told Haley what he wanted to hear. The historical Toby was not even born with the name Kunta Kinte—that genealogical lineage was pure fiction. While Haley's Africa was not a caricature on the order of Tarzan's over-ripe jungle, it was a half-conscious or self-conscious distortion: he converted Gambia into a place mirroring middle America, as a land of many villages. The actual village of his reputed ancestors, as Haley admitted, was a British trading post, not the symbolic West African "Eden" it was portrayed as, a pristine world to constitute for history-hungry African Americans a reverse Plymouth Rock.[5]

If that were the extent of the author's crimes, it would be bad enough. But Haley's attempts at research actually exposed far more serious errors. The birthdates of Kunta Kinte's American progeny were wrongly given, and Haley attributed to his family tree the names of people to whom he was unrelated. Neither the white nor the black families archived in *Roots* matched existing historical records.

As to his descent from the white Lea family of North Carolina, Haley completely invented a villainous cracker character named Tom Lea, who raped Kunta Kinte's daughter, Kizzy (Haley's alleged direct ancestor), and betrayed his own mulatto son, "Chicken George," by selling off his family. This could not have occurred, because the historical Thomas Lea was already dead by that time. And Lea was not in fact Haley's "po' cracker," but a prosperous landowner with sixteen thousand acres and numerous slaves; some of his relatives held prestigious political offices.

The class element in *Roots* was, in this way, as wrong on the American side as on the African. Nor was there a shred of evidence that Haley's lost Gambian ancestors were of an elite bloodline, and Toby/Kunte Kinte a breed and a class above the African American field hands who did the most backbreaking labor in the U.S. South. Yet for Haley, Kunta Kinte in America had to be fashioned as a man who honored the memory of his proud African ancestors; and in spite of his enslaved condition, he and his family had to set themselves apart from their low-class cracker relatives.[6]

Let us be clear, then. Besides being a fabrication of his family's history, Haley's book applied a kind of logic that was downright conservative. He construed himself as one of an African nobility, and he held that ancestry said a lot about what a person could become—and pass on. *Roots* was too good to be true, which was why Haley, who pitched his story to the networks before he had even written it, was eventually exposed as a hoaxer and a hustler.[7]

Haley's *Roots* demonstrated how easy it was to invent a pedigree. Fictional family trees were all the rage. James A. Michener, arguably the most popular of twentieth-century historical fiction writers, produced a primarily white version of *Roots* in his novel *Chesapeake* (1978).

Michener followed several families of varying class backgrounds and tied their destinies to a landscape dotted with geese and blue herons. The white trash lineage he covers originates with one Timothy Turlock, whom Michener describes as "small, quick, sly, dirty of dress and habit," and the father of "six bastards." After an undistinguished life in England, Turlock was unceremoniously dumped on the Eastern Shore of Maryland in the 1600s, and lived in a swamp.[8]

Multiple generations later, little had changed for the Turlock clan. Amos Turlock was a toothless crank living in a trailer in the 1970s. As one reviewer put it, "feral marshlanders" anchored the entire narrative. The Turlocks remained one with their terrain. Amos surrounded his trailer with tacky statuary of Santa and the Seven Dwarfs; he derived the greatest pleasure in finding his way around the game warden and ranging about with his extra-long (illegal) Twombly gun that he used to hunt geese. The Turlocks of Michener's historical reinvention were all cunning—savage survivalists.[9]

As sweeping narratives and small-screen histories accompanied the nation's bicentennial celebrations of 1976, it should come as no surprise, then, that the founders themselves provided a dynastic saga worthy of a miniseries. *The Adams Chronicles* traced the path of a crusty New England farmer, John Adams, to the presidency, and carried forward with his descendants, three generations' worth. The *Chronicles* led up to the accomplished Henry Adams, a strong-minded historian whose life crossed into the twentieth century.

In his introduction to the PBS treatment's companion book, Professor Daniel Boorstin, the newly appointed Librarian of Congress, recast John Adams as an oxymoron: a "self-made aristocrat." His well-known "vanity," his "independence from public opinion" morphs into an "Adams tradition," redefining class arrogance as an admirable family trait. There were no Turlocks in these *Chronicles,* so the rabble-rouser Samuel Adams stood in for the "slippery" side of the family. "Plain" John Adams was contrasted with his social climber of a cousin, who insisted on being chauffeured in a fancy carriage when he attended the Continental Congress.[10]

Amid the reconstruction of classes taking place in the 1970s, the political status of twentieth-century ethnics endured a series of changes, beginning with President Nixon's attempts to appeal to a different breed of "forgotten Americans" than those embraced by FDR's New Deal. Those whom Nixon wished to connect with were the "White Lower Middle Class" identified by Pete Hamill in a 1969 *New York* magazine article. They were the alienated "rabble," and Nixon promised to embrace the "Silent Majority" as the backbone of America—hardworking and true. Michael Novak, in *The Rise of the Unmeltable Ethnics* (1972), took the argument one step further, claiming that ethnic Americans were better Americans, because they understood the traditional values of loyalty, love of the flag, and hard work, and they did not expect government to provide unfair special assistance (as they imagined blacks were doing).[11]

The welfare system was one of the issues dividing Americans at this time. Some Nixon supporters acknowledged that there were hardworking people among welfare recipients who only occasionally took government assistance; but there were others, less deserving, whom they saw as permanently trapped in a cycle of dependence. Critics of welfare tended to see the issue as a racial one, but the reality was different. Among the "forgotten masses" were an estimated 17.4 million poor whites, and the majority of them lived in the South. In 1969, women took the lead in the welfare rights movement when a group of the disaffected in Beaufort, South Carolina, refused to be silent over delays in receiving their food stamps. One Mrs. Frazier, who had organized a day care program, led the "welfare mothers" in a visually powerful protest. At the same time as a group of wealthy women were holding their annual Beaufort historic homes and gardens tour, she organized a tour of poor homes. In the larger national debate, though, Nixon's supporters were seen angrily complaining about how welfare "breeds weak people." Poverty was once again being blamed on questionable breeding, and hard work was proclaimed as the means through which strong families put down solid roots and achieved upward mobility. To Frazier, welfare and day care were necessary if one were to be able to hold a job and feed a family. Starvation was a real danger—indeed the poor in South Carolina were still battling parasites like hookworm.[12]

During the ethnic revival that urbanites celebrated in the 1970s, hardworking Greeks and Italians and Chinese propped up family tradition, as neighborhood restaurants in Chinatowns grew in popularity. The celebratory impulse over ethnic cooking was a middle-class phenomenon, and poverty was softened when it could be seen through the hazy glow of times gone by. The ethic of hard work itself was now engrafted onto ethnic and family genealogical trees. Past poverty was no encumbrance; roots, whatever they were, were not a stain upon the present. In summing up Irving Howe's *World of Our Fathers* (1976), an affectionate story of the ethnic life of Jews on the Lower East Side of Manhattan, one reviewer concluded, "Everybody wants a ghetto to look back on."[13]

When it led to social mobility, ethnic identity was seen as a positive attribute. Unappealing (or un-American) idiosyncracies were cleaned up; the food, literature, music, and dress promoted; and the whole ethnicity set apart from the diseased and dirty huddled masses who came through Ellis Island. Heritage, like historic memory itself, is always selective. Ethnics and poor folk can be admired from afar, or from a temporal distance, as long as doing so ensures the supremacy of the middle class in the narrative. People can choose to treasure those parts of their heritage that they see as favorable and wish to keep, jettisoning what unpleasant truths they would prefer to forget.

The same impulses would soon be used to refashion the redneck and embrace white trash as an authentic heritage. It was moonshiners known for trippin' whiskey and outrunnin' the law who started the rough and wild sport of stock car racing. By the seventies, with money from Detroit automobile companies and celebrity drivers, an outlaw sport had become NASCAR, the tamer pastime of arriviste middle-class Americans. Meanwhile, country crooners Johnny Russell and Vernon Oxford released the hit singles "Rednecks, White Socks, and Blue Ribbon Beer" (1973) and "Redneck! (The Redneck National Anthem)" (1976). Vernon Oxford defined "redneck" as "someone who enjoys country music and likes to drink beer." In 1977, the year Elvis died, the new queen of country rock music, Dolly Parton, was featured in the elite fashion magazine *Vogue.* "Redneck chic" (the cleaned-up redneck) reached Hollywood in the 1981 film *Urban Cowboy,* in which Jersey boy John Travolta took on the role of hard-hat-wearing, honky-tonk-loving Texas two-stepper Buford Davis. In 1986, Ernest Matthew Mickler's *White Trash Cooking* was published, celebrating low-down lingo and rural recipes. When Mickler, a country singer as well as a caterer, gave his book to his seventy-two-year-old aunt, she remarked, "Well, that's what they call us, ain't it?"[14]

The transition to white trash acceptance or accommodation was not as smooth as it might seem. While Dolly Parton made over-the-top "floozydom" fashionable, and combined the burlesque of blonde bombshells Marilyn Monroe and Jayne Mansfield with Daisy Mae of *Li'l Abner* fame, her public identity did not escape the taint of white trash degradation. "You have no idea how much it costs to make someone look this cheap," Parton told a reporter in 1986. The Hollywood blockbuster *Deliverance* lacked even an ounce of delicacy, but offered up instead one of the most devastating portraits of rude hillbillies since the eugenics movement faded from view. White middle-class readers of the novel and film audiences wrote fan mail to author James Dickey, praising the four intrepid Atlanta adventurers as if they were old-time pioneers overcoming wilderness dangers while escaping the clutches of white trash savages. A former student of Dickey's wrote fawningly to his mentor, apparently oblivious to the dehumanizing tone of his letter. He was an ardent backwoods hiker, he said, "though I carry no bow and there are no rednecks awaiting me at the top for me to stalk and kill." He could not differentiate, in moral terms, between the thrill of taking on the mountains and the thrill of sending mountain men to their deaths.[15]

Class hostility persisted. Many southern suburbanites had no sympathy for the white trash underclass in their section. They drew a sharp class line between the lower-class rednecks and the "upscale rednecks." Lillian Smith, a Southern novelist and civil rights activist, identified the places where these toxic feelings stewed. Like the blue-collar ethnics in northern cities who switched their allegiance to the Republican Party, marginally middle-class southerners hated the "weak, lazy, good-for-nothing ones who whine all month until the relief check comes in." Seeing themselves as hardworking and self-reliant, the upwardly mobile sons of white trash parents believed, as Smith put it, that "he is responsible for himself and himself alone." The same self-made man who looked down on white trash others had conveniently chosen to forget that his own parents escaped the tar-paper shack only with the help of the federal government. But now that he had been lifted to respectability, he would pull up the social ladder behind him.

So suburban white animosity toward blacks was repeated in the treatment of poor whites. Smith found that the formerly poor southern white and the upwardly mobile immigrant population had something in common: "What everyone has always wanted in this country, what most came here for, was to get away from all those others who smell bad, are sleeping in a shanty, and are eating fatback and are going to loaf tomorrow because there is no job to go to." Moving up meant staying ahead of those still trapped in the "poverty ditch." But rather than help others escape destitution, this new addition to the middle class deeply resented a government that wasted money on the poor.[16]

Democrat Robert Byrd of West Virginia fit this mold. Newly elected as the Senate whip in 1971 by beating the patrician Edward Kennedy, he was, as the *New York Times Magazine* quoted, the "po white kid that could climb to the seat of the mighty and whip millionaires." An orphan, a former butcher and grocer who boasted having Lyndon Johnson as his patron, Byrd made his mark by attacking welfare, rioters, and communism. He hired investigators to kick cheaters off the welfare rolls in Washington, DC. Rioters, he declared with marked callousness, deserved to be mowed down, and looters shot on sight "swiftly and mercilessly." Byrd made himself one of the most hated men in the Senate, where he was compared to Dracula, Jekyll and Hyde, and Uriah Heep—the obsequious, greedy, upwardly mobile clerk in Charles Dickens's *David Copperfield*. After Byrd became whip, one top Senate aide remarked that Democrats would now have to look up at the "pinched Mephistophelian features of a redneck who made good."

Byrd referred to people on welfare as "fornicating deadbeats." He even appeared unsympathetic to children obtaining government assistance: if they were merely hungry, but not starving, they did not merit aid. As a former member of the Ku Klux Klan, Byrd conveniently distinguished welfare recipients in the District of Columbia (mostly black) from the deadbeats of his home state of West Virginia. Thus he made no effort to root out welfare cheaters among the mountain whites; they were his ticket into politics. In his first run for office, he courted the hillbilly crowd by playing fiddle tunes in the backseat of a car as he went from shack to shack. Reenacting the old tale of the Arkansas traveler, he cleverly played both roles in the nineteenth-century drama: the poor white and the ambitious politician. The *New York Times* declared Byrd to be the "embodiment of poor white power." He was Lillian Smith's angry redneck, who had "hacked his way out of the bushes" of poverty. As a symbol of political intolerance, he was as ruthless as they came.[17]

At the other end of the spectrum was the Georgian Jimmy Carter, a liberal Democrat who, when elected in 1970, appeared on the cover of *Time* as one of the "new southern governors." Though decades removed from odious southern politicians like James Vardaman and Eugene Talmadge, Carter still had to run a "redneck" campaign in order to win. He could not ignore the example of Alabama governor George Wallace, who could ignite the white man's rage. To capture the votes of blue-collar and rural voters, Carter painted his equally liberal opponent Carl Sanders as a corporate lawyer out of touch with the average man. Nicknaming Sanders "Cuff Link Carl," Carter's staff devised a television commercial with a closed country club door and a voice-over saying, "People like us aren't invited. We're too busy working for a living." Carter's team circulated the ugliest pictures of their candidate they could find in order to make him look like a poor country boy—in some he was riding a tractor. His money came from the honest trade of peanut farming, and from a warehousing operation—or so the logic went. Jimmy Carter was not one of the "Big Wigs" in Atlanta or Washington.[18]

During the runoff election, Sanders's team went on the offensive, producing flyers with photographs of the run-down homes of the tenants on Carter's peanut farm. The flyer's caption played off Carter's own slogan: "Isn't it time someone spoke up for these people?" The most damning of the opposition flyers had Carter climbing into bed with a racist leader. Here Carter was drawn as a clownish, barefoot redneck—the absurdity exacerbated by his polka-dotted suit. The point was that he was a leopard who could change his spots, manipulating his class identity just enough to satisfy politically conservative voters. The attack was not far from the truth: Carter was okay with alienating black voters in the primary, but in the general election he shifted, toning down his redneck appeal.[19]

As a politician, Carter was forced to endure a screening of *Deliverance* in Atlanta in 1972. He remained wary of its promoters' claim that the film was good for the state. Indeed, James Dickey and Jimmy Carter were two Georgians who had absolutely nothing in common. Carter was a Baptist and had a teetotaler wife, while Dickey was an outrageous alcoholic and an egomaniac, born to wealth. Haunted by insecurity after a pampered and effeminate youth, Dickey reinvented himself as the child of hillbillies—one of the many lies he told about himself. His North Georgia relatives were actually large landowners, whose past holdings included a considerable number of slaves.[20]

Dickey's novel, published in 1970, was a tortured exploration of lost manhood, an attempt to recover his "inner hillbilly." On the surface, the novel (and film) is about four men on a canoe trip in Appalachia. When the chubby bachelor Bobby (Ned Beatty) is raped in the movie by one of the mountain men, he is called a "sow" and told by his attacker to "squeal like a pig." In the psychosexual thriller, the dandified city folk aren't merely given their comeuppance; they are forced to rediscover their primal instincts. Dickey saw this as a good thing, and his hero ends up a stronger man. In one interview, the novelist admitted that the lure of the backcountry was to him the possibility of one's becoming a "counter-monster," behaving as men did who lived in remote parts, "doing whatever you felt compelled to do to survive." In the novel and film alike, the city men commit two murders, conceal the death of one of their traveling companions, Ronny Cox's character Drew, and make a pact never to reveal what happened on their ill-fated trip. Rechristened as blood brothers, the surviving trio carry their dark secrets away with them.[21]

Drew had to die. He was the only one of the four Atlanta businessmen who showed any compassion for rural people. He reached out to the idiot-savant teenager after their banjo-and-guitar duet. (Lonnie, the character in the novel, was supposed to be an albino.) The film's message was clear: sympathy was a sign of weakness that city boys had to overcome. Only by resorting to violence and taking a vicarious plunge into the uncensored psyche of the backwoodsman could they recover their feral redneck roots.[22]

Dickey's story had its giant appeal because the search he described found expression elsewhere in American society. NASCAR offered the same kind of allure, as Tom Wolfe wrote in *Esquire*. Men without inhibitions who lived for the momentary pleasure of danger had no fear of the consequences of their actions. North Carolinian driver Junior Johnson was not just a "hero a whole people or class can identify with," he was a "rare breed" who had gone from whiskey running in the isolated hills and hollows of his home state to stock car racing. He had it all: money, a

split-level house, a poultry business. He might have exchanged his overalls for a windbreaker with the collar up, and "Slim Jim" white pants, but
this "breed of old boy" proved something major by driving at 175 miles
per hour with a kind of madness that was "raw and hillbilly." That was
the appeal.[23]

The macho star of *Deliverance*, Burt Reynolds, went on to make a
southern-accented film that was an homage to the stock car racer's way
of life. In *Smokey and the Bandit* (1977), Reynolds's character lived for
the chase and ran from the law, while his female companion (played by
Sally Field) was a runaway bride—both of them rejecting civilization's
restraints. The Reynolds of this film was a modern-day squatter like good
old Sug, respected because he refused to knuckle down and join the daily
grind of working to get ahead. *Smokey and the Bandit* was the second
highest grossing film in 1977, but most of its popularity was in the South
and Midwest. Adding to the mix, in 1979, CBS launched *The Dukes of
Hazzard,* the plots of which revolved around rebel moonshiners decked
out in a bright red racing car, and a sexy kissing cousin named Daisy,
whose trademark was her high-cut jean shorts. Denver Pyle was cast as
Uncle Jesse, known for his overalls and countrified homilies; Pyle had
previously played Briscoe Darling Jr., the surly father of a musical hillbilly clan in *The Andy Griffith Show*.[24]

Wannabe bandits were among the thousands of spectators at
NASCAR who launched into rebel yells, drank too much, and ogled the
floozy on the float with her "big blonde hair and blossomy breasts" and
cheap Dallas Cowgirl outfit. They embraced a certain species of
freedom—the freedom to be a boor, out in the open and without regrets.
The "upscale rednecks," the rising white trash middle class, identified
with these hillbilly racers, men who had escaped the overalls and gained
as much respect as could be had in accepting wads of cash from Detroit.
Class structure had not changed appreciably for the rural poor: money
may have made a hillbilly or two reputable, but those left in the hills
were not reaping any social benefits. "Upscale rednecks" had no trouble
spotting those below them in their rearview mirrors.[25]

Jimmy Carter's presidency seemed to offer a break from past southern politicians. He was a born-again Christian and navy officer (with
training in nuclear physics) who predicated his 1976 campaign on his
refusal to lie to the voters. In the early days of the campaign, he gave an

unusual stump speech to elementary school children in New Hampshire, proclaiming that the United States could have a "government as good and as honest and as decent and as competent and as compassionate and as filled with love as the American people." Here was a sentimental democrat, a gospel-infused Christian populist, leaps and bounds from the anger-fueled populism of the old (redneck) South.[26]

Of all his predecessors, Carter probably came closest to Frank Clement's clean-cut demeanor, but he mostly kept his religious views to personal statements. He was no gyrating entertainer like Clement, nor (at five foot seven) was he a giant-sized jokester like "Big Jim" Folsom. He preferred to compare himself to Yale graduate and Tennessee liberal Estes Kefauver. The campaign rhetoric contained a "log cabin" story that captured the family's rise, but it left out the fact that Jimmy grew up with a tennis court in the backyard. He did express southern pride, though, gaining the support of country rock groups such as the Allman Brothers. His political handlers were sure to fashion a radio ad for the pickup truck crowd: "We've been the butt of every bad joke for a hundred years. Don't let the Washington politicians keep one of *us* out of the White House." The closest Carter came to acknowledging cracker roots was when he quoted the words of his supporter (his future United Nations ambassador) Andrew Young that he was "white trash made good." That made the peanut farmer Jimmy Carter "reformed" white trash. As a black congressman from Georgia, Young was suggesting that it was possible for the old hostility between poor blacks and whites to be overcome.[27]

As much as he rose above the dirty politics of the Nixon years, Carter's Sunday school teacher persona could go only so far. His image problem was cleverly summed up by fellow Georgian Roy Blount Jr. in the book *Crackers* (1980). Rather than find his inner redneck as James Dickey had, Carter ran on everything he wasn't: "He wasn't a racist, an elitist, a sexist, a Washingtonian, a dimwit, a liar, a lawyer . . . an ideologue, a paranoid, a crook." He was always in denial. By taking the "meanness and hambone out of the redneck," Blount reasoned, Carter was left without "force or framework." And no matter how liberal, how tolerant and accommodating he appeared, Carter's redneck shadow followed him. In that shadow the media lay in wait, preoccupied with Jimmy's toothy grin, his strange duel with a swamp rabbit, and, most notably, his redneck doppelgänger—brother Billy.[28]

Carter was the perfect candidate of the seventies, because he was someone who came to politics with "roots." He ran as the man from tiny Plains, as one who loved the land, loved his kin, and treasured his local community. That simple heritage was his calling card, and as a profile in the *Christian Science Monitor* concluded, "Few cling to their roots with more tenacity." Like Alex Haley, he was obsessed with his family's genealogy. He successfully cultivated his "common man" origins until a British publication on the peerage released a startling twenty-three-page finding on the Carter family lineage in 1977. Instead of descending from indentured servants, the president had one of the most significant family histories in the English-speaking world: he was related to both George Washington and the queen of England. The *New York Times* projected that his fellow Americans would find this discovery "amusing." It tempered the British announcement with a reminder to readers that some of the Carters in old England were poachers, the American equivalent of would-be moonshiners. Noble blood or hillbilly moonshiners? A spokesman for the British study, *Debrett's Peerage,* invoked eugenic thinking when he claimed that the Carter family had produced "intelligent to brilliant" people. The family line had its share of "sleepers," the expert confided, and it was from those less successful branches that Jimmy's brother Billy had acquired his less fine attributes.[29]

That said, Billy Carter was no sleeper. He became a redneck luminary, and tourists poured into the Carters' hometown of Plains looking for autographs and photographs with the down-home celebrity. He began producing his own beer, Billy Beer, and hired an agent to coordinate talks he gave around the country. He was known for voicing ornery, uncensored opinions. Billy smoked five packs of Pall Malls a day, and his code name on the CB radio was "Cast Iron," for his iron-gutted ability to drink anything and a lot of it. He was no "Holy Roller," no celebrant of the "Lost Cause." When asked what side he would have fought on in the Civil War, Billy joked, "I'd probably hid out in the swamp." In 1981, after his brother left office, Billy was peddling mobile homes.[30]

Roy Blount said he wished that Jimmy had a bit more of Billy in him, a little more irreverence and sass: "The first Cracker President should have been a mixture of Jimmy and Billy, . . . Billy's hoo-Lord-what-the-hell-get-out-the-way attitude heaving up under Jimmy's prudent righteousness—or Jimmy's idealism heaving up under Billy's sense of human limitations—and forming a nice-and-awful compound like life in Georgia." Blount's Cracker President would have "a richer voice, and a less dismissable smile."[31]

There was probably more redneck in Jimmy than Blount realized. When speechwriter Bob Shrum resigned from the Carter team in 1976, he exposed a less compassionate candidate. The man who publicly advocated for miners when he spoke before a labor audience told Shrum privately that "he opposed increased black-lung benefits for miners, because 'they chose to be miners.'" Seemingly lacking an understanding of class conditions, Carter right then revealed a mean streak a mile wide. Should miners suffer because they accepted the dangers of the job? He showed his mean side again in 1977 when he endorsed the Hyde Amendment for restricting Medicaid payments to poor women seeking abortions. In answer to a question from Judy Woodruff of NBC, the president did not defend his position on strictly moral grounds, but made a class argument instead: "Well, as you know, there are many things in life that are not fair, that wealthy people can afford and poor people can't. But I don't believe that the federal government should take action to try to make these opportunities exactly equal, when there is a moral factor involved." He basically held that the federal government should be able to deny poor women benefits because they were poor. The wealthy could do as they please, and the poor had to be disciplined. Carter was prone to the fatalistic view: poor women deserve their destiny, and coal miners must endure black-lung disease. In effect, the message was: don't expect equality or compassion if you can't help yourself.[32]

America's love affair with Jimmy Carter of Plains, Georgia, faded fairly rapidly. By 1979, his declining popularity was summed up in the parable of the swamp rabbit. It was a story the media refused to let go of, in part because the president's staff refused to release images of the encounter until pressed. Carter told his own tale of the swamp adventure. Paddling a canoe, he saw a wild rabbit chasing his small craft and "baring his teeth." He thought it was curious, and also funny. Reporters turned it into a modern version of the frontiersman's vaunted boasting session. Instead of "Daniel Boone wrestling with bears," one journalist chided, Carter was taking on "Peter Rabbit." Others had the president sparring with Banzai Bunny, or the killer rabbit of Monty Python fame.

It became a metaphor for a wimpy presidential leadership style, feeding the legend of the country boy who turned coward in what should have been familiar terrain—the marshy wilds of the Georgia backcountry. Jimmy Carter was not the hero of *Deliverance;* he was closer to Jimmy Stewart of *Harvey,* a feebleminded man unable to prove that the supernatural bunny existed or quash a story that made him look like a country bumpkin.[33]

In 1980, Carter lost to Ronald Reagan, a man who understood precious little about southern culture, but knew all he needed to about image making. His White House took on the trappings of a glamorous Hollywood set. Reagan could play the Irishman when he visited Ballyporeen, County Tipperary; he could wear a cowboy hat and ride a horse, as he did in one of his best-known films, *Santa Fe Trail.* The "acting president" had a skill few politicians possessed in that he was trained to deliver moving lines, look good for the camera, and project the desired tone and emotion. Since true eloquence had died with the advent of television, Reagan was less the "great communicator" his worshippers claimed than he was an actor with carefully honed "media reflexes." He came to office rejecting everything Carter stood for: the rural South, the common man, the image of the down-home American in bare feet and jeans. Reagan looked fantastic in a tuxedo. A rumor made the rounds in 1980 that Nancy Reagan was telling her friends that the Carters had turned the White House into a "pigsty." In her eyes, they were white trash, and every trace of them had to be erased.[34]

In a 1980 newspaper piece, one prominent Reagan supporter with strong conservative credentials made a rather dubious argument about rednecks. Patrick Buchanan charged that urban blacks had been lured into the poverty trap by government, and that black men had been shorn of the pride that came from being family providers. His hope was that they might switch their support to Reagan and form a new "Black Silent Majority." Casting the poor as pawns of the "professional povertarians," Buchanan revived the old attack against Rexford Tugwell of the New Deal for being the poor man's puppeteer. The most remarkable of Buchanan's prescriptions was that urban blacks should see their way to imitating the rednecks whose pickups featured a Reagan bumper sticker and whose sleeves sported the American flag (he should have said

Confederate). Putting poor blacks and rednecks in the same boat, Buchanan made bureaucracy the enemy of all.[35]

If Jimmy Carter's election made one of Roy Blount's friends cry out, "We ain't trash no more," that feeling was sadly deflated by 1987. That year's biggest public scandal was the fall of Reverend Jim Bakker. Rising from obscurity, Bakker and his wife, Tammy Faye, had built a televangelist empire out of the Charlotte, North Carolina, PTL ("Praise the Lord/ Pass the Love") Television Network that was estimated to reach thirteen million homes; they also opened the highly profitable twenty-three-hundred-acre Heritage USA Christian theme park. Along with Liberty University founder Jerry Falwell and Christian Broadcasting Network (CBN) founder Pat Robertson, Bakker had joined leading conservative religious leaders who made an appearance at the Reagan White House in 1984. Three years later, after an FBI investigation (in which the PTL was known as the "Pass-the-Loot Club"), he was convicted of all twenty-four charges of fraud and conspiracy. The judge was so disgusted that he sentenced the unscrupulous pastor to forty-five years in prison. In the end, he served a five-year term.[36]

Bakker was described as a "Bible school dropout," and his story revealed a man who not only fleeced his followers, but led a grossly extravagant life. He owned numerous homes, a 1953 Rolls-Royce, a sleek houseboat, and closets filled with expensive suits. Jim and Tammy Faye had gone from living in a trailer to amassing salaries and bonuses in the millions of dollars.[37]

Bakker's ministry preached the white trash dream of excess. In one 1985 program, he defended the extravagant style of his Christian amusement park hotel: "The newspaper people think we should still be back in the trash. . . . They really think Christians ought to be shabby, tacky, crummy, worthless people because we threaten them when we have things as nice as they have." In admitting his overindulgences, Bakker crooned, "I'm excessive. Dear Lord, I'm excessive. . . . God is a great God. He deserves my best." The second-rate hustler was a real-life version of Andy Griffith's role as Lonesome Rhodes in *A Face in the Crowd*. Or as one reporter claimed after watching untold hours of the Bakkers' show, their prosperity theology and living-room preaching had "the cheesy feel of *Petticoat Junction*."[38]

Greed was just the backstory. Tammy Faye, who became known for the makeup that oozed down her cheeks as she wept along with her flock, had to be carted off to rehab for an addiction to tranquilizers. Meanwhile, her reverend husband was paying hush money to the church secretary, a young woman he had used sexually seven years earlier. Jessica Hahn told her story to *Playboy*. And if that kind of exposure was not enough, the same church official who had arranged for Bakker's motel meeting with Hahn confessed that he had had three separate homosexual encounters with the TV pastor.[39]

The tabloid exploitation of the Bakker affair may have augured the official birth of "reality TV." One can directly trace the unholy line from the out-of-control Bakkers to the gawking at rural Georgian white trashdom in TLC's *Here Comes Honey Boo Boo*. Both the preacher's perversions and the underage beauty contestant's shenanigans tapped into the public's attachment to the tawdry behavior of the American underclass. (Tammy Faye later starred in the reality show *The Surreal Life* in 2004.) The people whom the Praise the Lord Ministry conned were mainly poor whites; the majority of the program's viewers were born-again, with less than a high school education, and were, most pitifully, unemployed. As one staffer revealed, PTL sent out appeals for money on the first of the month, when the Social Security and welfare checks were arriving. Critics of evangelical hypocrisy vented their rage, and one outraged editorialist attacked President Reagan himself for bringing "white trash front and center" when he entertained Bakker and other televangelists at the White House and told Americans they could learn from them about "traditional American values." The Bakkers appeared on television day and night, "dressed like pimps," massacring the English language and defiling religion.[40]

The Bakkers were not even native to the South. Tammy Faye was born into a poor family of eight children in a small rural town in Minnesota, in a house without indoor plumbing. Her parents were Pentecostal preachers. Jim, the son of a machinist, came from Michigan. They relocated to North Carolina because it was where they knew a market existed for their Pentecostal religious message. Tammy Faye was the charismatic heart of the show, singing, crying, and thriving on her gaudy reputation, "à la Liberace," as one religious scholar has concluded. Her physical appearance projected a class identity: frosted blonde hair, thick makeup,

tanned skin, loud, colorful dresses, and trademark fake eyelashes. She
was the picture of nouveau riche femininity.[41]

In this way only, she shared a persona with the Tennessean Dolly
Parton. The country singer known for her "voluptuously overflowing
body," garish outfits, big blonde wig—what one scholar has called "exces-
sive womanliness." Dolly's grandfather was a Pentecostal preacher. Like
Tammy Faye, the singer liked to buy her clothes at the cheaper stores.
Her image, as Parton confessed in her autobiography, expressed the
desire of poor white trash girls to see themselves as magazine models.
She explained, "They didn't look at all like they had to work in the fields.
They didn't look like they had to take a spit bath in a dishpan. They didn't
look as if men and boys could just put their hands on them any time they

The "excessive womanliness" of
Dolly Parton captured in a stand-up
poster of her in a Nashville music
store. This photograph appeared
in *Esquire* in 1977.

Esquire

felt like it, and with any degree of roughness they chose." Poverty, for a female, went beyond the wretchedness of having no money.[42]

Here lies a clue to the real appeal Tammy Faye had among her fans, who vicariously enjoyed the exhibitionism and excess. Parton's style could be seen as a burlesque—a hooker on the outside and a sweet country girl on the inside; similarly, Tammy Faye's drag queen look was embraced by the gay community. She was one of very few conservative evangelicals to show sympathy for gay men who were dying of AIDS. She also became for true believers a real-life Christian Cinderella story; one PTL partner made a handcrafted doll of her (marketed for adults, not children) that sold for $675. The Tammy Barbie was a fairy-tale princess with a large heart, adorned, as well, with exaggerated eyelashes.[43]

Yet this fairy tale did not have a happy ending. The media storm made the couple appear completely pathetic; Tammy gained little sympathy as a naïve wife. (Her kookiness probably saved her from indictment.) There was something almost gothic in the exaggerated white trash image of Tammy Faye Bakker. She achieved the American dream not because of

The seductive and materialistic message of prosperity theology. Tammy Faye Bakker on the cover of her album *Don't Give Up*.

Tammy Faye Bakker, *Don't Give Up* (1985)

her beauty, education, or talent, but because of having fashioned a cable TV personality that refused to partake of the fine manners of her social betters. Tammy Faye was the rejection of everything Pat Loud (of *An American Family*) and middle-class propriety stood for: emotional restraint, proper diction, subdued dress, and obvious refinement. Nor was she rustic, or the embodiment of old-fashioned yeoman simplicity. She embraced her garish self from head to toe. Her tawdry excess made her beloved among her poor white fans and unredeemable in the eyes of middle America.

The irony is that her white trash "roots" were hardly pure, if not wholly contrived. Her fake eyelashes and thick coat of makeup were part of a strange masquerade, consistent with the renegotiation of class identity that came with the expansion of mass media in the 1980s and 1990s. She said she borrowed her style of eyelashes from Lucille Ball . . . and Minnie Mouse. "In terms of broadcast hours," Roger Ebert claimed, "she lived more of her life on live TV than perhaps anyone else in history." Her public self appeared a composite of bad clichés—she was no closer to projecting authenticity than *The Beverly Hillbillies*. Tammy Faye was campy (mostly by accident), and more than anything else a creature of the surreal world of television that she loved.[44]

CHAPTER TWELVE
Outing Rednecks

Slumming, Slick Willie, and Sarah Palin

A dangerous chasm in the classes is alive and well in the United
States of America. Don't let anybody tell you it's not.
—Carolyn Chute, *The Beans of Egypt, Maine* (revised, 1995)

The Bakker scandal was not enough to stop the stampede toward
white trash and redneck chic that prevailed in the eighties and nine-
ties. Margo Jefferson in *Vogue* called the new rage "slumming." One of
the most surprising confessions in this vein came from John Hillerman,
the American actor who played the prim and proper English butler Jonathan Quayle Higgins III on *Magnum, P.I.* Hillerman said that when he
received fan mail from England, where he was claimed as one of their
own, he wrote back, "I hate to disappoint you, but I'm a redneck from
Texas."[1]

A growing chorus sought to clean up the image, to make "redneck" a
term of endearment. Lewis Grizzard, who made a name for himself as a
redneck journalist, thought it was time to stop mocking rednecks. He
praised the 1993 antidiscrimination ordinance in Cincinnati that made
hillbilly a protected class, and he hoped that Atlanta would pass a similar
law for rednecks in anticipation of the 1996 Summer Olympics. In Florida, a man was charged under the Hate Crime Statute in 1991 for defam-
ing a policeman by calling him a cracker. For Grizzard, "redneck" meant
"agriculturalist," a person like his father who worked outside and acquired
an uneven tan before there was sunscreen. He was wrong, of course, as
the long chronology catalogued here has shown.[2]

A certain ambiguity remained. Redneck, cracker, and hillbilly were
simultaneously presented as an ethnic identity, a racial epithet, and a
workingman's badge of honor. A North Carolina journalist neatly
summed up the identity confusion: "If you think you're a redneck, you
think you're hardworking, fun-loving and independent. If you don't think
you're a redneck, you think they're loud, obnoxious, bigoted and shallow."

Added to the article was a pop quiz featuring questions about NASCAR, food, and TV's *Hee Haw,* as if by a simple computation right answers could distinguish the "real Bubbas from the wanna-bes."[3]

To be sure, breeding remained paramount in considerations of identity. In 1994, one irate journalist insisted that the Georgia politician Newton Leroy Gingrich was no redneck: he was born in Pennsylvania, had no southern accent, had served as a college professor, and got elected to Congress by suburbanites of Atlanta, many of them Yankees. This newsman's expertise came from the fact that he was "kin to a great many of that breed." Besides, he chided, "Gingrich wouldn't last half an hour in a room of genuine rednecks." You were a dyed-in-the-wool redneck or you weren't. By this measure, neither Gingrich nor David Duke, the former Klan member who ran for governor of Louisiana in 1991, was a redneck. Duke was disqualified because he loved un-American Nazi salutes. Submitting to plastic surgery to make himself too pretty was also out of character. "No good ole Southern boy would dream of such a thing. It's unmasculine, un-Southern." This was the view of Jeffrey Hart, a conservative intellectual from Dartmouth College and former speechwriter for Presidents Nixon and Reagan.[4]

Redneck was no longer the exclusive province of country singers. It had become part of the cultural lingua franca, a means of sizing up public men, and a strangely mutated gender and class identity. Nor were women silent in this debate. Two prominent female writers earned acclaim in the modern genre of white trash fiction. In the tradition of William Faulkner and James Agee, Dorothy Allison and Carolyn Chute offered unsparing accounts of rural poverty. Allison creatively reconstructed the conditions she knew from her early years in *Bastard Out of Carolina* (1992), while Chute, a working-class, college-educated writer from Portland, told of trailer trash in rural Maine in her breakout book, *The Beans of Egypt, Maine* (1985). What set these writers apart was that they wrote from *within* their class, not as outside observers; they were outing themselves, and knew precisely how to describe poor women's experiences. Class and sexuality remained their dominant themes, and neither sugarcoated her subjects as good ol' girls. What they showed instead was that women cannot wear "white trash" or "redneck" as a badge of honor.[5]

Allison is the better writer. That said, a spare prose may have been intentional for Chute. She captures events as they are happening, offering few insights into the inner life of her white trash subjects. The Beans are a sprawling extended tribe who take over the underbelly of Egypt. They are an assorted lot. There is Beal and his mother, Merry Merry Bean, the latter of whom is crazy and kept locked in a tree house. Reuben is a violent drunk who ends up in prison; Auntie Roberta pops out babies like the rabbits she skins and eats. Reuben's girlfriend, Madeline, endures beatings at his hand. The characters' only talents are shooting and procreating. Beal sleeps with Roberta, and some of her children may be his. She, meanwhile, would never win any awards for mothering, allowing her babies to roam at will and to spit, hiss, and swallow pennies. Beal rapes (or doesn't rape) his neighbor Earlene Pomerleau, who becomes his wife, though he continues to sleep at his aunt's. Madeline parades around in flimsy halters that let her breasts fall out.[6]

Earlene is a step ahead of the Beans in class terms, at once disgusted by and attracted to them. She compares her first sexual encounter with Beal to being mauled by a bear. She is horrified by his large feet. As she completes the sex act, she "pictures millions of possible big Bean babies, fox-eyed, yellow-toothed, meat-gobbling Beans." Beal injures his eye at work, loses his job, and is racked by pain and a range of physical disabilities, but still he forbids Earlene to get food stamps. He refuses to go to a hospital until he is finally carried away by rescue workers. "I ain't worth a piss," the broken man says, scowling. He dies in a hail of police bullets after shooting out the windows of a wealthy family's home. Earlene watches him fall, the gun clasped in his hand.[7]

The Beans are waste people. Their women are breeders. They talk about Bean blood, and they all look alike. Earlene's father damns the Beans as uncivilized predators: "If it runs, a Bean will shoot it. If it falls, a Bean will eat it." Earlene's father is superior to these "tackiest people on earth," he believes, because they inhabit an old trailer, while he built his own house. As to the womenfolk, he singles out Roberta, muttering that there should be a law that after nine children with no husband, "you get the knife," that is, "tyin' the tubes." And when Reuben is taken away by the police, he voices the hope that they will "hog-tie the rest of the heathens." What he means is: round up the children and exterminate them before they become "full-blown Beans."[8]

In *The Beans of Egypt, Maine,* class warfare is played out at the lowest level. The middle class has no meaningful presence in the book: all that distinguishes the Pomerleaus from the Beans is Gram's religious discipline and the fact that Earlene's dad possesses artisan skills. Class is vividly shown when Earlene's father insists on patrolling the driveway dividing the two properties. He commands Earlene, "Don't go over on the Beans' side of the right-of-way. Not ever!" But of course she does. He loses his daughter to the other side.[9]

Chute's reception as a writer was often conflated with the life she led. With some condescension, she was praised for her "apparent ignorance of literary tradition," which magically preserved a "vigorous originality." Though compared to Faulkner, she had not read a single one of his novels until after reviewers noted the similarity between her *Beans of Egypt* and the Mississippian's work. A reviewer for *Newsweek* saw her characters as "candidates for compulsory sterilization," where "malevolent infants of doubtful paternity litter the floor." In interviews, Chute talked about her impoverished past, and insisted that she retained a personal bond with "my people." She explained, "Your material is what you live."[10]

Her husband, Michael, an illiterate laborer, was a conduit to "her people." The stories he told of rural characters influenced her writing. She herself had worked on a potato farm, in chicken processing, and in a shoe factory. Growing up in a working-class neighborhood in a suburb of Portland, she dropped out of high school, later taking classes at the University of Southern Maine. Her father was from North Carolina, which gave her southern roots. All of this contributed to the deeply political underpinnings of her books. She rejected the idea that anyone could escape the cycle of poverty—not if it meant leaving one's "homeland," "family," and "roots." The tribal nature of poor whites was their strength. The sense of place and of land was their only ballast.[11]

Over the next fifteen years, Chute's politics sharpened. In 1985, she did not call herself a redneck, but by 2000 she did. She lived off the grid, without modern plumbing, and until 2002 without a computer; she continued to wear work boots and bandanas. By now, "redneck" was a symbol of working-class populism for Chute. She organized her own Maine militia group, supported gun rights, and became an outspoken critic of corporate power. There was, she wrote in a postscript to the revised version of *The Beans of Egypt* in 1995, a "dangerous chasm in the classes

[that] is alive and well in the United States of America." The Beans were no longer ordinary people trying to survive; they were symbols of an approaching class war and a "crumbling" American dream.[12]

Dorothy Allison displayed just as much of an interest in class as Chute. She tells the story of difficult and sometimes violent relationships between men and women. Her female characters are less likely victims, swept up in circumstances, in the manner of Chute's female Beans; Allison's women have more material resources and greater support from their family members. But both writers depict emotionally stunted poor white men and recognize that everyday burdens fall more heavily on their women.[13]

In Allison's *Bastard Out of Carolina,* young Anne "Bone" Boatwright endures physical and sexual abuse at the hands of her mother's second husband, Daddy Glen Waddell. In the town of Greenville, South Carolina, as it is for the Beans of Egypt, Maine, the Boatwrights are despised. Daddy Glen's festering hatred of Bone comes from deeply lodged feelings of humiliation. He comes from a middle-class family, and he is the one member who never amounted to anything. He is a manual laborer and longs for a home like those of his brothers, one a dentist, the other a lawyer. "Nothing I do goes right," he grouses. "I put my hand in the honey jar and it comes out shit." He is jealous of Earle Boatwright's prowess with women too. Unlike the Beans, though, the Boatwright men tend to be affectionate and protective of the women and children in their extended family.[14]

Allison is fascinated by the thin line that separates the stepfather's family from the mother's; they might have more money, but they're shallow and cruel. Her cousins whisper that their car is like "nigger trash." Like Chute's Pomerleaus, they feel compelled to snub those below them. It is shame that keeps the class system in place.[15]

By the end of the novel, Bone frees herself from Glen, and in the process loses out to him when her psychically damaged mother decides to abandon the family and take off for California with him. In running away, her mother repeats the strategy of crackers a century earlier: to flee and start over somewhere else. Ruminating on her mother's life—pregnant at fifteen, wed then widowed at seventeen, and married a second time to Glen by twenty-one—Bone wonders whether she herself is equipped to make more sensible decisions. She won't condemn her mother, because she doesn't know for certain that she will be able to avoid some of the same mistakes.[16]

The lesson here is that the choices people make are both class- and gender-charged. Allison's story serves as a reminder that many more people—women especially—remain trapped in the poverty into which they are born; it is the exception who becomes, like the author Allison, a successful person capable of understanding the poor without condemning. The American dream is double-edged in that those who are able to carve out their own destiny are also hard-pressed not to condemn those who get stuck between the cracks. As it is with the character Scout in *To Kill a Mockingbird*, an awareness of the routine nature of injustice is most forcefully depicted when it is seen through the eyes of a child.

As the literary canon took on a new dimension with the rise of a talented generation of white trash writers, Americans returned another southerner to the White House in 1993. With Bill Clinton, the national spotlight focused once more on the uneasy relationship between class identity and American democracy. The boy from modest beginnings in Hope, Arkansas, had won a Rhodes Scholarship, was a Yale Law School graduate, and served as the governor of his state—in short, the American dream. William Jefferson Clinton was a perfect example of what his namesake, the man from Monticello, had formulated in 1779: raking from the rubbish a deserving youth who could eventually join the nation's aristocracy of talent. In his Fourth of July speech in his first year as president, Clinton recounted the story of how thirty years earlier he had met President Kennedy in the Rose Garden of the White House, shaking his hand, standing in awe as a "boy from a small town in Arkansas, with no money and no political connections."[17]

The Clinton saga was a blend of Charles Dickens and Dorothy Allison. He did not grow up in a financially secure middle-class nuclear family of the fifties. Rather, his father had died three months before he was born, and his mother left him in the care of grandparents and great-grandparents while she attended nursing school. "The strength of our family could not be measured by the weight of our wallets," he proudly declared on Independence Day in 1993. But as the public learned from his mother, Virginia, there was a darker side to Bill's childhood. In the biographical film shown during the Democratic National Convention, Clinton's fractured roots were exposed. He may have taken the name of his stepfather, but as a fourteen-year-old found he had to stand up to him. Roger Clinton was a car dealer and a gambler; he drank too much, and he became violent. One day, Bill quietly told him, "Don't ever, ever lay your hands on my mother again." But like Chute's and Allison's treatment of their male characters, he was not without compassion, saying of his stepfather's problem, "He didn't think enough of himself." He had internalized that sense of white trash shame.[18]

On the campaign trail, Clinton quoted Jefferson, and staged his ceremonial inaugural journey to Washington from the top of Jefferson's "little mountain." At the Republican convention, ex-president Reagan had taken the opportunity to question the pretensions of the boy from Hope, dismissing the idea that Clinton was the heir of either Kennedy or Jefferson. In a classic quip, he modified lines that the Texan Lloyd Bentsen had used against Dan Quayle of Indiana in the 1988 vice presidential debate, after the latter had compared himself to a young, untested JFK, with whom Bentsen had served. "Senator," Bentsen bellowed, "you're no Jack Kennedy." With mock gravity, Reagan deployed his own version of Bentsen's iconic putdown, this time applying the sentiment to then-governor Clinton. "I knew Thomas Jefferson," Reagan said. "He was a friend of mine. And, Governor, you're no Thomas Jefferson."[19]

What, then, was Bill Clinton? He embodied certain stereotypes: his cholesterol-rich dining habits, the wife-beating story about his mother, and allusions to dirt-poor shacks in the Arkansas hills. To add fuel to the fire, a grinning, still-campaigning Clinton was photographed with an Illinois (not Arkansas) mule named George, and a mule named Bill got press when it strolled down Pennsylvania Avenue as part of the Clinton inauguration parade.[20]

Arkansas was ranked forty-seventh in per capita income in 1992, and its legacy as a state scarred by "redneck benightedness" lingered on. By calling on a Jefferson or a Kennedy in his speeches, Clinton was attempting to distance himself from his home state and class background. His mentor had been Arkansas senator J. William Fulbright, a liberal champion of education and a statesman of real note, but he still needed national icons for his presidential run. Even in 2004, as a popular and productive ex-president, Clinton was still trying to balance the extremes of his upbringing and his ambition, as Texas pundit Molly Ivins felt when she reviewed his thick memoir: "You just have to stand back and admire the sheer American dream arc of this hopelessly hillbilly kid."[21]

Bill Clinton was not a hillbilly, nor a redneck, but he did claim at the Democratic National Convention to have a "little bit of Bubba" in him. *Bubba Magazine* was issued in his honor, and the first cover displayed a photograph of Clinton wearing a cap and holding a beer. In the words of humorist David Grimes of the *Sarasota Herald-Tribune,* this act of self-identification put Clinton in a long line of Bubba presidents, including Andrew Jackson, Lyndon Johnson (the biggest Bubba of them all), and Jimmy Carter, the last of whom "felt extremely guilty about it."

Clinton's election did what the earlier nonelite southern presidents could not, turning crackers and rednecks into something that mainstream America could embrace. The Texas-born New York editor of *Bubba Magazine* described Bubba as someone who was patriotic, religious, enjoyed a dirty joke, but "cut across socioeconomic groups" in expressing an identity. Bubba wasn't regionally based, then, and defied stereotypes about cultural upbringing normally associated with an ethnic identity. To be a Bubba was to adopt a leisure self, a thing put on and worn like a pair of dungarees or a trucker's cap. Take off your suit and tie and dress down à la redneck—one might call it white trash slumming. It was just one more attempt to downplay class by anointing (and electing) Bubba as the new common man. Or so innovators in democratic parlance preferred as the Clinton era took shape.[22]

Clinton acquired other, less folksy nicknames, of course. "Slick Willie" was a slur that dogged him all the way from Arkansas to the White House. Of the issues that attached to him—smoking marijuana (with or without inhalation), dodging the draft, an alleged affair—Clinton issued denials, offered earnest-seeming explanations, but always came across as somewhat less than forthright. Here he was portrayed as a smooth talker, even a con man—"Slick Willie" was a name with southern and rural flavor. There was in Clinton's rise the backdrop of a tawdry southern novel, as Paul Greenberg of the *Arkansas Democrat* discovered: Clinton's finesse at verbal dodges suggested a man ducking into all the available rabbit holes. It was Greenberg who first bestowed the ignominious title on the boy from Hope back in 1980. Another syndicated columnist saw something deeply southern in the moniker: it suggested the liberal politician's reflex—in the South, honesty could derail a career.[23]

Clinton could not help but be defined by his origins. Even with his gift for gab, he was never as polished or, well, as slick as Reagan, who was known as the "Teflon-coated president." In his first year in office, when Clinton appeared momentarily to fumble, an editorialist wrote that Slick Willie was looking more like Sheriff Andy Griffith's sidekick Barney Fife. Image was everything, and politicians were always fair game, no matter how shallow, fleeting, or obnoxious the label pasted on them in print or cartoon was. The game in the 1990s was to find an image that placed Bill Clinton in a more favorable light and brushed the dirt from his jeans. What might be Clinton's "Old Hickory" moment? As it turned out, he was saved by Elvis.[24]

Clinton was not in the least reticent about cultivating the Elvis image. He sang one of the King's songs on a New York City news program, and during an interview with Charlie Rose jokingly appealed to the press, "Don't Be Cruel." What really did it for him, though, was an appearance on *The Arsenio Hall Show* playing his saxophone rendition of "Heartbreak Hotel." Clinton had revived the old southern political strategy—as Jimmy Carter could not do—of singing and swinging his way into office. His vice president, Al Gore of Tennessee, regaled the Democratic National Convention by confessing that the moment at hand represented the fulfillment of his longtime wish to be the warm-up act for Elvis. As he made his final campaign swing, Clinton added a line to his speeches, parodying himself by telling each audience that he was communing with Elvis. Incumbent president George H. W. Bush was so annoyed with reporters' love affair with the Arkansas Elvis that his staff hired an Elvis impersonator to crash the Democrat's campaign appearances. Clinton took it all in stride and invited his own Elvis performer to the inauguration.[25]

"Elvis is America," explained one member of Clinton's staff. The fifties that Reagan had tried to recapture with nostalgic images of small-town U.S.A. was once again associated with fun-loving teenagers—less political than their parents. Clinton-the-marijuana-smoking-draft-dodger was in this way extracted from the dangerous sixties and rebranded as a child of the less contentious fifties. He wished to build a bridge to the southern working class, to make himself a son of the South in the best

SEEN AS 'WHITE TRASH'

Maybe some hate Clinton because he's too Southern

Even at the start of the presidential campaign, 'Bubba' and Arkansas jokes jammed the airways. The 'Slick Willie' motif emerged and stuck. 'Hee-haute' cuisine made the rounds.

By BILL MAXWELL

Bill Jeff with a Georgia mule: Just too down home?

In 1994, Bill Clinton's controversial reputation as white trash was reinforced by a campaign photograph of him with an Illinois mule.

"Seen as 'White Trash': Maybe Some Hate Clinton Because He's Too Southern," Wilmington, North Carolina, *Star-News*, June 19, 1994

way imaginable. Being an Elvis fan was a more neutral place to be within a divided electorate—a youthful role that played much better than Bubba, and a hipper way for Clinton to channel his southern-boy image.[26]

No amount of amiability, however, could quell the hatred of conservative Republicans on losing the White House. Beltway reporters said they had never seen such vitriol before. The attacks on President Clinton seemed disrespectful of the office, highly personal, and relentless. In 1994, journalist Bill Maxwell of Florida, an African American, said he thought he knew why. He saw something familiar in the tone of the Clinton bashing, and it had to do with his being seen as white trash. Reagan press aide David Gergen and the effusive speechwriter Peggy Noonan saw their President Reagan as a transcendent father figure, partaking of the family feeling inspired by a British king. To Reagan's admirers, Clinton was unworthy, an impostor whose upbringing besmirched the office: the prince had been replaced by the pauper.[27]

To Maxwell's mind, Clinton's earthiness, his southernness, was seen as being bred into him from his mother, Virginia. She had published a memoir, and her story was grim: her mother was a drug addict, her childhood was one of deprivation, and she was married four times. Her appearance borrowed from trailer trash: "skunk stripe in her hair, elaborate makeup, colorful outfits and racing form in hand." (Traces of Tammy Faye hung about her.) In the eyes of his enemies, said Maxwell, Clinton was his mother's son, a kind of bastard breed that fell short of representing the right "pedigree for a U.S. president."[28]

By the time the Monica Lewinsky scandal broke in 1998, Clinton's enemies were primed to portray the flawed president as a character in a Tennessee Williams play. "Slick Willie" had finally been caught in a tawdry sexual escapade suited to a trailer park—he had befouled the Oval Office. Independent counsel Kenneth Starr claimed that his official investigation was not about sex, but about perjury and the abuse of power, yet his final report mentioned sex five hundred times. *Harper's Magazine* contributing editor Jack Hitt claimed that Starr was intent on writing a "dirty book," recording (and relishing) every trashy detail of a sad soap opera. President Clinton's legal team countered that Starr's sole purpose was to embarrass the president. This was white trash outing on the grand national stage. Impeachable offenses demanded the "gravest wrongs" against the Constitution, or "serious assaults on the integrity of the process of government," if they were to rise to the standard of "high crimes and misdemeanors." By recording every salacious detail, Starr was trying to equate high crimes with low-class lewdness.[29]

Conservatives were apoplectic at the thought that Clinton's misdeeds could be compared with those of Thomas Jefferson—the DNA of the third president's male line was tested the same year as the Lewinsky story broke. Science could now determine that the master of Monticello (or at least a Jefferson male with regular access to her—and who else could that be?) fathered the children of the Monticello slave Sally Hemings, the much younger half sister of Jefferson's deceased wife. Distraught commentators twisted the facts of the case, offering up an odd collection of rationales in order to exonerate the third president from charges of immorality. One, Sally was beautiful (and Monica was cheap). Two, Clinton was an adulterer (and Jefferson was a widower of long standing). Three, Jefferson was a brilliant man whose words elevated him above his bodily urges (and the merely glib Clinton was unable to rise above his unimpressive origins). To conflate the impulses of Jefferson and Clinton was a leveling that upright Americans should not countenance.[30]

Another editor saw the Lewinsky episode differently. After Clinton survived the impeachment ordeal and emerged stronger and more popular, he looked for explanations. If hating Clinton was irrational, then so was loving him. It was the "Elvis principle," the journalist concluded, that subliminal desire all Americans have for kings. JFK had Camelot; Reagan was Hollywood royalty; Clinton and Elvis ("the King" to his millions of fans) were "rags to riches" monarchs. The kind of kings Americans looked up to were men with a hard-to-explain sex appeal and a gentle hubris. The point was that a little white trashiness could be a blessing in disguise. In the appearance-driven world of modern American politics, arrogance of style carried weight, and repressed, suit-and-tie candidates such as Walter Mondale or Michael Dukakis were not in the same league as Clinton. To exude that redneck chic—to have a little Bubba—was better than being a dull, invisible, cookie-cutter politician indistinguishable from the pack.[31]

Figuring out Clinton remained a favorite pastime. In 1998, looking on with horror at the trumped-up presidential adultery scandal, the novelist Toni Morrison drew her own conclusions. The violation of privacy, the ransacking of the presidential office when he was "metaphorically seized and body searched" was for her the kind of treatment black men faced. No matter "how smart you are, how hard you work," you will be "put in your place." Clinton had overreached. He was "our first black president," Morrison mused. The "tropes of blackness" were apparent in his upbringing in a single-parent and poor household, and in his working-class ways, his saxophone playing and love for junk food. This Clinton really was Elvis-like. He was not the redneck Elvis who still had devotees in the 1990s, but the "Hillbilly Cat" Elvis of the 1950s, the youth who transgressed the boundaries between black and white—something that was only possible to do in comfort among the lower ranks of southern society.[32]

Clinton's title of "first black president" was reaffirmed at the 2001 Congressional Black Caucus Dinner. When Barack Obama ran for president in 2007, Andrew Young, the Carter adviser who had been a friend to Dr. Martin Luther King Jr., said that Clinton was "every bit as black as Barack." How strange was that: the son of a Kenyan was less black than a Bubba from Arkansas? Young was treating blackness as a cultural identity, and Obama's childhood in Hawaii and Jakarta lacked Dixie roots. Kathleen Parker of the *Washington Post,* a southerner, saw confusion in figurative language, writing that all one had to do was to replace the sax with a banjo and Clinton became a pastiche of "white-trash tropes." Journalist Joe Klein pushed the trope further in *Primary Colors* (1996), his thinly veiled novel about Clinton, who is called Jack Stanton in the book. Stanton violates the sexual taboo, sleeping with an underage black female, fathering an illegitimate child. In the Mike Nichols film based on Klein's book, President Bubba was played by the unpolished John Travolta, instead of someone like the squeaky clean Tom Hanks. Was this fellow Stanton a symbol of blackness, or was he trailer trash?[33]

Clinton's embarrassing second term evidently wasn't read as a cautionary tale among Republicans, who plunged ahead with their own (effectively) white trash candidate in 2008, Alaska governor Sarah Palin. The devastatingly direct Frank Rich of the *New York Times* referred to the Republican ticket as "Palin and McCain's Shotgun Marriage." Did the venerable John McCain of Arizona, ordinarily a savvy politician, have a lapse in judgment here? *Slate* produced an online video of Palin's hometown of Wasilla, painting it as a forgettable wasteland, a place "to get gas and pee" before getting back on the road. Wasilla was elsewhere described as the "punch line for most redneck jokes told in Anchorage." Erica Jong wrote in the *Huffington Post*, "White trash America certainly has allure for voters," which explained the photoshopped image of Palin that appeared on the Internet days after her nomination. In a stars-and-stripes bikini, holding an assault rifle and wearing her signature black-rimmed glasses, Palin was one-half hockey mom and one-half hot militia babe.[34]

News of the pregnancy of Palin's teenage daughter Bristol led to a shotgun engagement to Levi Johnston, which was arranged in time for the Republican National Convention. *Us Weekly* featured Palin on the cover, with the provocative title, "Babies, Lies, and Scandal." Maureen Dowd compared Palin to Eliza Doolittle of *My Fair Lady* fame, in getting prepped for her first off-script television interview. Could there be any more direct allusion to her questionable class origins? The Palin melodrama led one journalist to associate the Alaska clan with the plot of a Lifetime television feature. The joke was proven true to life two years later, when the backwoods candidate gave up her gig as governor and starred in her own reality TV show, titled *Sarah Palin's Alaska.*[35]

Palin's candidacy was a remarkable event on all accounts. She was only the second female of any kind and the first female redneck to appear on a presidential ticket. John McCain's advisers admitted that she had been selected purely for image purposes, and they joined the chorus trashing the flawed candidate after Obama's historic victory. Leaks triggered a media firestorm over Palin's wardrobe expense account. An angry aide categorized the Palins' shopping spree as "Wasilla hillbillies looting Neiman Marcus from coast to coast."[36]

The Alaskan made an easy and attractive target. Journalists were flabbergasted when she showed no shame in displaying astounding lapses in knowledge. Her bungled interview with NBC host Katie Couric represented more than gotcha journalism: Palin didn't just misconstrue facts; she came across as a woman who was unable to articulate a single complex idea. (The old cracker slur as "idle-headed" seemed to fit.) But neither did Andrew Jackson run as an "idea man" in an earlier century, and it was his style of backcountry hubris that McCain's staffers had been hoping to revive. Shooting wolves from a small plane, bragging about her love of moose meat, "Sarah from Alaska" positioned herself as a regular Annie Oakley on the campaign trail.

It was not enough to rescue her from the mainstream (what she self-protectively called "lamestream") media. Sarah Palin did not have a self-made woman's résumé. She could not offset the "white trash" label as the Rhodes Scholar Bill Clinton could. She had attended six unremarkable colleges. She had no military experience (à la navy veteran Jimmy Carter), though she did send one son off to Iraq. Writing in the *New Yorker,* Sam Tanenhaus was struck by Palin's self-satisfied manner: "the certitude of being herself, in whatever unfinished condition, will always be good enough."[37]

Maureen Dowd quipped that Palin was a "country-music queen without the music." She lacked the self-deprecating humor of Dolly Parton—not to mention the natural talent. The real conundrum was why, even more than how, she was chosen: the white trash Barbie was at once visually appealing and disruptive, and she came from a state whose motto on license plates read "The Last Frontier." The job was to package the roguish side of Palin alongside a comfortable, conventional female script. In the hit country single "Redneck Woman" (2004), Gretchen Wilson rejected Barbie as an unreal middle-class symbol—candidate Palin's wardrobe bingeing was her Barbie moment.

Her Eliza Doolittle grand entrance came during the televised debate with Senator Joe Biden of Delaware. As the nation waited to see what she looked like and how she performed, Palin came onstage in a little black dress, wearing heels and pearls, and winked at the camera. From the neck down she looked like a Washington socialite, but the wink faintly suggested a gum-chewing waitress at a small-town diner. Embodying these two extremes, the fetching hockey mom image ultimately lost out to what McCain staffers identified as both "hillbilly" and "prima donna." She was a female Lonesome Rhodes—full of spit and spittle, and full of herself.[38]

Sex formed a meaningful subtext throughout Palin's time of national exposure. In terms of trash talk, daughter Bristol Palin's out-of-wedlock pregnancy was handled rather differently from Bill Clinton's legendary philandering. Bloggers muddied the waters by spreading rumors about Sarah's Down syndrome child, Trig: "Was he really Bristol's?" they asked. A tale of baby swapping was meant to suggest a new twist on the

Steve Brodner's caricature of Sarah Palin as the celebrity-seeking hillbilly, which appeared in the *New Yorker* in 2009.

New Yorker, December 7, 2009

Palin's supporters identify with her: she represents the erasure of any distinction between the governing and the governed.

backwoods immorality of inbred illegitimacy. Recall that it was Bill Clinton's mother, Virginia, whose pedigree most troubled the critics. The legacy held: the rhetoric supporting eugenics (and the sterilization laws that
followed) mainly targeted women as tainted breeders.[39]

Sarah Palin's *Fargo*esque accent made her tortured speech patterns
sound even worse. Former TV talk show host Dick Cavett wrote a scathing satirical piece in which he dubbed her a "serial syntax killer" whose
high school English department deserved to be draped in black. He
wanted to know how her swooning fans, who adored her for being a
"mom like me," or were impressed to see her shooting wolves, could
explain how any of those traits would help her to govern.

We had been down this road before as citizens and voters. "Honest
Abe" Lincoln was called an ape, a mudsill, and Kentucky white trash.
Andrew Jackson was a rude, ill-tempered cracker. (And like Palin, his
grammar was nothing to brag about.) The question loomed: At what
point does commonness cease to be an asset, as a viable form of populism, and become a liability for a political actor? And should anyone
be shocked when voters are swept up in an "almost Elvis-sized following," as Cavett said Palin's supporters were? When you turn an election
into a three-ring circus, there's always a chance that the dancing bear
will win.[40]

By the time of the 2008 election, Americans had been given a thorough taste of the new medium of reality TV, in which instant celebrity
could produce a national idol out of a nobody. In *The Swan,* working-
class women were being altered through plastic surgery and breast
implants to look like, say, a more modest, suburban Dolly Parton. While
American Idol turned unknowns into overnight singing sensations, the
attention-craving heiress Paris Hilton consented to filming an updated
Green Acres in *The Simple Life,* moving into an Arkansas family's rural
home. Donald Trump's *The Apprentice,* billed as a "seductive weave of
aspiration and Darwinism," celebrated ruthlessness. In these and related
shows, talent was secondary; untrained stars were hired to serve voyeuristic interests, in expectation that, as mediocrities, they could be
relied on to exhibit the worst of human qualities: vanity, lust, and greed.
In 2008, Palin underwent an off-camera "Extreme Makeover"—to borrow a title from one of the more popular such shows. McCain campaign
advisers bought into the conceit of reality TV, which said that anyone

could be turned into a pseudo-celebrity; in this instance, their experiment had the effect of reshaping national politics.[41]

After 2008, a new crop of TV shows came about that played off the white trash trope. *Swamp People, Here Comes Honey Boo Boo, Hillbilly Handfishin', Redneck Island, Duck Dynasty, Moonshiners,* and *Appalachian Outlaws* were all part of a booming industry. Like the people who visited Hoovervilles during the Depression, eyeing the homeless as if they were at the zoo, television brought the circus sideshow into American living rooms. The modern impulse for slumming also found expression in reviving the old stock vaudeville characters. One commentator remarked of the highly successful *Duck Dynasty*, set in Louisiana, "All the men look like they stepped out of the Hatfield-McCoy conflict to smoke a corncob pipe." The Robertson men were kissing cousins of the comic Ritz Brothers in the 1938 Hollywood film *Kentucky Moonshine.*[42]

Reality programming subsists on emotion-producing competition and outright scandal. The long-running *Here Comes Honey Boo Boo* was canceled in 2014, but only after it was discovered that Mama June Shannon was dating a convicted child molester; she next revealed that the father of two of her daughters was an entirely different convicted sex offender who had been caught in a sting on NBC's voyeuristic *To Catch a Predator.* Though her young daughter Honey Boo Boo was the headliner, June was the real star of the show, the new face of white trash. No longer emaciated and parchment colored, as white trash past was imagined, she

Kissing cousins. The comic Ritz Brothers from *Kentucky Moonshine* (1938) and their heirs, the male cast of *Duck Dynasty*, the highly popular A&E reality TV show.

was a grossly overweight woman and the antithesis of the typical mom who prettified her grade-school daughter and dragged her to child beauty pageants. June claimed to have had four daughters by three different men, one whose name she claimed she could not remember. Her town of McIntyre, in rural Georgia, is a place of stagnant poverty: one-quarter of its households are headed by single females, and in 2013 the median family income in McIntyre was $18,243.[43]

As the gap between rich and poor grew wider after 2000, conservatives took the lead in white trash bashing. In *Black Rednecks and White Liberals* (2005), the economist and Hoover Institute fellow Thomas Sowell connected the delinquency of urban black culture to redneck culture. The book begins with a quote dating to 1956: "These people are creating terrible problems in our cities. They can't or won't hold a job, they flout the law constantly and neglect their children, they drink too much and their moral standards would shame an alley cat." His assumption was that readers would associate the quote with a conventional racist attack. But it was aimed at poor whites living in Indianapolis, and reflected "undesirable" southern whites who lived in northern cities.

Sowell contended that there has been an unchanging subculture going back centuries. Relying on Grady McWhiney's *Cracker Culture* (1988), a flawed historical study that turned poor whites into Celtic ethnics (Scots-Irish), Sowell claimed that the bad traits of blacks (laziness, promiscuity, violence, bad English) were passed on from their backcountry white neighbors. In Sowell's odd recasting of the hinterlands, a good old eye-gouging fight was the seed of black machismo. Reviving the squatter motif, he downplayed the influence of slavery, and substituted for it a eugenic-like cultural contagion that spread from poor whites to blacks. He further argued that white liberals of the present day are equally to blame for social conditions, having abetted the destructive lifestyle of "black rednecks" through perpetuation of the welfare state.[44]

Another conservative blaming the poor for their problems is Charlotte Hays, whose 2013 book *When Did White Trash Become the New Normal?* was a "Southern Lady's" gossipy screed against obesity, bad manners, and the danger of national decline when society takes its "cues" from the underclass. Hays expressed her horror that *Here Comes Honey Boo Boo* attracted more viewers than the 2012 Republican National Convention. In her best imitation of a snooty matron complaining, "You can't get good help anymore," the author/blogger's senses were affronted whenever and wherever she saw the disappearance of the rules of politeness. That a depressed minimum wage keeps millions in poverty is of no concern: she writes that the colonists at Jamestown and Plymouth understood that hard work might still require "a little starving." If she was talking about the actual Jamestown, she should have said "a lot of starving" and a little cannibalism. Hays represents a good many people who persist in believing that class is irrelevant to the American system. It is, she insists, manners (alas, no longer practiced by one's social inferiors) that determine the health of a civilization. "A gentleman is defined," Hays writes, "in a way that a janitor could be considered one if he strove to do the right thing."[45]

Sowell and Hays were responding to the cultural shift that began in the 1970s. Hays wished to banish identity politics entirely, which is why she mocked all kinds of white trash slumming. In its place, she imagined reviving old-fashioned manners—as if it were possible for class identity to be hidden under a veneer of false gentility. She wanted the pretense of equality, but offered nothing for closing the wealth gap. Sowell reimagined what Alex Haley started, in attempting to rewrite race as an ethnic identity and heritage—that is, something transmitted culturally from one generation to the next. With his revisionist pen, he cut the tie to Africa, the roots forged by Haley, and replaced the noble African American progenitor with a debased cross-pollinating power: degenerate crackers of white America.

A corps of pundits exist whose fear of the lower classes has led them to assert that the unbred perverse—white as well as black—are crippling and corrupting American society. They deny that the nation's economic structure has a causal relationship with the social phenomena they highlight. They deny history. If they did not, they would recognize that the most powerful engines of the U.S. economy—slaveowning planters and land speculators in the past, banks, tax policy, corporate giants, and compassionless politicians and angry voters today—bear considerable responsibility for the lasting effects on white trash, or on falsely labeled "black rednecks," and on the working poor generally. The sad fact is, if we have no class analysis, then we will continue to be shocked at the numbers of waste people who inhabit what self-anointed patriots have styled the "greatest civilization in the history of the world."

America's Strange Breed

━━━⟫◦◦◦⟪━━━

The Long Legacy of White Trash

Two persistent problems have rumbled through our "democratic" past. One we can trace back to Franklin and Jefferson and their longing to dismiss class by touting "exceptional" features of the American landscape, which are deemed productive of an exceptional society. The founders insisted that the majestic continent would magically solve the demographic dilemma by reducing overpopulation and flattening out the class structure. In addition to this environmental solution, a larger, extremely useful myth arose: that America gave a voice to all of its people, that every citizen could exercise genuine influence over the government. (We should note that this myth was always qualified, because it was accepted that some citizens were more worthy than others—especially those whose stake in society came from property ownership.)

The British colonial imprint was never really erased either. The "yeoman" was a British class, reflecting the well-established English practice of equating moral worth to cultivation of the soil. For their part, nineteenth-century Americans did everything possible to replicate class station through marriage, kinship, pedigree, and lineage. While the Confederacy was the high mark—the most overt manifestation—of rural aristocratic pretense (and an open embrace of society's need to have an elite ruling over the lower classes), the next century ushered in the disturbing imperative of eugenics, availing itself of science to justify breeding a master class. Thus not only did Americans *not* abandon their desire for class distinctions, they repeatedly reinvented class distinctions. Once the government of the United States began portraying itself as "leader of the free world," the longing for a more regal head of state was advanced. The Democrats swooned over Kennedy's Camelot, and Republicans ennobled the Hollywood court of Reagan.

American democracy has never accorded all the people a meaningful voice. The masses have been given symbols instead, and they are often empty symbols. Nation-states traditionally rely on the fiction that a head of state can represent the body of the people and stand in as their proxy; in the American version, the president must appeal broadly to shared values that mask the existence of deep class divisions. Even when this strategy works, though, unity comes at the price of perpetuating ideological deception. George Washington and Franklin Roosevelt were called fathers of the country, and are now treated as the kindly patriarchs of yore; Andrew Jackson and Teddy Roosevelt descend to us as brash, tough-talking warriors. Cowboy symbols stand tall in the saddle and defend the national honor against an evil empire, as Reagan did so effectively; more recently, the American people were witness to a president dressed in a pilot jumpsuit who for dramatic effect landed on an aircraft carrier. That, of course, was George W. Bush, as he prematurely proclaimed an end to combat operations in Iraq. Left out of our collective memory, meanwhile, are corporate puppet presidents such as William McKinley, who was in the pocket of Big Steel and a host of manufacturing interests. When presidential candidate Mitt Romney in 2012 responded to a heckler with the line "Corporations are people, my friend," he inadvertently became the new McKinley. The "1 percent" were his constituency, and wearing blue jeans did little to loosen his buttoned-up image.

Power (whether social, economic, or merely symbolic) is rarely probed. Or if it is, it never becomes so urgent a national imperative as to require an across-the-board resolution, simultaneously satisfying a moral imperative and pursuing a practical cause. We know, for instance, that Americans have forcefully resisted extending the right to vote; those in power have disenfranchised blacks, women, and the poor in myriad ways. We know, too, that women historically have had fewer civil protections than corporations. Instead of a thoroughgoing democracy, Americans have settled for democratic stagecraft: high-sounding rhetoric, magnified, and political leaders dressing down at barbecues or heading out to hunt game. They are seen wearing blue jeans, camouflage, cowboy hats, and Bubba caps, all in an effort to come across as ordinary people. But presidents and other national politicians are anything but ordinary people after they are elected. Disguising that fact is the real camouflage that distorts the actual class nature of state power.

The theatrical performances of politicians who profess to speak for an

"American people" do nothing to highlight the history of poverty. The tenant farmer with his mule and plow is not a romantic image to retain in historic memory. But that individual is as much our history as any war that was fought and any election that was hotly contested. The tenant and his shack should remain with us as an enduring symbol of social stasis.

The underclass exists even when they don't rise to the level of making trouble, fomenting rebellions, joining in riots, or fleeing the ranks of the Confederacy and hiding out in swamps, where they create an underground economy. Those who do not disappear into the wilderness are present in towns and cities and along paved and unpaved roads in every state. Seeing the poor, whether it is in the photographs of a Walker Evans or a Dorothea Lange, or in comical form on "reality TV," we have to wonder how such people exist amid plenty. As she cast her eyes upon southern trailer trash in the middle of World War II, the *Washington Post* columnist Agnes Meyer asked, "Is this America?"

Yes, it is America. It is an essential part of American history. So too is the backlash that occurs when attempts are made to improve the conditions of the poor. Whether it is New Deal polices or LBJ's welfare programs or Obama-era health care reform, along with any effort to address inequality and poverty comes a harsh and seemingly inevitable reaction. Angry citizens lash out: they perceive government bending over backward to help the poor (implied or stated: undeserving) and they accuse bureaucrats of wasteful spending that steals from hardworking men and women. This was Nixon's class-inflected appeal, which his campaign staff packaged for the "Silent Majority." In the larger scheme of things, the modern complaint against state intervention echoes the old English fear of social leveling, which was said to encourage the unproductive. In its later incarnation, government assistance is said to undermine the American dream. Wait. Undermine *whose* American dream?

Class defines how real people live. They don't live the myth. They don't live the dream. Politics is always about more than what is stated, or what looms before the eye. Even when it's denied, politicians engage in class issues. The Civil War was a struggle to shore up both a racial *and* a class hierarchy. The Confederacy was afraid that poor whites would be drawn in by Union appeals and would vote to end slavery—because slavery was principally a reflection of the wealthy planters' self-interest.

Today as well we have a large unbalanced electorate that is regularly convinced to vote against its collective self-interest. These people are told that East Coast college professors brainwash the young and that Hollywood liberals make fun of them and have nothing in common with them and hate America and wish to impose an abhorrent, godless lifestyle. The deceivers offer essentially the same fear-laden message that the majority of southern whites heard when secession was being weighed. Moved by the need for control, for an unchallenged top tier, the power elite in American history has thrived by placating the vulnerable and creating for them a false sense of identification—denying real class differences wherever possible.

The dangers inherent in that deception are many. The relative few who escape their lower-class roots are held up as models, as though everyone at the bottom has the same chance of succeeding through cleverness and hard work, through scrimping and saving. Can Franklin's "nest egg" produce Franklin the self-made man? Hardly. Franklin himself needed patrons to rise in his colonial world, and the same rules of social networking persist. Personal connections, favoritism, and trading on class-based knowledge still grease the wheels that power social mobility in today's professional and business worlds. If this book accomplishes anything it will be to have exposed a number of myths about the American dream, to have disabused readers of the notion that upward mobility is a function of the founders' ingenious plan, or that Jacksonian democracy was liberating, or that the Confederacy was about states' rights rather than preserving class and racial distinctions. Sometimes, all it took was a name: before becoming known as a Reconstruction-era southern white who identified with black uplift or Republican reforms, the scalawag was defined as an inferior breed of cattle. The scalawag of today is the southern liberal who is painted by conservative ideologues as a traitor to the South for daring to say that poor whites and poor blacks possess similar economic interests.

And that is how we return to the language of breeding, so well understood in an agrarian age, so metaphorically resonant in the preindustrial economy in which restrictive social relations hardened. If the republic was supposedly dedicated to equality, how did the language of breeds appeal as it did? To speak of breeds was to justify unequal status among white people; it was the best way to divide people into categories and deny that class privilege exists. If you are categorized as a breed, it means you can't control who you are and you can't avert your appointed destiny.

Breeding. The erstwhile experts in this socially prescriptive field of study interpolated from the science and widespread practices of animal husbandry. The mongrel inherited its (or his or her) parent's incapacities, they said, just as towheaded children with yellowish skin were produced through living on bad soil and inbreeding. In these ways, negative traits were passed on. Scrubland produced a rascally herd of cattle—or people. Breeding determined who rose and who fell. The analogy between human and animal stock was ever present. As Jefferson wrote in 1787, "The circumstance of superior beauty is thought worthy of attention in the propagation of our horses, dogs, and other domestic animals; why not in that of man?"

Under a related form of logic, Manifest Destiny became a desirable means to open land routes and squeeze bad breeds out of the country, presumably through Mexico. In 1860, Daniel Hundley imagined that poor white trash would magically march right out of the United States. The old English idea of colonization required that the poor had to be dumped somewhere. The population had to be drained, strained, or purged. The very same thinking fed social Darwinism and eugenics: if tainted women bred with regular people, they would undermine the quality of future stock. Either nature would weed out inferior stock or a human hand would have to intervene and engage in Galton's notion of controlled breeding, sterilizing the curs and morons among the lowest ranks.

It was just as easy to ignore inequality by claiming that certain breeds could never be improved. As W. E. B. Du Bois explained in 1909, southern politicians were lost in the vacuity of illogic. They had fallen to arguing that any form of social intervention was pointless, because man could not repel nature's force; some races and classes were invariably stuck with their inferior mental and physical endowments. The South's claim to be protecting the public good by endorsing the existing regime that rewarded the already privileged was inherently antidemocratic. Blaming nature for intractable breeds was just a way to rationalize indifference.

While President Reagan loved to invoke the image of the "City upon a Hill," his critics were quick to point out that membership in that shining city was restricted, as much in the twentieth century as it had been in the seventeenth. Under Reaganomics, tax rates for the moneyed class were drastically cut. Governor Mario Cuomo of New York related the problem in memorable fashion as keynote speaker at the 1984 Democratic National Convention: "President Reagan told us from the beginning that he believed in a kind of Social Darwinism, survival of the fittest . . . [that] we should settle for taking care of the strong, and hope that economic ambition and charity will do the rest. Make the rich richer, and what falls from the table will be enough for the middle class and those who are trying desperately to work their way into the middle class." Cuomo's stark language echoed Du Bois, his anti-Darwinian inflection a reminder of the mind-set that justified dividing stronger from weaker breeds. It wasn't enough to preserve the status quo; inequality could be expanded, the gap widened between classes, without incident and without tearing the social fabric. In 2009, the 1 percent paid 5.2 percent of their income in state and local taxes, while the poorest 20 percent paid 10.9 percent. States penalized the poor with impunity.[1]

Class has never been about income or financial worth alone. It has been fashioned in physical—and yes, bodily—terms. Dirty feet and tallow faces remain signs of delinquency and depravity. To live in a shack, a "hovel," a "shebang," or in Shedtown or in a trailer park, is to live in a place that never acquires the name of "home." As transitional spaces, unsettled spaces, they contain occupants who lack the civic markers of stability, productivity, economic value, and human worth.

Job opportunities for all—the myth of full employment—is just that, a myth. The economy cannot provide employment for everyone, a fact that is little acknowledged. In the sixteenth century, the English had their "reserve army of the poor" who were drummed into the military. Modern America's reserve army of the poor are drummed into the worst jobs, the worst-paid positions, and provide the labor force that works in coal mines, cleans toilets and barn stalls, picks and plucks in fields as migrant laborers, or slaughters animals. Waste people remain the "mudsills" who fill out the bottom layer of the labor pool on which society's wealth rests. Poor whites are still taught to hate—but not to hate those who are keeping them in line. Lyndon Johnson knew this when he quipped, "If you can convince the lowest white man he's better than the best colored man, he won't notice you're picking his pocket. Hell, give him somebody to look down on, and he'll empty his pockets for you."

We are a country that imagines itself as democratic, and yet the majority has never cared much for equality. Because that's not how breeding works. Heirs, pedigree, lineage: a pseudo-aristocracy of wealth still finds a way to assert its social power. We see how inherited wealth grants status without any guarantee of merit or talent. To wit: would we know of Donald Trump, George W. Bush, Jesse Jackson Jr., or such Hollywood names as Charlie Sheen and Paris Hilton, except for the fact that these, and many others like them, had powerful, influential parents? Even some men of recognized competence in national politics are products of nepotism: Albert Gore Jr., Rand Paul, Andrew Cuomo, and numerous Kennedys. We give children of the famous a big head start, deferring to them as rightful heirs, a modern-day version of the Puritans' children of the Elect.

In Thomas Jefferson's formulation, nature assigned classes. Nature demanded a natural aristocracy—what he termed an "accidental aristoi." The spark of lust would direct the strong to breed with the strong, the "good and wise" to marry for beauty, health, virtue, and talents—traits that would be bred forward. One significant difference between Jefferson's master class and the eugenicists of the early twentieth century was the former's singular focus on the male making his selection, and the latter's urging the middle-class woman to carefully inspect the pedigree of the man she hoped to marry. Marriage has always been connected to class status: today's online dating services are premised on the eugenic notion that a person can find the perfect match—a match presumed to be based on shared class and educational interests. In 2014–15, a series of television commercials for eHarmony.com was sending the same message: that no "normal" middle-class applicant has to be stuck with a tawdry (i.e., lower-class) loser. And as the historian Jill Lepore has pointed out in the New Yorker, the entrepreneurial Dr. Paul Popenoe began his career as a leading authority on eugenics, before moving on to marriage counseling, and eventually launching computer dating in 1956. Some dating services have been quite blatant: the website Good Genes promised to help "Ivy Leaguers" find potential spouses with "matching credentials," by which was meant a similar class pedigree.[2]

The rule of nature was supposed to supplant artificial aristocracy with meritocracy. At the same time, though, it allowed people to associate human failures with different strains and inferior breeds, and to assign a certain inevitability to such failure. If, in this long-acceptable way of thinking, nature ruled, nature also needed a gardener. The human scrub grass had to be weeded from time to time. That is why squatters were used as the first wave of settlers to encroach on Indian lands, then were chased off the land when the upscale farmers arrived; in time, policing boundaries extended to segregation laws, and after that to zoning laws, separating the wheat from the chaff in the creation of modern suburbia. Class walls went up in the way property values were modulated in carefully planned towns and neighborhoods.

It was easy for nineteenth-century Americans to equate animals and humans. Stallions were like elite planters, and naturally given the best pastures; the weak tackies, like white trash, lazed about the marshlands. While it is not discussed very often, our society still measures human worth by the value of the land people occupy and own. The urban ghettos, no less than the trailer parks on devalued land on the city's edges, are modern representations of William Byrd's Dismal Swamp: an unsafe, uncivilized wasteland that is allowed to fester and remain unproductive.

Location is everything. Location determines access to a privileged school, a safe neighborhood, infrastructural improvements, the best hospitals, the best grocery stores. Upper- and middle-class parents instruct their children in surviving their particular class environment. They give them the appropriate material resources toward this end. But let us devote more thought to what Henry Wallace wrote in 1936: what would happen, he posed, if one hundred thousand poor children and one hundred thousand rich children were all given the same food, clothing, education, care, and protection? Class lines would likely disappear. This was the only conceivable way to eliminate class, he said—and what he didn't say was that this would require removing children from their homes and raising them in a neutral, equitable environment. A dangerous idea indeed!

We have always relied—and still do—on bloodlines to maintain and pass on a class advantage to our children. Statistical measurement has shown convincingly that the best predictor of success is the class status of one's forebears. Ironically, given the American Revolutionaries' hatred for Old World aristocracies, Americans transfer wealth today in the fashion of those older societies, while modern European nations provide considerably more social services to their populations. On average, Americans pass on 50 percent of their wealth to their children; in Nordic countries, social mobility is much higher; parents in Denmark give 15 percent of their total wealth to their children, and in Sweden parents give 27 percent. Class wealth and privileges are a more important inheritance (as a measure of potential) than actual genetic traits.[3]

Lest we relegate discredited ideas to the age in which they flourished, we can admit that eugenic thinking is not quite dead either. The poor can starve "a little," says Charlotte Hays, and there are surely others who feel the same way. The innocuous-sounding term "fertility treatment" enables the wealthy to breed their own kind, buying sperm and eggs at "baby centers" around the country. Abortion and birth control, meanwhile, are for evangelical conservatives a violation of God's will that all people should be fruitful and multiply, and yet this same fear of unnatural methods of reproduction does not engender opposition to fertility clinics. Antiabortion activists, like eugenicists, think that the state has the right to intervene in the breeding habits of poor single women.

Poor women lost state-funded abortions during the Carter years, and today they are proscribed from using welfare funds to buy disposable diapers. To modern conservatives, women are first and foremost breeders. This was tellingly displayed during the Republican primary debates in 2012, when candidates boasted about the size of their families, each trying to outdo the last, as the camera panned across the podium. The Republicans were mimicking the pride of the winners of the "fitter family" contests held at county fairs in the early twentieth century. A reporter joked that Jon Huntsman's and Mitt Romney's children should breed, "creating a super-race of astonishingly beautiful Mormons." There remains in America a cultural desire to breed one's "own kind." As with the nepotistic practices that continue in a variety of fields, class is reproduced in ways that are not dissimilar to the past.[4]

Some things never change. More than one generation has deluded itself by buying into the notion of an American dream. A singular faith exists today that is known and embraced as American exceptionalism, but it dates back centuries to the projections made and policies put in place when the island nation of Great Britain began to settle the American continent. It was Richard Hakluyt's fantastic literature that graduated to a broader colonial drive for continental domination. The same ideology fueled the theories of Benjamin Franklin, Thomas Paine, and Thomas Jefferson. (Meanwhile, London economist William Petty's idea of political arithmetic gave force to a long fascination with demographic growth.) Teddy Roosevelt had a dream, too, of rewarding parents with large families, encouraging eugenically sound marriages, and recognizing the American as the healthiest member of the Anglo-Saxon family.

This brings us to the slavery/free labor corollary. It was James Oglethorpe in Georgia who first put into practice a sensitive and sensible idea: allowing slavery to thrive would retard economic opportunity and undermine social mobility for average white men and their families. In this way, racial dominance was intertwined with class dominance in the southern states, and the two could never be separated as long as a white ruling elite held sway over politics and rigged the economic system to benefit the few. We now know, of course, that slavery and repression of African American talent was tragically wrong. So why do we continue to ignore the pathological character of class-centered power relations as part of the American republic's political inheritance? If the American dream were real, upward mobility would be far more in evidence.

Let's get it right, then. Because there was never a free market in land, the past saw as much downward as upward mobility. Historically, Americans have confused social mobility with physical mobility. The class system tracked across the land with the so-called pioneering set. We need to acknowledge that fact. Generally, it was the all-powerful speculators who controlled the distribution of good land to the wealthy and forced the poor squatter off his land. Without a visible hand, markets did not at any time, and do not now, magically pave the way for the most talented to be rewarded; the well connected were and are preferentially treated.

Liberty is a revolving door, which explains the reality of downward mobility. The door ushers some in while it escorts others out into the cold. It certainly allows for, even encourages, exploitation. Through a process of rationalization, people have long tended to blame failure on the personal flaws of individuals—this has been the convenient refrain of Republicans in Congress in the second decade of the twenty-first century, when former Speaker of the House John Boehner publicly equated joblessness with personal laziness. Another former Speaker of the House, Newt Gingrich, captured headlines at the end of 2011 when he seemed ready to endorse Jefferson's Revolutionary-era solution to poverty by making schools into workhouses. Gingrich: "You have a very poor neighborhood. You have students that are required to go to school. They have no money, no habit of work. . . . What if they became assistant janitors, and their job was to mop the floor and clean the bathroom?" It was only in the midst of the Great Depression that the country fully appreciated the meaning of downward mobility. At that time, when a quarter of the nation was thrown out of work, the old standby of blaming the individual no longer convinced anyone.[5]

For the most part, daily injustices in average people's lives go ignored. But that does not mean that poor people are numb to the condition of their own lives. Politicians have been willfully blind to many social problems. Pretending that America has grown rich as a largely classless society is bad history, to say the least. The "1 percent" is the most recently adopted shorthand for moneyed monopoly, bringing attention to the ills generated by consolidated power, but the phenomenon it describes is not new. Class separation is and has always been at the center of our political debates, despite every attempt to hide social reality with deceptive rhetoric. The white poor have been with us in various guises, as the names they have been given across centuries attest: Waste people. Offscourings. Lubbers. Bogtrotters. Rascals. Rubbish. Squatters. Crackers. Clay-eaters. Tackies. Mudsills. Scalawags. Briar hoppers. Hillbillies. Low-downers. White niggers. Degenerates. White trash. Rednecks. Trailer trash. Swamp people.

They are blamed for living on bad land, as though they had other choices. From the beginning, they have existed in the minds of rural or urban elites and the middle class as extrusions of the weedy, unproductive soil. They are depicted as slothful, rootless vagrants, physically scarred by their poverty. The worst ate clay and turned yellow, wallowed in mud and muck, and their necks became burned by the hot sun. Their poorly clothed, poorly fed children generated what others believed to be a permanent and defective breed. Sexual deviance? That comes from cramped quarters in obscure retreats, distant from civilization, where the moral vocabulary that dwells in town has been lost. We think of the left-behind groups as extinct, and the present as a time of advanced thought and sensibility. But today's trailer trash are merely yesterday's vagrants on wheels, an updated version of Okies in jalopies and Florida crackers in their carts.

They are renamed often, but they do not disappear. Our very identity as a nation, no matter what we tell ourselves, is intimately tied up with the dispossessed. We are, then, not only preoccupied with race, as we know we are, but with good and bad breeds as well. It is for good reason that we have this preoccupation: by calling America not just "a" land of opportunity but "the" land of opportunity, we collectively have made a promise to posterity that there will always exist the real potential of self-propulsion upward.

Those who fail to rise in America are a crucial part of who we are as a civilization. A cruel irony is to be found in the aftermath of the Hollywood film *Deliverance,* a gruesome adventure that exploited the worst stereotypes of white trash and ignored the poverty that existed in the part of the country where the movie was made. One actor stands out who was not a trained actor at all: Billy Redden. He played the iconic inbred character who sat strumming the banjo. He was fifteen when he was plucked from a local Rabun County, Georgia, school by the filmmakers because of his odd look (enhanced with makeup). He didn't play the banjo, so a musician fingered from behind, and the cameraman did the rest. Interviewed in 2012 to mark the fortieth anniversary of the film, Billy said he wasn't paid much for his role. Otherwise, the fifty-six-year-old said, "I wouldn't be working at Wal-Mart right now. And I'm struggling really hard to make ends meet."[6]

The discomfort middle-class Americans feel when forced to acknowledge the existence of poverty highlights the disconnect between image and reality. It seems clear that we have made little progress since James Agee exposed the world of poor tenant farmer in 1941. We still today are blind to the "cruel radiance of what is." The static rural experience is augmented by the persistence of class-inflected tropes and the voyeuristic shock in televised portraits of degenerate beings and wasted lives in the richest country that has ever existed. And what of Billy Redden? In 1972, a country boy was made up to fit a stereotype of the retarded hillbilly, the idiot savant. Today his mundane struggle to survive can satisfy no one's expectations, because his story is ordinary. He is neither eccentric nor perverse. Nor does he don a scraggly beard, wear a bandanna, or hunt gators. He is simply one of the hundreds of thousands of faceless employees who work at a Wal-Mart.

White trash is a central, if disturbing, thread in our national narrative. The very existence of such people—both in their visibility and invisibility—is proof that American society obsesses over the mutable labels we give to the neighbors we wish not to notice. "They are not who we are." But they are who we are and have been a fundamental part of our history, whether we like it or not.

NOTES

Preface to the Paperback Edition

1. "The Minefield: Donald Trump Represents Triumph of Class Over Identity," ABC News, November 9, 2016, www.abc.net.au/news/2016-11-10/minefield -trump-represents-triumph-of-class-over-identity/8012354.
2. Alex Griswold, "Bernie Sanders: Democrats Need to Move Beyond 'I'm a Woman, Vote for Me,'" Mediae.com, November 21, 2016, http://www.medi aite.com/online/bernie-sanders-democrats-need-to-move-beyond-im-a-woman -vote-for-me/; Peter Daou and Tom Watson, "Reality Check: Working Families Like Mine Don't Give a Damn About Hillary's Emails," September 25, 2015, http://www.hillarymen.com/latest/working-families-dont-give-a-damn -about-hillary-clintons-emails; Valentina Zarya, "Clinton's Pledge to Cap Child Care Costs at 10% of Income Would Be a Game-Changer," Fortune (May 11, 2016); April Ryan, "List of Black Women Supporting Hillary Clinton Grows," Essence.com (February 23, 2016).
3. On Sanders, see Margaret Talbot, "The Populist Prophet," New Yorker (October 12, 1015).
4. Mark Lilla, "The End of Identity Liberalism," New York Times, November 18, 2016.
5. For the gander pull, see John Mayfield, "The Theatre of Public Esteem: Ethics and Values in Longstreet's Georgia Scenes," Georgia Historical Quarterly 75, no. 3 (Fall 1991): 566–89, esp. 579–80; on Jeff Davis's tactics, see Dexter Marshall, "Some New Member of the United States Senate," New Orleans Times-Picayune, January 26, 1908.
6. Kenneth P. Vogel and Eli Stokols, "Trump Rejects New Adviser's Push to Make Him 'Presidential,'" Politico, April 26, 2016; and Nancy Isenberg, "Dismissing Trump Fans as White Trash Gets Our Class System All Wrong," Daily Beast, July 29, 2016.
7. See Arthur Brisbane, "William Randolph Hearst," North American Review 183, no. 599 (September 21, 1906): 519–25; Hearst also reveled in his "outsider status." See David Nasaw, The Chief: William Randolph Hearst (Boston: Houghton Mifflin, 2000), 169, 172, 192; also see Frank Kent, "The Psychology of Voting," Forum (December 1924): 810–11; on Trump rallies, see Jared Yates Sexton, "American Horror Story," New Republic (June 15, 2016).
8. Ross Douthat, "The Meaning of Trump," New York Times, July 28, 2015; Russell Berman, "Why Are Voters Drawn to Donald Trump?" Atlantic (April 8, 2016).
9. Nate Silver, "How Obama Really Won the Election," Esquire (January 14, 2009), http://www.esquire.com/news-politics/a5496/how-obama-won-0209.
10. On the word "classy," see Adam Rosen, "In the Age of Trump, What Does It Mean to Be 'Classy'?" Wilson Quarterly 40, no. 1 (Winter 2016); Aaron Oster, "Donald

Trump and WWE: How the Road to the White House Began at 'WrestleMania,'"
RollingStone.com, February 1, 2016, http://www.rollingstone.com/sports/features/
donald-trump-and-wwe-how-the-road-to-the-white-house-began-at-wrestle
mania-20160201.

11. James Parton, *Life of Andrew Jackson*, 3 vols. (New York: Mason Brothers,
1860), 1: vii.

12. Eric Bradner, "Donald Trump: No Apology on 'Blood' Remark Amid GOP
Backlash," CNNPolitics.com, August 10, 2015, http://www.cnn.com/2015/08/09/
politics/donald-trump-blood-comment-response-2016-sotu/.

13. Andrew Burstein, *America's Jubilee: How in 1826 a Generation Remembered
Fifty Years of Independence* (New York: Alfred A. Knopf, 2001), 171–80; Henry
Adams, *John Randolph* (Boston, 1882), 170–71; and Robert Dawidoff, *The
Education of John Randolph* (New York: W. W. Norton and Company, 1979).

14. "Remarks by the President in Farewell Address," White House Office of the
Press Secretary, January 10, 2017, https://obamawhitehouse.archives.gov/the
-press-office/2017/01/10/remarks-president-farewell-address; Lisa R. Pruitt,
"The Geography of Class Culture Wars," *Seattle University Law Review* 34,
no. 3 (Spring 2011): 767–814, esp. 792–93; "Inaugural Address: Trump's Full
Speech," CNN.com, January 21, 2017, http://www.cnn.com/2017/01/20/politics/
trump-inaugural-address/. Camilla L. Ryan and Kurt Bauman, *Educational
Attainment in the United States: 2015* (P. 20–578) (Washington, DC: U.S. Census Bureau, March 2016), 1–2, http://www.census.gov/content/dam/Census/
library/publications/2016/demo/p20-578.pdf.

15. "Inaugural Address: Trump's Full Speech"; Edwards also exposed the myth
of the self-made man, pointing out how class mobility is romanticized by
Americans. In 2007, he used as his example the movie *The Pursuit of Happy-
ness*, which told the story of a homeless man who became a millionaire stock-
broker. See John Edwards, "Ending Poverty: The Great Moral Issue of Our
Time," *Yale Law & Policy Review* 25, no 2 (Spring 2007): 337–48.

16. On the idea of Trump supporters feeling cheated and disinherited, see Sarah
Sobieraj, "With a Snarl, Trump Ratifies His Supporters' Rage," *New York
Times*, August 9, 2016; Arlie Russell Hochschild, *Strangers in Their Own Land:
Anger and Mourning on the American Right* (New York: The New Press, 2016),
61, 139–45, 151, 215–16, 218, 236; and James Davison Hunter and Carl
Desportes Bowman, *The Vanishing Center of American Democracy: The
2016 Survey of American Political Culture* (Charlottesville: The Institute for
Advanced Studies in Culture, 2016), 43–46; for the desire to shore up the
boundary between the "settled working class" and the "hard living" (the newer
categories for redneck and white trash), see Pruitt, "The Geography of the
Class Culture Wars," 795–97, 800. This anger over lesser Americans cutting
in line can be traced back to Reconstruction. As I discuss in chapter 8,
ex-Confederates deeply resented the Freedmen's Bureau and other civil rights
legislation that elevated free blacks and poor whites over former elites.

17. Douglas Ernst, "Joe Biden Says Democrats 'Don't Associate' with 'Difficulty'
of White Working Class," *Washington Times*, October 26, 2016, http://m
.washingtontimes.com/news/2016/oct/26/joe-biden-says-democrats-dont
-associate-with-diffi/.

18. Danielle Paquette, "How a Rust Belt Teenager Feels About a Future Under Donald Trump," *Washington Post*, January 20, 2017; also see Wilfred M. McClay, "A Distant Elite: How Meritocracy Went Wrong," *The Hedgehog Review: Critical Reflections on Contemporary Culture* 18, no. 2 (Summer 2016): 36–49.
19. "Inaugural Address: Trump's Full Speech," CNN.com.
20. Connor Kilpatrick, "Burying the White Working Class," *Jacobin*, May 13, 2016; Nancy Isenberg, "Five Myths About Class in America," *Washington Post*, July 1, 2016.

Preface

1. Harper Lee, *To Kill a Mockingbird* (New York: HarperCollins, 1960; anniversary publication, 1999), 194–95.
2. See twelve photos in "KKK Rallies at South Carolina Statehouse in Defense of Confederate Flag," NBC News, July 19, 2015; and "Paula Deen: 'Why, of Course, I Say the N-Word, Sugar. Doesn't Everybody?,'" Thesuperficial.com, July 19, 2013; and for calling Deen a "66-year-old, White trash, trailer park, backwards-ass, country-fried peckerwood," see "Paula Deen's Southern-Fried Racist Fantasies," *The Domino Theory by Jeff Winbush*, June 20, 2013.

Introduction: Fables We Forget By

1. Charles Murray, *Coming Apart: The State of White America, 1960–2010* (New York: Crown Forum, 2012), 4–5.
2. *The Adventures of Ozzie and Harriet* first aired in 1952, while *The Honeymooners* began in 1951. Murray, *Coming Apart*, 8–9.
3. See Francis J. Bremer, "Would John Adams Have Called John Winthrop a Founding 'Father'?," *Common-Place* 4, no. 3 (April 2004).
4. Sacvan Bercovitch, "How the Puritans Won the American Revolution," *Massachusetts Review* 17, no. 4 (Winter 1976): 597–630, esp. 603. Also see Michael P. Winship, "Were There Any Puritans in New England?," *New England Quarterly* 74, no. 1 (March 2001): 118–38, esp. 131–38; and Peter J. Gomes, "Pilgrims and Puritans: 'Heroes' and 'Villains' in the Creation of the American Past," *Proceedings of the Massachusetts Historical Society* 95 (1983): 1–16, esp. 2–5, 7.
5. The final version of the monument was eighty-one feet high. See James F. O'Gorman, "The Colossus of Plymouth: Hammatt Billings National Monument to the Forefathers," *Journal of the Society of Architectural Historians* 54, no. 3 (September 1995): 278–301.
6. Roger Cushing Aikin, "Paintings of Manifest Destiny: Mapping a Nation," *American Art* 14, no. 3 (Autumn 2000): 84–85.
7. Matthew Dennis, *Red, White, and Blue Letter Days: An American Calendar* (Ithaca, NY: Cornell University Press, 2002), 85, 87, 101; Ann Uhry Abrams, *The Pilgrims and Pocahontas: Rival Myths of American Origin* (Boulder, CO: Westview Press, 1999), 5, 26. Also see Flora J. Cooke, "Reading Lessons for Primary Grades: History, Series I, 'The Pilgrims,'" *Course of Study* 1, no. 5

(January 1901): 442–47; and John H. Humins, "Squanto and Massasoit: A Struggle for Power," *New England Quarterly* 60, no. 1 (March 1987): 54–70.

8. On the aura of mystery surrounding Roanoke, see Kathleen Donegan, *Seasons of Misery: Catastrophe and Colonial Settlement in Early America* (Philadelphia: University of Pennsylvania Press, 2014), 23–24, 67; Karen Ordahl Kupperman, "Roanoke Lost," *American Heritage* 36, no. 5 (1985): 81–90.

9. In 1803, William Wirt, a future U.S. attorney general and a protégé of Thomas Jefferson, called Pocahontas the "patron deity" of Jamestown. George Washington Parke Custis, the grandson of Martha Washington, wrote the play *Pocahontas* in 1830. Mary Virginia Wall, in her play *The Daughter of Virginia Dare* (1908), made Dare the consort of Powhatan and the mother of Pocahontas. Southern writer Vachel Lindsay published his ode to Virginia as America's birthplace, "Our Mother, Pocahontas," in 1917. See Jay Hubbard, "The Smith-Pocahontas Story in Literature," *Virginia Magazine of History and Biography* 65, no. 3 (July 1957): 275–300.

10. See Edward Buscombe, "What's New in the New World?," *Film Quarterly* 62, no. 3 (Spring 2009): 35–40; Michelle LeMaster, "Pocahontas: (De)Constructing an American Myth," *William and Mary Quarterly* 62, no. 4 (October 2005): 774–81; Kevin D. Murphy, "Pocahontas: Her Life and Legend: An Exhibition Review," *Winterthur Portfolio* 29, no. 4 (Winter 1994): 265–75. On women and nature, see Sherry Ortner, "Is Female to Male as Nature Is to Culture?" in *Women, Culture, and Society*, eds. Michelle Zimbalist Rosaldo and Louise Lamphere (Stanford, CA: Stanford University Press, 1974), 68–87; Anne Kolodny, *The Land Before Her: Fantasy and Experience of the American Frontier, 1630–1860* (Chapel Hill: University of North Carolina Press, 1984): 3–5; and Susan Scott Parrish, "The Female Opossum and the Nature of the New World," *William and Mary Quarterly* 54, no. 3 (July 1997): 476, 502–14.

11. Hubbard, "The Smith-Pocahontas Story," 279–85. Smith mentioned the rescue briefly in his first book, published in 1608, but only elaborated on the episode in his 1624 *Generall Historie of Virginia, New England, and the Summer Isles . . .*; see Karen Ordahl Kupperman, ed., *Captain John Smith: A Select Edition of His Writings* (Chapel Hill: University of North Carolina Press, 1988), 57–73. Ralph Hamor described her as "one of rude education, manners barbarous and cursed generation," and he saw the union as "meerely for the good and honour of the Plantation"; see Hamor, *A True Discourse of the Present State of Virginia* (London, 1615; reprint ed., Richmond: Virginia Historical Society, 1957), 24, 63. On the popular Scottish ballad, see Rayna Green, "The Pocahontas Perplex: The Image of Indian Women in American Culture," *Massachusetts Review* 16, no. 4 (Autumn 1975): 698–714, esp. 698–700.

12. Buscombe, "What's New in the New World?," 36; Murphy, "Pocahontas: Her Life and Legend," 270.

13. Nancy Shoemaker, "Native-American Women in History," *OAH Magazine of History* 9, no. 4 (Summer 1995): 10–14; and Green, "The Pocahontas Perplex," 704.

14. On the use of coercion and punishment to uphold the lower ranks of labor force (mostly children and adolescents) in New England, see Barry Levy, *Town Born: The Political Economy of New England* (Philadelphia: University

of Pennsylvania Press, 2013), 61–72. Even William Bradford in his *Of Plymouth Plantation* attempted to erase the dead by using political arithmetic to show that the "increase" of children outnumbered the dead; see Donegan, *Seasons of Misery*, 119, 135–36, 138, 153–54; Richard Archer, *Fissures in the Rock: New England in the Seventeenth Century* (Hanover and London: University of New Hampshire Press, 2001), 44, 50, 59–63.

15. Donegan, *Seasons of Misery*, 70, 74–76, 78, 100–103 (cannibalism), 108–10. On the English sharing the Spanish desire for gold, see Constance Jordan, "Conclusion: Jamestown and Its North Atlantic World," in *Envisioning an English Empire: Jamestown and the Making of the North Atlantic World*, eds. Robert Appelbaum and John Wood Sweet (Philadelphia: University of Pennsylvania Press, 2005), 280–81.

16. François Weil, "John Farmer and the Making of American Genealogy," *New England Quarterly* 80, no. 3 (September 2007): 408–34, esp. 431; Francesca Morgan, "Lineage as Capital: Genealogy in Antebellum New England," *New England Quarterly* 83, no. 2 (June 2010): 250–82, esp. 280–82; Michael S. Sweeney, "Ancestors, Avotaynu, Roots: An Inquiry into American Genealogical Discourse" (Ph.D. dissertation, University of Kansas, 2010), 41.

17. Francis J. Bremer, "Remembering—and Forgetting—Jonathan Winthrop and the Puritan Founders," *Massachusetts Historical Review* 6 (2004): 38–69, esp. 39–42. On legal standing, see Christopher Tomlins, *Freedom Bound: Law, Labor, and Civic Identity in Colonizing English America, 1580–1865* (New York: Cambridge University Press, 2010), 119–20. On the new City Hall, see David Glassberg, "Public Ritual and Cultural Hierarchy: Philadelphia Civic Celebration at the Turn of the Century," *Pennsylvania Magazine of History and Biography* 107, no. 3 (July 1983): 421–48, esp. 426–29. On Plymouth Rock, see Abrams, *The Pilgrims and Pocahontas*, 6; and Gomes, "Pilgrims and Puritans," 6. In his 1820 oration, the lawyer Daniel Webster described the rock as the "first lodgement, in a vast extent of country, covered with a wilderness, and peopled by roving barbarians"; see John Seelye, *Memory's Nation: The Place of Plymouth Rock* (Chapel Hill: University of North Carolina Press, 1998), 75.

18. On English notions of eliminating the poor, see E. P. Hutchinson, *The Population Debate: The Development of Conflicting Theories up to 1900* (Boston: Houghton Mifflin, 1967), 37, 44, 52, 123–24; Timothy Raylor, "Samuel Hartlib and the Commonwealth of Bees," in *Culture and Cultivation in Early Modern England*, eds. Michael Leslie and Timothy Raylor (New York: St. Martin's, 1992), 106.

19. Abbot Emerson Smith, *Colonists in Bondage: White Servitude and Convict Labor in America, 1607–1776* (Chapel Hill: University of North Carolina Press, 1947): 5, 7, 12, 20, 67–85, 136–51; A. Roger Ekirch, "Bound for America: A Profile of British Convicts Transported to the Colonies, 1718–1775," *William and Mary Quarterly* 42, no. 2 (April 1985): 184–222; Abbott Emerson Smith, "Indentured Servants: New Light on Some of America's 'First' Families," *Journal of Economic History* 2, no. 1 (May 1942): 40–53; A. L. Beier, *Masterless Men: The Vagrancy Problem in England, 1560–1640* (London: Methuen, 1985), 162–64; Tomlins, *Freedom Bound*, 21, 76–77; Farley Grubb, "Fatherless and Friendless: Factors Influencing the Flow of English Emigrant Servants,"

Journal of Economic History 52, no. 1 (March 1992): 85–108. On "Egyptian bondage," see Marilyn C. Baseler, *"Asylum for Mankind": America, 1607–1800* (Ithaca, NY: Cornell University Press, 1998), 99–101. On "Little Bess" Armstrong, see Emma Christopher, *A Merciless Place: The Fact of British Convicts After the American Revolution* (New York: Oxford University Press, 2010), 32.

20. Baseler, *"Asylum for Mankind,"* 35–40, 75; Tomlins, *Freedom Bound,* 504; Beier, *Masterless Men,* 95; Sir Josiah Child, *A Discourse on Trade* (London, 1690), 172–73; John Combs, "The Phases of Conversion: A New Chronology for the Rise of Slavery in Virginia," *William and Mary Quarterly* 68, no. 3 (July 2011): 332–60.

Chapter One: Taking Out the Trash: Waste People in the New World

1. See Peter C. Mancall, *Hakluyt's Promise: An Elizabethan's Obsession for an English America* (New Haven, CT: Yale University Press, 2007), 3, 6–8, 25, 31, 38, 40, 102.

2. Ibid., 8, 63, 76–77; D. B. Quinn, ed., *The Voyages and Colonizing Enterprises of Sir Humphrey Gilbert,* 2 vols. (London: Hakluyt Society, 1940), 1:102; Kenneth R. Andrews, *Trade, Plunder and Settlement: Maritime Enterprise and the Genesis of the British Empire, 1480–1630* (Cambridge: Cambridge University Press, 1984), 30–31, 200–201, 218, 294–99.

3. Mancall, *Hakluyt's Promise,* 3–4, 92–100, 158, 184–94, 218, 221–31; E. G. R. Taylor, "Richard Hakluyt," *Geographical Journal* 109, no. 4–6 (April–June 1947): 165–71, esp. 165–66; Kupperman, *Captain John Smith,* 3–4, 267. On Smith's borrowing from Hakluyt, see David B. Quinn, "Hakluyt's Reputation," in *Explorers and Colonies: America, 1500–1625* (London and Ronceverte, WV: Hambledon Press, 1990), 19.

4. Mancall, *Hakluyt's Promise,* 72, 92, 128–29, 139, 183–84; David B. Quinn and Alison M. Quinn, eds., *A Particular Discourse Concerning the Greate Necessite and Manifolde Commodyties That Are Like to Growe to This Realm of Englande by the Westerne Discoveries Lately Attempted. Written in the Year 1584. By Richard Hackluyt of Oxforde. Known as Discourse of Western Planting* (London: Hakluyt Society, 1993), xv, xxii. Hereafter cited as "Discourse of Western Planting."

5. Hakluyt, "Discourse of Western Planting," 8, 28, 31, 55, 116, 117, 119. Michel de Montaigne's "Of Cannibals" (1580) was translated into English in 1603; see Lynn Glaser, *America on Paper: The First Hundred Years* (Philadelphia: Associated Antiquaries, 1989), 170–73; and Scott R. MacKenzie, "Breeches of Decorum: The Figure of a Barbarian in Montaigne and Addison," *South Central Review,* no. 2 (Summer 2006): 99–127, esp. 101–3.

6. For Virginia as Raleigh's bride, see "Epistle Dedicatory to Sir Walter Ralegh by Richard Hakluyt, 1587," in *The Original Writings and Correspondence of the Two Richard Hakluyts,* ed. E. G. R. Taylor, 2 vols. (London: Hakluyt Society, 1935), 2:367–68; also see Mary C. Fuller, *Voyages in Print: English Travel to America, 1576–1624* (New York: Cambridge University Press, 1995), 75.

7. Tomlins, *Freedom Bound,* 114–18, 135–38, 143–44; and John Smith, *Advertisements: Or, The Pathway to Experience to Erect a Plantation* (1831), in *The*

Complete Works of Captain John Smith (1580–1631), ed. Philip L. Barbour, 3 vols. (Chapel Hill: University of North Carolina Press, 1986), 3:290.

8. For the manure reference, see Smith, *The Generall Historie of Virginia, New England, and the Summer Isles . . .* (1624) and John Smith, *Advertisements for the Unexperienced Planters of New England, or Any Where* (1631) in Barbour, *The Complete Works of Captain John Smith*, 2:109; 3:276. According to the *Oxford English Dictionary*, "waste" when connected to the land meant several things: (1a) uninhabited or desolate region, desert, or wilderness; (1b) a vast expanse of water, empty space in the air, or land covered with snow; (2) a piece of land not cultivated or used for any purpose, lying in common (not owned privately); and (3) a devastated region. The legal definition is "any unauthorized act of a tenant for a freehold estate not of inheritance, or for any lesser interest, which tends to the destruction of the tenement, or otherwise to the injury of the inheritance." This means a tenant, not an owner of the land, who damages the property and decreases its value. "Wasteland" referred to land in its uncultivated or natural state, or land (usually surrounded by developed land) "not used or unfit for cultivation or building and allowed to run wild."

9. Hakluyt, "Discourse of Western Planting," 115. For the language of agrarian improvement, see Andrew McRae, *God Speed the Plough: The Representation of Agrarian England, 1500–1660* (Cambridge: Cambridge University Press, 1996), 13, 116, 136–37, 162, 168.

10. Hakluyt, "Discourse of Western Planting," 28; also see the elder Hakluyt's "Inducements to the Liking of the Voyage Intended Toward Virginia" (1585), in Taylor, *The Original Writings*, 2:331; and McRae, *God Speed the Plough*, 168. Timothy Sweet, "Economy, Ecology, and Utopia in Early Colonial Promotional Literature," *American Literature* 71, no. 3 (September 1999): 399–427, esp. 407–8. Hakluyt's list of tasks (down to plucking and packing feathers) was borrowed from George Peckham's *A True Reporte of Late Discoveries and Possession, Taken in the Right of the Crowne of Englande of the Newfound Landes: By That Valiant and Worthye Gentleman, Sir Humphrey Gilbert, Knight*. Hakluyt later included the relevant passage: Richard Hakluyt, *The Principall Navigations Voiages and Discoveries of the English Nation* (London, 1589), eds. David Beers Quinn and Raleigh Ashlin Skelton, 2 vols. (reprinted facsimile, London: Cambridge University Press, 1965), 2:710–11.

11. Hakluyt, "Discourse of Western Planting," 28, 120, 123–24. On using the colonies to unburden England of idle children of the poor, see Hakluyt the elder, "Inducements for Virginia," in Taylor, *The Original Writings*, 2:330; Gilbert, "A Discourse of a Discoverie for a New Passage to Cataia" (London, 1576), in Quinn, *The Voyages and Colonizing Enterprises of Sir Humphrey Gilbert*, 1:161; and Peckham, "A True Report," in Hakluyt, *Principall Navigations*, 2:710–11.

12. Hakluyt, "Discourse of Western Planting," 28.

13. John Cramsie, "Commercial Projects and the Fiscal Policy of James VI and I," *Historical Journal* 43, no. 2 (2000): 345–64, esp. 350–51, 359.

14. Walter I. Trattner, "God and Expansion in Elizabethan England: John Dee, 1527–1583," *Journal of the History of Ideas*, vol. 25, no. 1 (January–Ma 1964): 17–34, esp. 26–27; Beier, *Masterless Men*, 56, 149–50, 168.

15. Hakluyt, "Discourse of Western Planting," 28. Gilbert made the same argument of settling needy men instead of sending them to the gallows; see "A Discourse of a Discoverie for a New Passage to Cataia," in Quinn, *The Voyages and Colonizing Enterprises of Sir Humphrey Gilbert*, 1:160–61. Under Roman law, men, women, and children could become slaves if they were captives of war. Captives were given their lives in return for serving as slaves; see Peter Temin, "The Labor Market of the Early Roman Empire," *Journal of Interdisciplinary History* 34, no. 4 (Spring 2004): 513–38, esp. 534. A French scholar has noted that in English ethnography, the term "rubbish men" was used to describe debt slavery; see Alain Testart, "The Extent and Significance of Debt Slavery," *Revue Française de Sociologie* 43, no. 1 (2002): 173–204, esp. 199.

16. Hakluyt, "Discourse of Western Planting," 31–32, 120. On the children of beggars being put into service, see A. L. Beier, "'A New Serfdom': Labor Laws, Vagrancy Statutes, and Labor Discipline in England, 1350–1800," in *Cast Out: Vagrancy and Homelessness in Global Perspective*, eds. A. L. Beier and Paul Ocobock (Athens: Ohio University Press, 2009), 47.

17. Beier, *Masterless Men*, 158–60; C. S. L. Davies, "Slavery and Protector Somerset: The Vagrancy Act of 1547," *Economic History Review* 19, no. 3 (1966): 533–49.

18. See William Harrison, "Chapter IX: Of Provisions Made for the Poor" (1577 and 1857), in *Elizabethan England: From "A Description of England," by William Harrison (in "Holinshed's Chronicles")*, edited by Lothrop Withington, with introduction by F. J. Furnivall (London: The W. Scott Publishing Co., 1902), 122–29, esp. 122; and Patrick Copland, *Virginia's God Be Thanked, or A Sermon of Thanksgiving for the Happie Successe of the Affayres in Virginia This Last Yeare. Preached by Patrick Copland at Bow-Church in Cheapside, Before the Honourable Virginia Company, on Thursday, the 18. of April 1622* (London, 1622), 31.

19. Beier, *Masterless Men*, 43; Copland, *Virginia's God Be Thanked*, 31; John Donne, *A Sermon upon the Eighth Verse of the First Chapter of the Acts of the Apostles. Preached to the Honourable Company of the Virginia Plantation, 13, November 1622* (London, 1624), 21. Though John White tried to counter this negative image, he acknowledged that it was widely believed the "Colonies ought to be Emunctories or Sinkes of States; to drayne away the filth"; see John White, *The Planters Plea, or the Grounds of Plantations Examined and Usuall Objections Answered* (London, 1630), 33. For the elder Hakluyt's phrase of "offals of our people," see his "Letter of Instruction for the 1580 Voyage of Arthur Pet and Charles Jackman," in Hakluyt, *Principall Navigations*, 1:460. The idea of draining off the poor into the colonies can be traced back to ancient Rome. Cicero described the poor as "'*dordem urbis et faecem*, the poverty stricken scum of the city,' who should be 'drained off to the colonies'"; see Paul Ocobock, introduction in Beier and Ocobock, *Cast Out*, 4.

20. Harrison, *Elizabethan England*, 122. Harrison's allusion to the poor as unbounded and haphazardly dispersed matched how the English thought of wastelands. A writer in 1652 described "those many and wild vacant *Wast-Lands* scattered up and down this Nation, be not suffered to lye longer (like deformed *Chaos*) to our discredit and disprofit"; see *Wast Land's Improvement, or Certain Proposals Made and Tendered to the Consideration of the*

*Honorable Committee Appointed by Parliament for the Advance of Trade,
and General Profits of the Commonwealth . . .* (London, 1653), 2.

21. William Harrison contended that while some believe that a "brood of cattle"
was far better than the "superfluous augmentation" of the poor, he pointed
out that the poor were necessary in times of war. They alone would form a
"wall of men" if England was invaded. See Harrison, *Elizabethan England*,
125; Beier, *Masterless Men*, 75–76.

22. Nicholas P. Canny, "Ideology of English Colonization: From Ireland to Amer-
ica," *William and Mary Quarterly* 30, no. 4 (October 1973): 575–90, esp. 589–
90; and Canny, "The Permissive Frontier: The Problem of Social Control in
English Settlements in Ireland and Virginia," in *The Western Enterprise: English
Activities in Ireland, the Atlantic, and America, 1480–1650*, eds. K. R. Andrews,
N. P. Canny, and P. E. H. Hair (Detroit: Wayne State University Press, 1979),
17–44, esp. 18–19. Also see Linda Bradley Salamon, "Vagabond Veterans: The
Roguish Company of Martin Guerre and *Henry V*," in *Rogues and Early Modern English Culture*, eds. Craig Dionne and Steve Mentz (Ann Arbor: University
of Michigan Press, 2004), 261–93, esp. 265, 270–71; and Roger B. Manning,
"Styles of Command in Seventeenth Century English Armies," *Journal of Military History* 71, no. 3 (July 2007): 671–99, esp. 672–73, 687.

23. Craig Dionne, "Fashioning Outlaws: The Early Modern Rogue and Urban Culture," and Salamon, "Vagabond Veterans," in Dionne and Mentz, *Rogues and Early
Modern English Culture*, 1–2, 7, 33–34, 267–68, 272–73; Harrison, *Elizabethan
England*, 127–28; Beier, *Masterless Men*, 93–94; Claire S. Schen, "Constructing
the Poor in Early Seventeeth-Century London," *Albion: A Quarterly Journal Concerned with British Studies* 32, no. 3 (Autumn 2000): 450–63, esp. 453.

24. As Hakluyt wrote, "If frontier wars there chance to arise, and if thereupon we
shall fortify, yet will occasion the training up of our youth in the discipline of
war and make a number fit for the service of the wars and for the defense of
our people there and at home"; see "Discourse of Western Planting," 119–20,
123. Other colonial promoters argued that colonial service was a substitute
for military service and that it would provide the necessary discipline for the
idle poor. Christopher Carleill made this argument based on his own military
experience in the Low Country wars; see Carleill, *A Breef and Sommarie
Discourse upon the Entended Voyage to the Hethermoste Partes of America:
Written by Captain Carleill in April 1583* (1583), 6. For soldiers as cannon
fodder, see Salamon, "Vagabond Veterans," 271; and Sweet, "Economy, Ecology, and Utopia in Early Colonial Promotional Literature," 408–9.

25. No scholar has recognized the connection between training the children of
the poor and treating them as recycled waste.

26. On the laws passed against defecating in the streets and punishments for
blasphemy and stealing vegetables, see "Articles, Lawes, and Orders, Divine,
Politique, and Martiall for the Colony of Virginia: First Established by Sir
Thomas Gates. . . . May 24, 1610," in *For the Colonial in Virginia Britannia.
Lavves, Diuine, Morall, and Martiall, &c. Alget qui non Ardet. Res nostrae
subinde non sunt, quales quis optaret, sed quales esse possunt* (London,
1612), 10–13, 15–17; also see Kathleen M. Brown, *Foul Bodies: Cleanliness in
Early America* (New Haven, CT: Yale University Press, 2009), 61–64. On the

man murdering and eating his wife, see *A True Declaration of the Estate of the Colonie in Virginia, with a Confutation of Such Scandalous Reports as have Tended to the Disgrace of So Worthy an Enterprise* (London, 1610), 16; and John Smith, *The Generall Historie of Virginia, New England, and the Summer Isles . . .* (1624), in Barbour, *The Complete Works of Captain John Smith,* 2:232–33; Donegan, *Seasons of Misery,* 103.

27. Donne, *A Sermon upon the Eighth Verse of the First Chapter of the Acts of the Apostles,* 19.

28. Karen Ordahl Kupperman, "Apathy and Death in Early Jamestown," *Journal of American History* 66, no. 1 (June 1979): 24–40, esp. 24–27, 31; and Wesley Frank Craven, *The Virginia Company of London, 1606–1624* (Williamsburg: Virginia 350th Anniversary Celebration Corporation, 1957), 22–28, 32–34. On the promise of finding gold, see David Beers Quinn, *England and the Discovery of America, 1481–1620* (New York: Knopf, 1974), 482–87. For a popular satire about the lure of quick riches and gold chamber pots to be found in the New World, see George Chapman, *Eastward Hoe* (London, 1605; reprint, London: The Tudor Facsimile Texts, 1914), 76. For "sluggish idlenesse," see *A True Declaration of the Estate of the Colonie* (1610), 19. For "beastiall sloth" and "idleness," see Virginia Company, *A True and Sincere Declaration of the Purpose and End of the Plantation Begun in Virginia* (London, 1610), 10.

29. Hakluyt, "Discourse on Western Planting," 28. Hakluyt took this idea from Gilbert, who advised having the children of the poor trained in "handie craftes" so they could make "trifles" to be sold to the Indians; see Gilbert, "A Discourse of a Discoverie for a New Passage to Cataia" (1576), in Quinn, *The Voyages and Colonial Enterprises of Sir Humphrey Gilbert,* 1:161. Also see Canny, "The Permissive Frontier," 25, 27–29, 33. And on prohibitions against gaming, rape, and trading with sailors, see "Articles, Lawes, and Orders . . . Established by Sir Thomas Gates," 10–11, 13–14.

30. On Thomas More's *Utopia* (1516), see Joan Thirsk, "Making a Fresh Start: Sixteenth-Century Agriculture and the Classical Inspiration," in Michael Leslie and Timothy Raylor, eds., *Culture and Cultivation in Early Modern England: Writing and the Land* (Leicester and London: Leicester University Press, 1992), 22.

31. On Rolfe and tobacco, see Philip D. Morgan, "Virginia's Other Prototype: The Caribbean," in *The Atlantic World and Virginia, 1550–1624,* ed. Peter C. Mancall (Chapel Hill: University of North Carolina Press, 2007), 362; and Edmund S. Morgan, "The Labor Problem at Jamestown, 1607–1618," *American Historical Review* 76, no. 3 (June 1971): 595–611, esp. 609.

32. See Manning C. Voorhis, "Crown Versus Council in the Virginia Land Policy," *William and Mary Quarterly,* 3rd ser., 3, no. 4 (October 1946): 499–514, esp. 500–501; and Edmund S. Morgan, *American Slavery, American Freedom: The Ordeal of Colonial Virginia* (New York: Norton, 1975), 93–94, 171–73. Morgan quotes Jamestown planter John Pory, who wrote that "our principall wealth . . . consisteth in servants." See Morgan, "The First American Boom," *William and Mary Quarterly* 28, no. 2 (1971): 169–98, esp. 176–77.

33. See Tomlins, *Freedom Bound,* 31–36, 78–81; Mary Sarah Bilder, "The Struggle over Immigration: Indentured Servants, Slaves, and Articles of Commerce," *Missouri Law Review* 61 (Fall 1996): 758–59, 764; and Warren M. Billings, "The

Law of Servants and Slaves in Seventeenth Century Virginia," *Virginia Magazine of History and Biography* 99, no. 1 (January 1991): 45–62, esp. 47–49, 51.

34. Morgan, "The First American Boom," 170, 185–86, 198; Schen, "Constructing the Poor in Early Seventeenth-Century London," 451; Billings, "The Law of Servants and Slaves," 48–49. On high death tolls for indentured servants, see Martha W. McCartney, *Virginia Immigrants and Adventurers: A Biographical Dictionary* (Baltimore: Genealogical Publishing Company, 2007), 14; and Smith, *The Generall Historie of Virginia, New England, and the Summer Isles . . .* , in Barbour, *The Complete Works of Captain John Smith*, 2:255.

35. Dr. John Pott paid the ransom for her release from the Indians with a few pounds of trade beads; he also claimed that her dead husband owed him three years of work on his indenture. See McCartney, *Virginia Immigrants and Adventurers*, 258; and "The Humble Petition of Jane Dickenson Widdowe" (1624), in *Records of the Virginia Company of London*, ed. Susan M. Kingsbury, 4 vols. (Washington, DC: Government Printing Office, 1906–35), 4:473; also see Canny, "The Permissive Frontier," 32.

36. Smith, *The Generall Historie of Virginia, New England, and the Summer Isles . . .* (1624), in Barbour, *The Complete Works of Captain John Smith*, 2:388. *The Merchant of Venice* was published in 1600. Under Roman law, not only war captives but debtors and abandoned children could be made slaves. Children born to slaves could be slaves too. In Jamestown, children born to debtors could be made slaves. See Temin, "The Labor Market of the Early Roman Empire," 513–38, esp. 524, 531.

37. See David R. Ransome, "Wives for Virginia, 1621," *William and Mary Quarterly* 48, no. 1 (January 1991): 3–18, esp. 4–7. The sex ratio was roughly four to one during the early years of Virginia; see Virginia Bernhard, "'Men, Women, and Children' at Jamestown: Population and Gender in Early Virginia, 1607–1610," *Journal of Southern History* 58, no. 4 (November 1992): 599–618, esp. 614–18. On the shipping of cattle and cows as emissaries of Englishness, see Virginia DeJohn Anderson, "Animals into the Wilderness: The Development of Livestock Husbandry in the Seventeenth-Century Chesapeake," *William and Mary Quarterly* 59, no. 2 (April 2002): 377–408, esp. 377, 379. The idea of sending women as breeders to the colonies was not new. In 1656, Cromwell had shipped off two thousand young women of England to Barbados in "order that by their breeding they should replenish the white population." See Jennifer L. Morgan, *Laboring Women: Reproduction and Gender in New World Slavery* (Philadelphia: University of Pennsylvania Press, 2004), 74–75.

38. William Berkeley, *A Discourse and View of Virginia* (London, 1663), 2, 7, 12.

39. Samuel Eliot Morrison, "The Plymouth Company and Virginia," *Virginia Magazine of History and Biography* 62, no. 2 (April 1954): 147–65; Donegan, *Seasons of Misery*, 119.

40. Tomlins, *Freedom Bound*, 23, 54–56; Alison Games, *Migration and Origins of the English Atlantic World* (Cambridge, MA: Harvard University Press, 1999), 25, 48, 53; T. H. Breen and Stephen Foster, "Moving to the New World: The Character of Early Massachusetts Migration," *William and Mary Quarterly* 30, no. 2 (April 1973): 189–222, esp. 194, 201; Nuala Zahedieh,

"London and the Colonial Consumer in the Late Seventeenth Century," *Economic History Review* 42, no. 2 (May 1994): 239–61, esp. 245.

41. See his "General Observations" (1629), in *John Winthrop Papers*, 6 vols. (Boston: Massachusetts Historical Society, 1928–), 2:111–15; Edgar J. A. Johnson, "Economic Ideas of John Winthrop," *New England Quarterly* 3, no. 2 (April 1930): 235–50, esp. 245, 250; Francis J. Bremer, *John Winthrop: America's Forgotten Founder* (New York: Oxford University Press, 2003), 152–53, 160–61, 174–75, 181, and footnote 9 on 431–32.

42. John Winthrop, "A Model of Christian Charity" (1630), *Collections of the Massachusetts Historical Society*, 3rd ser., 7 (Boston, 1838), 33; Scott Michaelson, "John Winthrop's 'Modell' Covenant and the Company Way," *Early American Literature* 27, no. 2 (1992): 85–100, esp. 90; Lawrence W. Towner, "'A Fondness for Freedom': Servant Protest in Puritan Society," *William and Mary Quarterly* 19, no. 2 (April 1962): 201–19, esp. 204–5.

43. Norman H. Dawes, "Titles of Symbols of Prestige in Seventeenth-Century New England," *William and Mary Quarterly* 6, no. 1 (January 1949): 69–83; David Konig, *Law and Society in Puritan Massachusetts: Essex County, 1629–1692* (Chapel Hill: University of North Carolina Press, 1979), 18–19, 29–30, 92; *John Winthrop Papers*, 4, 54, 476; Bremer, *John Winthrop*, 355.

44. Towner, "'A Fondness for Freedom,'" 202; Tomlins, *Freedom Bound*, 254–55; Bremer, *John Winthrop*, 313.

45. Tomlins, *Freedom Bound*, 56, 255–56, 258. Fourteen was the age of discretion in Massachusetts law, and most did not arrive at adulthood until the age of twenty-one. See Ross W. Beales Jr., "In Search of the Historical Child: Adulthood and Youth in Colonial New England," *American Quarterly* 27, no. 4 (April 1975): 379–98, esp. 384–85, 393–94, 397. Massachusetts first required youth to reside in families and work for them without compensation when land grants were distributed in 1623; laws were passed in Massachusetts, Connecticut, and Rhode Island that "all single persons had to reside with families." See William E. Nelson, "The Utopian Legal Order of Massachusetts Bay Colony, 1630–1686," *American Journal of Legal History* 47, no. 2 (April 2005): 183–230, esp. 183; and Archer, *Fissures in the Rock*, 106.

46. Tomlins, *Freedom Bound*, 307, 310; Philip Greven, *Four Generations: Population, Land, and Family in Colonial Andover, Massachusetts* (Ithaca, NY: Cornell University Press, 1970), 75, 81–83, 125, 132, 135, 149.

47. Winthrop's first two wives died in childbirth. His last wife gave birth a year before he died. Bremer, *John Winthrop*, 90–91, 102–3, 115, 314, 373.

48. Cotton Mather, *A Good Master Well Served* (Boston, 1696), 15–16, 35–36, 38; Towner, "'A Fondness for Freedom,'" 209–10; Robert Middlekauf, *The Mathers: Three Generations of Puritan Intellectuals, 1596–1728* (New York: Oxford University Press, 1971), 195.

49. William Perkins, "On the Right, Lawful, and Holy Use of Apparel" in *The Whole Treatise of the Cases of Conscience Distinguished into Three Books* (Cambridge, England, 1606); Louis B. Wright, "William Perkins: Elizabethan Apostle of 'Practical Divinity,'" *Huntington Library Quarterly* 2, no. 2 (January 1940): 171–96, esp. 177–78; Stephen Innes, *Creating the Commonwealth: Economic Culture of Puritan New England* (New York: Norton, 1998), 101–3. In

1651, officials in Massachusetts Bay Colony declared their "utter detestation & dislike that men and women of meane condition, education & callings should take upon theme the garb of the gentlemen"; see Leigh Eric Schmidt, "'A Church-Going People Are a Dress-Loving People': Clothes, Communication, and Religious Culture in Early America," *Church History* 58, no. 1 (March 1989): 36–51, esp. 38–39. During King Philip's War, the court charged "38 wives and maids and 30 young men . . . for wearing silk and that in a flaunting manner"; see Laurel Thatcher Ulrich, *The Age of Homespun: Objects and Stories in the Creation of an American Myth* (New York: Knopf, 2001), 125; and Konig, *Law and Society in Puritan Massachusetts*, 148. And on the anxiety over parents and masters indulging children and servants, see Edmund Morgan, *The Puritan Family: Religious and Domestic Relations in Seventeenth-Century New England* (Westport, CT: Greenwood Press, 1966), 149.

50. For the privileges that church members had in court proceedings, see Thomas Haskell, "Litigation and Social Status in Seventeenth-Century New Haven," *Journal of Legal Studies*, no. 2 (June 1978): 219–41. On Mary Dyer, see Carla Gardina Pestana, "The Quaker Executions as Myth and History," *Journal of American History* 80, no. 2 (September 1992): 441–69, esp. 441, 460–64; and David D. Hall, *Worlds of Wonder, Days of Judgment: Popular Religious Belief in Early New England* (Cambridge, MA: Harvard University Press, 1990), 172–74, 186. Excommunication in England could result in severe penalties of barring the person from receiving an inheritance or restricting the right to sue. In New England, at least initially, excommunication only led to disenfranchisement. In 1638, the courts established harsher punishments: if a person did not repent or seek readmission within six months of excommunication, he or she could be fined, jailed, banished, or "further." See Konig, *Law and Society in Puritan Massachusetts*, 32.

51. Archer, *Fissures in the Rock*, 44, 50, 59–63, endnote 5, 180; Robert J. Dinkin, "Seating the Meetinghouse in Early Massachusetts," *New England Quarterly* 43, no. 3 (September 1970): 450–64, esp. 453–54.

52. Kathryn Zabelle Derounian, "The Publication, Promotion, and Distribution of Mary Rowlandson's Indian Captivity Narrative in the Seventeenth Century," *Early American Literature* 23, no. 3 (1988): 239–62. On Rowlandson's embrace of English class and material symbols, see Nan Goodman, "'Money Answers All Things': Rethinking Economic Cultural Exchange in the Captivity Narrative of Mary Rowlandson," *American Literary History* 22, no. 1 (Spring 2010): 1–25, esp. 5.

53. Mary Rowlandson, *The Sovereignty and Goodness of God, Together with the Faithfulness of His Promises Displayed: Being a Narrative of Captivity and Restoration of Mrs. Mary Rowlandson and Related Documents*, ed. Neil Salisbury (Boston: Bedford Books, 1997), 1, 16, 26, 75, 79, 83, 86, 89, 96–97, 103; Ulrich, *The Age of Homespun*, 59; Teresa A. Toulouse, "'My Own Credit': Strategies of (E)valuation in Mary Rowlandson's Captivity Narrative," *American Literature* 64, no. 2 (December 1992): 655–76, esp. 656–58; Tiffany Potter, "Writing Indigenous Femininity: Mary Rowlandson's Narrative of Captivity," *Eighteenth-Century Studies* 36, no. 2 (Winter 2003): 153–67, esp. 154.

54. See Increase Mather, *Pray for the Rising Generation, or a Sermon Wherein Godly Parents Are Encouraged, to Pray and Believe for Children* (Boston, 1678), 12, 17; Hall, *Worlds of Wonder,* 148–55; Gerald F. Moran, "Religious Renewal, Puritan Tribalism, and the Family in Seventeenth-Century Milford, Connecticut," *William and Mary Quarterly* 36, no. 2 (April 1979): 236–54, esp. 237–38, 250–54; Bremer, *John Winthrop,* 314–15; Lewis Milton Robinson, "A History of the Half-Way Covenant" (Ph.D. dissertation, University of Illinois, 1963).

55. Hakluyt wrote two different dedications: one emphasized Virginia as a nubile bride, and the other as a child, with Queen Elizabeth as her godmother overseeing the gossips (midwives) assisting in the birth of a child. Samuel Purchas repeated the same marital allusion, writing that Virginia's "lovely looks" were "worth the wooing and loves of the best husband." See "Epistle Dedicatory to Sir Walter Ralegh by Richard Hakluyt, 1587," *De Orbe Novo Petri Martyris,* in Taylor, *The Original Writings,* 2:367; and "To the Right Worthie and Honourable Gentleman, Sir Walter Ralegh," in *A Notable Historie Containing four Voyages Made by Certayne French Captaynes into Florida* (London, 1587), [2]. Raleigh used a similar allusion about Guiana, that she hath "yet to lose her Maidenhead." See Sir Walter Ralegh, *The Discovery of the Large, Rich, and Beautiful Empire of Guiana, with a relation of the Great and Golden City of Manoa (which the Spaniards call El Dorado), etc. performed in the Year 1595,* edited by Sir Robert H. Schomburgk (London, 1848), 115; also see Louis Montrose, "The Work of Gender in the Discourse of Discovery," *Representations* 33 (Winter 1991): 1–41, esp. 12–13; Fuller, *Voyages in Print,* 75; and Morgan, "Virginia's Other Prototype," 360.

56. See Rachel Doggett, Monique Hulvey, and Julie Ainsworth, eds., *New World Wonders: European Images of the Americas, 1492–1700* (Washington, DC: Folger Shakespeare Library/Seattle: University of Washington Press, 1992), 37; Edward L. Bond, "Sources of Knowledge, Sources of Power: The Supernatural World of English Virginia, 1607–1624," *Virginia Magazine of History and Biography* 108, no. 2 (2000): 105–138, esp. 114.

57. See Jack Dempsey, ed., *New England Canaan by Thomas Morton of "Merrymount"* (Scituate, MA: Digital Scanning, 2000), 283–88; Karen Ordahl Kupperman, "Thomas Morton, Historian," *New England Quarterly* 50, no. 4 (December 1977): 660–64; Michael Zukerman, "Pilgrims in the Wilderness: Community, Modernity, and the May Pole at Merrymount," *New England Quarterly* 50, no. 4 (December 1977): 255–77; John P. McWilliams Jr., "Fictions of Merry Mount," *American Quarterly* 29, no. 1 (Spring 1977): 3–30.

58. He was first marooned on the Isle of Shoals (New Hampshire) after his arrest in 1628, and then shipped back to England. He returned to New England in 1629 and was banished again to England in 1630. He returned once more in 1643, only to be arrested the next year; he was released in 1645 on the condition that he go out of the jurisdiction, so he headed to Maine and died soon after. For the best overview of his life, see Jack Dempsey, *Thomas Morton of "Merrymount": The Life and Renaissance of an Early American Poet* (Scituate, MA: Digital Scanning, 2000).

59. Morton believed that special water used by the Indians (the "crystal fountain") cured barrenness; see Dempsey, *New English Canaan*, 7, 26–27, 53–55, 70, 90, 92, 120–21, 135–36, 139. For the best analyses of Morton's writings, see Michelle Burnham, "Land, Labor, and Colonial Economics in Thomas Morton's *New English Canaan*," *Early American Literature* 41, no. 3 (2006): 405–28, esp. 408, 413–14, 418, 421, 423–24; and Edith Murphy, "'A Rich Widow, Now to Be Tane Up or Laid Downe': Solving the Riddle of Thomas Morton's 'Rise Oedipeus,'" *William and Mary Quarterly* 55, no. 4 (October 1996): 755–68, esp. 756, 759, 761–62, 765–67.

60. Hamor, *A True Discourse of the Present State of Virginia*, 20; Hakluyt, "Epistle Dedicatory to Sir Walter Ralegh by Richard Hakluyt, 1587," 2:367–68. Lawson also emphasized the "wonderful increase" of sheep and cattle, which he described as "fat"—another word used to describe their abundant fertility; see John Lawson, *A New Voyage to Carolina*, with introduction by Hugh Talmage Lefler (reprint of 1706 London ed., Chapel Hill: University of North Carolina Press, 1967), 87–88, 91, 196. John Smith repeated this notion that Indian women "are easily delivered of childe." See Smith, *The Generall Historie of Virginia, New England, and the Summer Isles . . .* (1624) 2:1165. On New World images of fertility in general, see Parrish, "The Female Opossum and the Nature of the New World," 475–514, esp. 502–6, 511. The Romans claimed that barbarian and nomadic women "give birth with ease," and this idea readily translated to Native women in the New World. See Morgan, *Laboring Women*, 16–17.

61. Tomlins, *Freedom Bound*; Alsop also referred to Mary-land as having a "natural womb (by her plenty)," which gave forth several different kinds of animals. The land's "superabounding plenty" he compared to a woman's pregnant belly. If "copulative marriage" involved women coming to "market with their virginity," Alsop contrasted virgins with prostitutes or doxies, who "rent out" their wombs, and to spinsters who had let their wombs become "mouldy"; see George Alsop, *A Character of the Province of Maryland* (London, 1666), in *Narratives of Early Maryland, 1633–1684*, ed., Clayton G. Hall (New York: Charles Scribner's Sons, 1910), 340–87, esp. 343–44, 348, 358. Also see *A Brief Description of the Province of Carolina on the Coasts of Floreda* (London, 1666), 9–10.

62. On the marriage fraud to secure land, see Morgan, "The First American Boom," 189–90. Historian Carole Shammas has noted that the colonies of Virginia and Maryland were more generous to widows, which benefited men who married them, encouraging a "lively marriage market in widows"; see Shammas, "English Inheritance Law and Its Transfer to the Colonies," *American Journal of Legal History* 31, no. 2 (April 1987): 145–63, esp. 158–59. On high mortality rates and remarriage, see Lorena Walsh, "'Till Death Do Us Part': Marriage and Family in Seventeenth-Century Maryland," in *The Chesapeake in the Seventeenth Century: Essays on Anglo-American Society*, eds. Thad W. Tate and David L. Ammerman (Chapel Hill: University of North Carolina Press, 1979), 126–52. Widows were routinely made the executrix of their husband's estates, and most women remarried one year and never longer than two years after a husband's death; see James R. Perry, *The Formation of*

a *Society on Virginia's Eastern Shore, 1615–1655* (Chapel Hill: University of North Carolina Press, 1990), 41, 79, 81.

63. T. H. Breen, "A Changing Labor Force and Race Relations in Virginia, 1660–1710," *Journal of Social History* 7, no. 1 (Autumn 1973): 3–25, esp. 10. For "ye scum of the country," leveling language, and the charge that Bacon attracted the idle, or those in debt, see "William Sherwood's Account" and "Ludlow's Account," in "Bacon's Rebellion," *Virginia Magazine of History and Biography* 1, no. 2 (October 1893): 169, 171, 183. For Bacon's followers as "Vulgar and Ignorant," and "lately crept out of the condition of Servants," see "A True Narrative of the Late Rebellion in Virginia, by the Royal Commissioners, 1677," in *Narratives of the Insurrections, 1675–1690,* ed. Charles M. Andrews (New York: Charles Scribner's Sons, 1915), 110–11, 113. On comparing the rebels to swine, see William Sherwood, "Virginias Deploured Condition, Or an Impartiall Narrative of the Murders comitted by the Indians there, and of the Sufferings of his Maties Loyall Subjects under the Rebellious outrages of Mr Nathaniell Bacon Junr: to the tenth day of August Anno Dom 1676 (1676)," in *Collections of the Massachusetts Historical Society,* vol. 9, 4th ser. (Boston: Massachusetts Historical Society, 1871): 176.

64. Stephen Saunders Webb, *1676: The End of American Independence* (New York: Knopf, 1984; reprint ed., Syracuse, NY: Syracuse University Press, 1995), 16, 34, 41, 66; Tomlins, *Freedom Bound,* 39–41, 425.

65. In Bacon's manifesto, he made it clear that the Berkeley faction had formed a powerful "Cabal" that protected the "Darling Indians" over the lives of its English settlers. Bacon's rebels also protested against the governor's policy that forbade military action against Indians without an express order from Berkeley. See Nathaniel Bacon, "Proclamations of Nathaniel Bacon," *Virginia Magazine of History and Biography* 1, no. 1 (July 1893): 57–60; and Webb, *1676,* 7, 74.

66. On "Land lopers," see Sherwood, "Virginias Deploured Condition," 164. For unfair taxes and "Grandees" that "engrosse all their tobacco into their own hands," see "A True Narrative of the Late Rebellion," 108, 111; also see Peter Thompson, "The Thief, a Householder, and the Commons: Language of Class in Seventeenth Century Virginia," *William and Mary Quarterly* 63, no. 2 (April 2006): 253–80, esp. 264, 266–67. For the mixture of taxes, debts, and declining tobacco prices as the economic causes of the rebellion, see Warren M. Billings, "The Causes of Bacon's Rebellion: Some Suggestions," *Virginia Magazine of History and Biography* 78, no. 4 (October 1970): 409–35, esp. 419–22, 432–33. And for the importance of land issues and abuses of the council in the aftermath of the rebellion, see Michael Kammen, "Virginia at the Close of the Seventeenth Century: An Appraisal by James Blair and John Locke," *Virginia Magazine of History and Biography* 74, no. 2 (April 1966): 141–69, esp. 143, 154–55, 157, 159–60.

67. Bacon died on October 26, 1676; Berkeley died on July 9, 1677. As Kathleen Brown notes, Bacon's death by the bloody flux suggested that he was "defeated by his own body's corruption"; see Brown, *Foul Bodies,* 67. The lice may have been just as important, as it associated Bacon with the meaner sort and animals that carried lice. One account recorded that he had the "Lousy disease; so that swarmes of Vermyne that bred in his body he could not destroy

but by throwing his shirts into the fire." See "A True Narrative of the Late Rebellion," 139; Wilcomb E. Washburn, "Sir William Berkeley's 'A History of Our Miseries,'" *William and Mary Quarterly* 14, no. 3 (July 1957): 403–14, esp. 412; and Wilcomb E. Washburn, *The Governor and the Rebel: A History of Bacon's Rebellion in Virginia* (Chapel Hill: University of North Carolina Press, 1957), 85, 129–32, 138–39.

68. Andrews, *Narratives of the Insurrections*, 20. On white aprons, see Mrs. An. Cotton, "An Account of Our Late Troubles with Virginia. Written in 1676," in *Tracts and Other Papers, Principally Relating to the Origin, Settlement, and Progress of the Colonies of North America, from the Discovery of the Country to the Year 1776*, ed. Peter Force, 4 vols. (Washington, DC, 1836–46), 1:8. In another account the women were called guardian angels, and Aphra Behn in her play on Bacon's Rebellion alludes to the women being used as a truce to avoid combat; see "The History of Bacon's and Ingram's Rebellions, 1676," in Andrews, *Narratives of the Insurrections*, 68; and Behn, *The Widow Ranter, or, The History of Bacon in Virginia. A Tragi-Comedy* (London, 1690), 35; also see Washburn, *The Governor and the Rebel*, 80–81; Terri L. Snyder, *Brabbling Women: Disorderly Speech and the Law in Early Virginia* (Ithaca, NY: Cornell University Press, 2003), 33–34; and Webb, *1676*, 20–21.

69. On Lydia Chisman, see "The History of Bacon's and Ingram's Rebellions," in Andrews, *Narratives of the Insurrections*, 81–82. On Elizabeth Bacon's later marriages, see "Bacon's Rebellion," 6. On the confiscation and return of the estates to widows of the rebels, see Washburn, *The Governor and the Rebel*, 141–42; and Wilcomb E. Washburn, "The Humble Petition of Sarah Drummond," *William and Mary Quarterly* 13, no. 13 (July 1956): 354–75, esp. 356, 358, 363–64, 367, 371. Lyon G. Tylor, "Maj. Edmund Chisman," *William and Mary Quarterly* 1, no. 2 (October 1892): 89–98, esp. 90–91, 94–97; Susan Westbury, "Women in Bacon's Rebellion," in *Southern Women: Histories and Identities*, eds. Virginia Bernhard, Betty Brandon, Elizabeth Fox-Genovese, and Theda Perdu (Columbia: University of Missouri Press, 1992), 30–46, esp. 39–42.

70. Webb, *1676*, 102, 132–63.

71. See Behn, *The Widow Ranter*, 3, 12, 42, 45, 48; Jenny Hale Pulsipher, "'The Widow Ranter' and Royalist Culture in Colonial Virginia," *Early American Literature* 39, no. 1 (2004): 41–66, esp. 53–55; and Snyder, *Brabbling Women*, 11–12, 117, 122–23.

72. Jane D. Carson, "Frances Culpeper Berkeley," in *Notable American Women, 1607–1950*, ed. Edward James et al., 3 vols. (Cambridge, MA: Harvard University Press, 1971), 1:135–36; Snyder, *Brabbling Women*, 19–25.

73. Kathleen M. Brown, *Good Wives, Nasty Wenches, and Anxious Patriarchs: Gender, Race, and Power in Colonial Virginia* (Chapel Hill: University of North Carolina Press, 1996), 129–33; Tomlins, *Freedom Bound*, 455, 457–58.

74. Morgan, *Laboring Women*, 77–83; Anderson, "Animals into the Wilderness," 403.

75. For the quotation see Francis Bacon, *The Two Books of Francis Bacon, of the Proficience and Advancement of Learning, Divine and Human* (London, 1808), 72; for a different interpretation of this quotation, see Parrish, "The Female Opossum and the Nature of the New World," 489.

76. Turk McClesky, "Rich Land, Poor Prospects: Real Estate and the Formation of a Social Elite in Augusta County, Virginia, 1738–1770," *Virginia Magazine of History and Biography* 98, no. 3 (July 1990): 449–86; John Combs, "The Phases of Conversion: A New Chronology for the Rise of Slavery in Virginia," *William and Mary Quarterly* 68, no. 3 (July 2011): 332–60; Emory G. Evans, *A "Topping People": The Rise and Decline of Virginia's Old Political Elite, 1680–1790* (Charlottesville: University of Virginia Press, 2009), 1–30.

Chapter Two: John Locke's Lubberland: The Settlements of Carolina and Georgia

1. On the words Jefferson borrowed from Locke, see John Locke, *Two Treatises of Government,* ed. Peter Laslétt (Cambridge: Cambridge University Press, 1988), 523, 415. For the idea that Locke should be read by everyone, men, women, and children, see advertisement for Locke's *Second Treatise on Government,* in *Massachusetts Evening Gazette,* March 4, 1774; also see *Boston Evening Gazette,* October 19, 1772; and *New London Gazette,* October 9, 1767. Locke's major critic (and of his "disciples") was Welsh clergyman Josiah Tucker; see Josiah Tucker, *A Series of Answers to Certain Popular Objections, Against Separating from the Rebellious Colonies, and Discarding Them Entirely; Being the Concluding Tract of the Dean of Gloucester, on the Subject of American Affairs* (Gloucester, UK, 1776), in *Four Tracts on Political and Commercial Subjects* (Gloucester, 1776; reprint ed., New York, 1975), 21–22, 102–3. On Locke's involvement in the slave trade, see David Armitage, "John Locke, Carolina, and the *Two Treatises of Government,*" *Political Theory* 32, no. 5 (October 2004): 602–27, esp. 608; James Farr, "Locke, Natural Law, and New World Slavery," *Political Theory* 36, no. 4 (August 2008): 495–522, esp. 497; Wayne Glausser, "Three Approaches to Locke and the Slave Trade," *Journal of the History of Ideas* 51, no. 2 (April–June 1990): 199–216, esp. 200–204; George Frederick Zook, "The Royal Adventurers in England," *Journal of Negro History* 4, no. 2 (April 1919): 143–62, esp. 161.

2. Shaftesbury referred to Carolina as "my darling" in a 1672 letter to another proprietor, Sir Peter Colleton; see Langdon Cheves, ed., *The Shaftesbury Papers and Other Records Relating to Carolina* (Charleston: South Carolina Historical Society, 1897), 416; also see L. H. Roper, *Conceiving Carolina: Proprietors, Planters, and Plots, 1662–1729* (New York: Palgrave Macmillan, 2004), 15.

3. Armitage, "John Locke, Carolina, and the *Two Treatises of Government,*" 603, 607–8; and Armitage, "John Locke, Theorist of Empire?," in *Empire and Modern Political Thought,* ed. Sankar Muthu (Cambridge: Cambridge University Press, 2015), 7. For the important role of the secretary, see Herbert Richard Paschal Jr., "Proprietary North Carolina: A Study in Colonial Government" (Ph.D. dissertation, University of North Carolina, 1961), 145; and Barbara Arneil, *John Locke and America: The Defense of English Colonialism* (Oxford: Clarendon Press, 1996), 1–2, 21–22, 24–26, 43–44.

4. See "Concessions and Agreement Between the Lords Proprietors and Major William Yeamans and Others" (January 7, 1665) and *The Fundamental*

Constitutions of Carolina (July 21, 1669), in *North Carolina Charters and Constitutions, 1578–1698,* ed. Mattie Erma Edwards Parker (Raleigh, NC: Carolina Charter Tercentenary Commission, 1963), 122–23, 129, 133.

5. Ibid., 107, 112, 129–30, 132, 137–42, 145; Charles Lowry, "Class, Politics, Rebellion, and Regional Development in Proprietary North Carolina, 1697–1720" (Ph.D. dissertation, University of Florida, 1979), 38–39; Paschal, "Proprietary North Carolina: A Study in Colonial Government," 216, 229, esp. 236–37.

6. Parker, *The Fundamental Constitutions of Carolina,* 129, 134; *The Fundamental Constitutions of Carolina,* in *Locke: Political Essays,* ed. Mark Goldie (Cambridge: Cambridge University Press, 1997), 162; Farr, "Locke, Natural Law," 498–500; Thomas Leng, "Shaftesbury's Aristocratic Empire," in *Anthony Ashley Cooper, 1621–1681,* ed. John Spurr (Surrey, UK: Ashgate, 2011), 101–26; Shirley Carter Hughson, "The Feudal Laws of Carolina," *Sewanee Review* 2, no. 4 (August 1894): 471–83, esp. 482.

7. Parker, *The Fundamental Constitutions of Carolina,* 129, 136–37.

8. On Leet-men, see David Wootton, ed. and introduction, *John Locke: Political Writings* (New York: Penguin, 1993), 43; and John Locke, "An Essay on the Poor Law" (1697) and "Labour" (1661), in Goldie, *Locke: Political Essays,* 192, 328.

9. See Daniel W. Fagg Jr., "St. Giles' Seigniory: The Earl of Shaftesbury's Carolina Plantation," *South Carolina Historical Magazine* 71, no. 2 (April 1970): 117–23, esp. 123; and Shaftesbury to Mr. Andrew Percival, May 23, 1674, in *Collections of the South Carolina Historical Society,* vol. 5 (Charleston: South Carolina Historical Society, 1897), 5:443–44.

10. Thomas Woodward to Proprietors, June 2, 1665, in *The Colonial Records of North Carolina,* ed. William L. Saunders (Raleigh: Hale, 1886), 1:100–101. Hereafter cited as *CRNC.* Lindley S. Butler, "The Early Settlement of Carolina: Virginia's Southern Frontier," *Virginia Magazine of History and Biography* 79, no. 1, Part One (January 1971): 20–28, esp. 21, 28. On the influx of squatters, see Robert Weir, "'Shaftesbury's Darling': British Settlement in the Carolinas at the Close of the Seventeenth Century," in *The Oxford History of the British Empire,* vol. 1, *The Origins of the Empire: British Overseas Enterprise to the Close of the Seventeenth Century,* ed. Nicolas Canny (Oxford: Oxford University Press, 1998), 381.

11. For Locke's and Shaftesbury's dismissal of settlers who were "Lazy or debauched," see Locke's Carolina Memoranda, and Lord Ashley to Joseph West, December 16, 1671, *Collections of the South Carolina Historical Society,* 5:248, 366.

12. See Richard Waterhouse, *A New World Gentry: The Making of a Merchant and Planter Class in South Carolina, 1670–1770* (New York: Garland, 1989), 62–63, 71, 74; and Lori Glover, *All Our Relations: Blood Ties and Emotional Bonds Among the Early South Carolina Gentry* (Baltimore: Johns Hopkins University Press, 2000), 87–88.

13. Theo. D. Jervey, "The White Indentured Servants of South Carolina," *South Carolina Historical and Genealogical Magazine* 12, no. 4 (October 1911): 163–71, esp. 166. Slaves were 72 percent of the population by 1740, and then declined to around 50 percent of the population over the next forty years; see Tomlins, *Freedom Bound,* 436–37. Fears of the high rates of importing slaves began in the 1690s, and the recruitment of Leet-men, to offset this

imbalance, was still part of the equation; see Brad Hinshelwood, "The Carolinian Context of John Locke's Theory," *Political Theory* 4, no. 4 (August
2013): 562–90, esp. 579–80.

14. Noeleen McIlvenna, *A Very Mutinous People: The Struggle for North Carolina, 1660–1713* (Chapel Hill: University of North Carolina Press, 2009), 1,
13, 162; Kirsten Fischer, *Suspect Relations: Sex, Race, and Resistance in
Colonial North Carolina* (Ithaca, NY: Cornell University Press, 2002), 24; A.
Roger Ekirch, *"Poor Carolina": Politics and Society in Colonial North Carolina, 1729–1776* (Chapel Hill: University of North Carolina Press, 1981),
xviii–xix, 24. For "useless lubbers," see Hugh Talmage Lefler, ed., *A New
Voyage to Carolina by John Lawson* (Chapel Hill: University of North Carolina Press, 1967), 40.

15. See "From the *Gentlemen's Magazine*," *Boston Evening-Post*, February 5,
1739. Italics in the original.

16. See *Oxford English Dictionary*, 467; and William Shakespeare's poem "The
Passionate Pilgrim" (1598), line 201.

17. Sharon T. Pettie, "Preserving the Great Dismal Swamp," *Journal of Forestry*
20, no. 1 (January 1976): 28–33, esp. 29, 31; McIlvenna, *A Very Mutinous People*, 18. There are other estimates of the size of the swamp. Alexander Crosby
Brown believes the swamp in the colonial era was between six hundred and one
thousand square miles; see Brown, *The Dismal Swamp Canal* (Chesapeake:
Norfolk County Historical Society of Chesapeake, Virginia, 1970), 17.

18. William Byrd, "The Secret History of the Dividing Line" (hereafter SH) and
his revised version, "The History of the Dividing Line Betwixt Virginia and
North Carolina, Run in the Year of Our Lord, 1728" (hereafter HDL), in *The
Prose Works of William Byrd of Westover: Narratives of a Virginian* (Cambridge, MA: Belknap Press of Harvard University Press, 1966), 19–20, 63, 70,
190, 196–97, 199, 202.

19. For swamps having no fixed borders, and wetlands as transitional zones, see
William Howarth, "Imagining Territory: Writing the Wetlands," *New Literary History* 30, no. 3 (Summer 1999): 509–39, esp. 521. For the ongoing
boundary dispute, see Lowry, "Class, Politics, Rebellion," 31, 45–46.

20. Byrd, HDL, 202; Charles Royster, *The Fabulous History of the Dismal
Swamp Company* (New York: Knopf, 1999), 6–7, 82–83, 89–91, 98–99, 117,
287–88, 292–93, 299–301, 340, 342–43. Though Byrd's full "History of the
Dividing Line" was not published until 1841, a shorter excerpt circulated to
promote the company; see "A Description of the Dismal Swamp in Virginia,"
The Mail, or Claypoole's Daily Advertiser, March 15, 1792.

21. Hugh T. Lefler and William S. Powell, *Colonial North Carolina: A History*
(New York: Charles Scribner's Sons, 1973), 81–86; Lindley Butler, *Pirates,
Privateers, and Rebel Raiders of the Carolina Coast* (Chapel Hill: University
of North Carolina Press, 2000), 4–8, 30, 39–41, 46, 52–56, 60, 68; Marcus
Rediker, "'Under the Banner of the King of Death': The Social World of
Anglo-American Pirates, 1716–1726," *William and Mary Quarterly* 38, no. 2
(April 1981): 203–27, esp. 203, 205–6, 218–19; David Cordingly, *Under the
Black Flag: The Romance and the Reality of Life Among the Pirates* (New
York: Harvest, 1995), 18–19, 198–202.

22. Webb, *1676*, 26, 98; Jacquelyn H. Wolf, "Proud and the Poor: The Social Organization of Leadership in Proprietary North Carolina, 1663–1729" (Ph.D. dissertation, University of Pennsylvania, 1977), 28–29. For the proprietors wanting more compact settlements, see Lord Ashley to Governor Sayle, April 10, 1671, Lord Ashley to Sir John Yeamans, April 10, 1671, and Lord Ashley to Sir John Yeamans, September 18, 1671, in *Collections of the South Carolina Historical Society*, 5: 311, 314–15, 344; Barbara Arneil, "Trade, Plantations, and Property: John Locke and the Economic Defense of Colonialism," *Journal of the History of Ideas*, vol. 55, no. 4 (October 1994): 591–609, esp. 607; McIlvenna, *A Very Mutinous People*, 31, 33; Lowry, "Class, Politics, Rebellion," 33–34, 45–46, 80–81.

23. Jacquelyn Wolf has calculated that 309 grantees owned 49 percent of all land grants. From 1663 to January 1729, the number of land grants recorded was 3,281. Out of this number, 2,161 were grants of two or more to the same person. By 1730, the total population was 36,000, and it has been estimated that between 3,200 and 6,000 were slaves. See Wolf, "The Proud and the Poor," 25–28, 150–51, 157, 172–73; Fischer, *Suspect Relations*, 27. Charles Lowry, using land records instead of tithables, has calculated a lower population figure of 13,887 whites and 3,845 slaves. Contemporary observers in 1720 felt there were no more than 500 slaves in North Carolina. See Lowry, "Class, Politics, Rebellion," 8–9, 79–80, 84, 113, 115–17, 122–23; McIlvenna, *A Very Mutinous People*, 23, 133–34. For the minister's comments on sloth, see "Mr. Gordon to the Secretary, May 13, 1709," in Saunders, *CRNC*, 1:714; and "Petition to Governor and Council, February 23, 1708/9," in *The Colonial Records of North Carolina*, ed. Robert J. Cain, vol. 7, *Records of the Executive Council, 1664–1734* (Raleigh: Department of Cultural Recourses, North Carolina Division of Archives and History, 1984), 431.

24. Because of the possible defect in the first charter, a second charter was issued in 1665. See "Charter to the Lord Proprietors of Carolina" (June 30, 1650), in Parker, *North Carolina Charters and Constitutions*, 90; Wolf, "The Proud and the Poor," 69; McIlvenna, *A Very Mutinous People*, 49–50, 97–99. On the effort of Berkeley to acquire Albemarle, see Cain, *Records of the Executive Council*, 7:xix. For putting Carolina under stricter controls, see "Mr. Randolph's Memoranda About Illegal Trade in the Plantations, Mentioned in the Foregoing Presentment," November 10, 1696, and another report by Randolph, dated March 24, 1700, in Saunders, *CRNC*, 1:464–70, 527.

25. See Saunders, *CRNC*, 1:xxi; Mattie Erma E. Parker, "Legal Aspects of 'Culpeper's Rebellion,'" *North Carolina Historical Review* 45, no. 2 (April 1968): 111–27, esp. 118–20, 122–24; McIlvenna, *A Very Mutinous People*, 56–57, 65–66.

26. See "Answer of the Lords Proprietors of Carolina Read the 20 Nov. 1680" and "Petition of Thomas Miller to the King, November 20, 1680," in Saunders, *CRNC*, 1:303, 326–28; and Parker, "Legal Aspects of 'Culpeper's Rebellion,'" 111–27, esp. 111–12; Lowry, "Class, Politics, Rebellion," 49.

27. On the controversy surrounding Thomas Miller, see "Affidavit of Henry Hudson, January 31, 1679," and "Carolina Indictment of Th. Miller Received from Ye Comm. Of Ye Customes the 15 July 1680," in Saunders, *CRNC*, 1:272–74,

313–17; and Lindley S. Butler, "Culpeper's Rebellion: Testing the Proprietors," in *North Carolina Experience: An Interpretative and Documentary
History*, eds. Lindley S. Butler and Alan D. Watson (Chapel Hill: University
of North Carolina Press, 1984), 53–78, esp. 56–57. On the scarcity of landgraves and caciques in North Carolina, see Paschal, "Proprietary North Carolina," 184.

28. Wolf, "The Proud and the Poor," 68, and footnote 29 on 172; Paschal, "Proprietary North Carolina," 179; McIlvenna, *A Very Mutinous People*, 73, 80,
146; Lefler and Powell, *Colonial North Carolina*, 54; Lowry, "Class, Politics,
Rebellion," 49, 96–97. On Governor Spotswood waging war on North Carolina, and the connection to the Tuscarora Indians, see "Colonel Spotswood to
the Board of Trade, July 25, 1711," in Saunders, *CRNC*, 1:782.

29. "Journal of John Barnwell," *Virginia Magazine of History and Biography* 6,
no. 1 (July 1898): 442–55, esp. 451; on Barnwell's treachery, see "Colonel
Spotswood to the Board of Trade, July 26, 1752," in Saunders, *CRNC*, 1:862.
Barnwell was accompanied by around five hundred Yamassee and other
Indian allies. Their interest in attacking the Tuscaroras was also spurred on
by the desire to capture slaves. See Lowry, "Class, Politics, Rebellion," 98–99.

30. See "Governor Spotswood to the Earl of Rochester, July 30, 1711," in Saunders,
CRNC, 1:798; Lord Culpeper to the Board of Trade, December 1681, British
Public Record Office, class 1, piece 47, folio 261, Library of Congress, Washington, DC; and Barbara Fuchs, "Faithless Empires: Pirates, Renegadoes, and
the English Nation," *ELH* 67, no. 1 (Spring 2000): 45–69, esp. 50–51.

31. See Byrd, SH and HDL, 19, 66, 195; Philip Ludwell and Nathaniel Harrison,
"Boundary Line Proceedings, 1710," *Virginia Magazine of History and Biog-
raphy* 5 (July 1897): 1–21. It appears that Byrd wrote and revised his two
texts between 1729 and 1740. Although the more polished "History of the
Dividing Line" was not published until 1841, he did circulate the text among
friends and other curious people. See Kenneth A. Lockridge, *The Diary, and
Life, of William Byrd II of Virginia, 1674–1744* (Chapel Hill: University of
North Carolina Press, 1987), 127, 142–43; and Louis B. Wright and Marion
Tinling, eds., *William Byrd of Virginia: The London Diary (1717–1721) and
Other Writings* (New York: Oxford University Press, 1958), 39–40.

32. See William Byrd to Charles Boyle, Earl of Orrery, July 25, 1726, in "Virginia
Council Journals, 1726–1753," *Virginia Magazine of History and Biography*
32, no. 1 (January 1932): 26–27; and Robert D. Arner, "Westover and the
Wilderness: William Byrd's Images of Virginia," *Southern Literary Journal* 7,
no. 2 (Spring 1975): 105–23, esp. 106–7.

33. Byrd, SH, 66, 81; HDL, 182. For another discussion of the "knights-errant"
allusion, see Susan Scott Parrish, "William Byrd and the Crossed Languages
of Science, Satire, and Empire in British America," in *Creole Subjects in the
Colonial Americas: Empires, Texts, and Identities*, eds. Ralph Bauer and Jose
Antonio Mazotti (Chapel Hill: University of North Carolina Press, 2009),
355–72, esp. 363.

34. Byrd, HDL, 182, 204–5. The idea of women doing all the work and "husbands lie snoring in bed" is a much older theme. Thomas More alluded to this
dysfunctional gender pattern in *Utopia*, where he felt all men and women

should be engaged in productive labor. See Thomas More, *Utopia,* eds. George M. Logan and Robert M. Adams (Cambridge: Cambridge University Press, 1989; rev. ed., 2011), 51.

35. Byrd, SH, 143; HDL, 311–12. According to the *Oxford English Dictionary,* "bogtrotting" was first used in 1682, and was associated not only with the Irish but with people who were poor and lived near marshes.

36. Byrd, HDL, 196. Scholars have recognized Byrd's reference to Lubberland and sloth, but failed to trace its roots to the folktale of Lawrence Lazy, which circulated orally and was first published in English in 1670. The influence on Byrd is that his lazy Carolinians sit in the corner like Lazy Lawrence. For the history of the folktale, see J. B. Smith, "Toward a Demystification of Lazy Lawrence," *Folklore* 107 (1996): 101–5; also see Susan Manning, "Industry and Idleness in Colonial Virginia: A New Approach to William Byrd," *Journal of American Studies* 28, no. 2 (August 1994): 169–90; and James R. Masterson, "William Byrd in Lubberland," *American Literature* 9, no. 2 (May 1937): 153–70. Byrd was also influenced by "An Invitation to Lubberland," which appeared as a broadside in 1685. In this long verse, Lubberland is a land of plenty where one can "lead a lazy life free from labour" and "everyone do's what he pleases." See *An Invitation to Lubberland, with an Account of the Great Plenty of That Fruitful Country* (London, ca. 1685).

37. Byrd, HDL, 192, 196; SH, 59–61, 63. Wild boars cannibalize shoats and young pigs, and they eat everything, including newborn cattle. They are predators, and are willing to eat carrion and manure. Byrd's theory about pork was probably influenced by John Lawson's 1709 account of North Carolina. Lawson discussed how various Indians suffered from yaws, and he discussed pork as a "gross food," spreading juices through the body. See Lefler, *A New Voyage to Carolina,* 25; it was a common assumption among the English that to be noseless reduced a person to the state of an animal, because it was believed that man was the only creature with a nose. English jest books were filled with nasty jokes about noseless people. See Simon Dickie, "Hilarity and Pitilessness in the Mid-Eighteenth Century: English Jestbook Humor," *Eighteenth-Century Studies* 37, no. 1, Exploring Sentiment (Fall 2003): 1–22, esp. 2–3.

38. Byrd, HDL, 160–61, 221–22, 296. Byrd felt the Indians were healthy and strong, and less debilitated by the European disease of lewdness; see Fischer, *Suspect Relations,* 75–77. Lawson argued that men should marry Indian women rather than spend "four or five years Servitude," in which they might suffer sickness and die. Both Lawson and Byrd argued that intermarriage was a better method of conquest than bloodshed. See Lefler, *A New Voyage to Carolina,* 192, 244, 246. Byrd did purchase 100,000 acres west of "Lubberland," hoping to create a more stable community of Swiss-German settlers to offset the dangerous wastrels he observed on the expedition. By the end of his life, he had acquired 179,440 acres. See Lockridge, *The Diary, and Life, of William Byrd,* 140; Wright and Tinling, *William Byrd of Virginia,* 41.

39. For the account of Reverend John Urmston, who was in North Carolina from 1711 to 1720, see "Mr. Urmston's Letter," July 7, 1711, in Saunders, *CRNC,* 1:770; for Governor Johnson's remarks, see Ekirch, *Poor Carolina,* 67; and for

the later traveler, see J. F. D. Smyth, Esq., *A Tour of the United States of America* (Dublin, 1784), 64–65.

40. Smyth, *A Tour of the United States of America*, 65.

41. *A Voyage to Georgia: Begun in the Year 1735, by Francis Moore,* Georgia Historical Society, Savannah.

42. For the motto, see Mills Lane, ed., *General Oglethorpe's Georgia: Colonial Letters, 1733–1743* (Savannah, GA: Beehive Press, 1990), xviii. On the first group of settlers, see E. M. Coulter and A. B. Saye, eds., *A List of the Early Settlers of Georgia* (Athens: University of Georgia Press, 1949), xii, 111. Oglethorpe took on the unusual role of "gossip," helping pregnant women to give birth; see Mr. Benjamin Ingham's journal of his voyage to Georgia, 1736, in Egmont Papers, Philips Collection, University of Georgia, vol. 14201, 442–43; and Joseph Hetherington to Mr. Oglethorpe, March 22, 1733/34, in Lane, *General Oglethorpe's Georgia,* 138.

43. On emulation, see James Edward Oglethorpe, *Some Account of the Design for the Trustees for Establishing Colonies in America,* eds. Rodney M. Baine and Phinizy Spalding (Athens: University of Georgia Press, 1990), 31–32. On Oglethorpe's sacrifices for the community, and giving up the soft bed, see Samuel Eveleigh to the Trustees, April 6, 1733, in Lane, *General Oglethorpe's Georgia,* 1:13; and Governor Johnson to Benjamin Martyn, July 28, 1733, and Mr. Beaufain to Mr. Simond, January 23, 1733/34, and Extract of a letter from Georgia, March 7, 1735/36, Egmont Papers, vol. 14200, 36, 62; vol. 14201, 314.

44. Oglethorpe, *Some Account of the Design,* 51; Rodney E. Baine, "General James Oglethorpe and the Expedition Against St. Augustine," *Georgia Historical Quarterly* 84, no. 2 (Summer 2000): 197–229, esp. 197–98. On the military design of Savannah, see Turpin C. Bannister, "Oglethorpe's Sources for the Savannah Plan," *Journal of the Society of Architectural Historians* 20, no. 2 (May 1961): 47–62, esp. 60–62.

45. Oglethorpe wanted Georgia to allow men to "labour at a decent maintenance," and he calculated the labor value of wives and eldest sons to offset the needs for servants and slaves; see James Oglethorpe, *A New and Accurate Account of the Provinces of South-Carolina and Georgia* (London, 1733), 39, 42–43; also see Philip Thicknesse to his mother, November 3, 1736, in Lane, *General Oglethorpe's Georgia,* 1:281; Rodney Baine, "Philip Thicknesse's Reminiscences of Early Georgia," *Georgia Historical Quarterly* 74, no. 4 (Winter 1990): 672–98, esp. 694–95, 697–98. For the citizen-soldier idea, see Benjamin Martyn, *An Account, Showing the Progress of the Colony* (London, 1741), 18. For Oglethorpe's views on women and cleanliness, see Oglethorpe, *Some Account of the Design,* 23, 26, 29–31. On the problem of female slaves, see Betty Wood, *Slavery in Colonial Georgia, 1730–1775* (Athens: University of Georgia Press, 1984), 18. From 1732 to September 1741, 45.4 percent of the settlers sent on charity were "Foreign Protestants"; see Coulter and Saye, *A List of the Early Settlers,* x.

46. James Oglethorpe to the Trustees, August 12, 1733, in Egmont Papers, vol. 14200, 38–39.

47. See Colonel William Byrd to Lord Egmont, July 12, 1736, in "Colonel William Byrd on Slavery and Indentured Servants, 1736, 1739," *American*

Historical Review 1, no. 1 (October 1895): 88–99, esp. 89. On John Colleton, see J. E. Buchanan, "The Colleton Family and Early History of South Carolina and Barbados, 1646–1775" (Ph.D. dissertation, University of Edinburgh, 1989), 33.

48. James Oglethorpe to the Trustees, January 17, 1738/9, Egmont Papers, vol. 14203, 143.

49. "The Sailors Advocate. To Be Continued." (London, 1728), 8, 10–17; and Julie Anne Sweet, "The British Sailors' Advocate: James Oglethorpe's First Philanthropic Venture," *Georgia Historical Quarterly* 91, no. 1 (Spring 2007): 1–27, esp. 4–10, 12.

50. John Vat to Henry Newman, May 30, 1735, and Patrick Tailfer and Others to the Trustees, August 27, 1735, in Lane, *General Oglethorpe's Georgia*, 1:178, 225.

51. "Oglethorpe State of Georgia," October 11, 1739, (Introductory Discourse to the State of the Colony of Georgia), Egmont Papers, vol. 14204, 35; and "The Sailors Advocate," 12; Wood, *Slavery in Colonial Georgia*, 66; Coulter and Saye, *A List of the Early Settlers*, 106–11.

52. On the small number of Indian slaves, see Rodney M. Baine, "Indian Slavery in Colonial Georgia," *Georgia Historical Quarterly* 79, no. 2 (Summer 1995): 418–24. On debtors and economic vulnerability, see Oglethorpe, *Some Account of the Design*, 11–12; Oglethorpe, *A New and Accurate Account*, 30–33; and Rodney M. Baine, "New Perspectives on Debtors in Colonial Georgia," *Georgia Historical Quarterly* 77, no. 1 (Spring 1993): 1–19, esp. 4.

53. See Milton L. Ready, "Land Tenure in Trusteeship Georgia," *Agricultural History* 48, no. 3 (July 1974): 353–68, esp. 353–57, 359.

54. See Translation of Reverend Mr. Dumont's Letter to Mr. Benjamin Martyn, May 21, 1734, Egmont Papers, vol. 14207. Dumont wrote from Rotterdam, and represented a community of French Vaudois.

55. See Oglethorpe, *A New and Accurate Account*, 73–75. In his other promotional tract, he used a similar argument about the Roman colonies, noting that only men with land married and had children; see Oglethorpe, *Some Account of the Design*, 6, 9–10, 40.

56. James Oglethorpe to the Trustees, January 16, 1738/9, and James Oglethorpe to the Trustees, January 17, 1738/9, in Egmont Papers, vol. 14203, 142–43.

57. Wood, *Slavery in Colonial Georgia*, 67.

58. For the attempted murder, see "New York. Jan. 9. We Hear from Georgia," *Boston Gazette*, January 22, 1739.

59. Alan Gallay, "Jonathan Bryan's Plantation Empire: Land, Politics, and the Formation of a Ruling Class in Colonial Georgia," *William and Mary Quarterly* 45, no. 2 (April 1988): 253–79, esp. 253, 257–60, 275.

Chapter Three: Benjamin Franklin's American Breed: The Demographics of Mediocrity

1. *Poor Richard, 1741. An Almanack for the Year of Christ 1741, . . .* By Richard Saunders (Philadelphia, 1741), in *The Papers of Benjamin Franklin*, ed. Leonard W. Labaree et al., 40 vols. (New Haven, CT: Yale University Press, 1959–), 2:292. Hereafter cited as *Franklin Papers*.

2. On Silence Dogood and Franklin's creation of literary disguises, see Albert Furt-wangler, "The Spectator's Apprentice," in *American Silhouettes: Rhetorical Identities of the Founders* (New Haven, CT: Yale University Press, 1987), 15–34, esp. 28–30; R. Jackson Wilson, *Figures of Speech: American Writers and the Literary Marketplace from Benjamin Franklin to Emily Dickinson* (New York: Johns Hopkins University Press, 1989), 21–65. On Dingo, see David Waldstreicher, *Runaway America: Benjamin Franklin, Slavery, and the American Revolution* (New York: Hill & Wang, 2004), 50–52, 220. On the financial success of the *Pennsylvania Gazette,* see Charles E. Clark and Charles Wetherell, "The Measure of Maturity: The *Pennsylvania Gazette,* 1728–1765," *William and Mary Quarterly* 46, no. 2 (April 1989): 279–303, esp. 291. On the wide reach of his almanacs, see William Pencak, "Politics and Ideology in 'Poor Richard's Almanack,'" *Pennsylvania Magazine of History and Biography* 116, no. 2 (April 1992): 183–211, esp. 195–96. On his retirement, see Benjamin Franklin, *The Autobiography,* with introduction by Daniel Aaron (New York: Vintage, 1990), 116.

3. Carl Van Doren, *Benjamin Franklin* (New York: Viking, 1938), 170–71, 174–80, 195–96, 210–15, 220, 223–24. On his proposals for his academy, see George Boudreau, "'Done by a Tradesman': Franklin's Educational Proposals and the Culture of Eighteenth-Century Philadelphia," *Pennsylvania History* 69, no. 4 (Autumn 2002): 524–57. On Pennsylvania Hospital, see William H. Williams, "The 'Industrious Poor' and the Founding of the Pennsylvania Hospital," *Pennsylvania Magazine of History and Biography* 97, no. 4 (October 1973): 431–43. On his reception in Europe, see J. L. Heilbron, "Benjamin Franklin in Europe: Electrician, Academician, and Politician," *Notes and Records of the Royal Society of London* 61, no. 3 (September 22, 2007): 353–73, esp. 355; and L. K. Mathews, "Benjamin Franklin's Plans of Colonial Union," *American Political Science Review* 8, no. 3 (August 1914): 393–412.

4. For his arguments about human impulses shaped by pleasure and pain, see Franklin, "A Dissertation on Liberty and Necessity, Pleasure and Pain" (London, 1725), in *Franklin Papers,* 1:57–71, esp. 64, 71; also see Joyce Chaplin, *Benjamin Franklin's Political Arithmetic: A Materialist View of Humanity* (Washington, DC: Smithsonian Institution Libraries, 2006), 12–16.

5. Peter Kalm, *Travels into North America; Containing Its Natural History, and a Circumstantial Account of Its Plantations and Agricultural in General, with the Civil, Ecclesiastical and Commercial State of the Country, the Manners of the Inhabitants, and Several Curious and Important Remarks on Various Subjects,* trans. John Reinhold Forster, vol. 1 (Warrington, UK, 1770), 1:305–6; Benjamin Franklin to Samuel Johnson, August 23, 1750, *Franklin Papers,* 4:40–42, esp. 42.

6. For "uneasy in rest," see "A Dissertation on Liberty," *Franklin Papers,* 1:64. For the English as "stirrers abroad," see the dedication in Hakluyt, *Principall Navigations,* 1:[2].

7. Franklin, "Observations Concerning the Increase of Mankind" (1751), *Franklin Papers,* 4:225–34, esp. 228. This manuscript was first published in 1755; see William F. Von Valtier, "The Demographic Numbers Behind Benjamin Franklin's Twenty-Five-Year Doubling Period," *Proceedings of the American Philosophical Society* 155, no. 2 (June 2011): 158–88, esp. 160–61, footnote 9.

8. Franklin, "Observations Concerning the Increase of Mankind," *Franklin Papers,* 231. On the value of marrying young, also see Franklin to John Alleyne, August 9, 1768, *Franklin Papers,* 3:30–31, 15:184.

9. "The Speech of Miss Polly Baker," April 15, 1747, *Franklin Papers,* 3:123–25. One writer has suggested that Polly Baker was based on a real woman, an Eleanor Kellog, who was tried in Worcester, Massachusetts, in 1745 for having her fifth bastard child. See Max Hall, *Benjamin Franklin and Polly Baker: The History of a Literary Deception* (Pittsburgh: University of Pittsburgh Press, 1960; rev. ed., 1990), 94–98.

10. For the punishment for bachelors, see "To All Married Men to Whom These Presents Shall Come," *New-York Gazette,* March 20, 1749, reprinted in the *Boston Evening Post,* April 7, 1749; also see "From an Epistle from a Society of Young Ladies," *New-York Evening Post,* October 28, 1751; and a call to tax bachelors, *Boston Evening Post,* August 4, 1746; Franklin wrote elsewhere that "a single Man has not nearly the Value he would have in that State of Union"; see Franklin, "Old Mistresses Apologue," June 25, 1745, *Franklin Papers,* 3:30–31.

11. William H. Shurr, "'Now, God, Stand Up for Bastards': Reinterpreting Benjamin Franklin's Autobiography," *American Literature* 64, no. 3 (September 1992): 435–51, esp. 444. On Franklin's "pronatalist convictions," see Dennis Hodgson, "Benjamin Franklin on Population: From Policy to Theory," *Population and Development Review* 17, no. 4 (December 1991): 639–61, esp. 640–41.

12. Franklin, "Observations Concerning the Increase of Mankind," *Franklin Papers,* 4:231–32. See excerpts from Locke's "Atlantis" writings (1678–79) in Goldie, ed., *Locke: Political Essays,* xxvi, 255–59.

13. Franklin, "The Interest of Great Britain Considered (1760)," *Franklin Papers,* 9:59–100, esp. 73–74, 77–78, 86–87, 94.

14. Franklin to Peter Collinson (1753), *Franklin Papers,* 5: 158–59; and "Information to Those Who Would Remove to America," by Dr. Franklin, *Boston Magazine* (October 1784), 505–10. Franklin, "The Interest of Great Britain Considered (1760)," *Franklin Papers,* 9:86.

15. Franklin, *The Autobiography,* 13–25. For runaway servants, see Marcus Rediker, "'Good Hands, Stout Heart, and Fast Feet': The History and Culture of Working People in Early America," *Labour/Le Travail* 10 (Autumn 1982): 123–44, esp. 141; *The Infortunate: The Voyage and Adventures of William Moraley, an Indentured Servant* (1743), eds. Susan E. Klepp and Billy G. Smith, 2nd ed. (University Park: Pennsylvania State University Press, 2005), xvii–xviii, xxv–xxvi, 16, 26, 41, 51, 72–74, 78–79, 87–88, 97.

16. Billy G. Smith, "Poverty and Economic Marginality in Eighteenth-Century America," *Proceedings of the American Antiquarian Society* 132, no. 1 (March 1988): 85–118, esp. 100–103, 105, 113; Gary B. Nash, "Poverty and Poor Relief in Pre-Revolutionary Philadelphia," *William and Mary Quarterly* 33, no. 1 (January 1976): 3–30, esp. 12–13. On infant mortality rates, see Susan E. Klepp, "Malthusian Miseries and the Working Poor in Philadelphia, 1780–1830," in *Down and Out in Early America,* ed. Billy G. Smith (University Park: Pennsylvania State University Press, 2004), 63–92, esp. 64.

17. Jack Marietta, *The Reformation of American Quakerism, 1748–1783* (Philadelphia: University of Pennsylvania Press, 1984), 21–24, 28, 51, 65; Jean R.

Soderlund, "Women's Authority in Pennsylvania and New Jersey Quaker Meetings, 1680–1760," *William and Mary Quarterly* 44, no. 4 (October 1987): 722–49, esp. 743–44.

18. See Frederick B. Tolles, "Benjamin Franklin's Business Mentors: The Philadelphia Quaker Merchants," *William and Mary Quarterly* 4, no. 1 (January 1947): 60–69; J. A. Leo Lemay, *The Life of Benjamin Franklin*, vol. 1, *Journalist, 1706–1730* (Philadelphia: University of Pennsylvania Press, 2005), 1:238, 258, 268, 458–59, and vol. 2, *Printer and Publisher, 1730–1747* (Philadelphia: University of Pennsylvania Press, 2005), 2:322–23; Jacquelyn C. Miller, "Franklin and Friends: Franklin's ties to Quakers and Quakerism," *Pennsylvania History* 57, no. 4 (October 1990): 318–36, esp. 322–26.

19. On the rise of the non-Quaker elite, see Stephen Brobeck, "Revolutionary Change in Colonial Philadelphia: The Brief Life of the Proprietary Gentry," *William and Mary Quarterly* 33, no. 3 (July 1976): 410–34, esp. 413, 417–18, 422–23; Thomas M. Doerflinger, "Commercial Specialization in the Philadelphia Merchant Community, 1750–1791," *Business History Review* 57, no. 1 (Spring 1983): 20–49, esp. 22, 28, 46.

20. See Robert F. Oaks, "Big Wheels in Philadelphia: Du Simitière's List of Carriage Owners," *Pennsylvania Magazine of History and Biography* 95, no. 3 (July 1971): 351–62, esp. 351, 355. On Franklin's horse and carriage, see Lemay, *The Life of Benjamin Franklin*, 2:320–21, and footnote 36 on 594; and see "Appendix 2: Franklin's Residences and Real Estate to 1757" and "Appendix 8: Franklin's Wealth, 1756," in Lemay, *The Life of Benjamin Franklin*, vol. 3, *Soldier, Scientist, and Politician, 1748–1757* (Philadelphia: University of Pennsylvania Press, 2008), 3:599–602, 630–34. Franklin acquired other signs of elite status, such as a coat of arms and fine furniture, and he continued to purchase what he called "my Fancyings" while in England and Europe for his new home (which he began building in 1764) in Philadelphia; see Edward Cahill, "Benjamin Franklin's Interiors," *Early American Studies* 6, no. 1 (Spring 2008): 27–58, esp. 44–46.

21. Lemay, *The Life of Benjamin Franklin*, 2:320.

22. *Pennsylvania Gazette*, January 20, 1730, in *Franklin: Writings*, ed. J. A. Leo Lemay (New York: Library of America, 1987), 139. Approximately seventy-three thousand Europeans traveled to British North America during the 1730s, and at least seventeen thousand arrived in Philadelphia's port. Nearly one of every three passengers disembarking in Philadelphia during the 1730s was an indentured servant, and an additional five hundred imported slaves joined them at the bottom of the social ladder. The largest influx of convict laborers from Britain occurred during the mid-eighteenth century. Philadelphians were concerned about absconding servants; see *Pennsylvania Gazette*, July 2, 1751.

23. See *Boston News Post-Boy*, December 4, 1704; for fans, see [Boston] *Weekly Rehearsal*, May 14, 1733; for buttons, see *New-York Gazette, or Weekly Post-Boy*, June 15, 1747.

24. [Boston] *Weekly Rehearsal*, March 20, 1732; see Jenny Davidson, *Breeding: A Partial History of the Eighteenth Century* (New York: Columbia University Press, 2009), 137–43; Boudreau, "Done by a Tradesman," 529.

25. Williams, "The 'Industrious Poor' and the Founding of the Pennsylvania Hospital," 336–37, 339, 441–42; Franklin to Peter Collinson, May 9, 1753, and

"'Arator': On the Price of Corn, and the Management of the Poor" (1766), *Franklin Papers*, 4:479–86, esp. 479–80; 13:510–15.

26. Franklin to Peter Collinson, May 9, 1753, *Franklin Papers*, 4:480–82.

27. "To the Author of the Letter on the Last *Pennsylvania Gazette*," *Pennsylvania Gazette*, May 15, 1740; Franklin, *Plain Truth: or, Serious Considerations on the Present State of the City of Philadelphia and Province of Pennsylvania. By a Tradesman of Philadelphia* (Philadelphia, 1747), and "Form of Association," *Pennsylvania Gazette*, December 3, 1747, in *Franklin Papers*, 3:180–212, esp. 198–99, 201, 211; "Extracts from Plain Truth," *New-York Gazette, or Weekly Post-Boy*, December 14, 1747.

28. *Plain Truth*, and "Form of Association," in *Franklin Papers*, 3:198, 209, 211.

29. "Petition to the Pennsylvania Assembly Regarding Fairs" (1731), *Franklin Papers*, 1:211; *Pennsylvania Gazette*, November 18, 1731, and Waldstreicher, *Runaway America*, 94; Franklin, *The Autobiography*, 34–35.

30. On the inability to "wash out the stain of servility," see "From the Reflector: Of Ambition and Meanness," *Boston Evening Post*, March 2, 1752; on the meaner sort at the heels of those above them, see *The New-York Weekly Journal*, March 3, 1734. In England, there was actually more social mobility among the commercial classes; see Neil McKendrick, John Brewer, and John Harold Plumb, eds., *Birth of a Consumer Society: The Commercialization of Eighteenth-Century England* (Bloomington: Indiana University Press, 1982), 20.

31. "From a Paper entitled COMMON SENSE. The First Principles of Religion for Preserving Liberty," *Pennsylvania Gazette*, February 12, 1741.

32. Franklin to Benjamin Franklin Bache, September 25, 1780, *Franklin Papers*, 33:326.

33. Franklin to Peter Collinson, May 9, 1753, *Franklin Papers*, 4:480–82.

34. Ibid.; Franklin to Peter Collinson [1753?], *Franklin Papers*, 5:158–59.

35. On the impact of Paine's pamphlet, see Trish Loughan, "Disseminating *Common Sense*: Thomas Paine and the Problem of the Early National Best Seller," *American Literature* 78, no. 1 (March 2006): 1–28, esp. 4, 7, 12, 14. On Paine's background, see John Keane, *Tom Paine: A Life* (Boston: Little, Brown, 1995), 62, 73–74, 79, 84; J. C. D. Clark, "Thomas Paine: The English Dimension," in *Selected Writings of Thomas Paine*, eds. Ian Shapiro and Jane E. Calvert (New Haven, CT: Yale University Press, 2014), 538; John Brewer, *The Sinews of Power: War, Money and the English State, 1688–1783* (Cambridge, MA: Harvard University Press, 1900), 104–5, 222–30; Edward Larkin, "Inventing an American Public: Paine, the 'Pennsylvania Magazine,' and American Revolutionary Discourse," *Early American Literature* 33, no. 3 (1998): 250–76, esp. 254, 257, 261; and Robert A. Ferguson, "The Commonalities of *Common Sense*," *William and Mary Quarterly* 57, no. 3 (July 2000): 465–504, esp. 487–89, 502.

36. Thomas Slaughter, ed., *Common Sense and Related Writings by Thomas Paine* (Boston: Bedford/St. Martin's, 2001), 79; Thomas Paine, "Agrarian Justice, Opposed to Agrarian Law, and to Agrarian Monopoly," (1797), in Shapiro and Calvert, *Selected Writings of Thomas Paine*, 555, 557.

37. On his theory of commerce and nations, he wrote, "It is the commerce and not the conquest of America, by which England is to be benefited, and that

would in a great measure continue, were the countries independent of each other as France and Spain; because many articles, neither can go to a better market"; see Slaughter, ed., *Common Sense*, 89–90, 110.

38. Slaughter, *Common Sense*, 86, 89, 100, 113. Adam Smith offered a similar rebuke of the English financial system, highlighting its enormous debts and repeated engagement in costly wars in *The Wealth of Nations* (1776).

39. See Slaughter, *Common Sense*, 89, 100, 102–4. On Pennsylvania selling wheat and flour to southern Europe, see T. H. Breen, "An Empire of Goods: The Anglicization of Colonial America, 1760–1776," *Journal of British Studies* 25, no. 4 (October 1986): 467–99, esp. 487. The magazine for which Paine became the chief editor, the *Pennsylvania Magazine; or, American Monthly Museum,* published a chart of exports (tonnage and value) from Philadelphia's port for the years 1771 to 1773; see *Pennsylvania Magazine; or, American Monthly Museum* (February 1775), 72.

40. Paine wrote, "The *mercantile* and reasonable part in England, will be still with us; because peace *with* trade, is preferable to war *without* it"; see Slaughter, *Common Sense*, 114. On the debates in the Continental Congress on free trade in 1775 and 1776, see Staughton Lynd and David Waldstreicher, "Free Trade, Sovereignty, and Slavery: Toward an Economic Interpretation of the American Revolution," *William and Mary Quarterly* 68, no. 4 (October 2011): 597–630, esp. 610, 624–30. The British "friends of America" who supported independence did so because they wanted to ensure that a strong alliance was sustained between Great Britain and America, for both economic and political reasons. See Eliga H. Gould, *The Persistence of Empire: British Political Culture in the Age of the American Revolution* (Chapel Hill: University of North Carolina Press, 2000), 165.

41. See Thomas Paine, "A Dialogue Between the Ghost of General Montgomery Just Arrived from the Elysian Fields; and an American Delegate, in the Wood Near Philadelphia" (1776), which was published in newspapers and in a later edition of *Common Sense*; see Philip Foner, ed., *The Complete Writings of Thomas Paine*, 2 vols. (New York: Citadel, 1945), 2:91. He expanded on this notion of commercial transatlantic alliances in his later writing; see Thomas Paine, *Rights of Man, Part the Second. Combining Principle and Practice*, second edition (London, 1792), 82–88; and Thomas C. Walker, "The Forgotten Prophet: Tom Paine's Cosmopolitanism and International Relations," *International Studies Quarterly* 44, no. 1 (March 2000), 51–72, esp. 59–60. Paine also explored the nature of mutual affections and voluntary commerce through the analogy of American Indian marriages; and the detrimental influence of titles in encouraging the "over-awed superstitious vulgar"; see "Reflections on Titles," *Pennsylvania Magazine; or, American Monthly Museum* (May 1775), 209–210; and "The Old Bachelor, No. IV. Reflections on Unhappy Marriages," *Pennsylvania Magazine; or, American Monthly Museum* (June 1775), 263–65.

42. Slaughter, *Common Sense*, 112–14. Paine noted that there were three ways for the rebellion to go: declaring independence by "the legal voice of the people in Congress; by military power; by a mob: It may not always happen that our soldiers are citizens, and the multitude are reasonable men."

43. Slaughter, *Common Sense,* 79, 83–84, 102, 105; Keane, *Tom Paine,* 74.

44. Paine's ship docked in Philadelphia on November 30, 1774. He published the first run of *Common Sense* on January 10, 1776. See Keane, *Tom Paine,* 84; also see "To the Honorable Benjamin Franklin, Esq.," March 4, 1775, in Foner, *Complete Writings,* 1132. Paine recommended Goldsmith's *History of the World* to his readers in the *Pennsylvania Magazine,* and he included a poem and portrait of the Irish writer; see "List of New Books," and "Retaliation; a Poem, by Dr. Goldsmith," *Pennsylvania Magazine; or, American Monthly Museum* (January 1775), 40, 42; also see Oliver Goldsmith, *History of Earth and Animated Nature; abridged.* By Mrs. Pilkington (Philadelphia, 1808), 16–22. The first edition of Goldsmith's book appeared in eight volumes, published in London in 1774.

45. Linné first published his *General System* in 1735, where he simply laid out the four groups of *Homo sapiens* based on continents and colors; by 1758, he ascribed a series of traits. The 1735 edition was only eleven folio pages long; the 1758 edition was over three thousand pages. Buffon in his *Histoire Naturalle* (1749) preferred "race" to Linné's more stagnant "variety." Buffon viewed human races as particular stocks, lineages, in which traits were passed down through succeeding generations. See Sir Charles Linné, *A General System of Nature, Through the Three Grand Kingdoms of Animals, Vegetables, and Minerals; Systematically Divided into Their Several Classes, Orders, Genera, Species, and Varieties, with Their Habitations, Manners, Economy, Structure, and Peculiarities,* trans. William Turton, M.D. (London, 1802), 1; also see Nicholas Hudson, "From 'Nation' to 'Race': The Origins of Racial Classification in Eighteenth-Century Thought," *Eighteenth-Century Studies* 29, no. 3 (1996): 247–64, esp. 253.

46. See Joseph Priestley, *An Address to Protestant Dissenters of All Denominations, on the Approaching Election of Members of Parliament, with Respect to the State of Public Liberty in General, and of American Affairs in Particular* (London, 1774), 9; "Free Thoughts on Monarchy and Political Superstition," *St. James Chronicle or the British Evening Post,* January 22–25, 1774; and for the reprint of this piece in American newspapers, see *Dunlap's Pennsylvania Packet or, the General Advertiser,* April 25, 1774; it also appeared in *The Norwich Packet and the Connecticut, Massachusetts, New Hampshire and Rhode Island Weekly Advertiser,* May 12, 1774. For Franklin's friendship with Priestley, see Verner W. Crane, "The Club of Honest Whigs: Friends of Liberty and Science," *William and Mary Quarterly* 23, no. 2 (April 1966): 210–33, esp. 231.

47. Slaughter, *Common Sense,* 87–90, 94, 99, 104, 110; James V. Lynch, "The Limits of Revolutionary Radicalism: Tom Paine and Slavery," *Pennsylvania Magazine of History and Biography* 123, no. 5 (July 1999): 177–99.

48. Slaughter, *Common Sense,* 88, 90, 92–93, 99; Keane, *Tom Paine,* 42–45. On Canada, see Paine, *Letter Addressed to the Abbe Raynal, on the Affairs of North America: in Which the Mistakes in the Abbe's Account of the Revolution of America Are Corrected and Cleared Up* (1782), in Foner, *Complete Writings,* 2:258.

49. Slaughter, *Common Sense,* 100, 104–5.

50. Ibid., 87–88, 93–94, 110; and for the legal precept of waste on a pending lawsuit, see Book 2, chapter 14, "Of Waste," in Sir William Blackstone, *Commentaries on the Laws of England* (London, 1765–66).

51. Slaughter, *Common Sense,* 113–14.

52. See Paine, "A Dialogue Between the Ghost of General Montgomery" (1776) and *Letter Addressed to the Abbe Raynal, on the Affairs of North America* (1782), in Foner, *Complete Writings,* 2:92, 243. Paine also published the dialogue in *Dunlap's Pennsylvania Packet,* February 19, 1776.

Chapter Four: Thomas Jefferson's Rubbish: A Curious Topography of Class

1. For Jefferson's use of the phrases "empire of liberty" and "empire for liberty," see Thomas Jefferson to George Rogers Clark, December 25, 1780, *Papers of Thomas Jefferson,* ed. Julian Boyd et. al., 40 vols. to date (Princeton, NJ: Princeton University Press, 1950–), 4:237; Thomas Jefferson to James Madison, April 27, 1809, in *The Papers of Thomas Jefferson: Retirement Series,* ed. J. Jefferson Looney, 11 vols. to date (Princeton, NJ: Princeton University Press, 2005–), 1:69. Hereafter cited as *PTJ* and *PTJ-R.* Andrew Burstein and Nancy Isenberg, *Madison and Jefferson* (New York: Random House, 2010), 388–90. Also see John Murrin, "The Jeffersonian Triumph and American Exceptionalism," *Journal of the Early Republic* 20, no. 1 (Spring 2000): 1–25.

2. John E. Selby, *The Revolution in Virginia, 1775–1783* (Williamsburg, VA: Colonial Williamsburg Foundation, 1988), 26–32; Michael McDonnell, "Jefferson's Virginia," in *A Companion to Thomas Jefferson,* ed. Francis D. Cogliano (Chichester, UK: Wiley-Blackwell, 2012), 16–31, esp. 21–22. On Jefferson's slaves, see Lucia Stanton, *"Those Who Labor for My Happiness": Slavery at Thomas Jefferson's Monticello* (Charlottesville: University of Virginia Press, 2012), 56. Jefferson grew tobacco and wheat, but tobacco was his principal cash crop; see Barbara McEwan, *Thomas Jefferson: Farmer* (Jefferson, NC: McFarland & Co., 1991), 2–3, 39–42, 45–46.

3. Thomas Jefferson to John Jay, August 23, 1785, and Thomas Jefferson to Francis Willis, July 15, 1796, *PTJ,* 8:426, 29:153; and Thomas Jefferson, *Notes on the State of Virginia,* ed. William Peden (Chapel Hill: University of North Carolina Press, 1955), 164–65. For an excellent overview of Jefferson's troubled career as a farmer, see Lucia Stanton, "Thomas Jefferson: Planter and Farmer," in Cogliano, *A Companion to Thomas Jefferson,* 253–70.

4. See Thomas Jefferson to Thomas Leiper, February 23, 1801, *PTJ,* 8:210–12, 33:50. On Jefferson's design for the moldboard plough, see Thomas Jefferson to Sir John Sinclair, March 23, 1798, *PTJ* 30: 197–209; the original memorandum, "Description of a Mouldboard of the Least, & of the Easiest and Most Certain Construction," is located at the Massachusetts Historical Society, along with an undated drawing of the plough, MSi5 [electronic edition]. Thomas Jefferson Papers: An Electronic Archive, Boston, MA: Massachusetts Historical Society, 2003, thomasjeffersonpapers.org; and August C. Miller Jr., "Jefferson as an Agriculturalist," *Agricultural History* 16, no. 2 (April 1942): 65–78, esp. 70, 71–72, 75.

5. On English notions of husbandry and improvement, see Joan Thirsk, "Plough and Pen: Writers in the Seventeenth Century," *Social Relations and Ideas: Essays in Honour of R. H. Hilton* (Cambridge: Cambridge University Press, 1983), 295–318, esp. 297–98, 316; Benjamin R. Cohen, *Notes from the Ground: Science, Soil, and Society in the American Countryside* (New Haven, CT: Yale University Press, 2009), 18, 20, 25. On early modern English husbandry, see McRae, *God Speed the Plough*, 203–4, 206, 208, 210; George Washington to William Pierce, 1796, in *The Writings of Washington from the Original Manuscript Sources, 1744–1799,* ed. John C. Fitzpatrick, 39 vols. (Washington, DC: Government Printing Office, 1931–44), 34:451; and Jefferson, *Notes on the State of Virginia,* 85; Miller, "Jefferson as an Agriculturalist," 69, 71–72.

6. Jefferson described slaves as "confined to tillage"; see Jefferson, *Notes on the State of Virginia,* 139.

7. See Kevin J. Hayes, "The Libraries of Thomas Jefferson," in *A Companion to Thomas Jefferson,* 333–49; Burstein and Isenberg, *Madison and Jefferson,* 558. On Jefferson's literary training and epicureanism, see Andrew Burstein, *The Inner Jefferson: Portrait of a Grieving Optimist* (Charlottesville: University of Virginia Press, 1995), 16–17, 32, 34, 129, 133; and Burstein, *Jefferson's Secrets: Death and Desire at Monticello* (New York: Basic Books, 2005), 162, 165–66. On his purchase of wines and luxuries in France, see Herbert E. Sloan, *Principle and Interest: Thomas Jefferson and the Problem of Debt* (Charlottesville: University of Virginia Press, 1995), 25, and note 84 on 259–60, and *Jefferson's Memorandum Books: Accounts, with Legal Records and Miscellany, 1767–1826,* eds. James A. Bear Jr. and Lucia C. Stanton (Princeton, NJ: Princeton University Press, 1997), 671, 686, 717, 724, 728, 734, 741–42, 807. On training his slave James Hemings as a French chef, see Annette Gordon-Reed, *The Hemingses of Monticello: An American Family* (New York: Norton, 2008), 164–65, 209.

8. Thomas Jefferson to Charles Wilson Peale, April 17, 1813, *PTJ-R,* 6:69.

9. On cultivators having a "deposit for substantial and genuine virtue," see Jefferson, *Notes on the State of Virginia,* 164.

10. Michael A. McDonnell, *The Politics of War: Race, Class, and Conflict in Revolutionary Virginia* (Chapel Hill: University of North Carolina Press, 2007), 27, 93, 95, 109, 119, 227–29, 258–61, 275, 277–78, 306–7, 389–94; John Ferling, "Soldiers for Virginia: Who Served in the French and Indian War?," *Virginia Magazine of History and Biography* 94, no. 3 (July 1986): 307–28; Thomas Jefferson to Richard Henry Lee, June 5, 1778, *PTJ,* 2:194.

11. Thomas L. Humphrey, "Conflicting Independence: Land Tenancy and the American Revolution," *Journal of the Early Republic* 28, no. 2 (Summer 2008): 159–82, esp. 170; L. Scott Philyaw, "A Slave for Every Soldier: The Strange History of Virginia's Forgotten Recruitment Act of 1 January 1781," *Virginia Magazine of History and Biography* 109, no. 4 (2001): 367–86, esp. 371.

12. Stanley Katz, "Thomas Jefferson and the Right to Property in Revolutionary America," *Journal of Law and Economics* 19, no. 3 (October 1976): 467–88, esp. 470–71.

13. Holly Brewer, "Entailing Aristocracy in Colonial Virginia: 'Ancient Feudal Restraints' and Revolutionary Reform," *William and Mary Quarterly* 54, no. 2 (April 1997): 307–46; Christopher Michael Curtis, *Jefferson's Freeholders*

and the Politics of Ownership in the Old Dominion (New York: Cambridge University Press, 2012), 21–26, 56, 72, 75–76.

14. Curtis, *Jefferson's Freeholders*, 56, 72.

15. Humphrey, "Conflicting Independence," 180–81.

16. The bill was first presented in 1778, again in 1780, and in 1785, where it passed the House but died in the Senate. See "A Bill for the More General Diffusion of Knowledge" (1778), *PTJ*, 2:526–35; and Jennings L. Wagoner Jr., *Jefferson and Education* (Charlottesville, VA: Monticello Monograph Series, 2004), 34–38.

17. Jefferson, *Notes on the State of Virginia*, 146. Bunyan had two references to muck; one was the muck-rake, which was an emblem for covertness, the other was that of a bad crop turned into muck in his *Book for Boys and Girls*. See Roger Sharrock, "Bunyan and the English Emblem Writers," *Review of English Studies* 21, no. 82 (April 1945): 105–16, esp. 109–10, 112.

18. "A Bill for Support of the Poor," *PTJ*, 2:419–23. This bill was not passed until 1785.

19. Georges-Louis Leclerc, Comte de Buffon, *Natural History, General and Particular, by the Count de Buffon, Translated into English*, 8 vols. (2nd. ed., London, 1785), 3:104, 134–36, 190.

20. Ibid., 3:57–58, 61–62, 129–30, 192–93.

21. Jefferson, *Notes on the State of Virginia*, 7–8, 10, 19, 21–22, 43–54, 58–65, 79, 226–31, 253–54.

22. Thomas Jefferson to the Marquis de Chastellux, June 7, 1785, *PTJ*, 8:185–86.

23. Thomas Jefferson to G. K. van Hogendorp, October 13, 1785, and Thomas Jefferson to John Jay, August 23, 1785, *PTJ*, 8:426, 633; on chorography, see McRae, *God Speed the Plough*, 231–261.

24. "Report of the Committee, March 1, 1784," *PTJ*, 6:603; C. Albert White, *A History of the Rectangular Survey System* (Washington, DC: Government Printing Office, 1983), 11, 512; William D. Pattison, *Beginnings of the American Rectangular Land Survey System, 1784–1800* (Chicago: University of Chicago Press, 1957), 42–45, 63–65; Peter Onuf, "Liberty, Development, and Union: Visions of the West in the 1780s," *William and Mary Quarterly* 43, no. 2 (April 1986): 179–213, esp. 184.

25. J. Hector St. John de Crèvecoeur, *Letters from an American Farmer*, ed. Susan Manning (New York: Oxford University Press, 1997), xi–xiii, 15, 25, 27–28, 41–42, 45–47. For the excerpt of the farmer placing his son on the plough, see "Pleasing Particulars in Husbandry &c. [From Letters from J. Hector St. John, a Farmer in Pennsylvania, to his Friend in England]," *Boston Magazine* (July 1986), 285–91, esp. 285; also see Thomas Philbrick, "Crevecoeur as New Yorker," *Early American Literature* 11, no. 1 (Spring 1976): 22–30; and St. John Crèvecoeur to Thomas Jefferson, May 18, 1785, *PTJ*, 8:156–57.

26. Answers to Démeunier's First Queries, January 24, 1786, *PTJ*, 10:16.

27. On importing Germans into Virginia, see Thomas Jefferson to Richard Claiborne, August 8, 1787, *PTJ*, 16:540. On using Germans to train slaves, see Thomas Jefferson to Edward Bancroft, January 26, 1789, *PTJ*, 14:492, 35:718–21.

28. McDonnell, *The Politics of War*, 439, 455, 480–82; Woody Holton, "Did Democracy Cause the Recession That Led to the Constitution?," *Journal of American History* 92, no. 2 (September 2005): 442–69, esp. 445–46.

29. John Ferling, *Whirlwind: The American Revolution and the War That Won It* (New York: Bloomsbury, 2015), 320–21; Charles Royster, *A Revolutionary People at War: The Continental Army and the American Character, 1775–1783* (Chapel Hill: University of North Carolina Press, 1979), 353–57.

30. "Jefferson's Reply to the Representations of Affairs in America by British Newspapers" [before November 20, 1784], *PTJ*, 7:540–45; Wallace Evan Davies, "The Society of Cincinnati in New England, 1783–1800," *William and Mary Quarterly* 5, no. 1 (January 1948): 3–25, esp. 3, 5.

31. Thomas Jefferson to Abigail Adams, February 22, 1787, *PTJ*, 11:174–75; Thomas Jefferson to James Madison, January 30 and February 5, 1787, in *The Republic of Letters: The Correspondence Between Thomas Jefferson and Madison, 1776–1826*, ed. James Morton Smith, 3 vols. (New York: Norton, 1994), 1:461; Burstein and Isenberg, *Madison and Jefferson*, 146–48, 168; Woody Holton, *Unruly Americans and the Origins of the Constitution* (New York: Hill & Wang, 2007), 145–48, 155, 159; and David P. Szatmary, *Shays' Rebellion: The Making of an Agrarian Insurrection* (Amherst: University of Massachusetts Press, 1980), 66.

32. Abigail Adams to Thomas Jefferson, September 10, 1787, *PTJ*, 12:112. For Shays living in a sty, see "To the Printer," *American Recorder, and Charlestown Advertiser*, January 19, 1787. For the description of Shaysites as "ragamuffins," see the account of Reverend Bezaleel Howard of Springfield (September 1787), reprinted in Richard D. Brown, "Shays Rebellion and Its Aftermath: A View from Springfield, 1787," *William and Mary Quarterly* 40, no. 4 (October 1983): 598–615, esp. 602. For a description of Shaysites as "Abroad in rags like wolves to roam," see *New Haven Gazette, and Connecticut Magazine*, January 25, 1787.

33. "Jefferson's Observations on Démeunier's Manuscript," *PTJ*, 10:52.

34. Curtis, *Jefferson's Freeholders*, 97, 101.

35. Fredrika J. Teute and David S. Shields, "The Court of Abigail Adams," and "Jefferson in Washington: Domesticating Manners in the Republican Court," *Journal of the Early Republic* 35 (Summer 2015): 227–35, 237–59, esp. 229–30, 242, 246; Charlene M. Boyer Lewis, *Elizabeth Patterson Bonaparte: An American Aristocrat in the Early Republic* (Philadelphia: University of Pennsylvania Press, 2012), 12, 16, 20, 23, 29.

36. Peter Shaw, *The Character of John Adams* (Chapel Hill: University of North Carolina Press, 1976), 227, 230, 232–33.

37. See Simon Newman, "Principles or Men? George Washington and the Political Culture of National Leadership, 1776–1801," *Journal of the Early Republic* 12, no. 4 (Winter 1992): 447–507.

38. Burstein and Isenberg, *Madison and Jefferson*, 262, 381; Jean Edward Smith, *John Marshall: Definer of a Nation* (New York: Henry Holt, 1996), 12; John C. Rainbolt, "The Alteration in the Relationship Between the Leadership and Constituents in Virginia, 1660–1720," *William and Mary Quarterly* 27, no. 3 (July 1970): 411–34, esp. 418–22. Elite Virginians disliked vain displays of learning and dress as signs of the nouveau riche, which is why men like Jefferson and John Marshall dressed beneath their station. This class perspective is captured in Robert Munford's satirical play *The Candidates* (1770); see Jay B. Hubbell

and Douglas Adair, "Robert Munford's 'The Candidates,'" *William and Mary Quarterly* 5, no. 2 (April 1948): 217–57, esp. 233–35, 240–42; on Jefferson and his sheep, see Stanton, "Thomas Jefferson: Planter and Farmer," 264.

39. Jefferson, *Notes on the State of Virginia*, 86–87, 138–40.

40. See "A Bill Declaring What Persons Shall Be Deemed Mulattos," *PTJ*, 2:476; and Thomas Jefferson to Francis C. Gray, March 4, 1815, *PTJ-R*, 8:310–11. On Jefferson's method for breeding sheep, see "Notes on Breeding Merino Sheep," enclosure in Thomas Jefferson to James Madison, May 13, 1810, and Thomas Jefferson to William Thorton, May 24, 1810; and "Petition of Albemarle County Residents to the Virginia General Assembly" [before December 19, 1811], *PTJ-R*, 2:390, 2:413, 4:346; and *Thomas Jefferson's Farm Book: With Commentary and Relevant Extracts from Other Writings*, ed. Edwin Morris Betts (Charlottesville: University of Virginia Press, 1999), 111–41. Jefferson's argument was repeated in an 1816 essay by Dr. Parry; he applied the same pattern of animal crossing to humans and designated four stages of mixed-race types: the first cross produces a mulatto, the second a quadroon, the third a mestizo, and the fourth a quinteroon. He claimed that the quinteroon was an "almost perfect white" that was free of the "taint of the Negro." He also stressed that this worked only with white men and mixed-race women. The "converse would take place in the mixture of white female with male Negroes," that is, the children would breed back to a perfect black. See Dr. C. H. Parry, "On the Crossing the Breeds of Animals," *Massachusetts Agricultural Repository and Journal* (June 1, 1816): 153–58; also Buffon, *Natural History*, 3:164–65; and Andrew Curran, "Rethinking Race History: The Role of the Albino in the French Enlightenment Life Sciences," *History and Theory* 48 (October 2009): 151–79, esp. 171.

41. William Short to Thomas Jefferson, February 27, 1798, *PTJ*, 30:150.

42. Jefferson believed that racial mixing improved blacks. He wrote, "The improvement of the blacks on body and mind, in the first instance of their mixture with the whites, has been observed by everyone, and proves that their inferiority is not the effect merely of condition of life." See Jefferson, *Notes on the State of Virginia*, 141; Stanton, *"Those Who Labor for My Happiness,"* 64–65, 178–79, 197, 224; and Gordon-Reed, *The Hemingses of Monticello,* 41, 49, 80, 86, 100–101, 661–62.

43. See Thomas Jefferson to Joel Yancy, January 17, 1819, and Thomas Jefferson to John W. Eppes, June 30, 1820, in *Thomas Jefferson's Farm Book,* 43, 46. Jefferson measured the price of female slaves by their breeding capacity. In discussing a slave woman whom a relative considered selling, he described her as one who had "ceased to breed." See Thomas Jefferson to William O. Callis, May 8, 1795, *PTJ,* 28:346.

44. John Adams to Thomas Jefferson, August [14?], November 15, 1813, in *The Adams-Jefferson Letters: The Complete Correspondence Between Thomas Jefferson and Abigail and John Adams,* ed. Lester J. Cappon (Chapel Hill: University of North Carolina Press, 1959), 365–66, 397–402.

45. Thomas Jefferson to John Adams, October 28, 1813, *The Adams-Jefferson Letters,* 387–88; Jefferson, *Notes on the State of Virginia,* 140; Burstein, *Jefferson's Secrets,* 167–68.

46. Thomas Jefferson to John Adams, October 13, 1813, *The Adams-Jefferson Letters,* 387–89.

47. Thomas Jefferson to William Wirt, August 5, 1815, *PTJ-R,* 8:642–43. Jefferson had described the "class of artificers" as "panders," prone to vice; see Thomas Jefferson to John Jay, August 23, 1785, *PTJ,* 8:426; and *Notes on the State of Virginia,* 165. Jefferson also used the word "yeomanry" to represent the nonelite classes in the United States; see Thomas Jefferson to James Monroe, May 5, 1793, and Thomas Jefferson to James Madison, May 5, 1793, *PTJ,* 25:660–61.

48. John Adams to Thomas Jefferson, November 15, 1813, *The Adams-Jefferson Letters,* 401.

Chapter Five: Andrew Jackson's Cracker Country: The Squatter as Common Man

1. See John R. Van Atta, *Securing the West: Politics, Public Lands, and the Fate of the Old Republic, 1785–1850* (Baltimore: Johns Hopkins University Press, 2014), 17–18, 23.

2. See Malcolm J. Rohrbough, *The Land Office Business: The Settlement and Administration of American Public Lands, 1789–1837* (Belmont, CA: Wadsworth, 1990), 6; Eliga H. Gould, *Among the Powers of the Earth: The American Revolution and the Making of a New World Empire* (Cambridge, MA: Harvard University Press, 2012), 12.

3. While the concept of the southern backcountry began in the colonial period, its existence as a distinct area that was different from the East Coast settlement continued after the Revolution as new frontiers emerged during the early republic. See Robert D. Mitchell, "The Southern Backcountry: A Geographical House Divided," in *The Southern Backcountry: Interdisciplinary Perspectives on Frontier Communities,* eds. David C. Crass, Steven D. Smith, Martha A. Zierden, and Richard D. Brooks (Knoxville: University of Tennessee Press, 1998), 1–35, esp. 27.

4. Van Atta, *Securing the West,* 14, 18.

5. For the 1815 definition of squatter, see John Pickering, "Memoir of the Present State of the English Language in the United States, with a Vocabulary Containing Various Words Which Has Been Supposed to Be Peculiar to This Country," *Memoirs of the American Academy of Arts and Sciences* (January 1, 1815), 523. Pickering cited the Englishman Edward Augustus Kendall for his account of how the word squatter was used in America; see Kendall, *Travels Through the Northern Part of the United States in the Years 1807 and 1808* (New York, 1809), 160; also see Nathaniel Gorham to James Madison, January 27, 1788, *The Papers of James Madison,* 10:435–36. The *Oxford English Dictionary* incorrectly identifies Madison as first using the term, but Madison merely repeated verbatim in a letter to George Washington what Gorham had written to him. See also Madison to Washington, February 3, 1788, *The Papers of James Madison,* 10:463. For the article on Pennsylvania "squatlers," see "Philadelphia, August 10," *The* [Philadelphia] *Federal, and Evening Gazette,* August 10, 1790. On the Phelps-Gorham Purchase that

involved around six million acres in western New York, see William H. Stiles, "Pioneering in Genesee County: Entrepreneurial Strategy and the Concept of Central Place," in *New Opportunities in a New Nation: The Development of New York After the Revolution,* eds. Manfred Jonas and Robert W. Wells (Schenectady, NY: Union College Press, 1982), 35–68.

6. See Kendall, *Travels,* 160–62; Alan Taylor, "'A Kind of War': The Contest for Land on the Northeastern Frontier, 1750–1820," *William and Mary Quarterly* 46, no. 1 (January 1786): 3–26, esp. 6–9; and for the case of Daniel Hildreth in Lincoln County Supreme Court in Massachusetts, see "Various Paragraphs," *Columbian Centinel. Massachusetts Federalist,* October 18, 1800.

7. Kendall made the point that "squatters were not peculiar to Maine," and then mentioned Pennsylvania. See Kendall, *Travels,* 161–62. For the various proclamations, see *Proclamation, by Honorable George Thomas, Esq. Lieutenant Governor and Commander in Chief of the Province of Pennsylvania . . .* (October 5, 1742); and *Proclamation, by Honorable James Hamilton, Lieutenant Governor and Commander in Chief of the Province of Pennsylvania . . .* (July 18, 1749); and *Proclamation, by the Honorable John Penn, Esq., Lieutenant Governor and Commander in Chief of the Province of Pennsylvania* (September 23, 1766); and for the emphasis on the death penalty, see *Proclamation, by the Honorable John Penn, Esq., Lieutenant Governor and Commander in Chief of the Province of Pennsylvania . . .* (February 24, 1768). There were the equivalent of squatters in Great Britain, vagrants who lived in forests and marshes—the wastelands of manorial estates, as well as people who lived on property they did not own after the 1666 fire in London. See the broadside warning of ejectment: *This Court Taking into Consideration, the Utmost Time for Taking Down and Removing All Such Sheds, Shops, and Other Like Buildings, Which Have Been Erected Since the Late Dismal Fire . . .* (London, 1673); also see A. L. Beier, *Masterless Men,* 9, 19, 73–74.

8. Eric Hinderaker, *Elusive Empires: Constructing Colonialism in the Ohio Valley, 1763–1800* (Cambridge: Cambridge University Press, 1997), 239–40, 244, 246; Holly Mayer, "From Forts to Families: Following the Army into Western Pennsylvania, 1758–1766," *Pennsylvania Magazine of History and Biography* 130, no. 1 (January 2006): 5–43, esp. 13, 21, 23–24, 36–38, 40.

9. On Colonel Henry Bouquet, see Bouquet to Anne Willing, Bedford, September 17, 1759, in *The Papers of Colonel Henry Bouquet,* ed. Sylvester E. Stevens et al., 19 vols. (Harrisburg: Pennsylvania Historical Commission and Works Progress Administration, 1940–44), 3:371–72, 4:115–16.

10. For various meanings of "squat" and "squatting," see *Oxford English Dictionary;* Melissa J. Pawlikowski, "'The Ravages of a Cruel and Savage Economy': Ohio River Valley Squatters and the Formation of a Communitarian Political Economy, 1768–1782" (paper presented at the Society of Historians of the Early American Republic, July 17, 2011, in possession of the author). On Hottentots, see "The Voyage of Peter Kolben, A.M., to the Cape of Good Hope; with an Account of the Manners and Customs of Its Inhabitants," *The Pennsylvania Herald, and General Advertiser,* July 21, 1786. For a Cherokee woman sitting squat on the ground, see "A True Relation of the Unheard of Sufferings of David Menzies, Surgeon Among the Cherokees; Deliverance in

South-Carolina," *The Boston Post-Boy and Advertiser,* March 6, 1767. For British soldiers and their fighting style, see "Annapolis, in Maryland, July 15," [Boston] *Weekly News-Letter,* August 19, 1756; "New-York, March 27," *The New-York Gazette: or, The Weekly Post-Boy,* March 27, 1758; "Extract of a Letter from Ticonderoga, July 31," *Pennsylvania Gazette,* August 9, 1759; also see John K. Mahon, "Anglo-American Methods of Indian Warfare, 1675–1794," *Mississippi Valley Historical Review* 45, no. 2 (September 1958): 254–75. For the importance of the legal meaning of standing, see Tomlins, *Freedom Bound,* 119–20.

11. The colonial official also emphasized that "they enjoyed engaging in cruelty," were horse stealers, and tried to stir up war by propagating "idle stories"; see Captain Gavin Cochrane to Lord Dartmouth, June 22, 1767, in M. Mathews, "Of Matters Lexicographical," *American Speech* 34, no. 2 (May 1959): 126–30. On southern crackers, see Mr. Simpson and Mr. Barnard, Address Presented to Governor James Wright in March 1767, in *The Colonial Records of the State of Georgia,* ed. Allen D. Chandler, 26 vols. (Atlanta, 1904), 14:475–76; and Mr. James Habersham to Governor James Wright, in *The Letters of James Habersham 1756–1775,* in *The Collections of the Georgia Historical Society,* 15 vols. (Savannah, 1904), 6:204; also cited in Delma E. Presley, "The Crackers of Georgia," *Georgia Historical Quarterly* 60, no. 2 (Summer 1976): 102–16, esp. 102–3. For the cracker eye-gouger, see "Extracts of the Letter from a Camp Near Seneca, August 18," *Pennsylvania Ledger,* October 26, 1776 (this report was republished in numerous papers in Rhode Island, Connecticut, and Massachusetts).

12. Woodmason also called them "banditti, profligates, reprobates, and the lowest scum of the Earth." He further noted that the people were intended to "set down as a barrier between the Rich planters and Indians." See Richard Hooker, ed., *The Carolina Backcountry on the Eve of the Revolution: The Journal and Other Writings of Charles Woodmason, Anglican Itinerant* (Chapel Hill: University of North Carolina Press, 1953), 25, 27, 31–32, 52–54, 60–61, 154.

13. For the reference to "cracking traders" used by Ensign Alexander Cameron, a British agent in South Carolina, who was describing white poachers in a letter to Captain Gavin Cochrane, dated February 3, 1765, see John L. Nichols, "Alexander Cameron, British Agent Among the Cherokee, 1764–1781," *South Carolina Historical Magazine* 97, no. 2 (April 1996): 94–114, esp. 95, 97. Cameron appears to be the first person to use "cracking traders" before Cochrane called them crackers. Cameron was a native of Scotland, and first came to America as a soldier with General James Oglethorpe in 1738. For the term "louse cracker" (nasty, slovenly fellow), see *New-England Courant,* February 22–March 5, 1722. For the definition of "louse cracker," see John Ebers, *The New and Complete Dictionary of England and German Language,* vol. 2 (Leipzig, 1798), 363. For a "joke cracker," as a person who wastes time, see "Cursory Thoughts," *Vermont Gazette,* August 5, 1805. On nasty insults resembling smelly firecrackers, see *Lloyd's Evening Post,* May 15–17, 1765. For a cracker as liar, or teller of marvelous tales, see "No. CXXXIV. Kit Cracker, a Great Dealer in the Marvelous, Describes Himself and His

Adventures to the Observer," in Richard Cumberland, *The Observer: Being a Collection of Moral, Literary and Familiar Essays* (London, 1791), 86–95.

14. For "crack brained people" acting like crazy animals, see "No. III, To the Editors of the Charleston Courier," *United States Gazette,* June 13, 1804; also see "crack brained son" in *The Providence Gazette, and Country Journal,* January 3, 1768; and for a parody of haymakers and crack-brained drinkers, see "Attention Haymaker!," *Thomas's Massachusetts Spy, or Worcester Gazette,* July 20, 1796. For the use of the term "crack-brained" by prominent Georgia trustee the Earl of Egmont, see Robert G. McPherson, ed., *The Journal of the Earl of Egmont, Abstract of the Trustees Proceedings for Establishing the Colony of Georgia, 1732–1738* (Athens: University of Georgia Press, 1962), 59. Reverend Woodmason also referred to a "crack'd the brain" North Carolinian; see Hooker, *The Carolina Backcountry,* 62; for "crack brained," also see *Oxford English Dictionary;* and see Thomas Tusser, *Five Hundred Points of Good Husbandry* (1573; reprint ed., Oxford, 1848), 93.

15. For the reference to their "delight in cruelty" and "lawless set of rascals," see Gavin Cochrane to Lord Dartmouth, June 27, 1766, in Mathews, "Of Matters Lexicographical," 127. On "rascal" as rubbish, camp followers, and lean and inferior animals, see *Oxford English Dictionary;* for "rascal" as "trash," see Edward Philips, *A New World of Words: or A General Dictionary* (London, 1671), n.p.

16. Benjamin Rush, "An Account of the Progress of Population, Agriculture, Manners, and Government in Pennsylvania, in a Letter to a Friend in England," in *Essays, Literary, Moral, Philosophical* (Philadelphia, 1798), 214, 224–25. In 1816, the governor of the Michigan Territory described French settlers in the same way, as adopting the ways of Indians, living with periods of trade and then long periods of indolence, and neglecting their farms. They also were ignorant of "the common acts of domestic life." He warned that until there was a new migration of people, the territory would be plagued with "indigent helpless people." See Governor Lewis Cass to Secretary of War, May 31, 1816, in *The Territorial Papers of the United States,* vol. 10, *The Territory of Michigan, 1805–1820,* ed. Clarence Edwin Carter (Washington, DC: Government Printing Office, 1942), 642–43. The same idea of purging the poor accompanied the migration of wealthier settlers into the western states. See John Melish (who wrote on Kentucky), *Travels in the United States of America in the Years 1806 & 1807, and 1809, 1810, & 1811,* 2 vols. (Philadelphia, 1812), 2:204.

17. On land speculators and class power, see Lee Soltow, "Progress and Mobility Among Ohio Propertyholders, 1810–1825," *Social Science History* 7, no. 4 (Autumn 1983): 405–26, esp. 410, 412–15, 418, 420; Andrew R. L. Cayton, "Land, Power, and Reputation: The Cultural Dimension of Politics in the Ohio Country," *William and Mary Quarterly* 47, no. 2 (April 1990): 266–86, esp. 278; Rudolf Freud, "Military Bounty Lands and the Origins of the Public Domain," *Agricultural History* 20, no. 1 (January 1946): 8–18, esp. 8. For the relocation of the top-down social structure from Virginia to Kentucky, and the rise of the merchant class, see Craig T. Friend, "Merchants and Markethouses: Reflections on Moral Economy in Early Kentucky," *Journal of the*

Early Republic 17, no. 4 (Winter 1997): 553–74, esp. 556–57, 572. On elite speculators using kinship networks to advance their class power, see Marion Nelson Winship, "The Land of Connected Men: A New Migration Story from the Early Republic," *Pennsylvania History* 64 (Summer 1997): 88–104, esp. 90, 97.

18. On old soldiers, see Peter Onuf, "Settlers, Settlements, and New States," in *The American Revolution: Its Character and Limits,* ed. Jack Greene (New York: New York University Press, 1987), 171–96, esp. 180–82. For Jefferson's policy on squatters, see Thomas Jefferson to Secretary of War, April 8, 1804, in *The Territorial Papers of the United States,* vol. 13, *The Territory of Louisiana-Missouri, 1803–1806,* ed. Clarence Edwin Carter (Washington, DC: Government Printing Office, 1948), 13:19; and Thomas Jefferson to Albert Gallatin, November 3, 1808, in *The Territorial Papers of the United States,* vol. 7, *The Territory of Indiana, 1800–1810,* ed. Clarence Edwin Carter (Washington, DC: Government Printing Office, 1939), 7:610–11; also see Bethel Saler, *The Settlers' Empire: Colonialism and State Formation in America's Old Northwest* (Philadelphia: University of Pennsylvania Press, 2015), 48–50, 54; Van Atta, *Securing the West,* 77–78.

19. On wretchedness and a poor and feeble population, see Mathew Carey, *Essays on Political Economy, or, The Most Certain Means of Promoting Wealth, Power, Resources, and Happiness of Nations: Applied to the United States* (Philadelphia, 1822), 177, 376. On public education and the poor, see Andrew R. L. Cayton, *The Frontier Republic: Ideology and Politics in the Ohio Country, 1780–1825* (Kent, OH: Kent State University Press, 1986), 77, 144–45; Van Atta, *Securing the West,* 110–12, 118, 210.

20. On landlessness and limited mobility, see Gary Edwards, "'Anything . . . That Would Pay': Yeoman Farmers and the Nascent Market Economy on the Antebellum Plantation Frontier," in *Southern Society and Its Transformation, 1790–1860,* eds. Susanna Delfino, Michele Gillespie, and Louis M. Kyriakoudes (Columbia: University of Missouri Press, 2011), 102–30, esp. 108, 110; Craig Thompson Friend, "'Work & Be Rich': Economy and Culture on the Bluegrass Farm," in *The Buzzel About Kentuck,* ed. Craig Thompson Friend (Lexington: University Press of Kentucky, 1999), 124–51, esp. 128–33. For land agents discouraging tenancy, see Robert P. Swierenga, "The 'Western Land Business': The Story of Easley & Willingham, Speculators," *Business History Review* 41, no. 1 (Spring 1967): 1–20, esp. 12, 16; Rohrbough, *The Land Office Business,* 170–71, 175–76, 235–36. On the difficulty of tenants becoming large landowners (as compared to sons of the rich inheriting wealth), see Soltow, "Progress and Mobility," 423.

21. For the scandal swirling around Jackson's divorce, see Norma Basch, "Marriage, Morals, and Politics in the Election of 1828," *Journal of American History* 80, no. 3 (December 1993): 890–918; also see John Ward, *Andrew Jackson: Symbol for an Age* (New York: Oxford University Press, 1953), 54–55; and Andrew Burstein, *The Passions of Andrew Jackson* (New York: Knopf, 2003), 11, 170, 172.

22. For "Old Hickory" as a strong tree, see "Ode to the Fourth of July," *Salem* [MA] *Gazette,* July 15, 1823; and for Jackson's nickname meaning he was

"tough, unyielding, and substantial," see "Old Hickory," *Haverhill* [MA] *Gazette and Patriot,* August 7, 1824.

23. See Wilson's poem "The Pilgrim," and "Extract of a Letter from Lexington," *The Port-Folio* (June 1810): 499–519, esp. 505, 514–15. On Wilson, see R. Cantwell, *Alexander Wilson: Naturalist and Pioneer* (Philadelphia: J. B. Lippincott, 1961). Wilson applied the same criteria to studying birds and squatters; he wrote that the "character of the feathered race" could be determined by "noting their particular haunts, modes of constructing their nests"; see Edward H. Burtt Jr. and William E. Davis Jr., *Alexander Wilson: The Scot Who Founded American Ornithology* (Cambridge, MA: Belknap Press of Harvard University Press, 2013), 11.

24. Wilson, "Extract of a Letter from Lexington," 519. For the symbolic meaning of homes in securing territorial claims, also see Anna Stilz, "Nations, States, and Territory," *Ethics* 121, no. 3 (April 2011): 572–601, esp. 575–76.

25. Cornelia J. Randolph to Virginia J. Randolph (Trist), August 17, 1817, *PTJ-R*, Thomas Jefferson Foundation, Charlottesville, VA. I would like to thank Lisa Francavilla of the Retirement Series for alerting me to this letter.

26. See "Measuring for a Bed," *New Bedford* [MA] *Mercury,* February 12, 1830 (reprinted from the *Baltimore Emerald*); also see "Sporting in Illinois," *Spirit of the Times; A Chronicle of Turf, Agriculture, Field Sports, Literature, and Stage* (July 14, 1838): 169; and Ludwig Inkle, "Running from the Indians," *Magnolia; or Southern Monthly* (August 1841): 359–62. esp. 360.

27. See John M. Denham, "The Florida Cracker Before the Civil War as Seen Through Travelers' Accounts," *Florida Historical Quarterly* 72, no. 4 (April 1994): 453–68, esp. 460, 467–68; and Inkle, "Running from the Indians."

28. For a cracker shouting and squealing, see "The Tobacco Roller," [Augusta, GA] *Southern Sentinel,* November 6, 1794. For the Mississippi squatter as a screamer, see "Taking the Mississippi," *Maine Farmer,* October 26, 1848. For Hoosier anecdotes, see "A Forcible Argument," *New Hampshire Centinel,* June 15, 1837; "The Hoosier Girls," [Charleston, SC] *Southern Patriot,* October 12, 1837; "Hoosier Poetry," [New Orleans] *Daily Picayune,* July 26, 1838; *Barre* [MA] *Weekly Gazette,* November 2, 1838; "From the National Intelligencer," *Macon Georgia Telegraph,* April 7, 1840.

29. See John Finley, "The Hoosier's Nest," *Indiana Quarterly Magazine of History* 1, no. 1 (1905): 56–57; also see William D. Pierson, "The Origins of the Word 'Hoosier': A New Interpretation," *Indiana Magazine of History* 91, no. 2 (June 1995): 189–96.

30. "Cracker Dictionary," *Salem* [MA] *Gazette,* Mary 21, 1830; also see "Southernisms," *New Hampshire Patriot & State Gazette,* July 27, 1835; and "The Gouging Scene," *Philadelphia Album and Ladies Literary Portfolio,* September 25, 1830; and both "jimber-jawed" and "gimbal-jawed" were derived from "gimbal," meaning hinge or joint, and thus meant a protruding and loose jaw, see *Oxford English Dictionary.*

31. "Cracker Dictionary." Another writer defined a "squatter" with the motto of "'here to-day—gone in a moment'"; see "Original Correspondence," *Boston Courier,* November 25, 1830.

32. M. J. Heale, "The Role of the Frontier in Jacksonian Politics: David Crockett and the Myth of the Self-made Man," *Western Historical Quarterly* 4, no. 4 (October 1973): 405–23, esp. 405–9, 417; James R. Boylston and Allen J. Wiener, *David Crockett in Congress: The Rise and Fall of the Poor Man's Friend* (Houston: Bright Sky Press, 2009), 2–3.

33. Cynthia Cumfer, "Local Origins of National Indian Policy: Cherokee and Tennessee Ideas About Sovereignty and Nationhood, 1790–1811," *Journal of the Early Republic* 23, no. 1 (Spring 2003): 21–46, esp. 25, 31; Heale, "The Role of the Frontier in Jacksonian Politics," 416–17; and "Premium on Fecundity," [Haverhill, MA] *Essex Gazette*, April 3, 1830.

34. *Davy Crockett's Almanack of 1837* (Nashville, 1837), 40–43; Heale, "The Role of the Frontier in Jacksonian Politics," 408; James Atkins Shackford, *David Crockett: The Man and the Legend* (Chapel Hill, NC: University of North Carolina Press, 1956), 68–69, 136, 144; Alexander Saxton, *The Rise and Fall of the White Republic: Class Politics and Mass Culture in Nineteenth-Century America* (London: Verso, 1990), 78, 83; Boylston and Wiener, *David Crockett in Congress*, 16. On Crockett's advocacy for the poor man over the rich speculator, see "Remarks of Mr. Crockett, of Tennessee," *United States Telegraph*, May 19, 1828; "Congressional Canvas," [Columbia, SC] *Columbia Telescope*, June 12, 1829; and "Col. David Crockett, of Tennessee," *Daily National Intelligencer*, June 22, 1831; and "Cracker Dictionary."

35. See "There Are Some Queer Fellows in Congress," [Fayetteville, NC] *Carolina Observer*, March 20, 1828. On Crockett's popularity, surpassing the government, Black Hawk, or a "caravan of wild varmints," see an excerpt from his biography (supposedly written by Crockett), "Preface of Hon. David Crockett's Biography," *United States Telegraph*, February 22, 1834. On the comparison to the trained bear, see "The Indian Question," *Raleigh Register, and the North Carolina Gazette,* July 1, 1834; for Frederick Douglass's comparison of Crockett to the harlequin, see "Meeting in New York," *The North Star,* June 8, 1849, and Todd Vogel, *Rewriting White: Race, Class and Cultural Capital in Nineteenth-Century America* (New Brunswick, NJ: Rutgers University Press, 2004), 25.

36. *Davy Crockett's Almanack of 1837*, 8, 17.

37. For Crockett's speech in defense of poor squatters, see Guy S. Miles, "Davy Crockett Evolves, 1821–1824, *American Quarterly* 8, no. 1 (Spring 1956): 53–60, esp. 54–55; also see Melvin Rosser Mason, "'The Lion of the West': Satire on Davy Crockett and Frances Trollope," *South Central Bulletin* 29, no. 4 (Winter 1969): 143–45; also see Walter Blair, "Americanized Comic Braggarts," *Critical Inquiry* 4, no. 2 (Winter 1977): 331–49.

38. For alienating his Tennessee colleagues, see "Col. David Crockett, of Tennessee." For his opposition to the Indian Removal Bill, see "The Indian Question." For refusing to be Jackson's dog, see "Politics of the Day," *Daily National Intelligencer*, March 30, 1831; and "Col. Crockett. From the Boston Journal," *Indiana Journal*, May 31, 1834; also see Megan Taylor Shockley, "King of the Wild Frontier vs. King Andrew I: Davy Crockett and the

Election of 1831," *Tennessee Historical Quarterly* 56, no. 3 (Fall 1997): 158–69, esp. 161–62, 166.

39. On the defection of his friends and allies, see Burstein, *The Passions of Andrew Jackson,* 209–11.

40. For "hardy sons of the West," see "Old Hickory," [Haverhill, MA] *Gazette and Patriot,* August 7, 1824. On the "Old Hickory" name for tough, fibrous wood associated with the Tennessee tree of the frontier, see Harry L. Watson, *Liberty and Power: The Politics of Jacksonian America* (New York: Hill & Wang, 1990; rev. ed., 2006), 77.

41. See "Emigration to the Westward," [Boston] *Independent Chronicle,* September 11, 1815; also see broadside "Unparalleled Victory" (Boston, 1815). For Jackson celebrating the British death toll, see "Address, Directed by Maj. General Jackson to Be Read at the Head of Each Corps Composing the Line Below New Orleans, January 24, 1815," *Albany Argus,* February 28, 1815 (this address was widely published in many newspapers around the country). For the poem on Jackson's bloody victory in New Orleans, see "The River Mississippi," *American Advocate and Kennebec Advertiser,* March 25, 1815; Burstein, *The Passions of Andrew Jackson,* 125.

42. Burstein, *The Passions of Andrew Jackson,* 5, 121, 138. On Daniel Webster's 1824 account of Jefferson's remarks on Jackson, see Kevin J. Hayes, ed., *Jefferson in His Own Time: A Biographical Chronicle of His Life, Drawn from Recollections, Interviews, and Memoirs by Family, Friends, and Associates* (Iowa City: University of Iowa Press, 2012), 99.

43. For an excerpt from Jesse Benton's pamphlet attacking him as "Boisterous in ordinary conversation," see "From the Georgia Constitutionalist," [Charleston, SC] *City Gazette and Commercial Daily Advertiser,* October 22, 1824. For "A Backwoodsman and a Squatter," see "Foreign Notices of American Literature," *Literary Gazette,* March 3, 1821.

44. For the "rude instinct of masculine liberty," see a review of Achille Murat's *Essay on the Morality and Politics of the United States of North America* (1832), *North American Quarterly Magazine* (March 1838): 103–19, esp. 107. The author Achille Murat was a close friend of Jackson ally John Coffee and had lived in Florida for several years.

45. David S. Heidler and Jeanne T. Heidler, *Old Hickory's War: Andrew Jackson and the Quest for Empire* (Baton Rouge: Louisiana State University Press, 2003), 87–108.

46. Jackson was accused in the British press of exterminating the Indians and introducing savage principles into the character of the American people; his execution of the two British citizens was seen as another "atrocity." See "From the *Liverpool Courier* of Aug. 18," *Commercial Advertiser,* October 3, 1818; also see Isaac Holmes, *An Account of the United States of America, Derived from Actual Observation, During a Residence of Four Years in That Republic* (London, 1824), 83; "American Justice!! The Ferocious Yankee Gen.! Jack's Reward for Butchering Two British Subjects!," Tennessee State Museum Collection, Nashville; Heidler and Heidler, *Old Hickory's War,* 154–57; and David S. Heidler, "The Politics of National Aggression: Congress and the

First Seminole War," *Journal of the Early Republic* 13, no. 4 (Winter 1993): 501–30, esp. 504–5.

47. "White Savages," *Thomas's Massachusetts Spy, and Worcester Gazette,* September 9, 1818. For Seminoles' distrust of violent crackers, see "From Darien Gazette," [Windsor] *Vermont Journal,* June 28, 1819. For Indians only attacking "cracker houses," see "Seminole—First Campaign. Extracts from the Journal of a Private," *New Hampshire Gazette,* May 9, 1827.

48. On Jackson's outburst to Adams, "D—m Grotius! D—m Puffendorf! D—m Vatell! This Is Mere Matter Between Jim Monroe and Myself!," see Ward, *Andrew Jackson: Symbol for an Age,* 63. On Jackson threatening to cut off the ears of some senators, see "Mr. Lacock's Reply," *Nile's Weekly Register,* April 3, 1819.

49. F. P. Prucha, "Andrew Jackson's Indian Policy: A Reassessment," *Journal of American History* 56, no. 3 (December 1969): 527–39, esp. 529; Waldo S. Putnam, *Memoirs of Andrew Jackson; Major General in the Army of the United States and Commander in Chief of the Division of the South* (Hartford, CT, 1818), 310. John Eaton, one of his most devoted allies and the author of his biography, admitted that Jackson had an irritable and hasty temper, which brought him into many disputes. This point was considered well known in the aftermath of the Seminole War. See "The Life of Andrew Jackson," *Western Review and Miscellaneous Magazine* (September 1819): 87–91, esp. 87. For his "fiery and impetuous" temper and his disregard for "legal construction," see "General Andrew Jackson," *National Register,* August 5, 1820; and for his lack of civility, see "The Presidency," *Eastern Argus,* October 7, 1823. For Clay's insult of "military chieftain," see his letter published in the *Daily National Intelligencer,* February 12, 1825. Jackson's defenders claimed he had a duty to protect the life of every frontier settler, and that his policy was premised on protecting future emigrations; violence was the only way to deal with the savage foe. See "Defense of Andrew Jackson: Strictures on Mr. Lacock's Report on the Seminole War," *Niles Weekly Register,* March 13, 1819.

50. On Indian removal, see Michael Morris, "Georgia and the Conversation over Indian Removal," *Georgia Historical Quarterly* 91, no. 4 (Winter 2007): 403–23, esp. 405, 419. Jackson denied that Indians had any right of domain and rejected Indian claims to "tracts of country on which they have neither dwelt or made improvements"; see Prucha, "Andrew Jackson's Indian Policy: A Reassessment," 532. On squatters in Alabama, see Van Atta, *Securing the West,* 186–87; and Rohrbough, *The Land Office Business,* 163.

51. On the Dickinson duel, see Burstein, *The Passions of Andrew Jackson,* 56–57; "Col. Benton and Col. Jackson," *Daily National Journal,* June 30, 1828. For the 1824 account of Jackson's duel with Dickinson, see "Traits in the Character of General Jackson," *Missouri Republican,* September 13, 1824.

52. *Some Account of Some of the Bloody Deeds of Gen. Andrew Jackson* (broadside, Franklin, TN, 1818); also see "Reminiscences; or an Extract from a Catalogue of General Jackson's 'Juvenile Indiscretions,' from the Age of 23 to 60," *Newburyport Herald,* July 1, 1828.

53. See Andrew Jackson to John Coffee, June 18, 1824, in *Correspondence of Andrew Jackson,* ed. John Spencer Bassett, 6 vols. (Washington, DC, 1926–34),

3:225–26; and Matthew Warshauer, "Andrew Jackson as 'Military Chieftain' in the 1824 and 1828 Presidential Elections: The Ramifications of Martial Law on American Republicanism," *Tennessee Historical Quarterly* 57, no. 1 (Spring/Summer 1998): 4–23.

54. See "The Presidency" and "General Jackson," *Louisville Public Advertiser,* January 14, 1824, and October 22, 1822.

55. See "Sketch of a Debate: Seminole War," *City of Washington Gazette,* February 5, 1819.

56. See "The Beau and the Cracker," *Columbian Museum and Savannah Advertiser,* October 7, 1796; and *To a Woodman's Hut* (New York, 1812). The plot may be older, for it shares certain similarities with "A Dialogue Between a Noble Lord, and a Poor Woodman" (1770); Joseph Doddridge's story was printed in his *Logan. The Last of the Race of Schikellemus, Chief of the Cayuga Nation* (1823), as cited in Cecil D. Eby, "Dandy Versus Squatter: An Earlier Round," *Southern Literary Review* 20, no. 2 (Fall 1987): 33–36, esp. 34.

57. A popular anecdote circulated during the 1824 campaign that described a humorous encounter between the general and a "pert Macaroni" (dandy) in Philadelphia. See "Anecdote of General Jackson," *Raleigh Register, and North Carolina State Gazette,* February 13, 1824.

58. For the Crockett-like response to coffin handbills, see John Tailaferro, *Account of Some of the Bloody Deeds of GENERAL JACKSON, Being a Supplement to the "Coffin Handbill"* (broadside, Northern Neck, VA, 1828). On Jackson as "homebred," see "General Jackson," *Maryland Gazette and the State Register,* January 22, 1824. On Jackson being from a common family, see "Jackson's Literature," *United States' Telegraph,* March 8, 1828. For other articles focusing on his commonness and lack of education, see "The Presidency," [Portland, ME] *Eastern Argus,* October 7, 1823; "Something Extraordinary," *Raleigh Register, and North Carolina State Gazette,* August 6, 1824; and "General Jackson," *National Advocate,* March 10, 1824.

59. For a cracker supporter of Jackson, see *New Orleans Argus,* August 21, 1828 (this piece came from the *Darien Gazette* in Georgia and was widely reprinted in New Hampshire, Connecticut, and New York newspapers); and "The Backwoods Alive with Old Hickory," *Louisville Public Advertiser,* February 27, 1828.

60. See "Jackson Toasts," *Newburyport Herald,* June 22, 1828; and "Humorous Sketch," *Norwich Courier,* April 1, 1829; "Barney Blinn" (from the Augusta *Georgia Chronicle*), *New London Gazette,* December 19, 1827. For a song titled "Ode to General Jackson," in which he cut the British with his saber, "knock'd off all their legs," but retained the eternal devotion of his supporters even if he was "shot through the head," see Charles Mathews, *The London Mathews; Containing an Account of the Celebrated Comedian's Journey to America . . .* (Philadelphia, 1824), 33–34. For a satire of a typical Jackson man having no trouble with the fact that Jackson was a "blundering, half-taught, ignoramus," see "The Subjoined Communication," *New-England Galaxy and United States Literary Advertiser,* November, 7, 1828.

61. "Mr. Jefferson's Opinion of Gen. Jackson—Settled," *Indiana Journal,* January 3, 1828.

62. For the happy-marriage defense of Rachel Jackson, see *New Hampshire Patriot & State Gazette,* April 23, 1827. The accidental bigamy defense was published widely in newspapers; for example, see [Portland, ME] *Eastern Argus,* May 8, 1827. For exposing the fallacy of the accidental bigamy story, see Burstein, *The Passions of Andrew Jackson,* 28–33, 227–28, 241–48; and Ann Toplovich, "Marriage, Mayhem, and Presidential Politics: The Robards-Jackson Backcountry Scandal," *Ohio Valley History* 5 (Winter 2005): 3–22.

63. For Jackson robbing another man of his wife, see "From Harrisburgh, Pa.," *New Orleans Argus,* May 17, 1828; and Charles Hammond, "The Character of Andrew Jackson," in *Truth's Advocate and Monthly Anti-Jackson Advocate* (Cincinnati, 1828), 216.

64. See Basch, "Marriage, Morals, and Politics in the Election of 1828," 903; Charles Hammond, "View of General Jackson's Domestic Relations," *Truth's Advocate and Monthly Anti-Jackson Advocate,* 5; "Dana vs. Mrs. Jackson," *Richmond Enquirer,* May 4, 1827; and "Dana vs. Mrs. Jackson," *New Hampshire Patriot & State Gazette,* May 21, 1827. On Dana, see James D. Daniels, "Amos Kendall: Kentucky Journalist, 1815–1829," *Filson Historical Quarterly* (1978): 46–65, esp. 55–56. And for Rachel's log cabin immorality, see "Mrs. Jackson," *Richmond Enquirer,* May 4, 1827. Jackson himself was attacked as a mulatto, when a rumor was spread that his mother was a British camp follower who had shacked up with a black man. The story focused on Jackson's questionable pedigree, what *"stock or race"* Jackson had sprung from. See "Rank Villainy and Obscenity," *Charleston* [SC] *Mercury,* August 22, 1828.

65. For the washerwoman reference and the snide comment on her "healthy tanned complexion," see Lynn Hudson Parsons, *The Birth of Modern Politics: Andrew Jackson, John Quincy Adams and the Election of 1828* (New York: Oxford University Press, 2009), 189; for her pronunciation, see "British Scandal," *Salem Gazette,* April 15, 1828; for her favorite song, "Possum Up a Gum Tree," see "Mrs. Jackson," *New Bedford* [MA] *Mercury,* December 5, 1828; and for attacks hastening her death, see "Mrs. Jackson," [Portland, ME] *Eastern Argus Semi-Weekly,* February 24, 1829.

66. See "The Game of Brag," *Richmond Enquirer,* February 29, 1840. For the talkative country politician, see George Watterston, *Wanderer in Washington* (Washington, DC, 1827), 3. For Jackson as the "Knight of New Orleans," see "Toasts at a Celebration in Florida," *Orange County Patriot, or the Spirit of Seventy-Six,* March 14, 1815. For Jackson as the savior of his country, see John Eaton, *Letters of Wyoming to the People of the United States, on the Presidential Election, and in Favor of Andrew Jackson* (Philadelphia, 1824), 12. And for Jackson as the "Matchless hero! Incomparable man! . . . The records of chivalry, the pages of history do not furnish a more exalted character than that!," see William P. Van Ness, *A Concise Narrative of General Jackson's First Invasion of Florida, and of His Immortal Defense of New-Orleans; with Remarks. By Aristides* (Albany, NY, 1827), 29–30. Also see "Mr. J. W. Overton's Address," *Carthage Gazette,* June 9, 1815. In 1824, supporters of Adams claimed they were not "part of the boisterous boasting part of the population," but by 1832 they too were bragging about their candidate; see "Presidential," *Middlesex Gazette,* June 23, 1824; for Henry Clay and his

Party as braggarts, see "Henry Clay," *Richmond Enquirer*, August 21, 1832; for the term "electioneering rag," see "To the Editor of the Globe," *Richmond Enquirer*, August 31, 1832; for the "game of brag" used by newspapers to defend Clay's strength in the election, see "Put Up Your Cash!," *Rhode Island Republican*, October 2, 1832; on bragging and elections, see "From the National Intelligencer," *The Connecticut Courant*, May 25, 1835; for a poem mocking the failure of the Whig Party's bragging, see "The Whigs Lament, After the Election in '35," *New Hampshire Patriot & State Gazette*, June 1, 1835; on Whigs and the game of brag, see "General Harrison," *Richmond Enquirer*, July 29, 1836; and "Pennsylvania," *Richmond Enquirer*, September 27, 1836. After visiting the United States, Englishwoman Francis Trollope wrote, "Every American is a braggadocio. He is always boasting." See "Leaves from Mrs. Trollope's Journal," *Connecticut Mirror*, September 1, 1832.

67. See "A Challenge. The Walnut Cracker, vs. the Knight of the Red Rag," *Pendleton Messenger*, August 2, 1820; this story was originally published in a Tennessee paper and reprinted here in a Pendleton, South Carolina, newspaper. This was a duel to be waged over an infringement of the boundary lines between the states. In issuing his challenge, Walnut Cracker, "instead of a glove," sends him the heads of several men he had bitten off.

68. John R. Van Atta, "'A Lawless Rabble': Henry Clay and the Cultural Politics of Squatters' Rights, 1832–1841," *Journal of the Early Republic* 28, no. 3 (Fall 2008): 337–78; and for Clay's remarks taken from his 1838 speech in the Senate, also see "The Squatter in the White House," *Mississippian*, September 6, 1844; Rohrbough, *The Land Office Business*, 162–63, 169–75, 235–36. For a favorable portrait of squatters and the preemption debate, which was originally published in the *New York Post*, see "The Squatters," *Mississippian*, March 24, 1837, and "The Squatters," *Wisconsin Territorial Gazette and Burlington Advertiser*, July 10, 1837.

69. Michael E. Welsh, "Legislating a Homestead Bill: Thomas Hart Benton and the Second Seminole War," *Florida Historical Quarterly* 27, no. 1 (October 1978): 157–72, esp. 158–59; Van Atta, *Securing the West*, 181, 226–28.

70. See "Public Exhibition. Mammoth Hog, Corn Cracker. 'Kentucky Against the World,'" [New Orleans] *Daily Picayune*, June 3, 1840; Gustav Kobbe, "Presidential Campaign Songs," *The Cosmopolitan* (October 1888), 529–35, esp. 531; and Robert Gray Gunderson, *The Log-Cabin Campaign* (Lexington: University of Kentucky Press, 1957), 1, 8, 75–77, 102–3, 110–15. In a fake campaign biography of Martin Van Buren, supposedly written by Davy Crockett, Van Buren is mercilessly mocked as a strange hermaphroditic breed; see David Crockett, [Augustin Smith Clayton] *The Life of Martin Van Buren* (Philadelphia, 1835), 27–28, 79–81; and J. D. Wade, "The Authorship of David Crockett's 'Autobiography,'" *Georgia Historical Quarterly* 6, no. 3 (September 1922): 265–68.

71. John S. Robb, "The Standing Candidate; His Excuse for Being a Bachelor," in *Streaks of Squatter Life, or Far West Scenes* (Philadelphia, 1847), 91–100. Robb's story also appeared in newspapers; see "The Standing Candidate," *Cleveland Herald*, March 19, 1847, and "Old Sugar! The Standing Candidate," *Arkansas State Democrat*, June 4, 1847. For another story of the generous squatter (like the older backwoodsman story) opening his home to the traveler

(and disabusing readers that squatters might be violent men), see "Sketches of Missouri," [Hartford, CT] *New-England Weekly Review,* January 22, 1842.

72. See Daniel Dupre, "Barbecues and Pledges: Electioneering and the Rise of Democratic Politics in Antebellum Alabama," *Journal of Southern History* 60, no. 3 (August 1994): 479–512, esp. 484, 490, 496–97. For the fear of squatters making violent threats against rival bidders, see "Land Sales," *New Hampshire Sentinel,* August 13, 1835.

73. Alexander Keyssar, *The Right to Vote: The Contested History of Democracy in the United States* (New York: Basic Books, 2000), 26, 50–52; Marc W. Kruman, "The Second Party System and the Transformation of Revolutionary Republicanism," *Journal of the Early Republic* 12, no. 4 (Winter 1992): 509–37, esp. 517; Robert J. Steinfeld, "Property and Suffrage in the Early Republic," *Stanford Law Review* 41 (January 1989): 335–76, esp. 335, 363, 375; Thomas E. Jeffrey, "Beyond 'Free Suffrage': North Carolina Parties and the Convention Movement of the 1850s," *North Carolina Historical Review* 62, no. 4 (October 1985): 387–419, esp. 415–16; Fletcher M. Green, "Democracy in the Old South," *Journal of Southern History* 12, no. 1 (February 1946): 3–23.

74. For Jackson drafting restrictions, see "An Impartial and True History of the Life and Service of Major General Andrew Jackson," *New Orleans Argus,* February 8, 1828. On Florida, see Herbert J. Doherty Jr., "Andrew Jackson on Manhood Suffrage: 1822," *Tennessee Historical Quarterly* 15, no. 1 (March 1956): 57–60, esp. 60. Harold Syrett put it best: "Jackson did not once espouse a policy that was designed to aid the majority or to weaken the control of the minority over government"; see Harold C. Syrett, *Andrew Jackson, His Contribution to the American Tradition* (New York, 1953), 22. Liberia's universal suffrage lasted nine years, before new restrictions were imposed in 1848. The United States was not the first country to grant women the right to vote either; that honor went to New Zealand in 1893. Suffrage restrictions targeting blacks, women, and the poor continued until the Voting Rights Act of 1965, and even now the United States disenfranchises the poor. See Adam Przeworski, "Conquered or Granted? A History of Suffrage Extensions," *British Journal of Political Science* 39, no. 2 (April 2009): 291–321, esp. 291, 295–96, 314.

75. For the contrasting portraits of "country crackers" listening to a speech by George McDuffie, see *Augusta Chronicle and Georgia Advertiser,* August 18, 1827. Henry Clay was attacked for calling settlers "squatters," which meant a "term, denoting infamy of life or station"; see "Distinctive Features of Democracy—Outlines of Federal Whiggism—Conservative Peculiarities," *Arkansas State Gazette,* October 19, 1842.

76. For a story of President John Quincy Adams meeting a "backwoodsman," see "Letter to the Editor of the New-York Spectator," *Connecticut Courant,* January 27, 1826; and James Fenimore Cooper, *Notions of the Americans; Picked up by a Traveling Bachelor,* 2 vols. (London, 1828), 1:87.

77. Sarah Brown, "'The Arkansas Traveller': Southwest Humor on Canvas," *Arkansas Historical Quarterly* 40, no. 4 (Winter 1987): 348–75, esp. 349–50. For a similar perspective, in which poor Georgia crackers are entertained with barbecues but remain trapped in a life of destitution and ignorance, see "A Georgia Cracker," *Emancipator,* March 26, 1840.

Chapter Six: Pedigree and Poor White Trash:
Bad Blood, Half-Breeds, and Clay-Eaters

1. One of the earliest uses of "poor white trash" appeared in 1822 from George-town, DC. This was a report on a "very novel and whimsical trial [that] came on in our Circuit court on Thursday last, Nancy Swann a lady of color whose might powers of witchcraft have made de black niggers, and the poor white trash tremble"; see *Bangor* [ME] *Register*, August 1, 1822. In the earliest printed reference, the writer remarked that he had never heard "white trash" used in this way; see "From the Chronicle Anecdotes," [Shawnee] *Illinois Gazette*, June 23, 1821. The argument that poor whites were more miserable than slaves emerged in debates over the Missouri Compromise; see "Slavery in the New States," *Hallowell* [ME] *Gazette*, December 8, 1819. And for poor white laboring classes as "rude and uncultivated than slaves themselves," also see "Maryland," *Niles Weekly Register*, December 15, 1821. For a satirical piece in which a black man is horrified to hear that white trash are marrying into free black circles, see *Baltimore Patriot and Mercantile Advertiser*, April 12, 1831. For the description of poor white trash at the funeral of Andrew Jackson in Washington City, see *New York Herald*, June 30, 1845.

2. Emily P. Burke, *Reminiscences of Georgia* (Oberlin, OH, 1850), 205–6; "Sandhillers of South Carolina," *Christian Advocate and Journal*, August 1, 1851; "The Sandhillers of South Carolina," *Ohio Farmer*, January 1, 1857; "Clay for Food," *Ballou's Pictorial Drawing-Room Companion*, July 1, 1858; "Clay-eaters. From Miss Bremer's 'Homes of the New World,'" *Youth's Companion* (September 21, 1854): 88; "Poor Whites of the South," *Freedom's Champion*, April 11, 1863; "Poor Whites in North Carolina," *Freedom's Record*, November 1, 1865.

3. George M. Weston, *The Poor Whites of the South* (Washington, DC, 1856), 5; Eric Foner, *Free Soil, Free Labor, Free Men: The Ideology of the Republican Party Before the Civil War* (New York: Oxford University Press, 1970; rev. ed., 1995), 42, 46–47.

4. Daniel Hundley, *Social Relations in Our Southern States*, ed. William J. Cooper Jr. (1860; reprint ed., Baton Rouge: Louisiana State University Press, 1979), xv, 251, 254, 258.

5. Harriet Beecher Stowe, *Dred: A Tale of the Great Dismal Swamp*, ed. Robert S. Levine (1856; reprint ed., Chapel Hill: University of North Carolina Press, 2000), 106–7, 109, 190–91, 400; also see Allison L. Hurst, "Beyond the Pale: Poor Whites as Uncontrolled Contagion in Harriet Beechers Stowe's *Dred*," *Mississippi Quarterly* 63, no. 3–4 (Summer/Fall 2010): 635–53; and Hinton Rowan Helper, *The Impending Crisis of the South: How to Meet It*, ed. George M. Fredrickson (1857; reprint ed., Cambridge, MA: Belknap Press of Harvard University Press, 1968), ix, 32, 44–45, 48–49, 89, 110, 381. *The Impending Crisis* sold 13,000 copies in 1857; a new and enlarged version was published in 1860, and it sold over 100,000 copies, and Helper reported that it sold as many as 137,000 copies by May 1860. See David Brown, *Southern Outcast: Hinton Rowan Helper and "The Impending Crisis of the South"* (Baton Rouge: Louisiana State University Press, 2006), 1, 130, 148, 182.

6. The treaty with Mexico added 339 million acres, Oregon 181 million, and the Gadsden Purchase 78 million. On the war, see Thomas Hietala, *Manifest Design: American Exceptionalism and Empire,* rev. ed. (Ithaca, NY: Cornell University Press, 2003), 2, 10, 36, 40–42, 49, 52–53, 81–83, 200–201, 230–31, 251; Amy Greenberg, *A Wicked War: Clay, Polk, and Lincoln and the 1846 Invasion of Mexico* (New York: Knopf, 2012), 25, 55, 61–63, 67, 78–79, 84–85, 95, 100, 104, 259–61; Jesse S. Reeves, "The Treaty of Guadalupe-Hidalgo," *American Historical Review* 10, no. 2 (January 1905): 309–24; Jere W. Robinson, "The South and the Pacific Railroad, 1845–1855," *Western Historical Quarterly* 5, no. 2 (April 1974): 163–86.

7. On the increasing popularity of this ideology, see Reginald Horsman, *Race and Manifest Destiny: The Origins of American Racial Anglo-Saxonism* (Cambridge, MA: Harvard University Press, 1981), 183, 208–9, 224–28, 236–37. Franklin's theory still carried weight in the antebellum period. One writer claimed that the rate of increase doubles every twenty-three years, though what made the argument different from Franklin was the insistence that out of a population of seventeen million, "14,000,000 were of the Anglo-Saxon race." See "America," *Weekly Messenger* (December 7, 1842): 1502–3; also see "Progress of the Anglo-Saxon Race," *Literary World* (July 26, 1851): 72–73; and for Anglo-Saxons (United States and Great Britain) conquering the world by their population and their language, see "The Anglo-Saxon Race," *Christian Observer,* March 22, 1860.

8. "The Education of the Blood," *American Monthly Magazine* (January 1837): 1–7, esp. 4.

9. See "Spurious Pedigrees" and "American Blood," *American Turf Register and Sporting Magazine* (June 1830 and November 1836): 492–94 and 106–7; John Lewis, "Genealogical Tables of Blooded Stock," *Spirit of the Times: A Chronicle of the Turf, Agriculture, Field Sports, Literature and the* Stage (January 14, 1837): 380; and "From Our Armchair: The Races," *Southern Literary Journal and Magazine of Arts* (March 1837): 84–86.

10. Alexander Walker's book was republished in Philadelphia in 1853; also see "Intermarriage," *British and Foreign Medical Review or Quarterly Journal of Practical Medicine and Surgery* 7 (April 1839): 370–85. Orson Fowler echoed Jefferson, writing, "Farmers take extra pains to see that their sheep, calves, colts, and even pigs, should be raised from first rate stock, yet pay no manner of regard to the parentage of their prospective children." Fowler also divided the races, and he argued that both the Indian and African would naturally succumb to the superior Caucasian race. See Orson Squire Fowler, *Hereditary Descent: Its Laws and Facts Applied to Human Improvement* (New York, 1848), 36, 44, 66–69, 80, 92, 100, 125, 127, 135. For another example of this new advice literature, see Dr. John Porter, *Book of Men, Women, and Babies: The Laws of God Applied to Obtaining, Rearing, and Developing of Natural, Healthful, and Beautiful Humanity* (New York, 1855), 25, 28–29, 73, 79, 110, 193; also see "Remarks on Education," *American Phrenological Journal,* November 1, 1840; and for the same language of "attending to pedigree" used for cattle breeding, see "Essay upon Livestock," *Farmer's Register; a Monthly Magazine,* February 28, 1838; also see "Our

Anglo-Saxon Ancestry," *Philanthropist,* December 8, 1841; and for hereditary thinking in general, see Charles Rosenberg, *No Other Gods: On Science
and American Social Thought* (Baltimore: Johns Hopkins University Press,
1961), 28, 31–32, 34, 40, 42; also see Robyn Cooper, "Definition and Control:
Alexander Walker's Trilogy on Woman," *Journal of the History of Sexuality* 2,
no. 3 (January 1992): 341–64, esp. 343, 345, 347–48.

11. Lawrence published *Lecture on Physiology, Zoology, and the Natural History of Man* in 1819. On the different schools of thought to which Lawrence
and Nott belonged, see John Haller Jr., "The Species Problem: Nineteenth-
Century Concepts on Racial Inferiority in the Origins of Man Controversy,"
American Anthropologist 72 (1970): 1319–29. For Nott's argument on mulattoes as hybrids, and his insistence that the present-day "Anglo-Saxon and
negro races" are "distinct species," see J. C. Nott, "The Mulatto a Hybrid—
Probable Extermination of the Two Races If the Whites and Blacks Are
Allowed to Intermarry," *Boston Medical and Surgical Journal,* August 16,
1843; also see Reginald Horsman, *Josiah Nott of Mobile: Southerner, Physi-
cian, and Racial Theorist* (Baton Rouge: Louisiana State University Press,
1987).

12. See "Literary Notices," *Northern Light,* September 2, 1844; Horsman, "Scientific Racism and the American Indian at Mid-Century," *American Quarterly* 27, no. 2 (May 1975): 152–68.

13. "Inaugural Address 1836," in *First Congress—First Session. An Accurate
and Authentic Report of the Proceedings of the House of Representatives. From the 3d of October to the 23d of December,* by M. J. Favel (Columbia, TX, 1836), 67; Sam Houston to Antonio Santa Anna, March 21, 1842, in
Writings of Sam Houston, 1813–1863, eds. Amelia W. Williams and Eugene
C. Barker, 8 vols. (Austin, TX, 1938), 2:253; also see Charles Edward Lester,
Sam Houston and His Republic (New York, 1846), 103.

14. For Houston's inauguration ceremony and speech, see *First Congress—First
Session. An Accurate and Authentic Report of the Proceedings of the House
of Representatives,* 57, 65–69. There were negative reports of Houston as
a "base, and lost man," living in exile with Indians, until the Texas Revolution; see "General Houston," *Rural Repository,* July 16, 1836. Colonel Mirabeau Lamar, a former Georgia politician, was also praised in the press as "a
statesman, a poet, and a warrior," and the "beau ideal of Southern chivalry";
see "A Modern Hero of the Old School," *Spirit of the Times,* June 18, 1836.
Lamar called for "an exterminating war upon their warriors, which will admit
no compromise and have no termination except in their total extinction." He
had no intention of waiting until nature took its course. See Gary Clayton
Anderson, *The Conquest of Texas: Ethnic Cleansing in the Promised Land,
1820–1875* (Norman: University of Oklahoma Press, 2005), 174; also see
Mark M. Carroll, *Homesteads Ungovernable: Families, Sex, Race and the
Law in Frontier Texas, 1823–1860* (Austin: University of Texas Press, 2001),
23–24, 33–38, 43; Peggy Pascoe, *What Comes Naturally: Miscegenation
Law and the Making of Race in America* (New York: Oxford University Press,
2009), 18, 21.

15. On Gideon Lincecum, see Mark A. Largent, *Breeding Contempt: The History of Coerced Sterilization in the United States* (New Brunswick, NJ: Rutgers University Press, 2011), 11–12.

16. Carroll, *Homesteads Ungovernable,* 3–5, 11–13, 17–19.

17. Ibid., 42, 46. For the speeches of James Buchanan and Levi Woodbury, see appendix to *Congressional Globe,* Senate, 28th Congress, 1st Session, June 1844, 726, 771. Also see Horsman, *Race and Manifest Destiny,* 217. And for the mongrel notion that the "Spaniards grafted themselves on the conquered and debased aborigines, and the mongrel blood became dull and indolent," see Brantz Mayer, *Mexico as It Was and as It Is* (New York, 1844), 333.

18. William W. Freehling, *The Road to Disunion: Secessionists at Bay, 1776–1854* (New York: Oxford University Press), 419; Greenberg, *A Wicked War,* 69–70; Hietala, *Manifest Design,* 5, 26–34, 40–43, 50. For Benjamin Rush's theory, see chapter 5 of this book. For Robert Walker's speech on Texas annexation, see appendix to *Congressional Globe,* Senate, 28th Congress, 1st Session, June 1844, 557; Robert Walker, *Letter of Mr. Walker, of Mississippi, Relative to the Annexation of Texas* (Washington, DC, 1844), 14–15; Horsman, *Race and Manifest Destiny,* 215–17; and Stephen Hartnett, "Senator Robert Walker's 1844 Letter on Texas Annexation: The Rhetorical Logic of Imperialism," *American Studies* 38, no. 1 (Spring 1997): 27–54, esp. 32–33. For Nott's misuse of census data, see C. Loring Brace, "The 'Ethnology' of Josiah Clark Nott," *Journal of Urban Health* 50, no. 4 (April 1974): 509–28; and Albert Deutsch, "The First U.S. Census of the Insane (1840) and Its Use as Pro-Slavery Propaganda," *Bulletin of the History of Medicine* 15 (1944): 469–82.

19. Speech on Texas annexation by alexander Stephens, Appendix of *Congressional Globe,* 28th Congress, 2nd Session, House of Representatives, January 25, 1845, 313. Walker turned Texas into an organic body, with "veins and arteries," that had to be reunited with the United States to heal the wounds of a "mutilated state." See *Letter of Mr. Walker,* 9; Horsman, *Race and Manifest Destiny,* 218.

20. On marital annexations, see Nancy Isenberg, *Sex and Citizenship in Antebellum America* (Chapel Hill: University of North Carolina Press, 1998), 140; James M. McCaffrey, *Army of Manifest Destiny: The American Soldier in the Mexican War, 1846–1848* (New York: New York University Press, 1992), 200; and on Cave Johnson Couts, see Michael Magliari, "Free Soil, Unfree Labor: Cave Johnson Couts and the Binding of Indian Workers in California, 1850–1867," *Pacific Historical Review* 73, no. 3 (August 2004): 349–90, esp. 359, 363–65. On Polk's relationship with Couts, see Greenberg, *A Wicked War,* 69. The war unleashed a flood of racist propaganda; see Lota M. Spell, "The Anglo-Saxon Press in Mexico, 1846–1848," *American Historical Review* 38, no. 1 (October 1932): 20–31, esp. 28, 30.

21. On Texas riffraff, see Carroll, *Homesteads Ungovernable,* 4, 79, 84–86. For half-breeds and "mongrel dandyism," see Charles Winterfield, "Adventures on the Frontier of Texas and California: No. III," *The American Review; A Whig Journal of Politics, Literature, Art and Science* (November 1845): 504–17. Americans described the population of California as a "mongrel

race," a composite of the worst traits of the "arrogance of the Spanish and the laziness of Indians"; see "California in 1847 and Now," *Ballou's Pictorial Drawing-Room Companion,* February 6, 1858.

22. For Native Americans used as indentured servants, see Margliari, "Free Soil, Unfree Labor," 349–58. On using Indians as slave and servant labor, see "California—Its Position and Prospects," *United States Magazine and Democratic Review* (May 1849): 412–27. The same kinds of appeals were made to recruit marriageable women to Florida; see *New Bedford Mercury,* September 4, 1835. Novelist Eliza Farnham wrote promotional literature for recruiting women to California; see her *California, Indoor and Outdoor, How We Farm, Mine, and Live Generally in the Golden State* (New York, 1856); also see Nancy J. Taniguchi, "Weaving a Different World: Women and the California Gold Rush," *California History* 79, no. 2 (Summer 2000): 141–68, esp. 142–44, 148. For the French caricature, see *Le Charivari,* ca. 1850, Picture Collection, California State Library. On importing women to California ending spinsterhood, see "A Colloquial Chapter on Celibacy," *United States Magazine and Democratic Review* (December 1848): 533–42, esp. 537. On the sex ratio imbalance in California, claiming there were three hundred men to every woman, see "Letters from California: San Francisco," *Home Journal,* March 3, 1849.

23. See Sucheng Chan, "A People of Exceptional Character: Ethnic Diversity, Nativism, and Racism in the California Gold Rush," *California History* 79, no. 2 (Summer 2000): 44–85; Hinton Rowan Helper, *The Land of Gold: Reality Versus Fiction* (Baltimore, 1855), 264.

24. Helper, *Land of Gold,* 264; Brown, *Southern Outcast,* 25–26.

25. Helper, *Land of Gold,* 166, 214, 221–22, 268, 272–73, 275. Helper also used the old allusion to Indians disappearing like melting snow; see Laura M. Stevens, "The Christian Origins of the Vanishing Indian," in *Mortal Remains: Death in Early America,* eds. Nancy Isenberg and Andrew Burstein (Philadelphia: University of Pennsylvania Press, 2003), 17–30, esp. 18.

26. Helper, *Land of Gold,* 38–39, 47, 92, 94, 96, 111.

27. Ibid., 121–30. Helper's description of the defeated bull becomes a model for how he described defeated poor whites in the southern states. He wrote that in the South the free white laborer is "treated as if he was a loathsome beast, and shunned with utmost disdain . . . he is accounted as nobody, and would be deemed presumptuous, if he dared open his mouth, even so wide to give faint utterance to a three-lettered monosyllable, like yea or nay, in the presence of the august knight of the whip and the lash"; see *The Impending Crisis,* 41.

28. Helper, *Land of Gold,* 150, 152–60, 180–82, 185; Helper, *The Impending Crisis,* 42, 49, 89, 102–3, 101–11.

29. Foner, *Free Soil, Free Labor, Free Men,* 166; Richard H. Sewell, *A House Divided: Sectionalism and Civil War, 1848–1865* (Baltimore: Johns Hopkins University Press, 1988), 52–55; also see John Bigelow, *Memoir of the Life and Public Services of John Charles Fremont* (New York, 1856), 50–53.

30. On poor whites as refugees and exiles, see "Slavery and the Poor White Man," *Philanthropist,* May 31, 1843. On slavery depopulating the earth of her white inhabitants, and creating a class and political hierarchy in the South between the slaveowners and the "vassels to slaveowners," see "Slavery and the Poor

White Men of Virginia," *National Era,* January 11, 1849. On "land-sharks," see Helper, *The Impending Crisis,* 151.

31. On David Wilmot, see Foner, *Free Soil, Free Labor, Free Men,* 60, 116; Jonathan H. Earle, *Jacksonian Antislavery and the Politics of Free Soil, 1824–1854* (Chapel Hill: University of North Carolina Press, 2004), 1–3, 27–37, 123–39; also see "Slavery," *Workingman's Advocate,* June 22, 1844; and "Progress Towards Free Soil," and "The Homestead," *Young America,* January 17, February 21, 1846. On the defeat of the Homestead Bill of 1854, see Gerald Wolff, "The Slavocracy and the Homestead Problem of 1854," *Agricultural History* 40, no. 2 (April 1966): 101–12.

32. See report of speech in "Slavery in Kentucky," *Philanthropist,* May 5, 1841. Wilmot privately used the arguments of blood to attack the southern white slaveholder, claiming that "men born and nursed by white women are not going to be ruled by men who were brought up on the milk of some damn Negro wench!" In the theory of the time, as stated earlier, the quality of bloodlines was passed through a mother's milk. For the Wilmot quote, see Earle, *Jacksonian Antislavery,* 131.

33. On Frémont's acceptance speech, see Bigelow, *Memoir of the Life and Public Services of John Charles Fremont,* 458; also see "America vs. America," *Liberator,* July 22, 1842; and Helper, *The Impending Crisis,* 42, 121, 149, 376.

34. Helper, *The Impending Crisis,* 67–72, 90–91; Weston, *The Poor Whites of the South;* and on how southerners used the agricultural address to lament southern decline, see Drew Gilpin Faust, "The Rhetoric and Ritual of Agriculture in Antebellum South Carolina," *Journal of Southern History* 45, no. 4 (November 1979): 541–68.

35. For the description of "Hard-scratch," see Warren Burton, *White Slavery: A New Emancipation Cause Presented to the United States* (Worcester, MA, 1839), 168–69; and Henry David Thoreau, "Slavery in Massachusetts," in *Reform Papers,* ed. Wendell Glick (Princeton, NJ: Princeton University Press, 1973), 109; and for a discussion of this point, see Jennifer Rae Greeson, *Our South: Geographic Fantasy and the Rise of National Literature* (Cambridge, MA: Harvard University Press, 2010), 207.

36. Stowe, *Dred,* 105–6, 190–93.

37. Jeff Forret, *Race Relations at the Margins: Slaves and Poor Whites in the Antebellum Southern Countryside* (Baton Rouge: Louisiana State University Press, 2006), 112; Timothy James Lockley, *Lines in the Sand: Race and Class in Lowcountry Georgia, 1750–1860* (Athens: University of Georgia Press, 2001), 115, 129, 164.

38. Forret, *Race Relations at the Margins,* 29, 97, 105, 112; and for Gregg's speech, see Helper, *The Impending Crisis,* 377; also see Tom Downey, "Riparian Rights and Manufacturing in Antebellum South Carolina: William Gregg and the Origins of the 'Industrial Mind,'" *Journal of Southern History* 65, no. 1 (February 1999): 77–108, esp. 95; and Thomas P. Martin, "The Advent of William Gregg and the Grantville Company," *Journal of Southern History* 11, no. 3 (August 1945): 389–423.

39. On New Orleans laborers and poor white men and women in the fields, see Helper, *The Impending Crisis,* 299–301; also see Seth Rockman, *Scraping*

By: Wage Labor, Slavery, and Survival in Early Baltimore (Baltimore: Johns Hopkins University Press, 2009).

40. On the class barriers to social mobility among poor whites, see Charles C. Bolton, *Poor Whites of the Antebellum South: Tenants and Laborers in Central North Carolina and Northeast Mississippi* (Durham, NC: Duke University Press, 1994), 14, 25, 27–29, 53, 67, 69, 94; and Stephen A. West, *From Yeoman to Redneck in the South Carolina Upcountry, 1850–1915* (Charlottesville: University of Virginia Press, 2008), 28–39, 43–44. On the declining opportunities for nonslaveholding whites, see Gavin Wright, *The Political Economy of the Cotton South: Households, Markets, and Wealth in the Nineteenth Century* (New York: Norton, 1978), 24–42.

41. Stowe, *Dred*, 27, 37, 109, 194.

42. See William Cooper's introduction in Hundley, *Social Relations in Our Southern States*, xv–xx.

43. Hundley, *Social Relations in Our Southern States*, xxxii–xxxiii, 27–29, 31, 34–36, 40–41, 43–44, 60, 70–71, 82, 91, 198, 226, 239, 251, 255–57.

44. Stowe, *Dred*, 81, 83, 86–87, 89–90, 99, 107–9, 190–94, 400, 543, 549.

45. "Curious Race in Georgia," *Scientific American*, July 31, 1847. Emily Pillsbury of New Hampshire took a teaching position at the Savannah Female Orphan Asylum in 1840 and stayed in the South for nine years. She married the Reverend A. B. Burke while there, but he died and she left for Ohio. See Burke, *Reminiscences of Georgia*, 206. For the "abnormal classes in the slave states," also see "Selections: Manifest Destiny of the American Union," *Liberator*, October 30, 1857 (reprinted from the English publication the *Westminster Review*).

46. On white trash women as a wretched specimen of maternity, see "Up the Mississippi," *Putnam's Monthly Magazine of American Literature, Science, and Art* (October 1857): 433–56, esp. 456. On their strange complexion and hair, see Burke, *Reminiscences of Georgia*, 206; "Sandhillers of South Carolina," *Christian Advocate and Journal*, August 7, 1851; "The Sandhillers of South Carolina," *Ohio Farmer*, January 31, 1857; "Clay-Eaters," *Ballou's Pictorial Drawing-Room Companion*, July 31, 1858. On clay-eating infants, see "The Poor Whites of the South," *Freedom's Champion*, April 11, 1863; and Hundley, *Social Relations in Our Southern States*, 264–65.

47. Isabella D. Martin and Myrta Lockett Avary, eds., *A Diary from Dixie, as Written by Mary Boykin Chesnut* (New York, 1905), 400–401.

48. Hammond also claimed that mulattoes existed primarily in the cities and resulted from sex between northerners/foreigners and blacks. He called them "mongrels." On Hammond, see Drew Gilpin Faust, *James Henry Hammond and the Old South: A Design for Mastery* (Baton Rouge: Louisiana State University Press, 1982), 278–82; and James H. Hammond, *Two Letters on Slavery in the United States, Addressed to Thomas Clarkson, Esq.* (Columbia, SC, 1845), 10–11, 17, 26, 28. On others in the proslavery intelligentsia, see Drew Gilpin Faust, "A Southern Stewardship: The Intellectual and Proslavery Argument," *American Quarterly* 31, no. 1 (Spring 1979): 63–80, esp. 67, 73–74; and Laurence Shore, *Southern Capitalists: Politics and Ideology in*

Antebellum South Carolina (Chapel Hill: University of North Carolina Press, 2000), 43.

49. On Tucker, see Faust, "A Southern Stewardship," 74. On the *Richmond Enquirer,* see "White Slavery—The Privileged Class," *National Era,* January 24, 1856. And on the Republican reaction to this conservative southern defense of slavery, see "Charles Sumner's Speech," *Ohio State Journal,* June 19, 1860. Also see Hundley, *Social Relations in Our Southern States,* 272. Peter Kolchin has argued that proslavery defenders turned to defending servitude without regard to complexion; see Kolchin, "In Defense of Servitude: Proslavery and Russian Pro-Serfdom Arguments, 1760–1860," *American Historical Review* 85, no. 4 (October 1980): 809–27, esp. 814–17.

50. The decision was issued on March 6, 1857. Justice Taney insisted that the Declaration of Independence did not refer to slaves or descendants of the African race. He argued that there was no distinction between the slave and free black or mulatto, and that a "stigma" and "deepest degradation" was forever applied to the whole race. This "impassable barrier" was in place by the time of the Revolution and the federal Constitutional Convention. He further insisted that the black race was set apart by "indelible marks." He upheld the idea that Dred Scott was a "Negro of African descent; his ancestors were of pure African blood." See *Scott v. Sandford,* 19 How. 393 (U.S., 1856), 396–97, 403, 405–7, 409–10, 419. On the importance of pedigree, see James H. Kettner, *The Development of American Citizenship, 1608–1870* (Chapel Hill: University of North Carolina Press, 1978), 326, 328. Taney had rejected the authority of the Northwest Ordinance in an earlier 1851 decision, which he then used in the *Dred Scott* decision; see William Wiecek, "Slavery and Abolition Before the Supreme Court," *Journal of American History* 65, no. 1 (June 1978): 34–58, esp. 54, 56. Taney was able to insist that there was no difference between slaves and free blacks because he placed all the descendants of the entire race into one single category—again proving the importance of pedigree. Also see Dan E. Fehrenbacher, *Slavery, Law, and Politics: The Dred Scott Case in Historical Perspective* (New York: Oxford University Press, 1981), 187–98.

Chapter Seven: Cowards, Poltroons, and Mudsills: Civil War as Class Warfare

1. See the account of the arrival and speech of President Jefferson Davis in Montgomery, Alabama, in the *Charleston* [SC] *Mercury,* February 19, 1861, in *Jefferson Davis, Constitutionalist: His Letters, Papers and Speeches,* ed. Dunbar Rowland, 10 vols. (Jackson: Mississippi Department of Archives and History, 1923), 5:47–48.

2. Thomas Jefferson saw national unity as rooted in shared cultural values and national stocks. He wrote that too many immigrants would turn America into a "heterogeneous, incoherent, distracted mass." He wished for the U.S. government to be "more homogeneous, more peaceable, more durable" by limiting immigrants. See Jefferson, *Notes on the State of Virginia,* 84–85.

Others used the "one flesh trope," such as the writer who argued that all the southern slave states were metaphorically married and "no Yankee shall put asunder"; see *Richmond Examiner,* October 19, 1861.

3. Davis used "degenerate sons" in four speeches and "degenerate descendants" in another. For his February 18, 1861, speech, see Rowland, ed., *Jefferson Davis,* 5:48; for other references, see ibid., 4:545; 5:4, 391; 6:573.

4. For Davis's speech of December 26, 1862, see "Jeff Davis on the War: His Speech Before the Mississippi Legislature," *New York Times,* January 14, 1863.

5. See "Speech of Jefferson Davis at Richmond" (taken from the *Richmond Daily Enquirer,* January 7, 1863), Rowland, *Jefferson Davis,* 5:391–93.

6. On the importance of demonizing the enemy, see Jason Phillips, *Diehard Rebels: The Confederate Culture of Invincibility* (Athens: University of Georgia Press, 2007), 40–41.

7. On masking divisions within the Confederacy, see Paul Escott, *After Secession: Jefferson Davis and the Failure of Confederate Nationalism* (Baton Rouge: Louisiana State University Press, 1978); and George C. Rable, *The Confederate Republic: A Revolution Against Politics* (Chapel Hill: University of North Carolina Press, 1994), 27; Michael P. Johnson, *Toward a Patriarchal Republic: The Secession of Georgia* (Baton Rouge: Louisiana State University Press, 1977), 41. On southerners fighting for the Union, see William W. Freehling, *The South vs. the South: How Anti-Confederates Shaped the Course of the Civil War* (New York: Oxford University Press, 2001), xiii. On class strife, see David Williams, *Rich Man's War: Class, Caste, and Confederate Defeat in the Lower Chattahoochee Valley* (Athens: University of Georgia Press, 1998); and Wayne K. Durrill, *War of Another Kind: Southern Community in Great Rebellion* (New York: Oxford University Press, 1990). And on dissent in the South during the war, see Victoria E. Bynum, *The Long Shadow of the Civil War: Southern Dissent and Its Legacies* (Chapel Hill: University of North Carolina Press, 2010); and Daniel E. Sutherland, ed., *Guerrillas, Unionists, and Violence on the Confederate Homefront* (Fayetteville: University of Arkansas Press, 1999).

8. The *New York Herald* reprinted the quote and claimed that the article came from the *Muskogee Herald* in Alabama. The *New York Herald* writer complained that this was one of many attacks that could be found in numerous southern newspapers in Virginia, Mississippi, Louisiana, South Carolina, and Alabama. See "Ridiculous Attacks of the South upon the North, and Vice Versa," *New York Herald,* September 16, 1856.

9. For the banner of "greasy mechanic," see "Great Torchlight Procession! Immense Demonstrations," *Boston Daily Atlas,* October 1856.

10. Speech of Jefferson Davis at Aberdeen, Mississippi, May 26, 1851, in Rowland, *Jefferson Davis,* 2:73–74. He made a similar argument in a speech before the Mississippi legislature, November 16, 1858; see ibid., 3:357. This idea was widely used in the South by ruling elites to reaffirm the allegiance of poor whites; see Williams, *Rich Man's War,* 28; and William J. Harris, *Plain Folk and Gentry in a Slave Society: White Liberty and Black Slavery in Augusta's Hinterlands* (Middletown, CT: Wesleyan University Press, 1985), 75.

11. "Offscourings," which can be traced back to English insults aimed at vagrants, was a vicious slur. It meant fecal waste—dispelling the worst remains from the lining of the intestines. On urban roughs and the Union army, see Lorien Foote, *The Gentlemen and the Roughs: Violence, Honor, and Manhood in the Union Army* (New York: New York University Press, 2010). On immigrants, see Tyler Anbinder, "Which Poor Man's Fight? Immigrants and Federal Conscription of 1863," *Civil War History* 52, no. 4 (December, 2006): 344–72. On Union men as worse than "Goths and Vandals," see "The Character of the Coming Campaign," *New York Herald,* April 28, 1861. The Confederacy refused to recognize black soldiers as soldiers, or as prisoners of war, and promised death to any Union officer commanding such troops; see Dudley Taylor Cornish, *The Sable Arm: Black Troops in the Union Army, 1861–1865* (1956; reprint ed., Lawrence: University Press of Kansas, 1987), 158–63, 178.

12. James Hammond, Speech to the U.S. Senate, March 4, 1858, *Congressional Globe*, 35th Congress, 1st Session, Appendix, 71; also see Faust, *James Henry Hammond and the Old South,* 374.

13. Hammond, Speech to the U.S. Senate, 74. The equation of the Republican Party (and its philosophy) with a socialist revolution was common among southern writers; see Harris, *Plain Folk and Gentry,* 138; and Manisha Sinha, *The Counter-Revolution of Slavery: Politics and Ideology in Antebellum South Carolina* (Chapel Hill: University of North Carolina Press, 2000), 191, 223–29.

14. For "Red Republicans," see "The War upon Society—Socialism," *De Bow's Review* (June 1857): 633–44. On black Republicans making slaves the equals of poor whites, see Williams, *Rich Man's War,* 47; also see Arthur Cole, "Lincoln's Election an Immediate Menace to Slavery in the States?," *American Historical Review* 36, no. 4 (July 1931): 740–67, esp. 743, 745, 747. For the threat of amalgamation, see George M. Fredrickson, "A Man but Not a Brother: Abraham Lincoln and Racial Equality," *Journal of Southern History* 41, no. 1 (February 1975): 39–58, esp. 54. And for race-mixing charges during Lincoln's reelection campaign, see Elise Lemire, *"Miscegenation": Making Race in America* (Philadelphia: University of Pennsylvania Press, 2002), 115–23.

15. Alexander Stephens, "Slavery the Cornerstone of the Confederacy," speech given in Savannah, March 21, 1861, in *Great Debates in American History: States Rights (1798–1861); Slavery (1858–1861),* ed. Marion Mills Miller, 14 vols. (New York, 1913), 5:287, 290.

16. For Wigfall's remarks, see "Proceedings of the Confederate Congress," *Southern Historical Society Papers* (Richmond, VA, 1959), 52:323. For the bootblack reference, see "Latest from the South," [New Orleans] *Daily Picayune,* February 15, 1865. For class components of his speech, see "The Spring Campaign—Davis' Last Dodge," *New York Daily Herald,* February 9, 1865. Also see Edward S. Cooper, *Louis Trezevant Wigfall: The Disintegration of the Union and the Collapse of the Confederacy* (Lanham, MD: Fairleigh Dickinson University Press, 2012), 137–40.

17. Williams, *Rich Man's War,* 184. On conscription, see Albert Burton Moore, *Conscription and Conflict in the Confederacy* (New York, 1924), 14–18, 34, 38, 49, 53, 67, 70–71, 308. On desertion and the unequal burden of military

service, see Scott King-Owen, "Conditional Confederates: Absenteeism Among Western North Carolina Soldiers, 1861–1865," *Civil War History* 57 (2011): 349–79, esp. 377; Rable, *The Confederate Republic*, 294; and Jaime Amanda Martinez, "For the Defense of the State: Slave Impressment in Confederate Virginia and North Carolina" (Ph.D. dissertation, University of Virginia, 2008). Some Georgians thought that arming slaves would dispel the cries of "rich man's war and poor man's fight" and convince white deserters to rejoin the Confederate ranks; see Philip D. Dillard, "The Confederate Debate over Arming Slaves: View from Macon and Augusta Newspapers," *Georgia Historical Quarterly* 79, no. 1 (Spring 1995): 117–46, esp. 145.

18. On the attitudes and policy of Union generals, see Mark Grimsley, *The Hard Hand of War: Union Military Policy Toward Southern Civilians, 1861–1865* (New York: Cambridge University Press, 1995); and *Ulysses S. Grant: Memoirs and Selected Letters* (New York: Library of America, 1990), 148–49. Grant used the same five-to-one reference in a letter written during the war. He also voiced a similar view amid the war that the "war could be ended at once if the whole Southern people could express their unbiased feeling untrammeled by leaders." See Grant to Jesse Root Grant, August 3, 1861, and Grant to Julia Dent Grant, June 12, 1862, in ibid., 972, 1009. On Hinton Rowan Helper, *Land of Gold* (1855), see chapter 6 of this book.

19. *The Irrepressible Conflict. A Speech by William H. Seward, Delivered at Rochester, Monday, Oct 25, 1858* (New York, 1858), 1–2.

20. See "The Destinies of the South: Message of His Excellency, John H. Means, Esq., Government of the State of South-Carolina, . . . November 1852," *Southern Quarterly Review* (January 1853): 178–205, esp. 198; also see James Hammond, *Governor Hammond's Letters on Southern Slavery: Addressed to Thomas Clarkson, the English Abolitionist* (Charleston, SC, 1845), 21; Jefferson Davis, "Confederate State of America—Message to Congress, April 29, 1861," in *A Compilation of the Messages and Papers of the Confederacy*, ed. James D. Richardson, 2 vols. (Nashville: United States Publishing Co., 1906), 1:68; and Christa Dierksheide and Peter S. Onuf, "Slaveholding Nation, Slaveholding Civilization," in *In the Cause of Liberty: How the Civil War Redefined American Ideals*, eds. William J. Cooper Jr. and John M. McCardell Jr. (Baton Rouge: Louisiana State University Press, 2009): 9–24, esp. 9, 22–23.

21. "The Union: Its Benefits and Dangers," *Southern Literary Messenger* (January 1, 1861): 1–4, esp. 4; and "The African Slave Trade," *Southern Literary Messenger* (August 1861): 105–13; also see Rable, *The Confederate Republic*, 55. On the reaction to Helper's book, see Brown, *Southern Outcast;* and Williams, *Rich Man's War*, 31–32.

22. See *Memoir on Slavery, Read Before the Society for the Advancement of Learning, of South Carolina, at Its Annual Meeting at Columbia. 1837. By Chancellor Harper* (Charleston, SC, 1838), 23–24. On lower literacy rates and fewer opportunities for the poor to receive a common school education in the South, see Carl Kaestle, *Pillars of the Republic: Common Schooling and American Society, 1780–1860* (New York, 1893), 195, 206; James M. McPherson, *Drawn with the Sword: Reflections on the American Civil War* (New

York: Oxford University Press, 1996), 19. Estimates on illiteracy vary widely. McPherson chose the lower number of a three-to-one margin in illiteracy rates between slave and northern states. Wayne Flynt noted that the 1850 federal census announced that illiteracy rates among whites were 20.3 percent in the slave states, 3 percent in the middle states, and .42 percent in New England. That makes it over 40:1 with New England and 7:1 for the middle states. See Wayne Flynt, *Dixie's Forgotten People: The South's Poor Whites* (Bloomington: Indiana University Press, 1979), 8. On the call for a Confederate publishing trade, see Michael T. Bernath, *Confederate Minds: The Struggle for Intellectual Independence in the Civil War South* (Chapel Hill: University of North Carolina Press, 2013).

23. See "The Differences of Race Between the Northern and Southern People," *Southern Literary Messenger* (June 1, 1860): 401–9, esp. 403. On patrician rule in the South, see Frank Alfriend, "A Southern Republic and Northern Democracy," *Southern Literary Messenger* (May 1, 1863): 283–90. On tempting the poor, see "Message of Gov. Joseph E. Brown," November 7, 1860, in *The Confederate Records of Georgia,* ed. Allen D. Candler, 5 vols. (Atlanta, 1909–11), 1:47; William W. Freehling and Craig M. Simpson, *Secession Debated: Georgia Showdown in 1860* (New York: Oxford University Press, 1992); Bernard E. Powers Jr., "'The Worst of All Barbarism': Racial Anxiety and the Approach of Secession in the Palmetto State," *South Carolina Historical Magazine* 112, no. 3/4 (July–October 2011): 139–56, esp. 151; Harris, *Plain Folk and Gentry,* 134. And on vigilante societies and "Minute Men" companies, see West, *From Yeoman to Redneck,* 68–69, 76–81, 84, 91–92. Northern observers in the southern states wrote that many poor whites opposed secession but felt "forced to maintain silence." See "The Poor Whites at the South—Letter from a Milwaukee Man in Florida," *Milwaukee Daily Sentinel,* April 15, 1861. Alfriend repeated the same argument as Governor Brown, that the Lincoln administration would win over the poor whites by "all the glozing arts at the command of himself and his adroit advisers, he will flatter the vanity and pamper the grasping and indolent propensities of the people for federal bounties and cheap lands," and that the Republican message will peculate down to the "lower strata of Southern society." He also predicted that what awaited the South was either a war of conquest or a class war: "If not conquest, it will be civil war, not between the North and South, but between the slaveholder and the non-slaveholder backed by the North." See "Editor's Table," *Southern Literary Messenger* (December 1, 1860): 468–74, esp 472.

24. James D. B. De Bow was a South Carolinian who relocated to New Orleans to publish his own periodical. At first titled the *Commercial Review of the South and West,* it later became *De Bow's Review.* Although early in his career he advocated public education and industrialization in the South, he fully embraced the secessionist rhetoric that "cotton is King" and slavery was the major source of the South's superiority. De Bow published *The Interest in Slavery of the Southern Non-Slaveholder* as a pamphlet in 1860, and then republished the piece as articles in the *Charleston Mercury* and *De Bow's Review.* See James De Bow, "The Non-Slaveholders of the South: Their

Interest in the Present Sectional Controversy Identical with That of Slave-holders," *De Bow's Review*, vol. 30 (January 1861): 67–77; Eric H. Walther, "Ploughshares Come Before Philosophy: James D. B. De Bow," in *The Fire-Eaters* (Baton Rouge: Louisiana State University Press, 1992), 195–227; and Sinha, *The Counter-Revolution of Slavery*, 234. Governor Joseph Brown of Georgia made a similar appeal to poor whites; he praised the high wages in the South, and warned that if slavery was eliminated poor whites would lose legal and social status and slaves would plunder those living in the mountain-ous region of the state—a region known for a high proportion of poorer non-slaveholders. Elite secessionists praised his appeal and felt it was "well calculated to arouse them" to the cause of secession and would fortify their minds against all appeals that might "array the poor against the wealthy." See Johnson, *Toward a Patriarchal Republic*, 49–51.

25. Rable, *The Confederate Republic*, 32–35, 40–42, 50–51, 60–61; Johnson, *Toward a Patriarchal Republic*, 63–65, 110, 117–23, 153, 156; William C. Davis, *Jefferson Davis: The Man and His Hour* (Baton Rouge: Louisiana State University Press, 1991), 308; Stephanie McCurry, *Confederate Reckoning: Power and Politics in the Civil War South* (Cambridge, MA: Harvard University Press, 2010), 51, 55, 63, 75, 81; and G. Edward White, "Recovering the Legal History of the Confederacy," *Washington and Lee Legal Review* 68 (2011): 467–554, esp. 483. The *Southern Literary Messenger* felt that consti-tutional reform should restrict the franchise from "classes incapable of exer-cising it judicially," thus freeing the Confederate government from the "mercy of lawless and untutored majorities"; see "Editor's Table," 470; also see Richard O. Curry, "A Reappraisal of Statehood Politics in West Virginia," *Journal of Southern History* 28, no. 4 (November 1962): 403–21, esp. 405. And on Unionists in East Tennessee and their fear of secessionists imposing an elitist government, see Noel L. Fisher, "Definitions of Victory: East Tennessee Unionists in the Civil War and Reconstruction," in Sutherland, ed., *Guerrillas, Unionists, and Violence on the Confederate Homefront* (Fayetteville: University of Arkansas Press, 1999), 89–111, esp. 93–94.

26. Simms feared that the border states would promote manufacturing and thus increase the poor white population. See William Gilmore Simms to William Porcher Miles, February 20, 24, 1861, in *The Letters of William Gilmore Simms*, eds. Mary C. Simms Oliphant, Alfred Taylor Oldell, and T. C. Dun-can Miles, 5 vols. (Columbia: University of South Carolina Press, 1952–56), 4:330, 335; Alfriend, "A Southern Republic and Northern Democracy"; also see "The Poor Whites to Be Dis-Enfranchised in the Southern Confederacy," *Cleveland Daily Herald*, February 2, 1861. The editor of the *Southern Confederacy*, T. S. Gordon of Florida, defended not only the rejection of Jeffer-son's notions of the rights of man, but the idea that his generation had the right to "think for themselves" and disregard the "opinions of their forefa-thers"; see a reprint of Gordon's article in "Bold Vindication of Slavery," *Liberator*, March 22, 1861; and Rable, *The Confederate Republic*, 50, 55–56.

27. For the slaveowners' House of Lords, see Augusta *Chronicle and Sentinel*, February 9, 1861. While Ruffin called the masses the "swinish multitude," Georgia conservatives called them the mob or "domestic foes"; see William

Kauffman Scarborough, ed., *The Diary of Edmund Ruffin*, 3 vols. (Baton Rouge: Louisiana State University Press, 1972–89), 2:167–71, 176, 542; Rable, *The Confederate Republic*, 42; Johnson, *Toward a Patriarchal Republic*, 101, 130–31, 143, 178–79, 184; McCurry, *Confederate Reckoning*, 43; see reprint and discussion of editorial published in the *Charleston* [SC] *Mercury* in "Seceding from Secession," *New York Times*, February 25, 1861. For another example of secessionists viewing the three-fifths compromise as a usurpation of southern rights, see "National Characters—The Issues of the Day," *De Bow's Review* (January 1861); on race as a "title of nobility," see "Department of Miscellany . . . The Non-Slaveholder of the South," *De Bow's Review* (January 1, 1861).

28. "The Southern Civilization; or, the Norman in America," *De Bow's Review* (January/February 1862).

29. See John F. Reiger, "Deprivation, Disaffection, and Desertion in Confederate Florida," *Florida Historical Quarterly* 48, no. 3 (January 1970): 279–98, esp. 286–87; Escott, *After Secession*, 115, 119; Reid Mitchell, *Civil War Soldiers* (New York: Viking, 1988), 160; "The Conscription Bill. Its Beauty," *Southern Literary Messenger* (May 1, 1862): 328; and Harris, *Plain Folk and Gentry*, 153. On using the slur "Tartar," see James D. Davidson to Greenlee Davidson, February 12, 1861, in Bruce S. Greenawalt, "Life Behind Confederate Lines in Virginia: The Correspondence of James D. Davidson," *Civil War History* 16, no. 3 (September 1970): 205–26, esp. 218; also see Williams, *Rich Man's War*, 122; Bessie Martin, *Desertion of Alabama Troops in the Confederate Army: A Study in Sectionalism* (New York: Columbia University Press, 1932), 122.

30. On the twenty-slave exemption, see Williams, *Rich Man's War*, 132; Escott, *After Secession*, 95; also see King-Owen, "Conditional Confederates," 351, 359, 377–78. James Phelan measured patriotism in class terms: he wrote that the "pride of intellect, position, and education will only acutely feel its necessity and spring with alacrity to the post of such danger and sacrifice." The poor white farmers lacked those qualities. See James Phelan to Jefferson Davis, May 23, 1861, in *The War of Rebellion: A Compilation of the Official Records of the Union and Confederate Armies*, 130 vols. (Washington, DC: Government Printing Office, 1880–1901), Series IV, 1:353, also see Escott, *After Secession*, 115; Rable, *The Confederate Republic*, 156, 190–91; Harris, *Plain Folk and Gentry*, 64; Jack Lawrence Atkins, "'It Is Useless to Conceal the Truth Any Longer': Desertion of Virginia Soldiers from the Confederate Army" (M.A. thesis, Virginia Polytechnic Institute, 2007), 41–42.

31. Class-conscious men felt that honor and service displayed that they were the "right breed of people"; see Lee L. Dupont to his wife, February 27, 186[1 or 2], Dupont Letters, Lowndes-Valdosta Historical Society, as quoted in David Carlson, "The 'Loanly Runagee': Draft Evaders in Confederate South Georgia," *Georgia Historical Quarterly* 84, no. 4 (Winter 2000): 589–615, esp. 597. William Holden, the editor of the *Raleigh Weekly Standard* in North Carolina, became a vociferous critic of conscription. He wrote, "We are not willing to see any one white child starve to death on account of this war, while the negroes are fat and sleek." See *Raleigh Weekly Standard*, July 1, 1863, as

quoted in Rable, *The Confederate Republic*, 190–91. On "dog catchers," see John Beauchamp Jones, *A Rebel Clerk's Diary at the Confederate Capital*, 2 vols. (Philadelphia, 1866), 2:317; also see an editorial from the *Richmond Whig*, reprinted in "The Rebel Army and the Rebel Government," *Philadelphia Inquirer*, January 24, 1862.

32. Robert E. Lee to President Jefferson Davis, August, 17, 1863, in *The Wartime Papers of Robert E. Lee* (Boston: Little, Brown, 1961), 591; also see Atkins, "Desertion among Virginia Soldiers," 47–48; Harris, *Plain Folk and Gentry*, 179–80. North Carolina's desertion rates may have been closer to Virginia's numbers, but it is extremely difficult to get an accurate estimate; see Richard Reid, "A Test Case of the 'Crying Evil': Desertion Among North Carolina Troops During the Civil War," *North Carolina Historical Review* 58, no. 3 (July 1981): 234–62, esp. 234, 237–38, 247, 251, 253, 254–55. For retaliation against Confederates who joined the Union, see Lesley J. Gordon, "'In Time of War': Unionists Hanged in Kinston, North Carolina, February 1864," in Sutherland, *Guerrillas, Unionists, and Violence*, 45–58; Bynum, *The Long Shadow of the Civil War*, 28, 43–46; see Victoria E. Bynum, *The Free State of Jones: Mississippi's Longest Civil War* (Chapel Hill: University of North Carolina Press, 2001).

33. On Georgia deserters and the defiant wives of renegades, see Carlson, "The 'Loanly Runagee,'" 600, 610–13; and Harris, *Plain Folk and Gentry*, 180–81.

34. For the joke, see *Houston Tri-Weekly Telegraph*, December 23, 1864. Drawing on the work of James Scott, *Weapons of the Weak: Everyday Forms of Resistance* (1985), Katherine Guiffre points out that powerless groups often engage in everyday acts of rebellion—gossiping, malingering, petty theft—instead of extreme acts, such as fomenting a large-scale uprising; see Katherine A. Guiffre, "First in Flight: Desertion as Politics in the North Carolina Confederate Army," *Social Science History* 21, no. 2 (Summer 1997): 245–63, esp. 249–50, 260. I argue that jokes served a similar purpose, making light of what the ruling elite saw as acts of treason, cowardice, or mutiny.

35. Historians debate the estimates of men who served in the Confederate army. For the most recent estimates, see McCurry, *Confederate Reckoning*, 152. On desertion, see Mark A. Weitz, *More Damning Than Slaughter: Desertion in the Confederate Army* (Lincoln: University of Nebraska Press, 2005); and Reid, "A Test Case of the 'Crying Evil,'" 234, 247. For the best study on the problem of disaffection among conscripts, substitutes, and those who enlisted late in the war (two groups often ignored in studies of Confederate soldiers' motivation), see Kenneth W. Noe, *Reluctant Rebels: The Confederates Who Joined the Army After 1860* (Chapel Hill: University of North Carolina Press, 2010), 2, 7, 88–89, 94–95, 108, 113–14, 178, 190. As Noe notes, conscripts and substitutes, the men most likely to be disaffected, are also the two cohorts about whom historians have the least knowledge of their personal feelings. It is difficult to track down the correspondence of these men. Class also determines who was literate enough to write—so historians who rely on personal letters inevitably reflect a class bias. For the lower-class origins of substitutes and the difficulty identifying them, also see John Sacher, "The Loyal Draft Dodger? A Reexamination of Confederate Substitution," *Civil War History*

57, no. 2 (June 2011): 153–78, esp. 170–73. For another example of festering resentment, Sergeant William Andrews of the First Georgia Volunteers wrote after Lee's surrender, "While it is a bitter pill to have to come back into the Union, don't think there is much regret at the loss of the Confederacy. The treatment that the soldiers have received from the government in various ways put them against it." See David Williams, Teresa Crisp Williams, and David Carlson, *Plain Folk in a Rich Man's War: Class and Dissent in Confederate Georgia* (Gainesville: University Press of Florida, 2002), 194.

36. Williams et al., *Plain Folk in a Rich Man's War*, 25–29, 34–36; also see "Cotton Versus Corn," *Philadelphia Inquirer*, May 4, 1861.

37. See Teresa Crisp Williams and David Williams, "'The Woman Rising': Cotton, Class, and Confederate Georgia's Rioting Women," *Georgia Historical Quarterly* 86, no. 1 (Spring 2002): 49–83, esp. 68–79; on the riot in Richmond, see Michael B. Chesson, "Harlots or Heroines? A New Look at the Richmond Bread Riot," *Virginia Magazine of History and Biography* 92, no. 2 (April 1984): 131–75; for two accounts of the Richmond bread riot of 1863, see Mary S. Estill, "Diary of a Confederate Congressman, 1862–1863," *Southwestern Historical Quarterly* 39, no. 1 (July 1935): 33–65, esp. 46–47; and Jones, April 2, 1863, *A Rebel Clerk's Diary*, 1:285–87; also see Williams, *Rich Man's War*, 99, 100–101, 114–15; Escott, *After Secession*, 122. As Lebergott argued, because the Confederacy failed to collect sufficient taxes, it was forced to rely on impressments, which often targeted the weakest members of society: farms run by women whose husbands were soldiers. This practice encouraged desertions and heightened women's anger toward the government. See Stanley Lebergott, "Why the South Lost: Commercial Purpose in the Confederacy, 1861–1865," *Journal of American History* 79, no. 1 (June 1983): 58–74, esp. 71–72. In defense of the Confederacy, some reports insisted that the Richmond protest was not a "bread riot," and that the cause was crime, not want; see "Outrageous Proceedings in Richmond," *Staunton Spectator*, April 7, 1863; but in the same newspaper, another article argued that class conflict was going to destroy the Confederate cause, see "The Class Oppressed," *Staunton Spectator*, April 7, 1863.

38. "Pity the Poor Rebels," *Vanity Fair*, May 9, 1863.

39. Entries for July 26, 27, 1863, Lucy Virginia French Diaries, 1860, 1862–1865, microfilm, Tennessee State Library and Archives, Nashville; Stephen V. Ash, "Poor Whites in the Occupied South, 1861–1865," *Journal of Southern History* 57, no. 1 (February 1991): 39–62, esp. 55.

40. On government officials dining on delicacies while soldiers were suffering, see Jones, September 22, 1864, *A Rebel Clerk's Diary*, 2:290; and on snubbing Varina Davis, see Jones, March 19, 1865, *A Rebel Clerk's Diary*, 2:453.

41. "The Drum Roll," *Southern Field and Fireside*, February 18, 1864; and Anne Sarah Rubins, *The Shattered Nation: The Rise and Fall of the Confederacy, 1861–1868* (Chapel Hill: University of North Carolina Press, 2005), 88. The same theme of the loss of class privilege (wives forced to clean the "slops of the bed chamber") appeared in the *Richmond Daily Whig*, February 12, 1865; see George C. Rable, "Despair, Hope, and Delusion: The Collapse of Confederate Morale Re-Examined," in *The Collapse of the Confederacy*, eds.

Mark Grimsley and Brooks D. Simpson (Lincoln: University of Nebraska Press, 2001), 129–67, esp. 149–50; and "Items of Interest," *Houston Daily Telegraph,* December 21, 1864.

42. See "Sketches from the Life of Jeff. Davis," *Macon Daily Telegraph,* March 12, 1861. For southern papers calling Lincoln a drunken sot, see "The News," *New York Herald,* May 21, 1861. For Lincoln derided as the "Illinois ape," see Josiah Gilbert Holland, *The Life of Abraham Lincoln* (Springfield, MA, 1866), 243; also see "A Bad Egg for the Lincolnites," *The Macon Daily Telegraph,* September 18, 1861, and *Richmond Examiner,* October 19, 1861. On Davis's and Lincoln's shared birthplace of Kentucky, see "News and Miscellaneous Items," *Wisconsin Patriot,* March 30, 1861. For Hunter's opinion of Lincoln, see Letter from Salmon Portland Chase, October 2, 1862, in *Diary and Correspondence of Salmon Portland Chase,* eds. George S. Denison and Samuel H. Dodson (Washington, DC: American Historical Association, 1903), 105. And for the slur against midwesterners, see John Hampden Chamberlayne, *Ham Chamberlayne—Virginia: Letters and Papers of an Artillery Officer in the War for Southern Independence, 1861–1865* (Richmond, VA, 1932), 186. Chamberlayne also criticized people in Maryland for their free-labor ethos and Yankee blood. He described them as having low character, "with the education of common schools, with Dutch instincts dashed with Yankee blood." He dismissed them for only working to make money, believing that the man "is worthiest who most unremittingly toils with his hands, or if with his brains, he must dry them up with years of mechanic toil over Day Book & Ledger." See ibid., 105.

43. "The Presidential Campaign," *New York Herald,* June 8, 1860.

44. "The Educated Southerner," "The Effect of Bull Run upon the Southern Mind," "Anti-Mortem Sketches," and Charles Godfrey Leland, "North Men, Come Out!," *Vanity Fair,* May 6, August 17, August 21, and September 28, 1861. On *Vanity Fair,* which was published from December 31, 1859, to July 4, 1863, see James T. Nardin, "Civil War Humor: The War in Vanity Fair," *Civil War History* 2, no. 3 (September 1956): 67–85, esp. 67; also see "The Bad Bird and the Mudsill," *Frank Leslie's Illustrated Newspaper,* February 21, 1863.

45. "A Soldier's Speech," *Wooster* [OH] *Republican,* November 12, 1863. One essay argued that mudsills were the backbone of the economy; see "Who Are the Mudsills?," *American Farmer's Magazine,* August 1858. Garfield was less generous in his assessment of Confederate deserters. He described them as "men of no brains who had been scared into the rebel army and whose lives were not worth to the county what the bullet would cost to kill them"; see Harry James and Frederick D. Williams, eds., *The Diary of James Garfield,* 4 vols. (East Lansing: Michigan State University, 1967–1981), 1:65, and Mitchell, *Civil War Soldiers,* 33. For another rousing defense of northern mudsills, see the poem "Northmen, Come Out!," with the stanzas, "Out in your strength and let them know / How working men to work can go. / Out in your might and let them feel / How mudsills strike when edged with steel"; see Charles Godfrey Leland, "Northmen, Come Out!," *Hartford Daily Courant,* May 6, 1861, originally published in *Vanity Fair.* Northerners also reported on "secesh nabobs" paying high prices for "mudsill substitutes"; see *Hartford Daily Courant,* December 20, 1861.

46. Grimsley, *The Hard Hand of War,* 15–16, 56, 68–70. Halleck was an expert on international law, and the principle of occupying armies taxing disloyal citizens was laid out in Emmerich de Vattel's 1793 treatise *The Law of Nations.* This practice was not new to the Civil War, but what was different was the decision to target the rich. See W. Wayne Smith, "An Experiment in Counterinsurgency: The Assessment of Confederate Sympathizers in Missouri," *Journal of Southern History* 35, no. 3 (August 1969): 361–80, esp. 361–64; Louis S. Gerteis, *Civil War St. Louis* (Lawrence: University of Kansas Press, 2001), 172–76. And on guerrilla warfare shaping these policies, see Daniel E. Sutherland, "Guerrilla Warfare, Democracy, and the Fate of the Confederacy," *Journal of Southern History* 68, no. 2 (May 2002): 259–92, esp. 271–72, 280, 288; and Michael Fellman, *Inside War: The Guerrilla Conflict in Missouri During the American Civil War* (New York: Oxford University Press, 1989), 88, 94, 96.

47. John F. Bradbury Jr., "'Buckwheat Cake Philanthropy': Refugees and the Union Army in the Ozarks," *Arkansas Historical Quarterly* 57, no. 3 (Autumn 1998): 233–54, esp. 237–40. Estimates vary on the total number of southern refugees. Stephen Ash claims that nearly 80,000 white refugees had entered Federal lines by 1865. Elizabeth Massey contends that 250,000 were displaced by the war and the majority were women. See Stephen V. Ash, *When the Yankees Came: Conflict and Chaos in the Occupied South, 1861–1865* (Chapel Hill: University of North Carolina Press, 1999); Stephen V. Ash, *Middle Tennessee Society Transformed, 1860–1870: War and Peace in the Upper South* (Knoxville: University of Tennessee Press, 1988); and Mary Elizabeth Massey, *Women in the Civil War* (Lincoln: University of Nebraska Press, 1966), 291–316.

48. Grimsley, *The Hard Hand of War,* 108; and Smith, "An Experiment in Counterinsurgency," 366; Jacqueline G. Campbell, "There Is No Difference Between a He and a She Adder in Their Venom: Benjamin Butler, William T. Sherman, and Confederate Women," *Louisiana History: Journal of the Louisiana Historical Association* 50, no. 1 (Winter 2009): 5–24, esp. 12, 15, 18–19. Marion Southwood not only commented on the wealthy hiding assets but emphasized that it was the elites who "turned up their aristocratic noses" at the thought of assenting to the oath of allegiance; see Marion Southwood, *"Beauty and Booty": The Watchword of New Orleans* (New York, 1867), 123, 130–33, 159. The same rule of punishing rude women and subjecting disloyal women to confiscation was established by General Halleck in Missouri; see Gerteis, *Civil War St. Louis,* 174. Confederates described the destruction of elite property in class terms: as one account wrote, men from the "dunghill" of the North holding "saturnalias round the princely mansions of the Southern planters"; see "Rebel (Yankee Definition)," *Houston Tri-weekly Telegraph,* November 18, 1864. In Maryland, when one Virginia slaveowner demanded the return of his slaves, a dozen Union soldiers threw the man onto a blanket and tossed him up in the air. One sergeant described the slaveowner as "a perfect specimen of a Virginia gentleman," and he was pleased to think that man must have been horrified to be humiliated and unmanned by "Union soldiers—northern mudsills." See James Oakes, *Freedom National: The Destruction of Slavery in the United States, 1861–1865* (New York: W. W. Norton, 2012), 365.

49. Hans L. Trefousse, *Andrew Johnson: A Biography* (New York: Norton, 1989), 19, 21–23, 43, 55, 138, 152, 155–56, 168, 179; Ash, *Middle Tennessee Society Transformed,* 107, 159–60; also see Rufus Buin Spain, "R. B. C. Howell, Tennessee Baptist, 1808–1868" (M.A. thesis, Vanderbilt University, 1948), 105–7. It is interesting that Johnson planned to have all citizens take the loyalty oath and would begin with the wealthiest class, then ministers, doctors, and measured secessionist sympathies according to a class scale; see ibid., 101, 104–6.

50. Grimsley, *The Hard Hand of War,* 169, 202–3; and Debra Reddin van Tuyll, "Scalawags and Scoundrels? The Moral and Legal Dimensions of Sherman's Last Campaigns," *Studies in Popular Culture* 22, no. 2 (October 1999): 33–45, esp. 38–39. Soldiers blamed South Carolina for the war, and thought of its political elite as the very symbol of tyranny and arrogance. They looked forward to wreaking vengeance on the capital—where they vandalized property, set fire to buildings, and targeted the homes of the elites. See Charles Royster, *The Destructive War: William Tecumseh Sherman, Stonewall Jackson, and the Americans* (New York: Knopf, 1991), 4–5, 19–21.

51. Grimsley, *The Hard Hand of War,* 173–74, 188; Burstein and Isenberg, *Madison and Jefferson,* 204–5.

52. Hallock Armstrong to Mary Armstrong, April 8, 1865, in *Letters from a Pennsylvania Chaplain at the Siege of Petersburg, 1865* (published privately, 1961), 47.

53. Letter from William Wheeler, April 1, 1864, in *Letters of William Wheeler of the Class of 1855* (Cambridge, MA: H. G. Houghton & Co., 1875), 444–46; Grimsley, *The Hard Hand of War,* 173–74; John D. Cox, *Traveling South: Travel Narratives and the Construction of American Identity* (Athens: University of Georgia Press, 2005), 165, 174–76. And for the indistinguishable quality of shanties of poor white or blacks, see George H. Allen, *Forty-Six Months with the Fourth R. I. Volunteers in the War of 1861 to 1865: Comprising a History of Marches, Battles, and Camp Life, Compiled from Journals Kept While on Duty in the Field and Camp* (J. A. & R. A. Reid Printers, 1887), 219; also see "Confederate Prisoners at Chicago," *Macon Daily Telegraph,* February 14, 1863; Mitchell, *Civil War Soldiers,* 42, 95, 97; Diary of Robert Ransom, *Andersonville Diary, Escape, and List of the Dead, with Name, Co., Regiment, Date of Death and No. of Grave in Cemetery* (Auburn, New York, 1881), 71.

54. On marching through mud, fighting swamps and rebels, see Manning Ferguson Force, "From Atlanta to Savannah: The Civil War Journal of Manning F. Force, November 15, 1864–January 3, 1865," *Georgia Historical Quarterly* 91, no. 2 (Summer 2007): 185–205, esp. 187–90, 193–94. And on muddy mass graves, see Drew Gilpin Faust, *The Republic of Suffering: Death and the American Civil War* (New York: Random House, 2008), 73–75.

55. Phillips, *Diehard Rebels,* 56, 62. Confederates also hoped that the New York City draft riots were a sign of class revolution in the North; see "Important News from the North" and another report in the *Richmond Enquirer,* July 18, 1863; also see A. Hunter Dupree and Leslie H. Fischel Jr., "An Eyewitness Account of the New York City Draft Riots, July, 1863," *Mississippi Valley Historical Review* 47, no. 3 (December 1960): 472–79, esp. 476.

56. "Recent News by Mail," *Philadelphia Inquirer,* April 14, 1861.

Chapter Eight: Thoroughbreds and Scalawags:
Bloodlines and Bastard Stock in the Age of Eugenics

1. W. E. B. Du Bois, "The Evolution of the Race Problem," *Proceedings of the National Negro Conference* (New York, 1909), 142–58, esp. 148–49.
2. Ibid., 147–48, 152–54, 156.
3. Ibid., 153–54, 157.
4. Charles Darwin, *The Descent of Man* (London, 1871), 2:402–3. Galton's major publications were an article, "Hereditary Talent and Character" (1865), and books *Hereditary Genius* (1869), *Inquiry into Human Faculty* (1883), and *Natural Inheritance* (1889); see Mark H. Haller, *Eugenics: Hereditarian Attitudes in American Thought* (New Brunswick, NJ: Rutgers University Press, 1963), 4–6, 8–12. Also see Richard A. Richards, "Darwin, Domestic Breeding and Artificial Selection," *Endeavour* 22, no. 3 (1988): 106–9; and for the importance of animal breeding in shaping Darwin's theory of natural selection, see Robert J. Roberts, "Instinct and Intelligence in British Natural Theology: Some Contributions to Darwin's Theory of Evolutionary Behavior," *Journal of the History of Biology* 14, no. 2 (Autumn 1981): 193–230, esp. 224–25.
5. "Plebein [*sic*] Aristocracy," *Independent* (May 24, 1864); and Heather Cox Richardson, *West from Appomattox: The Reconstruction of America After the Civil War* (New Haven, CT: Yale University Press, 2007), 17–20.
6. For a typical example of a free-labor economy for poor whites and free slaves, see "The Emancipation and Free Labor Question in the South," *New York Herald*, May 18, 1865; also see Heather Cox Richardson, *The Death of Reconstruction: Race, Labor, and Politics in the Post–Civil War North, 1865–1901* (Cambridge, MA: Harvard University Press, 2004), 21–22, 24–25, 34, 39, 42.
7. The newspapers focused on the stipulation that exempted the elite class from the amnesty: "All persons who have voluntarily participated in said rebellion and the estimated value of whose taxable property is over $20,000"; see "President Johnson's Plan of Reconstruction in Bold Relief," *New York Herald,* May 31, 1865; "President Johnson and the South Carolina Delegation," *Philadelphia Inquirer,* June 26, 1865. And for an article pointing out how all the New York newspapers stressed this point, see "The New York Press on the President's Talk with the South Carolina Delegation," *Daily Ohio Statesman,* July 6, 1865. Also see Andrew Johnson, "Proclamation 134—Granting Amnesty to Participants in the Rebellion, with Certain Exceptions," May 29, 1865; and "Interview with South Carolina Delegation, June 24," in *The Papers of Andrew Johnson, May–August 1865,* ed. Paul H. Bergeron (Knoxville: University of Tennessee Press, 1992), 8:128–29, 280–84.
8. On Johnson's decision to pardon the elites because he needed their support, see Eric Foner, *Reconstruction: America's Unfinished Revolution, 1863–1877* (New York: Harper & Row, 1988), 191. Johnson pardoned 13,500 out of the 15,000 who applied; see Richardson, *The Death of Reconstruction,* 16.
9. For Johnson's view of a racial war of extermination, see "The Negro Question—Dangers of Another 'Irrepressible Conflict,'" *New York Herald,* July 12, 1865; also see [San Francisco] *Evening Bulletin,* July 31, 1865. On

Johnson's opinion that Negro suffrage would breed a race war between the freedmen and poor whites, see "The President upon Negro Suffrage," *Philadelphia Inquirer,* October 25, 1865; also see "Interview of George L. Stearns," October 3, 1865," *The Papers of Andrew Johnson,* 9:180.

10. See the remarks by Senators David Schenck, Henry S. Lane, John P. Hale, and Reverdy Johnson, *Congressional Globe,* 38th Congress, 2nd Session, 959, 984–85, 989; and Congressman Green Clay Smith, *Congressional Globe,* 39th Congress, 1st Session, 416; also see Paul Moreno, "Racial Classification and Reconstruction Legislation," *Journal of Southern History* 61, no. 2 (May 1995): 271–304, esp. 276–77, 283–87; and Michele Landis Dauber, "The Sympathetic State," *Law and History Review* 23, no. 2 (Summer 2005): 387–442, esp. 408, 412, 414–15.

11. For "loafing whites," see "North Carolina: Blacks and Whites Loafing," *New York Times,* May 28, 1866; and "From Over the Lake. Barancas—Gens. Steel and Ashboth—The Seen and Unseen—The Refugee Business, Etc., Etc.," *New Orleans Times,* March 9, 1865. On poor white refugees and children, see "Poor White Trash," *Independent* (September 7, 1865): 6; Daniel R. Weinfield, "'More Courage Than Discretion': Charles M. Hamilton in Reconstruction-Era Florida," *Florida Historical Quarterly* 84, no. 4 (Spring 2006): 479–516, esp. 492; and William F. Mugleston and Marcus Sterling Hopkins, "The Freedmen's Bureau and Reconstruction in Virginia: The Diary of Marcus Sterling Hopkins," *Virginia Magazine of History and Biography* 86, no. 1 (January 1978): 45–102, esp. 100. It was also reported that North Carolina had the highest number of "white trash," and most of the cases adjudicated by the Freedmen's Bureau involved this class. See "Affairs in the Southern States: North Carolina," *New York Times,* March 22, 1865.

12. "From the South: Southern Journeyings and Jottings," *New York Times,* April 15, 1866; Sidney Andrews, *The South Since the War* (Boston, 1866); Whitelaw Reid, *After the War: A Tour of the Southern States* (London, 1866); John T. Trowbridge, *The South: A Tour of Its Battlefields and Ruined Cities* (Hartford, CT: 1866). Andrews's book was known for providing a "portraiture of the poor whites" that was "painfully true to nature"; see "New Books," *Philadelphia Inquirer,* April 23, 1866. His portrait of the typical poor white as physically stunted and displaying "insipidity in his face, indecision in his step, and inefficiency in his whole bearing" was reprinted verbatim in "Poor Whites of North Carolina, Wilmington, October 14," *Freedmen's Record. Organ of the New England Aid Society* (November 1, 1865): 186–87.

13. Gilmore's allusion to a fungus was identical to social Darwinist Herbert Spencer's argument that "whatever produces a diseased state in one part of the community, must inevitably inflict injury upon all other parts"; see Spencer, *Social Statistics, or, The Conditions Essential to Human Happiness Specified and the First of Them Developed* (London, 1851), 456. Edward Kirke (pseudonym of James Roberts Gilmore), *Down in Tennessee, and Back by Way of Richmond* (New York, 1864), 104, 184, 188–89. Excerpts from Gilmore's book were printed in the newspapers; see "The White Population in the South. 'Poor Whites'—'Mean Whites'—And the Chivalry," *New Hampshire*

Sentinel, November 10, 1864; "The Common People of the South" *Circular* (September 26, 1864): 222–23; "From 'Down in Tennessee.' The 'Mean Whites' of the South," *Friends' Review* (October 15, 1864): 101–2. Gilmore also published an article; see J. R. Gilmore, "The Poor Whites of the South," *Harper's New Monthly Magazine* (June 1, 1864): 115–24.

14. Andrews wrote, "I should say that the real question at issue in the South is, not 'What shall be done with the negro? but 'What shall be done with the white?'" Andrews, *The South Since the War*, 224. The variation on Andrews's phrase quoted in the text, which added "poor white," appeared in a Colorado newspaper article (reprinted from the *Chicago Republican*), "The Rising Race in the South," *Miner's Register*, January 12, 1866. The same question was raised in the *Christian Advocate and Journal:* "It is not the negro who calls for pity, he can take care of himself; it is the ignorant, landless, clay-colored, hope-abandoned whites that demand and yet defy relief"; see Reynard, "A Vacation Tour in the South and West: Hell Opens Her Mouth," *Christian Advocate and Journal* (August 24, 1865), 266.

15. A writer for the *New York Times* argued that poor whites had had the vote for eighty years and remained "improvident, ignorant and debased" and the "easy dupes of designing leaders"; see "The Suffrage Question," *New York Times*, February 13, 1866; also see "The Poor Whites," *Miner's Register*, October 18, 1865; Reid, *After the War*, 59, 221, 247–50, 255, 302–3, 325, 348; Andrews, *The South Since the War*, 335–36. On freedmen having a greater desire for education than poor whites, see "A Dominant Fact of the Southern Situation," *New York Times*, August 10, 1865. On rapid educational progress of freedmen, see "Condition of the South," *New York Times*, August 27, 1867. On the equal need for education of poor whites, see "The Education of Poor Whites," *New York Times*, October 5, 1865. On neatness and thriftiness and preparation for the franchise among the freedmen, see Trowbridge, *The South*, 220, 458, 589; also see Stephen K. Prince, *Stories of the South: Race and Reconstruction and Southern Identity* (Chapel Hill: University of North Carolina Press, 2014), 28. On freedmen's superiority to poor whites in brains and muscle, see "The Negro, Slave and Free," *Hartford Daily Courant*, March 6, 1865. On loyalty of the freedman and distrust of poor whites, see "Governing and Governed" and "Two Reasons," *New Orleans Tribune*, June 8, 1865, August 27, 1865; "Reconstruction," *Wilkes Spirit of the Times*, August 26, 1865; "Reconstruction and Negro Suffrage," *Atlantic Monthly* 16, no. 94 (August 1865): 238–47, esp. 245; also see Richardson, *The Death of Reconstruction*, 32–37.

16. For "inert," see "The Poor Whites," *Miner's Register*, October 18, 1865. For deformed and idiotic, see Gilmore, *Down in Tennessee*, 187. For "thoughtless," "fumbling," and the "moony glare" of the lunatic, see "The Poor White Trash," *New Orleans Tribune*, September 1, 1865. For poor whites ranked on the lowest level in Darwin's evolutionary scale, see "From the South: Southern Journeyings and Jottings," *New York Times*, April 7, 1866; also see "The Poor Whites," *The Congregationalist*, September 22, 1865. For belonging to the "genus Homo," but "from long effects of long generations of ignorance,

neglect, degradation and poverty, it has developed few of the higher qualities
of the race to which it belongs," see J. S. Bradford, "Crackers," *Lippincott's
Magazine*, vol. 6 (November 1870): 457–67, esp. 457.

17. For "dangerous class," see "The Poor Whites," *Miner's Register*, October 18,
1865. On intermarrying, incest, and wife selling, see Gilmore, *Down in Tennessee*, 184, 187. On mothers conniving illicit liaisons for daughters and poor
white women having sex with black men, see "The Low-Down People," *Putnam's Magazine* (June 1868): 704–13, esp. 705–6. On filthy refugees in box-
cars, see Reid, *After the War*, 248; also see W. De Forest, "Drawing Bureau
Rations," *Harper's Monthly Magazine* 36 (May 1868): 792–99, esp. 794, 799.
On Herbert Spencer, see Robert J. Richards, *Darwin and the Emergence of
Evolutionary Theories of Mind and Behavior* (Chicago: University of Chicago Press, 1987), 303–4; Spencer first used "survival of the fittest" in his
Principles of Biology (London, 1864), 1:444, 455. On the popularity of Dar-
win and Spencer, see "The Theory of Natural Selection," *The Critic* (Novem-
ber 26, 1859), 528–30; "Natural Selection," [New Orleans] *Daily Picayune*,
January 9, 1870. And for an article underscoring Darwin's tree analogy, and
that the harsh law of natural selection meant that certain branches have
"decayed and dropped off," see "Review of Darwin's Theory of the Origins of
Species by Means of Natural Selection," *American Journal of Science and the
Arts* (March 1860): 153–84, esp. 159.

18. "The Low-Down People," *Putnam's Magazine of Literature, Science, Art and
National Interests* (June 1868): 704–16. On the importance of *The Jukes*, see
Nicole Hahn Rafter, *White Trash: The Eugenic Family Studies, 1877–1919*
(Boston: Northeastern University Press, 1988), 2–3, 6–7.

19. See Sanford B. Hunt, "The Negro as Soldier," *Anthropological Review* 7 (January 1869): 40–54, esp. 53; also see John S. Haller Jr., *Outcasts from Evolution: Scientific Attitudes of Racial Inferiority, 1859–1900* (Urbana: University
of Illinois Press, 1971), 20–32.

20. "Mongrel" came from various sources: animal and plant breeding, evolutionary science, racist arguments for miscegenation and amalgamation, and older
theories of conquest (barbarian and Mongol hordes became "mongrel hordes"),
and the English slur of "mongrel pup" for a lower-class man without any pedigree. For free blacks as a spurious and mongrel race, see "Free Blacks of the
North," [Fayetteville, NC] *Carolina Observer*, October 7, 1858. On the mongrel party voting themselves down to the level with degraded Negroes, see
"Correct Likeness of the Union Party," [Millersburg, OH] *Holmes County
Farmer*, October 5, 1865; and "Mexico and the Indians—Two More 'Twin
Relics' for the Next New Party," *New York Herald*, June 28, 1867. On preserving the "best blood" from "admixture of baser blood," see "Our People,"
New-Orleans Times, November 24, 1865. And since mongrels were often
identified as dogs without any known pedigree, see "Strange Dog," [New
Orleans] *Daily Picayune*, June 12, 1866. On the famous English mongrel pup
rhyme ("Of mongrel, pup, ay, whelp and hound, / And curs of low degree"),
see "Letter from Mobile," *Daily Picayune*, August 16, 1866. On comparing
the South to the mongrel republic of Mexico, see "The Future of the Freemen," *New-Orleans Times*, October 22, 1865; "Southern Self-Exile—Mexico

and Brazil," *Richmond Examiner,* April 14, 1866; "The Mongrel Republics of America," *Old Guard,* September 1867, 695–702; "Editor's Table," *Old Guard* (September 1868): 717–20. And for mongrel hordes, see "Speech of Gen. Geo. W. Morgan," *Daily Ohio Statesman,* October 5, 1865. Also see Elliott West, "Reconstructing Race," *Western Historical Quarterly* 34, no. 1 (Spring 2003): 6–26, esp. 11; Haller, *Outcasts from Evolution,* 72–73, 82; John G. Menke, *Mulattoes and Race Mixture: American Attitudes and Images, 1865–1918* (Ann Arbor, MI: UMI Research Press, 1979), 51, 60–61, 101–2; Forrest G. Wood, *Black Scare: The Racist Response to Emancipation and Reconstruction* (Berkeley: University of California Press, 1968), 65–70. For the long-standing English slur for a dog "without a breed," see Neil Pemberton and Michael Worboys, *Mad Dogs and Englishmen: Rabies in Britain, 1830–2000* (New York: Palgrave, 2007), 30–31. And on the Greek etymology of the word "mongrel" meaning "lust" and "an outrage on nature," see Warren Minton, "Notes. On the Etymology of Hybrid (Lat. Hybrida)," *American Journal of Philology* (October 1, 1884): 501–2.

21. On the carpetbagger and his black valise, see Ted Tunnell, "'The Propaganda of History': Southern Editors and the Origins of the 'Carpetbagger' and the 'Scalawag,'" *Journal of Southern History* 72, no. 4 (November 2006): 789–822, esp. 792. For the theme of race traitor and treason, see Hyman Rubin III, *South Carolina Scalawags* (Columbia: University of South Carolina Press, 2006), xvi; Foner, *Reconstruction,* 297.

22. On President Johnson's veto of the Civil Rights Act described as rejecting "mongrel citizenship," see "Veto of Civil Rights Bill," [Harrisburg, PA] *Weekly Patriot and Union,* April 5, 1866; also see Francis S. Blair Jr. to Andrew Johnson, March 18, 1866, and the Veto of the Civil Rights Bill, March 27, 1866, in Bergeron, *The Papers of Andrew Johnson,* vol. 10, *February–July 1866,* 10:270, 312–20. Johnson was more explicit in his Annual Message to Congress, December 3, 1867, in which he contended the two races could never subject be to "amalgamation or fusion of them into one homogeneous mass"— and to try to force this on the South would "Africanize half the country." Johnson's attack on mongrel citizenship in his veto of the Civil Rights Act echoed the speeches of Edgar Cowan in the Senate, who had raised the danger of gypsies, Chinese, and Indians gaining citizenship from the act. See Senate, *Congressional Globe,* 39th Congress, 1st Session, May 30, 1866, 2890–91. Johnson was personally invested in the idea of "fitness." He wrote that section of the veto. See John H. Abel Jr. and LaWanda Cox, "Andrew Johnson and His Ghost Writers: An Analysis of the Freedmen's Bureau and Civil Rights Veto Messages," *Mississippi Valley Historical Review* 48, no. 3 (December 1961): 460–79, esp. 475.

23. In one term, Johnson vetoed twenty-nine legislative bills, far more than Jackson or any previous president; during the period from Washington to the Civil War, all the presidents combined had vetoed only fifty-nine acts of Congress. On the revolutionary significance of the Fourteenth Amendment, see Robert J. Kraczorowski, "To Begin the Nation Anew: Congress, Citizenship, and Civil Rights After the Civil War," *American Historical Review* 92, no. 1 (February 1987): 45–68, esp. 45; and see Wood, *Black Scare,* 111–13. On Johnson's

obstruction leading to impeachment, especially his opposition to the Fourteenth Amendment and control of the military, see Michael Les Benedict,
The Impeachment and Trial of Andrew Johnson (New York: Norton, 1973),
49; and Hans L. Trefousse, *Impeachment of a President: Andrew Johnson,
the Blacks, and Reconstruction* (New York: Fordham University Press, 1999),
41–48, 54.

24. For "pride of caste" and "pride of race," see "Extension of Suffrage," *Macon
Daily Telegraph,* October 28, 1865. For women protecting bloodlines, see
"Our People," *New-Orleans Times,* November 24, 1865. Senator Montgomery Blair, brother of Francis Blair Jr., in a speech at a large Democratic rally
in New York City, argued that only abandoned women would marry black
men; see "The New York Campaign," *New York Herald,* October 19, 1865;
and F. Fleming, ed., "The Constitution and the Ritual of the Knights of the
White Camelia," in *Documents Relating to Reconstruction* (Morgantown,
WV, 1904), 22, 27. On the Knights of the White Camelia and racial purity,
also see "Arkansas," *New York Herald,* October 31, 1868. On treating a
mixed-race child as bastard progeny, see "Miscegenation," *Georgia Weekly
Telegraph,* February 27, 1870.

25. On Blair's fondness for Darwin's *Origins of Species,* see Foner, *Reconstruction,*
340. On his speeches, see "General Blair's Letter to General George Morgan,
July 13, 1868" and "Speeches of Horatio Seymour and Francis P. Blair, Jr.,
Accepting the Nominations, July 10, 1868," in Edward McPherson, *The Political History of the United States of America During the Period of Reconstruction (from April 15, 1865, to July 15, 1870)* . . . (Washington, DC, 1880),
369–70, 381–82; "General Blair's Speeches," [Alexandra, LA] *Louisiana Democrat,* September 2, 1868; "Blair on the Stump," *New York Times,* August 9,
1868. On the Georgia case, see *Scott v. State,* 39 Ga. 321 (1869). For coverage
of the case, see "Social Status of the Blacks," *New York Herald,* June 27, 1869;
also see Charles Frank Robinson III, *Dangerous Liaisons: Sex and Love in the
Segregated South* (Fayetteville: University of Arkansas Press, 2003), 24, 37–38;
Pascoe, *What Comes Naturally,* 20; James R. Browning, "Anti-Miscegenation
Laws in the United States," *Duke Bar Journal* 1, no. 1 (March 1951): 26–41,
esp. 33. For the theory that mongrel mixtures exaggerate the vices of both
races, see "The Philosophy of Miscegenation," *New-Orleans Times,* January 4,
1867. It is just as important to understand that Democratic politicians supported laws against amalgamation in order to curb the "waywardness" of low-
down whites for degrading Saxon blood; see "Remarks of Thomas Orr, in the
Senate, on the Bill to Prevent the Amalgamation of the African with the White
Race in Ohio," [Columbus, OH] *Crisis,* February 28, 1861.

26. Hyman argues that violence was the key to the dismantling of the Republican
Party, including targeted assaults against scalawags who were political leaders;
see Hyman, *South Carolina Scalawags,* xvi, xxv, 41, 45, 48. Republican vice
presidential candidate Schuyler Colfax gave a powerful speech in the defense
of scalawags, and stressed the vicious threats made against them; see "Political
Intelligence," *New York Herald,* October 8, 1868. For hanging scalawags, see
"The Rebel Press," [Raleigh, NC] *Tri-Weekly Standard,* 1868. The editor of
the *Atlanta Constitution* argued that the inauguration of a Democratic

president would be a signal for hanging scalawags and carpetbaggers; see George C. Rable, *But There Was No Peace: The Role of Violence in the Politics of Reconstruction* (Athens: University of Georgia Press, 1984), 69. On the trial for the murder of radical Republican Mr. Ashburn, the defense attorney—none other than former governor Joseph Brown—used the scalawag slur to justify the attack; see "The Ashburn Tragedy," *Georgia Weekly Telegraph,* July 17, 1868. On the KKK targeting scalawags, see "Editorial," *Daily Memphis Avalanche,* June 7, 1868. On calls to shoot scalawags, see "Reconstruction Convention," *Daily Austin Republican,* July 22, 1868. And for a Republican election poem mocking the Democratic Party's campaign: "Then let's shoot and stab and kill, / The men who dare their thoughts to tell / If we lack the power, we have the will / To drive the scalawags, down to hell"; see "Democratic Principles," *Houston Union,* May 7, 1869. On assassinations of prominent Republican politicians in 1868, also see Foner, *Reconstruction,* 342.

27. For an account of the stereotypical black man "Cuffy" kissing a scalawag, see "'I Salute You, My Brother,'" [Memphis, TN] *Public Ledger,* May 7, 1868; and "A Scalawag Senator Invites a Darkey to His House," [Atlanta] *Daily Constitution,* July 3, 1868. For scalawags as "piebald," "mangy," "slarapery" (meaning flabby-headed or feebleminded) and "stinkee," see "Arkansas," "News in Brief," and "The Scalawag," *Daily Avalanche,* May 20, June 24, August 27, 1868; "Ye Stinkee and the Perry House," *Georgia Weekly Telegraph,* March 27, 1868. For "slaves of the scalawag white trash," see "Mississippi," *New York Herald,* August 12, 1868. On inciting Negroes with "low-flung" speeches, a comment made by Judge Carlton after observing a Republican gathering in Virginia, see "Meeting at Music Hall Last Night," [Albany, IN] *Daily Ledger,* October 31, 1868. On the role as party operatives, see "Carpet Baggery and Scalawagerie," *New-Orleans Times,* August 16, 1868; Foner, *Reconstruction,* 297.

28. "The Autobiography of a Scalawag," *Boone County* [IN] *Pioneer,* March 13, 1868.

29. For reference to "low born scum and quondam slaves," see the poem "White Men Must Rule," published in the [Raleigh] *North Carolinian,* February 15, 1868, as quoted in Karen L. Zipf, "'The Whites Shall Rule the Land or Die': Gender, Race, and Class in North Carolina Politics," *Journal of Southern History* 65, no. 3 (August 1999): 499–534, esp. 525. For a specific call to return the hereditary elite to power in place of "mongrel Republicanism," see "Address of the Conservative Men of Alabama to the People of the United States," *Daily Columbus* [GA] *Enquirer,* October 1, 1867.

30. For Wade Hampton, see "The Week," *Nation* 7, no. 165 (August 27, 1868): 161; and "America," *London Daily News,* September 18, 1865. For scalawag as vagabond stock, see "Horse and Mule Market," [New Orleans] *Daily Picayune,* February 9, 1867. For carpetbaggers as the "offscourings of the North" and scalawags the "spewed up scum of the South," see "Feels Bad," [Raleigh, NC] *Tri-Weekly Standard,* May 14, 1868. The same theme was used again to sum up the failure of Reconstruction; see Charles Gayarre, "The Southern Question," *North American Review* (November/December 1877): 472–99, esp. 482–83.

31. For his speech, see "Bullock Ratification Meeting," *Georgia Weekly Telegraph,* March 27, 1868.

32. For motley breeds, see "Negro Suffrage," *Abbeville* [SC] *Press,* March 16, 1866; and that mongrels communicate all the vices and few of the virtues of the parent stock, see "Results of Miscegenation," *Pittsfield* [MA] *Sun,* March 16, 1865. For scalawag cattle as a low breed dragging down the rest to its level, see *New York Tribune,* October 24, 1854. One journalist made fun of the term "scalawag" as the "elegant language of refined Virginia gentleman," and observed that the word applied to all natives who were loyal or Republicans, regardless of their class background; see "Virginia," *New York Times,* July 27, 1868. Scholars who have studied actual "scalawags" have shown that they were not white trash, but they were of a lower class than either antebellum politicians in the South or their opponents who formed the Redeemer governments in the 1870s. Many had only a public school education. Many supported black suffrage, as James Baggett has argued, "to prevent conservatives, who were judged their betters, from ruling"; see Baggett, "Summing Up the Scalawags," and appendix Table 3, *The Scalawags: Southern Dissenters in the Civil War and Reconstruction* (Baton Rouge: Louisiana State University Press, 2003), 261–62; Hyman, *South Carolina Scalawags,* xxi, 27–28, 52; also see James Baggett, "Upper South Scalawag Leadership," *Civil War History* 29, no. 1 (March 1983): 53–73, esp. 58–60, 73. On the modest landholdings (and the majority as nonslaveholders), see Richard L. Hume and Jerry B. Gough, *Blacks, Carpetbaggers, and Scalawags: The Constitutional Conventions of Radical Reconstruction* (Baton Rouge: Louisiana State University Press, 2008), 6, 19, 262, 270.

33. On the importance of education uniting the North and South, see "National Help for Southern Education," "President Hayes's Speech," and "Education for the South," *New York Times,* January 31, September 2, December 17, 1880; Charles F. Thwing, "The National Government and Education," *Harper's New Monthly Magazine* 68 (February 1884): 471–76; Allen J. Going, "The South and the Blair Education Bill," *Mississippi Valley Historical Review* 44, no. 2 (September 1957): 267–90. Reverend A. D. Mayo was one of the strongest supporters of the Blair bill, and a vocal advocate of training poor whites in the South; see A. D. Mayo, "The Third Estate of the South," *Journal of Social Sciences* (October 1890): xxi–xxxii. On reconciliation stories, see Nina Silber, "'What Does America Need So Much as Americans?': Race and Northern Reconciliation with Southern Appalachia, 1870–1900," in *Appalachians and Race: The Mountain South from Slavery to Segregation,* ed. John Inscoe (Lexington: University of Kentucky Press, 2001): 245–58.

34. Mary Denison, *Cracker Joe* (Boston, 1887), 9–10, 17, 33, 97–198, 206, 233, 248–55, 314, 317, 320. For other reconciliation stories presenting positive portrayals of crackers, see "The Southern Cracker," *Youth's Companion* (May 13, 1875): 149–50; Charles Dunning, "In a Florida Cracker's Cabin; To the Mockingbird," *Lippincott's Magazine* (April 1882): 367–74; Zitella Cocke, "Cracker Jim," *Overland Monthly and Out West Magazine* 10, no. 55 (July 1887): 51–70.

35. William Goodell Frost, "University Extension in Kentucky" (September 3, 1898): 72–80, esp. 72, 80; also see Frost, "Our Contemporary Ancestors in the Southern Mountains," *Atlantic Monthly* 83 (March 1899): 311–19; and

James Klotter, "The Black South and White Appalachia," *Journal of American History* 66, no. 4 (March 1980): 832–49, esp. 840, 845. For less flattering portrayals, see Will Wallace Harvey, "A Strange Land and Peculiar People," *Lippincott's Magazine* 12 (October 1873): 429–38, esp. 431. Others stressed their isolation in the mountains, cut off from modern commerce, as the cause of their shiftlessness, lawlessness, ignorance, and clanlike vendettas; see James Lane Allen, "Mountain Passes of the Cumberland (with Map)," *Harper's New Monthly Magazine* 81 (September 1890): 561–76, esp. 562. Allen also stressed their distinctive physiognomy—their time warp style of living—which gave them a "general listlessness," angular bodies "without great muscular robustness," and "voices monotonous in intonation"; see James Lane Allen, "Through the Cumberland Gap on Horseback," *Harper's New Monthly Magazine* 73 (June 1886): 50–67, esp. 57.

36. Davis of Arkansas served from 1901 to 1913; Tillman, who also served as a senator, was first elected governor of South Carolina in 1890; Vardaman was Mississippi governor from 1904 to 1908, then senator from 1913 to 1919. See Stephen Kantrowitz, *Ben Tillman and the Reconstruction of White Supremacy* (Chapel Hill: University of North Carolina Press, 2000); William F. Holmes, *White Chief: James Kimball Vardaman* (Baton Rouge: Louisiana State University Press, 1970); Albert D. Kirwan, *Revolt of the Rednecks: Mississippi Politics, 1876–1925* (Lexington: University of Kentucky Press, 1951), 145–47, 152–53, 160–61. And on Jeff Davis, see Richard L. Niswonger, "A Study in Southern Demagoguery: Jeff Davis of Arkansas," *Arkansas Historical Quarterly* 39, no. 2 (Summer 1980): 114–24. For the story of the term "redneck" involving Guy Rencher, see "Mississippi Campaign Reaches Noisy Stage," [New Orleans] *Daily Picayune,* July 11, 1911. For rednecks in the Mississippi swamps, see Hunt McCaleb, "The Drummer," *Daily Picayune,* April 2, 1893. On rednecks in the Boer War, see "Dashing Sortie by British," [Baltimore] *Sun,* December 11, 1899. One article noted that the Boers called the British and Americans "damned rednecks"; see "The News from Ladysmith," *New York Daily Tribune,* November 2, 1899. On Guy Rencher, see Dunbar Rowland, *The Official and Statistical Register of the State of Mississippi, 1908,* vol. 2 (Nashville, 1908): 1156–57. On one of the earliest usages of "redneck" in Mississippi politics, on August 13, 1891, see Patrick Huber and Kathleen Drowne, "Redneck: A New Discovery," *American Speech* 76, no. 4 (Winter 2001): 434–43. For the folk rhyme "I Would Rather Be a Negro Than a Poor White Man," see Thomas W. Talley, *Negro Folk Rhymes: Wise and Otherwise* (New York, 1922), 43. For the dating of the rhyme, see Archie Green, "Hillbilly Music: Source and Symbol," *Journal of American Folklore* 78, no. 309 (July–September 1965): 204–28, esp. 204.

37. On the "coon-flavored President," see *Biloxi Herald,* April 22, 1903; "Vardaman at Scranton," [New Orleans] *Daily Picayune,* June 24, 1903. For "coon-flavored miscegenationist," see "Correspondence: A Mississippian on Vardaman," *Outlook,* September 12, 1903; also see "Lynch Law, and Three Reasons for Its Rule," [New Orleans] *Times-Picayune,* March 21, 1904; "Southern Democrats Berate President," *New York Times,* October 19, 1901; J. Norrell, "When Teddy Roosevelt Invited Booker T. Washington to Dinner," *Journal of*

Blacks in Higher Education, no. 63 (Spring 2009): 70–74; and Dewey W. Grantham Jr., "Dinner at White House: Theodore Roosevelt, Booker T. Washington, and the South," *Tennessee Historical Quarterly* 17, no. 2 (June 1958): 112–30, esp. 114–18.

38. For Roosevelt's comment on Vardaman's "foul language" as "kennel filth which the foulest New York blackguard would not dare to use on the stump," and his "unspeakable lowness," see Theodore Roosevelt to Lyman Abbott, October 7, 1903, Theodore Roosevelt Papers, Manuscript Division, Library of Congress, Washington, DC. He voiced similar views in a letter to the muck-raking journalist Ray Stannard Baker; see Roosevelt to Ray Stannard Baker, June 3, 1908, in *The Letters of Theodore Roosevelt,* ed. Elting Morison, 8 vols. (Cambridge, MA: Harvard University Press, 1951–54), 6:1046–48. For controversy over Vardaman's dog insult, see "The Vardaman Campaign," *Macon Telegraph,* August 31, 1903; "It Is Not Denied," "And This Man Wants to Be Governor!," *The Biloxi Daily Herald,* July 31, August 5, 1903; and two untitled articles in *The Biloxi Daily Herald,* July 22, August 1, 1903; "Vardaman Wrote It," *New York Times,* August 16, 1904.

39. On rednecks and hillbillies, see "Vardaman, the Saint," [Gulfport, MS] *Daily Herald,* March 3, 1911. On "dirty" democracy and the people, see "Vardaman at Scranton," [New Orleans] *Daily Picayune,* June 24, 1903. On Vardaman as a "medicine man," see William Alexander Percy, *Lanterns on the Levee: Recollections of a Planter's Son* (Baton Rouge: Louisiana State University Press, 1973; originally published 1941), 143.

40. See John M. Mecklin, "Vardamanism," *Independent* (August 31, 1911): 461–63. On the symbolic meaning of the "cracker cart" or "*critter-kyarts*" as the cracker's usual form of transportation, see "Work Among the 'Poor Whites,' or 'Crackers,'" *Friends' Review* (March 22, 1888): 532–33. For an African American newspaper's pointed criticism of Vardaman's racism, see "That Devilish Old Vardaman," *Topeka Plaindealer,* August 15, 1913. On the problem of poor white illiteracy in Mississippi, see S. A. Steel, "A School in the Sticks: Problem of White Illiteracy," *Zion's Herald,* December 30, 1903; and "Governor Vardaman on the Negro," *Current Literature* 36, no. 3 (March 1904): 270–71. On the importance of pitting poor whites against blacks, see John Milton Cooper Jr., "Racism and Reform: A Review Essay," *Wisconsin Magazine of History* 55, no. 2 (Winter 1971): 140–44; and Kirwan, *Revolt of the Rednecks,* 212.

41. Percy, *Lanterns on the Levee,* 148–49.

42. For accounts of Roosevelt's visit and speech, see "President Denounces Rape and Lynching," [Columbia, SC] *State,* October 26, 1905; "Gala Day in Little Rock. President on Race Problem," *Charlotte Daily Observer,* October 26, 1905; "Twelve Doves of Peace Hover over Roosevelt," *Lexington Herald,* October 26, 1905. On rebuking Davis, see "The President's Most Important Speech," *Macon Telegraph,* October 29, 1905; "Governor Jefferson Davis," *Morning Olympian,* December 6, 1905; "Can't Train with Roosevelt Now," *Fort Worth Telegram,* December 6, 1905. For comment that Roosevelt avoided being shot by Vardaman, see "Vardaman Outwitted," *New York Times,* November 1, 1905; and William B. Gatewood Jr., "Theodore Roosevelt and Arkansas, 1901–1912," *Arkansas Historical Quarterly* 32, no. 1

(Spring 1973): 3–24, esp. 18–19; also see Mrs. Wallace Lamar, "Roosevelt Wrongs His Mother's Blood," *Macon Telegraph,* October 26, 1905; and Henry Fowler Pringle, "Theodore Roosevelt and the South," *Virginia Quarterly Review* 9, no. 1 (January 1933): 14–25.

43. On Roosevelt's view of Washington's educational project, see Theodore Roosevelt to L. J. Moore, February 5, 1900, in Morison, *The Letters of Theodore Roosevelt,* 2:1169; Thomas G. Dyer, *Theodore Roosevelt and the Idea of Race* (Baton Rouge: Louisiana State University Press, 1980), 97.

44. Theodore Roosevelt to Cecil Arthur Spring-Rice, August 11, 1899, in Morison, *The Letters of Theodore Roosevelt,* 2:1053; Roosevelt, "The World Movement," in *The Works of Theodore Roosevelt,* ed. Herman Hagdorn (New York: Charles Scribner's Sons, 1924), 14:258–85; Dyer, *Theodore Roosevelt and the Idea of Race,* 39, 42, 64, 148; also see David H. Burton, "The Influence of the American West on the Imperialist Philosophy of Theodore Roosevelt," *Arizona and the West* 4, no. 1 (Spring 1962): 5–26, esp. 10–11, 16.

45. Roosevelt, of course, wrote an account of his Amazon expedition; see Theodore Roosevelt, *Through the Brazilian Wilderness* (New York, 1914). For a detailed account of his trip, see Candice Millard, *River of Doubt: Theodore Roosevelt's Darkest Journey* (New York: Doubleday, 2005). And for the best discussion of Roosevelt's rugged masculinity, see Gail Bederman, *Manliness and Civilization: A Cultural History of Gender and Race in the United States, 1880–1917* (Chicago: University of Chicago Press, 1995), 170–215.

46. On the composition of the Rough Riders, see Gary Gerstle, "Theodore Roosevelt and the Divided Character of American Nationalism," *Journal of American History* 86, no. 3 (December 1999): 1280–1307, esp. 1282–83, 1286–87.

47. Frederic Remington, "Cracker Cowboys of Florida," *Harper's New Monthly Magazine* 91, no. 543 (August 1895): 339–46, esp. 339, 341–42, 344; for a similar portrait, see "Florida Crackers and Cowboys," [San Francisco] *Daily Evening Bulletin,* May 5, 1883.

48. Theodore Roosevelt to Owen Wister, April 27, 1906, *The Letters of Theodore Roosevelt,* 5:226–28; "Br'er Vardaman," *Biloxi Herald,* January 21, 1902.

49. Roosevelt took the concept of "race suicide" from University of Wisconsin professor Edward Ross; see Theodore Roosevelt to Marie Van Horst, October 18, 1902. This letter became the "famous race suicide letter," and was reprinted as the introduction to Van Horst's book *The Woman Who Toils* (New York: Doubleday, Page & Co., 1903); also see Theodore Roosevelt, "On American Motherhood," March 13, 1905, speech given before the National Congress of Mothers, in *[Supplemental] A Compilation of the Messages and Speeches of Theodore Roosevelt, 1901–1905,* ed. Alfred Henry Lewis, vol. 1 (Washington, DC: Bureau of National Literature and Art, 1906), 576–81; Dyer, *Theodore Roosevelt and the Idea of Race,* 15, 147, 152–55, 157; Laura L. Lovett, *Conceiving the Future: Pronatalism, Reproduction, and the Family in the United States, 1890–1938* (Chapel Hill: University of North Carolina Press, 2007), 91–95. The majority of fearmongers who worried about "race suicide" never based their claims on statistical data; see Miriam King and Steven Ruggles, "American Immigration, Fertility, and Race Suicide at the Turn of the Century," *Journal of Interdisciplinary History* 20, no. 3 (Winter 1990): 347–69, esp. 368–69.

50. Report of the Eugenics Section of the American Breeders' Association, in Harry H. Laughlin, *Scope of the Committee's Work,* Eugenics Record Office Bulletin, No. 10A (Cold Spring Harbor, Long Island, NY), 16, as quoted in Julius Paul, "Population 'Quantity' and 'Fitness for Parenthood' in the Light of State Eugenic Sterilization Experience, 1907–1966," *Population Studies* 21, no. 3 (November 1967): 295–99, esp. 295; also see Theodore Roosevelt to Charles Davenport, January 3, 1913, Charles Benedict Davenport Papers, American Philosophical Society, Philadelphia (Digital Library, #1487); and Theodore Roosevelt, "Twisted Eugenics," *Outlook* (January 3, 1914): 30–34; Dyer, *Theodore Roosevelt and the Idea of Race,* 158–60.

51. For his criticism of the new income tax and for his other proposals for mothers, see Theodore Roosevelt, "A Premium on Race Suicide," *Outlook* (September 27, 1913); Roosevelt also supported the idea of a "very high tax on the celibate and childless"; see Kathleen Dalton, *Theodore Roosevelt: A Strenuous Life* (New York: Vintage Books, 2004), 312; also see "Mother's Pensions in America," *Journal of the American Institute of Criminal Law and Criminology* 9, no. 1 (May 1918): 138–40, esp. 139. On "fit" mothers, see Jessica Toft and Laura S. Abrams, "Progressive Maternalist and the Citizenship Status of Low-Income Single Mothers," *Social Science Review* 78, no. 3 (September 2004): 447–65, esp. 460. Some jurists saw the pensions as working similarly to eugenics, preventing "the child's poverty" from reaching a "menacing state"; see Susan Sterett, "Serving the State: Constitutionalism and Social Spending, 1860s–1920s," *Law and Social Inquiry* 22, no. 2 (Spring 1997): 311–56, esp. 344.

52. "Eugenic Mania," *Pacific Medical Journal* (October 1, 1915): 599–602; Steven Selden, "Transforming Better Babies into Fitter Families: Archival Resources and the History of the American Eugenics Movement, 1908–1930," *Proceedings of the American Philosophical Society* 149, no. 2 (June 2005): 199–225; Daniel J. Kelves, *In the Name of Eugenics: Genetics and the Uses of Human Heredity* (New York: Knopf, 1985), 59–62, 91–92; Matthew J. Lindsay, "Reproducing a Fit Citizenry: Dependency, Eugenics, and the Law of Marriage in the United States, 1860–1920," *Law and Social Inquiry* 23, no. 3 (Summer 1998): 541–85; Mark A. Largent, *Breeding Contempt: The History of Coerced Sterilization in the United States* (New Brunswick, NJ: Rutgers University Press, 2008), 13–95.

53. Kelves, *In the Name of Eugenics,* 44–46, 103; Anne Maxwell, *Picture Imperfect: Photography and Eugenics, 1870–1940* (Brighton: Sussex Academic Press, 2008), 111; Matthew Frye Jacobson, *Barbarian Virtues: The United States Encounters Foreign Peoples at Home and Abroad, 1876–1917* (New York: Hill & Wang, 2000), 157–58; Jan A. Witkowski, "Charles Benedict Davenport, 1866–1944," in *Davenport's Dream: 21st Century Reflections on Heredity and Eugenics,* eds. Jan. A Witkowski and John R. Inglis (Cold Spring Harbor, NY: Cold Spring Harbor Laboratory Press, 2008), 47–48; Barbara A. Kimmelman, "The American Breeders' Association: Genetics and Eugenics in an Agricultural Context, 1903–13," *Social Studies Science* 13, no. 2 (May 1983): 163–204.

54. Davenport wrote his brother in 1924 that if immigrants were allowed to overrun the country, in two hundred years New York and the North would be transformed into Mississippi. Here he used southern backwardness as his model for the menace of foreign immigration. See Charles Davenport to

William Davenport, February 11, 1924, Box 33, Charles Benedict Davenport Papers, 1876–1946, American Philosophical Society, as cited in Kelves, *In the Name of Eugenics*, 94. He saw the failure to segregate the sexes in the poorhouse as primarily a southern problem; see Davenport, *Heredity in Relation to Eugenics* (New York: Henry Holt & Co., 1911), 67, 70–71, 74, 182, 200. On Mississippi, see Edward J. Larson, *Sex, Race, and Science: Eugenics in the Deep South* (Baltimore: Johns Hopkins University Press, 1995), 81, 92. Davenport wanted to use the U.S. Census to collect data on human bloodlines and use that information to identify in each county the "centers of feeblemindedness and crime and know who each hovel brings forth"; see Davenport, *Heredity in Relation to Eugenics*, 1, 80–82, 87–90, 211–12, 233–34, 248–49, 255, 268. Eugenicist and sociologist Edward Ross (who coined the term "race suicide") also believed that migration to the city produced a different and better breed. He argued that long-skulled people moved to the city, while the broad-skulled and mentally inferior stayed in the countryside; see Edward Ross, *Foundations of Sociology* (New York, 1905), 364.

55. On Davenport's reference to women with big hips, and for a reference to horse breeding, see *Heredity in Relation to Eugenics*, 1, 7–8. For Alexander Graham Bell's argument at the Fourth Annual Convention of the American Breeders' Association, see "Close Divorce Doors If Any Children. Prof. Alexander Graham Bell Considers Plan to Produce Better Men and Women," *New York Times*, January 30, 1908; W. E. D. Stokes, *The Right to Be Well Born, or Horse Breeding in Its Relations to Eugenics* (New York, 1917), 8, 74, 76, 199, 256; also see "W. E. D. Stokes on Eugenics," *Eugenical News* 2, no. 2 (February 1917): 13. On the focus on "human thoroughbreds" and the "unborn," also see "A Perfect Race of Men: According to Prof. Kellar the Success of Eugenics Depends on Rules Made by Custom," *New York Times*, September 27, 1908. It was Mary Harriman's daughter, also named Mary, both a student of eugenics and a horse lover, who encouraged her mother to donate money to Davenport's Eugenics Record Office. Her brother William Averell Harriman was a horse breeder, and the daughter Mary also bred cattle. See Persia Campbell, "Mary Harriman Rumsey," *Notable American Women, 1607–1950: A Biographical Dictionary*, vol. 1, eds. Edward T. James, Janet Wilson James, and Paul Boyer (Cambridge, MA: Belknap Press of Harvard University Press, 1971): 208–9.

56. A Michigan legislator proposed a measure for killing by electricity children considered hopeless cases; see S. T. Samock, "Shall We Kill the Feeble-Minded?," *Health* (August 1903): 258–59. W. Duncan McKim, M.D., Ph.D., called for a method of elimination of the very weak and very vicious by carbonic acid gas asphyxiation in his *Heredity and Human Progress* (New York, 1900), 188–93. On executing the grandfather, see Kelves, *In the Name of Eugenics*, 92. For a similar argument that degeneracy should be stopped at the grandfather, see John N. Hurty, M.D., "Practical Eugenics," *Journal of Nursing* 12, no. 5 (February 1912): 450–53. On sterilization laws and categories, see Paul, "Population 'Quantity' and 'Fitness for Parenthood,'" 296; and Paul Popenoe, "The Progress of Eugenic Sterilization," *Journal of Heredity* 25, no. 1 (January 1934): 19–27, esp. 20. On Taussig, see Thomas C. Leonard,

"Retrospectives: Eugenics and Economics in the Progressive Era," *Journal of Economic Perspectives* 19, no. 4 (Autumn 1905): 207–24, esp. 214.

57. For examples of the argument that whites, especially white women, had an instinctual aversion to blacks, see an article by the chancellor of the University of Georgia, Walter B. Hill, "Uncle Tom Without a Cabin," *Century Magazine* 27, no. 6 (1884): 862; Reverend William H. Campbell's book, *Anthropology for the People: A Refutation of the Theory of the Adamic Origins of All Races* (Richmond, 1891), 269; "The Color Line," *New York Globe,* June 1883; "Race Amalgamation," *American Economic Association. Publications* (August 1896): 180; and "The Psychology of the Race Question," *Independent* (August 13, 1903): 1939–40; Ellen Barret Ligon, M.D., "The White Woman and the Negro," *Good Housekeeping* (November 1903): 426–29, esp. 428; and Mencke, *Mulattoes and Race Mixture,* 105, 107–8; also see Stokes, *The Right to Be Well Born,* 86, 222–24, 230. On checking husbands before marriage, see Mrs. John A. Logan, "Inheritance, Mental and Physical," *Philadelphia Inquirer,* April 24, 1904. On eugenic marriages, see "Wants to Be a Eugenic Bride," *New York Times,* November 3, 1913. On a novel about eugenic marriage (*Courtship Under Contract: The Science of Selection*), see "Book Reviews," *Health* (February 1911): 43. On a eugenic school for female orphans in Louisiana, see "Quits Society for Eugenics," *New York Times,* August 29, 1913. On a eugenic registry, see "Superman a Being of Nervous Force . . . Eugenic Registry Plan Would Develop a Race of Human Thoroughbreds, It Is Argued—Elimination of the Unfit," *New York Times,* January 11, 1914; and Selden, "Transforming Better Babies into Fitter Families," 206–7, 210–12. On the important role of women in the eugenics movement, see Edward J. Larson, "'In the Finest, Most Womanly Way': Women in the Southern Eugenics Movement," *American Journal of Legal History* 39, no. 2 (April 1995): 119–47.

58. By 1928, nearly four hundred colleges and universities were offering eugenics courses; see Steven Selden, *Inheriting Shame: The Story of Eugenics and Racism in America* (New York: Teachers College Press, 1999), 49. Goddard classified morons as having the mental age from eight to twelve; see Henry H. Goddard, "Four-Hundred Feeble-Minded Children Classified by the Binet Method," *Journal of Psycho-Asthenics* 15, no. 1–2 (September and December, 1910): 17–30, esp. 26–27. On the moron and sexual deviance, see Edwin T. Brewster, "A Scientific Study of Fools," *McClure's Magazine* 39, no. 3 (July 1912): 328–34. On the fecundity of feebleminded women, see "The Unfit," *Medical Record* (March 4, 1911): 399–400; and Martin W. Barr, M.D., "The Feebleminded a Sociological Problem," *Alienist and Neurologist* (August 1, 1913): 302–5. On feebleminded girls as a menace to society, see "The Menace of the Feebleminded," *Colman's Rural World* (June 25, 1914): 8. On female morons becoming prostitutes or slovenly housekeepers with hordes of children, see George S. Bliss, M.D., "Diagnosis of Feebleminded Individuals," *Alienist and Neurologist* (January 1, 1918): 17–23; also see Kevles, *In the Name of Eugenics,* 77, 107; Davenport, *Heredity in Relation to Eugenics,* 233–43; and Wendy Kline, *Building a Better Race: Gender, Sexuality, and Eugenics from the Turn of the Century to the Baby Boom* (Berkeley: University of California Press, 2005), 20–29.

59. On the continuing fears of miscegenation, see William Benjamin Smith, *The Color Line: A Brief in Behalf of the Unborn* (New York, 1905), 5, 8, 11–14, 17–18, 74; Robert W. Shufeldt, M.D., *The Negro: A Menace to American Civilization* (Boston, 1907), 73–74, 77–78, 103–4, 131. Between 1907 and 1921, Congress proposed twenty-one bills against miscegenation; see Robinson, *Dangerous Liaisons*, 82.

60. For Goddard using the same metaphors as Reconstruction writers for white trash, see Henry Herbert Goddard, *The Kallikak Family: A Study in the Heredity of Feeble-Mindedness* (New York, 1912), 66, 71–72. On reducing taxpayers' burden, an argument used in Indiana, which passed one of the first sterilization laws in 1907, see "Feeble-Minded Women," *Duluth News Tribune,* March 12, 1904; Davenport, *Heredity in Relation to Eugenics,* 259; Kline, *Building a Better Race,* 49, 53; Kelves, *In the Name of Eugenics,* 72. On morons as needed for manual laborers, see Lewis M. Terman, *The Measurement of Intelligence* (Boston: Houghton Mifflin, 1916), 91. This was the argument of Albert Priddy, superintendent of the asylum involved in the *Buck v. Bell* case; see Gregory Michael Dorr, *Segregation's Science: Eugenics and Society in Virginia* (Charlottesville: University of Virginia Press, 2008), 132.

61. On the Chamberlain-Kahn Bill passed by Congress in 1918, for detaining suspected prostitutes, see Kristin Luker, "Sex, Social Hygiene, and the State: The Double-Edged Sword of Social Reform," *Theory and Society* 27, no. 5 (October 1998): 601–34, esp. 618–23; Christopher Capozzola, "The Only Badge Needed Is Your Patriotic Fervor: Vigilance, Coercion, and the Law in World War I America," *Journal of American History* 88, no. 4 (March 2002): 1354–82, esp. 1370–73; Kline, *Building a Better Race,* 46–47; Aine Collier, *The Humble Little Condom: A History* (Amherst, NY: Prometheus Books, 2007), 185, 187. On the draft, see Jeanette Keith, *Rich Man's War, Poor Man's Fight: Race, Class and Power in the Rural South During the First World War* (Chapel Hill: University of North Carolina Press, 2004), 43, 70–71, 73–75.

62. On the army filled with morons, and calls for intelligence tests for voting, see "Are We Ruled by Morons?," *Current Opinion* 72, no. 4 (April 1922): 438–40. For southern poor whites and blacks receiving lower scores, especially those from the Deep South, see M. F. Ashley Montagu, "Intelligence of Northern Negroes and Southern Whites in the First World War," *American Journal of Psychology* 58, no. 2 (April 1945): 161–88, esp. 165–67, 185–86; also see Daniel J. Kevles, "Testing the Army's Intelligence: Psychologists and the Military in World War I," *Journal of American History* 55, no. 3 (December 1968): 565–81, esp. 576; Dorr, *Segregation's Science,* 110; and James D. Watson, "Genes and Politics," in Witkowski and Inglis, *Davenport's Dream,* 11.

63. Hookworm was identified as the reason for stunted bodies among World War I draftees; see M. W. Ireland, Albert Love, and Charles Davenport, *Defects Found in Drafted Men: Statistical Information Compiled from the Draft Records* (Washington, DC, 1919), 34, 265. For clay-eating as a white trash addiction, see (the ironically titled) "They Eat Clay and Grow Fat," *Philadelphia Inquirer,* November 26, 1895; and "The Clay Eaters," *Fort Worth Register,* January 12, 1897. On hookworm and stunted bodies, see Marion Hamilton Carter, "The Vampires of the South," *McClure's Magazine* 33, no. 6

(October 1909): 617–31; J. L. Nicholson, M.D., and Watson S. Rankin, M.D., "Uncinariasis as Seen in North Carolina," *Medical News* (November 19, 1904): 978–87; H. F. Harris, "Uncinariasis; Its Frequency and Importance in the Southern States," *Atlanta Journal-Record of Medicine*, June 1, 1903; "Uncinariasis, the Cause of Laziness," *Zion's Herald*, December 10, 1902; "The Passing of the Po' 'White Trash': The Rockefeller Commission's Successful Fight Against Hookworm Disease," *Hampton-Columbia Magazine*, November 1, 1911. On white trash diseases, see James O. Breeden, "Disease as a Factor in Southern Distinctiveness," and Elizabeth W. Etheridge, "Pellagra: An Unappreciated Reminder of Southern Distinctiveness," in *Disease and Distinctiveness in the American South*, eds. Todd L. Savitt and James Harvey Young (Knoxville: University of Tennessee Press, 1988), 1–28, 100–19, esp. 14–15, 104. On the army's discovery that southern recruits had a "poorer degree of physical development," see Natalie J. Ring, *The Problem of the South: Region, Empire, and the New Liberal State, 1880–1930* (Athens: University of Georgia Press, 2012), 79.

64. See S. A. Hamilton, "The New Race Question in the South," *Arena* 27, no. 4 (April 1902): 352–58; also see "Science and Discovery: The Coming War on Hookworm," *Current Literature* 17, no. 6 (December 1909): 676–80; E. J. Edwards, "The Fight to Save 2,000,000 Lives from Hookworm," *New York Times*, August 28, 1910; John Ettling, *The Germ of Laziness: Rockefeller Philanthropy and Public Health in the New South* (Cambridge, MA: Harvard University Press, 1981); Andrew Sledd, "Illiteracy in the South," *Independent*, October 17, 1901, 2471–74; Richard Edmonds, "The South's Industrial Task: A Plea for Technical Training of Poor White Boys," an address before the Annual Convention of Southern Cotton Spinners' Association at Atlanta, November 14, 1901 (Atlanta, 1901). On education and reforming poor whites, see Bruce Clayton, *The Savage Ideal: Intolerance and Intellectual Leadership in the South, 1890–1914* (Baltimore: Johns Hopkins University Press, 1972), 114–15, 119, 140. On millwork endangering white women and children, see Elbert Hubbard, "White Slavery in the South," *Philistine* (May 1902): 161–78; "Child Labor in the South," *Ohio Farmer* (February 3, 1906): 121; Louise Markscheffel, "The Right of the Child Not to Be Born," *Arena* 36, no. 201 (August 1906): 125–27; Owen R. Lovejoy, assistant secretary of the National Child Labor Committee, "Child Labor and Family Disintegration," *Independent* (September 27, 1906): 748–50. On tenant farmers as the new vagrants, see Frank Tannenbaum, *Darker Phases of the South* (New York, 1924), 131–35; also see Ring, *The Problem of the South*, 25–26, 62–63, 121, 125–26, 135–36. The poor whites were also a greater target because blacks had been disenfranchised in many southern states. The uneducated cracker still had political power, which many elite southerners found troubling. See Charles H. Holden, *In the Great Maelstrom: Conservatives in Post–Civil War South Carolina* (Columbia: University of South Carolina Press, 2002), 65, 80.

65. Dorr, *Segregation's Science*, 122–23, 129, 132; Paul Lombardo, "Three Generations, No Imbeciles: New Light on *Buck v. Bell*," *New York University Law Review* 60, no. 1 (April 1965): 30–60, esp. 37, 45–50.

66. See David Starr Jordan and Harvey Ernest Jordan, *War's Aftermath: A Preliminary Study of the Eugenics of War as Illustrated by the Civil War of the United States and the Late Wars in the Balkans* (Boston: Houghton Mifflin, 1914), 63; Dorr, *Segregation's Science,* 54–55, 57, 59, 62, 65; Gregory Michael Dorr, "Assuring America's Place in the Sun: Ivey Foreman Lewis and the Teaching of Eugenics at the University of Virginia, 1915–1953," *Journal of Southern History* 66, no. 2 (May 2000): 257–96, esp. 264–65.

67. In addition to focusing on their immoral sexual relations and high fecundity, he emphasized how most of their teachers ranked the children as "feebleminded," "stupid," and "hopeless." He also delineated the degree of inbreeding, mostly second cousins mating and marrying. He identified four "fountain heads," or male progenitors; one was Joseph Brown, a white man, who married a full-blooded Indian. He described their "stock" as better than if not equal to the common whites of Virginia. The Wins themselves recognized those of pure white blood as having "clar blood." See Arthur H. Estabrook and Ivan E. M. McDougle, *Mongrel Virginians: The Win Tribe* (Baltimore: Williams & Wilkins Company, 1926), 13–14, 23, 119, 125, 145–46, 154–57, 160–66, 181, 203–5.

68. Estabrook included in his book a copy of the 1924 proposed law and an explanation of it; see Estabrook, *Mongrel Virginians,* 203–5. Virginia's 1924 Racial Integrity Act also had the "Pocahontas exception" that protected elite families (descendants of John Rolfe) from being considered racially tainted; see Richard B. Sherman, "'The Last Stand': The Fight for Racial Integrity in Virginia in the 1920s," *Journal of Southern History* 54, no. 1 (February 1988): 69–92, esp. 78; Dorr, *Segregation's Science,* 145–46.

69. On the law prohibiting the mixing of blacks and whites in public venues, see Sherman, "'The Last Stand,'" esp. 83–84. For the opinion of Justice Oliver Wendell Holmes, see *Buck v. Bell,* 274 U.S. 200 (1927), 208.

70. Harry Laughlin used Albert Priddy's words in his disposition for the 1924 trial when he described the Buck family as "belong[ing] to the shiftless, ignorant, and worthless class of anti-social whites of the South." In 1914, in a report to the governor, Priddy had defended sterilization for the feebleminded by equating heredity defects with antisocial behavior (crime, prostitution, drunkenness) among the "non-producing and shiftless persons, living on public and private charity." See Lombardo, "Three Generations, No Imbeciles," 37, 49–50, 54; Dorr, *Segregation's Science,* 129–30, 132, 134. Eugenic promoters published the court's decision to justify the expansion of sterilization; see Popenoe, "The Progress of Eugenic Sterilization," 23–26. For Carrie Buck's pedigree chart, used in the trial, see "Most Immediate Blood-Kin of Carrie Buck. Showing Illegitimacy and Hereditary Feeblemindedness" (circa 1925), the Harry H. Laughlin Papers, Truman State University, Lantern Slides, Brown Box, 1307, accessed from Image Archive on the American Eugenics Movement, Dolan DNA Center, Cold Spring Harbor Laboratory (#1013), http://www.eugenicsarchive.org.

71. Lewis M. Terman dismissed the influence of environment and saw class as an accurate outcome of hereditary ability. He wrote, "Common observation would itself suggest that social class to which the family belongs depends less

on chance than on the parents' native qualities of intellect and character." For his class arguments, see Terman, *The Measurement of Intelligence,* 72, 96, 115. Terman worried more about the low birthrates among the talented class, and doing everything possible to increase this class; see Lewis Madison Terman, "Were We Born That Way?," *The World's Work* 44 (May–October 1922): 655–60. Terman's intelligence scale was more elitist; he grouped the most severely mentally deficient into one category of the "intellectually feeble," and then used borderline, inferior, average, superior, very superior, select, very select, and genius. It was the top of the scale that mattered most to him; see Terman, "The Binet Scale and the Diagnosis of Feeble-Mindedness," *Journal of the American Institute of Criminal Law and Criminology* 7, no. 4 (November 1916): 530–43, esp. 541–42; also see Mary K. Coffey, "The American Adonis: A Natural History of the 'Average American' Man, 1921–32," in *Popular Eugenics: National Efficiency and American Mass Culture in the 1930s,* eds. Susan Currell and Christina Cogdell (Athens: Ohio University Press, 2006), 185–216, esp. 186–87, 196, 198. Other eugenicists like popular lecturer Albert E. Wiggam feared that if intelligent and beautiful women (as if those traits were united in one class) did not breed, "the next generation will be both homely and dumb"; see R. le Clerc Phillips, "Cracks in the Upper Crust," *Independent* (May 29, 1926): 633–36.

72. On C. W. Saleeby and his new book *Woman on Womanhood,* see "Urging Women to Lift the Race," *New York Times,* November 19, 1911; for a satire of eugenic feminism, of women running down men, replacing marriage for love with the "cold-blooded selection" of the best based on "scientific propagation," see Robert W. Chambers, "Pro Bono Publico: Further Developments in the Eugenist Suffragette Campaign," *Hampton's Magazine* (July 1, 1911): 19–30; and William McDougall, *National Welfare and Decay* (London, 1921), 9–25. McDougall did a similar study comparing the intellectual capacity of English private schools (children of educated elite) and primary schools (children of shopkeepers and artisans) and arrived at the same conclusion as Terman: there was a marked superiority of the children of the educated elite. See Reverend W. R. Inge, "Is Our Race Degenerating?," *The Living Age* (January 15, 1927): 143–54.

73. Steven Noll, *Feeble-Minded in Our Midst: Institutions for the Mentally Retarded in the South, 1900–1940* (Chapel Hill: University of North Carolina Press, 1995), 71. For the importance of targeting delinquent white girls of the poorer class for sterilization in North Carolina in the 1920s, see Karen L. Zipf, *Bad Girls at Samarcand: Sexuality and Sterilization in a Southern Juvenile Reformatory* (Baton Rouge: Louisiana State University Press, 2016), 3, 66–67, 73, 83–84, 150–52, 154.

74. See Sherwood Anderson, *Poor White* (New York: B. W. Huebsch, Inc., 1920), 3–8, 11–14, 18; Stephen C. Enniss, "Alienation and Affirmation: The Divided Self in Sherwood Anderson's 'Poor White,'" *South Atlantic Review* 55, no. 2 (May 1990): 85–99; Welford Dunaway Taylor and Charles E. Modlin, eds., *Southern Odyssey: Selected Writings of Sherwood Anderson* (Athens: University of Georgia Press, 1997); and on Anderson's focus on people building walls, often class barriers, see Percy H. Boynton, "Sherwood Anderson," *North American Review* 224, no. 834 (March–May 1927): 140–50, esp. 148.

75. Anderson, *Poor White*, 29, 43, 55, 56, 62, 72, 80, 118–21, 127–28, 156, 169, 171–72, 190–91, 227–28, 230–31, 253–54, 299.

76. Ibid., 136, 260, 271, 277, 332, 342, 345, 357, 367–71.

77. For the idea of "childish impotence," "arrested development of the social class," "spiritual stagnation," and that the South had "buried its Anglo-Saxons," see Tannenbaum, *Darker Phases of the South*, 39–42, 56, 70, 117–19, 183; William Garrott Brown, *Lower South in American History* (New York, 1902), 266; Edgar Gardner Murphy, *The Problems of the Present South* (New York, 1909), 123; also see Ring, *The Problem of the South*, 139, 148, 152. Ira Caldwell published a five-part series in 1929 for *Eugenics: A Journal of Race Betterment* on a poor white family that he called "The Bunglers." It was his own family study in the tradition of *The Jukes*. See Ashley Craig Lancaster, "Weeding out the Recessive Gene: Representations of the Evolving Eugenics Movement in Erskine Caldwell's 'God's Little Acre,'" *Southern Literary Journal* 39, no. 2 (Spring 2007): 78–99, esp. 81.

78. Erskine Caldwell, *The Bastard* (New York, 1929), 13–14, 16, 21, 28.

79. Ibid., 21–23, 141–42, 145–46, 165–66, 170, 175, 177, 198–99.

80. For articles debating aristocracy, see Robert N. Reeves, "Our Aristocracy," *American Magazine of Civics* (January 1896): 23–29; Harry Thurston Peck, "The New American Aristocracy," *The Cosmopolitan* (October 1898): 701–9; Harry Thurston Peck, "The Basis for an American Aristocracy," *Independent* (December 22, 1898): 1842–45; "Is America Heading for Aristocracy?," *The Living Age* (September 21, 1907): 757–60; Charles Ferguson, "A Democratic Aristocracy," *The Bookman: A Review of Books and Life* (October 1917): 147–48. In favor of an aristocracy of talent, see James Southall Wilson, "The Future of Aristocracy in America," *North American Review* (January 1932), 34–40. And for an inbred civil servant class, see James Edward Dunning, "An Aristocracy of Government in America," *Forum* (June 1910): 567–80. There were also critics of creating this master class; see "Modern Biology as the Enemy of Democracy," *Current Opinion* 49, no. 3 (September 1920): 346–47; on the new power of science and expertise, see JoAnne Brown, *The Definition of a Profession: The Authority of Metaphor in the History of Intelligence Testing, 1900–1930* (Princeton, NJ: Princeton University Press, 1992), 41.

81. On the flapper, see Corra Harris, *Flapper Anne* (Boston: Houghton Mifflin, 1926). It was serialized in *Ladies' Home Journal* in 1925; see Betsy Lee Nies, *Eugenic Fantasies: Racial Ideology and the Literature and Popular Culture of the 1920s* (New York: Routledge, 2010), 41.

Chapter Nine: Forgotten Men and Poor Folk: Downward Mobility and the Great Depression

1. David M. Kennedy, *The American People in the Great Depression: Freedom from Fear: Part I* (New York: Oxford University Press, 1999), 86–87, 89.

2. See U.S. National Emergency Council, *Report on Economic Conditions in the South. Prepared for the President by the National Emergency Council* (Washington, DC: Government Printing Office, 1938), 1; Will W. Alexander, "Rural Resettlement," *Southern Review* 1, no. 3 (Winter 1936): 528–39, esp.

529, 532, 535, 538. As another expert explained, rural rehabilitation did not mean a return to the status quo, but giving farmers the means to sustain and improve their standard of living; see Joseph W. Eaton, *Exploring Tomorrow's Agriculture: Co-Operative Group Farming—A Practical Program of Rural Rehabilitation* (New York: Harper & Brothers, 1943), 4–7.

3. Matthew J. Mancini, *One Dies, Get Another: Convict Leasing in the American South, 1866–1928* (Columbia: University of South Carolina Press, 1996), 2–3, 23, 37–38; Edward L. Ayers, *Vengeance and Justice: Crime and Punishment in the Nineteenth-Century American South* (New York: Oxford University Press, 1985), 185–222.

4. Robert E. Burns, *I Am a Fugitive from a Georgia Chain Gang*, foreword by Matthew J. Mancini (Athens: University of Georgia Press, 1997), vi–ix. By 1932, nearly a third of the population of convicts were white, a tripling since 1908; see Alex Lichtenstein, "Chain Gangs, Communism, and the 'Negro Question': John L. Spivak's Georgia Nigger," *Georgia Historical Quarterly* 79, no. 3 (Fall 1995): 633–58, esp. 641–42.

5. On Warner Brothers, see Andrew Bergman, *We're in the Money: Depression America and Its Films* (Chicago: Ivan R. Dee, 1971), 92.

6. Lewis W. Hine, *Men at Work: Photographic Studies of Modern Men and Machines* (New York, 1932), frontispiece; also see Kate Sampsell Willmann, "Lewis Hine, Ellis Island, and Pragmatism: Photographs as Lived Experience," *Journal of the Gilded Age and Progressive Era* 7, no. 2 (April 2008): 221–52, esp. 221–22.

7. Amity Shlaes, *The Forgotten Man: A New History of the Great Depression* (New York: Harper Perennial, 2008), 129; Roger Daniels, *The Bonus March: An Episode of the Great Depression* (Westport, CT: Greenwood, 1971); John Dos Passos, "The Veterans Come Home to Roost," *New Republic* (June 29, 1932): 177–78. One account noted that there were a large number of farmers; see Mauritz A. Haligren, "The Bonus Army Scares Mr. Hoover," *Nation* 135 (July 27, 1932): 73. On burning the shantytown, see "The Bonus Army Incident," *New York Times*, September 16, 1932. On the reaction to Hoover calling Bonus Army men criminals, see Harold N. Denny, "Hoover B.E.F. Attack Stirs Legion Anew," *New York Times*, September 13, 1932; John Henry Bartlett, *The Bonus March and the New Deal* (Chicago: M. A. Donohue & Co., 1937), 13; and Donald J. Lisio, "A Blunder Becomes a Catastrophe: Hoover, the Legion, and the Bonus Army," *Wisconsin Magazine of History* 51, no. 1 (Autumn 1967): 37–50.

8. Charles R. Walker, "Relief and Revolution," *Forum and Century* 88 (August 1932): 73–79.

9. Edward Newhouse, *You Can't Sleep Here* (New York: Macaulay, 1934), 103–4, 112.

10. On thirties writers, see David P. Peeler, *Hope Among Us Yet: Social Criticism and Social Solace in Depression America* (Athens: University of Georgia Press, 1987), 167–68, 171; Tom Kromer, *Waiting for Nothing* (New York, 1935), 186; and Arthur M. Lamport, "The New Era Is Dead—Long Live the New Deal," *Banker's Magazine* (June 1933): 545–48.

11. See the photographs "The Flood Leaves Its Victims on the Bread Line" and "Tennessee Puts a Chain Gang on Its Levees," *Life* 2, no. 7 (February 15, 1937): 9, 12–13.

12. "Muncie, Ind. Is the Great U.S. 'Middletown': And This Is the First Picture Essay of What It Looks Like," *Life* 2 (May 10, 1937): 15–25; also see Sarah E. Igo, "From Main Street to Mainstream: Middletown, Muncie, and 'Typical America,'" *Indiana Magazine of History* 101, no. 3 (September 2005): 239–66, esp. 244–45, 255, 259–60. As one writer noted, the popular understanding of the American standard of living was "mouthed about by everyone, but defined by none," and at the "present time the American Standard of Living is probably nothing more than a set of values which the majority of people place on things they *wish* they had"; Elmer Leslie McDowell, "The American Standard of Living," *North American Review* 237, no. 1 (January 1934): 71–75, esp. 72.

13. "The American Collapse," *The Living Age* (December 1, 1929): 398–401; on the Egyptian tomb theme, see Virgil Jordan, "The Era of Mad Illusions," *North American Review* (January 1930): 54–59.

14. See William Stott, *Documentary Expression and Thirties America* (Chicago: University of Chicago Press, 1973), 62–63, 67–68, 212. And on the importance of erosion to Roy Stryker's photographic agenda, see Stuart Kidd, "Art, Politics and Erosion: Farm Security Administration Photographs of the Southern Land," *Revue française d'études américaines*, rev. ed. (1986): 67–68; Arthur Rothstein, "Melting Snow, Utopia, Ohio," February 1940, Library of Congress, Prints and Photographs Division, Washington, DC; and Peeler, *Hope Among Us Yet*, 148.

15. On waste, see Herbert J. Spinden, "Waters Flow, Winds Blow, Civilizations Die," *North American Review* (Autumn 1937): 53–70; Russell Lord, "Behold Our Land," *North American Review* (Autumn 1938): 118–32; on the chaotic groundswell, also see Russell Lord, "Back to the Land?," *Forum* (February 1933): 97–103, esp. 99, 102. Spinden was an archeologist who specialized in Mayan art and was curator of American Indian art and culture at the Brooklyn Museum from 1929 to 1951. See Regna Darnell and Frederic W. Gleach, eds., *Celebrating a Century of the American Anthropological Association: Presidential Portraits* (New York, 2002), 73–76. Dorothea Lange and Paul Taylor, *An American Exodus: A Record of Human Erosion* (New York: Reynal & Hitchcock, 1939), 102. Engineer and WPA consultant David Cushman Coyle published a powerful little book titled *Waste*, which offered this statement in his opening chapter, "Mud": "Wherever man touches this land, it breaks down and washes away. If he builds a cabin, the track to his door becomes a devouring gully. . . . This land shrinks and withers under the touch of man"; see *Waste: The Fight to Save America* (Indianapolis: Bobbs-Merrill, 1936), 5–6. He also had a chapter titled "Human Erosion," and described working people "moving into the slums or into shacks built of rubbish—sliding down and down, at last to the relief line"; see ibid., 57. This little book became a key campaign tool in Roosevelt's 1936 reelection campaign in Indiana; see James Philip Fadely, "Editors, Whistle Stops, and Elephants: The Presidential Campaign in Indiana," *Indiana Magazine of History* 85, no. 2 (June 1989): 101–37, esp. 106.

16. See Carleton Beals, "Migs: America's Shantytown on Wheels," *Forum and Century* 99 (January 1938): 10–16, esp. 11–12; "'I Wonder Where We Can Go Now,'" *Fortune* 19, no. 4 (April 1939): 91–100, esp. 91, 94; Paul Taylor, "The Migrants and California's Future: The Trek to California and the Trek in California" [ca. 1935], in Taylor, *On the Ground in the Thirties* (Salt Lake City: Peregrine Smith Books, 1983), 175–84, esp. 175–77, 179; Charles Poole, "John Steinbeck's 'The Grapes of Wrath,'" in "Books of the Month," *New York Times,* April 14, 1939; "'The Grapes of Wrath': John Steinbeck Writes a Major Novel About Western Migrants," *Life* 6, no. 23 (June 5, 1939): 66–67; Woody Guthrie, "Talking Dust Bowl Blues" (1940); Frank Eugene Cruz, "'In Between a Past and Future Town': Home, the Unhomely, and 'The Grapes of Wrath,'" *Steinbeck Review* 4, no. 2 (Fall 2007): 52–75, esp. 63, 73; Michael Denning, *The Cultural Front: The Laboring of American Culture in the Twentieth Century* (London: Verso, 1997), 259; Vivian C. Sobchack, "The Grapes of Wrath (1940): Thematic Emphasis Through Visual Style," *American Quarterly* 31, no. 5 (Winter 1979): 596–615.

17. Paul K. Conkin, *Tomorrow a New World: The New Deal Community Program* (Ithaca, NY: Cornell University Press, 1959), 26, 30; William H. Issel, "Ralph Borsodi and the Agrarian Response to Modern America," *Agricultural History* 41, no. 2 (April 1967): 155–66; Ralph Borsodi, "Subsistence Homesteads: President Roosevelt's New Land and Population Policy," *Survey Graphic* 23 (January 1934): 11–14, 48, esp. 13; and Borsodi, "Dayton, Ohio, Makes Social History," *Nation* 136 (April 19, 1933): 447–48, esp. 448. On Dayton, Ohio, also see John A. Piquet, "Return of the Wilderness," *North American Review* (May 1934): 417–26, esp. 425–26; Charles Morrow Wilson, "American Peasants," *The Commonweal* 19 (December 8, 1933): 147–49; and Pamela Webb, "By the Sweat of the Brow: The Back-to-the-Land Movement in Depression Arkansas," *Arkansas Historical Quarterly* 42, no. 4 (Winter 1983): 332–45, esp. 337.

18. Webb, "By the Sweat of the Brow," 334. One observer concluded that "many of these would-be farmers are not farmers and most of them may be expected to return to city jobs when prosperity returns"; see W. Russell Taylor, "Recent Trends in City and County Population," *Journal of Land and Public Utility Economics* 9, no. 1 (February 1933): 63–74, esp. 72.

19. Richard S. Krikendall, *Social Scientists and Farm Politics in the Age of Roosevelt* (Ames: Iowa State University Press, 1982), 12–14; and M. L. Wilson, "The Fairway Farms Project," *Journal of Land and Public Utility Economics* 2, no. 2 (April 1926): 156–71, esp. 156; Roy E. Huffman, "Montana's Contributions to New Deal Farm Policy," *Agricultural History* 33, no. 4 (October 1959): 164–67; also see "A Hope and a Homestead" (Washington, DC: Government Printing Office, 1935), 6, 8–10; and M. L. Wilson, "The Subsistence Homestead Program," *Proceedings of the Institute of Public Affairs* 8 (1934): 158–75.

20. M. L. Wilson, "A New Land-Use Program: The Place of Subsistence Homesteads," *Journal of Land and Public Utility Economics* 10, no. 1 (February 1934): 1–12, esp. 6–8; Wilson, "Problem of Poverty in Agriculture," *Journal of Farm Economics* 22, no. 1, Proceedings Number (February 1940): 10–29, esp. 20; *Farm Tenancy: Report of the President's Committee* (Washington, DC: Government Printing Office, 1937), 4.

21. Wilson, "A New Land-Use Program," 2–3, 11–12; "A Hope and a Home-stead," 4; *Farm Tenancy: Report of the President's Committee*, 5.

22. Arthur F. Raper, *Preface to Peasantry: A Tale of Two Black Belt Counties* (Chapel Hill: University of North Carolina Press, 1936), 61, 172, 218, 405; also see Rupert B. Vance, *Human Factors in Cotton Culture: A Study in Social Geography of the American South* (Chapel Hill: University of North Carolina Press, 1929), 153, 248, 279; *Farm Tenancy: Report of the President's Committee*, 3, 5–7, 9.

23. Harold Hoffsommer, "The AAA and the Cropper," *Social Forces* 13, no. 4 (May 1935): 494–502, esp. 494–96, 501; Raper, *Preface to Peasantry*, 61, 75, 157–59, 173, 405; Vance, *Human Factors in Cotton Culture*, 161–62, 168, 201, 204, 215, 259, 307–8; Wilson, "A New Land-Use Program," 9, 12; Wilson, "Problem of Poverty in Agriculture," 14–17, 21; Wilson, "The Problem of Surplus Agricultural Population," *International Journal of Agrarian Affairs* 1 (1939): 37–48, esp. 41–43; Wilson, "How New Deal Agencies Are Affecting Family Life," *Journal of Home Economics* 27 (May 1935): 274–80, esp. 276–78.

24. Henry A. Wallace, "The Genetic Basis of Democracy" (February 12, 1939), in Henry A. Wallace, *Democracy Reborn*, ed. Russell Lord (New York: Reynal and Hitchcock, 1944), 155–56.

25. Wilson, "Problem of Poverty in Agriculture," 20, 23, 28; Wallace, "Chapter VII: The Blessing of General Liberty," in *Whose Constitution? An Inquiry into the General Welfare* (New York: Reynal and Hitchcock, 1936), 102–3.

26. John Corbin, "The New Deal and the Constitution," *Forum and Century* 90, no. 2 (August 1933): 92–97, esp. 94–95; Wilson, "Problem of Poverty in Agriculture," 17. Though he was the drama critic for the *New York Times*, Corbin spent four years studying history, which led to his biography of George Washington, *Washington: Biographic Origins of the Republic* (New York: Charles Scribner's Sons, 1930); also see David M. Clark, "John Corbin: Dramatic Critic (Lincoln: University of Nebraska Press, 1976). For the importance of the word "readjustment," see "President's Address to the Farmers," *New York Times*, May 15, 1935.

27. Wallace, "Chapter VIII: Soil and the General Welfare," in *Whose Constitution*, 109, 115–17.

28. Wallace, "Chapter IX: Population and the General Welfare," in *Whose Constitution*, 122–24, 126. The full quote from the film is, "Rich fellas come up an' they die, an' their kids ain't no good and they die out, but we keep a-comin'. We're the people that live. They can't wipe us out, they can't lick us. We'll go on forever, Pa, cos we're the people." Steinbeck wrote, "We ain't gonna die out. People is goin' on—changin' a little, maybe, but goin' right on." See *The Grapes of Wrath* (New York: Penguin, 2014), 423.

29. Conkin, *Tomorrow a New World*, 128–30, 142–45; Richard S. Kirkendall, *Social Scientists and Farm Politics in the Age of Roosevelt* (Columbia: University of Missouri Press, 1966); Kennedy, *The American People in the Great Depression*, 208–10; Fred C. Frey and T. Lynn Smith, "The Influence of the AAA Cotton Program upon the Tenant, Cropper, and Laborer," *Rural Sociology* 1, no. 4 (December 1936): 483–505, esp. 489, 500–501, 505; Warren C. Whatley, "Labor for the Picking: The New Deal in the South," *Journal of*

Economic History 43, no. 4 (December 1983): 905–29, esp. 909, 913–14, 924, 926–29; Jack T. Kirby, *Rural Worlds Lost: The American South, 1920–1960* (Baton Rouge: Louisiana State University Press, 1987), 65–74; George Brown Tindall, *The Emergence of the New South, 1913–1945* (Baton Rouge: Louisiana State University Press, 1967), 409.

30. Kirkendall, *Social Scientists and Farm Politics,* 109–11; Sidney Baldwin, *Poverty and Politics: The Rise and Decline of the Farm Security Administration* (Chapel Hill: University of North Carolina Press, 1968), 92–96, 117–19. On migratory workers, see Paul Taylor, "What Shall We Do with Them? Address Before the Commonwealth Club of California" (April 15, 1938); and "Migratory Agricultural Workers on the Pacific Coast" (April 1938), reprinted in Taylor, *On the Ground in the Thirties,* 203–20.

31. R. G. Tugwell, "Resettling America: A Fourfold Plan," *New York Times,* July 28, 1935. For Tugwell's criticism of Jefferson, see "'Through Our Fault' Is the Waste of Land," *Science New Letter* 30, no. 800 (August 8, 1936), 85–86; Tugwell, "Behind the Farm Problem: Rural Poverty, Not the Tenancy System, but the Low Scale of Life, Says Tugwell, Is the Fundamental Question," *New York Times Magazine,* January 10, 1937, 4–5, 22; and Rexford G. Tugwell, "The Resettlement Idea," *Agricultural History* 33, no. 4 (October 1959): 159–64, esp. 160–61. On the unromantic portrait of farming, see Rexford G. Tugwell, Thomas Munro, and Roy E. Stryker, *American Economic Life and the Means of Its Improvement* (New York, 1930), 90; also see Baldwin, *Poverty and Politics,* 87–88, 105–6, 163–64.

32. Tugwell, "Behind the Farm Problem," 22, and "The Resettlement Idea," 162; Baldwin, *Poverty and Politics,* 111.

33. Baldwin, *Poverty and Politics,* 113–14; Roger Biles, *The South and the New Deal* (Lexington: University of Kentucky Press, 1994), 64; Howard N. Mead, "Russell vs. Talmadge: Southern Politics and the New Deal," *Georgia Historical Review* 65, no. 1 (Spring 1981): 28–45, esp. 36, 38, 42.

34. On "parlor pink," see Paul Mallon, "Tugwell," and in the same paper, see "Tugwellism," [Steubenville, OH] *Herald Star,* June 13, 1934. On his "carefully-studied informality," see "Tugwell Defends 'New Deal' Earnestly; Ignore Red Scare," [Burlington, NC] *Daily Times-News,* April 24, 1934. On "a dream walking," see "Tugwell Meets His Critics," *Oelwein* [IA] *Daily Register,* June 11, 1934; also see "Sick of Propertied Czars at 24, Tugwell Homes Dreamy Economics," *Kansas City Star,* August 31, 1936; and "Tugwell Named to Fill New Post," *New York Times,* April 25, 1934.

35. On Huey Long's hillbilly image, see James Rorty, "Callie Long's Boy Huey," *Forum and Century,* August 1935, 74–82, 126–27, esp. 75, 79–80, 127. On Long as a defender of "poor white trash," see eulogies in "Friends Applaud Memory of Long in Senate Talks," [New Orleans] *Times-Picayune,* January 23, 1936. For Long's failure to help the poor in Louisiana, see Anthony J. Badger, "Huey Long and the New Deal," *New Deal/New South: An Anthony J. Badger Reader* (Fayetteville: University of Arkansas Press, 2007), 1–30, esp. 1, 5–7, 21–25. On Long's rustic clown role, see J. Michael Hogan and Glen Williams, "The Rusticity and Religiosity of Huey P. Long," *Rhetoric and Public Affairs* 7, no. 2 (Summer 2004): 149–171, esp. 151, 158–59. On

politicians claiming to be one with the plowmen or "plain old country boy[s]," see Roger Butterfield, "The Folklore of Politics," *Pennsylvania Magazine of History and Biography* 74, no. 2 (April 1950): 164–77, esp. 165–66. On Ed "Cotton" Smith using Vardaman's tricks, see Dan T. Carter, "Southern Political Style," in *The Age of Segregation: Race Relations in the South, 1890–1954*, ed. Robert Haws (Jackson: University Press of Mississippi, 1978), 45–67, esp. 51. On friends telling Tugwell to affect a homely democratic manner, see Arthur Krock, "In Washington: Senator Smith Certainly 'Put On a Good Show,'" *New York Times*, June 12, 1934.

36. For the most vicious attack, see Blair Bolles, "The Sweetheart of the Regimenters: Dr. Tugwell Makes America Over," *American Mercury* 39, no. 153 (September 1936): 77–86, esp. 84–85. On criticism of the New Deal, see "What Relief Did to Us," *American Mercury* 38, no. 151 (July 1936): 274–83, esp. 283; H. L. Mencken, "The New Deal Mentality," *American Mercury* 38, no. 149 (May 1936): 1–11. For endorsing eugenics over relief, see Mencken, "The Dole for Bogus Farmers," *American Mercury* 39, no. 156 (December 1936): 400–407; also see Cedric B. Cowing, "H. L. Mencken: The Case of the 'Curdled' Progressive," *Ethics* 69, no. 4 (July 1959): 255–67, esp. 262–63.

37. On Tugwell's slogan "nothing is too good for these people," see Rodney Dutcher, "Behind the Scenes in Washington," [Biloxi, MS] *Daily Herald*, September 12, 1937. Bolles wrote another critical article on FDR as an extravagant spender; see "Our Uneconomic Royalist: The High Cost of Dr. Roosevelt," *American Mercury* 43, no. 171 (March 1938): 265–69.

38. See "Mission of the New Deal by Rexford G. Tugwell," *New York Times*, May 27, 1934; "Address Delivered at the National Conference of Social Work, Kansas City, May 21, 1934," in Rexford Tugwell, *The Battle for Democracy* (New York: Columbia University Press, 1935), 319. Tugwell defended the theory of a flexible Constitution and the role of government mediating imbalances in class power; see "Design for Government" and "The Return to Democracy," ibid., 12–13, 204–5; also see Simeon Strunsky, "Professor Tugwell Defines the Battle for Democracy," *New York Times*, January 6, 1935.

39. For Tugwell's defense of the loans, see Tugwell, "The Resettlement Idea," 161. For the popularity of the program, see Tindall, *The Emergence of the New South*, 423–24; also see Eleanor Roosevelt, "Subsistence Farmsteads," *Forum and Century* 91, no. 4 (April 1934): 199–202; Wesley Stout, "The New Homesteaders," *Saturday Evening Post* 207, no. 5 (August 4, 1934): 5–7, 61–65, esp. 7, 64; and Conkin, *Tomorrow a New World*, 116–17.

40. For the impact of Arthurdale, see testimony of C. B. Baldwin in *Congressional Committee on Non-Essential Services*, May 18, 1943, 4307; also see Linda T. Austin, "Unrealized Expectations: Cumberland, the New Deal's Only Homestead Project," *Tennessee Historical Quarterly* 68, no. 4 (Winter 2009): 433–50, esp. 443–44. On the Alabama communities, see Charles Kenneth Roberts, "New Deal Community-Building in the South: The Subsistence Homesteads Around Birmingham, Alabama," *Alabama Review* 66, no. 2 (April 2013): 83–121, esp. 91, 95–96, 99, 102, 110, 114–16; and Jack House, "547 Homesteaders in District Now Enjoy More Abundant Life," *Birmingham News-Age Herald*, May 9, 1943. I want to thank Charles Roberts for sending me this article.

41. For images of homesteader and plow, see Frank L. Kluckhorn, "Subsistence Homestead Idea Spreading," *New York Times*, December 9, 1934; also see Carl Mydans, "Homestead, Penderlea, North Carolina" (August 1936), and Arthur Rothstein, "Plowing a Field at Palmerdale, Alabama. New Homestead in Background" (February 1937), Library of Congress, Prints and Photographs Division, FSA/OWI Collection, LC-USF33-T01-00717-M2, LC-USF34-005891-E; and Roberts, "New Deal Community-Building in the South," 91.

42. On Penderlea, see Gordon Van Schaack, "Penderlea Homesteads: The Development of a Subsistence Homesteads Project," *Landscape Architecture* (January 1935): 75–80, esp. 80. On the discontents of the residents, see Thomas Luke Manget, "Hugh MacRae and the Idea of the Farm City: Race, Class, and Conservation in the New South, 1905–1935" (M.A. thesis, Western Carolina University, 2012), 154–57; and Harold D. Lasswell, "Resettlement Communities: A Study of the Problems of Personalizing Administration" (1938), in Series II: Writings, Box 130, Folders 135–39, Harold Dwight Lasswell Papers, Yale University, New Haven, CT; Conkin, *Tomorrow a New World*, 290–91.

43. On the lack of a cooperative agricultural culture in the South, see Charles M. Smith, "Observations on Regional Differentials in Cooperative Organization," *Social Forces* 22, no. 4 (May 1944): 437–42, esp. 437, 439, 442. On visitors to the Greenbelt town, see Gilbert A. Cam, "United States Government Activity in Low-Cost Housing, 1932–1938," *Journal of Political Economy* 47, no. 3 (June 1939): 357–78, esp. 373. On prefabrication, see Greg Hise, "From Roadside Camps to Garden Homes: Housing and Community Planning for California's Migrant Work Force, 1935–1941," *Perspectives in Vernacular* 5 (1995): 243–58, esp. 243, 249; also see Conkin, *Tomorrow a New World*, 171–72; Philip K. Wagner, "Suburban Landscapes for Nuclear Families: The Case of the Greenbelt Towns in the United States," *Built Environment* 10, no. 1 (1984): 35–41, esp. 41; and Will W. Alexander, "A Review of the Farm Security Administration's Housing Activities," *Housing Yearbook, 1939* (Chicago: National Association of Housing Officials, 1939), 141–43, 149–50. Only Huey Long protested the exclusion, and led a one-man filibuster in the Senate. On the exclusion of agricultural workers from Social Security, see Mary Poole, *The Segregated Origins of Social Security: African Americans and the Welfare State* (Chapel Hill: University of North Carolina Press, 2006), 33, 39, 41, 43, 45, 94; and Earl E. Muntz, "The Farmer and Social Security," *Social Forces* 24, no. 3 (March 1946): 283–90.

44. On the special committee that put together the *Farm Tenancy* report, Henry Wallace was the chairman, and Will W. Alexander, R. G. Tugwell, M. L. Wilson, and Howard Odum were members, while Arthur Raper's work was cited; see *Farm Tenancy: Report of the President's Committee*, 28, 87.

45. See Harvey A. Kantor, "Howard W. Odum: The Implications of Folk, Planning, and Regionalism," *American Journal of Sociology* 79, no. 2 (September 1973): 278–95, esp. 279–80; and Dewey W. Grantham Jr., "The Regional Imagination: Social Scientists and the American South," *Journal of Southern History* 34, no. 1 (February 1968): 3–32, esp. 14–17.

46. Kantor, "Howard W. Odum," 283. For Johnson's reliance on Odum's work, see Gerald W. Johnson, *The Wasted Land* (Chapel Hill: University of North Carolina Press, 1937), esp. 6–7. On Johnson's education and role as editor of the *Baltimore*

Evening Sun, see review of "The Wasted Land," *Social Forces* 17, no. 2 (December 1938): 276–79; also see Louis Mazzari, "Arthur Raper and Documentary Realism in Greene County, Georgia," *Georgia Historical Quarterly* 87, no. 3/4 (Fall/Winter 2003): 389–407, esp. 396–97; Stuart Kidd, *Farm Security Administration Photography, the Rural South, and the Dynamics of Image-Making, 1935–1943* (Lewiston, NY: Edward Mellon Press, 2004), 50, 152–53; and Mary Summer, "The New Deal Farm Programs: Looking for Reconstruction in American Agriculture," *Agricultural History* 74, no. 2 (Spring 2000): 241–57, esp. 248–50.

47. Johnson, *The Wasted Land,* 6–11, 21, 24–30; Howard Odum, *Southern Pioneers in Social Interpretation* (Chapel Hill: University of North Carolina Press, 1925), 25; Howard Odum, "Regionalism vs. Sectionalism in the South's Place in the National Economy," *Social Forces* 12, no. 3 (March 1934): 338–54, esp. 340–41; Broadus Mitchell, "Southern Quackery," *Southern Economic Journal* 3, no. 2 (October 1936): 143–47, esp. 146.

48. See Odum, "Regionalism vs. Sectionalism in the South's Place in the National Economy," esp. 339, 345; Mitchell, "Southern Quackery," 145; and William B. Thomas, "Howard W. Odum's Social Theories in Transition, 1910–1930," *American Sociologist* 16, no. 1 (February 1981): 25–34, esp. 29–30; also see Odum's assessment of southern regionalism in "The Regional Quality and Balance of America," *Social Forces* 23, no. 3, *In Search of the Regional Balance in America* (March 1945): 269–85, esp. 276–77, 279–80.

49. See Howard K. Menhinick and Lawrence L. Durisch, "Tennessee Valley Authority: Planning in Operation," *Town Planning Review* 24, no. 2 (July 1953): 116–45, esp. 128–30, 142; and F. W. Reeves, "The Social Development Program of the Tennessee Valley Authority," *Social Science Review* 8, no. 3 (September 1934): 445–57, esp. 447, 449–53. For the importance of sociology in the planning process, see Arthur E. Morgan, "Sociology and the TVA," *American Sociological Review* 2, no. 2 (April 1937): 157–65; William E. Cole, "The Impact of the TVA upon the Southeast," *Social Forces* 28, no. 4 (May 1950): 435–40; Daniel Schaffer, "Environment and TVA: Toward a Regional Plan for the Tennessee Valley, 1930s," *Tennessee Historical Quarterly* 43, no. 4 (Winter 1984): 333–54, esp. 342–43, 349–50, 353; and Sarah T. Phillips, *This Land, This Nation: Conservation, Rural America, and the New Deal* (New York: Cambridge University Press, 2007), 80, 89, 96–98, 100, 105–7.

50. On the class and caste system (here he meant family and kinship in which inclusion was measured by intermarriage; this notion of caste was separate from the race–sex caste system), see Howard W. Odum, "The Way of the South," *Social Forces* 23, no. 3, 258–68, esp. 266–67. Odum also believed that regions had a "folk personality" or "biography," quoting Carl Sandburg to express the powerful hold of folk culture: "the feel and the atmosphere, the layout and the lingo of a region, of breeds of men, of customs and slogans, in a manner and air not given in regular history"; see Odum, ibid., 264, 268; also see Arthur T. Raper and Ira de A. Reid, "The South Adjusts—Downward," *Phylon* 1, no. 1 (1st quarter, 1940): 6–27, esp. 24–26.

51. In this collection of letters, nine of the forty-six used the word "shiftless"; others used related terms. Benjamin Burke Kendrick and Thomas Abernathy thought "shiftless" would be a better term than "poor white." See B. B.

Kendrick to Howard Odum, March 10, 1938, and Thomas Abernathy to Odum, April 6, 1938. For "fuzzy," see Charles Sydnor to Odum, March 12, 1939; for others on "shiftless," also see Frank Owsley to Odum, March 27, 1938, Haywood Tearce to Odum, March 19, 1938, A. B. Moore to Odum, April 29, 1938, Earle Eubank to Odum, March 23, 1938, Read Bain to Odum, January 21, 1938, D. B. Taylor to Odum, January 25, 1938; and on "indolent, shiftless class," see Dudley Tanner to Odum, January 25, 1938. See Howard Washington Odum Papers, 1908–82, Folder 3635, Special Collections, Wilson Library, University of North Carolina, Chapel Hill.

52. The word "shiftless" goes back to the 1500s meaning helpless, without resources, lazy, without a shift or shirt; see *Oxford English Dictionary.* On the shiftless behavior of Virginia planters and Louisiana slaves, see Frederick Law Olmsted, *The Cotton Kingdom: A Traveller's Observations on Cotton and Slavery in the American Slave States* (New York, 1861), 106, 373. For "shiftless" as a New England term, see "Shiftless," *Ohio Farmer,* December 17, 1896; also see "'Farmer Thrifty' and 'Farmer Shiftless,'" *Maine Farmer,* June 4, 1870. On the typical shiftless tavernkeeper, see Gail Dickersin Spilsbury, "A Washington Sketchbook: Historic Drawings of Washington," *Washington History* 22 (2010): 69–87, esp. 73. On shiftless deserting husbands, and a bill passed in New York in 1897 called the "Shiftless Fathers Bill," see Michael Willrich, "Home Slackers: Men, the State, and Welfare in Modern America," *Journal of American History* 87, no. 2 (September 2000): 460–89, esp. 469. On eugenics and "shiftless," see Irene Case and Kate Lewis, "Environment as a Factor in Feeble-Mindedness: The Noll Family," *American Journal of Sociology* 23, no. 5 (March 1918): 661–69, esp. 662; Leonard, "Retrospectives: Eugenics and Economics in the Progressive Era," 220; Kelves, *In the Name of Eugenics,* 48–49; and Davenport, *Heredity in Relation to Eugenics,* 81–82. On the shiftlessness of poor whites in fiction, and the association of shiftlessness with tenancy and transiency, see William J. Flynt, *Poor but Proud: Alabama's Poor Whites* (Tuscaloosa: University of Alabama Press, 1989), ix, 63, 90, 160, 293. On shiftless vagabonds, see "Causes of Poverty," *Genesee Farmer and Gardner's Journal,* March 10, 1832; Todd Depastino, *Citizen Hobo: How a Century of Homelessness Shaped America* (Chicago: University of Chicago Press, 2003), 15, 102; and W. J. Cash, *The Mind of the South* (New York: Knopf, 1941), 22–24.

53. See movie review, which describes Stepin Fetchit as the "sluggard of the tale, the ebony creature whose distaste for work" is emphasized; "Hearts in Dixie" (1929), *New York Times,* February 28, 1929; and D. Bogle, *Toms, Coons, Mulattoes, Mammies, and Bucks: An Interpretative History of Blacks in American Films* (New York: Continuum, 1994), 8; also see Ira de A. Reid to Howard Odum, February 2, 1938, Howard Washington Odum Papers.

54. See M. Swearingen to Howard Odum, June 13, 1938. On "social scum living like Negroes," see Frederic L Paxon to Odum, March 18, 1938. On no clear line of demarcation between black and poor white homes, see Ulin W. Leavell to Odum, January 27, 1938. On poor whites being above Negroes "in only one respect, the matter of color," see L. Guy Brown to Odum, February 6, 1938. On "looked down upon by all Negroes," see A. C. Lervis to Odum, February 2, 1938. On working like blacks and living side by side with blacks, see W. A.

Schiffley to Odum, February 7, 1938. On "briar hoppers," see Earle Eubank to Odum, March 23, 1938, Howard Washington Odum Papers.

55. Raymond F. Bellamy to Howard Odum, January 21, 1938, Howard Washington Odum Papers.

56. B. O. Williams to Howard Odum, February 9, 1938, Howard Washington Odum Papers.

57. James Agee and Walker Evans, *Let Us Now Praise Famous Men* (1941; reprint ed., Boston: Houghton Mifflin, 2001), 5–6, 8–9.

58. Ibid., 70–73, 127, 137, 164–65, 183–84, 205–6, 231–39. On the ninety-three pages of detailed description of the material culture, see Michael Trinkley, "'Let Us Now Praise Famous Men'—If Only We Can Find Them," *Southeastern Archeology* 2, no. 1 (Summer 1983): 30–36. On Agee's distrust of the writer's investment in the documentary process, see James S. Miller, "Inventing 'Found' Objects: Artifactuality, Folk History, and the Rise of Capitalist Ethnography in 1930s America," *Journal of American Folklore* 117, no. 466 (Autumn 2004): 373–93, esp. 387–88.

59. Agee and Walker, *Let Us Now Praise Famous Men*, 184–85. As one reviewer at the time observed, Agee reveals as much about himself (and the things about ourselves that he represents) as about his subject, which was its "chief social documentary value"; see Ruth Lechlitner, "Alabama Tenant Families," review of *Let Us Now Praise Famous Men, New York Herald Tribune Books,* Sunday, August 24, 1941, 10; and for a discussion of this point, see Paula Rabinowitz, "Voyeurism and Class Consciousness: James Agee and Walker Evans, 'Let Us Now Praise Famous Men,'" *Cultural Critique* 21 (Spring 1992): 143–70, esp. 162.

60. Only around three hundred copies of *Let Us Now Praise Famous Men* were sold in 1941; see Stott, *Documentary Expression and Thirties America,* 264; also see Donald Davidson, *The Attack on Leviathan: Regionalism and Nationalism in the United States* (Chapel Hill: University of North Carolina Press, 1938), 308; Tindall, *The Emergence of the New South*, 594; and Edward S. Shapiro, "Donald Davidson and the Tennessee Valley Authority: The Response of a Southern Conservative," *Tennessee Historical Quarterly* 33, no. 4 (Winter 1974): 436–51, esp. 443.

61. Jennifer Ritterhouse, "Dixie Destinations: Rereading Jonathan Daniels' *A Southerner Discovers the South*," *Southern Spaces* (May 20, 2010).

62. Jonathan Daniels, *A Southerner Discovers the South* (New York: Macmillan, 1938), 31, 140, 148, 299–305. For the gully becoming a tourist site, see Paul S. Sutter, "What Gullies Mean: Georgia's 'Little Grand Canyon' and Southern Environmental History," *Journal of Southern History* 76, no. 3 (August 2010): 579–616, esp. 579, 582–83, 585–86, 589–90.

63. Daniels, *A Southerner Discovers the South*, 25, 58.

64. Ibid., 345.

65. Ibid., 346.

Chapter Ten: The Cult of the Country Boy:
Elvis Presley, Andy Griffith, and LBJ's Great Society

1. Randall Woods, *LBJ: Architect of American Ambition* (New York: Free Press, 2006), 458; Bobbie Ann Mason, *Elvis Presley: A Life* (New York: Viking,

2002), 105; Karal Ann Marling, "Elvis Presley's Graceland, or the Aesthetic of Rock 'n' Roll Heaven," *American Art* 7, no. 4 (Autumn 1933), 99; Michael T. Bertrand, *Race, Rock, and Elvis* (Urbana and Chicago: University of Illinois Press, 2005), 224.

2. Jack Gould, "TV: New Phenomenon: Elvis Presley Rises to Fame as Vocalist Who Is Virtuoso of Hootchy-Kootchy," *New York Times,* June 6, 1956. For the zoot suit reference, see Jules Archer, "Stop Hounding Teenagers!: Elvis Presley Defends His Fans and His Music," *True Story* (December 1956): 18–20, 22–24, 26, 28. "Elvis Presley: What? Why?," *Look Magazine* (August 7, 1956): 82–85; Candida Taylor, "Zoot Suit: Breaking the Cold War's Dress Code," in *Containing America: Cultural Production and Consumption in 50s America,* eds. Nathan Abrams and Julie Hughes (Edgbaston, Birmingham, UK: University of Birmingham Press, 2000), 64–65; Karal Ann Marling, *As Seen on TV: The Visual Culture of Everyday Life in the 1950s* (Cambridge, MA: Harvard University Press, 1994), 169–70; and Michael Bertrand, "I Don't Think Hank Done It That Way: Elvis, Country Music, and the Reconstruction of Southern Masculinity," in *A Boy Named Sue: Gender and Country Music,* eds. Kristine M. McCusker and Diane Pecknold (Jackson: University Press of Mississippi, 2004), 59–85, esp. 59, 62, 66, 73, 75, 84.

3. On the difficulties of overcoming his southern identity, see Joe B. Frantz, "Opening a Curtain: The Metamorphosis of Lyndon B. Johnson," *Journal of Southern History* 45, no. 1 (February 1979): 3–26, esp. 5–7, 25.

4. On his inaugural address, see "The President's Inaugural Address, January 20, 1965," in *Public Papers of the Presidents of the United States: Lyndon B. Johnson: Containing the Public Messages, Speeches, and Statements of the President, 1965 (in Two Books), Book I—January 1 to May 31, 1965* (Washington, DC: Government Printing Office, 1966), 71–74, esp. 73; Carroll Kilpatrick, "Great Society, World Without Hate," *Washington Post,* January 21, 1965.

5. Dale Baum and James L. Hailey, "Lyndon Johnson's Victory in the 1948 Texas Senate Race: A Reappraisal," *Political Science Quarterly* 109, no. 4 (Autumn 1994): 595–13, esp. 596, 613; Robert A. Caro, *The Years of Lyndon Johnson: Means of Ascent* (New York: Knopf, 1990), xxxii, 211, 218, 223, 228, 232, 238, 259–64, 268, 300; on Johnson's crucial role in promoting NASA and shaping Kennedy's space policy, see Andreas Reichstein, "Space—The Last Cold War Frontier?" *Amerikastudien/American Studies* 44, no. 1 (1999): 113–36.

6. For the theme of brotherhood over divisiveness, see "Address to the Nation upon Proclaiming a Day of Mourning Following the Death of Dr. King, April 5, 1968," and his proclamation, in *Public Papers of the Presidents, Book I—January 1 to June 30, 1968–1969,* 493–95.

7. John O'Leary and Rick Worland, "Against the Organization Man: *The Andy Griffith Show* and the Small-Town Family Ideal," in *The Sitcom Reader,* eds. Mary M. Dalton and Laura R. Linder (Albany: SUNY Press, 2005), 73–84, esp. 80–82; also see syndicated columnist for the National Enterprise Association Erskine Johnson, "Andy Griffith Drops Yokel Role for Semi-intellectual," *Ocala Star-Banner,* October 2, 1960.

8. On Gomer Pyle, see "Comedies: Success Is a Warm Puppy," *Time* (November 10, 1967): 88; Anthony Harkins, "The Hillbilly in the Living Room: Television

Representations of Southern Mountaineers in Situation Comedies, 1952–1971," *Appalachian Journal* 29, no. 1/2 (Fall–Winter 2002): 98–126, esp. 106. The *New York Times* writer described Jim Nabors's character as a "hillbilly," with an "attractive awkwardness and naiveté," who "merely assumes that everyone in the Marines is as friendly as the folks back home." See Jack Gould, "TV: Freshness in Old Military Tale," *New York Times,* September 26, 1964.

9. See the cover of *Saturday Evening Post* (February 2, 1963); "Hope Quips Convulse Convention," *Billboard: The International Music-Record Newsweekly* (April 13, 1963), 41; Hal Humphrey, "Last Laugh on Ratings," *Milwaukee Journal,* November 16, 1963; also see Harkins, "The Hillbilly in the Living Room," 112, 114; Jan Whitt, "Grits and Yokels Aplenty: Depictions of Southerners on Prime-Time Television," *Studies in Popular Culture* 19, no. 2 (October 1996): 141–52, esp. 148.

10. Richard Warren Lewis, "The Golden Hillbillies," *Saturday Evening Post* (February 2, 1963): 30–35, esp. 34. Paul Henning produced, directed, and cowrote every episode of *The Beverly Hillbillies;* see Henning's interview in Noel Hoston, "Folk Appeal Was Hooterville Lure," [New London, CT] *Day,* August 10, 1986. The most influential Hollywood gossip columnist came to the defense of *The Beverly Hillbillies,* along with conservative women's groups; see Hedda Hopper, "Hollywood: Hillbillies Take Off," [New Orleans] *Times-Picayune,* March 23, 1964. Irene Ryan, who played Granny, offered this defense of the show: "When I was a kid I worked through the Ozarks, where our characters are supposed to be from. They are terribly funny, warm people, but up to now nobody ever really got 'em down on paper. Our show did"; see Muriel Davidson, "Fame Arrived in a Gray Wig, Glasses and Army Boots," *TV Guide* (September 7, 1963): 5–7, esp. 5.

11. On the connection between *The Beverly Hillbillies* and the Joads, see John Keasler, "TV Synopsis: Unappreciated Art Form," *Palm Beach Post,* May 30, 1970.

12. On the Davy Crockett craze, see Steven Watts, *The Magic Kingdom: Walt Disney and the American Way of Life* (Columbia: University of Missouri Press, 1997), 313–22, esp. 318, 320–21. While the six-foot-five Parker was called handsome and compared to Jimmy Stewart, Buddy Ebsen was dismissed as "greasy and gamey"; see Bosley Crowther, "Screen Disney and the Coonskin Set," *New York Times,* May 26, 1955. For Parker's "aw-shucks school of acting" like Gary Cooper and Jimmy Stewart, see "Meet Fess Parker," *St. Petersburg Times,* December 24, 1954. For photograph of LBJ and Fess Parker, see "Davy Crockett and Old Betsey," [Santa Ana, CA] *Register,* April 1, 1955.

13. Harkins, "The Hillbilly in the Living Room," 100–101, 114; and Paul Harvey, "The Beverly Hillbillies," *Lewiston* [ME] *Evening Journal,* October 26, 1968; the same article by the syndicated columnist circulated in the South. For a synopsis of Barney's failure in the big city, see "Reunion to Bring Barney Fife Back," *New York Times,* November 20, 1965.

14. Hal Humphrey, "Viewing Television: Theory of the 'Hillbillies,'" [New Orleans] *Times-Picayune,* January 13, 1963. Another critic saw the stories of the

top ten television shows as relying on the "rube" versus the "city slicker," or the older cracker motif of the beau versus the backwoodsman. He called *The Beverly Hillbillies* "vigorous vulgarians," the characters in *The Andy Griffith Show* "oafs," and Gomer Pyle a "slob." See Arnold Hano, "TV's Topmost— This Is America?," *New York Times*, December 26, 1965.

15. Marling, "Elvis Presley's Graceland," 74, 79–81, 85, 89.

16. For Elvis becoming a "country squire," see "Presley Buys $100,000 Home for Self, Parents," [New Orleans] *Times-Picayune*, March 24, 1957. On Nixon's trip, see "'Made in U.S.A.'—In Red Capital," *U.S. News & World Report* (August 3, 1959): 38–39; Stephen J. Whitfield, *The Culture of the Cold War* (Baltimore: Johns Hopkins University Press, 1991), 72–73; Elaine Tyler May, *Homeward Bound: American Families in the Cold War* (New York: Basic Books, 1988), 10–12.

17. "By Richard Nixon," *New York Times*, July 25, 1959.

18. Charles Hillenger, "Disneyland Dedication: Vice-President and Other Celebrrities Help Open Six New Attractions at Park," *Los Angeles Times*, June 15, 1959; Mary Ann Callan, "Says Pat Nixon: 'It's American Dream,'" *Los Angeles Times*, July 27, 1960; James McCartney, "Campaign Push Starts for Pat: Republicans Feel Pat Nixon May Hold the Key to the Election," *Pittsburgh Press*, September 1, 1960; Patricia Conner, "Women Are Spotlighted in 1960 Presidential Campaign," *Lodi* [CA] *News-Sentinel*, November 1, 1960; Marylin Bender, "Home and Public Roles Kept in Cheerful Order," *New York Times*, July 28, 1960; also Martha Weinman, "First Ladies—In Fashion, Too? This Fall the Question of Style for a President's Wife May Be a Great Issue," *New York Times*, September 11, 1960.

19. Becky M. Nicolaides, "Suburbia and the Sunbelt," *OAH Magazine of History* 18, no. 1 (October 2003): 21–26; Eric Larrabee, "The Six Thousand Houses That Levitt Built," *Harper's Magazine* 197, no. 1180 (September 1948): 79–88, esp. 79–80, 82–83; Boyden Sparkes, "They'll Build Neighborhoods, Not Houses," *Saturday Evening Post* (October 28, 1944): 11, 43–46. For Levittown as a "vast housing colony," see "New Model Homes to Be Opened Today," *New York Times*, April 3, 1949; Kenneth T. Jackson, *Crabgrass Frontier: The Suburbanization of the United States* (New York: Oxford University Press, 1985), 234–37; and Thomas J. Anton, "Three Models of Community Development in the United States," *Publius* 1, no. 1 (1971): 11–37, esp. 33–34.

20. Sparkes, "They'll Build Neighborhoods," 44. Though the Levitts removed the restrictive covenant, they continued to discriminate against black families; see "Housing Bias Ended," *New York Times*, May 29, 1949; and James Wolfinger, "'The American Dream—For All Americans': Race, Politics, and the Campaign to Desegregate Levittown," *Journal of Urban History* 38, no. 3 (2012): 230–52, esp. 234. For the Norfolk housing facility, see Larrabee, "The Six Thousand Houses That Levitt Built," 80; Jackson, *Crabgrass Frontier*, 234.

21. For the symbolic weight given the barbecue, see Kristin L. Matthews, "One Nation over Coals: Cold War Nationalism and the Barbecue," *American Studies* 50, no. 3/4 (Fall/Winter 2009): 5–34, esp. 11, 17, 26; and A. R. Swinnerton, "Ranch-Type Homes for Dudes," *Saturday Evening Post* (August 18,

1956): 40. Also see Lois Craig, "Suburbs," *Design Quarterly* 132 (1986): 1–32, esp. 18; Ken Duvall, "Sin Is the Same in the City or the Suburb," *Toledo Blade,* December 6, 1960. On "Fertile Acres," see Harry Henderson, "The Mass-produced Suburbs: I. How People Live in America's Newest Towns," *Harper's Magazine* 207, no. 1242 (November 1953): 25–32, esp. 29. On lawn mowing as husbandry, see Dan W. Dodson, "Suburbanism and Education," *Journal of Educational Sociology* 32, no. 1 (September 1958): 2–7, esp. 4; Scott Donaldson, "City and Country: Marriage Proposals," *American Quarterly* 20, no. 3 (Autumn, 1968): 547–66, esp. 562–64; and Harry Henderson, "Rugged American Collectivism: The Mass-produced Suburbs, II.," *Harper's Magazine* (December 1953): 80–86.

22. Frederick Lewis Allen, "The Big Change in Suburbia," *Harper's Magazine* 208, no. 1249 (June 1954): 21–28. On the way class reinforced racial segregation, see "Economic Factors May Keep Suburbia Segregated," [Lexington, KY] *Dispatch,* June 19, 1968. On Mahwah and Westchester, see Dodson, "Suburbanism and Education," 5–6. On the class strategies of zoning, see Carol O'Connor, *A Sort of Utopia: Scarsdale, 1891–1981* (Albany: SUNY Press, 1983), 30–42, 159–65; also Lizabeth Cohen, *A Consumer's Republic: The Politics of Mass Consumption in Postwar America* (New York: Knopf, 2003), 202–8, 231; and Becky M. Nicolaides, "'Where the Working Man Is Welcomed': Working-class Suburbs in Los Angeles, 1900–1940," *Pacific Historical Review* 68, no. 4 (November 1999): 517–59, esp. 557. On neat lawns and gardens as class markers, see William Dobriner, *Class in Suburbia* (Englewood Cliffs, NJ: Prentice Hall, 1963), 23.

23. See Wolfgang Langewiesche, "Everybody Can Own a House," *House Beautiful* (November 1956): 227–29, 332–35; Jackson, *Crabgrass Frontier,* 205, 235, 238.

24. Because home construction relied heavily on banks and other such institutions, lenders had tremendous power in reinforcing racial and class stratification; see "Application of the Sherman Act to Housing Segregation," *Yale Law Journal* 63, no. 6 (June 1954): 1124–47, esp. 1125–26. For the residents' obsession with property values, see Henderson, "Rugged American Collectivism," 85–86; Cohen, *A Consumer's Republic,* 202, 212–13. For lack of variety in suburbs, see Sidonie Matsner Gruenberg, "The Challenge of the New Suburbs," *Marriage and Family Living* 17, no. 2 (May 1955): 133–37, esp. 134; David Reisman, "The Suburban Dislocation," *Annals of the American Academy of Political and Social Science* 314 (November 1957): 123–46, esp. 134. For Lewis Mumford's critique, see Penn Kimball, "'Dream Town'—Large Economy Size: Pennsylvania's New Levittown is Pre-Planned Down to the Last Thousand Living Rooms," *New York Times,* December 14, 1952; and Vance Packard, *The Status Seekers: An Exploration of Class Behavior in America and the Hidden Barriers That Affect You, Your Community, Your Future* (New York: David McKay Co., 1959), 28.

25. On the Bucks County Levittown, see "Levitt's Design for Steel Workers' Community," *New York Times,* November 4, 1951; David Schuyler, "Reflections on Levittown at Fifty," *Pennsylvania History* 70, no. 1 (Winter 2003): 101–9, esp. 105. On the trailer park, see Don Hager, "Trailer Towns and

Community Conflict in Lower Bucks County," *Social Problems* 2, no. 1 (July 1954): 33–38; and Andrew Hurley, *Diners, Bowling Alleys, and Trailer Parks: Chasing the American Dream* (New York: Basic Books, 2001), 195–96.

26. For one of the first references to trailer trash in reference to war workers, see Mary Heaton Vorse, "And the Workers Say . . . ," *Public Opinion Quarterly* 7, no. 3 (Autumn 1943): 443–56. For the homemade trailers as "monstrosities," see Harold Martin, "Don't Call Them Trailer Trash," *Saturday Evening Post* 225, no. 5 (August 2, 1952): 24–25, 85–87; Allan D. Wallis, "House Trailers: Innovation and Accommodation in Vernacular Housing," *Perspectives in Vernacular Architecture* 3 (1989): 28–43, esp. 30–31, 34; "Trailers for Army Areas," *New York Times,* March 19, 1941; Carl Abbott, *The New Urban America: Growth and Politics in the Sunbelt Cities* (Chapel Hill: University of North Carolina Press, 1981), 107–10; Hurley, *Diners, Bowling Alleys, and Trailer Parks,* 203; "Trailers for Army Areas," *New York Times,* March 19, 1941; and see Lucy Greenbaum, "'Trailer Village' Dwellers Happy in Connecticut Tobacco Field," *New York Times,* April 13, 1942.

27. See "Agnes Ernest Meyer" (1887–1970), in *Notable American Women: The Modern Period,* eds. Barbara Sicherman and Carol Hurd Green (Cambridge, MA: Harvard University Press, 1980), 471–73; and Agnes E. Meyer, *Journey Through Chaos* (New York, 1944), x.

28. Meyer, *Journey Through Chaos,* ix, 373–74.

29. Ibid., 196–99, 210, 216.

30. See Alexander C. Wellington, "Trailer Camp Slums," *Survey* (1951): 418–21. For trailer camps and idle wastelands as part of the fringe zone around Flint, Michigan, see Walter Firey, *Social Aspects to Land Use Planning in the Country-City Fringe: The Case of Flint, Michigan* (East Lansing: Michigan State College, 1946), 8, 32, 42, 52, 54. "Photograph of Mobile Homes, Described as 'Squatters,' in Winkelman, Arizona" (1950), Arizona Archives and Public Records, Arizona State Library. For earlier references to trailerites as squatters and the trailer as the "family kennel," see "200,000 Trailers," *Fortune* 15, no. 3 (March 1937): 105–11, 214, 200, 220, 222, 224, 226, 229, esp. 105–6, 220. The squatter allusion continued to hold sway; see Keith Corcoran, "Mobile Homes Merit More Respect," [Schenectady, NY] *Daily Gazette,* April 14, 1990.

31. See John E. Booth, "At Home on Wheels: Trailer Exhibition Stresses Comfortable Living," *New York Times,* November 16, 1947; Virginia J. Fortiner, "Trailers a la Mode," *New York Times,* April 27, 1947; "Trailers: More and More Americans Call Them Home," *Newsweek* (July 7, 1952): 70–73, esp. 70; Martin, "Don't Call Them Trailer Trash," 85. Some six thousand trailers were being used on college campuses in 1946; see Milton Mac Kaye, "Crisis at the Colleges," *Saturday Evening Post* 219 (August 3, 1946): 9–10, 34–36, 39, esp. 35.

32. Allan D. Wallis, *Wheel Estate: The Rise and Decline of Mobile Homes* (New York: Oxford University Press, 1991), 116. On zoning restrictions, see Emily A. MacFall and E. Quinton Gordon, "Mobile Homes and Low-Income Rural Families." (Washington, DC, 1973), 38–40; Robert Mills French and Jeffrey K. Hadden, "An Analysis of the Distribution and Characteristics of Mobile

Homes in America," *Land Economics* 41, no. 2 (May 1965): 131–39; Lee Irby, "Taking Out the Trailer Trash: The Battle over Mobile Homes in St. Petersburg, Florida," *Florida Historical Quarterly* 79, no. 2 (Fall 2000): 181–200, esp. 188, 194–96; Hurley, *Diners, Bowling Alleys, and Trailer Parks,* 235–41, 254, 256, 258.

33. Dina Smith, "Lost Trailer Utopias: *The Long, Long Trailer* (1954) and Fifties America," *Utopian Studies* 14, no. 1 (2003): 112–31.

34. "Trailers Gaining in Popularity in U.S. but Urban Planner Asserts Community Opposition Is Growing," *New York Times,* July 17, 1960; "Mobile Homes—Today's Name for Residence on Wheels," *Sarasota Herald-Tribune,* January 19, 1961. *Vickers v. Township Comm. of Gloucester Township,* 37 N.J. 232, 265, 181 A.2d 129 (1962), dissenting opinion at 148–49; for a discussion of the case, see Richard F. Babcock and Fred P. Bosselman, "Suburban Zoning and the Apartment Boom," *University of Pennsylvania Law Review* 11, no. 8 (June 1963): 1040–91, esp. 1086–88; also see "Would Forbid Trailer Parks: Council Group Acts," *Milwaukee Journal,* December 14, 1954.

35. Anthony Ripley, "Mobile Home 'Resorts' Make 'Trailer Park' a Dirty Word," *New York Times Magazine,* May 31, 1969, 25, 48; "Fess Parker's Dollars Ride on Wheels," [Bowling Green, KY] *Park City Daily,* November 11, 1962—a news story written by Erskine Johnson, Hollywood correspondent, for the NEA; also see "Giant Man, with a Giant Plan," *Tuscaloosa News,* March 28, 1969; and "Fess Parker Rides Again," [Fredricksburg, VA] *Free Lance-Star,* October 3, 1970.

36. Morris Horton, "There's No Crack in Our Picture Window," *Trailer Topics* (May 1957): 7, 74, 76; Agnes Ash, "Trailer Owners Staying Put," *Miami News,* July 24, 1960; also see "The Mobile Home Isn't So Mobile Any More," *Business Week* (March 16, 1957): 44–46.

37. Douglas E. Kneeland, "From 'Tin Can on Wheels' to the Mobile Home," *New York Times Magazine,* May 9, 1971. In 1941, a white community in Detroit had erected a wall between themselves and a black community in order to receive FHA approval for mortgages; see Jackson, *Crabgrass Frontier,* 209.

38. See "A Sociologist Looks at an American Community," *Life* (September 12, 1949): 108–19; Robert Mills French and Jeffrey K. Hadden, "Mobile Homes: Instant Suburbia or Transportable Slums?," *Social Problems* 16, no. 2 (Autumn 1968): 219–26, esp. 222–25; Bailey H. Kuklin, "House and Technology: The Mobile Home Experience," *Tennessee Law Review* 44 (Spring 1977): 765–844, esp. 809, 814; MacFall and Gordon, "Mobile Homes and Low-Income Rural Families," 46. On the high depreciation rate of trailers, see Jack E. Gaumnitz, "Mobile Home and Conventional Home Ownership: An Economic Perspective," *Nebraska Journal of Economics and Business* 13, no. 4, Midwest Economics Association Papers (Autumn 1974): 130–43, esp. 130, 142. One of the worst trailer parks in Denver was described as follows: "Called 'Peyton Place,' many of the trailer pads are empty. One is littered with an old porcelain toilet bowl from some forgotten departure. The place is for sale and the sign, in misspelled English, read 'vacancy'"; see Ripley, "Mobile Home 'Resorts,'" 48.

39. For prostitutes in trailers at military and defense installations, see "Syphilis and Defense," *New York Times*, November 29, 1941. Even before the war, there were rumors of a "rolling bordello" traveling between trailer camps in Florida, and racy stories in newspapers, such as that of a man traveling with both his wife and his mistress; see "200,000 Trailers," 220, 229. For the association of trailers with immoral behavior, see Kuklin, "House and Technology," 812–13; also Alan Bérubé and Florence Bérubé, "Sunset Trailer Park," in *White Trash: Race and Class in America*, eds. Annalee Newitz and Matt Wray (New York: Routledge, 1997), 19; Orrie Hitt, *Trailer Tramp* (Boston: Beacon, 1957). Similar titles included: Loren Beauchamp, *Sin on Wheels: The Uncensored Confessions of a Trailer Camp Tramp* (1961) and Glenn Canary, *The Trailer Park Girls* (1962). On the cover of *Cracker Girl*, it read, "She was his property; to keep, to beat, to use"; see Harry Whittington, *Cracker Girl* (Stallion Books, 1953). The psychologist Harold Lasswell listed "trailer nomadism" along with other sources of degeneracy, such as alcoholism, drugs, gambling, and delinquency; see Harold Lasswell, "The Socio-Political Situation," *Educational Research Bulletin* 36, no. 3 (March 13, 1957): 69–77, esp. 75.

40. "The Mobile Home Market," *Appraiser's Journal* 40, no. 3 (July 1972): 391–411, esp. 397; and "Planners Approve City Trailer Parks for the Homeless," *New York Times*, March 23, 1971.

41. Cohen, *A Consumers' Republic*, 202–8, 228, 231, 240–41, 404. On the migration from rural to metropolitan areas, see Pete Daniel, "Going Among Strangers: Southern Reactions to World War II," *Journal of American History* 77, no. 3 (December 1990): 886–911, esp. 886, 898. On television and tribalism, see H. J. Skornia, "What TV Is Doing to America: Some Unexpected Consequences," *Journal of Aesthetic Education* 3, no. 3 (July 1969): 29–44.

42. Counts was working for the afternoon *Arkansas Democrat* when he took the picture, which made his photograph the first to appear. Johnny Jenkins published a similar photograph the next day in the *Arkansas Gazette*. See Karen Anderson, *Little Rock: Race and Resistance at Central High School* (Princeton, NJ: Princeton University Press, 2010), 2; Peter Daniel, *Lost Revolutions: The South in the 1950s* (Chapel Hill: University of North Carolina Press, 2000), 262; David Margolick, *Elizabeth and Hazel: Two Women of Little Rock* (New Haven, CT: Yale University Press, 2011), 1–2, 36–37, 59–61, 63, 152–54.

43. Margolick, *Elizabeth and Hazel*, 38–39, 41. On the rural white migration into Little Rock, see Ben F. Johnson III, "After 1957: Resisting Integration in Little Rock," *Arkansas Historical Quarterly* 66, no. 2 (Summer 1007): 258–83, esp. 262.

44. Margolick, *Elizabeth and Hazel*, 70–71, 88.

45. Benjamin Fine, "Students Unhurt," *New York Times*, September 24, 1957; Fletcher Knebel, "The Real Little Rock Story," *Look*, November 12, 1957, 31–33, esp. 33; Margolick, *Elizabeth and Hazel*, 37, 105; Daniel, *Lost Revolutions*, 263; and Phoebe Godfrey, "Bayonets, Brainwashing, and Bathrooms: The Discourse of Race, Gender, and Sexuality in the Desegregation of Little Rock's Central High," *Arkansas Historical Quarterly* 62, no. 1 (Spring 2003):

42–67, esp. 45–47; and Belman Morin, "Arkansas Riot Like Explosion," [Spokane, WA] *Spokesman Review,* September 23, 1957.

46. For Guthridge's remarks, see "Some Bitterness," *Arkansas Gazette,* September 1, 1957; C. Fred Williams, "Class: The Central Issue in the 1957 Little Rock School Crisis," *Arkansas Historical Quarterly* 56, no. 3 (Autumn 1997): 341–44; Graeme Cope, "'Everybody Says All Those People. . .Were from out of Town, but They Weren't': A Note on Crowds During the Little Rock Crisis," *Arkansas Historical Quarterly* 67, no. 3 (Autumn 2008): 245–67, esp. 261.

47. Roy Reed, *Faubus: The Life and Times of an American Prodigal* (Little Rock: University of Arkansas Press, 1997), 358; "The South: What Orval Hath Wrought," *Time* (September 23): 1957, 11–14, esp. 12–13. Also see Williams, "Class: The Central Issue," 344; "Orval's Iliad and Odyssey," *Life* (September 23, 1957): 28–35; Anderson, *Little Rock,* 68; and Don Iddon, "Faubus of Little Rock: 'The President Underestimated the Ruthless Ambition of This Hillbilly Who So Far Has Always Won in the End,'" [London] *Daily Mail,* September 26, 1957.

48. Benjamin Fine, "Militia Sent to Little Rock; School Integration Put Off," *New York Times,* September 3, 1957; "Speech of Governor Orval E. Faubus, September 2, 1957," http://southerncolloqrhetoric.net/resources/Faubus570902 .pdf. The original speech is located in the Orval Eugene Faubus Papers, 1910– 1994, Series 14, Box 496, University of Arkansas, Fayetteville, AK; and David Wallace, "Orval Faubus: The Central Figure at Little Rock Central High School," *Arkansas Historical Quarterly* 39, no. 4 (Winter 1980): 314–29, esp. 324.

49. Anthony Lewis, "President Sends Troops to Little Rock, Federalizes Arkansas National Guard; Tells Nation He Acted to Avoid Anarchy," *New York Times,* September 25, 1957. On Faubus manufacturing the myth of violence, see "Arkansas," *Time* (September 30, 1957): 17–19; "Little Rock Sputnik Is Burning Itself Out," *Washington African American,* October 22, 1957.

50. John Chancellor, "Radio and Television Had Their Own Problems in Little Rock Coverage," *Quill* (December 1957): 9–10, 20–21; Jack Gould, "TV: Reality in the South," *New York Times,* September 26, 1957; Harold R. Isaacs, "World Affairs and U.S. Race Relations: A Note on Little Rock," *Public Opinion Quarterly* 22, no. 3 (Autumn 1958): 364–70, esp. 366–67; and "A Historic Week of Civil Strife," *Life* (October 7, 1957): 37–48, esp. 38–39.

51. For local journalists calling them rednecks, see Cope, "'Everybody Says All Those People,'" 246–47, 267. For "many in overalls," see Chancellor, "Radio and Television," 9. For the "rednecked man," see Homer Bigart, "School Is Ringed: Negroes Go to School in Little Rock as Soldiers Guard the Area," *New York Times,* September 26, 1957. For the women in the Nashville mob, see "The South: What Orval Hath Wrought," 12, 15. For the crowd as white trash, see Stewart Alsop, "Tragedy in the Sunshine at Little Rock," *Victoria Advocate,* September 26, 1957 (reprinted from the *New York Herald Tribune*). Another portrayal of the mob as a "motley crowd of poor whites" is in the syndicated columnist Bob Considine's "Anatomy of the Mob—II," *St. Petersburg Times,* September 16, 1957; Considine, "The Anatomy of Violence—1: Mob Actions Help Cause of Integration," *Milwaukee Sentinel,*

September 14, 1957. On calling women "slattern housewives" and "harpies," see Considine, "Riffraff of Little Rock Is Giving City Bad Name," *Milwaukee Sentinel*, September 12, 1957. An African American newspaper claimed that Governor Faubus had inflamed a mob of "Arkansas hillbillies"; see "Ring Out the False, Ring in the True," *Baltimore Afro-American*, December 29, 1959.

52. "Eisenhower Address on Little Rock Crisis," *New York Times*, September 25, 1957; Jack Gould, "Little Rock: Television's Treatment of Major News Developments Found Superficial" and "The Face of Democracy," *New York Times*, September 15 and 26, 1957; Richard C. Bedford, "A Bigger Bomb," *Journal of Higher Education* 29, no. 3 (March 1958): 127–31; Daniel, *Lost Revolutions*, 267; and "Tragedy at Little Rock," *Times Literary Supplement*, August 28, 1959, 491.

53. On his political success in Arkansas, see Reed, *Faubus*, 251, 352, 357; Daniel, *Lost Revolutions*, 283; Paul Greenberg, "Orval Faubus Finally Blurts Out Truth of His Defiance That Led to the Racial Crisis in Little Rock in 1957," [Washington, DC] *Observer-Reporter*, June 1, 1979; "The Faubus Victory," *Lakeland* [FL] *Ledger*, July 30, 1958; "Faubus Unperturbed by Crisis," [Hopkinsville] *Kentucky New Era*, September 20, 1957; Anderson, *Little Rock*, 77; Thomas F. Pettigrew and Ernest Q. Campbell, "Faubus and Segregation: An Analysis of Arkansas Voting," *Public Opinion Quarterly* 24, no. 3 (Autumn 1960): 436–47. Faubus had Jeff Davis in mind, because he wanted to be the "first Arkansas governor since Jeff Davis to be elected to a third term." In the end, Faubus served six terms from 1955 to 1967. He also defended his actions based on polls. See Wallace, "Orval Faubus," 319, 326; and "Segregation Wins on Arkansas Poll," *New York Times*, January 29, 1956; "The Mike Wallace Interview: Guest Orval Faubus," September 15, 1957, transcript, Harry Ransom Center, University of Texas at Austin.

54. Gilbert Millstein, "Strange Chronicle of Andy Griffith," *New York Times*, June 2, 1957; "A Face in the Crowd," *Berkshire* [MA] *Eagle*, June 6, 1957.

55. Millstein, "Strange Chronicle of Andy Griffith."

56. On the film *Wild River*, see Henry Goodman, "Wild River by Elia Kazan," *Film Quarterly* 13, no. 4 (Summer 1960): 50–51; Robert Murray and Joe Heumann, "Environmental Catastrophe in Pare Lorentz's 'The River' and Elia Kazan's 'Wild River': The TVA, Politics, and Environment," *Studies in Popular Culture* 27, no. 2 (October 2004): 47–65, esp. 55. And on the controversy in Cleveland over Gum Hollow, see "Southern Pride Ends Movie Roles for 'White Trash,'" *Ocala Star-Banner*, November 15, 1959.

57. On the aggressive marketing campaign, see syndicated article by Hollywood correspondent Erskine Johnson, "'Bayou' Film, Bust in 1957, Released Under New Title," [Florence, AL] *Times Daily*, December 11, 1962; and Jim Knipfel, "The Brooklyn Cajun: Timothy Carey in 'Poor White Trash,'" *The Chiseler*, chiseler.org/post/6558011597/the-brooklyn-cajun-timothy-carey-in-poor-white (2011). On the advertising campaign, see [Hopkinsville] *Kentucky New Era*, October 9, 1961; and "Compromise with Sin," *Lewiston* [ME] *Daily Sun*, June 23, 1962.

58. Lisa Lindquist Dorr has shown that the politics surrounding rape were more complicated. In her study of Virginia, the reputations of the white woman and the accused black man were taken into account. So the film and Lee's novel,

for dramatic effect, paint a much more skewed picture. This serves to make the white trash characters even more insidious, because the Ewells demand the protection of the code of honor without deserving it. See Lisa Lindquist Dorr, *White Women, Rape, and the Power of Race in Virginia, 1900–1960* (Chapel Hill: University of North Carolina Press, 2004), 79, 115–19.

59. In the novel, Lee offers this scathing portrait of the Ewells: "No economic fluctuations changed their status—people like the Ewells lived as guests of the country in prosperity as well as in the depths of the depression. No truant officers could keep their numerous offspring in school; no public health officer could free them from congenital defects, various worms, and diseases indigenous to their filthy surroundings. . . . The Ewells gave the dump a thorough gleaning every day, and the fruits of their industry (those that were not eaten) made the plot of land around their cabin look like the playhouse of an insane child." Lee also has Atticus Finch offer a different definition of white trash, one decoupled from poverty, as anyone, rich or poor, who tried to cheat a black man or treat him unfairly; see Harper Lee, *To Kill a Mockingbird* (New York: HarperCollins, 1999; originally published 1960), 194–95, 253.

60. Though the film muted its eugenic theme, one reviewer saw Bob Ewell as a "degenerate father" and the daughter as a "poor white trash type"; see syndicated columnist Alice Hughes, "A Woman's New York," *Reading Eagle,* February 23, 1963. The *New York Times* called the portrayals of Bob and Mayella Ewell "almost caricatures"; see Bosley Crowther, "Screen: 'To Kill a Mockingbird,'" *New York Times,* February 15, 1963. For the tangled career of John Frederick Kasper, the paid agitator from New Jersey, see John Egerton, "Walking into History: The Beginning of School Desegregation in Nashville," *Southern Spaces* (May 4, 2009).

61. An African American newspaper gave this description of the film *Poor White Trash:* "There are no Emily Post rules to raw life, and 'Poor White Trash' creates none in this story of a people whose way of life has stood still while time has marched on and left them in a world apart"; see "'Poor White Trash' in Neighborhood Runs," *Baltimore Afro-American,* September 22, 1962. On Sloan Wilson's *The Man in the Gray Flannel Suit* (1955) and the dangers of losing one's individuality, see Anna Creadick, *Perfectly Normal: The Pursuit of Normality in Postwar America* (Amherst: University of Massachusetts Press, 2010), 77, 86–87. Jeans and a white T-shirt was not only the outfit of James Dean in *Rebel Without a Cause* (1955), but also the dress of angry poor white men protesting desegregation in Nashville in 1957. See "The South: What Orval Hath Wrought," 15.

62. Daniels, *A Southerner Discovers the South,* 183, 175, 179.

63. See "redneck" and "hillbilly," in *Dialect Notes, Vol. II, Part IV, Publications of the American Dialect Society* (New Haven, CT, 1904), 418, 420. The Hatfields ruthlessly killed women as well as men, breaking a key taboo of civilized behavior; see "So Ends a Mountain Feud," *Kansas City Times,* January 30, 1921. On myth about the feud, see Altina L. Waller, "Feuding and Modernization in Appalachia: The Hatfields and McCoys," *Register of the Kentucky Historical Society* 87, no. 4 (Autumn 1989): 385–404, esp. 399, 401–2; Hal Boyle, "Arkansas Ends Hillbilly Myth," *Tuscaloosa News,* May 29, 1947. On a critique of "hillbillydom" from the *Arkansas Gazette,* see "Hillbillies in

Action," *Tuscaloosa News*, August 12, 1940. On the woman having "her number," see Mandel Sherman and Thomas R. Henry, *Hollow Folk* (New York, 1933), 26. A review of *Hollow Folk* described them as "degenerate," and though "the inhabitants of our own race, theirs is a primitive culture"; see Robert E. L. Paris, "Hollow Folk," *American Journal of Sociology* 39, no. 2 (September 1933): 256.

64. Frank S. Nugent, "The Screen: 'Mountain Justice,' A Hill-Billy Anthology Is Shown at the Rialto—A New Film at the Cine Roma," *New York Times*, May 13, 1937; Sharon Hatfield, "Mountain Justice: The Making of a Feminist Icon and a Cultural Scapegoat," *Appalachian Journal* 23, no. 1 (Fall 1995), 26–47, esp. 28, 33, 35, 37, 42.

65. On hillbilly bands, comic strips, and *Kentucky Moonshine*, see Anthony Harkins, *Hillbilly: A Cultural History of an American Icon* (New York: Oxford University Press, 2004), 86–87, 103–13, 124–36, 154–55, 161–62. On Minnie Pearl, see Pamela Fox, "Recycled Trash: Gender and Authenticity in Country Music Autobiography," *American Quarterly* 50, no. 2 (1998): 234–66, esp. 253–54. For the connection between "radio rubes" like Minnie Pearl and the vaudeville circuit, see Bill C. Malone, "Radio and Personal Appearances: Sources and Resources," *Western Folklore* 30, no. 3, Commercialized Folk Music (July 1971): 215–25, esp. 216–17.

66. "The Hillbilly in Huey Long's Chair," *Milwaukee Journal*, January 4, 1946. Davis had a bachelor's degree in history and taught history at Dodd College for women, but had an M.A. thesis in psychology; his thesis, which he earned in 1927, was on the rather racist topic of intellectual differences among whites, blacks, and mulattoes. He sang songs with his band on the campaign trail. His greatest hit was "You Are My Sunshine." He refused to run a negative campaign. He ran for governor and won one term in 1944–48, and another in 1960–64. He rode his horse up the capitol steps in 1963. On Davis, see Angie Reese, "Jimmie Davis: From Sharecropper's Cabin to the Governor's Mansion" (M.A. thesis, Southeastern Louisiana University, 1995), 1, 4–9, 14–16, 30, 99.

67. See William C. Pratt, "Glen H. Taylor: Public Image and Reality," *Pacific Northwest Quarterly* 60, no. 1 (January 1969): 10–16; "O'Daniel Writes Own Songs for Vote Campaign" and "Biscuit Passing Pappy," [New Orleans] *Times-Picayune*, July 25 and August 14, 1938; "Hill-Billy Sense," *Cleveland Gazette*, September 10, 1938; P. McEvoy, "Pass the Biscuits, Pappy," *Reader's Digest*, October 1938, 9–12. On Dewey Short, see "Hillbilly 'Demosthenes,'" *Milwaukee Journal*, August 3, 1942.

68. See W. R. Crocker, "Why Do Americans Dislike the English?," *Australian Quarterly* 21, no. 1 (March 1949): 27–36, esp. 31–33. Crocker made references to both Jimmy Davis and Pappy O'Daniel.

69. On the time-warp theme, see Brooks Blevins, "In the Land of a Million Smiles: Twentieth-Century Americans Discover the Arkansas Ozarks," *The Arkansas Historical Quarterly* 61, no. 1 (Spring 2000): 1–35, esp. 2, 20, 24. On the classless myth, see speech by Supreme Court justice Hughes on the hill folk of Appalachia in "Merit Not Birth America's Basis," [Columbia, SC] *State*, February 25, 1915. On the theme that mountain people practiced true equality, a place where "pride of birth and social standing meant nothing," see

the advertisement for a movie based on the 1903 classic mountain novel *The Little Shepherd of Kingdom Come*, in *Lexington Herald*, March 21, 1920. By the fifties, the egalitarian theme had become more pronounced; see Julia McAdoo, "Where the Poor Are Rich," *American Mercury* (September 1955): 86–89; also see Brooks Blevins, "Wretched and Innocent: Two Mountain Regions in the National Consciousness," *Journal of Appalachian Studies* 7, no. 2 (Fall 2001): 257–71, esp. 264–65. On the "Park Avenue Hillbilly," see Mark Barron, "Broadway Notes," [New Orleans] *Times-Picayune*, July 23, 1950.

70. See promotion for Hillbilly Jamboree staring Red Smith and Elvis Presley, [New Orleans] *Times-Picayune*, September 1, 1955. For touring with Griffith in 1955, see Hedda Hopper, "Elvis Was Nice to Andy," *Times-Picayune*, February 6, 1957; and Goddard Lieberson, "'Country' Sweeps Country: Hillbilly Music Makers Have Parlayed a Blend of Blues, Spirituals and Folk Tunes into a $50-Million-Year Business," *New York Times*, July 28, 1957; Dick Kleiner, "Elvis Presley," *Sarasota Journal*, July 11, 1956; Vivian Boultinghouse, "The Guy with the Blue Suede Shoes," *Times-Picayune*, July 1, 1956; and Hedda Hopper, "Hollywood: Star Switch on Goodwin," *Times-Picayune*, August 2, 1956.

71. On Elvis's background in Tupelo, Mississippi, see Lloyd Shearer, "Elvis Presley," *Parade*, September 30, 1956, 8–13, esp. 11; and Michael T. Bertrand, "A Tradition-Conscious Cotton City: (East) Tupelo, Mississippi, Birthplace of Elvis Presley," in *Destination Dixie: Tourism and Southern History*, ed. Karen L. Cox (Gainesville: University of Florida Press, 2012), 87–109, esp. 87–88, 91–92, 95–97. On his female fans as mountain mules, see Jock Carroll, "Side-Burned Dream Boat of Red-Blooded Youth? This Reviewer (Male) Says I Like Elvis Presley," *Ottawa Citizen*, September 8, 1956.

72. Noel E. Parmenter Jr., "Tennessee Spellbinder: Governor Clement Runs on Time," *Nation* (August 11, 1956): 114–17, esp. 113, 116; "Democrats: Answer to Dick Nixon," *Newsweek* (July 23, 1956): 19–20; Harold H. Martin, "The Things They Say About the Governor!," *Saturday Evening Post* (January 29, 1955): 22–23, 48–51, 54–55, 58, esp. 22.

73. Martin, "The Things They Say About the Governor!," 22, 48; "Democrats: Answer to Dick Nixon," 20; Parmenter, "Tennessee Spellbinder," 117; "Democrats' Keynote," *Time* (July 23, 1956): 14. On Folsom, see Paul E. Deutschman, "Outsized Governor: 'Big Jim' Folsom Loathes Shoes and Grammar—But Loves Nature, Girls and Being Top Man in Alabama," *Life* (September 1, 1947): 59–65, esp. 59, 64–65; "'Clowning' Blamed in Folsom's Defeat" and "Politician in Squeeze: Gov. James E. Folsom," *New York Times*, June 6, 1948, and February 25, 1956; and Robert J. Norrell, "Labor at the Ballot Box: Alabama Politics from the New Deal to the Dixiecrat Movement," *Journal of Southern History* 57, no. 2 (May 1991): 201–34, esp. 230.

74. For the text of his address, see "Democratic National Convention: Keynote Address, by Frank Clement, Governor of Tennessee," *Vital Speeches of the Day*, vol. 22 (September 1, 1956): 674–79; and John Steinbeck, "'Demos Get Selves Voice in Clement'—Steinbeck," [New Orleans] *Times-Picayune*, August 15, 1956.

75. On Clement's later comment, see Robert E. Corlew III, "Frank Goad Clement and the Keynote Address of 1956," *Tennessee Historical Quarterly* 36,

no. 1 (Spring 1977): 95–107, esp. 107. There were other critical reviews of his performance, some calling his address mere "bombast," or a forensic exercise rather than real eloquence; see "The New Democrats: A Democratic Party of Youth and Energy," *Life* (August 27, 1957): 20–36, esp. 22; and George E. Sokolsky, "'A Torrent of Oratory,' *Gadsden Times,* August 17, 1956; also see memorandum from Horace Busby to Bill Moyers, July 29, 1964, in the appendix of Robert Mann, *Daisy Petals and Mushroom Clouds: LBJ, Barry Goldwater, and the Ad That Changed American Politics* (Baton Rouge: Louisiana State University Press, 2014), 122.

76. Hodding Carter, "Hushpuppies, Stew—and Oratory: Southern Politicians Must Be Showmen, Too, but Behind Their Act Is a Deadly Seriousness," *New York Times Magazine,* June 18, 1950; "The Politician as Bore," *Chicago Tribune,* March 23, 1956.

77. "Hillbilly Chivalry," *Chicago Tribune,* March 15, 1958.

78. On Estes Kefauver and "Big Jim" Folsom, see William G. Carleton, "The Southern Politician—1900 and 1950," *Journal of Politics* 13, no. 2 (May 1951): 215–31, esp. 220–21; Corlew, "Frank Goad Clement," 106–7; and for linking Clement's fall from prominence to his "corn-filled keynote speech," see "Politics: Ole Frank," *Time* (August 10, 1962): 13. On Johnson as the second most powerful man in the nation, see Stewart Alsop, "Lyndon Johnson: How Does He Do It?," *Saturday Evening Post* (January 24, 1959): 13–14, 38, 43, esp. 13–14. And on Johnson hanging Clay's portrait in the oval office, see "Portraits of Washington, Clay and Jackson on Walls," *New York Times,* March 2, 1964. On Johnson as a teacher, see John R. Silber, "Lyndon Johnson as Teacher," *Listener and BBC Television Review* 73 (May 20, 1965): 728–30.

79. On Johnson earning sympathy, see James Reston, "The Office and the Man: Johnson Emerges Grave and Strong as the Presidency Works Its Change," *New York Times,* November 28, 1963; Anthony Lewis, "Johnson Style: Earthy and Flamboyant," *New York Times,* November 24, 1963; "Lyndon Baines Johnson," *New York Times,* August 27, 1964. On his close associates rejecting the rural hick portrait, see the AP article that appeared in numerous newspapers: Arthur Edson, "Johnson Called Complex Person Mistaken as a 'Cornball'" *Milwaukee Journal,* December 28, 1963. On "digging down deeply," see "Johnson's Way," *New York Times,* April 26, 1964; and Russell Baker, "President's Manner, Like Jackson's, a Folksy One," *New York Times,* November 2, 1964. On his showmanship and deep emotions, see Marianne Means, "Despite His Informal Air, LBJ Seldom Shows Sensitive Side," *San Antonio Light,* October 10, 1965. The ambivalence over Johnson continued during his presidency. As one reporter wrote in 1968 on his accession to the presidency, "Just plain folksy or just plain corny, spontaneous or devious, inspiring persuader or ruthless arm-twister, Lyndon Baines Johnson was now firmly in the saddle"; see AP correspondent Saul Pett, "The Johnson Years: The Arc of Paradox," *Hutchinson* [KS] *News,* April 14, 1968.

80. See Lyndon Johnson, "Remarks in Johnson City, Tex., Upon Signing the Elementary and Secondary Education Bill, April 11, 1965," in *Public Papers of the Presidents: Johnson,* 412–14, esp. 414. On his echoes of Odum, see Lyndon B. Johnson, "My Political Philosophy," *Texas Quarterly* 1, no. 4 (Winter

1958): 17–22. On the strategic plan for winning over southern legislators, see William B. Cannon, "Enlightened Localism: A Narrative Account of Poverty and Education in the Great Society," *Yale Law and Policy Review* 4, no. 1 (Fall–Winter 1985): 6–60, esp. 39, 43; John A. Andrew III, *Lyndon Johnson and the Great Society* (Chicago: Ivan R. Dee, 1998), 120–21. On Lady Bird Johnson's visit without her husband, see Nan Robertson, "Mrs. Johnson Visits Poverty Area," *New York Times*, March 22, 1964.

81. On photographs, see "Johnson and the People," *New York Times*, May 3, 1964. On poor white images, also see "Johnson's Great Society—Lines Are Drawn," *New York Times*, March 14, 1965; and John Ed Pearce, "The Superfluous People of Hazard, Kentucky," *Reporter* 28, no. 1 (January 3, 1963): 33–35; Homer Bigart, "Kentucky Miners: A Grim Winter," *New York Times*, October 20, 1963; Robyn Muncy, "Coal-Fired Reforms: Social Citizenship, Dissident Miners, and the Great Society," *Journal of American History* (June 2009): 72–98, esp. 74, 90–95; and Ronald Eller, *Uneven Ground: Appalachia Since 1945* (Lexington: University Press of Kentucky, 2008), 20, 23–25, 30–32, 36–39; David Torstensson, "Beyond the City: Lyndon Johnson's War on Poverty in Rural America," *Journal of Policy History* 25, no. 4 (2013): 587–613, esp. 591–92, 596, 606.

82. On Johnson's hat, see "Random Notes from All Over: Johnson Says Aye to LBJ Hats," *New York Times*, February 17, 1964. On the poor, see Marjorie Hunter, "President's Tour Dramatized Issue" and "Johnson Pledges to Aid the Needy," *New York Times*, April 26, 1964, and September 21, 1964; Franklin D. Roosevelt, "State of the Union Address," January 11, 1944.

83. Bill Moyers, "What a Real President Was Like: To Lyndon Johnson the Great Society Meant Hope and Dignity," *Washington Post*, November 13, 1988. On manipulation of white trash pride in Faulkner's writing, see John Rodden, "'The Faithful Gravedigger': The Role of 'Innocent' Wash Jones and the Invisible 'White Trash' in Faulkner's *Absalom, Absalom!*," *Southern Literary Journal* 43, no. 1 (Fall 2010): 23–38, esp. 23, 26, 30–31; and Jacques Pothier, "Black Laughter: Poor White Short Stories Behind *Absalom, Absalom!* and *The Hamlet*," in *William Faulkner's Short Fiction*, ed. Hans H. Skei (Oslo: Solum Forlag, 1977), 173–184, esp. 173. Nearly thirty years after he wrote *A Southerner Discovers the South*, Jonathan Daniels wrote of the unfulfilled promise of the American dream in the South. The "New South" was still the Old South, poor whites and blacks remained poor together, and "none but the blind can believe that in the South the unfortunate and dispossessed are only of one color." See Daniels, "The Ever-Ever Land," *Harper's Magazine* (April 1965): 183–88.

84. For the Republican campaign attack film, see Nan Robertson, "G.O.P. Film Depicts 'Moral Decay,'" *New York Times*, October 21, 1964; and Mann, *Daisy Petals and Mushroom Clouds*, 94–95. On Billy Carter's famous comment, see "You'll Have to Pardon Billy," *Milwaukee Sentinel*, February 17, 1977; also see John Shelton Reed, *Southern Folk, Plain and Fancy: Native White Social Types* (Athens: University of Georgia Press, 1986), 38. On Malcolm X, see William E. Leuchtenburg, *The White House Looks South: Franklin D. Roosevelt, Harry Truman, and Lyndon B. Johnson* (Baton Rouge: Louisiana State University Press, 2005) 327.

85. On Elvis's Cadillac, see Joe Hyams, "Meet Hollywood's Biggest Spenders," *This Week Magazine,* February 25, 1962. The film's attack was based on stories about Johnson driving his car fast and drinking beer, but they added the references to him throwing cans out the window. On LBJ's wild driving and posing with a piglet, see "Presidency: 'Mr. President, You're Fun,'" *Time* (April 3, 1964): 23–24. On the symbolic meaning of freedom (escaping your ancestors) associated with cars in American culture, see Deborah Clark, *Driving Women: Fiction and Automobile Culture in Twentieth-Century America* (Baltimore: Johns Hopkins University Press, 2007), 165.

86. On Fulbright and McGovern, see Albert Lauterbach, "How Much Cutback for Consumers," *Challenge* 6, no. 7 (April 1958): 72–76, esp. 72; and Joseph Green, "Events & Opinions," *The Clearing House* 32, no. 8 (April 1958): 485–86; also "Presley Termed a Passing Fancy," *New York Times,* December 17, 1956. On Elvis's "orgiastic" dancing, see Bosley Crowther, "The Screen: Culture Takes a Holiday: Elvis Presley Appears in 'Love Me Tender,'" *New York Times,* November 16, 1956.

87. Robertson, "G.O.P. Film Depicts 'Moral Decay.'" Elvis's delinquent ways led a church congregation in Jackson, Florida, to pray for his soul; see "Elvis a Different Kind of Idol," *Life* (August 27, 1956): 101–9, esp. 108–9. Elvis was considered the idol of delinquent boys; see Martin Gold, *Status Forces in Delinquent Boys* (Ann Arbor, MI: Institute for Social Research, 1963), 104; and Eugene Gilbert, "Typical Presley Fan Is a 'C' Student; Aloof, Indifferent," [New Orleans] *Times-Picayune,* March 14, 1958. On Appalachians having no respect for working hard and striving to move up the ladder, see Roscoe Griffin, "When Families Move . . . from Cinder Hollow to Cincinnati," *Mountain Life and Work* (Winter 1956): 11–20, esp. 16, 18. On the lure of being lazy, see Damon Runyon, "My Old Home Town—The Passing of Crazy Bill," *Milwaukee Sentinel,* September 8, 1957; Eller, *Uneven Ground,* 26.

88. Harrington wrote, "But the real explanation of why the poor are where they are is that they made the mistake of being born to the wrong parents, in the wrong section of the country, in the wrong industry, or in the wrong racial or ethnic group. Once that mistake has been made, they could have been paragons of will and morality, but most of them would never have had a chance to get out of the other America." See Michael Harrington, *The Other America: Poverty in the United States* (Baltimore: Penguin, 1962), 21. Another researcher used a different set of analogies that emphasized inherited incapacities: he said the poor were "underendowed," "economic invalids," and possessed an "inadequate personal patrimony." See Oscar Ornati, "Affluence and the Risk of Poverty," *Social Research* 31, no. 3 (Autumn 1964): 333–46, esp. 341–45; and see Eller, *Uneven Ground,* 101.

89. John Kenneth Galbraith, *The Affluent Society,* 40th anniversary ed. (Boston: Houghton Mifflin, 1999), 235–37; Harrington, *The Other America,* 9–14, 18, 34.

90. Lewis H. Lapham, "Who Is Lyndon Johnson?," *Saturday Evening Post* (September 9, 1965): 21–25, 65–67, 70–72, esp. 66, 71. On the idiom of "big ones" as rich white folks and poor whites as craving land and respect, see Jack

Temple Kirby, "Black and White in Rural South, 1915–1954," *Agricultural History* 58, no. 3 (July 1984): 411–22, esp. 418; also see "Johnson's Rare Word: 'Caliche,' a Soil Crust," *New York Times,* January 5, 1965; "Politics Was Johnson's Work, Rest, and Relaxation," [Clearfield, PA] *Progress,* January 24, 1973; Ryan Greene, "Sideglances in the Mirror," *Gilmer* [TX] *Mirror,* May 26, 1966.

91. James Reston, "Paradox and Reason," *New York Times,* January 21, 1965.

92. Lyndon Johnson, "Remarks to Students Participating in the U.S. Senate Youth Program," February 5, 1965, *Public Papers of the Presidents: Johnson,* 148–51, esp. 150.

Chapter Eleven: Redneck Roots:
Deliverance, Billy Beer, and Tammy Faye

1. Mary Bernstein, "Identity Politics," *Annual Review of Sociology* 31 (2005): 47–74, esp. 49, 53, 64. As Mary Louis Adams argued, "It is important to note that identity politics encompass a celebration of the group's uniqueness as well as an analysis of its particular oppression"; see "There's No Place Like Home: On the Place of Identity in Feminist Politics," *Feminist Review,* no. 31 (Spring 1989): 22–33, esp. 25; and Douglas C. Rossinow, *The Politics of Authenticity: Liberalism, Christianity, and the New Left in America* (New York: Columbia University Press, 1998); Mathew D. Lassiter, *The Silent Majority: Suburban Politics in the Sunbelt South* (Princeton, NJ: Princeton University Press, 2006), 1, 3.

2. Joseph Bensman and Arthur J. Vidich, "The New Middle Classes: Their Culture and Life Styles," *Journal of Aesthetic Education* 4, no. 1 (January 1970): 23–39, esp. 24–25, 29.

3. Anne Roiphe, "'An American Family': Things Are Keen but Could Be Keener," *New York Times Magazine,* February 18, 1973, 8–9, 41–43, 45–47, 50–53, esp. 8, 47, 50–53.

4. Thomas Lask, "Success of Search for 'Roots' Leaves Alex Haley Surprised," *New York Times,* November 23, 1976; Paul D. Zimmerman, "In Search of a Heritage," *Newsweek* (September 27, 1976): 94–96. Even the Library of Congress classified the book as genealogy instead of fiction; see David Henige, "Class as GR Instead?," *American Libraries* 31, no. 4 (April 2000): 34–35.

5. The first compelling critique that exposed problems with his African research was Mark Ottaway, "Tangled Roots," *Sunday Times* (London), April 10, 1977, 17, 21. His conclusions were reconfirmed by an African scholar who explained that the griot, or family storyteller, was unreliable, and told the inquirer what he wanted to hear. (Haley failed to tape the interview, relied on only one informant, and when other information contradicted the story he wanted, he ignored it.) See Donald R. Wright, "Unrooting Kunta Kinte: On the Perils of Relying on Encyclopedic Informants," *History in Africa* 8 (1981): 205–17, esp. 206, 209–13. For Haley's response to Ottaway's criticism and his rationale for the unrealistic portrayal of Kinte's village, see Robert D. McFadden, "Some Points of 'Roots' Questioned: Haley Stands by the Book as a Symbol," *New York Times,* April 10, 1977. Professional historians had different

reactions to Haley's claims: Oscar Handlin of Harvard called the book a "fraud," and Professor Willie Lee Rose of Johns Hopkins University, an expert in slavery, concluded that the "anachronisms . . . are too numerous and chip away at the verisimilitude of central matters in which it is important to have full faith." See Israel Shenker, "Some Historians Dismiss Report of Factual Mistakes in 'Roots,'" *New York Times,* April 10, 1977.

6. For the most thorough exposition of research errors in *Roots,* coauthored by a historian and genealogist, see Gary B. Mills and Elizabeth Shown Mills, "'Roots' and the New 'Faction': A Legitimate Tool for Clio?," *Virginia Magazine of History and Biography* 89, no. 1 (January 1981): 3–26, esp. 6–19. On Haley's class bias (making his ancestors superior to other slaves), see Mills and Mills, "'Roots' and the New 'Faction,'" 25; and James A. Hijiya, "Roots: Family and Ethnicity in the 1970s," *American Quarterly* 30, no. 4 (Autumn 1978): 548–56.

7. For Haley as a hoaxer, see Stanley Crouch, "'The Beloved Fraud of 'Roots,'" *Garden City Telegram,* May 9, 2011; for timing of pitch to ABC, see obituary of Brandon Stoddard, who developed the *Roots* miniseries, *Washington Post,* December 29, 2014.

8. James A. Michener, *Chesapeake* (New York: Random House, 1978), 158–59, 161.

9. Ibid., 325, 803, 822, 826, 842–45, 854–55; Tom Horton, "Michener's 'Chesapeake' Revisited Novel," *Baltimore Sun,* October 24, 1997.

10. See Nancy Isenberg and Andrew Burstein, "Adamses on Screen," in *A Companion to John Adams and John Quincy Adams,* ed. David Waldstreicher (Malden, MA: Wiley-Blackwell, 2013), 487–509; Boorstin's introduction, in Jack Shepherd, *The Adams Chronicles: Four Generations of Greatness* (Boston: Little, Brown, 1975), xxxi; and Hijiya, "Roots," 551.

11. Pete Hamill, "The Revolt of the White Lower Middle Class," *New York* (April 14, 1969): 24–29; Philip Shabecoff, "A Blue-Collar Voter Discusses His Switch to Nixon," *New York Times,* November 6, 1972; Richard Nixon, "Address Accepting the Presidential Nomination at the Republican National Convention in Miami Beach, Florida, August 8, 1968," in John T. Woolley and Gerhard Peters, *The American Presidency Project at UC Santa Barbara,* http://presidency.ucsb.edu/ws/index.php?pid=25968; Scott J. Spitzer, "Nixon's New Deal: Welfare Reform for the Silent Majority," *Presidential Quarterly* 42, no. 3 (September 2012): 455–81, esp. 458–62, 471, 473, 477; Rick Perlstein, *Nixonland: The Rise of a President and the Fracturing of America* (New York: Scribner, 2008); Lassiter, *The Silent Majority,* 234, 236; Michael Novak, *The Rise of the Unmeltable Ethnics* (New York: Macmillan, 1972), 4, 30, 53, 60, 70–71, 81, 258–60; Matthew Frye Jacobson, *Roots Too: White Ethnics Revival in Post–Civil Rights America* (Cambridge, MA: Harvard University Press, 2006), 44–45, 190.

12. See Washington syndicated NEA (Newspaper Enterprise Association) columnist Bruce Biossat, "White Poor in US Forgotten Masses," *Gadsden* [AL] *Times,* September 14, 1969; Biossat, "Poor White Dilemma," *Sumter Daily Item,* May 24, 1967; "White Tar Heels Poor, Too," *Spring Hope* [NC] *Enterprise,* November 2, 1967; Marjorie Hunter, "To the Poor in South Carolina, Free Food Stamps Are a Source of Satisfaction and Embarrassment," *New York Times,* May 18, 1969. On the role of the welfare rights movement, see

Premilla Nadasen, *Welfare Warriors: The Welfare Rights Movement in the United States* (New York: Routledge, 2005); and Felicia Kornbluh, *The Battle for Welfare Rights: Politics and Poverty in Modern America* (Philadelphia: University of Pennsylvania Press, 2007); "The Work Ethic," *New York Times,* November 6, 1972; Gaylord Shaw, "Welfare Ethic Advocates Hits; Leads to Vicious Cycle of Dependency—Nixon," [New Orleans] *Times-Picayune,* September 4, 1972; also see "Transcript of the President's Labor Day Address," *New York Times,* September 7, 1971.

13. Marcus Klein, "Heritage of the Ghetto," *Nation* (March 27, 1976): 373–75, esp. 373.

14. On changes in NASCAR from the forties to the seventies, see Daniel, *Lost Revolutions,* 94–97, 108–10, 118–20. On Dolly Parton, see "People Are Talking About: Dolly Parton," *Vogue* (October 1, 1977): 300–301. On "redneck chic," see Patrick Huber, "A Short History of Redneck: The Fashioning of a Southern White Masculine Identity," *Southern Cultures* 1, no. 2 (Winter 1995): 145–66, esp. 159. On redneck country music, see Joe Edwards, "He's a Redneck," *Reading* [PA] *Eagle,* August 12, 1976; and Joe Edwards, "'Redneck' Doesn't Have to Be Offensive," *Gadsden* [AL] *Times,* March 25, 1983. On *White Trash Cooking,* see Sylvia Carter, "He's Proud to Be 'White Trash,'" *Milwaukee Journal,* December 29, 1986.

15. See Robert Basler, "Dolly Parton: Fittin' into Floozydom Comfortably," [Lafayette, LA] *Advertiser,* April 24, 1986; Emily Satterwhite, *Dear Appalachia* (Lexington: University of Kentucky Press, 2011), 131, 172, 174–75.

16. See Lillian Smith, "White Trash" (ca. 1964 or 1965) and "The Poor White's Future" (ca. 1964), Lillian Eugenia Smith Papers, Box 41, ms. 1283 A, and Box 43, ms. 1238 A, Hargrett Rare Book and Manuscript Library, University of Georgia Libraries, Athens; Huber, "A Short History of Redneck," 161.

17. Robert Sherrill, "The Embodiment of Poor White Power," *New York Times Magazine,* February 28, 1971. In 1968, a group of demonstrators from an Appalachian contingent of the Poor People's Campaign protested at his home in Arlington. See John Yago, "Poor Encountered a Slick Senator," *Charleston Gazette,* June 24, 1968; also see Sanford J. Ungar, "The Man Who Runs the Senate: Bobby Byrd: An Upstart Comes to Power," *Atlantic Monthly* (September 1975): 29–35, esp. 35; and Robert C. Byrd, *Robert C. Byrd: Child of the Appalachian Coalfields* (Morgantown: West Virginia University Press, 2005), 42, 53, 219–221, 223, 228, 235–37, 244–45.

18. See cover and "New Day A'Coming in the South," *Time* (May 31, 1971): 14–20, esp. 14–16. On Wallace, see Dan T. Carter, "Legacy of Rage: George Wallace and the Transformation of American Politics," *Journal of Southern History* 62, no. 1 (February 1996): 3–26, esp. 10–12, 26; Randy Sanders, "'The Sad Duty of Politics': Jimmy Carter and the Issue of Race in His 1970 Gubernatorial Campaign," *Georgia Historical Quarterly* 76, no. 3 (Fall 1992): 612–38, esp. 620–21, 623–25; and see James Clotfelter and William R. Hamilton, "Electing a Governor in the Seventies," in *American Governor in Behavioral Perspective,* eds. Thad Beyle and J. Oliver Williams (New York: Harper & Row, 1972), 32–39, esp. 34, 36.

19. Sanders, "'The Sad Duty of Politics,'" 632–33.

20. On Dickey inventing his mountain roots, see Satterwhite, *Dear Appalachia*, 149–50, 508–11; and Henry Hart, "James Dickey: The World as a Lie," *The Sewanee Review* 108, no. 1 (Winter 2000): 93–106; also Harkins, *Hillbilly*, 209. In his memoir, Dickey's son Christopher recounted his father's endless need to lie about his life; for a review of the memoir (*Summer of Deliverance: A Memoir of Father and Son*), see David Kirby, "Liar and Son," *New York Times*, August 30, 1998; on Dickey's egomania, see Benjamin Griffith, "The Egomaniac as Myth Maker" (review of *The One Voice of James Dickey: His Letters and Life, 1970–1997*), *Sewanee Review* 117, no. 1 (Winter 2009): vi–viii.

21. In the novel, Dickey describes Bobby as "plump and pink," and screaming and squalling. He also has Lewis voice the survivalist ethos that the four men must tap the instincts within themselves to endure their ordeal. As used goods, Bobby is unable to overcome the "taint" of his rape. See James Dickey, *Deliverance* (Boston: Houghton Mifflin, 1970), 54, 121–22, 126, 135, 167; also see Christopher Ricks, "Man Hunt," *New York Review of Books* 14, no. 8 (April 23, 1970), 37–40, esp. 40; Walter Clemmons, "James Dickey, Novelist," *New York Times*, March 22, 1970. On the sexualized nature of the trauma and the pact among the three survivors, see Linda Ruth Williams, "Blood Brothers," *Sight and Sound*, September 1994, 16–19. For a review that focused on "sodomy-inclined hillbillies," see Vincent Canby, "The Screen: James Dickey's 'Deliverance' Arrives," *New York Times*, July 31, 1972.

22. Not only does Drew show compassion, but he is the only one to defend the law over Lewis's primal code of survival. See Dickey, *Deliverance*, 68, 70, 137; Anil Narine, "Global Trauma at Home: Technology, Modernity, 'Deliverance,'" *Journal of American Studies* 42, no. 3 (December 2008): 449–70, esp. 466. On the idiot savant, see Hal Aigner, "'Deliverance' by John Boorman," *Film Quarterly* 26, no. 2 (Winter 1972–73): 39–41, esp. 41.

23. On discovery of this "rare breed," Wolfe writes, "There is Detroit, hardly able to believe itself, what it has discovered, a breed of good old boys from the fastness of the Appalachian hills and flats—a handful from this rare breed—who have given Detroit . . . speed . . . and the industry can present it to a whole generation as . . . yours." Tom Wolfe, "The Last American Hero Is Junior Johnson. Yes!" *Esquire* (March 1965): 68–74, 138, 142–48, 150–52, 154–55, esp. 71, 74, 147, 155.

24. Andrew Horton, "Hot Car Films & Cool Individualism or, 'What We Have Here Is a Lack of Respect for the Law,'" *Cinéaste* 8, no. 4 (Summer 1978): 12–15, esp. 14; and James Poniewozik, "What Did *The Dukes of Hazzard* Really Say About the South?," *Time* (July 2, 2015).

25. Wolfe, "The Last American Hero," 71, 74, 144.

26. James Wooten, *Dasher: The Roots and Rising of Jimmy Carter* (New York: Summit Books, 1978), 280, 346–47, 354–56; and James Wooten, "The Man Who Refused to Lose: James Earl Carter Jr.," *New York Times*, July 15, 1976.

27. For Carter on the kinship he felt for Justice Hugo Black and Estes Kafauver, see Anthony Lewis, "Jimmy Carter: Southern Populist," *Morning Record*, June 4, 1976. On Carter's "log cabin" campaign style, see Frank Jackman (of the *New York Daily News*), "Profile: Who Is Jimmy Carter?" [St. Petersburg, FL] *Evening Independent*, July 15, 1976. On the Allman Brothers benefits for

Carter, see Wayne King, "Rock Goes Back to Where It All Began: Rock Goes South," *New York Times,* June 20, 1976. On the radio ad, see Eli Evans, "The Natural Superiority of Southern Politicians," *New York Times,* January 16, 1977. For Carter describing himself as "white trash made good," see Charles Mohr, "Reporter's Notebook: Enigmatic Side of Carter," *New York Times,* July 1, 1976. Young's comment was aimed at the black community, where many of Carter's critics called him a "cracker" and "redneck." And Carter called himself a redneck; see Paul Delaney, "Many Black Democratic Leaders Voice Doubt: Fear and Distrust About Carter," *New York Times,* July 6, 1976. Other political observers saw Carter as the "new roots" of a new South, because he was not a redneck; see James Wolcott, "Presidential Aesthetics: You've Seen the Movie ('Nashville'), Now Meet the Candidate—Jimmy Carter," *Village Voice,* January 19, 1976.

28. Roy Blount Jr., *Crackers: This Whole Many Angled Thing of Jimmy, More Carters, Ominous Little Animals, Sad Singing Women, My Daddy and Me* (New York: Knopf, 1980), 210, 221. Norman Mailer wrote about the campaign film shown at the Democratic convention that covered the parodies of Carter's famous smile (such as Alfred E. Neuman on the cover of *Mad Magazine*); see Norman Mailer, "The Search for Carter," *New York Times Magazine,* September 26, 1976, 20–21, 69–73, 88–90, esp. 69. And there was even an Associated Press news story on Carter's dentist, see Fred Cormier, "That Famous Carter Grin Doesn't Need Toothpaste," *Ocala Star-Banner,* February 7, 1980.

29. On Carter's tenacity for his roots, see John Dillin, "Jimmy Carter: Forces in His Life," *Boca Raton News,* August 1, 1976 (reprinted from the *Christian Science Monitor*); Robert D. Hershey Jr., "Carter's Family Linked to Royalty by British Publication on Peerage," *New York Times,* August 12, 1977. For Carter's fascination with his own roots, also see Wooten, *Dasher,* 62. On the fact that the "details" of Carter's colonial Virginia heritage were as sketchy and improbable as Alex Haley's, see Douglas Brinkley, "A Time for Reckoning: Jimmy Carter and the Cult of Kinfolk," *Presidential Studies Quarterly* 29, no. 4 (December 1999): 778–97, esp. 781. And on the centrality of Carter's Georgia roots as crucial to his self-fashioning, see F. N. Boney, "Georgia's First President: The Emergence of Jimmy Carter," *Georgia Historical Quarterly* 72, no. 1 (Spring 1988): 119–32, esp. 119, 123.

30. See Phil Gailey, "Meet Billy Carter," [St. Petersburg, FL] *Evening Independent,* July 15, 1976; Huber, "A Short History of Redneck," 158. On selling mobile homes, see "Billy Carter," [Henderson, NC] *Times-News,* September 23, 1981; also see Stanley W. Cloud, "A Wry Clown: Billy Carter, 1937–1988," *Time* (October 10, 1988): 44.

31. Blount, *Crackers,* 93, 131–32.

32. On Shrum, see Mary McGrory, "Ex-Carter Speech Writer Says Jimmy Lies," *Boca Raton News,* May 9, 1976. On poor women, see David S. Broder, "Life Isn't Fair," *Telegraph,* July 25, 1977. Carter displayed the same dichotomy on welfare, calling for greater health care for poor rural women, yet emphasizing that government cannot "solve all our problems." As one *New York Times* reporter noted, Carter's Dixie conservatism was part of a tradition that

"embraces a certain fatalism about social inequalities and the natural pecking order more readily than do Northern liberals"; see Hendrick Smith, "Carter's Political Dichotomy: Beliefs Rooted in Southern Democratic Traditions Seem to Counteract His Compassion for the Poor," *New York Times,* July 16, 1977; and Andrew R. Flint and Joy Porter, "Jimmy Carter: The Re-Emergence of Faith-Based Politics and the Abortion Rights Issue," *Presidential Studies Quarterly* 35, no. 1 (March 2005): 28–51, esp. 39.

33. For a sample of the stories of the rabbit affair, see *Chicago Tribune*–New York News Syndicate writer Jack W. Germond and Jules Witcover, "Laughing with the President—Or at Him," *St. Petersburg Times,* September 1, 1979; "Banzai Bunny 'Just a Quiet Georgia Rabbit,'" *Montreal Gazette,* August 31, 1979; "Carter and Peter Rabbit," *Lewiston Evening Journal,* August 31, 1979; Louis Cook, "About the Rabbit . . . ," *Bangor Daily News,* August 31, 1979; Valerie Schulthies, "Monster Rabbits Strike Terror in Many a Heart," *Deseret News,* September 1, 1979; Ralph de Toledano, "The Great Rabbit Caper," *Lodi* [CA] *News-Sentinel,* September 20, 1979. For Carter telling the story, see "Questions Get Tough When Carter Meets the Press," *Palm Beach Post,* August 31, 1979; "A Tale of Carter and the 'Killer Rabbit'; President Orders Photograph," "Carter Describes Foe: 'Quiet Georgia Rabbit,'" and "Rabbit Photo Kept Secret," *New York Times,* August 29, August 31, and September 5, 1979. For a release of the "clearest picture" of the rabbit duel, see "The Famed Rabbit Attack," *Gainesville* [FL] *Sun,* June 23, 1981. Tom Paxton wrote a satirical song, titled "I Don't Want a Bunny Wunny," playing on the theme of a mock duel or battle: "President Carter saved the day; / Splashed with the paddle, rabbit swam away. / Jimmy was a hero, felt it in his bones, / Said in the words of John Paul Jones."

34. On Reagan's visit to Ireland, see Jacobson, *Roots Too,* 16–17. When Reagan gave a speech at the dedication of the Carter library, he called Carter's personal story the "story of the South," clearly the opposite of what Reagan stood for. On Reagan not understanding the South, see Frederick Allen, "Jimmy Carter, a Son of the South Who Bore the Region's Burdens," [Wilmington, NC] *Star-News,* October 5, 1986. On Reagan's acting skills and the Nancy Reagan "pigsty" rumor, see Bob Schieffer and Gary Paul Gates, *The Acting President* (New York: E. P. Dutton, 1989), 170, 181, 375. Kitty Kelley wrote that Nancy Reagan wanted "'a return of dignity,'" as if "the Carters had been jugheads in blue jeans who prodded cattle through the halls"; see Kitty Kelley, *Nancy Reagan: The Unauthorized Biography* (New York: Simon & Schuster, 1991), 296–97. On Reagan's "media reflexes," see Lance Morrow, "The Decline of Oratory," *Time* (August 18, 1980): 76, 78, esp. 76.

35. Patrick Buchanan, "Reagan Offers Hope to Blacks," *Chicago Tribune,* September 2, 1980.

36. Blount, *Crackers,* 5. On Bakker at the White House, see Dudley Clendinen, "Spurred by White House Parley, TV Evangelists Spread Word," *New York Times,* September 10, 1984. For the "Pass-the-Loot Club," see Sandy Grady, "Camera Double-Crossed Bakker," *Spokane Chronicle,* September 22, 1989. On the forty-five-year sentence, see June Preston, "Bakker Given 45 Years, $500,000 Fine for Fraud," *Schenectady Gazette,* October 25, 1989. By 1987,

the PTL broadcast on 165 local stations covering 85 percent of the national TV market; see Charles E. Shepard, *Forgiven: The Rise and Fall of Jim Bakker and the PTL Ministry* (New York: Atlantic Monthly Press, 1989), 239.

37. For the "Bible school dropout," see Preston, "Bakker Given 45 Years"; for the Bakkers' extravagant lifestyle, see Elizabeth LeLand, "Jim and Tammy Bakker Lived Life of Luxuriant Excess," *Ocala Star-Banner*, May 24, 1987; Richard N. Ostling, "Of God and Greed: Bakker and Falwell Trade Charges in Televangelism's Unholy Row," *Time* (June 8, 1987): 70–72, 74, esp. 72. On living in a trailer and later excesses, see Shepard, *Forgiven*, 35, 110, 133, 180, 201, 249, 264, 551.

38. On Jim Bakker's use of his poor class background in his religious message, see Richard N. Ostling, "TV's Unholy Row: A Sex-and-Money Scandal Tarnishes Electronic Evangelicalism," *Time* (April 6, 1987): 60–64, 67, esp. 62. On prosperity theology, see "Jim Bakker," in Randall Herbert Balmer, *Encyclopedia of Evangelicalism* (Waco, TX: Baylor University Press, 2004), 50–52; and Axel R. Schafer, *Countercultural Conservatives: American Evangelicalism from the Postwar Revival to the New Christian Right* (Madison: University of Wisconsin Press, 2011), 125. On the "cheesy" nature of the Jim and Tammy show, see Brian Siang, "Jim & Tammy Faye's Fall from Grace Is Perfectly Clear," *Philadelphia Inquirer*, April 8, 1987.

39. On Tammy's drug addiction, see "Tammy Bakker Treated," [New Orleans] *Times-Picayune*, 1986; and Ostling, "Of God and Greed," 72. On sex scandals and Hahn revelations, see Associated Press story, "Playboy Interview with Jessica Hahn," [Spartanburg, SC] *Herald Journal*, September 22, 1987; Horace Davis, "Hahn's Story—In Hahn's Words," *Lakeland* [FL] *Ledger*, October 9, 1987; "Fletcher Says Bakker Bisexual," *Gadsden* [AL] *Times*, December 5, 1988; "As He Faces Likely Indictment, New Sex Accusation: Bakker Says Christianity in Disarray," *Ellensburg* [WA] *Daily Record*, December 5, 1988; "Bakker Defrocked by Assemblies of God," *Lodi* [CA] *News-Sentinel*, May 7, 1987; Montgomery Brower, "Unholy Roller Coaster," *People*, September 18, 1989, 98–99, 102–4, 106, esp. 104; Mary Zeiss Stange, "Jessica Hahn's Strange Odyssey from PTL to Playboy," *Journal of Feminist Studies in Religion* 6, no. 1 (Spring 1990): 105–16, esp. 106; "The Jessica Hahn Story: Part 1," *Playboy*, November 1987, 178–80; "The Jessica Hahn Story: Part 2," *Playboy*, December 1987, 198; "Jessica: A New Life," *Playboy*, September 1988, 158–62.

40. On sending out the appeals for money on the first of the month, see Montgomery, "Unholy Roller Coaster," 106; Nicholas Von Hoffman, "White Trash Moves Front and Center," *Bangor Daily News*, April 8, 1987. Hoffman's editorial appeared alongside a cartoon of Satan meeting with his minions, holding a paper marked "T.V. Evangelicals." Satan is saying, "Then it's agreed. The hostile takeover will not be attempted. The enterprise in question being too sleazy for our consideration." For the typical viewers of televangelist shows, see Barry R. Litman and Elizabeth Bain, "The Viewership of Religious Television Programming: A Multidisciplinary Analysis of Televangelism," *Review of Religion* 30, no. 4 (June 1989): 329–43, esp. 338. For President Reagan cultivating televangelists, see Jeffrey K. Hadden, "The Rise and Fall of American

Televangelism," *Annals of the American Academy of Political and Social Science* 527 (May 1993): 113–30, esp. 126.

41. "Tammy Faye Bakker," in R. Marie Griffith, "The Charismatic Movement," in *Encyclopedia of Women and Religion in North America,* eds. Rosemary Skinner Keller and Rosemary Radford Reuther (Bloomington: University of Indiana Press, 2006), 463; Shepard, *Forgiven,* 6–7, 30–31, 152–53; and William E. Schmidt, "For Jim and Tammy Bakker, Excess Wiped Out a Rapid Climb to Success," *New York Times,* May 16, 1987.

42. Parton told Roy Blount that the reason for her outrageous appearance was that she had nothing as a child and, having acquired money, "I'm gonna pile it all over me." Roy Blount Jr., "Country's Angels," *Esquire* (March 1977): 62–66, 124–26, 131–32, esp. 126; Pamela Wilson, "Mountains of Contradictions: Gender, Class, and Region in the Star Image of Dolly Parton," *South Atlantic Quarterly* 94, no. 1 (Winter 1995): 109–34, esp. 110, 112, 125; Pamela Fox, "Recycled 'Trash': Gender and Authenticity in Country Music Autobiography," *American Quarterly* 50, no. 2 (June 1998): 234–66, esp. 258–59; Dolly Parton, *My Life and Other Unfinished Business* (New York: HarperCollins, 1994), 59.

43. Griffith, "Tammy Faye Bakker," 463. On the Tammy Faye Bakker dolls being sold for $675 at the Heritage USA gift shop, and for $500 from the doll maker herself, see "Tammy Faye Dolls Selling for $500," [Wilmington, NC] *Star-News,* May 19, 1987.

44. Roger Ebert, "Tammy Faye's Story Captured in Documentary," January 24, 2000, RogerEbert.com; Renee V. Lucas, "The Tammy Look: It's Makeup by the Numbers," Philly.com, April 8, 1987.

Chapter Twelve: Outing Rednecks: Slumming, Slick Willie, and Sarah Palin

1. Margo Jefferson, "Slumming: Ain't We Got Fun?," *Vogue* (August 1, 1988): 344–47; Mike Boone, "Magnum's Oh, So English Chum Higgins Is Really a Texas Redneck," *Montreal Gazette,* June 19, 1982.

2. Lewis Grizzard, "In Defense of Hillbillies and Rednecks," [Burlington, NC] *Times-News,* December 3, 1993. On Grizzard's reputation, see "Columnist Grizzard Dies After Surgery," [Schenectady, NY] *Daily Gazette,* March 22, 1984. For "redneck" becoming a term of endearment, see Clarence Page, "Getting to the Root of Redneck," *Chicago Tribune,* July 16, 1987; and Larry Rohter, "To Call a Floridian a 'Cracker' in Anger May Be a Crime," *New York Times,* August 19, 1991.

3. Celia Riverbark, "'Hey, Do You Know Me?': The Definition of Redneck Depends on Your Point of View," [Wilmington, NC] *Star-News,* August 23, 1993.

4. Stacy McCain, "One Thing Gingrich Is Not, Is a Redneck," *Rome* [GA] *News-Tribune,* November 27, 1994; and in syndicated column "Hart to Heart," Jeffrey Hart, "What's Behind David Duke?," *Gadsden* [AL] *Times,* October 31, 1991.

5. One reviewer of Chute's second book remarked, "If Ms. Chute's characters were Southern, we'd call them poor white trash"; see Mary Davenport, "Chute Novel Finds White Trash Up North," [Wilmington, NC] *Star-News,* May 29,

1988. Scholars have identified the genre as "Rough South," of which Allison has figured prominently, but the regional name is inaccurate given that Chute's subjects are rural families in Maine. For a discussion of the genre and how these novelists write from "within" their class, see Erik Bledsoe, "The Rise of Southern Redneck and White Trash Writers," *Southern Cultures* 6, no. 1 (Spring 2000): 68–90, esp. 68.

6. Carolyn Chute, *The Beans of Egypt, Maine* (New York: Ticknor & Fields, 1985), 10–11, 21, 23–25, 92, 100, 114–16, 122–24, 134–35, 156, 174, 189.

7. Ibid., 135–36, 165, 175, 177–79, 181, 192.

8. Ibid., 3, 46–47, 122, 116.

9. Ibid., 3.

10. See Peter S. Prescott, "A Gathering of Social Misfits: Six New Novels Take a Walk on Life's Weirder Shores," *Newsweek* (February 25, 1985): 86; and David Gates, "Where the Self Is a Luxury Item," *Newsweek* (June 13, 1988): 77. Chute emphasized that she was "so close to these people—they were my people"; see Ellen Lesser and Carolyn Chute, "An Interview with Carolyn Chute," *New England Review and Bread Loaf Quarterly* 8, no. 2 (Winter 1985): 158–77, esp. 161, 174. For other interviews highlighting her experiences with poverty, see Donald M. Kreis, "Life Better for 'Beans of Egypt' Author Carolyn Chute," *Lewiston* [ME] *Daily Sun*, March 6, 1985; and Katherine Adams, "Chute Dialogics: A Sidelong Glance from Egypt, Maine," *National Women's Studies Association Journal* 17, no. 1 (Spring 2005): 1–22.

11. Lesser and Chute, "An Interview with Carolyn Chute," 158, 160, 164–67, 177. For her husband as "coauthor," see Dudley Clendinin, "Carolyn Chute Found Her Love and Her Calling in Maine," *Gainesville* [FL] *Sun*, February 3, 1985. On the influence of her husband, see "Illiterate Mate Inspires Maine's Carolyn Chute," [Lewiston, ME] *Sun Journal*, September 16, 1991. For a realistic portrait of Maine poverty, see Leigh McCarthy, "Carolyn Chute Took a Bum Rap on Poverty," *Bangor* [ME] *Daily News*, September 24, 1985.

12. In 1985, Chute distinguished herself from rednecks. Doing public readings, she wrote, "gives me a chance to see some people that aren't [slaps her neck with her hand to indicate 'redneck.'] I wouldn't mind if rednecks showed up, that would be all right. I just don't like to see them brushing their teeth out my window." See Lesser and Chute, "An Interview with Carolyn Chute," 163. But in 2000, she wrote, "But being a redneck, working class—or, more accurately, the 'tribal class,'—I am proud of that." See "An Interview with Carolyn Chute," *New Democracy Newsletter* (March–April 2000), in Newdemocracy world.org; Charles McGrath, "A Writer in a Living Novel," *New York Times*, November 3, 2008; Carolyn Chute, *The Beans of Egypt, Maine: The Finished Version* (San Diego: Harcourt Brace & Co., 1995), 273, 275; Gregory Leon Miller, "The American Protest Novel in a Time of Terror: Carolyn Chute's Merry Men," *Texas Studies in Literature and Language* 52, no. 1 (Spring 2010): 102–28, esp. 103; Dwight Gardner, "Carolyn Chute's Wicked Good Militia," Salon.com, February 24, 1996.

13. Chute explains that Reuben Bean's immaturity comes from social disadvantages; he "was at a childish level, not in his intelligence but in his emotional development." See Lesser and Chute, "An Interview with Carolyn Chute," 169.

Chute also said in another interview that the minimum wage produces genuine male rage and that women were better able to endure than men. See "Chute's Book Is a Real American Classic," [Norwalk, CT] *Hour,* February 21, 1985.

14. Dorothy Allison, *Bastard Out of Carolina* (New York: Plume, 1992), 12, 22–24, 69, 80–81, 91, 98–99, 123.

15. Ibid., 102. Chute also talked about the shame of using food stamps. "But in the little stores they were kind of mean to us. Food stamps, you know, ugh. They come right out with it. I got to the point where I didn't want to go to the store anymore, I was so embarrassed. I really dreaded going. There was a lot of times when Michael and I were eligible for food stamps that we didn't go, because I felt so humiliated by it." See Lesser and Chute, "An Interview with Carolyn Chute," 169.

16. Allison, *Bastard Out of Carolina,* 309.

17. For his July Fourth speech, see William Jefferson Clinton, "What Today Means to Me," *Pittsburgh Post Gazette,* July 4, 1993.

18. Ibid. On Clinton standing up to his stepfather, see Ron Fournier, "Early Lessons Serve Him Well," *Beaver County* [PA] *Times,* January 20, 1993. On *The Man from Hope* film, see David M. Timmerman, "1992 Presidential Candidate Films: The Contrasting Narratives of George Bush and Bill Clinton," *Presidential Studies Quarterly* 26, no. 2 (Spring 1996): 364–73, esp. 367.

19. Mike Feinsilber, "But Others Say, 'You're No Thomas Jefferson,'" *Prescott* [AZ] *Courier,* January 17, 1993.

20. On describing Clinton as a poor sharecropper, see Todd S. Purdum, "If Kennedy's Musical Was 'Camelot,' What's Clinton's?," *New York Times,* January 17, 1993. See AP photograph of Clinton with the mule George in Centralia, Illinois, July 21, 1992, in Brian Resnick, "Campaign Flashback: Bill Clinton in Summer '92," *National Journal;* and Josh O'Bryant, "Well-Known Democratic Mule of Walker Dies," *Walker County* [GA] *Messenger,* May 14, 2008.

21. Roy Reed, "Clinton Country: Despite Its Image as a Redneck Dogpatch, Arkansas Has Long Been a Breeding Ground of Progressive Politics," *New York Times Magazine,* September 6, 1992; Peter Applebome, "Suddenly Arkansas's Being Noticed, but a First Glance Can Be Misleading," *New York Times,* September 26, 1992; Hank Harvey, "Arkansas Needs Clinton's Candidacy," *Toledo Blade,* October 4, 1992; Molly Ivins, "Clinton Still a Kid from Arkansas," [Wilmington, NC] *Star-News,* July 15, 2004; Randall Bennett Woods, *J. William Fulbright, Vietnam, and the Search for a Cold War Foreign Policy* (Cambridge: Cambridge University Press, 1998), 280.

22. David Grimes, "Put Bubba in White House," *Sarasota Herald-Tribune,* July 21, 1992; Nancy Kruh (*Dallas Morning News*) syndicated in [Spokane, WA] *Spokesman Review,* February 14, 1993; Michael Kelly, "A Magazine Will Tell All About Bubba," *New York Times,* February 4, 1993.

23. On Greenberg's use of "Slick Willie," see Paul Greenberg, "Truth Catches Slick Willie," *Tuscaloosa News,* February 19, 1992; Paul Greenberg, "Why Yes, I Did Dub Bill Clinton 'Slick Willie,' but Then, He Earned It," [Fredericksburg, VA] *Free Lance-Star,* June 28, 2004; "Just Why Is Slick Willy So Smooth?," [Burlington, NC] *Times-News,* April 6, 1992; Sandy Grady, "Clinton's Biggest Enemy Is Image of 'Slick Willie,'" *The Day* [New London, CT],

April 16, 1992; Martin Schram, "Wherever Bill Clinton Goes, Slick Willie Is Sure to Follow," *Rome* [GA] *News-Tribune,* April 6, 1992; Walter D. Myers, "'Slick Willie' Clinton Inherits the Woes of Tricky Dick," [Bend, OR] *Bulletin,* April 2, 1992.

24. See Schieffer and Gates, *The Acting President,* 180. Colorado congresswoman Patricia Schroeder gave Reagan the name "Teflon-coated president"; see Steven V. Roberts, "Many Who See Failure in His Policies Don't Blame Their Affable President," *New York Times,* March 2, 1984; Donald Kaul, "Slick Willie Starts to Look Like Barney Fife," [Wilmington, NC] *Star-News,* February 11, 1993.

25. On Clinton singing the Elvis song, see "Elvis Presley Sighting in Clinton Campaign," *Allegheny Times* [PA], April 3, 1992. Clinton's staff also used Paul Simon's song "Graceland" to introduce the candidate before his speeches; see "Elvis Running," *Ellensburg* [WA] *Daily Record,* April 3, 1992. For Elvis as the reporters' nickname for Clinton, see John King, "Slick Willie's Calling on Elvis," *Lodi* [CA] *News-Sentinel,* May 4, 1992; "Clinton Inaugural: He'd Invite Elvis," *Gainesville* [FL] *Sun,* May 1, 1992. For Clinton communing with the spirit of Elvis, see "Clinton Enjoying His Lead: He's Finding Time to Joke About Elvis," *Reading Eagle,* October 22, 1992. For an Elvis impersonator participating in the inaugural parade, see "'Elvis' to Perform in Grand Parade for Clinton," *New Straits Times* [Singapore], December 16, 1992. On Bush hiring an impersonator and *The Arsenio Hall Show,* see Daniel Marcus, *Happy Days and Wonder Years* (New Brunswick, NJ: Rutgers University Press, 2004), 156, 166–67.

26. For "Elvis is America," and the Elvis image as a way to attract more centrist voters, see "Elvis and Bill: Southern Boys with Thangs in Common" [Wilmington, NC] *Star-News* (reprinted from the *Economist*), August 18, 1996; and Marcus, *Happy Days,* 155, 158.

27. Bill Maxwell, "'Seen as 'White Trash': Maybe Some Hate Clinton Because He's Too Southern," [Wilmington, NC] *Star-News,* June 19, 1994. On Noonan gushing over Reagan and Pope John Paul II, two men she wrote books about, see Kenneth L. Woodward, "'John Paul the Great,' by Peggy Noonan," *New York Times,* December 18, 2005; Helen Eisenbach, "Looking for Mr. Right," *New York* (September 1, 2004); and on Gergen and Noonan seeing Reagan as a beloved father figure who transcended his party, see Marcus, *Happy Days,* 83; and Peggy Noonan, *What I Saw at the Revolution: A Political Life in the Reagan Era* (New York: Random House, 1990), 127.

28. Maxwell, "Seen as 'White Trash.'"

29. For the revival of the "Slick Willie" slur, see Jack Germond and Jules Witcover, "Clinton's Deposition Reveals Reputation as 'Slick Willie,'" *Reading* [PA] *Eagle,* March 12, 1998. William Rusher argued that Clinton was white trash, that with his "record of moral squalor and criminal misconduct, we must now add an essential tackiness straight out of the trailer parks of Arkansas"; see William Rusher, "White Trash in the White House," *Cherokee County* [GA] *Herald,* February 7, 2001; Jack Hitt, "Isn't It Romantic?," *Harper's Magazine* (November 1998): 17–20, esp. 17; "Second White House Response to Starr," *Washington Post,* September 12, 1998.

30. See Marianne Means, "But Bill Clinton's No Thomas Jefferson," [Wilmington, NC] *Star-News,* November 7, 1998; Thomas J. Lucente Jr. "No Comparison for Clinton and Jefferson," *Lawrence Journal-World,* November 20, 1998; Georgie Anne Geyer, "Clinton and Jefferson: An Odd Comparison," *Victoria Advocate,* November 12, 1998. There was a cartoon accompanying Geyer's article of Clinton calling Jefferson and telling him not to worry about the DNA evidence. "The People don't give a damn!" Also see Andrew Burstein, Annette Gordon-Reed, and Nancy Isenberg, "Three Perspectives on America's Jefferson Fixation," *Nation* (November 30, 1998): 23–28.

31. Jeffery Jackson, "Understanding Clinton: The King Is Dead; Long Live the King," *Nevada Daily Mail,* August 19, 1999.

32. See Toni Morrison, "The Talk of the Town," *New Yorker* (October 5, 1998): 31–32, esp. 32.

33. Kathleen Parker, "Democratic Race Seems to Be Bill vs. Oprah," *The Item,* December 1, 2007. Andrew Young also made the crude comment that Clinton had slept with more black women than Barack Obama. On Klein's *Primary Colors,* see Eric Lott, "The First Boomer: Bill Clinton, George W., and Fictions of State," *Representations* 84, no. 1 (November 2003): 100–122, esp. 101, 108, 111.

34. Frank Rich, "Palin and McCain's Shotgun Marriage," *New York Times,* September 7, 2008; Erica Jong, "The Mary Poppins Syndrome," *Huffington Post,* October 4, 2008; Eliza Jane Darling, "O Sister! Sarah Palin and the Parlous Politics of Poor White Trash," *Dialectical Anthropology* 33, no. 1 (March 2009): 15–27, esp. 19, 21. On Wasilla as a redneck town, see Jill Clarke of the Associated Press, "Alaskan Views of Clinton Reflect Those in the Lower 48," [Schenectady, NY] *Daily Gazette,* January 16, 1999.

35. Monica Davey, "Palin Daughter's Pregnancy Interrupts G.O.P. Convention Script," *New York Times,* September 2, 2008; Stephanie Clifford, "Readers See Bias in *Us Weekly*'s Take on Sarah Palin," *New York Times,* September 8, 2008; Maureen Dowd, "My Fair Veep," *New York Times,* September 10, 2008; David Firestone, "Sarah Palin's Alaskan Rhapsody," *New York Times,* December 9, 2010.

36. It was discovered that Palin had spent "tens of thousands" more than the disclosed $150,000 and that $20,000 to $40,000 had been used for her husband's clothes; see "Hackers and Spending Sprees," *Newsweek* (November 5, 2008); also see Darling, "O Sister! Sarah Palin," 24.

37. Sam Tanenhaus, "North Star: Populism, Politics, and the Power of Sarah Palin," *New Yorker* (December 7, 2009); 84–89, esp. 89.

38. Maureen Dowd, "White Man's Last Stand," *New York Times,* July 15, 2009; on Gretchen Wilson, see Nadine Rubbs, "'Redneck Woman' and the Gendered Poetics of Class Rebellion," *Southern Cultures* 17, no. 4 (Winter 2011): 44–77, esp. 56, and endnote 24 on page 69. For Palin as a hillbilly and prima donna, see Gail Collins, "A Political Manners Manual," *New York Times,* November 8, 2008.

39. Justin Elliot, "Trig Trutherism: The Definitive Debunker: Salon Investigates the Conspiracy Theory: Is Sarah Palin Really the Mother of Trig Palin?," Salon.com, April 22, 2011.

40. On her accent, see Jesse Sheildlower, "What Kind of Accent Does Sarah Palin Have? Wasillan, Actually," Slate.com, October 1, 2008; Dick Cavett, "The Wild Wordsmith of Wasilla," *New York Times*, opinionator.blogs.nytimes .com, November 14, 2008.

41. William Egginton, "The Best or Worst of Our Nature: Reality TV and the Desire for Limitless Change," *Configurations* 15, no. 2 (Spring 2007): 177–91, esp. 191; David Carr, "Casting Reality TV, No Longer a Hunch, Becomes a Science," *New York Times*, March 28, 2004; Jim Ruttenberg, "Reality TV's Ultimate Jungle: Simulated Presidential Politics," *New York Times*, January 9, 2004; also see Brenda R. Weber, *Makeover TV: Selfhood, Citizenship, and Celebrity* (Durham, NC: Duke University Press, 2009), 143–44.

42. *Duck Dynasty* was simply a modified version of *The Real Beverly Hillbillies*, a reality TV show that was canceled because of protests; see *Appalachian Journal* 31, no. 3/4 (Spring/Summer 2004): 438; Jonah Goldberg, "'Duck Dynasty,' Unreal Outrage," *New York Post*, December 20, 2013.

43. Mary Elizabeth Williams, "What Will It Take for TLC to Dump 'Honey Boo Boo'?," Salon.com, October 23, 2014; Jenny Kutner, "'Honey Boo Boo' Star Mama June Reveals Father of Two Daughters Is a Sex Offender," Salon.com, November 13, 2014.

44. Thomas Sowell, *Black Rednecks and White Liberals* (San Francisco: Encounter Books, 2005), 1, 5–9, 14–15, 29, 51; also see James B. Stewart, "Thomas Sowell's Quixotic Quest to Denigrate African American Culture: A Critique," *Journal of African American History* 91, no. 4 (Autumn 2006): 459–66. Grady McWhiney, *Cracker Culture: Celtic Ways of the Old South* (Tuscaloosa: University of Alabama Press, 1988). McWhiney's work was yet another example of the rush to turn poor whites into an ethnicity, and to deny that they were/are a class. McWhiney argued, "Cracker does not signify an economic condition; rather, it defines a culture." See *Cracker Culture*, xiv.

45. Charlotte Hays, *When Did White Trash Become the New Normal? A Southern Lady Asks the Impertinent Question* (Washington, DC: Regnery, 2013), 7, 9, 11, 45, 172; and Hays, "When Did White Trash Become Normal?," *New York Post*, November 2, 2013.

Epilogue: America's Strange Breed: The Long Legacy of White Trash

1. Carl Davis et al., *Who Pays? A Distributional Analysis of the Tax Systems of All 50 States*, 3rd. ed. (Washington, DC: Institute on Taxation and Economic Policy, 2009), 2.

2. Jill Lepore, "Fixed: The Rise of Marriage Therapy, and Other Dreams of Human Betterment," *New Yorker* (March 29, 2010).

3. See Sean McElwee, "The Myth Destroying America: Why Social Mobility Is Beyond Ordinary People's Control," Salon.com, March 7, 2015; and Lisa A. Keister and Stephanie Moller, "Wealth Inequality in the United States," *Annual Review of Sociology* 26 (2000), 63–81, esp. 72. As one scholar wrote, "If you want the American Dream, you'll have to go to Denmark." Also, Americans grossly underestimate wealth inequality, and if shown charts

comparing the United States' and Sweden's wealth distribution (though without identifying the countries), respondents overwhelming choose Sweden. See Tim Koechlin, "The Rich Get Richer: Neoliberalism and Soaring Inequality," *Challenge* 56, no. 2 (March/April 2013): 5–30, esp. 16–17, 20.

4. Bryce Covert, "The First-Ever Bill to Help Low-Income Moms Afford Diapers," *Think Progress*, August 13, 2014, thinkprogress.org. The large families celebrated by Republicans invited a comparison to our eugenic president Theodore Roosevelt and his six children; see Amy Bingham, "Presidential Campaign: Big GOP Families Lining Up to Fill White House," ABC News, June 21, 2011, abcnews.go.com. It was not only the number of children but the master-race looks of the Romney and Huntsman children that got attention. Scott Stossel, an editor of *Atlantic* magazine, joked on his Twitter feed, "Huntsman daughters and Romney sons should get together and breed." See Paul Harris, "Republican Candidates Seek Strength in Numbers to Show Off Family Values," *Guardian,* January 7, 2012.

5. Paul Krugman, "Those Lazy Jobless," *New York Times,* September 22, 2014; "Gingrich Says Poor Children Have No Work Habits," ABC News, December 1, 2011, abcnews.go.com.

6. "Billy Redden—Deliverance," YouTube, https://www.youtube.com/watch?v=PBgxdROTTrE; Cory Welles, "40 Years Later, 'Deliverance' Causes Mixed Feelings in Georgia," Marketplace.org, August 22, 2012; "Mountain Men: A Look at the Adaptation of James Dickey's Novel," *Atlanta Magazine,* September 2, 2011.

INDEX

Fallen Founder

The Life of Aaron Burr

Generations have been told that Aaron Burr was a betrayer— of Alexander Hamilton, of his country, of those who had nobler ideas. But in this eye-opening biography, Nancy Isenberg resurrects the Burr that time forgot: a loyal patriot, brilliant lawyer, and progressive Enlightenment intellectual who had the tremendous misfortune to make powerful enemies. *Fallen Founder* offers a fresh, provocative, and often surprising view of Burr and his fascinating era.

"Isenberg's meticulous biography reveals a gifted lawyer, politician, and orator who championed civility in government and even feminist ideals, in a political climate that bears a marked resemblance to our own."
—*The Washington Post*